COMMUNISM IN INDIA

GENE D. OVERSTREET

MARSHALL WINDMILLER

Communism
in India

1959

UNIVERSITY OF CALIFORNIA PRESS

BERKELEY AND LOS ANGELES

UNIVERSITY OF CALIFORNIA PRESS
BERKELEY AND LOS ANGELES
CALIFORNIA
CAMBRIDGE UNIVERSITY PRESS
LONDON, ENGLAND
© 1959 BY THE REGENTS OF THE UNIVERSITY OF CALIFORNIA

PUBLISHED WITH THE ASSISTANCE OF A
GRANT FROM THE FORD FOUNDATION

LIBRARY OF CONGRESS CATALOG CARD NUMBER: 58-12832
PRINTED IN THE UNITED STATES OF AMERICA

Foreword

This volume on the Communist movement in India by Gene D. Overstreet and Marshall Windmiller was written under the auspices of the
Modern India Project at the University of California, Berkeley. The
Modern India Project was established in the spring of 1954 to encourage research on Indian political parties, leadership, and issues. Financial support for the efforts of the project was granted by the Ford
Foundation, and the University of California undertook to provide
the institutional base from which the several researches of the project
could be carried on.

No set of ideas, institutions, or techniques of political action have
had a greater impact on world and national politics in recent years
than those reflected in the Communist movement. India, seeking national freedom and social welfare, was influenced by the ideas of Marx,
Engels, Lenin, and others of Marxian persuasion, as was the rest of the
world.

The main vehicle of these ideas was the Communist Party of India,
and no understanding of Indian history since World War I is possible
without an examination of this Party and its relation to world communism and Indian nationalism. The authors, both political scientists,
have analyzed this broad canvas of recent Indian history, emphasizing
the Communist Party of India, but giving due attention to the details
of Communist and non-Communist international influences on the
course of Indian communism.

The objectives of this study are twofold: to examine in detail the

Communist movement in India, historically and analytically; and to throw light on the complex arena of Indian and world Communist politics. In relation to the objectives of the Modern India Project, this is a study of a major Indian political party, in its world-wide as well as its national context; it constitutes an examination of one important group of political leaders in India; and it is concerned with a series of significant political issues that have arisen within the past four decades.

This study may be considered controversial on the grounds alone of its subject matter. However, the authors have gone to the sources painstakingly to assure themselves of accuracy. Those who have studied the Communist movement in various parts of the world will realize how difficult it is at times to discover truth where evidence is scanty and contemporary interpretation is carefully covered over with purposeful obscurantism.

This comprehensive, carefully detailed study should contribute to a better understanding of the form and process of Indian politics and of the world Communist movement.

Richard L. Park

Center for South Asia Studies
Institute of International Studies
University of California, Berkeley
September 1958

Acknowledgments

The authors take genuine pleasure in recalling the encouragement and assistance they have received in the course of their work from a great number of persons. To acknowledge our debt to them is therefore more than a dutiful gesture.

To Richard L. Park, director of the Modern India Project, University of California, we owe the opportunity to conclude the research and writing of this book. Its completion has depended in large measure on his support and its content has been improved by his counsel. We would also like to record our appreciation to the Ford Foundation not only for its support of the Modern India Project which made this study possible, but also for earlier fellowships, unrelated to this study, which enabled each of us to visit India and observe its government and politics at first hand.

This book is the result of library and field research in the United States, Europe, and India. Mr. Overstreet was in India from 1953 to 1955; Mr. Windmiller was there in 1953–1954 and again in 1955. The authors have pooled their skills and materials, which were in large degree complementary. In the preparation of the first draft, Mr. Overstreet wrote chapters 1, 8, 9, 10, 11, 12, 13, 15, 18, 19, 20 and the introduction and postscript, while Mr. Windmiller wrote chapters 2, 3, 4, 5, 6, 7, 14, 16, 17, 21 and the biographical chapter. Each chapter was subsequently revised after joint consultation, and the conclusions were written jointly.

Obvious errors of punctuation and spelling in cited material have

been corrected by the authors when this could be done without alter-
ing the meaning, and for consistency British spelling has been changed
to American forms. The spelling of Indian proper names has been
standardized with the use of those forms which appear to be most frequently used by the persons concerned.

Several persons have read the manuscript in whole or in part and it
has benefited much from their suggestions. They include Robert C.
North, Xenia Eudin, Jane Degras, Selig S. Harrison, Philip E. Mosely,
and John H. Kautsky.

In the course of our research we have received valuable advice and
suggestions from an uncounted number of persons. Specific mention is
due to Robert C. North, M. R. Masani, Philip Spratt, Jane Degras,
S. N. Tagore, Sibnath Banerjee, Violet Connolly, Joan V. Bondurant,
and Margaret W. Fisher.

Special mention should be made of those who have loaned us important documentary materials otherwise inaccessible. These include
Selig S. Harrison, Thomas A. Rusch, Philip J. Jaffe, J. P. Mitter. We
wish to thank the Institute of Pacific Relations for permission to use
material which originally appeared in its journal *Pacific Affairs*.

We thank the many librarians who have assisted us, among them
Walter H. Maurer of the Library of Congress, Inez Richardson and
Frances Bioletti of the Hoover Institute and Library, B. S. Kesavan of
the National Library, Calcutta, Shankar Shetty of the Yusuf Meherally
Library, Bombay, Anne H. Reed of the University of California.

To Patrick Wilson, librarian for South Asia Studies at the University of California, we owe a special debt for locating many documents
after we had given up the search, and for drawing to our attention important materials which we otherwise might have missed.

We are also greatly indebted to Toni Volcani who edited our first
draft and in the process taught each of us a great deal about the English language. Special thanks also go to Max E. Knight of the Editorial
Department of the University of California Press for additional editing
and for preparing the index.

Others who have aided us will, we hope, accept a general expression
of our appreciation. It remains only to be said that we alone are responsible for the accuracy of fact and correctness of interpretation
of all that is discussed in this book.

GENE D. OVERSTREET
MARSHALL WINDMILLER

Berkeley, Summer, 1958

Contents

PART 2

TABLES

I would say that the Communist Party is not a thing to be feared, yet it cannot be destroyed by any force or any violence. The Communist Party feeds and grows on force and violence. Truth, understanding, and an ability to measure this thing calmly and react in a democratic way—this will destroy it. This will leave it out of our scene, and it doesn't belong in this scene anymore.

Howard Fast, in an interview by Martin Agronsky, *The Progressive,* March, 1958.

ABBREVIATIONS

AICC	All-India Congress Committee
AIFSU	All-India Friends of the Soviet Union
AIKS	All-India Kisan Sabha
AIPC	All-India Peace Council
AIPWA	All-India Progressive Writers' Association
AIRF	All-India Railwaymen's Federation
AISF	All-India Students' Federation
AITUC	All-India Trade Union Congress
AMS	Andhra Mahasabha
BTLU	Bombay Textile Labor Union
CC	Central Committee
CPGB	Communist Party of Great Britain
CPI	Communist Party of India
CPSU	Communist Party of the Soviet Union
CSP	Congress Socialist Party
ECCI	Executive Committee of the Communist International
FSU	Friends of the Soviet Union
GKU	Girni Kamgar Union
KMPP	Kisan Mazdoor Praja Party
ICFA	India-China Friendship Association
IFTU	International Federation of Trade Unions
INTUC	Indian National Trade Union Congress
IPTA	Indian People's Theater Association
ISCS	Indo-Soviet Cultural Society

ITUF	Indian Trade Union Federation
MARS	Mahila Atma Raksha Samity
NFIW	National Federation of Indian Women
NUS	National Union of Students
PEPSU	Punjab and East Patiala States Union
PHQ	Party Headquarters
PPH	People's Publishing House
PPTUS	Pan-Pacific Trade Union Secretariat
PSP	Praja Socialist Party
RILU	Red International of Labor Unions
SPI	Socialist Party of India
WPP	Workers' and Peasants' Party

PART **1**

INTRODUCTION

The student of a political party in action is concerned not only with the nature of the party itself but also with the role of the party in its broader political context. He wants to understand the organizational structure, mode of operation, personnel, and program of the party, as well as how it acts upon, and in turn is acted upon by, its environment.

An observer of a Communist party is confronted with a special problem of analysis, for such a party functions not in one environment but in two. It is both an element of the international Communist community and an element of a national political community. It interacts with both of these contexts, and it is thus enmeshed in an exceedingly complex web of influences.

This study of the Communist Party of India (CPI) aims not only to describe the Party itself but also to relate it to its dual environment. Part I of the book recounts the development of the CPI, from about 1920 to 1958; Part II examines some of the main aspects of Indian Communist policy and practice, with emphasis on the recent period. Throughout the book an attempt is made to describe the CPI's relations with both communities to which it belongs, and to weigh their effects upon it.

This study is focused on the central, or all-India, aspect of the CPI. No attempt has been made to include a full examination of provincial (state) or local Communist policy or activity. However, these lower levels of Party organization receive some attention; they are of unusual significance in India, for the CPI reflects the heterogeneity of its national environment. The state and local Party units will provide a fruitful field of enquiry in the future.

Although many pages describe conditions in India or in the international Communist movement, this study does not present a comprehensive view of these environments in their totality. This book does not constitute a study of Indian politics as a whole, nor does it reflect an assumption that the CPI is the dominant factor in the Indian political scene.

The authors hope, however, that a study of the Indian Communist movement may contribute in some measure to fuller understanding both of Indian politics and of international communism. The fact that the CPI is related to both these environments provides an opportunity for two-way comparative analysis. By comparing the CPI with other Communist parties and observing how it deviates from the Communist norm, one may be aided in identifying certain characteristics of Indian politics. For example, it appears that factionalism based on charismatic leadership is more common in the CPI than in other Communist parties, and thus it may be inferred that this is a characteristic of Indian political behavior. On the other hand, by comparing the CPI with other Indian political parties, one may be aided in identifying qualities peculiar to Communist behavior. For example, it may be seen that the CPI has shown greater cohesiveness, arising from a common allegiance to an authoritative ideology, than have other Indian parties, from which it may be inferred that such cohesiveness is characteristic of Communist political behavior. These inferences are of course tentative, but they provide hypotheses for further study.

Problems of Analyzing Communist Literature

The internal affairs of a Communist party—that is, the processes whereby policy is made and communicated—are not normally a matter of public knowledge. The analyst must rely for information about the movement largely on official Party literature—literature in which policy is expressed in the jargon of conventional Communist theory. Thus official publications may seem designed to conceal Communist policy rather than to communicate it. But this literature does not necessarily obscure the real content or even the real motives of that policy, if it is properly interpreted.

The ostensible purpose of Communist theoretical literature is to provide a conceptual framework by which political and economic processes can be understood. In actuality its primary purpose is to surround a particular course of action with an aura of scientific correctness, and thereby to mobilize support for that specific plan among the Party rank and file, and its followers. Because the body of theoretical writing is so large and complex, only a priesthood in the Communist movement is really familiar with it. This priesthood is therefore armed with a potent means of influencing the rank and file, which is awed by the theory and by the intellects of those who are able to discourse learnedly about it. But the party membership is expected to be able to distill the essence of the proposed course of action from the theoretical jargon. And a non-Communist analyst may do the same, identifying the real content of policy in elaborate theoretical statements.

Further, a non-Communist may often identify the real motives of policy, by examining Communist polemical writings. Before a particular course of action is agreed upon by the top leadership in the international movement, or a single party, a debate may appear in the open publications. This debate is generally carried on in abstract terms. From careful analysis of such a debate, one may deduce the nature of the practical issues at stake and identify the contending factions. With a knowledge of the surrounding circumstances, it is possible to infer the nature of the process by which policy decisions are made in the Communist world.

But in order to "decode" this literature, it is necessary at the outset to have a reasonably clear understanding of the major policy alternatives which are provided in the ideology. At the most basic level, the level of strategy, two main alternatives may be identified: the anti-imperialist and anticapitalist strategies. Under the former, a Communist party aims at leading the four main classes of the community (the proletariat, peasantry, petty bourgeoisie, and bourgeoisie) against foreign imperialism. Under the latter, the Party aims at leading only three classes (proletariat, peasantry, and petty bourgeoisie) against domestic capitalism. These basic strategic aims are pursued by various tactical methods, including the united-front-from-above and the united-front-from-below, revolutionary and parliamentary action, and a wide range of programatic slogans.

Until recently at least, Communist policy in India has fluctuated between these two strategies, in one period supporting bourgeois nationalism against imperialism (as in the years 1935–1939 and 1945–1947) and in another period attacking bourgeois nationalism under the anticapitalist strategy (as in the years 1928–1934 or 1948–1950). These two strategies constitute the main categories by which Communist policy in India must be analyzed. But in recent years, there have been signs that a third strategy is emerging, both in the international Communist community and in the CPI itself. The theories of "people's democracy" and "new democracy," applied in Eastern Europe up to 1948 and in China since that time, are designed for a transition stage during which a Communist-led regime completes the bourgeois-democratic revolution and lays the basis for the subsequent achievement of socialism. During this transitional stage the appropriate strategy is the anti-imperialist variant, described above, in which the four main classes are united against foreign imperialism (and its domestic concomitants, feudalism and monopoly capitalism). But both in Eastern Europe and in China there has been a tendency to maintain the alliance of the four classes beyond this transitional stage into the socialist stage of development. The ultimate result may be a new strategy of uniting the four classes against, not imperialism, but capitalism itself. Such a strategy is not so quixotic as it may on first glance appear; in various underdeveloped countries of Asia, the business class has been persuaded or forced to support governmental programs containing elements of socialism. In India, as in China, the Communists may endeavor to "educate" the business class to socialism. But for the present, such a strategy has not received clear and mature expression.

Precise definition of these basic categories of policy is essential to systematic treatment of the main turns of Communist policy in India, and they are therefore discussed at greater length in chapter 1. It remains to be said here that, although the authors have adopted a somewhat different pattern of analysis, they have been considerably stimulated and aided in this task by John H. Kautsky's recent study of postwar Indian communism, *Moscow and the Communist Party of India.* Professor Kautsky's work should be consulted for a more detailed and in some respects contrasting account of the CPI in the period 1947–1953.

1 THE DUAL ENVIRONMENT
OF THE CPI

Although concrete attempts to plant the Russian flag there were abortive, India, the pivot of the British Empire, was for centuries an object of tsarist ambitions. Peter the Great tried by various expedients to open direct trade relations with the subcontinent and thereby to rival the British East India Company; unsuccessful in securing a land route, he eventually sent a small naval expedition, which soon turned back when the ships proved unseaworthy. Emperor Paul collaborated with Napoleon on plans for a joint military invasion of India; Paul dispatched an army of Don Cossacks, which foundered for lack of maps and supplies before it reached the borders of Russia.[1] In 1900, Russia signed a military convention with France, again agreeing to invade India; an expedition of 300,000 men was to be launched as soon as a railway could be built as far as Tashkent, but the railway was not completed in time.[2]

When the new Bolshevik regime came to power in Russia, therefore, it had ample historical precedent for at least an interest in India. The Bolsheviks were not long in showing this interest. They saw, no less than the tsars before them, that even a *threat* to British power in India would undermine British power the world over. By way of India, then, they could weaken an enemy who represented the chief obstacle to global revolution and the chief menace to the security of the Soviet

---

[1] George Vernadsky, *A History of Russia,* 3d. rev. ed. (New Haven: Yale University Press, 1951), pp. 104, 137.

[2] B. H. Sumner, *A Short History of Russia,* rev. ed. (New York: Harcourt, Brace and Company, 1949), 422 pp.

government itself. Moreover, apart from offering a weapon against Britain, India in itself presented an attractive object for the export of revolution. The spectacle of an oppressed colonial people was a strong stimulant to the revolutionary zeal of the Bolsheviks in these early years.

Writing of the prospect in India in 1919, one commentator, Kerzhentsev, showed both the calculation and the ardor that were characteristic of the Bolshevik outlook. India, he said, is the "most profitable" of the British colonies, and when it throws off the imperialist yoke Britain will be deprived of "huge revenue." But more than that, he said, when India rises up against imperialism it will ignite revolutions throughout the colonial world; Mesopotamia, Syria, Arabia, South Africa, Egypt, China, Tibet, Persia—all these, he said, will follow the Indian example. "In a word," he concluded, "the liberation of India from British domination will be a signal for a whole series of Asian countries to take up the struggle against imperialism." Britain has conquered and ruled India by "barbaric and insidious methods," he declared, and the country is ripe for revolution. "The revolutionary movement will grow increasingly stronger in the coming months." [3]

For the fulfillment of these aspirations, the Bolsheviks needed both a revolutionary plan and revolutionary agents. In the task of recruiting advance agents, they could not avail themselves of a large-scale rebel movement within the subcontinent—as they had done in Persia, where they joined forces with the guerrilla leader Mirza Kuchuk Khan for a military assault on the Iranian government in Teheran. But in India, they could find many active rebels among the case of frustrated émigrés scattered throughout the world. During World War I, these Indian groups had tended to look to Germany for support in their anti-British plots, and a number of them had received arms and money; but with the defeat of Germany they needed new sources of support. There was thus a natural mutuality of interest between them and the Bolsheviks.

Chief among these groups, perhaps, was an assorted émigré colony in Berlin, partially organized in the Berlin Committee led by Virendranath Chattopadhyaya and Bhupendranath Dutta. Another was the "Provisional Government of India" in Kabul, led by Mahendra Pratap, Barkatullah, and Obeidullah. In New York there was a branch of the Home Rule League led by Lala Lajpat Rai, and in California

---

[3] V. Kerzhentsev, *Angliiskii Imperializm* [English Imperialism] (Moscow: Izdatel'stvo vserossiiskogo tsentral'nogo ispolnitel'nogo komiteta sovetov R.K., K. i K. deputatov, 1919), 32 pp.

the Ghadr (Revolt) Party whose activities had prompted the San Francisco Conspiracy Case, and whose founder, Har Dayal, had moved on to Stockholm. In London there were several organized Indian groups, within which Shapurji Saklatvala was particularly prominent. In Japan there was a group around Rash Behari Bose, who had fled from India to escape trial in the Delhi-Lahore Conspiracy Case. And there was in Mexico the Indian émigré destined to be the first leader of communism in the subcontinent, M. N. Roy.[4]

There was considerable contact among these groups, but little co-ordination; their relations were characterized by enmity and intrigue. Describing the Berlin Indians, for example, Har Dayal wrote that "the greater part of their time and energy was spent in quarrelling among themselves and telling lies against one another." As he pointed out, "They had not much work; and idle hands always find mischief to do."[5] To recruit advance agents of revolution in India, then—and to mobilize the heterogeneous discontented elements of the Indian population—required above all a unifying plan of action.

In their initial approach to a revolutionary program for India, the Bolsheviks would naturally be influenced by two factors: one was their own system of political goals and methods, codified in Leninist strategy and tactics; the other was their reading of the Indian situation. Therefore, before proceeding to the origins of Communist policy and organization in India, it is necessary to consider these two backgrounds or "environments"—the basic ideas of the international Communist community and the basic features of the Indian political community—as they had both taken form in about 1920.

Leninist Strategy and Tactics

When Lenin and his comrades in the new Bolshevik elite of Soviet Russia first addressed themselves to the question of India, they brought to the task a dynamic doctrinal system, at once flexible and dogmatic.

Through a career of incessant interpretation of the changing forms of the Russian scene, Lenin had evolved a set of ideas on political strategy and tactics which were knit with the more general body of Marxist historical materialism. The precise extent to which these ideas were in fact influenced by Marxist philosophy on the one hand and by practical reality on the other, is a question which cannot be re-solved here. The fundamental tenets of Marxism provided a certain

---

[4] For information on these émigré groups see especially *Communism in India, 1924–1927* (Calcutta: Government of India Press, 1927), pp. 322–378.

[5] Har Dayal, *Forty-Four Months in Germany and Turkey* (London: P. S. King and Son, Ltd., 1920), p. 68.

"vision" of the broader outlines of history, but Lenin was an intensely practical man. Empirical flexibility was therefore an outstanding characteristic of his formulae for strategy and tactics.

Yet whatever may have been the origins of his ideas, Lenin sought persistently to rationalize them in terms of Marxist doctrine and to incorporate them into the general doctrinal framework. Once this was accomplished, the ideas became more or less sacrosanct. Since the doctrine was regarded as a "science," all its elements were assumed to be universally applicable. Communist leaders following Lenin therefore tended to impose preconceived ideas upon reality, out of doctrinaire fervor. And Lenin himself, when he turned his attention to India, appears to have viewed it through the lens of an established mode of interpretation.

In Leninist analysis the formulation of strategy and tactics in a given situation followed a series of fixed steps. The first step was to identify the historical *stage* which the society in question had attained. This was accomplished, in accordance with fundamental Marxist conceptions of the "iron laws" of historical development, by examining the primary economic factors in the situation—the prevailing level of technology and production, and the prevailing rules governing the relations of men to the productive process. A society might thus be identified as feudal, capitalist, or socialist.

Following logically upon this, the second step was to define the roles of the various *classes* in the society. Again, this depended on basic Marxist notions concerning the functions of the classes in the evolution of the productive process. Certain class relations were always characteristic of certain stages of development in any society, according to the materialist view of history.

The third step was to define the *basic aims* of the proletariat vis-à-vis these other classes. The proletariat would strive to crush its class enemies, to paralyze wavering classes, and to gain ascendancy over its class allies. Put in Communist terminology, its aims toward the various classes would be liquidation, neutralization, or hegemony. These basic aims make up an over-all framework for action, or strategy.

In this analytic process, the identification of historical (or "revolutionary") stages was obviously of fundamental importance, for a particular strategy corresponded to a particular stage and prevailed throughout that stage. Thus when Communists argue endlessly about the seemingly academic question of whether a particular country is feudal or capitalist—as they have frequently done at Comintern congresses or in doctrinal literature—they are in reality debating the premises of two alternative strategies. Concealed in the apparent hair-splitting are practical political points.

Looking upon the Russian scene as early as 1905, Lenin foresaw two main historical stages (setting aside the remotely distant third stage of utopian communism): a revolution against feudalism and a revolution against capitalism. For these two stages he proposed two basic strategies, which differed primarily in their aims with respect to the bourgeois class. These two fundamental strategic alternatives have formed the basis of Communist policy almost to the present day, applied in varying contexts and supported by varying tactics, and they therefore require clear definition.

The first stage of history described by Lenin—the stage which confronted him immediately—was the period of bourgeois-democratic revolution against the prevailing political, economic, and social order of feudal autocracy. But, paradoxically, in evaluating the roles of the various classes in this period, Lenin asserted that the Russian bourgeoisie was incapable of leading its own "bourgeois-democratic" revolution to fulfillment. The big bourgeoisie or monopoly capitalists would join forces with the autocracy at the beginning, he said, and the middle bourgeoisie would occupy a vacillating and unstable position, at times supporting the autocracy and at times opposing it. Only the three remaining classes—the proletariat, the poor peasantry, and the petty bourgeoisie—would struggle consistently for the full completion of this revolution and the total liquidation of feudalism; but in the meantime the middle bourgeoisie would support some revolutionary action. In the antifeudal stage of history, therefore, the Communists must endeavor to lead these four classes.

This strategy required the subtle and flexible aim of allying with the bourgeoisie in its "revolutionary" mood and opposing it in its "reactionary" mood. Since the bourgeois class would ultimately move over to an altogether counterrevolutionary position, the strategy called for using it so long as it was willing but also preparing the way for reducing it to political impotence. This aim Lenin called "neutralizing" the bourgeoisie, or "paralyzing" its "instability."

The antifeudal strategy, as he summed it up, is therefore as follows: the proletariat must gain hegemony over the poor peasantry and petty bourgoisie, neutralize the bourgeoisie, and liquidate the big bourgeoisie and feudal landlords. In his own words:

> The proletariat must carry to completion the democratic revolution, by allying to itself the mass of the peasantry [including its petty bourgeois element] in order to crush by force the resistance of the autocracy and to paralyze the instability of the bourgeoisie.[6]

---

[6] V. I. Lenin, *Two Tactics of Social Democracy in the Democratic Revolution* (Moscow: Foreign Languages Publishing House, 1950), p. 152.

At the climax of this first stage, the bourgeoisie would, in Lenin's view, strike a deal with the feudal autocracy and thus betray its own revolution. It would then be the duty of the proletariat to capture power with the petty bourgeoisie and poor peasantry, and begin the transition to the second, anticapitalist, revolution. This new provisional regime—the "revolutionary-democratic dictatorship of proletariat and peasantry"—would complete the bourgeois-democratic revolution, primarily through the redistribution of land which would liquidate feudalism in the countryside. After this intermediate period, it would then embark upon the building of socialism.

In the second stage, a fundamentally different set of relations would prevail among classes, and a new strategy would thus be required. The Communists now would endeavor to lead three classes: the proletariat, the poor peasantry, and the petty bourgeoisie. The petty bourgeoisie would constitute a vacillating and unreliable ally at this stage as had the bourgeoisie in the earlier stage. The anticapitalist strategy must therefore aim at the liquidation of the bourgeoisie, at neutralization of the petty bourgeoisie (including the middle peasantry), and at hegemony over the poor peasantry.

In Lenin's words,

> The proletariat must accomplish the socialist revolution, by allying to itself the mass of the semi-proletarian elements of the population [the poor peasantry] in order to crush by force the resistance of the bourgeoisie and to paralyze the instability of the peasantry and the petty bourgeoisie.[7]

For the pursuit of these two main sets of strategic goals, Lenin devoted himself wholeheartedly to the task of providing rules of political tactics. In Communist usage, "strategy" is the plan for winning a revolutionary war, and "tactics" is the plan for winning a revolutionary battle. Expressed another way, strategy defines the nature of the struggle among classes as a whole, while tactics defines the nature of the particular struggles among the political organizations of those classes. Strategy therefore means defining long-term aims of action, and tactics means the adoption of appropriate techniques of action, forms of organization, and political slogans.[8] The technique of action might be a general strike, an agrarian revolt, an urban insurrection, or a united-front-from-above or from-below. The form of organization might be an illegal or legal Communist party, a so-called workers and peasants party, or a "peace" front. Appropriate slogans might com-

---

[7] *Ibid.*, pp. 152–153.

[8] This paraphrases Stalin's definition of strategy and tactics, in J. Stalin, *The Foundations of Leninism* (Moscow: Foreign Languages Publishing House, 1950), pp. 114–115, 117.

prise a moderate or a militant political program. Tactics change with the ebb and flow of the revolutionary movement, within a given stage. The strategic aim of the Party toward a class may be pursued by a bewildering variety of short-run tactics, according to circumstances.

On the subject of tactics, Lenin's main theme was the need for expedient compromise, the need to fit tactical measures to the current political environment.

One manifestation of this was his insistence on combining legal and illegal, direct and indirect techniques of action. Communists must seize every opportunity for work among the masses, he asserted. They must participate, openly or secretly, in any organization through which they could influence the masses in any degree—not only trade unions and peasant associations but also parliaments and other political parties. They should not shrink from participation even in bourgeois political organizations, he said, so long as it contributed to the strengthening of the Party. While the Communist Party itself might of necessity be illegal, Communists must penetrate the other institutions of the body politic wherever possible.

In elaborating the techniques for action vis-à-vis other political organizations, Lenin described two main tactical devices which have prevailed to the present: action "from above" and action "from below." Action "from above" denotes a formal alliance with non-Communist organizations, and Lenin cited, as an illustration, the "provisional revolutionary government" in which Social Democrats would join with other parties. This tactic means exerting pressure on another organization through public collaboration with its leaders, and such action should be utilized, Lenin said, wherever "practical expedience" permitted. Action "from below" denotes an open attack on non-Communist organizations; it means exerting pressure on another organization, from within or without, by appealing to its constituents or members. This type of action must be resorted to "in any case," he stated.[9]

In summary, then, the preëminent purpose of tactics, according to Lenin, is the creation of a party which is the acknowledged vanguard of the proletariat. But tactics must also serve the purpose of securing influence over other political organizations, whenever they are willing, though they may be enemies on the morrow. Lenin hammered at this point with endless persistence.

The more powerful enemy can be vanquished only by exerting the utmost effort, and *without fail*, most thoroughly, carefully, attentively and skillfully using every, even the smallest, "rift" among the enemies, of every antagonism of interest among

---

[9] *Ibid.*, pp. 29–33.

the bourgeoisie of the various countries and among the various groups or types of bourgeoisie within the various countries, and also by taking advantage of every, even the smallest, opportunity of gaining a mass ally, even though this ally be temporary, vacillating, unstable, unreliable and conditional.[10]

Lenin's ideas on strategy and tactics reflected the peculiarities of the Russian scene, and particularly his contempt for the political capacities of the capitalist class there. Yet these concepts were incorporated into a general body of theory intended for universal application. Lenin's later proposals for strategy and tactics in the underdeveloped and colonial areas of the world, such as India, were in large part merely an extension of this established system of ideas.[11]

The Indian Environment

An attempt to survey the Indian political situation in about 1920 must begin with an examination of the nationalist movement, since the primary problem of Communist policy would be to define its attitude toward that political force.

The main instrument of Indian nationalism was the Indian National Congress, an amorphous organization embracing a wide variety of political creeds and factions which were united by a common aspiration for independence. The Congress was formed in 1885 and for several decades was the vehicle of a moderate leadership inspired by imported liberal ideology. The aim of the organization was merely to secure, by constitutional means, greater Indian participation in the existing system of government. It affirmed its loyalty to British rule, and it included a number of Englishmen in its top ranks. The British authorities viewed it with tolerance and even with sympathy.

Beginning about 1900, however, the Congress leadership was challenged by the rise of an extremist school of thought, led by such men as Tilak and Ghose, which combined Hindu revivalism with militant political activism. They sought to turn the Congress into a genuinely anti-imperialist instrument, and under their influence in 1907 the Congress adopted the goal of swaraj—self-government within the British Empire.

But because the Congress itself, extremists and moderates together, constituted a tiny band of intellectuals, it remained an elite organization. It was not until after World War I, with the advent of Gandhi on the Indian scene, that the Congress matured into a mass movement

---

[10] V. I. Lenin, *"Left-Wing" Communism, An Infantile Disorder* (Moscow: Foreign Languages Publishing House, 1950), p. 91. Emphasis in original.
[11] V. I. Lenin, *Two Tactics* . . . , p. 170.

with a revolutionary purpose. For Gandhi performed an indispensable function; he catalyzed the development of Indian nationalism by his ability to unite the uneducated peasants in the myriad villages of India with the Westernized elite. Born a Vaisya by caste and educated in England, he could have joined the tiny professional class and prospered as a lawyer; he commanded the respect of the business and professional elite, and under his leadership the Congress burgeoned, nourished by the financial aid and professional skills which this elite provided. But he retained an "Indian-ness" of thought and personality which endowed him with an unparalleled popular appeal as well; to the peasant he became the mahatma—the great soul—and the Congress became a genuinely popular political party.

Furthermore, Gandhi exercised an essential creative function, devising political tactics which were uniquely suited to the elements of his environment. There was little prospect of a successful appeal to arms against the British, and Gandhi proposed instead an appeal to conscience; with the weapon of *satyagraha*—nonviolent direct action—he made a virtue of Indian weakness.

Satyagraha included many forms of peaceable resistance to British rule. It included boycott of British goods, protest fasts against British authority, withdrawal from British organizations, and violation of British laws. These methods could be applied through mass action or a symbolic deed by a solitary leader.

But because mass action frequently degenerated into mob violence, there was a tendency to confine *satyagraha* to the action of a few selected martyrs. With his exacting insistence on nonviolence, Gandhi appeared to be as much concerned with inculcating virtue in his own people as with influencing the British, and he conceived his political methods as providing a school for training in self-discipline. Indeed, he called off the first great civil disobedience campaign of 1919–1920 because of a single violent outrage perpetrated by his followers.

Satyagraha was appropriate not only to the materials at hand, but also to the nature of the adversary. Since the British regime permitted a large measure of civil liberty, the nationalist movement was free to engage in peaceable political action without fear of extreme reprisal. So long as foreign rule remained "permissive," the Congress thrived on calculated martyrdom.

Moreover, the British proved amenable to an appeal to conscience. Though they did not fully satisfy the nationalist demands, neither did they wholly thwart them, and nationalist agitation was rewarded with gradual progress toward self-rule. Thus radicalism had little chance to flourish; so long as peaceable political action produced some result, a violent revolutionary program could not inspire overwhelming mass enthusiasm.

But in a sense, Gandhi's virtues also constituted his limitations. Certain of his ideas, keyed as they were to the traditionalist milieu of the semifeudal countryside, enabled him to arouse the benighted peasantry to political action; but at the same time they were an obstacle to material and social advancement. In the realm of social and economic philosophy, Gandhi was markedly antimodern, by Western standards; his ideal for India was a confederation of many small village communities, integrated in a common culture but economically and politically self-sufficient. In the realm of social policy, he deprecated the abolition of caste and urged that the traditional social hierarchy be retained—though at the same time he opposed untouchability. On the subject of economic policy, he set his face against technological progress, declaring that industrialization and urbanization brought greater evils than benefits in their train. He opposed the introduction of Western science in many fields such as medicine. He also opposed any form of coercion in the removal of economic inequalities, urging that the rich voluntarily become "trustees" and administer their excess wealth for the benefit of the poor. In any case, in Gandhi's credo the poor were the more fortunate, since to foreswear material goals was prerequisite to the higher goal of spiritual fulfillment.

Such an ideology was likely to dissatisfy at least one section of Indian society—the growing intellectual class produced by a British-style education. While this group did not necessarily wish to cast off all traditional values, it was nourished by Western ideas and ardently desired that India should attain social and economic progress equal to that of the industrial giants of the world. And this group was of crucial importance to India's future, since it exemplified the attitudes and possessed the skills necessary to modern government; when the British abdicated in India, the intellectual class would probably fall heir to the positions of power.

To some among this educated group, Socialist ideology was inherently attractive, for it offered not only a program of rapid economic, social, and political advancement but also an organic philosophy or view of life. For young men and women possessed of a will to believe and a will to act, but alienated from traditional values, socialism provided an alternative to Gandhism.

The malaise of the educated youth sought an outlet in various forms of political activity. One was a penchant for terrorism which developed in those areas, such as Bengal and Punjab, which had special grievances

against British rule. Terrorism was never more than a minor phenomenon, but it burst out sporadically—usually as clumsy acts of
violence on the part of teen-age conspirators.

But another, more profitable, arena of political activity lay before
the leftist intellectuals in the field of labor and peasant agitation.
Before 1920 there were almost no trade-union or peasant organizations. Though the Congress had worked among these oppressed classes
and tried to attract recruits, it had not made any systematic attempt
to develop class organizations which would form subsidiaries of the
nationalist movement. Indeed, Gandhi preached a philosophy of class
peace and collaboration and opposed any appeal to class interest. Thus
the field was open to those who, because of political ambition or personal conviction, chose to promote the self-consciousness and organization of the proletariat or the peasantry.

While the Congress under Gandhi was the primary nationalist
agency, there were other groups which could not readily be incorporated within its ranks. Though the Congress claimed to represent
all of India, and though Gandhi urged brotherhood among all religions, the Muslim minority of the subcontinent showed signs of
claiming for itself a separate political identity. The Muslim League
was founded in 1906, and it grew steadily in strength and assertiveness.
The Hindu-Muslim cleavage was not overcome in a single, united,
nationalist organization.

Furthermore, nationalism was not the sole political reality in India.
The subcontinent was divided into a variety of cultural-linguistic
regions, demarcated by about twelve major language groups. The people speaking these languages (for instance, the Bengalis, Marathis,
and Tamils) were ethnically distinct, their differences being rooted
in the ancient or medieval history of India. Hence while all Indians
were united at one level in demanding freedom from British rule,
they were divided at another level by cultural and political loyalties to
the subnations to which they belonged. Nationalism was a tender
growth, and a genuine sense of Indian nationhood was confined to
the few. Thus in Indian politics nationalism was challenged by regional
particularism.

Regional-linguistic loyalty expressed itself in a variety of ways, but
its main political manifestation was the demand that state boundaries
be redrawn in conformity with ethnic boundaries. The British had
ignored these ethnic divisions in drawing the political-administrative
map of India, and a linguistic group might be divided among as many
as four provinces. The demand for linguistically homogeneous provinces was but one evidence of a powerful desire for subnational au-

tonomy; the Indian nationalist leadership was therefore confronted with the delicate yet crucial task of devising a constitutional scheme that would satisfy both national and subnational ambitions.

There was, finally, another element which could not be easily incorporated within the Congress. The subcontinent—and the nationalist movement—was further divided by the distinction between British India and the princely states. British India contained three-quarters of the total population of India; the remainder inhabited the native states—562 separate kingdoms ranging in size from a few square miles to the vast and important states of Hyderabad and Kashmir. In the princely states, ruled by autocratic hereditary dynasties under British veto, nationalist consciousness and organization were slow to emerge. The Congress confined its activities to British India; the native states remained a largely unexploited field for political action, open to penetration by rivals of the Congress.

In summary, under Gandhi the Congress became a uniquely viable and effective nationalist organization, but it was not without political rivals and not without a certain vulnerability to political ideologies antagonistic to its own. In 1920, then, the Indian environment provided both obstacles and openings to the growth of a Communist movement. The capacity of the Communists to adjust to that environment—in so many ways distinctive—would in large measure determine their prospects.

Note.—For detailed information and valuable insights concerning the Indian environment as of 1955, see Myron Weiner, *Party Politics in India* (Princeton University Press, 1957), 319 pp.

2   INDIANS JOIN THE COMINTERN

In April, 1915, an Indian who had just returned after many years abroad made a speech in Madras to help the British recruit soldiers for the war against Germany. "I discovered," he said, "that the British Empire had certain ideals with which I have fallen in love." That same month another Indian left India to rendezvous with a ship bearing German arms that he planned to smuggle into India for a revolution against the British. Both men passionately desired self-government for their country, yet one was prepared to defend India's rulers against their enemy, and the other was conspiring with that enemy to bring about Britain's defeat.

Twenty-seven years later Britain, still ruling India, was once again locked in mortal combat with Germany. The same two Indians, after many years of struggle and sacrifice for the cause of Indian independence, again saw the British Empire in danger. But on this occasion the roles were reversed. He who had recruited soldiers now launched a movement that plunged the subcontinent into violence and chaos, and he who had conspired with Britain's enemy in 1915 now wrote pamphlets in support of the Allied (and thus Britain's) war effort. These two men were Mohandas Karamchand Gandhi and Manabendra Nath Roy.

Although guided by the same star—independence for India— Gandhi and Roy set very different courses. Both men had traveled in the Western world and both were deeply influenced by it. But only Roy actually became noticeably Westernized; Gandhi remained profoundly Indian. Until 1930, Roy conducted his struggle from abroad, using revolutionary techniques learned from experience in Europe. Gandhi, on the other hand, fought in India using ancient ideas that he adapted to modern conditions. Roy sought Indian independence through violent revolution; Gandhi led the masses in disciplined nonviolence.

It is appropriate to begin a study of Indian communism with some background on Roy, for between 1920 and 1928 he not only directed Indian Communist activity from abroad, but he also interpreted India to the Comintern and thus played a major role in determining its strategy for India and for other colonial areas. Roy's career in the Communist International was one of meteoric rise and rapid decline, and some knowledge of the reasons for this is necessary to any understanding of the development of communism in India during this period.

Roy, whose real name was Narendra Nath Bhattacharya, was born in the village of Arbalia, Bengal, in 1886.[1] Like many Bengali Brahmans he was attracted to politics in his teens, and before he was twenty he was deeply involved in the struggle for Indian independence. Bengal was a turbulent land at the beginning of the century; acid bulbs and homemade bombs—the weapons of terrorism—were standard equipment for hot-headed revolutionaries, but effective weapons for revolution were lacking. The outbreak of the European war in 1914 seemed to provide an opportunity for securing them.

To the Germans, India presented a formidable opening: if an armed revolution could be fomented in India, Britain would be obliged to withdraw troops from the European front to put it down, and could not send native Indian regiments to Europe. With this in mind the Germans invited to Berlin the Indian revolutionary Har Dayal, who was then in Switzerland and who had founded the Ghadr Party in California.[2] In Germany Har Dayal was asked to head what became known as the Berlin Indian Independence Committee. With the aid of this group the Germans hoped to smuggle arms into India.

In September, 1914, a German agent in the United States purchased 8,080 Springfield rifles, 2,400 carbines, 4,000,000 rounds of ammunition,

---

[1] The authors were unable to establish Roy's exact birth date with precision. A cousin has stated that Roy was born in the Bengali year 1293 (A.D. 1886–87), and the 1886 date is generally accepted. *Radical Humanist*, XVIII (Feb. 7, 1954), p. 78.

[2] For a detailed account of the Ghadr Party based on California police records, see: *Seventh Report: Un-American Activities in California*, [Senate] Fact-Finding Committee on Un-American Activities (Sacramento: California State Printing Office, 1953), pp. 213–246. Also useful is the CPI publication: Randhir Singh, *The Ghadar Heroes* (Bombay: People's Publishing House, 1945).

and assorted other weapons.[3] M. N. Roy records in his memoirs that by the end of the year word from the Berlin committee reached the revolutionaries in Bengal informing them that the Germans were ready to send arms and money.[4] An Indian emissary went to Berlin with word that the Germans should make delivery in Java, the nearest neutral country. Accordingly, German agents in America developed an elaborate plan for shipment in the steamship *Maverick*. The Ghadr Party participated in the plan and designated five of its members to accompany the shipment. The arms and the five Indians left San Diego on the *Annie Larsen,* which was to rendezvous with the *Maverick* at an island off the coast of lower California. But contact was never made for one of the ships failed to arrive at the appointed time and the other, not daring to linger, sailed on.[5]

The *Maverick* had set sail from San Pedro, California, in April, 1915. That same month M. N. Roy left India for Java.[6] But the *Maverick* did not appear, and in June Roy returned to India with some German money but no arms.[7] In August he again left India for Java. This time the *Maverick* was there. The arms, however, were not aboard her. Unwilling to return empty-handed a second time, Roy decided to stay abroad. He journeyed to China, Japan, and ultimately to the United States, arriving in San Francisco in late 1915, disguised as an Indian Christian theology student, Father Martin.[8]

M. N. Roy in America

Fearing arrest by the San Francisco police, Roy did not stay long, but instead went to Stanford University, about thirty miles to the south, where he had heard there were a number of Indian students,

---

[3] Giles Taylor Brown, *The Hindu-Conspiracy and the Neutrality of the United States, 1914–1917* (M.A. Thesis, University of California, History, 1941), p. 32.

[4] M. N. Roy, "Memoirs," *Radical Humanist,* XVII (Feb. 1, 1953), p. 54. Roy's memoirs ran serially in his own journal, *Radical Humanist,* from February 1, 1953, to September 5, 1954. Hereinafter they will be cited as *Roy Memoirs.*

[5] Brown, *The Hindu-Conspiracy . . . ,* pp. 40–52. See also John Price Jones and Paul Merrick Hollister, *The German Secret Service in America* (Boston: Small, Maynard & Co., 1918), pp. 264–267.

[6] Lt.-Col. Sir Cecil Kaye, *Communism in India* (Delhi: Government of India Press, 1926), p. 4.

[7] An undated telegram from Chandra Chakraberty, an Indian conspirator in New York, to the German foreign secretary, Zimmerman, states that Roy was accompanied to Java on his first trip by two other Indians and that a German agent in Java gave Roy 25,000 guilders. Quoted in: Earl E. Sperry, German Plots and Intrigues (Washington, D.C.: Committee on Public Information, 1918), p. 52.

[8] Kaye, *Communism in India,* p. 4, and *Roy Memoirs* (Feb. 22, 1943), p. 91. E. R., writing in the organ of the American Communist Opposition, states that Roy spent more than a year in the United States beginning in 1915. E. R., "M. N. Roy and Indian Communism," *Revolutionary Age,* II (Sept. 28, 1931), p. 3.

and others in the community who were sympathetic to Indian nationalism. Har Dayal had been on the faculty at Stanford for a short period,
and Dhan Gopal Mukherji, the younger brother of one of Roy's
friends in Bengal and later a well-known Indian novelist, was there
to welcome the traveler.

Except for noting that it was at Stanford that he adopted the name
M. N. Roy, Roy has little to say in his memoirs about this period.
Yet it was an important interlude, for it was then that Roy met Evelyn,
a young Stanford graduate, who fell in love with him. When Roy left
for New York after about two months on the West Coast, Evelyn went
with him. In New York, they contacted Indian nationalists and laid
plans to get to Germany in order to work with the Berlin Indian
Independence Committee.

The leader of the New York Indians at the time of Roy's arrival
was Dr. Chandra Chakraberty, a young Bengali intellectual who had
come to the United States around 1910. Chakraberty has written that
while he was negotiating with the captain of the famous German
cargo submarine, *Deutschland*, to take Roy to Germany, Roy was
arrested on a complaint telegraphed to New York by Evelyn's father.
According to Chakraberty, Evelyn defied her father, married Roy in
the jail, and the two were released.[9]

In his memoirs Roy states that in New York he became a close
friend of the revered Indian nationalist, Lala Lajpat Rai. At the
same time he began to circulate among American socialists and
anarchosyndicalists, for they were naturally sympathetic to the cause
of Indian independence. Roy says that it was during this period that
he began to read Marx in the New York Public Library. But Marxist
ideas evidently did not initially impress him, for his major writings
during the next two years do not reveal their influence.

If the Indians in the United States had not become so deeply involved with German agents it is likely that they could have continued
to work for Indian independence by collecting funds and writing
propaganda. But the United States, jealous of its neutrality, was put
on the alert for German conspiracies by frequent tips received from
British intelligence agents. On March 7, 1917, shortly before the

---

[9] Chandra Chakraberty, *New India* (Calcutta: Vijoyakrishna Bros., n.d. [1951]),
p. 34. Roy does not discuss his personal life in his memoirs, nor does he make any
mention of Evelyn who was not only his wife, but an important help in his work
until their separation in 1925. He refers to Chakraberty as "deceitful," "oily," and
"an imposter," and claims that he knew nothing of the *Deutschland* while he was
in New York. He says that Chakraberty made no effort to secure his passage on it.
Roy Memoirs (April 19, 1953), p. 186.

American entry into the war, the police arrested Chakraberty and his German contact in New York. Other arrests followed, and ultimately ninety-eight Germans and Indians were brought to trial in San Francisco in the famous Hindu Conspiracy Case.[10] Roy and his wife were questioned by the police but were not held.[11] Shortly after he was again picked up and was indicted for violating the immigration laws. This suggests that his connection with the German conspiracy at this point was limited or was well concealed. He was never brought to trial on the immigration charge because he and Evelyn fled to Mexico.[12]

In Mexico Roy wasted no time in getting in touch with the Germans. They believed that he could be useful not only in promoting revolution in India but also in maintaining contact with Indians in the United States. They accordingly put at his disposal a substantial amount of money. Roy mentions one sum of 50,000 pesos in gold coin,[13] and another of $50,000.[14] He dispensed this money, according to his own account, to various revolutionary comrades in amounts ranging from two to ten thousand dollars.

In Mexico Roy "learned to appreciate the good things in life." "My mode of living was not exactly proletarian," he recalls in his memoirs. His Mexico City residence was a "house in the plutocratic Colonia Roma, furnished with green satin-covered Louis XV furniture." The drawing room "was a longish room with several tall windows on the street, quite suitable for transformation into the semblance of an exclusive private chapel in a fashionable church." Roy took up riding, hired a language and chess tutor, frequented the fashionable cafes, and circulated in the higher levels of the capital's cosmopolitan society.[15]

He also made the acquaintance of a number of radical Americans —Charles Francis Phillips (alias Frank Seaman), Linn A. E. Gale, Michael Gold (alias Irwin Granich), Carleton Beals, Henry Glitenkamp—some of whom had fled to Mexico to escape the draft. With them he began to write for Mexican publications, taking Mexico's side in its grievances with the United States. The Mexican government

[10] A full account of the trial is contained in Brown, *The Hindu-Conspiracy . . .* , pp. 75–99.
[11] *New York American,* March 12, 1917, p. 1.
[12] *Roy Memoirs* (Feb. 15, 1953), pp. 79–80.
[13] *Ibid.* (May 10, 1953), p. 222.
[14] *Ibid.* p. 224.
[15] *Ibid.* (May 31, 1953), pp. 258–259; (June 7, 1953), p. 270; (June 14, 1953), pp. 282–283.

was naturally sympathetic to these activities, and Roy says that he became the unofficial adviser to President Carranza. He also published in Spanish some pamphlets and a 189-page book on India. The book was a typical nationalist polemic of the period, charging that before the advent of the British the Indians had been prosperous, united, and almost one hundred per cent literate.[16] Their present poverty, disunity, and backwardness were entirely due to the British policy of divide, rule, and exploit. Nowhere in the book does one find a trace of the Marxist system of thought to which Roy was later converted, although some hint of Socialist influence can be found in an article he wrote for *Gale's* magazine in August, 1919.[17]

Mexico was a remote outpost for conducting a revolution in India, and before very long Roy became discouraged in this aspect of his work. "After reaching Mexico," he recalls in his memoirs, "I was completely out of touch with India. For two years practically no news had reached me, and I was entirely ignorant of what might be happening at home." [18] With the defeat of Germany, which was then impending, he would no longer have political or financial support for work in India. Convinced he could do nothing for the liberation of India in the near future, he applied himself "wholeheartedly to the new fields of revolutionary activities which promised satisfaction" in Mexico itself.

During the summer of 1919 a movement developed among various leftist groups in Mexico City to form a national Socialist party. Roy took an active interest and began financing the small paper, *El Socialista*, of Francisco Cervantes Lopez. When the first national conference of the Mexican Socialist Party took place (August 25 to September 4, 1919) he underwrote the expenses and with his wife chaired several of the meetings. During the conference a dispute broke out over the seating of Luis Morones whom the left wing, led by Linn Gale, accused of being an agent of Samuel Gompers. Two votes were taken, both ending in a tie. On the third ballot, Roy, as chairman, voted to seat Morones, and from then on he was labeled as a rightist by the left wing. Shortly after the conference, Gale's faction

---

[16] In the book Roy says: "History teaches us that the Indian people under the Hindu monarchs were almost universally literate and educated. Daily reading of selections of the holy scripture was welcome obligation for the Hindus. So illiteracy was an almost unknown phenomenon among the Indian people during that period. Instruction was always free in India." M. N. Roy, *La India: su Pasado, su Presente y su Porvenir* (Mexico: 1918), p. 122.

[17] M. N. Roy, "Hunger and Revolution in India," *Gale's*, III (Aug. 1919), pp. 9, 25.

[18] *Roy Memoirs* (Aug. 30, 1953), p. 414.

held a rump session calling themselves the Communist Party of Mexico.[19]

While Gale's account of the conference is the most detailed of those available, it is highly polemical and contains enough internal contradictions to cast suspicion on points which cannot be corroborated from other sources. Gale charges that the original call for the conference was drafted by Roy and contained an endorsement of the Second International. He further states:

> Roy had never been a Socialist until two or three months previous and even then there was reason to doubt that he had been completely converted. On January 17, 1919, he wrote me: "Not being myself a Radical, I have no connection with any Radical group that would enable me to secure support for any undertaking."[20]

Gale says Roy's only interest before the conference had been to lecture and write on India. Carleton Beals, one of the Americans who knew Roy in Mexico, has written:

> Except for desiring Indian independence, he was in no sense a radical, for he believed firmly in child marriages, the caste system and most of the traditional evils that thus far have prevented India from achieving nationhood.[21]

Beals was under the impression that Roy was an Indian prince.

During September, the month of the Socialist conference, Mexico City had a visitor from the Soviet Union. He was F. Gruzenberg (later known as Michael Borodin), an agent of the Comintern posing as a Russian commercial representative. Borodin, noticing the Socialist coloration of the regular English-language page in the Mexican paper, *El Heraldo de Mexico,* paid a call on its editor, Charles Phillips. Phillips introduced Borodin to Roy, the two became good friends, and Borodin moved into Roy's home. "We learned from each other," says Roy; "in the beginning I was the gainer. He initiated me in the intricacies of Hegelian dialectics as the key to Marxism." [22]

Roy says that he invited President Carranza to dinner and introduced him to Borodin,[23] as a result of which the president made Mexican diplomatic facilities available to Borodin for communication with Moscow. Shortly thereafter, according to Roy, Borodin informed him that Lenin wanted him to come to Russia. Carleton Beals recalls:

> Borodin, I later discovered, had told Roy that if he would found a Communist party in Mexico, then get himself named delegate to the Third International

---

[19] Linn A. F. Gale, "Gompers Dominates Mexican Socialist Conference; Communist Party Organized," *Gale's,* III (Sept., 1919), pp. 7–8, 25.

[20] *Ibid.,* p. 8.

[21] Carleton Beals, *Glass Houses* (Philadelphia: Lippincott, 1938), p. 44.

[22] *Roy Memoirs* (Aug. 9, 1953), p. 379.

[23] *Ibid.* (Aug. 23, 1953), p. 402.

Congress in Moscow, he, Borodin, would assist him to promote Hindu independence, a bigger opportunity for Roy than remaining marooned in Mexico, far from the theater of activities.[24]

It was not easy to "found a Communist party," for Gale's group already called itself the Communist Party and was certainly less than friendly to Roy. Roy tried to get the Socialist Party to change its name, but failed, and according to Beals, he then "was obliged to secede with his little clique and form a second Communist Party— six members and a calico cat."[25] This group named Roy and Phillips as delegates to the Congress of the Communist International. Phillips left for Moscow via Cuba, and in November, 1919, Roy and his wife traveled to Spain on a Mexican diplomatic passport under the names of Mr. and Mrs. V. Garcia. From there they went overland to Berlin. They left behind them in Mexico three quarreling groups of radicals, two of which claimed recognition as the legitimate Communist Party of Mexico.

For Roy, Berlin was merely a stopover en route to Moscow. The Berlin Committee, which had directed the activities of exiled Indian nationalists while Germany was in the ascendancy, had now lost its main source of power, German gold. In passing through Berlin, Roy could afford to treat the Berlin Indians with considerable indifference. Though the most important member of the committee, Virendranath Chattopadhyaya, was in Stockholm, Roy met some of the other members, among them Bhupendranath Dutta and Champakraman Pillai. His memoirs indicate he had little use for any of them and was annoyed by their insistence on an accounting of the German money he had received in Mexico.[26] He was exceedingly interested in the German Communists, however, attended many meetings of the German Communist Party and became quite friendly with Heinrich Brandler and August Thalheimer. "I was immensely benefitted by the experience," he wrote. "Thalheimer took great pains to give me the English rendering of discussions. . . . They all treated me with kindness, affection and respect."[27]

The Second Congress of the Communist International

Gale's group in Mexico had also elected a delegation for the Comintern Congress, but none of the delegates had money to make the trip. As a consequence, credentials were given to Keikichi Ishimoto,

---

[24] Beals, *Glass Houses*, p. 50.
[25] *Loc. cit.*
[26] *Roy Memoirs* (Nov. 8, 1953), pp. 534–536.
[27] *Ibid.* (Oct. 18, 1953), p. 505.

a young Japanese who had visited Mexico a year before and had written from New York that he intended to go to Moscow. Gale sent Ishimoto a detailed report on the Mexican Communist movement hoping that its delivery in Moscow would discredit Roy.[28]

As to the way Roy was received in the Soviet capital, there is only his own account, published in his memoirs written many years later. He states that Lenin was cordial and that they had several private discussions on the question of strategy and tactics for colonial areas. It is not known whether Ishimoto ever reached Moscow; if he did, there is no evidence that his report hurt Roy.

At the Second Congress which met from July 19 to August 7, 1920, Roy and his wife, Evelyn, played a very active part. Roy was not the only Indian at the Congress, and in fact he represented Mexico, not India.[29] Phillips was also there, listed in the official account under his alias, Frank Seaman. The Indian delegation consisted of Abani Mukherji and a man listed as Acharya, presumably M. P. T. Acharya. Mukherji had known Roy in Bengal in 1914 and had been sent to Japan at about the time that Roy made his first trip to Java.[30] Acharya had left India in 1908 and had traveled in Europe and America. But of the Indians present at the Congress only Roy had a vote, accorded to him as head of the Mexican delegation. Evelyn Roy, Mukherji, and Acharya had only consultative votes. Both Roys (who used the name Allen at the Congress) served on the Colonial Commission, Roy representing Mexico, Evelyn representing British India.[31]

Lenin had already prepared and circulated his own formulation of policy on the colonial problem. But Roy, in his memoirs, states that

---

[28] For the text see "Report of Communist Party of Mexico to the Third International," *Gale's*, III (March, 1920), pp. 6–7, 26–27.

[29] Roy continued to travel on a Mexican passport as late as 1925. *Masses of India*, Nos. 2–3 (Feb.–March, 1925), p. 2.

[30] A. K. Hindi, *M. N. Roy, the Man Who Looked Ahead* (Ahmedabad: Modern Publishing House, 1938), p. 26.

[31] Information concerning Indian representation has been compiled from several official accounts of the Second Congress: *The Second Congress of the Communist International, Proceedings* (Moscow: Communist International, 1920), 500 pp.; *Der Zweite Kongress der Kommunistischen Internationale; Protokoll der Verhandlungen* . . . (Hamburg: Verlag der Kommunistischen Internationale, 1921), pp. 780–788; *Vtoroi kongress kommunisticheskogo internatsionala; stenograficheskii otchet* [Second Congress of the Communist International; Stenographic Report], (Petrograd: Izdatel'stvo kommunisticheskogo internatsionala, 1921), 682 pp.; and *Vtoroi kongress kominterna; protokoly kongressov kommunisticheskogo internatsionala* [Second Congress of the Comintern; Proceedings of the Congresses of the Communist International], (Moscow: Partiinoe Izdatel'stvo, 1934), pp. 619–625. Roy's use of the name "Allen" is curious, since Gale refers to an José Allen as international secretary of the Mexican Socialist Party after the two "Communist Parties" broke away. See *Gale's*, III (Sept., 1919), p. 7.

in their private conversations Lenin was so impressed with Roy's point of view that he asked Roy to draft an alternative thesis for the Colonial Commission. He further states that Lenin presented Roy's draft to the Commission with the declaration that prolonged discussion had made him doubtful of his own formulations.[32] Whether or not it was at Lenin's behest, Roy did write an alternative thesis and did submit it to the Congress. Because it embodied an entirely different evaluation of the revolutionary potential of the Indian middle class, Roy's thesis differed fundamentally with Lenin's. In the debates at the Congress, both theses were modified, and both were adopted. But even though word changes had softened the contradictions between the two documents, those contradictions remained leaving wide scope for conflicting interpretations in later years.[33]

Lenin's Strategy for Colonial Areas

The main point of disagreement between Lenin and Roy is embodied in Paragraph 11 of Lenin's preliminary draft:

11. In respect to the more backward countries and nations with prevailing feudal or patriarchal and patriarchal-peasant relations, it is necessary to bear in mind especially:

a) The necessity of all Communist parties to render assistance to the bourgeois-democratic liberation movement in such countries; especially does this duty fall upon the workers of such countries upon which the backward nations are colonially or financially dependent.[34]

Roy's disagreement is described in a contemporary Russian newspaper account as follows:

Comrade Roy arrives at the conclusion that it is necessary to eliminate from point 11 of the theses on the national problem the paragraph according to which Communist Parties must assist any bourgeois-democratic liberation movement in eastern countries. The Communist International should assist exclusively the institution and development of the Communist movement in India, and the Communist Party of India must devote itself exclusively to the organization of the broad popular masses for the struggle for the class interests of the latter.[35]

---

[32] Roy Memoirs (Jan. 24, 1954), p. 43.

[33] See The Second Congress of the Communist International, Proceedings, pp. 114–17 for Roy's thesis as amended by the Colonial Commission. By a curious accident, his unamended thesis was reproduced in most of the official documents until the error was noticed in 1934, thereby increasing the likelihood of conflicting interpretation. See Allen S. Whiting, Soviet Policies in China, 1917–1924 (New York: Columbia University Press, 1954), p. 56, and E. H. Carr, The Bolshevik Revolution, 1917–1923, III (London: Macmillan, 1953), p. 252 n.

[34] The Second Congress of the Communist International, Proceedings, p. 478.

[35] The Second Congress of the Communist International, as reported and interpreted by the official newspapers of Soviet Russia, United States Department of State (Washington: Government Printing Office, 1920), p. 43.

Roy finally succeeded in getting Lenin's wording modified, but only slightly. The critical paragraph as finally adopted reads as follows:

11. With regard to those states and nationalities where a backward, mainly feudal, patriarchal, or patriarchal-agrarian regime prevails, the following must be borne in mind: (1) All Communist Parties must give active support to the revolutionary movements of liberation, the form of support to be determined by a study of existing conditions, carried on by the party wherever there is such.[36]

The crucial change is in the elimination of the words "bourgeois-democratic liberation movement" and the substitution of "revolutionary movements of liberation." It was clear that to Lenin's mind the change was more apparent than real, for he declared in the debate, "There is no doubt that every nationalist movement can be only a bourgeois-democratic movement." [37] Such a movement, according to Lenin, was "revolutionary" so far as it opposed imperialism and campaigned for a democratic republic—the first of his revolutionary "stages."

Roy's Strategy and Tactics

Roy's disagreement with Lenin is apparent even in the amended version of his thesis adopted by the Congress. In it he argued that in the dependent countries there were "two distinct movements" which were growing farther apart each day. One was the "bourgeois-democratic nationalist movement, with a program of political independence under the bourgeois order," and the other was "the mass action of the poor and ignorant peasants and workers for their liberation from all sorts of exploitation." The former endeavors to control the latter, he said, and the Communist International should try to prevent this. The first and most necessary task, he argued, was to form Communist parties that would organize the peasants and workers and lead them to revolution and to the establishment of Soviet republics. The anti-imperialist struggle, he said, should not mean endorsing "the nationalist aspirations of the native bourgeoisie."

Lenin's theses had referred to "future proletarian parties" in the colonies and to the fact that the proletarian movement there was "still in its embryonic state." This implied that for the moment there were no important proletarian parties. Roy's thesis took the opposite view:

8) The real strength of the liberation movements in the colonies is no longer confined to the narrow circle of bourgeois democratic nationalists. In most of the colonies there already exist organized revolutionary parties which strive to be in

---

[36] *The Second Congress of the Communist International, Proceedings,* p. 574.
[37] *Ibid.,* p. 109.

close connection with the working masses. (The relation of the C.I. with the revolutionary movement in the colonies should be realized through the mediums of these
parties and groups, because they were the vanguard of the working class in their
respective countries.) They are not very large today, but they reflect the aspirations
of the masses and the latter will follow them to the revolution. The Communist
parties of the different imperialistic countries must work in conjunction with
these proletarian parties of the colonies, and through them give all moral and
material support to the revolutionary movement in general.

9) The revolution in the colonies is not going to be a communist revolution in
its first stages. But if from the outset the leadership is in the hands of a communist vanguard, the revolutionary masses will not be led astray.[38]

To sum up, Lenin and Roy disagreed on both strategy and tactics.
Lenin believed that bourgeois nationalist movements were characteristically revolutionary and that Communists should support
them. Roy believed that they were not revolutionary and, therefore,
were unworthy of support. Lenin wanted Communists to work with
bourgeois nationalist organizations because they were anti-imperialist
and because he believed there were no proletarian organizations of
any consequence at the time. Roy insisted that there were important
proletarian parties in the colonies and that Communists should work
with them in preference to bourgeois organizations. The differences
were fundamental and were to loom large when projected into the
future.

Why Roy Opposed Lenin

In view of his limited experience as a Marxist theoretician, it
is reasonable to inquire why, on the occasion of his first participation
in an international Communist gathering, Roy felt so strongly im-
pelled to oppose the theoretical formulations of the greatest Marxist
strategist of the Soviet Union. There is undoubtedly no simple answer
to this question. A major factor, no doubt, was his natural feeling
as an Asian that Asians were better able than Europeans to understand Asian conditions, and perhaps there was some resentment that
Lenin should presume to formulate strategy for such a vast area where
he had had no first-hand experience. There is no doubt that the
Russians regarded the Asian revolution primarily as ancillary to the
struggle in Europe, and Roy and other Asians frequently protested
against this emphasis on Europe, which to them resembled the very
imperialism that the Comintern was pledged to fight.

Though framed in general theoretical terms for application to all
colonial areas, Roy's arguments sprang primarily from his view of
the Indian situation. For aside from his brief tour of the Far East

[38] *Ibid.*, p. 578.

in 1915 en route to San Francisco, his own first-hand knowledge was limited to India and Mexico. And it is probable that, like many other Indians at the time, he was drawn to the Communist International not because of ideological convictions but rather because it provided political and financial support for his struggle against imperialism in India—as had the German government earlier.

Though now a Communist, Roy remained an Indian with his own definite views on India—extremist views, as is shown by his earlier allegiance to terrorism. Further evidence of this extremism can be found in his book on India written in Mexico. Though for the most part it reads like the typical anti-British tract of the period, it does have one characteristic that sets it apart—its emphasis on violence. "India will never be able to free herself from English rule by the good will of those same rulers"; Roy wrote, "the only method is bloody revolution, however desperate this appears in the present circumstances." [39] The moderate, parliamentary approach of the National Congress had been contemned by Roy and his terrorist companions, and it was certainly not out of character for Roy, once a Communist, to oppose a strategy that, in effect, credited the Congress with more revolutionary potential than any other Indian organization. How could he work with the mere "debating society," which he and his action-minded comrades had so despised?

Other, more practical considerations may also have played a part. Roy apparently had no important connections with the bourgeois Indian National Congress; his contacts were almost entirely with Bengali and Punjabi revolutionary groups, the latter having been made through Ghadr Party members in California. Moreover, as Roy recalls in his memoirs, he had been "completely out of touch with India" during his two years in Mexico. The Berlin Committee, on the other hand, had fairly good relations with the Congress. Virendranath Chattopadhyaya, its leader, was the brother of Sarojini Naidu, the most important woman in the Indian nationalist movement and a close follower of Gandhi. If the Comintern should decide to give direct support to the Indian National Congress, then Chattopadhyaya was in a better position to serve as the Comintern's agent than was Roy—assuming Chattopadhyaya was amenable, as in fact he proved to be.

Roy may have had an inkling in Berlin that the Chattopadhyaya group would approach the Communist International on this very basis. At any rate, British Intelligence later reported that in October, 1920, two months after the conclusion of the Second Congress, Chatto-

---

[39] Roy, *La India: su Pasado* . . . , pp. 174–175.

padhyaya did forward to the Communist International a detailed proposal for the organization of all Indian revolutionaries in Europe.[40]

Roy was able and exceedingly proud, and he had no desire to play second fiddle to Chattopadhyaya.[41] As long as the Comintern was inclined to support bourgeois nationalism, Chattopadhyaya would be a threat to his leadership. In his own interest, Roy might have been tempted to minimize the value of bourgeois nationalism to the Communists, and to play up the importance of the proletarian movement.

Certainly Lenin had no taste for working directly with bourgeois parties, but there was neither a Communist party in India nor any real organization of Indian Communists abroad. Moreover, he knew enough about Indian conditions to realize that it would take some time for Roy's "organized revolutionary parties" to develop into a real Communist party. According to a French Communist who attended the Second Congress:

> Patiently Lenin replied to him [Roy] explaining that for a longer or shorter period of time the Indian Communist Party would be a small party with but few members, having only weak resources, incapable of reaching, on the basis of its program and by means of its own activity, a substantial number of peasants and workers. On the other hand, on the basis of demands for national independence, it would become possible to mobilize large masses—experience had already demonstrated that amply—and it was only in the course of this struggle that the Indian Communist Party would forge and develop its organization to the point where it would be in a position, once the national demands were satisfied, to attack the Indian bourgeoisie.[42]

Whether Lenin realized it or not, his analysis of Indian conditions made Chattopadhyaya a more logical choice than Roy to head the Comintern effort in India.

Roy had a number of advantages, however, in his bid for a position of importance in the Comintern. First, he had the friendship and support of Michael Borodin. Second, he had gotten to Moscow

---

[40] Kaye, *Communism in India*, pp. 1–3.

[41] J. T. Murphy, a British Communist who met Roy at the Second Congress, describes him as "a tall fine figure of a man, with black hair and glittering eyes, a handsome Brahman. . . . Of all Indians I have met he was the most arrogant." J. T. Murphy, *New Horizons* (London: John Lane, The Bodley Head, 1941), p. 240. Commenting on this passage, Roy wrote in his memoirs: "It is true that I have always been rather stiff, if not arrogant. In the earlier days of my contact with modern ideas and modern culture, it was the expression of an inferiority complex. But in course of time, experience taught tolerance and modesty." *Roy Memoirs* (May 3, 1953), p. 210. An Indian Communist who knew Roy during this period and who later defected has written: "Self-important and ill-tempered in discussion, he was often vehement in seeking to impose his opinion upon others." Abdul Qadir Khan, *The Times* (London) Feb. 25, 1930, p. 16.

[42] Alfred Rosmer, "In Moscow in Lenin's Days: 1920–1921," *The New International*, XXI (Summer, 1955), p. 109.

first, while the Berlin revolutionaries had still not recovered from the confusion which resulted when the defeat of Germany terminated their financing. Third, and most important, Roy was a clever dialectician, accompanied by an equally clever wife, and he had enough knowledge of Marxism and of Indian conditions to convince the Russians that he was a Communist well-grounded in doctrine and a keen analyst of India's revolutionary potential. The debate on the colonial question gave him an excellent opportunity to demonstrate both qualities, and no doubt he acquired considerable prestige as the man who had forced the great Lenin to make concessions.

Yet despite his prominence at the Second Congress, Roy did not immediately become a member of the Executive Committee of the Communist International (ECCI). Although the official records show that he and the Dutch representative, Sneevliet (later known in China as Maring), tried to get the Congress to expand the Asian representation on the ECCI, which then included only one Asian, Sen Katayama, Roy states that he declined to accept membership on that body, but did allow himself to be coöpted onto the powerful five-man "Small Bureau," the supreme policy-making group of the Comintern.[43] The official records do not corroborate this, but do show that Roy became a candidate member of the ECCI at the Fourth Congress in 1922, and a full voting member in 1924 when he also joined the Presidium.

There are two possible explanations for Roy's delay in securing an influential position in the Comintern organization. The first concerns the delicate state of Anglo-Soviet relations brought about by British charges that the Russians were interfering in India. Roy may have been kept off the ECCI in order not to antagonize the British Foreign Office. The other possibility is that the Russians, at the time of the Second Congress, may not have been eager to channel all their efforts in India through him. This theory is supported by the fact that when Chattopadhyaya presented his proposal for organizing Indian revolutionaries in Europe, the Russians invited him to Moscow to discuss the plan in detail. There he met Lenin, who agreed to support the proposal if Chattopadhyaya could produce some sort of a mandate signed by leading Indian revolutionaries. Accordingly, he returned to Berlin to prepare evidence of his leadership. In February, 1921, the Russians requested him to bring to Moscow representatives of all organized Indian groups. Chattopadhyaya asked for a delay

---

[43] *Roy Memoirs* (Feb. 28, 1954), p. 98. The authors were unable to find corroborating evidence concerning Roys membership in this body. Jane Degras lists five members of the Small Bureau but does not mention Roy. Jane Degras, *The Communist International 1919–1943 Documents*, I (London: Oxford, 1956), p. 453.

until April, but by March had succeeded in assembling a group of Indians in Berlin. A Soviet representative then visited Berlin and returned to Moscow with a favorable report, whereupon money was sent to enable Chattopadhyaya's delegation to journey to the Russian capital.[44] But before discussing their visit, it is necessary to look at the activities of M. N. Roy while the negotiations with Chattopadhyaya were going on.

M. N. Roy's Mission to Tashkent

According to Roy's memoirs, one of the first projects of the ECCI's Small Bureau was to plan in detail a revolutionary strategy for Asia. The Bureau passed two resolutions: one, that a First Congress of Peoples of the East be held at Baku, and the other that a Central Asiatic Bureau of the Comintern be established in Tashkent. Roy writes that he opposed the idea of the Baku Congress, and he described it as "a wanton waste of time, energy and material resources." [45] He was, however, eager to see the Central Asiatic Bureau set up and operating. Preoccupied with this project, he declined to attend the Baku Congress and suggested that Abani Mukherji go instead.[46] The Central Asiatic Bureau was eventually established, and consisted of Roy, Georgi Safarov, and M. Sokolnikov, who acted as chairman.[47] Roy was anxious to go to Tashkent and, from among the Indian expatriates there, to recruit an army that would liberate India. These Indians were members of the Khilafat, a pan-Islamic movement having its origin in Muslim opposition to the Treaty of Sèvres which had destroyed the Caliphate of Turkey. During the 1920's the movement had taken hold among the Muslims of India and, due to Gandhi's support, had brought about a period of rare cooperation between Muslims and Hindus.

As part of their protest, Indian Muslims by the hundreds became *muhajirun* (pilgrims), leaving India in the hope either of joining Mustafa Kemal Pasha's army in Turkey or merely of taking up residence in a country ruled by a Muslim. Many went to Afghanistan whose amir had promised a cordial welcome, but finding conditions somewhat less than hospitable, they became a ragged, disillusioned lot. Roy hoped that enough of them would come to Tashkent to form an army of liberation.

---

[44] Kaye, *Communism in India,* pp. 1–2.

[45] *Roy Memoirs* (Feb. 28, 1954), p. 98.

[46] For a detailed account of the Baku Congress, see Carr, *The Bolshevik Revolution, 1917–1923,* III, pp. 260–268.

[47] *Roy Memoirs* (Feb. 28, 1954), p. 98.

Roy left Moscow for Tashkent with two trainloads of arms, gold bullion, and Indian currency.[48] With a few Indians (Pathans who had deserted from the Indian army), some Persians and other Middle Easterners he formed what he described as the first international brigade of the Red Army.

Shortly after his arrival in Tashkent word reached Roy that the Turkoman rebel forces had captured a band of Indian *muhajirun,* and were badly treating them. A Red Army detachment was dispatched to the area and managed to bring a group of about fifty of the *muhajirun* to Tashkent, on the promise that they would receive military training. Among them was Shaukat Usmani who was later to play an important part in the development of Indian communism. It is Usmani who has left the most detailed records of events in Tashkent.[49] He states that when he reached Tashkent he found two groups of "professional revolutionaries" there. One, led by M. N. Roy, included Abani Mukherji and Mohamed Ali. The other was headed by Abdul Rab, who was supported by M. P. T. Acharya and Khalil Bey (an uncle of Enver Pasha of Turkey). Of Usmani's band of *muhajirun* some, including Usmani, joined Roy, some joined Rab, and others formed a "neutralist" group.

Roy set out to indoctrinate his faction in Communist theory. "It was quite clear that before we could proceed to do anything fruitful with the emigrants," he recalls, "the educated minority should be differentiated from the fanatical mass. So to begin with, I set myself to the task of politically educating the educated few." [50] Some remained unmoved; others apparently responded with vigor, becoming as fanatically devoted to communism as they had been to the cause of the Khilafat. A considerable amount of bickering went on among all factions. The new Communist converts wanted to form an "Indian Communist Party"; Roy claims that though he did not favor the idea, he was forced to agree. Mohammed Shafiq became the first secretary of the Party, and Usmani took an active part in it.

Roy was assisted in his work in Tashkent by his wife Evelyn, whose role is mentioned by one of his Communist students, Abdul Qadir Khan, a man who later left the Communist movement and wrote about its activities for *The Times.* Khan recalls:

In so far as his [M. N. Roy's] Communistic convictions were honest, he derived them mainly from his gifted Californian wife, Evelyn Roy, a former friend and

---

[48] *Ibid.* (March 21, 1954), p. 138.
[49] See Shaukat Usmani, *Peshawar to Moscow* (Benares: Swarajya Publishing House, 1927), and his *I Met Stalin Twice* (Bombay: K. Kurian, 1953).
[50] *Roy Memoirs* (May 2, 1954), pp. 210–211.

colleague of the late Lala Lajpat Rai. She was very enthusiastic on such subjects as the fuller emancipation of the women of India, and she looked forward eagerly to a revolution in that country, of which she had no personal knowledge; but later she grew tired of the Indian revolutionaries abroad, and complained bitterly that they were never united in their aims, that they were jealous and suspicious of each other, and could not work together.[51]

The school at "India House" in Tashkent functioned for only a short period, and it is not possible to discover how many Indians were trained there. One writer familiar with events of the period fixes the number at 36, and it is not likely that there were many more than this.[52] Because of the quarreling and factionalism, it is doubtful whether anything of importance was accomplished. Many of the students wanted aviation training, and it was given to a few, although for what purpose it is difficult to imagine. When Roy was summoned to Moscow early in 1921 he took three of his students (Shaukat Usmani, Abdul Majid, and Abdul Kabir Sehrai) with him for further political training in Moscow. Abani Mukherji was left in charge in Tashkent.

Roy's Rivals Visit Moscow

Roy was called to Moscow to take part in the conference of Indian revolutionaries in Europe to which Chattopadhyaya's group had also been invited. The Russians apparently hoped to use this meeting to set up effective machinery for propaganda and organizational work in India. Chattopadhyaya's party was late in arriving, and during the delay Roy had ample time to discuss the situation with the Russians and to report on his activities in Tashkent. According to British Intelligence sources he argued that Chattopadhyaya was a nationalist, not a Communist, and that it was contrary to Communist principles to support nationalists. Had not the colonial theses of the Second Congress warned against this?

Chattopadhyaya arrived in Moscow in May accompanied by Bhupendranath Dutta, Nalini Gupta, G. A. K. Luhani, and a Maharashtrian named Khankoji. Also with the delegation was Agnes Smedley who had been associated with Chattopadhyaya for some time and who,

---

[51] *The Times* (London), Feb. 25, 1930, p. 16.

[52] Saumyendranath Tagore, *Historical Development of the Communist Movement in India* (Calcutta: Red Front Press, 1944), p. 3. This rare book was seen in Calcutta by Robert C. North who made a typewritten copy. Mr. North has made this copy available to the authors for which they would like to record their grateful acknowledgment. Although the book gives detailed information not found elsewhere, its strong bias against M. N. Roy together with several factual errors suggest that it should be used with caution.

Roy believed, was the "driving force" of the group.[53] Roy assumed that it was she who, with the assistance of Luhani, had prepared a document which contradicted Roy's "supplementary theses" of the Second Congress and on which the group was basing its arguments in Moscow. According to Roy, three of the Berlin Indians secured an interview with Lenin who referred them to Karl Radek, then general secretary of the Communist International. Radek suggested they present their thesis to the Third Congress of the Communist International, which was about to convene and which they could attend as nonvoting delegates. A commission was set up to hear their case, but they apparently failed in their bid for recognition and had no influence on the Congress. As a result, Roy claims that he was recognized as the Comintern's sole agent for India. Reporting on her husband's victory, Evelyn Roy wrote from Moscow to a correspondent in Paris:

> All work is to be carried on by the Communist Party which already exists here: here will be established the Bureau for our work and the training school for such of our people as wish to avail themselves of it. Classes have already been opened in the University and we have 17 students enrolled—the course will last three months, as they have already had some preliminary training with us. . . . All Nationalists are to seek help elsewhere: the International cannot aid Nationalist causes except through a Communist Party as intermediary. Every effort will be bent upon building up a strong Communist Party within the country [India] using those elements which we have outside who are really Communist, as preliminary workers. Headquarters will be here, and a journal issued.[54]

At the conclusion of the Third Congress, Chattopadhyaya's group was sent back to Berlin. One of them, Nalini Gupta, remained in Moscow and joined forces with Roy.

Radicalization of Indian Politics

During 1920 and 1921, while Comintern policy for India was being shaped in Moscow, the political scene in India was taking on an increasingly radical hue. The trade-union movement, which had been born immediately after the war, culminated in July, 1920, in the creation of the All-India Trade Union Congress under the presidency of Lala Lajpat Rai, the venerable Indian nationalist with whom M. N. Roy had been friendly in New York. News of the Soviet Union was beginning to interest Indian nationalists, and Marxist literature

---

[53] Shaukat Usmani states that M. P. T. Acharya and Abdul Rab were also in Moscow at this time. *Peshawar to Moscow*, p. 153.

[54] Kaye, *Communism in India*, pp. 6–7. For a description of the classes held in Moscow by Evelyn Roy for the 17 Indian students see Ernestine Evans, "Looking East from Moscow," *Asia*, XXII (Dec., 1922), pp. 972–976.

was finding its way to the bookshelves of the educated few. But most important, it was during this period that Gandhi launched his first big civil-disobedience campaign, which resulted in a massive, nation-wide protest against British rule. "A demoralized, backward, and broken-up people," wrote Jawaharlal Nehru in his autobiography, "suddenly straightened their backs and lifted their heads and took part in disciplined, joint action on a countrywide scale." There was "thunder in the air, and the atmosphere was tense and pregnant with revolutionary possibilities."

Then as the Indian earth trembled under the sandals of the millions who followed Gandhi, an incident occurred at Chauri Chaura, a little town in Uttar Pradesh. There on February 4, 1922, a mob burned a police station and killed a number of policemen. It was not the first episode of violence; there had been many others in several parts of India. But it was too much for the conscience of the Mahatma, and he suspended the entire movement at a moment when it might have become a full-scale revolution. The masses were confused by the de-cision, and the Congress leadership was resentful. "Civil resistance stopped," Nehru recalls, "and noncoöperation wilted away."

Although Gandhi's decision to halt civil disobedience caused a temporary lull in mass political activity, it stimulated a great deal of debate about the Mahatma's leadership and about techniques of winning independence from the British. These discussions helped to form an intellectual climate conducive to the spread of new theories and new ideas.

Sometime during the spring of 1921 a young Indian student by the name of Shripat Amrit Dange published a pamphlet entitled *Gandhi and Lenin*. It was a critical comparison of the two leaders in which the Indian came off second best. Dange's pamphlet came to the attention of one Ranchoddas Bhavan Lotvala, a wealthy Bombay flour-mill owner who had been interested in liberal causes. Lotvala arranged to meet the author, and was so impressed by the youth's intellectual abilities that he offered to subsidize his further study of Marxism. For several years thereafter Dange was Lotvala's protegé, and together they built up a library of Marxist literature, published translations of the Marxist classics, and actively disseminated Marxist interpretations of Indian affairs.[55] Lotvala was not mistaken in his appraisal, for Dange ultimately became a top leader in the Com-munist Party of India and today holds a position on the Politbureau, which he has occupied for several years.

---

[55] Indulal Yajnik, *Life of Ranchoddas Bhavan Lotvala* (Bombay: Atmaram Dixit, 1952), pp. 51–52.

Roy's Contacts with Indian Communists

Believing he had full Comintern support, Roy set out to make contact with Indian radicals like Dange. One of the first projects was to train a number of Indians who could be sent to India to carry out propaganda and organizational work. Several of the Tashkent students were brought to Russia and enrolled in the Communist University of Toilers of the East which had been established in Moscow in April, 1921. Evelyn Roy, in the letter already quoted, fixes their number at seventeen.

In September, 1921, Shaukat Usmani decided to return to India. This was apparently his own idea, and one which was disturbing to Roy who presumably had little confidence in him. Wishing to have an agent of his own choosing reach India first, Roy dispatched Nalini Gupta with £200 and instructions to form a Communist party in India, establish liaison with Gandhi and the Khilafat movement, and recruit Indian leaders for training in Moscow.[56] Gupta reached Colombo in November, 1921, and went on to Calcutta where he contacted Muzaffar Ahmed, one of the leaders among Roy's old terrorist comrades. Gupta apparently did not visit any other cities and left India in March, 1922, as a sailor on a liner which sailed from Calcutta.[57] Usmani covered more ground and visited Bombay in April, 1922.[58]

M. N. Roy's First Book

While Usmani and Gupta were in India, Roy was busy writing in Moscow. In line with his analysis of the role of bourgeois nationalists he began collecting material for a documented report on the "objective conditions" for revolution in India. In his memoirs Roy states that Lenin suggested the report be expanded into a book. Roy agreed, and enlisted the services of Abani Mukherji, recently returned from Tashkent, as collaborator. The book was finished in the fall of 1921 and was titled *India in Transition*. He and his wife returned to Berlin in April, 1922, and the book was published there.[59]

By contemporary standards, *India in Transition* was a stimulating piece of analysis and an effective piece of propaganda. Like most

---

[56] Kaye, *Communism in India,* pp. 7–8.

[57] Tagore says (*Historical Development of the Communist Movement in India,* p. 5) that Gupta visited S. A. Dange in Bombay, but Lt.-Col. Kaye, whose agents were watching him closely, makes no mention of it.

[58] Kaye, *Communism in India,* p. 15.

[59] M. N. Roy, *India in Transition* (Geneva: J. B. Target, 1922). The publisher and place of publication are false.

Communist literature it does not cite the sources of statistical data, much of which are in error. Roy places the blame for this on Muk-herji, particularly for the first chapter where faulty data give an exaggerated impression of the degree of capitalist development in India.[60]

The book begins by rejecting the notion, then prevalent among Communists, that India's economic and social structure was feudal. The significant political factor in India, it states, is the rising bourgeoisie, already well established. Permitted only limited participation in the economic opportunities afforded by increasing industrialization in India, the bourgeoisie has begun a political struggle against British imperialism. Parallel to the rise of bourgeois nationalism has been the increased impoverishment of the masses, which has intensely aroused their political consciousness. To prevent a union between the bourgeoisie and the masses, a union which might destroy British control, the imperialists have made political and economic concessions to the bourgeoisie in an effort to weaken the foundation for its nationalistic strivings. These concessions have caused the bourgeoisie to vacillate: on the one hand, the bourgeoisie wants a share in the exploitation of the masses, but it recognizes that much of its bargaining strength vis-à-vis the British lies in its ability to speak for the growing mass revolutionary sentiment. Thus it must maintain leadership ties with the masses. At the same time the bourgeoisie is haunted by the fear that the growing political effectiveness of the masses may eventually threaten its own existence. Thus it can be expected to compromise with imperialism and to relinquish any revolutionary role.

The most serious defect of Roy's book is its underestimation of Mahatma Gandhi's political potential. "The impending wane of Gandhism," Roy states, "signifies the collapse of the reactionary forces and their total elimination from the political movement." Gandhism he describes as "the acutest and most desperate manifestation of the forces of reaction." [61]

Roy's Activities in Berlin

Berlin, in those days, was a headquarters of a sort for many Indians living in Europe, and a good place to make contacts. It was logical for Roy and his wife to return there to set up a base for directing the Indian revolution. But in Berlin they were again challenged by Chattopadhyaya who, despite his defeat at the Third Congress, had by no means given up the idea of winning support from the

---

[60] *Roy Memoirs* (Aug. 22, 1954), p. 398.
[61] Roy, *India in Transition*, p. 205.

Comintern. Also in Berlin was Barkatullah, the former foreign minister of Mahendra Pratap's provisional Indian government, which had been set up in Kabul by the Germans during the war. Barkatullah joined forces with Chattopadhyaya who started an Indian News and Information Bureau in December, 1921, to carry on propaganda and revolutionary activity. Chattopadhyaya's Bureau contained two committees, one to direct revolutionary work, the other, consisting only of declared Communists, to work for the formation of a Communist party in India. A conference was planned for March, 1922, at which Chattopadhyaya hoped to challenge Roy's leadership of the Indian movement. Advertisements for the conference were placed in Indian newspapers.

Early in 1922, however, Barkatullah had organized an India Independence Party, and, according to British Intelligence, Soviet Foreign Minister Chicherin, who passed through Berlin on his way home from the Genoa conference, agreed to support the new group provided that Chattopadhyaya was excluded.[62] Thus although Roy was undoubtedly the primary leader of Comintern activity in India at the time he arrived in Berlin, other competitors were in the field and were receiving encouragement and money from the Russians. Whether Soviet aid to rival groups was intentional or the result of bureaucratic inefficiency, it scarcely encouraged harmony among the Berlin Indians who, since the days of Har Dayal, had shown an exceptional propensity for jealousy and petty bickering.

When Nalini Gupta returned to Europe in the spring of 1922, he, Abani Mukherji, and S. N. Kar (who had recently arrived from the United States) questioned Roy on finances, a course which probably did not endear them to him. Mukherji and Kar ultimately broke with Roy and joined Chattopadhyaya who, in turn, was deserted by Bhupendranath Dutta.

Regardless of these intrigues, Roy was able to accomplish a great deal in Berlin during 1922. He was well supplied with money, which enabled him to begin publishing a bimonthly paper called *The Vanguard of Indian Independence*. The paper appeared with remarkable regularity under different names until 1928 (see table on page 448). With the assistance of Indian seamen, Roy began to send the Comintern's *International Press Correspondence (Inprecor)* and *Vanguard* to India, copies of which were noticed by the British authorities in India in May, 1922. *Vanguard* was a great success and boosted Roy's prestige both in India and in Moscow. According to British Intelligence, *Amrita Bazar Patrika* of Calcutta was among the newspapers

---

[62] Kaye, *Communism in India*, p. 75.

influenced by *Vanguard*. Others included *Atma Sakti* of Calcutta, *In-dependent* of Allahabad, and *Nava Yuga* of Guntur (Madras presidency). Roy wrote most of the material for *Vanguard,* although Evelyn Roy wrote a number of articles under the pen name, Santi Devi. Both of them also contributed to *Inprecor.* By July, Roy had printed an English edition of *India in Transition,* and copies of it were seen in India in August.[63]

Communist Emissaries in India

Publishing Communist propaganda and smuggling it into India was only half of the job which faced Roy; an even more important task was that of building an organization in India which would distribute the material and form a Communist party. Neither Nalini Gupta nor Shaukat Usmani (who was still in India) had accomplished much, and Roy obviously had very little confidence in either of them. In fact one may assume that he didn't trust any of the Berlin Indians, for in August, 1922, he wrote to the Communist Party of Great Britain (CPGB) asking if they could send two Europeans to India, one to go to Calcutta and the other to Bombay. Roy would provide the money, although not enough for them to adopt a "European standard of living." [64]

The British Communists were able to supply only one emissary, Charles Ashleigh, a well-known Communist writer who had recently served a prison term in the United States in connection with strike activity. He had been released in February, 1922, and deported to England. The plan was for him to go to Bombay and Calcutta to contact Dange and Muzaffar Ahmed with whom Roy had been in touch by mail, and to arrange for an Indian delegation to the Fourth Congress of the Comintern. Ashleigh's mission was discovered by the British authorities, and when he arrived in Bombay on September 19, 1922, he was promptly taken into custody and notified that he would be deported. During the delay in deportation proceedings he did manage to contact Dange and other leftists in Bombay and deliver verbal messages. He was put on a ship destined for Marseilles on September 23.[65]

The failure of Ashleigh's mission was not the only disappointment. Most of the *muhajirun* that Roy had helped to train in Tashkent and Moscow had been arrested on their way home at the Indian frontier by the British authorities, and many of them confessed that they

---

[63] *Ibid.,* p. 36.
[64] *Ibid.,* p. 21.
[65] *Ibid.,* pp. 22–23.

had worked with the Communists only as a means of staying alive and getting back to India. Only one, Shaukat Usmani, did much work: he organized a few Communists in the United Provinces (now Uttar Pradesh).

Other small Communist groups were scattered around the country. In Madras, a small organization had formed around Singaravelu Chettiar, an elderly congressman with some knowledge of Marxism. S. A. Dange was the leader of the Bombay group, and Muzaffar Ahmed was in charge in Calcutta. The leader in Lahore was Ghulam Hussain, a former professor at Edwards Mission College in Peshawar, who had visited Kabul in March, 1922. Roy had contacted him there through a student named Khushi Mahomed.

Of these five groups the one in Bombay was the most important, chiefly because of S. A. Dange's organizing ability and the financial resources of his patron, R. B. Lotvala. In addition to the Rs.100,000 that he had provided to establish a Marxist publishing concern, he also set up a hostel and library for students of Marxism, and "helped to maintain a number of comrades who would devote themselves wholly to labor work." [66] The new publishing house took over an established Marathi language daily, *Induprakash,* running it on "radical and extremist lines," and in August, 1922, a weekly English-language journal, *Socialist,* was inaugurated under the editorship of S. A. Dange.

Muzaffar Ahmed had done a modest amount of propaganda work in Bengal; and Ghulam Hussain, in Lahore, started an Urdu paper called *Inquilab.* Hussain had received Rs.6,000 for this purpose in Kabul, either from Roy's agents or from the Soviet embassy. He received an additional Rs.16,000 after returning to India.[67]

Thus by the fall of 1922 M. N. Roy could justifiably claim that a foothold for communism had been established in India. Indian Communists were few and widely dispersed, and most of them had only the most elementary understanding of Marxism and world Communist strategy. Roy's contribution was that he drew them together both organizationally and ideologically, and linked them directly to the Communist International. The movement was not yet tight and well-disciplined, but it had potential. Recognizing this, the government of India began to intensify its efforts to suppress all Communist activity.

---

[66] Yajnik, *Life of Ranchoddas Bhavan Lotvala,* p. 54.

[67] Kaye, *Communism in India,* p. 13. It is Hussain's expenditures which figure in the British note to the Soviet government of May 8, 1923, the text of which is given in *The Times,* May 9, 1923, p. 11.

3 COMMUNIST ATTEMPTS TO CAPTURE THE NATIONALIST MOVEMENT

By the fall of 1922 M. N. Roy, working abroad, had brought together the components of a national organization in India. Five small Communist groups had been organized in as many major cities. It is important at this point to analyze the strategy that Roy outlined for these groups, and the methods he advised them to adopt for the promotion of revolution in India. This analysis will show that although Comintern policy for India was to take over the nationalist movement by capturing the Indian National Congress, Roy continued to oppose this policy and did his best to get the Comintern to abandon it. Failing in this, and in order to satisfy the Comintern that he was carrying out its policy, he was forced to attempt to gain influence in the Congress. But he did not cease trying to discredit the Congress in the eyes of the Comintern in the hope of bringing about a revision of its policy.

As was shown in chapter 2, Roy's first attack within the Comintern on bourgeois nationalist organizations like the Indian National Congress had come during his famous disagreement with Lenin at the Second World Congress. There Roy had argued that the Comintern should work through small "organized revolutionary parties" by which, in India, he apparently meant such terrorist groups as the Juguntar Party and the Anushilan Samiti in Bengal. Nevertheless, by December, 1921, it became clear that Roy wanted to influence— or at least to appear to be trying to influence—the bourgeois National Congress, against which he had argued so vigorously. In a manifesto

44

prepared for the 36th Annual Session of the Congress meeting in Ahmedabad he acknowledged that the Congress was "the leader of the movement for national liberation" and appealed for the adoption of a liberal economic program dedicated to raising the standard of living of the impoverished workers and peasants.[1] Only by working for the economic betterment of the masses, the manifesto stated, could the Congress hope to gain their support in the struggle for independence and thus become a real mass movement. This was a theme in much of Roy's published writing during the next year.

Tactics for Control of the Indian National Congress

Like the society from which it emerged, the Indian National Congress in the 1920's was a heterogeneous collection of groups and individuals with widely different philosophies and aims. Roy correctly looked upon the Congress, not as a tightly organized political party, but as "the traditional organ for the National struggle." [2] Within the Congress were blocs that competed for control of the entire organization, and organized factionalism was well established when Roy began to plan his tactical approach.

Roy's plan became apparent in a series of articles in *Advance Guard* (the name was changed from *Vanguard,* October, 1922, in the hope of circumventing police interception) during the summer and fall of 1922. The plan consisted of two main elements: First, those Indians who had already accepted Communist ideology were to form an opposition bloc in the Congress and try to capture the leadership. Second, congressmen with liberal social views were to be propagandized, through the pages of *Advance Guard,* in an attempt to convert them to communism; the frequent use of "we" and "our" in Roy's articles addressed to Congressmen indicates that he did not look upon the paper as an organ for Communist readers only.

He began by claiming that "Today the National Congress as a political organization is dead. Its corpse wants either to be buried or resurrected by a new breath of life." [3] Roy attributed this moribund condition to the lack of a definite economic program: "A political party is of no importance without a program," he said, "because in

---

[1] M. N. Roy and Evelyn Roy, *One Year of Non-Coöperation; from Ahmedabad to Gaya* (Calcutta: Communist Party of India, 1923), p. 11.

[2] *King-Emperor vs. Nalina Bhushan Das Gupta, Muhammad Shaukat Usmani, Muzaffar Ahmad, and Shripat Amrit Dange, in the High Court of Judicature at Allahabad, Criminal Side* (Allahabad: Superintendent Government Press [1924?]) Exhibit No. 5. This document will hereinafter be cited as Cawnpore Case Evidence.

[3] *The Advance Guard,* I (Oct. 1, 1922), p. 1.

that case it cannot count upon the conscious support of any social element."

If the Congress is to be a political party, it has to base itself on one or another of the three principal classes into which the present Indian society is divided. *It must either be the party of the landlords or of the propertied upper and middle classes or of the exploited workers and peasants.* Its program will show which class it represents.[4]

Thus the Congress had failed, so far, to identify itself with any social class. What was to be done about it? The answer was obvious:

. . . the revolutionary factions believing in mass action should form an Opposition Block within the Congress. . . . This Opposition Block, which will eventually grow into the revolutionary party of the people destined to be the leader of the final struggle, should put forth a program calculated to give fresh impetus to the waning enthusiasm of the masses and thus draw them into the political struggle.[5]

In a significant letter to S. A. Dange dated November 2, 1922, Roy revealed the inner structure of his plan, and the part the CPI was to play. The opposition bloc should be a legal mass party embracing all truly revolutionary elements; it should have a "non-offensive" name that would not raise the Communist bogey, but its political direction should be in the hands of "Communists and Socialists who alone can be the custodians of the interest of the toiling masses." However, an illegal Communist party should continue to exist side by side with this legal organization.[6]

Though the independence struggle, according to Roy, had been "deserted by the hesitating middle classes and betrayed by the compromising upper class," he was well aware that the Comintern line required him to work within the Congress. Therefore, he wrote, the new mass party which he proposed to create "must not part company with the National Congress, but bid for its leadership." [7] This was related to the second element of his plan: the attempt to influence those congressmen whose liberal views might make them amenable to Communist ideology.

Of the Congressmen whom Roy sought to influence the most important was Chitta Ranjan Das, a leading Bengali politician who in 1921 was president-elect of the Congress. C. R. Das was a liberal humanitarian, acutely conscious of the poverty of the Indian masses and eager to do something about it. He felt that the nationalist movement should promote the economic welfare of the people, and not

---

[4] *Ibid.* (Nov. 1, 1922), p. 3. Emphasis in original.
[5] *Ibid.* (Dec. 1, 1922), p. 2. Emphasis in original.
[6] Cawnpore Case Evidence, Exhibit No. 5.
[7] *Ibid.*, Exhibit No. 7c.

merely agitate for greater participation in government by a limited Indian elite. On December 10, 1921, shortly before the Ahmedabad Congress, he had been arrested and imprisoned by the British authorities for nationalist activity. He was released in July, 1922.

There is no doubt that Roy had great hopes of making a Communist or a fellow traveler out of Das, for during 1922 and 1923 Roy addressed articles and letters directly to him. The British authorities suspected at the time that the two were in direct communication, although they never produced any letters from Das to Roy.[8] Whether Roy actually had significant direct influence on Das is impossible to determine from the limited evidence available, but it is known that Roy's agents in Bengal contacted Das and supplied him with Roy's literature. It is worth noting too that there was considerable similarity between the ideas expressed by Das in some of his speeches and those contained in articles in *Vanguard.* For example, at a political conference in Dehra Dun on November 1, 1922, Das said:

> The Liberals fight shy of revolution. What is revolution but a part of that growth the totality of which we call evolution. . . . Revolution means complete change and we want complete change. I am sorry most of our non-coöperators are still enamoured of parliamentary Government.

> I do not want the sort of Swaraj [self-government] which will be for the middle class alone. . . . I want Swaraj for the masses, not for the classes. I don't care for the bourgeoisie. How few are they?[9]

Roy was also interested in another congressman, a man with the single name, Sampurnanand, who was active in the Congress organization in the United Provinces, and who later rose to the post of chief minister of that state (Uttar Pradesh) in 1954. Shaukat Usmani wrote to Roy in October, 1922, about Sampurnanand. "As he is an influential man in the Congress circle," said Usmani, "he promises to circulate the literature and books among his most trustworthy friends. That is what we want him to do." [10] During the same month Sampurnanand published a "Memorandum on the Congress Program" which, according to Roy's review of it in *Advance Guard,* apparently embodied a number of Roy's ideas. Roy described the document as "the clear voice of one of those true revolutionaries to whom belong the future leadership of our movement," and noted with ap-

---

[8] The Earl of Lytton, *Pundits and Elephants* (London: Peter Davies, 1942), p. 65, gives an unflattering evaluation of Das and charges that he had direct contact with the terrorists.

[9] *The Tribune* (Lahore), Nov. 4, 1922, p. 3.

[10] Sir Cecil Kaye, *Communism in India* (Delhi: Government of India Press, 1926), p. 30.

proval that Sampurnanand had quoted Lenin.[11] Usmani wrote Roy
about Sampurnanand again in February, 1923:

> Sampurnanand is not a Socialist much less a Communist. He is a good simple
> but revolutionary Nationalist. But I trust him and he promises help in advancing
> our work. He is sentimental but far from [Mani Lal] Shah or any other. I have every
> reason to recommend him to you—I have supplied him with immense literature and
> some books on revolutionary theories. He seems to be drawing more and more near
> our lines and days are not long that he will be a great enthusiast member of our
> party.[12]

The third man on whom Roy pinned his hopes for influence within
the Congress was Singaravelu Chettiar. He had some status in the
Congress and, as has been shown, considered himself a Communist.
He was in direct contact with Roy and worked hard to distribute
Roy's propaganda among Congress members.

It is likely that Roy and his agents, due to their revolutionary
optimism and their desire to establish their own political effectiveness, overestimated their direct influence over C. R. Das and Sampurnanand. By this time Socialist theories had found their way to
India from a number of sources and it was to be expected that some
prominent congressmen should have dabbled in them. Roy's prolific
pen made a considerable contribution to the broadcasting of these
ideas.

Roy's "Program"

The National Congress was to hold its 37th Annual Session at
Gaya on December 26, 1922. It was to be a crucial meeting, because,
as had been apparent for some months, a showdown between Gandhi
and C. R. Das was inevitable. It was at this meeting, also, that Roy
planned to put the Congress leadership to the test with his "Program
for the Indian National Congress."

The months preceding the Gaya Congress had been marked by
widespread debate throughout India between the followers of Gandhi
and of Das as to the form that noncoöperation should take. The discussion started when, in February, 1921, Gandhi called off his non-
coöperation campaign because of the violent turn it had taken at
Chauri Chaura. The debate eventually focused on the coming elections
for the new legislative councils, provided under the Montagu-Chelmsford reforms. Gandhi urged that the Congress boycott the elections
and have nothing to do with the councils; Das urged the Congress to
participate in the elections and enter the councils for the express

---

[11] *The Advance Guard*, I (Jan. 1, 1923), p. 1.
[12] Cawnpore Case Evidence, Exhibit No. 43.

purpose of wrecking them through noncoöperation at the governmental level. This question would have to be settled at the Gaya Congress.

While this debate was occupying the Congress during the summer and fall of 1922, Roy had been pointing out in *Advance Guard* articles the need for a definite program by which the Congress would show, once and for all, "which class it represents." It is not surprising, therefore, that just before the Gaya session Roy offered, through the pages of *Advance Guard,* a wide-ranging program that, if accepted, would align the Congress with the "exploited workers and peasants."

The "Program" was a comprehensive document which called for complete national independence, universal suffrage, abolition of landlordism, nationalization of public utilities, full rights for labor to organize, minimum wages in all industries, an eight-hour day, profit-sharing in industry, free compulsory education, the abolition of the standing army, and "arming of the entire people to defend the National Freedom." [13] Hundreds of copies of this issue of *Advance Guard* were sent to India for distribution among the delegates at Gaya. The British authorities intercepted 540 of them, but admitted that a large number got through.

Both the articles showing why a program was necessary, and the program itself, give the impression that Roy hoped the Congress would accept some elements of his ideology, at least. However, the November 2 letter to Dange proves that this was not, in fact, the case. For in telling Dange of his plan to draw up a program for the Gaya meeting, Roy explained:

It is needless to point out to you the object of such tactics. We want to liberate the movement from the domination of reactionary leadership. But it should be done by putting the present leadership to a test. The program we intend to bring forward will be such as to demand a certain revolutionary outlook on the part of those subscribing to it. Therefore, it is a foregone conclusion that the Congress as presently constituted will not adopt this program. And this failure of theirs will expose their true character. This will open before us the way for launching the call for a new party of the masses with its own leadership and own program having for its object the capture of the Congress, the traditional organ for the National struggle.[14]

This letter shows that Roy had no doubt as to the "true character" of the Congress, and was confident that it would reject his program. He intended his program to serve as a litmus paper by which he could conclusively show that the Congress was not red. The exposure of reactionary leadership by such methods was an approved Communist

---

[13] *The Advance Guard,* I (Dec. 1, 1922), p. 1.
[14] Cawnpore Case Evidence, Exhibit No. 5.

tactic and had been discussed many times by Zinoviev and others. Though Roy may have hoped this device would open the way for "a new party of the masses," his speech at the Fourth Comintern Congress a short time later suggests that he also hoped, by exposing the "true character" of the Congress, to persuade the Comintern to place less emphasis on capturing it.

The Fourth Comintern Congress

The Fourth World Congress of the Communist International met in both Moscow and Petrograd during November 7 to December 3, 1922. Invitations to the Congress had been issued to at least five Indians: Roy, Dange (delivered personally by Charles Ashleigh), Nalini Gupta, Chira Ranjan Das (the son of C. R. Das), and Subhas Chandra Bose, a radical Congressman. Roy's letter inviting the last two requested that they come with credentials from the Indian National Congress or some other legitimate group. But in the end only Roy attended, and thus he held India's only vote.[15]

The references to India in the speeches of Comintern leaders indicated that they were satisfied with Roy's work to date. The chairman of the Comintern, Zinoviev, said in his opening address:

> We have had valuable results in India. I can communicate to the Congress that the work of our comrades during the past few months has been crowned with success. Comrade Roy, with a group of friends, is issuing a periodical, whose task it is to smooth our way in India. Our comrades have been able to gather together the Communist elements in India. They have found entrance into the newspapers; they have entered the trade unions. I believe that this is a great step forward.[16]

Karl Radek was a little more cautious:

> In India we have already an ideological centre; I must say that Comrade Roy has succeeded in achieving a big piece of work during the last year in the Marxist interpretation of Indian conditions given in his admirable book, and also in his organ. In no other Eastern communist party has this kind of work been done. It certainly deserves to be supported by the Communist International. However, it must be admitted that as yet we have not done much in connection with the great trade union movement in India and the large number of strikes which convulsed the country. We have not yet understood to make use of the rights which our

---

[15] Kaye, *Communism in India*, pp. 27–28. That four Indians had been invited is confirmed by the report of the credentials committee; see: *Fourth Congress of the Communist International, Abridged Report* . . . (London: Communist Party of Great Britain, [1923?], p. 291.) Santokh Singh and Rattan Singh were reported to have attended on behalf of the California Ghadr Party, but there is no support for this in the official documents. British Intelligence reported that Jotin Mitra attended: *Communism in India, 1924–27*, p. 358.

[16] *Fourth Congress* . . . , p. 26.

British overlords are compelled to concede to us. The reception accorded there to Comrade Roy shows that there are some legal opportunities there. But we have not even taken the first steps as a practical workers' party, and all this means that: "It is a long way to Tipperary." [17]

Roy himself made only one speech in a plenary session of the Congress. It was in support of a draft thesis on the colonial question which he and other Asian delegates had prepared.[18] Arguing along conventional Leninist lines, Roy said that the nature of capitalist competition indicates that between imperialism and a section of the native bourgeoisie there is a potential conflict which can have revolutionary significance. To illustrate this point Roy drew certain conclusions from recent developments in Turkey:

Unless the bourgeoisie come into existence and become leaders of the society the national struggle cannot take place with all its revolutionary possibilities. So in all these countries, in proportion as the bourgeoisie is developing, the national struggle has become intensified. From this point of view, although we know there is danger of the colonial bourgeoisie always compromising with the imperial bourgeoisie, we must always on principle stand for them; that a bourgeois national movement in the colonial countries is objectively revolutionary, therefore it should be given support; but we should not overlook the fact that this objective force cannot be accepted as unconditional, and that particular historical reasons should be taken into consideration. The bourgeoisie becomes a revolutionary factor when it raises the standard of revolt against backward, antiquated forms of society—that is, when the struggle is fundamentally against the feudal order, the bourgeoisie leading the people. Then the bourgeoisie is the vanguard of the revolution.[19]

Thus Roy asserted his allegiance to the fundamental Marxist-Leninist thesis on the role of the bourgeoisie in the "democratic" stage of the revolution. He even went further, using the word "vanguard," a term which Lenin generally tried to reserve exclusively for the Communist Party. But it is important to note here Roy's emphasis on the circumstances in which the bourgeoisie is entitled to be called a revolutionary factor. It is revolutionary "when it raises the standard of revolt against backward, antiquated forms of society—that is, when the struggle is fundamentally against the feudal order, the bourgeoisie leading the people." Did Roy believe that this was, in fact, the case in India? This question is answered by the first sentence in his then recently-published *India in Transition*: "Contrary to the general notion, India is not under the feudal system." [20] And two months be-

---

[17] *Ibid.*, p. 224.
[18] *Ibid.*, pp. 208–211. This is an abridged account. Full text in *Advance Guard,* I (Jan. 15, 1923), pp. 2–3.
[19] *The Advance Guard,* I (Jan. 15, 1923), p. 3.
[20] M. N. Roy, *India in Transition* (Geneva: J. B. Target, 1922), p. 17.

fore, in *Labour Monthly,* he had written: "The nationalist bourgeoisie is not pitted against an old order of social production." [21]

In the rest of his speech Roy restated the thesis of *India in Transition;* namely, that in the economically more advanced colonial countries (*e.g.,* India), a segment of the bourgeoisie has a vested interest in the prevailing economic structure. Since this segment, according to the thesis, fears the chaos and anarchy that might result from the overthrow of foreign rule, it is willing to attenuate its patriotism in order to protect its economic interests.

In his speech Roy warned that the bourgeoisie "will go to a certain extent and then try to stop the revolution." And again:

. . . there comes a time when these people are bound to betray the movement and become a counter-revolutionary force. Unless we are prepared to train politically the other social element, which is objectively more revolutionary, to step into their places and assume the leadership, the ultimate victory of the nationalist struggle becomes problematical for the time being.[22]

The existence of Communist parties in the colonies, he argued, proved that

social factors are there, demanding political parties, not bourgeois political parties, but political parties which will express and reflect the demands, interests, aspirations of the masses of the people, peasants and worker, as against the kind of nationalism which merely stands for the economic development and the political aggrandisement of the native bourgeoisie. . . . We have to develop our parties in these countries in order to take the lead in the organization of [the united anti-imperialist front].[23]

On occasion Roy distinguished between the Indian National Congress leadership and the rank and file. For example, he had said that Chauri Chaura proved the Congress rank and file to be revolutionary, but their willingness to agree to suspension of the campaign he interpreted as showing their subservience to reactionary leadership. He was convinced that the Congress was dominated by the bourgeoisie and was therefore, as a whole, an instrument of the bourgeoisie. Thus in any discussion of the role of the bourgeosie in India, Roy was actually discussing the Congress and its policy. Indeed, the two words became practically interchangeable in Roy's writing during this period.

At the Fourth Congress, then, Roy was telling the Comintern that in India, at least, the bourgeoisie (*i.e.,* the Congress) had very little or no revolutionary utility, and that it was "the other social element" that the Comintern should support.

[21] M. N. Roy, "The Empire and the Revolution," *Labour Monthly,* III (Oct., 1922), p. 224.
[22] *The Advance Guard,* I (Jan. 15, 1923), p. 3.
[23] *Loc. cit.*

Roy failed to convince the Comintern that his analysis was correct. The thesis on the Eastern Question, as finally adopted, stated that the Communist International "supports all national revolutionary movements against imperialism." [24] But though the Comintern did not accept his arguments, it continued to support his leadership of the Indian movement. In his confidential report to the Colonial Commission, Roy stated that the Central Committee of the Communist Party of India, meeting in Bombay on September 5, had requested £120,000 from the Communist International: £35,000 was to be for Party work, £70,000 for support of labor organizations, and £15,000 for the *Socialist*. It was considerable exaggeration to refer to a "central committee," for the Indian Communists were not yet sufficiently well organized to have a central committee. Indeed, they were squabbling among themselves as to who should be leader, with no agreement in sight. Whether or not the Comintern knew this, by a vote of 18 to 3 the Colonial Commission approved the entire grant.[25] Comintern support was further evidenced in Roy's election to the ECCI as a candidate member.

The Gaya Congress

The British authorities had clearly become alarmed at the spread of Roy's propaganda, for they took special precautions to stop his publications at the ports of entry and, as has been mentioned, confiscated hundreds of copies of the December, 1922, *Advance Guard* containing Roy's program. Yet on December 21, five days before the Gaya Congress was to convene, Reuters news agency cabled Roy's entire program to the subscribing press in India, taking pains to identify it as the work of a Bolshevik.

Since Roy's literature was known to be proscribed in India, it is not surprising that some of the more sophisticated Indian nationalists began to wonder why the semiofficial Reuters agency had given his program such extensive publicity. The answer seems fairly obvious, and indeed was pointed out by some newspapers at the time: Reuters had publicized the program for the sole purpose of labeling it as Bolshevik. Even at this early date, Bolshevism had become a dangerous symbol to many Congressmen, a fact Roy recognized in recommending that his revolutionary party be given a "nonoffensive" name. Hence by branding the program a Bolshevik plot, the British could hope to discredit both the ideas contained in the program and any Indian

---

[24] *Resolutions & Theses of the Fourth Congress of the Communist International* (London: Communist Party of Great Britain [1923?]), p. 55.

[25] Kaye, *Communism in India*, p. 53.

leader who advanced them. Those most embarrassed would be C. R. Das and the other progressive leaders of the Congress whom Roy was trying to identify with his plans.[26]

Among the Communists who attended the Gaya Congress were S. A. Dange, Singaravelu Chettiar, and Mani Lal Shah. Before the Congress ended, Abani Mukherji arrived from Europe as the emissary of the India Independence Party, Roy's competitors in Berlin, with instructions to obtain recognition by the Congress. The British authorities suspected that Communist money was behind his trip, although in October Otto Kuusinen had issued a secret statement saying that the Comintern had no connection with or confidence in him.[27] Since one of Mukherji's principal aims was to discredit Roy it is not likely that his presence contributed much to unity and effectiveness among the Communists at Gaya. His main influence appears to have been with Mani Lal with whom he issued a manifesto.[28]

The Communists suffered a clear defeat at the Gaya Congress. Roy's program met with general hostility, and C. R. Das, the man on whom the Communists had counted most, not only retreated from his earlier socialist stand, but tended to take an anti-Bolshevik tone. He did argue, in his presidential address, against the "concentration of power in the hands of the middle class," but he omitted his earlier plea of Swaraj for the masses. Moreover, in urging the Congress to organize the workers and peasants he warned that "if the Congress fails to do its duty, you may expect to find organizations set up in the country by Laborers and Peasants detached from you, disassociated from the cause of Swaraj, which will eventually bring within the arena of the peaceful revolution class struggles and the war of special interests." [29] This, of course, was a clear reference to the Communists.

In the showdown between the Mahatma and Das the personality of Gandhi, rather than the merits of the arguments, determined the outcome; Das was defeated, and the Congress decided to boycott the elections and refrain from entering the new legislative councils. Nevertheless, Das had found enough support to encourage him to organize, with Motilal Nehru (Jawarhalal Nehru's father), his own party within

---

[26] This was Roy's own view. For a detailed description of the entire episode with many quotations from contemporary press comment, see: Roy and Roy, *One Year of Non-cöoperation* . . . , Chapter XI.

[27] Cawnpore Case Evidence, Exhibit No. 10b. Kaye, in *Communism in India*, p. 135, says that Mukherji was in Moscow as late as October, 1924. This would suggest that despite the Kuusinen statement, the Comintern continued to have dealings with him.

[28] Kaye, *Communism in India*, p. 77.

[29] P. C. Ray, *Life and Times of C. R. Das* (London: Oxford, 1927), p. 288.

the Congress; this new group, the Swaraj Party, participated in the elections with some success.

Although Roy had hoped the Congress would betray itself by rejecting his program, he could scarcely have wanted a reaction that would lose him what little influence he had. But this appears to have been the net result of his tactics. No doubt the Reuters dispatch played a major part in Das's retreat from socialism, and in the general hostility to Roy's program. It is an example of the brilliant maneuvers that helped a handful of clever Englishmen to rule over 300,000 Indians for almost 200 years. But the main cause of the Communist defeat at Gaya was inherent in Roy's tactical approach, at the crux of which was the question of violence.

Violence versus Nonviolence

Roy's writings suggest that the Communist attitude to violence may have been a factor in drawing him into the Comintern orbit. Communist theory endorsed violence, which was compatible with Roy's Bengali terrorist background, but it led him to a far more advanced ideological position since it deprecated individual acts of terrorism and advocated organized, full-scale, armed revolt.

That Roy regarded violent struggle to be essential is clear from his articles written as early as during his Mexican period, and there was hardly an issue of *Vanguard* that did not contain some sort of appeal for violent revolution. For example, in the June, 1922, issue of *Vanguard*, Roy said: "The government maintained by violence and brute force cannot be overthrown without violence and brute force." [30] And though political expedience might have suggested that he soft-pedal his theme in deference to the Gandhian ideal of nonviolence, Roy waged a head-on propaganda battle against nonviolent revolution; in December, 1922, he wrote:

We have repeatedly said and still say that a premature resort to voilent tactics may be playing into the hands of the enemy. But it is altogether erroneous to think that there can be such a thing as a "non-violent revolution," no matter how "peculiar and abnormal" the situation in India may be. The cult of nonviolence is inseparable from an anti-revolutionary spirit. Those who do not want a *revolution* in India can pin their hope on non-violent methods. Strictly nonviolent methods are hardly distinguishable from constitutional agitation, and no people on the face of the earth has ever made a revolution by constitutional methods.[31]

Another example of Roy's views is provided in the Comintern message to the Indian National Congress annual session at Gaya

---

[30] *The Vanguard of Indian Independence,* I (June 15, 1922), p. 5.
[31] *The Advance Guard,* I (Dec. 1, 1922), p. 2. Emphasis in original.

(signed by Humbert Droz, secretary of the presidium of the Fourth Comintern Congress). Typewritten copies of this manifesto, bearing corrections in Roy's handwriting, were intercepted by the British authorities in India, and Roy later published the entire text in *Advance Guard*. It contained these significant paragraphs:

British rule in India was established by force and is maintained by force; therefore it can and will be overthrown only by a violent revolution. We are not in favor of resorting to violence if it can be helped; but for self-defense, the people of India must adopt violent means, without which the foreign domination based upon violence cannot be ended. The people of India are engaged in this great revolutionary struggle. The Communist International is wholeheartedly with them.

The economic, social and cultural progress of the Indian people demands the complete separation of India from imperialist Britain. To realize this separation is the goal of revolutionary nationalism. This goal, however, cannot be attained by negotiation nor by peaceful means.[32]

Mahatma Gandhi, the symbol of nonviolence, was therefore anathema to Roy, particularly after Gandhi called off the 1920 noncoöperation campaign just when it might have become a full-scale revolution. It is hard to imagine anything that could have roused a Communist to greater anguish. Concerning this incident Roy wrote bitterly:

The national uprising which they [the government] had feared and prepared against during the last three months, was checked and thrown into rout by the good offices of Mr. Gandhi himself, whose incorrigible pacifism and dread of the popular energy could be counted upon to prevent the explosion. What government repression in all its varied forms had failed to accomplish, the agonized appeal of the Mahatma was able to effectuate. . . . That which arrests, tortures, floggings, imprisonments, massacres, fines and police-zoolums [oppression] could not quell—the blind struggles of a starving nation to save itself from utter annihilation—Mr. Gandhi by the simple magic of love and non-violence, reduced to impotence and inactivity. . . . The Congress had committed suicide by repudiating the revolutionary action of its own followers. A powerful revolutionary movement had been sacrificed on the altar of Gandhism.[33]

During 1922 *Vanguard* had carried a series of articles dealing with Gandhi. They were careful to point out the saintly character of the Mahatma and the importance of his contribution in uniting the masses, but they attacked his social theory and in general charged him with being a protector of the reactionary or traditional interests in Hindu society. Several of these articles, written by Evelyn Roy, were a persuasive and in some ways realistic appraisal of Gandhi's political role. (See chapter 21.) Indeed, in the Roys' attack on Gandhism there was

---

[32] "To the All India National Congress, Gaya, India," *ibid.* (Jan. 1, 1923), p. 3.
[33] Roy and Roy, *One Year of Non-coöperation* . . . , pp. 40–41.

much that could have been accepted by the bourgeois intellectuals whom they were addressing, and these articles might have had a considerable effect on Congress politics had it not been for their overemphasis on violence. But the Congress was too full of respectable middle-class elements and intellectuals to whom the idea of going to the barricades was completely repugnant; to preach violence to them was to lose their confidence, and to destroy the audience for radical economic ideas. Certainly Roy's attitude toward violence was an important factor in the alienation of C. R. Das who, in his presidential address at Gaya, had said:

I cannot refuse to acknowledge that there is a body of Indian opinion within the country as well as outside according to which non-violence is an ideal abstraction incapable of realization, and that the only way in which Swaraj can ever be attained is by the application of force and violence. I do not for a moment question the courage, sacrifice and patriotism of those who hold this view. I know that some of them have suffered for the cause which they believe to be true. But may I be permitted to point out that apart from any question of principle, history has proved over and over again the utter futility of revolutions brought about by force and violence. I am one of those who hold to non-violence on principle.[34]

Das was not the only one to be frightened by Roy's emphasis on violence. In his speech at Gaya even Roy's own man, Singaravelu, had felt obliged to endorse nonviolence. "That method has been disputed by our fellow communists abroad," he said in an obvious reference to Roy. "I told them that we have adopted that method as a practical necessity, and that I believe in that method. Therefore, they differ fundamentally as to method." [35]

It is quite possible, of course, that C. R. Das and Singaravelu were merely shrewd politicians, quick to adjust to the new climate of opinion created by Gandhi's exceptional qualities of leadership. Regardless of their own views on nonviolence, they may have decided that for the time being it was poor politics to oppose it. Roy was at a disadvantage in being far from the scene. He had seriously underestimated the impact of Gandhi and his ideology, and he may also have been mistaken in accepting the statements of Das and Singaravelu at face value.

At any rate, it is clear that by taking so explicit a stand in favor of violence Roy was placing himself and the Communists in opposition to Gandhi on an issue of primary importance to the latter. To be sure, the noncoöperation movement did generate a high potential for violence, as Chauri Chaura and other incidents proved, and there were,

[34] Ray, *Life and Times of C. R. Das,* pp. 267–268.
[35] *The Vanguard,* II (April 15, 1923), p. 3.

no doubt, many Congressmen who were prepared to allow violence to take its course while they paid lip service to the Mahatma's ideals. But to proclaim the virtue or the necessity of violence, or to be associated with anyone who did, was another matter entirely. This, Roy failed to recognize.

One should not, however, overlook the possibility that Roy advocated violence with the deliberate intention of frightening Congressmen into denouncing Bolshevism. Certainly this would be consistent with his desire to separate the reformists from the revolutionaries and, more important, to prove that the Congress as then constituted was hopelessly unrevolutionary. But whatever Roy's reasons for doing so, his blatant sanction of violence during this period alienated the average Congressman, and thus made it impossible for the Communists to harness the revolutionary dynamism generated by the peace-loving little man in the loincloth.

4   ORGANIZING THE VANGUARD

Gandhi's triumph at Gaya was a great blow to M. N. Roy and the Indian Communists. Roy's plan had failed. "We sought to strengthen the hand of the Left Wing, but only succeeded in frightening it," he admitted in *Inprecor*.[1] "It is, however, a gain," he added, for though he had alienated potential sympathizers in the process, he had succeeded in "exposing" the Congress leadership as unrevolutionary.

Now Roy's tactical aims became clearer. He still advocated the organization of a revolutionary party within the Congress, and he continued to hope that C. R. Das would lead it. His emphasis, however, was no longer on capturing the Congress, but on building the Indian Communist Party that would, while working both within and without the Congress, eventually capture the sole leadership of the national revolutionary movement.

With the issue of February 15, 1923, *Advance Guard* once again became *Vanguard*, and for the first time the words "Central Organ Communist Party of India" appeared on the masthead. The lead article of this issue was an editorial entitled "Ourselves," which outlined the new policy beginning with an appraisal of the Congress:

With all its desire to enlist the support of the masses, and with all its virtuous schemes of uplifting the downtrodden, the Congress as a body *will remain a bourgeois political organ.* It will never be able to lead the workers and peasants in the revolutionary struggle for national freedom. . . . Therefore the organization

---

[1] M. N. Roy, "The Indian National Congress," *Inprecor*, III (March 1, 1923) p. 127.

of a party of the workers and peasants has become an indispensable necessity.
The Communist Party of India is called upon by history to play this role. . . .
It is only under the banner of the Communist Party that the masses can be
organized and led into the national struggle as the first stage of a great revolutionary
movement for liberation. So, those who sincerely stand for the interests and
welfare of the toiling masses must swell the ranks of the Communist Party, the
leader of the workers and peasants—the *Vanguard* of National Revolution. . . .
We will fight as part of the National Congress; by fearless criticism, vigorous
agitation and constant propaganda we will endeavour to push the middle class
nationalists forward in the struggle; we will coöperate with every social element
that is objectively antagonistic to the imperialist domination; and we will stand
shoulder to shoulder with every political party so long as it carries on the struggle
against foreign domination.[2]

Taken at face value this article seemed to imply a shift. Whereas
previously Roy had advised the creation of a mass party with a "non-
offensive" name to operate parallel to an illegal Communist Party
and be controlled by it, here he appears to be suggesting that the
Communist Party itself become the mass organization.

In an "Open Letter to Chitta Ranjan Das and His Followers," in
the same issue of *Vanguard,* he wrote: "There is room for only three
parties in the Congress. Two are already in the field. You have to be
either the third, that is, the political expression of the working masses,
or nothing." According to Roy both the other two parties were the
instruments of the reformists and the reactionaries. It would be reasonable to conclude from this article that Roy was suggesting that Das
should head a new revolutionary party. Yet Das was the man whom
Roy regarded as a "sentimentalist and not a revolutionary" and whose
ideas, he said in a letter to Dange on March 8, 1923, were equally as
harmful as Gandhism.[3] Roy continued to try to influence Das at least
as late as June, 1923, when, under elaborate, but as usual ineffective
security arrangements, he wrote to him again from Berlin, asking him
to come to Europe and offering financial assistance. In the letter he
said that Das could "rally all the available revolutionary elements
within and without the Congress, thus marking the beginning of the
revolutionary mass party, which is the crying need of the day and
which will alone save the Congress." [4]

It is not unusual for a Communist to court a bourgeois leader for
whom he really has no respect. But for Roy it was imperative that he
get a foothold in the Congress, since this is what the Comintern wanted
him to do. The extent of his desperation is evident in an incident

---

[2] "Ourselves," *Vanguard of Indian Independence,* II (Feb. 15, 1923), pp. 1–2. Emphasis added.

[3] Cawnpore Case Evidence, Exhibit No. 21, p. 6.

[4] *Ibid.,* Exhibit No. 19, p. 38.

that took place early in 1923. Roy had received a letter from one
Baidyanath Biswas, on the letterhead of the Bengal Trade Union
Federation, offering to coöperate with Roy and to come to Europe
if Roy would send the necessary funds. Roy had already been informed
by Muzaffar Ahmed that Biswas was a police spy. Nevertheless Roy
wrote Ahmed on February 18, 1923, saying:

Baidyanath Biswas wishes to come here as representative of the Bengal Trade
Union Federation and the All India Trade Union Congress. But he will not
be able to come without passage expenses. I remember what you wrote about
Baidyanath. But for various other reasons it is necessary to bring him or someone
else of their organization here. I must contrive to effect an entry into all these
organizations, whatever be the means. Of course, nothing is gained by falling
into the hands of Government spies. But there is no reason to suppose that
Baidyanath or his co-workers are Government spies. The blame rests with those
big folks who sit at the top and are publishing names. These smaller ones at
the utmost want to be leaders. . . . I want Baidyanath to be brought here.[5]

Ahmed replied on March 21, 1923:

You must know that I did not write to you anything without knowing. There is
not the slightest doubt that Baidyanath Biswas is a permanent spy. As you have
warned us against Mukherji so it is our duty to warn you against such men. It
is within your power to heed us or not. By what have you been deluded? Is it
on seeing the name of Trade Union of Bengal? The "Bengal Trade Union
Federation" simply means a printed letter heading and a rubber stamp. There
is nothing else. How can there be a representative of it? I have written to you
time after time that more [than] 90 per cent of the Trade Unions here are
Government organizations. . . . If money be available, good men will be sent.
Do not make a mistake without understanding. . . . Brother, conduct yourself
with some circumspection. If you correspond with anybody and everybody, everything will be spoiled.[6]

Whether Biswas was actually a spy was not so important as the fact
that Roy's most able agent in Calcutta said he was. By showing such
scant regard for his advice, Roy could hardly have boosted the morale
of the best organizer he had in Northern India. That he was willing to
do this is a measure of the importance he attached to bringing some
nationalist leader to Europe.

Communication Problems

Roy was greatly handicapped in his work by inadequate facilities
for communication. News was slow in reaching him, and his correspondents were not the most accurate reporters or the most penetrating analysts. Indian politics, in 1923, was complicated, and difficult

---

[5] *Ibid.*, Exhibit No. 146, p. 9.
[6] *Ibid.*, Exhibit No. 15a, pp. 15–16.

to understand; added to this were the attempts of Abani Mukherji to undermine Roy's position, which further increased the factionalism and confusion. But perhaps most important was the remarkable efficiency of the British CID. The director of the Indian government's Intelligence Bureau said of Roy some years later:

His "contacts" with this country during the past few years have been tolerably well known, and his correspondence has been extensively read. It has been an unfailing source of information of proved accuracy as to the movements of men, money and literature, and the knowledge derived from it has been used more than once to the discomfiture of our enemies.[7]

Several times the British authorities intercepted money in such a way as to create suspicion of financial dishonesty between the sender and the receiver. Certainly the record of the CID during this period is an excellent example of how effectively a conspiratorial organization can be controlled by imaginative police work. There was evidently very little that went on among the Communists that the CID did not learn about sooner or later.

For a considerable period Roy tried to route all his correspondence to India through R. C. L. Sharma, a resident of Pondicherry, the French enclave on India's east coast. He assumed that mail addressed to the French possession would not be subject to examination by the British authorities, and Sharma was supposed to arrange to smuggle it into India by couriers. The assumption proved false, and whether through French coöperation or otherwise, Roy's correspondence did not escape the scrutiny of the British authorities.

With the exception of Muzaffar Ahmed and S. A. Dange, Roy's contacts in India were of a very low caliber. Sharma was hardly an ideal person to act as Roy's main communication link with India. Before he began working for Roy in January, 1923, he had offered his services as an informer to the British. He had even volunteered to go to Afghanistan and report on activities there. "As he was constitutionally incapable of playing straight," said the director of Intelligence a few years later, "he was not employed: He is now [1926] deeply committed to M. N. Roy, but would doubtless sell him reasonably cheaply." [8]

Roy had a little better luck in his correspondence with Singaravelu, in Madras, who was able to use the respected newspaper *The Hindu* as a cover address and thus avoid interception. This arrangement

---

[7] *Communism in India, 1924–27* (Calcutta: Government of India, 1927), p. 127.
[8] Sir Cecil Kaye, *Communism in India* (Delhi: Government of India, 1926), p. 91.

was ultimately discovered by the management and was terminated with an announcement on August 25, 1923.[9]

Organizational Difficulties in India

After the Gaya Congress there were two basic things that Roy wanted to accomplish. First, he wanted the Indian Communists from all over the country to meet and form an all-Indian organization. Second, he wanted to bring a small delegation of Indian Communists to Europe for a conference.

In February, 1923, Singaravelu issued a manifesto in preparation for the all-India conference recommended by Roy. He hoped to make his own recently formed Labor and Kisan Party in Madras the center of a new country-wide organization. Among those to whom copies of the manifesto were sent was Mani Lal Shah in the United Provinces. Mani Lal had returned to India from the Fiji Islands where he had been politically active in behalf of Indian immigrants. Back in India he had become involved in trade-union work and was in contact with various Communists and Socialists, among them Roy's enemy, Abani Mukherji.

When Mani Lal received Singaravelu's manifesto, he and Abani Mukherji made a few changes and reissued it in March as their own. They sent copies to Dange, Ghulam Hussain, and even to Roy and Singaravelu. The next month Hussain responded by issuing a circular letter calling for a meeting in Lucknow on June 30, 1923, "to organize Dr. Mani Lal's Manifesto Party." [10] When Singaravelu saw what was happening he protested in letters to both Roy and Hussain. "What you call Mani Lal's manifesto," he told Hussain, "was our draft manifesto originally framed by us." He also complained that his own call for a conference had been virtually ignored by the Communists scattered about India. S. A. Dange, for example, had not even answered Singaravelu's letters.

In Europe Roy received the Mani Lal manifesto and recognized that it had been plagiarized from Singaravelu. He also detected the hand of Abani Mukherji whom he knew to be working in India to take the leadership of the Communist movement away from him. It is not surprising, therefore, that he immediately denounced the Mani Lal document as "spurious" and gave his full support to Singaravelu. He wrote to Dange requesting him "very urgently to get in touch with Singaravelu without delay. . . . I am convinced he is the best

[9] *Ibid.*, p. 103.
[10] *Ibid.*, p. 79.

man available to be the figurehead of the legal party," he told Dange. "He provides us with an access into the ranks of the Congress which is very valuable. Through him we can lay our hands on the labor Sub-Committee [of the Congress]." [11]

Hoping that the confusion would be dispelled and that the Indian Communists would meet under Singaravelu's leadership, Roy sent a memorandum dated June 5, 1923 for the guidance of the conferees.

The memorandum made it clear that Roy had returned to his original idea of building two parties—a mass party to be called the Workers' and Peasants' Party (WPP), and an illegal Communist Party. The CP would be "the illegal apparatus of the legal mass party," and all members of the CP would automatically be members of the Workers' and Peasants' Party.[12] Roy urged that the new WPP should send a delegate to the Communist International. Formal affiliation would not be possible since the party would not be a true Communist party, but fraternal relations could be established.

In the realm of strategy Roy said that the new party should seek a "working alliance" with bourgeois nationalist parties "during the anti-imperialist struggle" using "every available opportunity for striking an agreement" in order to put pressure on the bourgeois nationalist movement and bring out its "revolutionary significance." Missing from the manifesto was any specific reference to the Congress Party or the necessity of capturing it.

In the realm of tactics Roy showed that he had learned a lesson from the Gaya experience. The Communists should "leave out of our propaganda the controversy of violence vs. nonviolence," he said. "That will be the best tactical move we can make without giving the lie to our program." But at the same time he maintained that the emancipation of the exploited "cannot be done by peaceful and non-violent means."

In the end, the all-Indian conference did not take place. The chief reason was the personal rivalry among the Communists in India. This rivalry was, in a sense, a reflection of the situation that existed in Berlin where Chattopadhyaya still cherished hopes of replacing Roy in the Comintern. If Mukherji, with Mani Lal's help, had been able to convene a conference it would have been a victory for Chattopadhyaya. If Singaravelu had succeeded, it would have been a victory for Roy. But both failed, and for several years the Indian Communists remained unable to form a single, unified, country-wide organization.

It is interesting that Roy backed Singaravelu without having seen

[11] Cawnpore Case Evidence, Exhibit No. 23, pp. 9–11.
[12] *Ibid.*, Exhibit No. 13, p. 29.

a copy of his manifesto, although, according to British Intelligence, Singaravelu did send Roy a copy.[13] Six months after the events just described, Roy wrote a comrade in India stating that he had endorsed the manifesto on the basis of what he had been told about it, and that when he actually saw it much later, he found it to be just as bad as the Mani Lal document. He was especially critical of its denunciation of Bolsheviks and foreign agents, for such remarks would make it difficult to get funds for the new party from the Comintern.[14]

Roy was in Moscow in June, 1923, to attend the third plenum of the enlarged ECCI, and his memorandum to the WPP conference was probably written there. It is not clear whether Roy was able at this plenum to convince the ECCI that it should no longer attempt to capture the Congress Party, but he apparently succeeded in getting its agreement that the WPP should exist separately. This can be deduced from the message which the ECCI sent to the projected WPP conference. Dated June 14, 1923, and signed by Kolarov it said:

It is clear that the workers and peasants on whose shoulder falls [sic] the greatest part of the burden of imperialist exploitation, can no longer remain an adjunct to bourgeois nationalism to act or keep quiet at its bidding. . . . the working class must come forward as an independent political force and take up the leadership.[15]

But the ECCI did not accept Roy's view of the bourgeoisie, for the message continued:

Indian bourgeoisie is a revolutionary factor, because its interests are objectively in conflict with imperialism. The struggle for national liberation is a revolutionary movement. In leading this movement the political party of the workers and peasants must act in coöperation with, and give fullest support to, the bourgeois parties in so far as they struggle against imperialism in some way or other.[16]

Government Measures Against the Communists

As has been mentioned, the government had already taken legal action against the Communist movement with the arrest and trial of nine of the returned *muhajirun* in the Peshawar Conspiracy Case. The police had been looking for Shaukat Usmani in this connection, and on May 31, 1923, when he went to a post office to pick up £25 sent by Roy, he was arrested. This action, no doubt, had an unsettling effect on the other leading Communists. Shortly thereafter Muzaffar Ahmed and Ghulam Hussain were also arrested and interned.

---

[13] Kaye, *Communism in India*, p. 84.
[14] *Ibid.*, p. 85.
[15] Cawnpore Case Evidence, Exhibit No. 15, p. 32.
[16] *Ibid.*, p. 33.

These arrests completed the demoralization of the Indian Communists. It was obvious that the authorities were cracking down. In July, 1923, they tightened up their censorship methods, and as a consequence no less than 1,485 copies of *Vanguard* of June 1 and 1,124 of June 15 were intercepted in Bombay.[17] Surveillance work was also stepped up to the extent that in July, Dange wrote Roy that he was taking the position of an "open organizer" because he was too strictly watched to form any illegal apparatus. "Elements for an illegal apparatus are absolutely lacking in the people about," he added. "Gandhism had destroyed the mentality and elements of secrecy." [18]

For the balance of 1923 the Communist movement in India remained crippled and disorganized. Roy admitted that his work had been "seriously hampered," but the greatest frustration was shown by his wife Evelyn. She wrote to a Bengal revolutionary in July, 1923, saying that the idea of British tyranny should be so impressed upon the upper classes as to "goad a few of them into fanaticism who will begin desultory acts of bloodshed. This will demoralize the Whites. . . . Let there be chaos; even that is better than the lifeless existence of the people." [19]

By December, 1923, it was obvious that the French authorities in Pondicherry were extending full coöperation to the British, for in that month they proscribed *Vanguard* and *Inprecor* and confiscated a trunk full of Communist literature addressed to Sharma. Sharma had offered to go to Europe if facilities were provided, and Roy had sent his agent, Sipassi, to Pondicherry with money and a Persian passport for Sharma. But no sooner had he arrived than the French authorities ordered him to leave, and interned Sharma in a small village some distance from the port.[20] Roy's main transmission line to India was thus completely broken.

In January, 1924, the government of India completed a brief on Communist activities in India, which it submitted to counsel for recommendations concerning legal action. The brief dealt with all members of

---

[17] Kaye, *Communism in India,* p. 99.

[18] Cawnpore Case Evidence, Exhibit No. 24, p. 11. Speaking of the nationalist movement as it was in 1921, Nehru wrote in his autobiography: "There was no more whispering, no round-about legal phraseology to avoid getting into trouble with the authorities. We said what we felt and shouted it out from the housetops. What did we care for the consequences? Prison? We looked forward to it; that would help our cause still further. The innumerable spies and secret-service men who used to surround us and follow us about became rather pitiable individuals as there was nothing secret for them to discover. All our cards were always on the table." Jawaharlal Nehru, *Toward Freedom* (New York: John Day, 1941), p. 69.

[19] Kaye, *Communism in India,* p. 97.

[20] *Ibid.,* p. 108.

the conspiracy, from Roy to those who had permitted the use of their addresses as covers for the active Communists, and contained detailed statements concerning Roy, Muzaffar Ahmed, Shaukat Usmani, Ghulam Hussain, S. A. Dange, Singaravelu Chettiar, R. C. L. Sharma, Nalini Gupta, S. D. Hasan, M. P. T. Velayudham (an associate of Singaravelu in Madras), Sampurnanand, Mani Lal, and Satya Bhakta (active in the United Provinces). The government counsel recommended prosecution of the first eight of these, but made no recommendations against the remaining five. It is significant that Abani Mukherji was not charged, and that he was able to return to Europe in March, 1924. The British were convinced that Mukherji had come to India "with the secret approval of the Communist International," and this seems confirmed by his subsequent visit to Moscow.[21] But they also knew that he was working against Roy, and it therefore seems likely that they felt it would be more damaging to the Communist movement to allow him to remain free to cause trouble for Roy. According to British Intelligence, Mukherji was enough of a nuisance to provoke Roy into expressing his determination to have Mukherji murdered if he should ever return to Berlin.[22]

The Cawnpore Conspiracy Case

On February 27, 1924, a complaint was filed in Cawnpore charging that Roy, Gupta, Ahmed, Usmani, Dange, Hussain, Sharma, and Singaravelu had "entered into a conspiracy to establish throughout British India a branch of a revolutionary organization known as the Communist International with the object of depriving the King of the Sovereignty of British India." [23] However, when the trial began in April, 1924, there were only four defendants: Gupta, Usmani, Dange, and Ahmed. Roy and Sharma were not in the country and could not be apprehended. Hussain had turned informer, and the charges against him were withdrawn. Singaravelu was certified to have been too ill to travel to the court from Madras, and was excused.

The Cawnpore trial began in April, and was concluded on May 20, 1924. Dange admitted that he had been in correspondence with Roy, but insisted that he had disapproved of Roy's program and was

---

[21] *Ibid.*, p. 121.

[22] *Ibid.*, p. 90. Kaye may have inferred too much from a letter from Roy to Nalini Gupta dated Berlin, August, 1923, in which he said: "Where is that Vagabond gone? Is he still in the country? If he comes here, I shall perform his sradh [death rites]." (Cawnpore Case Evidence, Exhibit No. 54, p. 5.) Under cross examination by counsel for the defense in the Cawnpore Conspiracy Case, Kaye denied that he had employed Abani Mukherji.

[23] Cawnpore Case Evidence, Introduction, p. 5.

not engaged in a conspiracy. The other defendants denied everything, but the evidence against them all—including correspondence in their handwriting—was so compelling that convictions were easily secured, and they were sentenced to four years' imprisonment. The effect of the trial was to cripple the Communist movement, for it removed the most effective Communist leaders from the political scene and it frightened off potential recruits with the threat of prosecution and imprisonment.

It is significant that when the Cawnpore Case was appealed to the High Court, the two appeal judges in a lengthy judgment handed down on November 10, 1924, described the conspiracy as "absurd and unbelievable" and in effect conceded that the scheme had never been a real threat to the security of the state.[24] The defendants had, however, acted "in the most serious spirit" and the appeal was denied.[25] Roy's reaction to the case was one of contempt for the defendants. "Poor fellows," he wrote in November, 1924. "If they could only have put up a better defense, four years in jail would have been worth while. We must have better Communists than this lot; and the defending Councils [sic]. By God, what fools! . . . With a better lot in the dock and less stupid heads at the Bar, the Cawnpore case could have been made an epochmaking event in our political history." [26]

Difficulties for Roy in Europe

While the law was being invoked against the Communists in India, Roy was having similar difficulties in Europe. In September, 1923, he realized that there was danger that the Germans would ask him to leave the country. Consequently, he made a trip around Europe visiting Zurich, Marseilles, Paris, Genoa, and Amsterdam for the purpose of finding a suitable place to set up headquarters and publish *Vanguard*. He was also seeking assistance from fraternal Communist parties in devising means of getting his publications through the British censorship screen, whose effectiveness was painfully evident to him.

When the Germans did expel him in January, 1924, Roy went to

---

[24] This statement appears in L. F. Rushbrook Williams, *India in 1924–25*, (Calcutta: Government of India, 1925), p. 100. That the Communists had not accomplished much before the Cawnpore Case was also the opinion of D. Petrie, director of the government of India's Intelligence Bureau in 1927. Said Petrie: "It may be accepted . . . that Roy's 'illegal party' was never capable of much mischief and had, in point of fact, accomplished but little when the Cawnpore prosecution cut short its activities." *Communism in India, 1924–27*, p. 70.

[25] Williams, *India in 1924–25*, p. 100.

[26] *Communism in India, 1924–27*, p. 96.

Zurich and had *Vanguard* published there. This arrangement apparently only continued for two months, however, for the last issue of the paper to be published from Zurich was probably that of March 1, 1924, since the Zentralbibliothek in Zurich declares its file, which ends with this issue, is complete.[27] From Zurich Roy addressed a letter (dated February 20, 1924) to Prime Minister Ramsey MacDonald inquiring if he could be granted amnesty for his early terrorist activity and permitted to return to India. This was before the Cawnpore Conspiracy Case, for when news of the case reached him Roy must have realized that his chances of getting back to India legally were nil.

According to British Intelligence, Roy transferred his headquarters from Zurich to Annecy in France, probably after the March 1 issue of *Vanguard*. Apparently he went to Moscow while Evelyn carried on *Vanguard* from France, for the same source also quotes a letter from him to Evelyn written from Moscow in March, 1924, in which he states that the Comintern had decided to give increased financial assistance to its "Near Eastern Section." "Almost unlimited funds have become available," he added.[28]

Sometime during the next three months Roy's headquarters were shifted again, this time to Paris. It is not clear whether Roy himself returned to France from Russia before the Fifth Comintern Congress, but it does seem fairly certain that he did not remain in the Soviet Union from March until June, for British Intelligence reported his visiting Berlin June 6, 1924, en route to Moscow, and the ECCI in Moscow specifically reports that no Indian delegate was present at its June 12 meeting.[29] Abani Mukherji, however, did arrive in Paris in March, 1924, and although it is not known how long he stayed there or with whom he met, it may be assumed that whatever he had to say about the Indian movement was not favorable to Roy. British Intelligence later reported Mukherji to have been in Berlin in August and in Moscow in October, 1924, missing Roy on both occasions.[30]

The Fifth Comintern Congress

Despite the fact that Mukherji had probably been undermining him in Paris, and Chattopadhyaya was unfriendly to him in Berlin,

---

[27] Sir Cecil Kaye states that *Vanguard* was later printed in Marseilles by Paul Senf, one of Roy's agents. In 1952 one of the authors consulted a file of *Vanguard* for 1924 in the New York Public Library. He drew the attention of the staff to its poor condition, and suggested that this valuable collection be microfilmed. No film was made, however, and the original was "discarded."

[28] *Communism in India, 1924–27*, p. 78.

[29] *Inprecor*, IV (June 18, 1924), p. 341.

[30] Kaye, *Communism in India*, p. 135.

Roy's prestige in the International was apparently in no way diminished, for when the Fifth Comintern Congress convened on June 17, 1924, he was elected a full member of the ECCI and a candidate member of its presidium.[31]

Sometime before the Fifth Congress was to convene the ECCI had issued a detailed report to be discussed within the various branches of the Comintern. The report's recommendations concerning India were limited to setting forth the tasks of the Indian Communist Party as:

> Restoration of the national liberation movement (abandoned by the big bourgeoisie) on a revolutionary basis; formation of a national peoples' party which is to comprise the urban petty-bourgeoisie, the pauperized intellectuals, the small clerks, the rebellious peasantry and the advanced workers; establishment of a proletarian class party.
>
> The Indian Communist Party must bring the trade union movement under its influence. It must reorganize it on a class basis and must purge it of all alien elements.[32]

This cautious recommendation did not say whether the "national peoples' party" should be formed within the Congress or separate from it, nor did the ECCI report review the question as to the type of liaison the Comintern should establish with such nationalist organizations as the Indian National Congress. This question had been raised four years earlier at the Second Congress, and it is evident, even from the official accounts of the Fifth Congress, that it had remained a subject for heated debate.

The ECCI offered its view of the matter in a resolution dealing with its report and prepared just before the Fifth Congress met. The resolution stated flatly that the ECCI should expand "direct contact" with the "national movements for emancipation." [33] In view of later developments, it seems obvious that the intention of the resolution, so far as it applied to India, was to establish direct relations between the ECCI and the Indian National Congress. But Roy opposed this completely. He told the Comintern delegates, at their twenty-first session:

> I must first point out that in the resolution on the report of the Executive, there is a clause which does not correspond with the theses passed by the Second Congress. My amendment was rejected [evidently in the Colonial Commission] on the ground that it was not in accord with these same theses, but I want

---

[31] *Inprecor*, IV (Aug. 12, 1924), p. 614.

[32] *From the Fourth to the Fifth World Congress* (London: Communist Party of Great Britain, 1924), p. 68.

[33] The preliminary draft is not available, but Roy quotes these phrases in his speech and they also appear in the final version as adopted by the Congress.

to prove that it is the resolution which does not correspond with the theses, and which is totally mistaken when considered in the light of the events that have taken place since the Second Congress. The resolution says, that in order to win over the people of colonial and semi-colonial countries, there must be a "further direct development of the direct contact of the Executive with the national movements for emancipation." It is true that we must always have a connection with these national movements, but it seems to have been overlooked that these connections have not always been successful.[34]

Roy then quoted from Lenin's Second Congress thesis which stated that the Comintern should support revolutionary movements in the colonies—

for the exclusive purpose of uniting the various units of the future proletarian parties and educating them to the consciousness of their specific tasks, that is, to the tasks of the struggle against the bourgeois democratic tendencies within their respective nationalities.[35]

"If this is our task," concluded Roy,

then we must have direct connection with the masses, but the resolution says that we must have direct connection with the national liberation movements. These include all sorts of classes and aims. We shall never progress if we stand by this vague formula; our failure hitherto has been due to theoretical confusion.[36]

The resolution as finally adopted included the phrase which Roy had tried to expunge. The key paragraph reads as follows:

18. In addition to winning the support of the peasant masses and of the oppressed national minorities, the Executive Committee, in its instructions, always emphasized the necessity for winning over the revolutionary movements for emancipation of the colonial peoples and for all peoples of the East so as to make them the allies of the revolutionary proletariat of the capitalist countries. This requires not only the extension of the direct contact between the Executive and the national emancipation movements of the Orient, but also very close contact between the sections in the imperialist countries with the colonies of those countries, and, in the first place, a constant struggle against the imperialist colonial policy of the bourgeoisie in every country. In this respect the activities are everywhere still very weak.[37]

It is quite possible that Roy saw the resolution as a threat to his position, since it called for that direct contact with the colonial nationalist movement which he himself had been unable to attain. The resolution posed, indeed, a double threat in its order to the Communist parties in the imperialist countries to establish "very close contact" with the political movements in the respective colonies. Thus in effect it directed the British Communist Party to participate more

---

[34] *Inprecor*, IV (July 25, 1924), p. 518.
[35] *Loc. cit.*
[36] *Loc. cit.*
[37] *Inprecor*, IV (Aug. 29, 1924), p. 647.

fully in Indian Communist affairs—and this, too, might well result in undermining Roy's position.

Roy had a much more difficult time at the Fifth Congress than he had had at previous congresses, for the threat implied by the resolution forced him to state his position more boldly than ever before. Despite concessions to the prevailing view, such as his earlier reference to the bourgeoisie as the "vanguard of the revolution," Roy's basic disagreement with Comintern strategy emerged so clearly that the chairman of the Colonial Commission, Manuilsky, was provoked into charging Roy with deviationism. Said Manuilsky, in his report to the plenary session:

> Some deviations were recorded by the Commission. Roy, as at the Second Congress, exaggerated the social movement [the Communist and pro-Communist forces] in the colonies to the detriment of the national movement. . . . He goes so far as to say that the national movement had lost its character of the united front of all the classes of an oppressed country, that a new period was beginning, in which the class struggle was becoming transported into the colonies. . . . In regard to the colonial question, Roy reflects the nihilism of Rosa Luxemburg. The truth is that a just proportion should be looked for between the social movement and the national movement. Can the right of self-determination become a contradiction to the interest of the revolution? Had Roy put the question in this manner, one could discuss it with him.[38]

Roy had failed at "winning over the revolutionary movements for emancipation" in India. Not only did the Congress Party pay no attention to him, but his own organization was virtually smashed by the Cawnpore Conspiracy Case, and by the clever police work of Sir Cecil Kaye. Without doubt he had hoped that his Workers' and Peasants' Party would develop into something in its own right that would impress the Comintern. Yet he had not even succeeded in his call for a conference. The extent to which Comintern officials knew of Roy's failure must remain a matter for conjecture, but the debates at the Fifth Congress do suggest that there was considerable dissatisfaction concerning the progress of the Indian movement. The Congress appointed a commission (which included, among others, Roy, Manuilsky, Stalin, and Katayama) to review the colonial question and prepare detailed recommendations.

In the three years that followed, Roy's retention of his eminent position in the Comintern was apparently not based on his contribution to the revolution in India.

---

[38] *Ibid.* (Aug. 12, 1924), p. 608. These sentences do not appear in the abridged report of the Fifth Congress published by the CPGB.

The Fifth Plenum of the ECCI

Roy returned to France after the Fifth Congress and was in Paris by August, 1924. The balance of that year was not very fruitful for him. News of the failure of the Cawnpore Case appeal reached Roy in November, and that same month he wrote in despair to an Indian comrade: "For some months we have been practically cut off from all contact, which must be revived without delay and by all means." [39] The crowning blow came on January 30, 1925, when Roy and his wife were arrested in Paris. Evelyn was released and allowed to remain in France, but Roy was deported to Luxembourg. He didn't remain there long, however, for by March 21, he was in Moscow for the meeting of the fifth plenum of the ECCI.

When the fifth plennum convened, it faced two important questions concerning India which had not been resolved at the Fifth Congress the previous summer. The first was the question of the attitude of the Comintern toward the Indian National Congress, and the second concerned the type of "direct contact" that should be maintained with it by the ECCI. The chairman of the Colonial Commission was "Dorsey," the American delegate, and his report to the full plenum is the only published description of the line agreed upon in the Commission. Said Dorsey:

In India, the reports of the delegates show that the movement is now in a process of transition, finding new forms and tactics to correspond with the real basic revolutionary nationalist movement in India. The old Gandhi movement of non-violence and non-coöperation has collapsed and was followed by the Swarajist Party with its policy of parliamentary obstruction. This Party has come to the point of collapse and is now tending to decompose into a small center group between the bourgeois parties on the one side and the revolutionary mass movement on the other. The masses of India are discontented with the Swarajist program of self-government. They are demanding separation from the British Government.

The Commission proposes the following policy for India: "The Commission is of the opinion that it is now necessary for the Communists to continue work in the National Congress and in the Left Wing of the Swaraj Party. All nationalist organizations should be formed into a mass revolutionary Party, an all-Indian anti-imperialist bloc. The slogan of the People's Party, having for the main points in its program: separation from the Empire, a democratic republic, universal suffrage and the abolition of feudalism—slogans put forward and popularized by the Indian Communists—is correct."

In its resolution the Commission instructs the Indian Communists to direct their efforts towards securing leadership over the masses of the peasantry, to

---

[39] Kaye, *Communism in India*, p. 139.

encourage the organization and amalgamation of trade unions, and to take over the leadership of all their struggles.[40]

It is evident from this quotation that Roy's strategical formulations were rejected once again. The Comintern still regarded the bourgeoisie as revolutionary and still wanted to work with the Indian National Congress. The plenum did, however, endorse the formation of a "mass revolutionary Party" but it indicated that it should be made up of "all nationalist organizations." The feeble efforts to organize a WPP that had been going on in India were a far cry from that.

Influence of British Communist Party

The resolution on the colonial question of the Fifth Comintern Congress had stated that there should be "very close contact between the sections [of the Comintern] in the imperialist countries with the colonies of those countries." Early in 1925 the CPGB began to act on these instructions by forming a Colonial Committee and by sending another emissary, Percy E. Glading, to India to survey the revolutionary situation. Roy opposed the trip. Glading arrived in India on January 30, 1925, visited a few big cities, and left on April 10. When he returned to England he reported to the CPGB that "no Indian Communist groups existed at all." [41]

During the spring of 1925 many overseas groups attempted to direct the Indian Communist movement. Roy was in Berlin as a result of his expulsion from France which, in his words, had "affected me rather seriously. It has dislocated our business." [42] His wife Evelyn remained at work in Paris, aided by a small group of Indians, most important of whom were G. A. K. Luhani and Mohammed Sipassi. In addition to publishing *Vanguard* (which changed its name on January 1, 1925 to *Masses of India*) she also worked with some French intellectuals, headed by Henri Barbusse, who organized themselves into a *Comité Pro-Hindou*. This group did some propaganda work in favor of Indian independence, but was ineffective in trying to secure a reversal of Roy's expulsion order.[43] In England, both the Colonial Committee of the CPGB (sometimes called the Colonial Department), and the Indian Bureau, a group of about twelve Indian leftists, mostly students residing in London, occupied themselves with Indian affairs. Shapurji Saklatvala, a Parsi who had been elected to the British Parlia-

---

[40] *Inprecor*, V (April 18, 1925), p. 513.

[41] *Communist Papers*. Parliamentary Publications, 1926, Vol. XXIII (Accounts and Papers, vol. 8), Command 2682 (London: HMSO, 1926), p. 84.

[42] *Communism in India, 1924–27*, p. 102.

[43] *Ibid.*, p. 92, states that the Comité established direct contact with Jawaharlal Nehru.

ment in 1922, was also active in the work of the CPGB and the Indian Bureau. With so many groups interested in the Indian movement, friction was bound to develop.

One important step taken during this period by the CPGB was the planning of an Oriental Conference to be held in Europe and attended by representatives from colonial areas. In June, 1925, Chaman Lall, G. Goswami, and N. M. Joshi, three moderate Indian trade unionists, attended the ILO conference in Geneva. On their way through London they were invited by the British Communists to attend the Oriental Conference. They agreed and named twenty-five other Indians to whom invitations might be sent.[44]

To discuss the proposed Oriental Conference and to clear up some of the confusion resulting from the multiplicity of Communist groups interested in India, the CPGB invited a small group of European Communists to meet in Amsterdam, July 11 and 12, 1925. Present were M. N. Roy, Evelyn Roy, Sneevliet, Gertrude Hessler, Khan (of the Indian Bureau), Glading, N. J. Uphadayaya (who had been organizing Indian seamen for the CPGB in London), and Clemens Dutt and R. W. Robson of the CPGB.[45] Robson prepared a detailed report of the Amsterdam meeting; the report was picked up by the British police when they later raided the CPGB headquarters, and was published in a British command paper along with other seized documents.

Robson's report indicates that there was serious conflict between Roy and the CPGB over the direction of Indian affairs: Roy, who had previously complained to the Comintern that the British Communists were not doing enough to organize the revolution in India, protested at Amsterdam that they were doing too much. He was irritated by the Glading visit, and was especially incensed at the British Communists over the Indian Bureau's allegations that letters given the CPGB for delivery to Roy had been opened and their contents altered. He was also vexed by the fact that the Oriental Conference had been planned without his knowledge.

Roy directly challenged Robson's statement that the CPGB should have the right to control work conducted in the British colonies. "This," said Roy, "smacks of Imperialism," and Evelyn Roy agreed.[46] He also claimed to have documentary evidence that Indian Communist groups did exist, but said they had been unable to make up their

---

[44] *Communist Papers*, p. 77.

[45] The magistrate of the Meerut Sessions Court believed "R. W. Robson" was the pseudonym of Graham Pollard. Meerut (UP). District Court. [Meerut Communist Conspiracy Case. Magistrate's order of committal to trial.] (Meerut: Saraswati Press, 1929?), p. 96. Hereinafter cited as Meerut Committal Order.

[46] *Communist Papers*, p. 83.

minds whether to reveal themselves to Glading before he left India.

Within a few months, however, the conflict between Roy and the CPGB was apparently resolved to the satisfaction of both, although how this was accomplished is not clear from the available documents. Many years later the magistrate who prepared the indictment in the Meerut Conspiracy Case concluded, from documents presented in evidence, that after the Amsterdam conference Roy went to Moscow and consulted the Comintern's Colonial Bureau, and that his role in the Indian movement was outlined in a letter to the CPGB written from Moscow on September 25, 1925.[47]

The Moscow decision did not establish clear lines of authority, but it did imply that the CPGB should not work independently of Roy; it also directed Roy and the other Indian Communists in Europe to constitute themselves a Foreign Bureau of the CPI, thus becoming an actual part of the Indian organization. Apparently it was also suggested at the time that Roy should visit England in order to work directly with the CPGB and the Indian Communists residing there. Roy never did this, however, for after the Cawnpore Case it was obvious that the British authorities would have arrested him had he entered British territory.

Another factor in lessening the friction between Roy and the British party may have been the efforts of Clemens Dutt, who apparently visited the Continent on occasion and established a friendly relationship with Roy. In fact he became a member of Roy's Foreign Bureau of the CPI while continuing as a member of the CPGB.[48] Roy appears to have realized that he needed the British Communists to help in re-

---

[47] The authors were unable to locate all printed volumes of documents used in the Meerut Case, and thus could not examine the text of No. P 2385, the key document in this instance. Like many others, it had to be reconstructed from fragmentary quotations scattered throughout the texts of the Sessions Court Judgment and the Committal Order. In this case there is an important discrepancy which may be due to a typographical error, of which there are many in all volumes. The Committal Order gives no date for P 2385 but says it was after the Amsterdam conference, which would make it 1925 (p. 97). The Sessions Court Judgment dates it 1924 (p. 69). The Committal Order version appears to be correct in the context of events of the period. A contradictory version, however, is presented in an official CPI history of the Party. "In this conference [at Amsterdam] M. N. Roy's attitude on behalf of the Colonial Bureau was criticized. A resolution was passed that the task of forming the Party in India should be taken over by the British Communist Party. From then onward, the British Communist Party looked after Indian Party affairs." (Chalasani Vasudeva Rao, *Bharatha Communist Party Nirvaana Charitrea* [Vijayawada: Praja Sakti Press, 1943]), p. 26.

[48] Meerut Sessions Judgment, p. 69. Roy's later disappointment with Dutt implies that he trusted him at this time. "I believed he was a decent sort," he wrote in *Fragments of a Prisoner's Diary; Letters from jail,* (Bombay: Indian Renaissance Assn., 1943), p. 10.

cruiting seamen as couriers, and in transmitting money to India; he could not, therefore, deprive them of all authority in determining Indian policy. In evaluating Roy's role during this period the Meerut Case judge said:

> Roy definitely wanted to keep the control or guidance of Communist activities in India in his own hands and was inclined to criticize the efforts of the CPGB as based on insufficient understanding of the problems. This view seems to have been partially accepted by the Communist International.[49]

This conclusion is supported by the available evidence.

Further Organizational Attempts in India

In 1924, shortly after the Cawnpore Conspiracy Case, a man in the United Provinces named Satya Bhakta had decided to organize a legal Communist party. He had concluded from the Cawnpore Case that to advocate communism was not in itself illegal, and that a Communist party could exist without engaging in activities which the government would regard as treasonable. Bhakta's party had not attracted much attention during 1924, but by the middle of 1925 Communist activity began to pick up. Nalini Gupta was released from jail in July, and Muzaffar Ahmed was discharged on grounds of poor health in September. They immediately resumed organizational work, and since nothing had been done while they were in jail, they were naturally interested in Bhakta's party. It was probably Ahmed who informed Roy of Bhakta's plan to hold a Communist conference in Cawnpore in December, 1925, concurrently with the annual session of the Indian National Congress. In October, *Masses of India* carried a Bombay dispatch which said: "It is premature to say what shape this 'Communist Party' will ultimately assume and how far it is going to be Communist in its program and actions." [50]

Articles appearing in *Masses of India* show that Roy was interested in Bhakta's group; he dispatched Jotin Mitra to India, ostensibly to get more information about it. It is possible, however, that Roy only wanted to get rid of Mitra, whom he regarded as stupid and useless.[51] If so, this was not a shrewd move, for Mitra was apparently instrumental in creating the impression among the Indian Communists that Roy could have rendered much greater financial assistance to the Indian movement than he had.

When the conference of Bhakta's "Indian Communist Party" convened on December 26, 1925, S. A. Dange and Shaukat Usmani were

---

[49] Meerut Sessions Judgment, pp. 69–70.
[50] "New Political Parties," *Masses of India,* I (Oct., 1925), p. 15.
[51] Cawnpore Case Evidence, Exhibit No. 28*B*, p. 20.

still in jail. Muzaffar Ahmed, had been released, however, and he attended along with C. K. Iyengar of Madras; K. N. Joglekar, S. V. Ghate, R. S. Nimbkar, and J. P. Bergerhotta from Bombay; and Abdul Majid from Lahore.[52] All these men were part of Roy's network, either in touch with him directly or through Dange, Ahmed, or Singaravelu. Bergerhotta was actually a police spy, although this was not discovered until 1929.[53]

To serve as chairman of the reception committee, Bhakta had recruited Maulana Hasrat Mohani, a well-known Congressman, president of the Muslim League, and chairman of the reception committee of the All-India Khilafat Congress which had convened in Cawnpore the previous day. Mohani had made a name for himself by proposing that, in contrast to the more moderate demands of Gandhi, the National Congress proclaim complete independence as its goal. The conference president was Singaravelu Chettiar, one of the men through whom Roy had previously hoped to penetrate the National Congress.

The conference suffered an initial setback when the Congress refused permission to hold the meeting in the *pandal* (tent-like enclosure) set up for annual session of the Congress. Another location was found, however, and about five hundred people attended, most of them workers and peasants who probably understood little of what was happening.[54] In their speeches to the delegates, both Mohani and Singaravelu made a particular point of emphasizing that the party was not connected with the Communist International. "Our organization is purely Indian," said Mohani. "Our relation with similar parties of other countries will be only that of sympathy and mental affinity to all these in general and to the Third International in particular." [55]

Singaravelu was even more specific:

> Indian Communism is not Bolshevism, for Bolshevism is a form of communism which the Russians have adopted in their country. We are not Russians. Bolsheviks and Bolshevism may not be needed in India. . . . We are one with the world communists but not with Bolsheviks.[56]

Ahmed and the Communists from Bombay knew that this line was not correct and must have argued against it.

The Party's executive committee met on December 28, 1925; it

---

[52] Meerut Sessions Judgment, p. 343.

[53] From Philip Spratt's handwritten annotations on Robert C. North's typewritten copy of Saumyendranath Tagore, *Historical Development of the Communist Movement in India.*

[54] J. Coatman, *India in 1925–26* (Calcutta: Government of India, 1926), pp. 195–196.

[55] Mitra, ed., *Indian Annual Register, 1925,* II, 367.

[56] *Ibid.,* p. 371.

consisted of Joglekar, Ghate, Nimbkar, Ahmed, Abdul Majid, Bergerhotta, and Iyengar. Bergerhotta and Ghate were elected general secretaries, and Ahmed and Iyenger were appointed secretaries for their
areas.[57] The available documentation of this meeting makes no mention of Bhakta and it is likely that he did not even attend, for it was
at about this time that he broke with the Communists. Roy had attacked Bhakta bitterly in *Masses of India,* and when a detailed report
of the conference reached him he strongly criticized the speeches of
Mohani and Singaravelu. Labeling them "childish," he wrote:

> Nothing can be more non-communistic than to say that the Indian working
> class will play its historic role in the struggle for national freedom and work out
> its own salvation independently of the international proletarian movement. Those
> who maintain and propagate this point of view are far from being Communists:
> they are veritable enemies of the Indian working class.[58]

While the Bhakta group was preparing for the conference in Cawnpore, other organizational activity had been taking place in Bengal.
On November 1, 1925, a "Labour Swaraj Party of the Indian National
Congress" was formed in Calcutta under the leadership of Quazi
Nazrul Islam, a well-known revolutionary poet. Saumyendranath
Tagore, who became active in this party during 1926, has implied
that Muzaffar Ahmed was one of the founders.[59] The official history
of the party does not mention his name among those who were the
original organizers, but does indicate that by August, 1926, he was
the editor of its official organ.[60]

The new party sought to attain Indian independence by organizing
workers and peasants, for whose interests it would fight in the legislatures, and its members were free to belong to the Swaraj Party. Word
of the new organization had reached Europe by February, 1926, for
in that month Roy's paper stated: "The *Masses of India* welcome the
Labour Swaraj Party and congratulate its promoters for their revolutionary courage in the attempt to break away from the politics of
vested interests." [61] The journal admitted, however, that it did not
know who formed the rank and file of the party or what its program
was.

On February 6, 1926, an All-Bengal Tenants Conference was held
at Krishnagar, at which it was decided to form the Peasants' and

---

[57] Meerut Sessions Judgment, p. 343.

[58] "The Indian Communists and the Communist International," *Masses of India,*
II (March, 1926), p. 6.

[59] Tagore, *Historical Development of the Communist Movement in India,* p. 6.

[60] *A Call to Action* (Calcutta: Workers' and Peasants' Party of Bengal, 1928), p.
49.

[61] "A Step in the Right Direction," *Masses of India,* II (Feb., 1926), p. ●

Workers' party of Bengal, which would absorb the Labour Swaraj Party.[62] The leadership was made up predominantly of middle-class intellectuals, and the total membership during the year 1926 remained at only about forty. The new party continued to publish the Bengali weekly, *Langal (Plough)*, which had been started by the Labour Swaraj Party on December 16, 1925, but after fifteen issues it was suspended on April 15, 1926 due to lack of funds.[63]

Thus in spite of considerable activity the Communist movement in India, during the first part of 1926, was still small, poorly organized, and generally ineffective. Personal jealousies and lack of money appear to have been the major impediments. British Intelligence reported that in January the Communists determined to approach Roy for money, planning to decide their relationship with him on the basis of whether or not it was forthcoming.[64] It didn't arrive, and at an informal meeting in Calcutta in April, 1926, strong indignation was expressed against Roy.[65] It was decided to send him a stiff letter, and, accordingly, Jotin Mitra wrote to Sipassi, Roy's chief lieutenant in Europe:

> You people do not realize our difficulties here. . . . The boss [Roy] and family are living as Princes . . . and the boys here—real, sincere workers—are starving. You hypocrites mean no business, you are simply exploiters. Your behaviour has created such a bad atmosphere against you that now, except a few of us, *all* in the Punjab, UP, Bombay and Bengal are losing confidence in you.[66]

It was at this time that Roy and Evelyn decided to end their relationship. Sometime in 1925 or 1926 they broke permanently. The exact date and reason are not clear, but they had been separated for some time due to Roy's expulsion from France. British Intelligence was under the impression she had returned to the United States around August, 1925, and an official report implies that her whereabouts were known until 1927.[67] Neither her name nor her pseudonym, Santi Devi, appears in any of the documents or literature relating to Indian communism after 1925.[68] There is no doubt that her departure was a great political loss to Roy. Not only had she written many articles for *Masses of India* and

---

[62] *A Call to Action*, p. 46. This ultimately became the Workers' and Peasants' Party of Bengal and hereinafter will be referred to as the Bengal WPP.

[63] *Ibid.*, p. 49.

[64] *Communism in India, 1924–27*, p. 10.

[65] *Ibid.*, p. 107.

[66] *Ibid.*, ellipsis in original. See also p. 109, which implies that another letter denouncing Roy was sent.

[67] *Ibid.*, pp. 153, 366.

[68] Evelyn Roy should not be confused with Ellen (Gottschalk) Roy who met Roy in 1929, married him after his release from an Indian prison in 1936, and remained his wife until his death.

Inprecor, she also had done much to interest Henri Barbusse and other French intellectuals in the cause of Indian independence.

During 1924–1925, then, Roy's influence in India sharply declined, while the Communist Party of Great Britain began to take over the direction of Indian Communist affairs.

5   THE "IMPERIALISM" OF THE CPGB

While the Communists in India squabbled over who would head their new party, the Communists in Europe continued to compete for the privilege of directing the movement from abroad. M. N. Roy and the CPGB apparently maintained an uneasy truce following the Amsterdam conference, but by the beginning of 1926 there was once again open disagreement over strategy and tactics. Because both Roy and the British Communists continued to publish their views (in their respective journals as well as in official Comintern publications), the Communists in India were confronted with conflicting advice which was of little help in solving their tactical and leadership problems. To complicate matters, both Roy and the CPGB had to formulate their proposals for India with due respect for the official Comintern line—a burden which weighed more heavily on Roy than on the CPGB, for he had never accepted the prevailing strategy that the Communists should coöperate with bourgeois nationalists. The contradiction between his own views and official Comintern policy was frequently reflected in his writing, as when he wrote for a Comintern publication in 1925:

Objectively, the Indian bourgeoisie are a revolutionary factor; but they are totally unconscious of this revolutionary role of theirs, and what is worse still, they are remarkably inclined towards counter-revolution, or rather, reaction.[1]

---

[1] M. N. Roy, "Anti-Imperialist Struggle in India," *Communist International* No. 6 [n.d.], p. 84.

The differences and similarities between the advice of Roy and that of the CPGB emerge most clearly in two books published in 1926. The first was *The Future of Indian Politics* by Roy, parts of which appeared in his journal, *Masses of India,* in April, 1926. The second was *Modern India* by Clemens Dutt's brother, R. Palme Dutt, who, with the publication of this book, assumed the role of adviser to the Indian Communists—a role in which he has continued to wield great influence to the present day. Both books were intended as study guides, both attempt a Marxist analysis of the class forces operating in India, and both outline strategy and tactics for the Indian Communist movement.

M. N. Roy's "The Future of Indian Politics"

In his book Roy renewed his criticism of the Indian nationalist movement, and pointed out "the separation of the Nationalist bourgeoisie from the revolutionary masses." [2] "The big bourgeoisie," he stated, "is practically eliminated from the struggle for national freedom."

Practically, the bourgeois bloc seeks to make a united front with the imperialist forces of law and order to make the country safe against any possible revolution. The middle class, which still makes the show of a parliamentary fight, is in hopeless political bankruptcy. . . . The future of Indian politics (of national liberation) will, therefore, be determined by the social forces which still remain and will always remain antagonistic to Imperialism even in the new era dominated by the "higher ideals of Swaraj within the Empire." These social forces are composed of the workers, peasantry and the petty bourgeoisie (small traders, artisans, employees, students, petty intellectuals, etc.).[3]

Since the entire social basis of the nationalist movement had changed, said Roy, new class alignments were necessary:

Both the leadership and organizational form will naturally be determined by the social character of the movement. The social elements that will henceforth compose the movement for national liberation are the petty intellectuals, artisans, small traders, peasantry, and the proletariat. In the existing condition of Indian society, these all belong to the oppressed and exploited class. The movement for national liberation will take place on the basis of the struggle between the exploiting and exploited classes. Henceforth the fight for national freedom in India becomes a class-struggle approximating to the final stage.[4]

Having thus dealt with strategy, Roy turned to tactics, especially as they involved organizational forms: "To play creditably its political role, the proletariat will, of course, have its own party—the Com-

---

[2] M. N. Roy, *The Future of Indian Politics* (London: R. Bishop, 1926), p. 78.
[3] *Ibid.,* p. 90.
[4] *Ibid.,* p. 95.

munist Party. But in that there will be no room for its democratic
allies." [5] The "democratic allies," he said, must be part of a broader
organization that would enable the revolutionary elements of the
different classes to come together in a common struggle against imperialism. "How to organize these forces of national revolution in a
democratic party is the immediate problem before the Indian revolutionaries," said Roy.[6] But he flatly stated that "None of the existing Nationalist parties can serve the purpose." Roy's democratic party
was to be a new Congress, minus its bourgeois element:

> The people's fight for freedom must be led by the party of the people—a
> party organization which will be broad enough for all the forces of national
> revolution. The proletariat will be in it, but it will not be a proletarian party,
> nominally or essentially. In this party the proletariat will stand side by side
> with the petty bourgeois and peasant masses, as the most advanced democratic
> class.[7]

In sum, *The Future of Indian Politics* argued that the existing political organizations in India were not revolutionary and that the
immediate need was the formation of a new mass party in which all
anti-imperialist elements could rally for the struggle for independence.

R. Palme Dutt's "Modern India"

Though the advice contained in Dutt's *Modern India* is similar
in many ways to that in *The Future of Indian Politics,* there are some
important differences. On the question of strategy, Dutt was less
ready to write off the bourgeoisie as unrevolutionary. "The fight
for national liberation," he said, "is a fight of many social strata—of
workers, of peasants, of the lower middle class, of the intelligentsia
and even of a section of the bourgeoisie." [8] On tactics, there was an
even greater divergence between the two books. "The immediate important task," said Dutt, "is to carry on a battle of clarification within
the existing movement and organizations. Within both the Congress
and the Swaraj Party, the Left Nationalist elements should gather
themselves round a popular national program." [9] Unlike Roy, Dutt
did not call for the immediate formation of a new mass party to replace the Congress. He was content to await developments. "When the
time comes," he said, "the new forces will have to find their form of

---

[5] *Ibid.,* p. 98.

[6] *Ibid.,* pp. 7–8.

[7] *Ibid.,* p. 114.

[8] R. Palme Dutt, *Modern India* (London: Communist Party of Great Britain,
1927), p. 129. The authors have been unable to locate a copy of the Indian edition.
Dutt states in the preface of the English edition that the text was revised.

[9] *Ibid.,* p. 148.

organization and expression. It is a matter of indifference how this will arise, whether through the existing forms of the Congress and the Swaraj Party or by a combination of these and other elements." [10] What to Roy was an "immediate problem," was to Dutt a "matter of indifference."

Modern India was originally published in India in the spring of 1926. When the English edition appeared the following year it contained a preface dated December 1, 1926, which indicated that Dutt had moved closer to Roy's stand on strategy:

> The Indian bourgeoisie is today a counter-revolutionary force: they fear the social revolution that would follow on national independence more than they desire independence; and therefore they have made their terms with the imperialists and are all supporters of the Empire.[11]

And on tactics:

> Only a new National movement, based on the workers and peasants, and with a political and social program expressing the interests of the masses, can bring new life. The conditions for this are ripe.[12]

By the end of 1926, then, it appears that there were no longer any great differences between Roy and the CPGB on either strategy or tactics.

Manifesto to the Indian National Congress

Early in December, the Dorrit Press in London (the same firm that had printed Roy's *Future of Indian Politics*), published *A Manifesto to the All-India National Congress,* by the Communist Party of India.[13] The document itself gives no evidence of authorship. Among the Communists in Europe, only Roy, Clemens Dutt, and Mohammed Sipassi had the authority to speak for the CPI. Roy, however, was in Moscow, and presumably had been there at least since November 22, 1926, when the seventh ECCI plenum convened. It is, of course, possible that the manifesto had been drawn up earlier with his approval.[14]

The manifesto resembles the document which Roy had prepared for the Gaya Congress four years earlier in that it is an appeal to the Congress to adopt a radical program. This suggests that, like its

---

[10] *Ibid.,* pp. 148–149.

[11] *Ibid.,* p. 17.

[12] *Ibid.,* p. 18.

[13] *A Manifesto to the All India National Congress* (London: Dorrit Press, [n.d., 1926?]). The manifesto is dated December 1, 1926, and the British Museum copy was acquired on December 13, 1926.

[14] Meerut Sessions Judgment, p. 89, implies that the manifesto was drawn up in India.

predecessor, the manifesto may have been issued in the firm belief that the Congress would reject the program, and would thus expose its bourgeois orientation. However, there is no corroborating evidence for this, as there was in the case of the Gaya manifesto.

The 1926 manifesto states that the National Congress is at a low ebb, that it "exists but in name," and that there is "little fundamental difference" between the various parties grouped within it. It must, the document argues, be "brought under the inspiring influence of a republican people's party." The manifesto gives no details regarding the organization of such a people's party, nor does it say whether the party should be inside or outside of the Congress. But by insisting that the Congress must be "brought under the influence" of a people's party, the manifesto demonstrates that its authors were not yet prepared to tell the Indian Communists to cut themselves off completely from the party of Gandhi and Nehru.

Communist Emissaries to India

It was before Roy and the CPGB were in substantial agreement on strategy and tactics that the CPGB began in earnest to take over the direction of the Communist movement in India. On April 30, 1926, George Allison, a Scottish coal miner and a member of the CPGB, arrived in Bombay.[15] One of his colleagues of this period recalls that he had been dispatched to India by the Red International of Labor Unions (RILU) for the purpose of stimulating trade union organization.[16] He apparently confined himself to trade union activities in India and did not come to the notice of the authorities until November, 1926, when his connection with known Communists was established through intercepted correspondence.[17] On January 22, 1927, Allison's forged passport (issued under his alias, Donald Campbell) was discovered in a police raid in Calcutta. Allison was arrested the next day, convicted, imprisoned, and ultimately deported from India.

The month before Allison was arrested the CPGB had dispatched another envoy to India. He was Philip Spratt, a 24-year-old Communist who had joined the party during his student days at Cambridge. "It was not as an expert that I was sent to India," Spratt modestly recalls in his memoirs. "I was chosen because I was unknown to the police, and my job was to be that of a messenger and re-

---

[15] Meerut Sessions Judgment, p. 92.
[16] Philip Spratt, *Blowing Up India* (Calcutta: Prachi Prakashan, 1955), p. 32.
[17] Meerut Sessions Judgment, p. 93.

porter." [18] Before leaving England, Spratt was taken in secrecy to meet the Comintern representative in London, a Russian named Petrovsky. Petrovsky's only instructions were that Spratt should write a pamphlet on China urging India to follow the example of the Kuomintang. In December, 1926, Clemens Dutt took Spratt to Paris where he met Mohammed Sipassi, Roy's chief lieutenant. After a few days in Paris Spratt left for India via Marseilles, traveling ostensibly as the representative of a London firm of foreign booksellers. He arrived in Bombay on December 30, 1926, and immediately became much more than a "messenger and reporter."

Spratt recalls that his mission was to contact Muzaffar Ahmed, S. V. Ghate, and other Indian Communists and instruct them to form a workers' and peasants' party, which would serve as a legal cover for Communist activity.[19] Documents adduced in the 1929 Meerut Conspiracy Case make it clear that one of his major aims was to place Communists in positions of leadership within the Congress organization. In notes for the guidance of a meeting which was to organize the Bombay WPP he lists the principal tasks of the new party as: "(1) obtaining representation in the National Congress Committees (2) getting program accepted and our delegates elected by the TUC (3) support for the textile paper (4) increase the membership (5) 'Hands off China Campaign.'" Then he adds, "The united front committee of the National Congress Committee, Swaraj Party, TU's, WPP should be formed for Bombay as soon as possible." [20] On February 8, 1927, the meeting was held at which the WPP of Bombay was formed.[21]

On January 14, 1927, another Communist visitor arrived in India. He was Shapurji Saklatvala, an Indian resident of London who had been elected to the British Parliament from a working-class constituency on a Communist ticket. Saklatvala's motives in making this visit are not clear, but it is not very likely that he was sent by the CPGB. Spratt, in his account of this period, thinks that there may have been some rivalry between the Dutt brothers and Saklatvala for influence with the Indian Communists, and recalls that when Clemens Dutt took him to meet Saklatvala, just before Spratt was to leave for India, Dutt had displayed "either contempt or dislike of Saklatvala." [22]

About the time Saklatvala left England for India, the Indian Com-

[18] Spratt, *Blowing Up India*, p. 29.
[19] *Loc. cit.*
[20] Meerut Sessions Judgment, p. 97.
[21] *Ibid.*, p. 98. See also Meerut Conspiracy Case Evidence, Exhibit No. P 420.
[22] Spratt, *Blowing Up India*, p. 36. See also Meerut Sessions Judgment, pp. 102–103.

munists, including Muzaffar Ahmed from Calcutta, had convened in
Bombay and drawn up plans for a Communist conference to be held
in Lahore in March. They decided to ask Saklatvala to preside over
the conference. But Saklatvala was not impressed with the Indian
Communists, and he not only declined their invitation but also criticized them in a letter which he released to the press. This generated
so much ill feeling and bad publicity that the Communists decided to
call off their Lahore conference.[23] By March, however, Saklatvala had
changed his attitude, for he summoned the Indian Communists to
Delhi and patched up his differences with them. At Delhi it was
decided to hold a general meeting in Bombay on May 29, 1927, at
which a constitution would be adopted and an executive committee
elected.[24]

In general, Saklatvala's tour was a personal triumph. He visited
several parts of India, and wherever he went he drew large crowds.
His speeches were extensively reported in the press, and in Calcutta
he was accorded an official welcome, an honor which the city had not
seen fit to bestow upon the visiting viceroy a short time earlier. He
also interviewed Mahatma Gandhi and engaged in a lengthy public
correspondence in an effort to convince Gandhi that his economic
theories were reactionary and that his assumption of spiritual leadership was a degenerative influence. By playing the role of a Mahatma,
Saklatvala charged, Gandhi was "ruining the mentality and the psychology of these villagers for another generation or two." "Politically
this career of yours is ruinous," he added, "and from a humanitarian
point of view its degenerating influence appears to me to be a moral
plague." [25]

However, his open attacks on Gandhi were resented by much of
the public, and by the time Saklatvala was ready to leave India his
popularity had waned considerably. When he finally sailed for England on April 9, 1927, the Bombay Municipal Corporation refused
to vote him a farewell address. Like other Communists before and
after him, Saklatvala discovered that Marxist "realism" was no match
for the religious revivalism of the Mahatma.

Another Communist emissary of this period was Fazl Elahi (alias
Qurban), a *muhajir* who had received training in Moscow and who
was one of Roy's most trusted comrades in Europe. He was apparently
dispatched to India to look after Roy's interests in the face of in-

---

[23] Meerut Sessions Judgment, p. 103.

[24] *Ibid.*, p. 151.

[25] Shapurji Saklatvala, *Is India Different?* (London: Communist Party of Great
Britain, 1927), p. 17.

creased activity by the CPGB. The authorities in India knew in advance of Elahi's mission, and kept him under surveillance as soon as he arrived in late December, 1926.[26] He appears to have been so disturbed by the arrest of George Allison that he accomplished very little, although he did visit Communists in Calcutta, Madras, Delhi, and Bombay. He was finally arrested on April 5, 1927, prosecuted at Peshawar under Section 121-A of the Indian Penal Code, and sentenced to five years imprisonment.[27]

The Communist conference took place on May 31, 1927, in Bombay. It was attended by most important Indian Communists, including S. A. Dange who had been released from prison on May 24.[28] S. V. Ghate was elected general secretary, and Muzaffar Ahmed, K. S. Iyengar, and S. A. Dange were elected to the presidium.[29]

The question of affiliation with the Comintern came up at this meeting in Bombay, and a resolution was passed which stated: "The CPI looks up to the CPs of the world as well as the International for lead and guidance in the work undertaken by this party in this country." [30] There is no indication in the available documents that the Indian Communists intended to request formal affiliation. But in view of the leadership of Philip Spratt, Ghate, Mirajkar, and others of known loyalty to the Comintern, it does not seem probable that there was any significant opposition to becoming a section of the International; more likely the Communists at Bombay were concerned about further government prosecutions and wanted to avoid any grounds for the accusation that they were members of an international conspiracy. This also seems to be why Dange, upon his release from prison, stated that he was an "Indian Communist" and not a "Bolshevik." Dange's remarks drew the fire of Roy's paper, *The Masses of India,* which objected to any suggestion that there was an Indian variety of communism. "A Communist movement in a country must be a national section of the international communist movement," said *Masses* in July, "otherwise it cannot be communist and may degenerate into anything. . . . It is absurd to seek for a special Indian variety of communism. An Indian who calls himself a communist must be a communist like the others in the rest of the world." [31] It is

---

[26] *Communism in India, 1924–27* (Calcutta: Govt. of Indian Press, 1927), p. 114.
[27] *Loc. cit.*
[28] Meerut Committal Order, p. 198. See also S. A. Dange, *Hell Found!* (Calcutta: Vanguard Literature Co., [n.d.]).
[29] Meerut Sessions Judgment, p. 155.
[30] *Loc. cit.*
[31] "An Indian Communist?" *Masses of India* III (July, 1927), pp. 1–2.

certain that the Indian Communist leaders subscribed to this; that *Masses* felt obliged to print such a rebuke indicates the extent to which its editors were out of touch with the Indian situation.[32]

The increased activity among Indian Communists during 1927 was due largely to the work of Philip Spratt, an able and dedicated worker who brought new energy to trade union and party work. He injected a much-needed dose of efficiency into the Indian movement, and to some extent security was tightened up and money from Europe was more successfully transmitted. Spratt was joined in September by another member of the CPGB, Benjamin F. Bradley. Bradley professed to be an engineer and was ostensibly in India as the representative of his brother's firm, the Crab Patent Underdrain Tile Company —a name which seems poorly calculated to avoid amused attention if not suspicion.[33] Together, Bradley and Spratt became the *de facto* leaders of the Indian Communist Party working, for the most part, through Ahmed, Mirajkar, and Ghate. "There was no intention to form a clique," Spratt recalls, "we just got together with the members we realized were unconditionally loyal to the CI, able to keep secrets and reasonably honest with money." [34] Under the leadership of Spratt and Bradley, the Communist movement began to gather the momentum that the Indians had been unable to achieve by themselves.

Roy Leaves the Scene

At almost the same time that the CPGB sent Spratt to India, the Comintern sent Roy on a mission to China. Thus it came about that during most of 1927, while Spratt and Bradley were reorganizing the Indian movement, Roy was as far from the scene as he could well be, and was completely out of touch with events in India. His absence from Europe gave the British Communists a free hand in Indian Communist affairs, and because it was during this period that they assumed virtual control of the Indian movement, it is interesting to examine the circumstances surrounding Roy's China mission.

Sometime in the fall of 1926 Roy had left Berlin and journeyed to Moscow for the seventh plenum of the ECCI, which met from November 22 to December 16.[35] China was the principal subject of discussion at the plenum; the general disagreement, as always, cen-

---

[32] Roy disclaims responsibility for the paper during the first eight months of 1927. M. N. Roy, *Our Differences* (Calcutta: Saraswaty Library, 1938), p. 28.

[33] Meerut Sessions Judgment, p. 162.

[34] From Philip Spratt's handwritten annotations on Robert C. North's type-written copy of Saumyendranath Tagore, *Historical Development of the Communist Movement in India*.

[35] *Inprecor*, VI (Oct. 28, 1926), p. 1221 reports Roy in Moscow on October 23, 1926.

tered on the role of the bourgeoisie, and in this instance, specifically on the role of the bourgeois Kuomintang.[36]

Chiang Kai-shek and his army, marching north, were consolidating Kuomintang power over most of China. The Chinese Communists were part of the Kuomintang, and were allied with its left wing against the bourgeois leadership. The Communists had also established considerable mass support for themselves in the countryside by organizing the peasants, but their efforts had gotten somewhat out of hand and there were spontaneous uprisings in which the peasants demanded that the lands be confiscated and turned over to the tillers. But because the landholding class dominated the Kuomintang and, through its officers, the Kuomintang army, the Communists could not support an agrarian revolution without risking almost certain expulsion from the Kuomintang.

The Chinese Communist delegates at the seventh plenum, together with the Comintern agents who had been in China and most of the other delegates, were in favor of continuing to maintain good relations with the Kuomintang, but Roy disagreed. In an account published twenty years later, Roy recalls that he was

alone to advocate the different point of view that the Chinese Revolution had reached a critical moment in which it must strike out a new course and a fetish should not be made of the alliance with the Kuomintang. The Executive of the CI adopted my point of view, which was opposed in the beginning by Stalin himself. But Stalin was brought around to my view and the Thesis adopted by the ECCI was drafted by me. Immediately afterwards, I left for China as the head of a new delegation of the CI.[37]

The official documents of the period corroborate only Roy's claim that he was suspicious of the Chinese bourgeoisie. In his speech to the full plenum on November 30, 1926, Roy said:

The policy of imperialism in China at this time is to find a possible modus vivendi with a section of the Chinese bourgeoisie. If the national bourgeoisie determine the progress and tactics of the revolution it will be sabotaged and weakened as a consequence of this new policy of imperialism. Therefore, it is very clear that when we talk about the united anti-imperialist front we have to keep the big bourgeoisie out of account. . . . A section of the bourgeoisie has moved further and further away from the revolution, and in proportion

---

[36] For a detailed description of the seventh-plenum debate on China see Robert C. North, *Moscow and Chinese Communists* (Stanford: Stanford University Press, 1953), pp. 91–92. The account of the Chinese political situation presented here is based primarily on North's book.

[37] M. N. Roy, *Revolution and Counter-Revolution in China* (Calcutta: Renaissance Publishers, 1946), p. 538 n. In an interview with Robert C. North, Roy acknowledged the collaboration of Bubnov and Bukharin. North, *Moscow and Chinese Communists*, p. 90.

as the revolutionary forces (the proletariat, the peasantry, the petty-bourgeoisie) become more and more revolutionary, the upper strata of the bourgeoisie will move more and more away from the revolution to the extent of making a united front with the imperialists against revolutionary China.[38]

If Roy was equating the "national bourgeoisie" with the Kuomintang, as it seems reasonable to assume he was, then he was indeed arguing against making a "fetish" of the Kuomintang. However, it is clear that such views carried very little weight in the Chinese Commission, for in his report to the full plenum, the chairman of the Commission, Tan Ping-shan, said:

> The Commission is unanimous against the demand of the Russian Opposition that the Communists should leave the Kuomintang. We are of the opinion that the relations between the Communist Party of China and the Kuomintang must be consolidated even more than heretofore.[39]

And the resolution itself as finally adopted (and which Roy claims to have written) stated:

> The point of view that the Communist Party must leave the Kuomintang is incorrect. The whole process of development of the Chinese revolution, its character and its perspectives demand that the Communists must stay in the Kuomintang and intensify their work in it.[40]

This was the main element of the policy that Roy was sent to China to help carry out.

By the time Roy arrived, early in 1927, events were moving so rapidly that an entirely new situation confronted the Chinese Communists. After completing his northern expedition, Chiang Kai-shek broke with the left wing of the Kuomintang and in April turned violently against the Communists, massacring them in the streets of Shanghai. The Communists remained in the good graces of the left wing of the Kuomintang branch which controlled the Wuhan area and whose leader, Wang Ching-wei, wanted to march against Chiang. Meanwhile, peasant uprisings in the Wuhan area had increased, much to the annoyance of the Wuhan Kuomintang leaders many of whom, despite their leftist orientation, belonged to the landowning class. The Communists faced a formidable dilemma: should they attempt to seize control in the area by leading the peasants in a full-scale agrarian revolution against the Wuhan Kuomintang, or should they support the latter in its proposed march against Chiang? Roy claims that he urged the Chinese Communists to support the

---

[38] *Inprecor*, VI (Dec. 30, 1926), p. 1604.
[39] *Ibid.*, VII (Jan. 27, 1927), p. 174.
[40] *Ibid.*, (Feb. 3, 1927), p. 233.

peasant revolution, but that Borodin, who was also in China as a representative of the Comintern, was in favor of supporting the Wuhan leaders in their march against Chiang. Roy referred the matter to Moscow. On June 1 he received a telegram from Stalin containing the remarkable instructions that he follow both courses at once. Apparently Borodin had greater influence with the Chinese Communists than did Roy, for they agreed to forego revolution and support the Kuomintang. But it was too late. Wang Ching-wei had become suspicious of the Communists; he purged them from the Wuhan Kuomintang and made his peace with Chiang Kai-shek.

It has been argued that Roy was to blame for Wang's defection, and the controversy over Roy's responsibility centers on the Stalin telegram. In instructing Roy and Borodin to support both the agrarian revolution and the Wuhan Kuomintang, Stalin had made it clear that support of the Wuhan group was to be only a temporary expedient. "The leadership of the Kuomintang," said Stalin, "must be freshened and reinforced by new leaders who have come to the fore in the agrarian revolution. . . . It is necessary to liquidate the unreliable generals immediately." [41]

Roy showed this telegram to Wang; whether or not Wang took it to mean that he himself was one of the "unreliable generals," he immediately turned against the Communists and joined forces with Chiang.

Roy's critics claim that he must surely have known what Wang's reaction would be, and that it was a colossal blunder to show the telegram to him. According to Roy, however, Wang already suspected that the Communists were ready to betray him by supporting the peasant revolution; Roy contended that he showed the message to Wang as a final, desperate effort to regain his confidence.[42]

Roy's China mission was a failure, but the fault was not his. The fault lay in the Comintern policy of preserving the Kuomintang alliance at the cost of weakening the Chinese Communist Party. Certainly the events in China seemed to confirm what Roy had been arguing ever since his debate with Lenin: that the bourgeois nationalists could not be trusted and that they would betray the revolution. Roy was in an excellent position to claim credit for prescience.

The fact that Roy had vigourously opposed the very policy which the Comintern was pursuing in China raises the question as to why he, of all people, was designated to carry it out. Roy himself wanted

---

[41] Quoted in North, *Moscow and Chinese Communists*, p. 106. North notes that there are different versions of the text of this message.

[42] *Ibid.*, p. 107.

to go to India, not to China, and agreed to accept the mission only after Stalin promised to send him to India if he was successful.[43] Why, then, was he sent? The fact that his mission coincided with the CPGB's major effort to take direction of the Communist movement in India suggests that Roy may have been sent to China in order to remove him from Europe and thus from participation in Indian affairs. Another event of the period supports this hypothesis: the Congress of Oppressed Nationalities, held in Brussels in February, 1927.

The Congress of Oppressed Nationalities

As has been shown in chapter 4, early in 1925 the CPGB had planned an Oriental Conference and had secured the coöperation of Chaman Lall, G. Goswami, and N. M. Joshi—three moderate Indian trade unionists. When Roy discussed this conference with the British Communists at their Amsterdam meeting, he opposed the idea vigorously and expressed resentment at British interference in Indian affairs. The British Communist, R. W. Robson, describes Roy's attitude in his report of the Amsterdam meeting:

Roy asked for a report regarding arrangements for the Oriental Conference and our relations with Goswami, Chaman Lall, Deep Singh and Joshi. I therefore reported what had been done in this connection consisting mainly so far as India was concerned in the dispatch of about 20 invitations to certain people in India, which invitations the four above referred to had signed as well as Horniman [Guy Horniman, editor of the *Bombay Chronicle* and staunch supporter of Indian nationalism]. Roy complained that vital information regarding this business was lacking, and that he had received no reports. He had been informed in Paris by Joshi that all four had been invited to Russia, Saklatvala being the intermediary. . . . The International does not consider it necessary to get into touch with these people but with the real revolutionaries. . . .

Roy also asked whether the Party had thought of consulting him regarding these invitations, and whether the Party was completely aware of the record of these four people, and did we think we were justified in relying on them? He then attacked their records, as did Evelyn Roy also. . . .

He [Roy] knew more about India than any of those four and had not been consulted. We were following a wrong policy. He wished to be in Moscow when these four nationalist leaders were there. He had been a pessimist regarding the Conference results and had not believed we would get real revolutionaries. The people we would reach through Chaman Lall and the rest of them would be of no use. There was no objection to them going to Moscow but he would expect to be informed when they set off. He wished it to be recorded as his opinion that the Oriental Conference would be futile; at the same time he offered all cooperation possible if the British Party considered it of any value.[44]

---

[43] Interview with a friend of Roy who accompanied him to China but who has requested anonymity.

[44] *Communist Papers*. Parl. Pubs. 1926, Vol. XXIII (Accounts and Papers, vol. 8), Cmd. 2682 (London: HMSO, 1926), pp. 85–86.

Robson also reports Evelyn Roy's statement that Chaman Lall had refused to see her when he passed through Paris, and in general this document makes it clear that Roy was not on good terms with these four men. They were the principal leaders of Indian trade unionism at that time, and were key members of the left wing of the Congress Party. Thus Roy's previously expressed hostility to them reinforces the hypothesis that he was sent to China to get him out of the way; so also does his statement concerning the futility of an Oriental Conference.

For Roy was alone in his opposition to the Oriental Conference and there is little doubt that the Comintern favored the project. Already, in March, 1926, and more than nine months before Roy was sent to China, Zinoviev had told an enlarged plenum of the ECCI:

During the last few years we have also been able to rely on a number of non-Party organizations. . . . But now there is a possibility of forming yet further organizations of this kind. . . .

Societies to fight against war, organizations against colonial atrocities and oppression of Eastern peoples are a new type of sympathizing mass organizations which in the immediate future come to our notice in many countries.[45]

While Roy was away in Moscow and in China, plans for the conference went ahead, and toward the end of 1926 invitations were sent to many prominent nationalists and trade unionists in India. Among those taking part in the planning was Virendranath Chattopadhyaya, Roy's old rival in Berlin.

From February 10 to 15, 1927, the conference, now called the Congress of Oppressed Nationalities, was held in Brussels, and was attended by 175 delegates from 37 countries.[46] There was little doubt even at the outset that the conference was Communist-inspired and that the organization which emerged from its deliberations, the League Against Imperialism, was actually a Communist front.

The Brussels conference is significant, as far as India is concerned, because it was attended by Jawaharlal Nehru, as an official delegate from the Indian National Congress. Nehru had left India in March, 1926, to accompany his ailing wife to Switzerland where she could undergo special medical treatment. He says in his autobiography:

Towards the end of 1926 I happened to be in Berlin, and I learned there of a forthcoming Congress of Oppressed Nationalities, which was to be held at Brussels. The idea appealed to me, and I wrote home, suggesting that the Indian National Congress might take official part in the Brussels Congress. My

---

[45] *Inprecor*, VI (April 8, 1926), p. 402.

[46] See *Labour Monthly*, IX (March, 1927), pp. 179–185; and Roger Baldwin's account in *The Nation*, CXXIV (April 13, 1927), pp. 397–398.

suggestion was approved, and I was appointed the Indian Congress representative for this purpose.[47]

Nehru also mentions meeting Chattopadhyaya, who became one of the three joint secretaries of the League. He speaks of him with marked affection and respect. "Popularly known as Chatto, he was a very able and a very delightful person," says Nehru. "Of the few [Indian exiles] I met," he adds, "the only persons who impressed me intellectually were V. Chattopadhyaya and M. N. Roy." [48]

Nehru agreed to serve on the Executive Committee of the League Against Imperialism and continued in this position until 1931. The Meerut Conspiracy Case records show that during this period Chattopadhyaya wrote to him frequently. Some of these letters were intercepted by the authorities and were never delivered, but Nehru does recall that he was able to "remain in distant touch with it [the League] by correspondence." [49]

All these circumstances—the CPGB's effort to gain control of the Indian movement, the importance attached to the Brussels conference by the Comintern, Roy's known opposition to the conference and his hostility toward important Indians who had agreed to participate, Chattopadhyaya's role in the preparations for the conference, and the incongruousness of the selection of Roy to help carry out the Comintern's China policy—strongly suggest that Roy was sent to China in order to deprive him of a role in Indian Communist affairs and to remove him from the scene of a conference organized by his rivals for people of whom he did not approve.

Saumyendranath Tagore in Moscow

The CPGB was able to take over the leadership of the Indian Communist movement with such ease partly because the Indian Communists were generally dissatisfied with Roy. As has been shown in chapter 4, discontent with Roy's leadership had begun to develop among Communists in India as early as the spring of 1926. In April, 1927, Saumyendranath Tagore, a leader of the Bengal Workers' and Peasants' Party, left India for Moscow in order to establish direct contact with the Comintern. Tagore arrived in Moscow in June, while Roy was still in China. Shortly after his arrival he had an interview with Ossip Piatnitsky, the treasurer of the Comintern. Tagore, writing in the third person, gives this account of the meeting:

---

[47] Jawaharlal Nehru, *An Autobiography* (London: John Lane, The Bodley Head, 1942), p. 161.
[48] *Ibid.*, pp. 153–154. Nehru met Roy for only "a brief half-hour" in the summer of 1927 when he visited Moscow for "three or four days." *Ibid.*, p. 154.
[49] *Ibid.*, p. 164.

Piatnitsky, the then General Secretary of the Central Committee of the Comintern, sent for Tagore and had a long talk regarding the work of the communists in India. It was evident from the talk that quite a different picture of the communist activities in India had been presented to the Comintern by M. N. Roy. Piatnitsky had an idea that there were hundreds of communists in India in those days. When Tagore told him about the actual number of communists in India in those days, which did not exceed more than a dozen, Piatnitsky was quite taken aback. He said that it seemed unbelievable, as Roy had reported the existence of hundreds of communists in India. Tagore told him in reply that Roy might have hidden these communists in the Himalayas, they were neither heard nor seen in India. It was also evident from the talk with Piatnitsky that the Comintern had given enormous sums to M. N. Roy for financing the Communist movement in India. Tagore informed Piatnitsky that hardly any money had been received in India and the growth of the Communist movement was tremendously handicapped due to the lack of money and literature. From Piatnitsky's words it was clear that enormous sums had been placed at the disposal of M. N. Roy for catering to all those needs of the communist movement in India.

When Tagore arrived in Moscow and submitted his reports to the Communist International and had the above-mentioned talk with Piatnitsky, M. N. Roy was then away in China. A month or more after Tagore's arrival in Moscow M. N. Roy returned to Moscow from China.

It was clear from the talks that Tagore had with Roy that Roy had already sensed the danger of exposure and was very keen on Tagore's early return to India.[50]

Tagore's two charges against Roy—that he had misappropriated funds and had misrepresented the size of the Communist apparatus in India—are corroborated to some extent by British Intelligence sources. A detailed intelligence report prepared in 1927 records that long lists of Indian Communists fell into the hands of British agents, but as each name was checked by the police it was found to be entirely fictitious. The report concludes:

In short, the whole consideration of these lists served to raise a doubt how far Roy was playing straight with Moscow, that is, whether he was dealing with them honestly, or whether he was making his living (and probably large expenses) out of them by representing that he had established in India a vastly larger organization than in reality existed.[51]

As for Tagore's allegation that "enormous sums had been placed at the disposal of M. N. Roy," this, too, is corroborated by British Intelligence. This source cites several different allocations by the Comintern for work in India—£120,000 in July, 1922; £120,000 in November, 1922; £2,000 in February, 1923.[52] It must be pointed out,

---

[50] Saumyendranath Tagore, *Historical Development of the Communist Movement in India* ([Calcutta?]: Red Front Press, 1944), pp. 10–11.

[51] *Communism in India, 1924–27*, p. 77.

[52] Sir Cecil Kaye, *Communism in India* (Delhi: Govt. of Indian Press, 1926), pp. 16, 53, 69.

however, that the accuracy and completeness of this information are not beyond question. Moreover, there is no indication of how much of the money allocated by the Comintern for work in India was disbursed by Roy himself. A considerable amount of money was sent to India by the Soviet embassy in Kabul, operating, it is assumed, independently of Roy who was in Berlin. On the other hand, it seems unlikely that Roy was not entrusted with substantial sums, for he was, after all, in charge of organizational work in India and did hold high office in the Comintern. And it should be remembered, as has already been noted, that he wrote Evelyn Roy in March, 1924, that "almost unlimited funds have become available." [53]

There is also little doubt that the amount of money that actually got through to the Indian Communists was rather small. Of this, a significant part went into private pockets and was never employed for revolutionary purposes. But even allowing for graft on the Indian side, it was natural for the Communists in India to hold Roy, as the leader of their movement and their link with the Comintern, responsible for their financial straits.

But although Roy, as the director of the Indian movement, might be held responsible for the financial difficulties of the Communists in India, it is not fair to accuse him of misappropriation of funds, on the basis of the evidence presently available. His work in Western Europe was undoubtedly very expensive. His publishing activities were costly, and he was obliged to travel extensively. Moreover, as an expatriate revolutionary he may have had to engage in a considerable amount of bribery, not only to ship his literature to India but also to assure his own freedom of movement. Nevertheless, if the Comintern did, in truth, place large sums of money at Roy's disposal, there can be little doubt that Tagore's report to Piatnitsky jeopardized his reputation.

Roy Returns to Europe

Roy left Hankow around August 8, 1927, and must have reached Moscow shortly thereafter. There he met Tagore and learned of the charges that had been made against him. He also learned the details of the bitter struggle then reaching a climax within the Russian Communist Party. The July CPSU plenum had sided with Stalin, and Trotsky and the opposition were in full retreat. Roy did not linger long in the Russian capital; he departed on October 3, 1927 for Berlin. That same month Trotsky and Zinoviev were expelled from the CPSU.

---

[53] *Communism in India, 1924–27,* p. 78.

In the past, Roy and Trotsky had been in agreement on at least one thing—their opposition to any strategy based on support of bourgeois nationalism in the colonial and semicolonial areas.[54] Hence Trotsky, like Roy, had opposed the Kuomintang alliance; when it resulted in disaster Trotsky seized upon it in his effort to discredit Stalin.

Roy, back in Berlin, knew that the Chinese fiasco had vindicated his stand, but to say so would put him on Trotsky's side in the life-or-death struggle with Stalin—and Trotsky had already been expelled from the Russian Party. Roy chose to support Stalin and Stalin's policy; soon after he resumed its editorship, *Masses of India* carried an unsigned article entitled "Revolution and Counter Revolution in China," which said: "Full support to the Wuhan group, Communist Party remaining in the Kuomintang, and Communists entering the nationalist revolutionary government were . . . perfectly correct and absolutely necessary tactics." [55] And to hammer home his point, Roy compiled a book of documents on the Chinese revolution which was later published in Russian from Moscow. In the introduction he said:

> The Opposition in the Russian Communist Party and its supporters in other countries said that the defeat of the Chinese revolution was caused by a mistaken and "opportunist" policy on the part of the Communist International. One can dispel these doubts and show the unsoundness of that accusation. . . . We shall . . . answer the question: was the policy of support of the Kuomintang, the policy of the Communist Party entering the Kuomintang and collaborating with it in the first stages of the revolution, a correct policy?
>
> All the results of that policy demonstrate the neccessity of a categorically affirmative answer. . . . Support of the left-wing of the KMT as the organ of struggle against imperialism and national reaction, including the traitorous bourgeoisie, became all the more necessary when the feudal-bourgeois elements turned against the revolution.[56]

Like Stalin, Roy placed the entire blame for the 1927 debacle on the Chinese Communist Party, completely absolving the Comintern and Stalin of any responsibility.

---

[54] Compare Trotsky's remarks on India and on the role of the bourgeoisie in his report to the Third Congress of the Communist International with Roy's statements on the bourgeoisie as quoted *passim* in chapters 3 and 4 of the present volume. Leon Trotsky, *The First Five Years of the Communist International* (New York: Pioneer Publishers, 1945), p. 223. A brief survey of the Trotsky papers held by the Houghton Library at Harvard University did not reveal any information on Roy or on his relationship with Trotsky. Lack of time prevented the authors from making an exhaustive search of this enormous file of letters and papers.

[55] "Revolution and Counter-revolution in China," *Masses of India*, III (Nov., 1927), p. 14.

[56] M. N. Roy, *Kitaiskaia Revoliutsiia* . . . [The Chinese Revolution], (Moscow-Leningrad: State Publishing House, 1929), pp. 3–10.

Roy's memoirs contain revealing comments about his relation with Trotsky. Roy describes Trotsky as "an unmitigated egoist . . . never impressed by anybody except Lenin, and that also not always out of conviction, but for political opportunism." "I could never be friendly with him," Roy says. "He defended his voluntary personal isolation with the armour of vanity and arrogance." But after these harshly critical remarks, Roy says:

Although disagreeing with his views as regard many grave issues, I was more attracted by his personality and I sympathized with him as the man who was fighting a single-handed battle against a powerful combination of the Old Bolshevik leaders. That attitude of mine deceived Trotsky into counting me as one of his supporters. On my part, I felt that his attitude toward me was less aloof than with many others, indeed, affectionate to a degree. . . . Ultimately I had to disappoint Trotsky by refusing to support him in the most crucial moment of his life. It was not a personal choice for me. The issue was political, and I had to make the choice on principle.[57]

In view of Roy's past writings and speeches on the colonial question, Trotsky can certainly be excused for having made the mistake—if indeed he did—of counting on Roy as a supporter. It is quite possible that Roy was both repelled and attracted by a man as complex as Leon Trotsky. But this is not enough to explain why, in a struggle that was to determine the whole course of Russian and Communist history, Roy failed to side with the principal proponent of his own long-held views. In demonstrating his loyalty to Stalin, Roy's repudiation of his previous stand was so complete as to demand fuller explanation than his memoirs provide.

[57] *Roy Memoirs* (Aug. 8, 1954), p. 379.

6 THE COMINTERN CHANGES COURSE

In China, the Communist movement had suffered a debacle. On Stalin's order the Chinese Communists had supported the Kuomintang to the point of neglecting their own political base in the countryside. Weakened by this policy, they were almost wiped out when the Kuomintang turned against them. The disastrous course of events in China was to have profound consequences for the Communist movement in India.

For many Communists who were interested in India, the events in China raised certain questions. Was not the class orientation of the Indian National Congress the same as that of the Kuomintang? And, if so, would not the Communists risk the same betrayal that had befallen their Chinese comrades, were they to support the Congress?

One of those who answered affirmatively was M. N. Roy. But this, of course, was no new idea for him; he had argued against supporting the Congress for years; if India and China were equated, the events in China could be cited in support of anti-Congress tactics. There was, however, one problem that had to be faced: in advising the Communists to shun the Congress, Roy could not imply that the Chinese Communists had made a mistake in failing to shun the Kuomintang. Whether true or not, to point this out would be to blame Stalin and to agree with Trotsky, and the former's star was rising while the latter's was in eclipse.

Immediately after Roy's return to Berlin, *Masses of India* carried an article "The Lessons of the Chinese Revolution," most probably written by Roy. The article carefully avoided criticism of the policy of supporting the Kuomintang, but it drew pointed conclusions concerning India:

> The lessons of these revolutionary and counter-revolutionary events in China are that the nationalist bourgeoisie in the colonial and semi-colonial countries are essentially counter-revolutionary; that the national revolution to be successful must be an agrarian revolution; that not only the big bourgeoisie, but even the petty bourgeoisie, in spite of their radical phrases, cannot and will not lead the agrarian revolution; that the petty bourgeoisie when placed in power by the support of the workers and peasants do not share and defend this power with the working class, but hand it over to the counter-revolutionary bourgeoisie; and that the working class operating through their independent political party (Communist Party) is the only guarantee for the success of national revolution.[1]

As by Roy's definition the Indian National Congress was a predominantly bourgeois organization with petty-bourgeois leadership, this was another version of his old argument against having anything to do with it.

The Theory of Decolonization

The Sixth World Congress of the Comintern was to convene in Moscow in July, 1928. In the discussion which preceded the Sixth Congress, and in the debates of the Congress itself, India occupied a prominent place. The disagreements were both strategical and tactical and focused on what became known as the theory of decolonization, a formulation subsequently associated with the name of M. N. Roy. Because of the prominence given to this theory in discussion during the year 1928, it is necessary to dispel some of the confusion which surrounded it at the time and which blurred the roles of the participants in the drama.

Roy's version of the origin of the theory is as follows:

> While I was away in China (1927) a new comrade [Tagore] from India came to Moscow. In his report he emphasized on [sic] the rapid development of modern industry in India. . . . In summarizing the debate on the report of the Indian delegate, Bukharin suggested that the Commission set up for examining the question should report on the process of such "decolonization." (He used the term for the first time, evidently in a tentative and relative sense.)
>
> On my return [from China] I was charged to draft a resolution on the basis of the preparatory work accomplished by the Commission. The resolution drafted by me, which was never formally accepted (not because there was any serious objection to it, but because of the waning of interest in the subject), subsequently became the main weapon against me. It was in that document that all my heresies were discovered, when subsequently it became necessary to find evidence in support of a verdict already secretly pronounced against me for some unknown crime.[2]

---

[1] "The Lessons of the Chinese Revolution," *Masses of India,* III (Sept.–Oct., 1927), pp. 19–20.

[2] M. N. Roy, *Our Differences* (Calcutta: Saraswaty Library, 1938), pp. 29, 30, 31.

Speaking of this resolution, Roy says that he "wrote it in Moscow and left it there." [3] However, he must have had a copy of it with him in Berlin for he claimed to be quoting from it extensively in an open letter he wrote to the Comintern in 1929.[4] Since most of this quoted material is also to be found in an article in *Masses,* for November, 1927, it seems reasonable to assume that the article was based on the resolution, if indeed it is not the actual resolution itself. Thus the article can be regarded as the first and most authoritative expression of the theory of decolonization.

The theory itself was not new, but there was novelty in the politico-economic argument with which Roy expressed it. He asserted that increased industrialization in India had created a manufacturing bourgeoisie which found itself competing with the imperialists in the exploitation of the masses. As it grew, the new bourgeoisie had demanded concessions from the imperialists, and in order to win them threatened to side with the masses. This created a revolutionary situation that frightened the imperialists, and as its revolutionary potential increased, the imperialists granted the concessions. The new bourgeoisie were thus brought nearer to running their own affairs—hence the term "decolonization." They were, moreover, drawn more and more into partnership with the imperialists in exploiting the masses; in exchange for the imperialist concessions, the bourgeoisie would dampen the revolutionary ardor of the masses and help imperialism maintain its foothold. "The new economic policy of British imperialism in India," said Roy, "sharpens the class differentiation and ripens the class struggle in the face of which nationalist struggle based upon capitalist antagonism loses its importance." [5]

All of this was, in fact, only a slightly different way of saying what Roy had always said, namely, that the bourgeoisie was not a revolutionary factor and could not be regarded as an ally in the revolution. The following quotations make this clear:

The National Congress, in the coming annual session, is going to declare peace with British imperialism. . . . The bourgeoisie are not only withdrawing themselves from the national revolution; the withdrawal is but a prelude to a definite stand against the national revolution together with British imperialism. . . . The bourgeois nationalist movement is split up into half a dozen parties all of which are opposed to a revolutionary struggle against imperialism. . . . It [the bourgeoisie] is no longer a revolutionary force. Not only from the point of view of the internal conditions of India; but from the point of view of the present

---

[3] *Ibid.,* p. *v.*

[4] *Ibid.,* pp. 32–33.

[5] "The Role of the Bourgeoisie in the National Revolution," *Masses of India,* III (Nov., 1927), p. 7.

world conditions also the Indian bourgeoisie is rallied on the side of the counter-revolution. It cannot and does not lead or participate in the struggle for national freedom. . . . Indian National Revolution has passed its bourgeois stage. It must still realize a program which, objectively and historically, is the program of bourgeois revolution; but it is no longer a bourgeois revolution, because it can and will succeed only by breaking the bounds of capitalist society.[6]

Contained in this theory were certain important tactical imperatives. By saying that the bourgeois nationalist movement was "split up into half a dozen parties all of which are opposed to a revolutionary struggle against imperialism," Roy was pointing not only at the Indian National Congress, but even at its more radical components. The only tactics justified by the theory of decolonization would be opposition to these bourgeois parties, for any other course would help the Indian bourgeoisie increase its share in the exploitation of the masses.

M. N. Roy's Assembly Letter

Since the debate preceding and during the Sixth Congress was as much concerned with tactical considerations as with strategy, it is necessary at this point to outline the tactics which Roy set forth for the Indian movement and which came to be linked with his decolonization theory. These tactics were communicated to the Indian Communists in a letter dated December 30, 1927, which later became known as the Assembly Letter when an intercepted copy was read into the record of the Indian Legislative Assembly.[7]

The main tactical advice in the Assembly Letter concerned organizational forms for the Indian movement, that is, how the Workers' and Peasants' Party and the Communist Party should be organized, and what their relations with Roy and with international communism should be. Roy favored the continued existence of both parties: the CPI should be illegal, and the WPP legal. "A Communist Party," he said, "can exist legally in India only if it abstains from the preparations to wage war against the King, that is, legality can be had at the expense of the very *raison d'être* of the CP." [8] The WPP, on the other hand, would be a legal party, serving as a "rallying ground of all the exploited social elements (proletariat, peasantry and petty bourgeoisie)." "The Communists," Roy continued, "should be in the WPP and by virtue of their being the conscious vanguard of the working class

---

[6] *Ibid.*, pp. 5–8.

[7] The complete text of the Assembly Letter was not available to the authors, but sufficiently detailed quotations are found in the Meerut trial documents and in the press to permit reconstruction of the central themes. See Meerut Sessions Judgment, pp. 186–189; Meerut Committal Order, pp. 66–69; *The Times* (London), Sept. 25, 1928; and *Statesman* (Calcutta), Aug. 18, 1928.

[8] Meerut Sessions Judgment, p. 186.

will be the driving force of the Party." [9] Commenting on the current situation, the letter warned:

> The present form of its organization obstructs the development of the WPP. It is too openly identified with the CP. This keeps away from it many revolutionary elements who would join it. . . . It is publicly known that practically all the members of the CC of the CP are the leaders of the WPP. Of course, in fact it should be so, but the cat has been unnecessarily let out of the bag by publishing the list of the CC of the CP. This mistake must be rectified as soon as possible.[10]

Next, Roy dealt with the question of international affiliation. The WPP should affiliate with the League Against Imperialism, he said, whereby it would have "the relations and aid" it needed but "will not be condemned of having connections with M. [Moscow]." The CPI, on the other hand, "must unquestionably be a section of the CI." And he added, "It is practically treated as such, but no formal request to this effect has yet come from our Party in India." [11]

Finally, Roy revealed his own competition with the CPGB for control of the Indian movement. He declared:

> The centers in Berlin and Paris are the agencies of the CI to look after the Indian affairs. The CP of India will have its relation with the CI through those centers and not through London. Any British comrade that may come to India comes to work there under the supervision and in accord with the CC of the CPI. He has no superior right, unless he comes with a mandate from the CI as its representative. No such representative has as yet been sent to India. So you know the position. . . . Indian Communists in emigration are members of the CPI and are automatically members of the WPP; we expect to be treated by the comrades at home as such. We should not be looked upon as outsiders who could serve you only as financial agents. As members of the same Party nationally and internationally, we must coordinate our efforts.[12]

This coördination, Roy said, should be accomplished through the Foreign Bureau of the CPI, whose existence had already been sanctioned at an earlier meeting of Communists in India. The Foreign Bureau would have three members, Roy, Clemens Dutt, and Mohammed Sipassi, and it would function as the organ through which the CI would guide the movement in India.

Obviously, Roy's primary purpose in issuing the Assembly Letter was to regain control of the Indian movement which, in his absence in China, had fallen more and more under the influence of the CPGB. The Letter was a thinly veiled attack on Spratt and Bradley who had become, in effect, the real leaders of the CPI and whose ties with their

---

[9] *Ibid.*, p. 187.
[10] Meerut Committal Order, pp. 66–67.
[11] Meerut Sessions Judgment, p. 188.
[12] *Ibid.*, p. 189.

compatriots in London were much closer than their relations with Roy. The letter also criticized Saumyendranath Tagore whose visit to Russia had hardly bolstered Roy's position in the Comintern.

Roy's Last Trip to Moscow

Having reasserted his claim to the leadership of the Indian Communist movement, Roy determined to attend the Ninth Plenum of the ECCI, scheduled to meet in Moscow in February, 1928. Despite the attacks made on him by Saumyendranath Tagore, he had reason to believe that a cordial reception awaited him, for he regarded Stalin as a personal friend, and a friend ought to be appreciative of the support Roy had given him on the China question.[13] Roy also had good personal relations with Bukharin who was at the time head of the Comintern and was closely allied with Stalin. And finally, Roy was still a member of the ECCI—no charges against him had ever been made by that body.

Roy arrived in Moscow on February 4, 1928, and immediately set about familiarizing himself with the complicated political situation.[14] He discussed China with Heinz Neumann who had been there after Roy left, and he wrote to a friend in western Europe: "We were more or less correctly informed about the Chinese question . . . there has been an unofficial conference of all the 'experts' to discuss the problem."

Roy attended the opening meeting of the plenum on February 9, and wrote the next day that it "threatens to be a rather long-drawn affair." On February 22 he went to bed with a pain in his ear that ultimately developed into a serious infection, evidently mastoiditis. Confined to bed and under a doctor's care, Roy was unable to attend all of the meetings of the plenum. He complained in a letter that he was out of touch with the proceedings and that "only important political things were communicated to me." "Who told you I am having political difficulties?" he wrote on March 6. "Nothing of the kind."

Roy had remained in Moscow long beyond the original four weeks

---

[13] Two of Roy's close friends of this period, Communists who knew him in Moscow in 1926, have told one of the authors that the friendship between Roy and Stalin was real and intimate, but neither remembers ever seeing the two men together. The authors have been unable to locate testimony on this friendship from anyone with first-hand knowledge, except from Roy himself.

[14] This account of Roy's visit to Moscow for the ninth plenum is based on letters which he wrote at the time to a friend in Western Europe. The present owner of the letters, who prefers to remain anonymous, has generously permitted the authors to examine them and has supplied additional information about the period.

he had planned on when he left Berlin, and his friends by this time
had become quite worried over his health and his political situation.
One of them was considering the advisability of going to Moscow to
see what could be done, and this idea was communicated to Roy. "I
like it less here than ever before," he replied on March 18. "I hate the
idea of your coming back with the risk of getting somehow entangled."
And then in a postscript he added the revealing comment: "From your
letter to ——— I find your views about coming here. They are correct,
and I hope you will carefully consider them if you decide to come."

With this indication that Roy was in serious difficulty, the friend
journeyed to Moscow from Berlin. Arriving in the Soviet capital,
this person discovered Roy's physical condition to be very serious and
suspected that he was being denied adequate medical care, perhaps
deliberately. With the aid of highly placed Russians, still friendly to
Roy, exit visas were secured. Then in a dramatic episode, Roy was
taken from the hospital and rushed to the airport where two seats
had been booked under fictitious names.[15] All went well and Roy
reached Berlin safely where proper medical care ultimately resulted
in his complete recovery.

The Controversy on Strategy and Tactics

Ironically, Roy's flight from Moscow took place during the very
month when the Comintern began to veer toward Roy's view of the
bourgeoisie. That month, March, 1928, the Russian position on the
Indian question was presented in an article by Eugene Varga, published in *Inprecor*. The starting point of Varga's argument was that
industrialization in India had been exaggerated by Roy and his supporters, and that British policy in recent years had been to arrest the
trend toward industrialization which it had permitted as an expedient
during the war. From this premise Varga drew certain conclusions
which were relevant to the critical question of the role of the bourgeoisie in Indian politics. The Indian bourgeoisie, he said, was in
opposition, but their struggles were "for an improvement of their position within the Empire" and were not a "revolutionary fight against
British imperialism." [16] It was the Indian proletariat which would
lead the nationalist struggle. By saying that the Indian bourgeoisie
was not in a revolutionary fight with British imperialism, Varga was

---

[15] Deruluft, a joint Russo-German airline, operated at this time between Moscow
and Berlin.

[16] E. Varga, "Economics and Economic Policy in the Fourth Quarter of 1927,"
Inprecor, VIII (March 14, 1928), p. 294.

removing the only reason for the Communists to make an alliance with it. It was what M. N. Roy had been saying all along. The Comintern was coming around to Roy's position.[17]

When Varga's formulations were brought up for discussion at the Comintern's Indian Commission which met in March and April, 1928, they were challenged by both the British and Indian members of that Commission.[18] The CPGB, which by now had more influence with the Indian Communists than had Roy, made public its disagreements with the developing trend in a long article by R. Palme Dutt in *Labour Monthly* in June, 1928.

Dutt conceded that there had been some change in Britain's policy toward Indian industrialization. "Today we are faced with a noticeable arrest in the development of the policy," he said. "The tone in relation to the National Movement is one of open contempt and indifference. There is a noticeable hardening against concessions and conciliation towards the Indian bourgeoisie." [19] But Dutt insisted that this did not mean there was no industrialization at all. "The whole character of the British policy of industrialization in India," he said, "is to secure industrialization *under British control*." [20]

Then he concluded:

From every sign of what is going on at present we can build with confidence on our diagnosis of the continuing capitalist and industrial evolution of India, with the accompanying political revolutionising consequences, and in particular on the growth, both in numbers and in consciousness, of the industrial proletariat, alongside the intensifying agrarian crisis.[21]

This discussion of whether industrialization was or was not increasing in India was only tangential to the main question, the attitude to be taken toward the Indian National Congress. In the debates on the decolonization theory, before and during the Sixth Congress, the real issue was generally buried in a bog of sophistry and could be detected only occasionally as, for example, when Dutt said in his article:

---

[17] That Roy had not changed his views is clear from an article appearing the following month in *Masses of India*. It said: "One thing is clear. The bourgeoisie—with all its elements from Right to Left—are drifting away from the main current of the national revolutionary struggle. The leaders of the Congress . . . have been trying consistently to suppress the revolutionary instincts of the masses and damp their revolutionary enthusiasm." "The Significance of Third February," *Masses of India*, IV (April, 1928), p. 9.

[18] See speech of R. Page Arnot, which traces the history of the discussion, in *Inprecor*, VIII (Oct. 30, 1928), p. 1421.

[19] R. Palme Dutt, "Notes of the Month," *Labour Monthly*, X (June, 1928), p. 326.

[20] *Ibid.*, p. 331. Emphasis in original.

[21] *Ibid.*, p. 334.

In general, and on all fundamental questions, the role of the Indian bourgeoisie since the collapse of the Non-Cooperation movement has evolved in the direction of becoming more and more clearly counter-revolutionary. . . . But at the same time, within this general framework of capitulation, there takes place a process of friction and antagonism which has recently grown sharper. . . . Thus the role of the bourgeoisie in the national struggle is not yet exhausted, and may even extend under certain conditions; but it remains permanently limited in scope by its fear and hostility towards any wider mass revolutionary movement, and, therefore, very dangerous to the real struggle against imperialism. It becomes the task of the mass movement to exploit to the maximum the opportunities presented by bourgeois resistance, as in the boycott of the Simon Commission, but under independent leadership.[22]

In other words, though the bourgeoisie was becoming counterrevolutionary, it still had a revolutionary role to play. And he demonstrated particular confidence in the petty bourgeoisie:

But if we turn to the rank and file of the Nationalist Movement, representing in the main the various elements of the petty-bourgeoisie, the sharpening of opposition [to imperialism] is much more conspicuous. Here an actual process of revolutionization is at work among a considerable section, following on the disillusionment after the collapse of Gandhi and Non-Cooperation, and on the economic hardships of the present period.[23]

ECCI View of India

In July, 1928, a month after the appearance of Dutt's article, the ECCI published a 508-page report which was to serve as a basis for the discussions preceding the Sixth Congress.[24] In addition to detailed accounts of organizational activities, the report contained separate chapters on all of the major countries of the world. It seems likely that the Indian section was the result of the deliberations of the Indian Commission which met in Moscow in March and April. Concerning the Indian bourgeoisie the ECCI report said:

For the purpose of getting nearer to the masses and utilizing their revolutionary orientation for its reformist policy, the bourgeoisie has improved the methods and slogans it used in 1919–1922. It has taken into consideration the increased political development of the broad masses. In this advanced stage of development it is no longer possible for the bourgeois parties to force themselves on the masses as the leaders of the national revolutionary struggle. Neither is it possible to impress them with the revolutionary slogans of independence unless they are accompanied by an effort at revolutionary actions. With the independence slogan the bourgeoisie endeavours to keep under the influence of the bourgeois leaders the Left nationalist elements composed of the mass of the petty bourgeoisie and the intelligentsia.

---

[22] *Ibid.*, pp. 334–335.

[23] *Ibid.*, p. 335.

[24] *The Communist International Between the Fifth and the Sixth World Congresses* (London: CPGB, 1928).

By keeping the leadership over the petty bourgeoisie and the intelligentsia in its hands, the bourgeoisie is endeavouring to establish a connection with the upper strata of the proletariat and the peasantry which it hopes to draw into its struggle. . . . Organizationally unseparated from the bourgeois political parties and politically led by them, the nationalist Left wing, with its slogans of independence, social equality and socialism, has evolved into an instrument, in the hands of the bourgeoisie, for the penetration and vicarious leadership of the broad working masses.[25]

Whereas Dutt appears to have been arguing that both the bourgeoisie and the petty bourgeoisie had a revolutionary part to play, the ECCI document emphasized the unreliable character of the petty bourgeoisie by stating that the bourgeoisie would try to dominate the petty bourgeoisie and use it as a tool to control the masses. All this apparently academic quarrel actually revolved around the future of the WPP in India, and this was made specific in the ECCI document. It said:

The main weak point of the Workers' and Peasants' Party is that, in practice, it is acting more as a Left wing of the Congress than as an independent political Party. The Workers' and Peasants' Party cannot develop into a party of mass national-revolutionary struggle unless it emancipates itself entirely from the influence of bourgeois politicians and becomes transformed into a bloc of the working class with all the exploited masses under the leadership of the proletariat. On the other hand, it is entirely out of the question that the Workers' and Peasants' Party should be a substitute for the Communist Party, the organization of which is absolutely necessary.[26]

Here then was the heart of the matter: should the Comintern promote the Workers' and Peasants' Party, or should it devote its attention exclusively to the formation of a Communist party? The leadership of the WPP was predominantly petty bourgeois. If the petty bourgeoisie was unreliable and subject to the influence of the bourgeoisie, then the WPP could not be genuinely revolutionary. Moreover, there was the danger that in supporting the WPP the Comintern might be guilty of promoting the hegemony of the petty bourgeoisie over the proletariat, a course so un-Marxian as to fill orthodox Communists with horror.[27]

Indian Delegates to the Sixth Congress

The Sixth World Congress of the Communist International met in Moscow from July 17 to September 1, 1928. There were six Indians

---

[25] *Ibid.*, pp. 468–469.

[26] *Ibid.*, p. 476.

[27] The question is raised in just this fashion by "Savdar" in his article, "Revoliutsionnyie dvizhenie Indii v sviazi s sobyitiiami v Kitae," (The Revolutionary Movement in India in Relation to Events in China), *Revoliutsionnyi Vostok* [The Revolutionary East], No. 2 (1927), pp. 96–107.

present—seven if one includes Clemens Dutt who was identified as representing India in the *Inprecor* reports of his speeches. The debates of the Congress were extensively reported in *Inprecor*, and the names of the Indian participants were given as Sikander Sur, Narayan, Mahmoud, Raza, Mazut, and Luhani. Sikander Sur was in reality Shaukat Usmani, and Narayan was Saumyendranath Tagore. Tagore lists the Indian delegation as Shaukat Usmani, Clemens Dutt, G. A. K. Luhani, Mohammed Shafiq, and himself.[28] He says that Habib Ahmad Nasim was chosen as the delegate to the Communist Youth Congress which met in Moscow at the same time. The Indian delegation had three deciding votes and three consultative votes. In the analysis presented here, the real names will be used to identify the various participants where they are positively known.[29]

Some word should be said about the legitimacy of the Indian delegation. Tagore had come to Moscow in the middle of 1927 with, in his words, "a mandate of the Workers' and Peasants' Party of Bengal, there being no Communist Party of India as yet." Philip Spratt disputes this, saying:

> There was a CPI, and Muzaffar Ahmed was a member of it, though it began to work only in 1927. I have never quite understood Muzaffar's relation to Tagore. Muzaffar was a stickler for CP correctness and prestige. I do not think he regarded Tagore as a member. Yet he was a party to sending Tagore to Moscow and at this time maintained a friendly attitude towards him.[30]

It is important to note that Tagore left India more than a year before the Sixth Congress and that he claimed a mandate from the WPP, not the CPI; the latter had its first important meeting only after he left.

Usmani's credentials were even more questionable. According to Tagore, Usmani went to Bombay in April, 1928. There he had a dispute with Benjamin Bradley over the party work, and shortly thereafter, he decided to go to Moscow to attend the Sixth Congress. Tagore reports:

> He informed his party comrades about his plan to leave for Moscow. Dange, the diplomat, supported him in private but expressed his helplessness to support

---

[28] Saumyendranath Tagore, *Historical Development of the Communist Movement in India* ([Calcutta?]: Red Front Press, 1944), p. 14.

[29] *Names as they appear in the debates:*   *Identification:*

Names as they appear in the debates:	Identification:
Sikander Sur	Shaukat Usmani
Narayan	Saumyendranath Tagore
Dutt	Clemens Dutt
Luhani	G. A. K. Luhani
Mahmoud	Mohammed Shafiq (?)
Raza (sometimes Rasur)	(?)
Mazut	Habib Ahmad Nasim (?)

[30] From Philip Spratt's hand written annotations on Tagore, *Historical Development of the . . .*

him openly. The triumvirate clique—Ghate, Muzaffar Amed and Joglekar—supported by the two satraps, Spratt and Bradley, tried their best to persuade Usmani to give up his proposed trip to Moscow. When they found that their persuasion had no effect on Usmani, they refused to give him a mandate from the party.[31]

Spratt's account differs on the point of whether Usmani made known his intentions before departure. He says:

> The VI World Congress had taken place in the summer of 1928. Without telling the rest of us, Shaukat Usmani decided to attend it, and went via Iran, taking three others with him. . . . The first I heard of their adventure was a cable from London asking whether Usmani represented the party. I replied no, which of course was true.[32]

Tagore corroborates the fact that the Indian Communists did not give Usmani a mandate. He says: "A letter had in the meantime reached the Comintern from the Indian party informing the Communist International that Usmani did not represent the party at all and that he represented none but himself." [33]

It is clear, therefore, that none of the Indian delegates had authority to speak for the Communists in India. Tagore, by his own testimony, represented only the WPP, not the CPI. Luhani had been associated with Roy in Europe, hardly a valid mandate in 1928. The same applies to Clemens Dutt, a member of Roy's Foreign Bureau of the CPI, but also a member of the CPGB. Usmani, and presumably his three companions, had specifically been disqualified by the Communists in India.[34] It is, therefore, most interesting that it was he who was elected to the Presidium of the Congress. There are two possible explanations for this. The most compelling one, as will be shown, emerges from an analysis of the debate wherein Usmani sided with the Russians against the CPGB on the critical question of the Workers' and Peasants' Party. The other explanation centers on the presence in Moscow of S. Srinivasa Iyengar, who had just completed a term as president of the Indian National Congress.

Iyengar, with Jawaharlal Nehru and Subhas Chandra Bose, was one of the leaders of the left wing in the Congress. At Madras in 1927, he had moved the resolution in favor of boycotting the Simon Com-

---

[31] Tagore reports: "Usmani stressed the necessity of concentrating more efforts on the organization of the party than on the trade unions. Bradley, who was specially deputed to India for trade union work, could not allow anyone to minimize the importance of his job." Tagore, *Historical Development of the* . . . , p. 13.

[32] Philip Spratt, *Blowing Up India* (Calcutta: Prachi Prakashan, 1955), p. 41.

[33] Tagore, *Historical Development of the* . . . , p. 14.

[34] Spratt states that Usmani's three companions were detained in the Soviet Union and ultimately shot as spies. Spratt, *Blowing Up India*, p. 42.

mission, and as a member of the Central Legislative Assembly he had sponsored a resolution protesting the use of Indian troops to maintain British holdings in China. Usmani, writing in 1953, makes an interesting reference to Iyengar:

I was released [from jail] in August, 1927. Many revolutionaries implored me to set out for Moscow again and seek some help from the Comintern. Before I left, I had important discussions with top-ranking political workers in the country. This chapter of my meetings with them should remain a closed secret for some more time to come. Many of them are dead now and others are occupying key positions in both parts of the subcontinent. I do not have their permission to publish even the gist of these talks. . . . Moscow at this time [summer 1928] had two visitors of note: Henri Barbusse [of the Comité Pro-Hindou in Paris, see p. 74], the famous French writer, and Mr. Srinivasa Iyengar. Mr. Iyengar had figured prominently in the talks I had in Delhi with important leaders before I left; but I soon learnt that his mission to Moscow failed. I knew it was bound to fail. I had several sessions with Bukharin, and it was clear as daylight to me that Bukharin did not at all favour the idea of giving any aid to the Indian revolutionaries. . . . Mr. Srinivasa Iyengar was going to have a meeting with Stalin and asked me whether I would accompany him, but I refused. He finally took Saumyendranath Tagore, grand-nephew of the great poet as interpreter. I knew it was no use seeing Stalin on military aid to India; and the meeting turned out exactly as I had thought.[35]

Usmani makes several references to his desire to instigate guerrilla warfare in India with Soviet help, and he implies that Iyengar's "mission" to the USSR was for similar purposes. Iyengar's biographer provides no corroboration for this, saying merely that Iyengar went to Russia "in order to observe communism in action." However, he adds, that "the great experiment in Russia, where a wretched and impoverished peasantry—so similar to the Indian peasantry—was heroically engaged in a colossal experiment, could not but make a lasting impression on Mr. Srinivasa Iyengar's sensitive mind. Inevitably he gravitated toward socialism." [36]

Iyengar's visit to Russia came only a year after that of his colleague, Jawaharlal Nehru. The evidence presently available is inadequate for speculation concerning the question raised by Usmani's testimony, namely, the possibility that leading Indian nationalists were seeking assistance from the Soviet Union. It does seem likely, however, that through Iyengar, Shaukat Usmani was able to represent himself as having important connections with the Indian National Congress, and that this enhanced his prestige with the Russians despite the fact that they were about to brand the Congress as counterrevolutionary.

---

[35] Shaukat Usmani, *I Met Stalin Twice* (Bombay: K. Kurian, 1953), pp. 22, 27.
[36] K. R. Srinivasa Iyengar, *S. Srinivasa Iyengar: The Story of a Decade of Indian Politics* (Mangalore: Basel Mission Press, 1939), p. 64.

Sixth Congress Debate on the Colonial Question

The Russian position on the Indian question was first set forth in the report of the Comintern general secretary, Bukharin. It was inconceivable, he argued, that the bourgeoisie would play a revolutionary role for any length of time. It might maneuver against British imperialism, but this was a far cry from the armed struggle against imperialism that had been waged by the bourgeoisie in China. He was especially critical of the Swarajists, but exempted from his attack "the various petty bourgeois parties or terroristic organizations." [37]

Bukharin's analysis was brief; the main report on the revolutionary movement in the various colonies was delivered by Otto Vilhelm Kuusinen who had been assigned this responsibility by the ECCI a few weeks before. Kuusinen apparently had specialized knowledge neither of the subject in general, nor of India in particular. But the report which he read to the Congress was focused, primarily, on India. "Why should Indian conditions be dealt with specially here?" Kuusinen asked. "Of course firstly, because of the enormous importance of India among the colonies, because of the class character of the colonial monopoly which is particularly noticeable in India, and also because I hold the view that a serious revolutionary crisis will develop in India in the not far distant future." [38]

Kuusinen's report amounts to a statement of the three-class strategy. He begins with an attack on the theory of the industrialization and consequent decolonization of India, using the arguments already developed by Varga and by the ECCI. Then he considers the role of the bourgeoisie:

> That the national bourgeoisie is raising a hue and cry is quite true. But it is important to understand the political character of the Indian bourgeoisie, *its national reformist policy*. That this policy is directed against the proletariat is as plain as that the bourgeoisie is the bourgeoisie. That the policy of the Indian bourgeoisie is not revolutionary, is also quite clear.[39]

His position on the petty bourgeoisie is ambiguous, but he concedes that "the urban petty bourgeoisie, and to a considerable extent the petty bourgeois intelligentsia can play an important role in the national movement." [40] Note that the reference is to the "national movement" and not to the revolution.

---

[37] *Inprecor*, VIII (July 30, 1928), p. 734.
[38] O. V. Kuusinen, "The Revolutionary Movement in the Colonies." *Inprecor*, VIII (Oct. 4, 1928), p. 1225.
[39] *Ibid.*, p. 1229. Emphasis in original.
[40] *Loc. cit.*

Next Kuusinen comes to the question of the workers' and peasants' parties. He says:

For a time, some comrades considered the advisability of "labour and peasant parties" as a substitute for such organizational forms [as Communist Parties]. It is now clearer than before that this form is not to be recommended, especially in colonial and semi-colonial countries. It would be an easy matter for the labor and peasant parties to transform themselves into petty-bourgeois parties, to get away from the Communists, thereby failing to help them to come in contact with the masses. To consider such parties as a substitute for a real Communist Party, would be a serious mistake. We are for a bloc with the peasantry, but we will not have anything to do with fusion of various classes.[41]

The principle opposition to the Kuusinen position came from the members of the British delegation, as one would expect in view of the controversy which had preceded the Congress. With the exception of J. T. Murphy, the entire British delegation took a firm stand against the Kuusinen thesis and opposed it to the end. They insisted that industrialization was continuing in India, albeit under British control, and that failure to recognize this fact would mean underestimating the role of the working class. How could it be argued, they said, that the proletariat was growing in India, if it was not conceded that industry was growing also, since the former is the product of the latter? [42]

The industrialization debate was only ancillary to the question of the role of the bourgeoisie. Clemens Dutt summarized the British viewpoint when he said: "The Indian bourgeoisie is a counter-revolutionary force, but that does not mean that we cannot use even it in the development of the mass revolution." [43] This question of the bourgeoisie touched on the attitude the Communists would take toward the Indian National Congress. Of even greater importance to the CPGB was the question of the Workers' and Peasants' parties, about which Dutt said:

The point I want to make is that the question of the Workers' and Peasants' Party cannot be dismissed with a phrase. . . . The characteristic feature of the Workers' and Peasants' Parties in the present stage of development in India is that they are forming an important route through which communists are finding their way to the masses.[44]

On the question of the Workers' and Peasants' parties, then, the lines were clearly drawn. The Russians wanted to liquidate them; the British

---

[41] *Ibid.*, pp. 1230–1231.
[42] See Bennet's speech in *Inprecor*, VIII (Oct. 17, 1928), p. 1320, and his sarcastic interruption of Mazut: "The industry does not develop but the proletariat grows?" *Ibid.* (Nov. 8, 1928), p. 1465.
[43] *Ibid.*, (Oct. 30, 1928), p. 1425.
[44] *Loc. cit.*

wanted to maintain them. It is now appropriate to examine the attitude of the Indian delegates on this important issue.

Among the Indians, Usmani and Tagore were the most active in the
debate. On the key issue of the WPP, Usmani, Raza, and Mazut sided
with the Russians. Agreeing with the draft thesis which, in effect,
called for the liquidation of the WPP, Usmani said: "The Workers' and
Peasants' parties exist owing to the wrong tactics and instructions of
the Comintern." [45] Raza added: "We must criticize the policy of the
Comintern in conducting the organization of the Workers' and Peasants' parties while altogether ignoring the organization of the Communist Party of India. This is just as absurd as to put the cart before
the horse. This policy must be revised." [46]

Tagore on the other hand tried to defend the WPP tactic under the
new strategy. He argued:

> It seems to me that some of the comrades are scared with the nightmare which
> is the result of their own irrational fantasy that the Workers' and Peasants'
> Party is a substitute of the Communist Party. Nobody has ever put forward that
> the Workers' and Peasants' Party would be a substitute for the Communist Party.
>
> The petty bourgeois elements in the country who have been proletarianized are
> sometimes more proletarian than the proletariat themselves. The petty bourgeois
> intelligentsia, the urban petty bourgeoisie, have to play a role in the revolutionary
> movement in the colonies. What should be the organizational expression of
> the anti-imperialist front of the petty bourgeois elements? Can we afford to swamp
> the Communist Party with such petty bourgeois elements? We cannot. On the
> other hand, the Communist Party of India should utilize the revolutionary
> energies of the petty bourgeoisie. I think it is clear that this anti-imperialist
> front can only take the organizational form of a Workers' and Peasants' Party
> composed of the urban intelligentsia and the petty bourgeois elements, under
> the leadership of the proletariat. . . . We have been able to take over some
> trade unions from the reformist leadership, to organize peasant unions; now
> we are told to liquidate all these Workers' and Peasants' Parties. This is pure
> and simple professorial dogmatism against which Lenin warned us so many times.[47]

Although Tagore's position on this tactical question was the same
as that of the CPGB, it would be wrong to conclude from this that he
approved the role the British Party was taking in Indian affairs. In
fact he took specific exception to a phrase in the draft program which
he felt implied that "the proletarian movement in India should march
under the leadership of the British Communist Party." "Nobody will
deny," he said, "that in the organic structure of British Imperialism
India and England are closely connected with each other and for the

---

[45] *Inprecor*, VIII (Nov. 8, 1928), p. 1473.
[46] *Ibid.*, p. 1454.
[47] *Ibid.* (Oct. 30, 1928), p. 1391.

same reason the Communist Parties of India and Britain are also organically linked up with each other for carrying out the Proletarian Revolution in these two countries, but this on no account means the subordination of the colonial party to the leadership of the party of the imperialist home country." [48] From the tone of Usmani's attack on the British position, it is obvious that he, also, did not relish CPGB leadership of India.

In terms of Indian realities, there is little doubt that the WPP had some potential, and that its liquidation would remove the most effective instrument then in existence for the propagation of Communist ideology on the subcontinent. Tagore's position is easily understandable, for since it was the WPP that he represented at the Sixth Congress, his own interests were involved. He had not been admitted to the CPI and even claimed that it did not exist.

But Usmani's opposition to the WPP is difficult to understand unless he had lent his services to the Russians, perhaps in the hope that he could step into Roy's shoes. "Comrades who have been here for about ten years," he said, in an obvious reference to Roy, "cannot properly deal with the situation." [49] In his recollections of this period, published in a pamphlet in 1953, Usmani mentions his election to the presidium, saying, "Unwillingly and unexpectedly—I did not deserve such an honor—I was pushed into the Presidium of the Comintern Congress, and found myself seated third from Stalin." [50]

Usmani was speaking the simple truth when he said that he did not deserve the honor of a place on the Presidium for, strictly speaking, he was not even eligible to participate in the Congress let alone hold an important office. He was probably also speaking the truth when he said that he was "pushed into the Presidium," and in view of his eulogy of Stalin (which is what his 1953 pamphlet amounts to), one may suspect that it was Stalin who did the pushing. Stalin may have thought that Usmani's connections with Iyengar and the Indian National Congress would be useful, but certainly, and more importantly, he wanted support in his demand for a new Comintern strategy—the leftist strategy signaled by Varga's articles, and strongly opposed by the CPGB. The British delegates based their arguments against this strategy on their experiences with the Indian movement; in opposing them Stalin might have assumed that an Indian, fresh from India, would be a helpful ally. And this is what Usmani became, attacking

---

[48] *Ibid.* (Sept. 25, 1928), p. 1203.
[49] *Ibid.* (Oct. 4, 1928), p. 1248.
[50] Usmani, *I Met Stalin Twice*, p. 23.

the British comrades with such vehemence that at one point in the debate he flayed their arguments as "nothing more than an open defense of imperialism!" [51]

The Russians were clearly bent on making "decolonization" an odious word. To do this, they ascribed to it a meaning which Roy certainly never intended, namely, the voluntary cessation of imperialist exploitation.

Perhaps to avoid the appearance of siding with Roy, the British delegation accepted the spurious Russian definition and roundly denounced decolonization. Yet in effect the British had accepted part of Roy's tactics, while the Russians were in the process of adopting his strategy.

This traffic in poorly defined scare words did not serve to make the Sixth Congress a monument to honest political debate, and one can understand how some of the participants got lost in the dialectical fog. One Russian, Lominadze, was candid enough to remark about the draft thesis: "I must say that I read a certain statement four times without understanding it, and yet theses are written for people who know much less than we delegates to this Congress." [52] The most straightforward remark about decolonization came from G. A. K. Luhani who told the Congress:

I consider it necessary to declare that I have nothing whatever to do with the so-called "decolonization of India" theory which Comrade Kuusinen described in his speech introducing the draft theses on the Revolutionary movement in the colonies and semi-colonies. What he, and some other comrades taking part in the discussion, said in this connection is a complete travesty and misrepresentation of what some of us wanted to convey in the provisional use of the term "decolonization." I emphasize that our use of the term was provisional; we always put the term in quotation marks. I repudiate entirely the interpretation which Comrade Kuusinen has given to our use of the term.

In order to dissipate the confusion which has been created with regard to the genesis of this point of view, I think a certain *mise en point* is called for. About a year ago at a meeting of the Political Secretariat of the ECCI, an Indian comrade made a report on the situation in India. In the report no mention was made either of the colonization or de-colonization of India. As a result of the discussion of the report, a special commission was, however, appointed to study, among other aspects of the Indian situation, the question of decolonization. The term "decolonization" was included in what I may call the terms of reference of the commission. So far as I am aware, it was the first occasion of the use of the term "decolonization" with reference to India. The special commission occupied itself with the questions as formulated. Materials were submitted to the commission embodying a certain point of view. There were several discussions held and I remember no serious divergence of opinion inside the commission, and, if I am

[51] *Inprecor*, VIII (Nov. 8, 1928), p. 1474.
[52] *Ibid.*, p. 1461.

not mistaken, the point of view was accepted as general groundwork. The materials of the commission, either in a manuscript or printed form, have been available for the last nine months. They contain the subject matter of the greater part of the present discussion on India—I have not the possibility here of raising the question whether the point of view is right or wrong, or whether it is Right or Left, and of formulating my response to the somewhat one-sided discussion. However, I want you to take note of the fact that the point of view has been presented to you, not in its original, but in its travestied form. Thus, our own formulation of the point of view in question is not before you. I must register my energetic protest against this method of controversy as, to put it mildly, unfair both to the delegates of the Congress and those whose point of view is being criticized.[53]

The New Colonial Thesis

Although it made some concessions to the British viewpoint, the colonial thesis which ultimately emerged from the Sixth Congress was, in the main, faithful to the Russian view, and strongly reflected the Chinese experience. It represented a three-class strategy, based upon the implicit assumption that the Indian revolution had reached the agrarian phase. The decline of bourgeois nationalism, according to the thesis, had enabled British imperialism "once more to return to its policy of hindering the industrial development of India." [54] It defines the poor peasantry and the petty bourgeoisie as the allies of the proletariat, stating that the "poor urban petty-bourgeoisie together with the petty-bourgeois intelligentsia" is "to a very considerable extent brought under the influence of the active revolutionary forces." [55] Among the class enemies of the revolution is the "trading bourgeoisie" which "directly serves the interests of imperialist capital," like the compradore bourgeoisie in China. The bourgeoisie itself, which reflects the interests of native industry, supports the national movement, declares the thesis, but manifests "a special vacillating compromising tendency which may be designated as national reformism." [56] This ambiguous statement actually meant that the bourgeoisie was no longer revolutionary; while it might still have a vestigial anti-imperialist impulse, it was now regarded as an enemy in the agrarian revolution. The main burden of the thesis, and of subsequent Communist policy, was a wholesale attack on the bourgeois enemy.

What should be the tactics of the Communists toward the bourgeoisie? They should reject the formation of any bloc with it, although

---

[53] *Ibid.,* p. 1472.

[54] "Theses on the Revolutionary Movement in the Colonies and Semi-Colonies," *Inprecor,* VIII (Dec. 12, 1928), p. 1660.

[55] *Ibid.,* p. 1665.

[56] *Loc. cit.*

they may make "temporary agreements" and "temporary unions" in connection with "definite anti-imperialist demonstrations." Communist parties, however, should "demarcate themselves in the most clear-cut fashion, both politically and organizationally, from all the petty-bourgeois groups and parties." [57] In all of their activities the Communists should criticize the "half-heartedness and vacillation of the petty-bourgeois groups," including the left wing of the Indian National Congress.

On the most important practical issue, the question of organizational forms, the colonial thesis follows the Russian view:

> Special "Workers' and Peasants' Parties," whatever revolutionary character they may possess, can too easily, at particular periods, be converted into ordinary petty bourgeois parties, and, accordingly, Communists are not recommended to organize such parties. The Communist Party can never build its organization on the basis of a fusion of two classes, and in the same way also it cannot make it its task to organize other parties on this basis, which is characteristic of petty bourgeois groups. . . . The union of all Communist groups and individual Communists scattered throughout the country into a single, illegal, independent and centralized party represents the first task of Indian Communists.[58]

The thesis makes even more explicit the mandate given the European Communist parties at the Fifth Congress. It states:

> [It is] obligatory for the Communist International to give an absolutely special attention to the tasks of building the Party in the colonial and semi-colonial countries. An especially great responsibility in this connection lies with the Communist Parties of the imperialist countries. This demands not only assistance in the matter of working out the correct political line, accurate analysis of experiences in the sphere of organization and agitation, but also systematic education of the Party ranks, the publication of a certain minimum of Marxist-Leninist literature and its translation into the languages of the different colonial countries, most active assistance in the matter of study and Marxist analysis of the economic and social problems of the colonies and semi-colonies, and in the creation of a Party press, etc.[59]

Although debate on the new line continued for some time after the Sixth Congress, this Congress did mark the beginning of a new strategy for India. From its long-held policy of supporting bourgeois nationalism the Comintern moved toward one of opposing it. The denunciation of the theory of decolonization, with which M. N. Roy's name had become associated, tended to obscure the fact that in essence the new line was that which Roy had advocated so vigorously since 1920. It was only on specific tactical questions that the Comintern

---

[57] *Ibid.*, p. 1668.
[58] *Ibid.*, pp. 1671, 1673.
[59] *Ibid.*, p. 1670.

differed with Roy. The Comintern wanted to liquidate the WPP, while Roy and the CPGB did not. Roy and the CPGB favored two parties, a legal WPP dominated by an illegal CPI; and there is little doubt that under the conditions then existing, both legal and political, this would have been the most effective approach. The WPP was, after all, a going concern, one which had been organized at the cost of considerable time and money. That it had some political potential was evidenced by the difficulty in liquidating it, as will be shown. But regardless of what would have been best for the Communist movement in India, the Russian view prevailed, and Comintern support was withdrawn from the WPP.

7   THE POLITICAL WILDERNESS

During 1928, while international communism was producing reams of obscure dialectical argument on the issue of bourgeois nationalist movements, Indian nationalism was beginning to stir in response to the growing unrest and political awareness in the Indian masses, and to the radical ideas for social and economic change of its rising young leaders.

Of these, the most important was Jawaharlal Nehru. Nehru's sympathies were clearly with the left. While in Europe he had accepted office in the Comintern-sponsored League Against Imperialism, and after his return from a tour of the Soviet Union he had expressed great admiration for the Russian experiment and for Socialist ideas in general.

At the Madras session of the National Congress, held in December, 1927, Nehru emerged as the leader of the Congress radicals, and it was through his efforts that the left wing won a major victory, the most significant element of which was the resolution demanding complete independence for India. In his autobiography Nehru writes, "I presented a bunch of resolutions to the Working Committee— resolutions on Independence, War Danger, association with the League Against Imperialism, etc.,—and nearly all of these were accepted and made into official Working Committee resolutions." [1] By presenting these resolutions, Nehru was carrying out an important part of the

---

[1] Jawaharlal Nehru, *An Autobiography* (London: John Lane, The Bodley Head, 1942), p. 167.

program of the League Against Imperialism; for example, the resolution on "War Danger" implied that Britain intended aggression against the USSR.

Nehru's proposals were "all almost unanimously adopted," he writes, but he "had an uncomfortable feeling that they were either not understood for what they were, or were distorted to mean something else." [2] This was apparently true of the resolution demanding Indian independence, for immediately after the Madras session the meaning of this resolution became a matter of controversy so serious that it soon split the Congress.

Among the Communists who attended the Madras session were Philip Spratt, R. S. Nimbkar, K. N. Joglekar, and a few others. They, of course, supported Nehru's resolution on the war danger and his proposal that the Congress affiliate with the League Against Imperialism. But doubtless because of Nehru's preëminence, they made little impact on the session. Their own resolution congratulating the Soviet Union on the anniversary of the Russian Revolution was rejected, and the Congress refused to endorse their call for protest strikes and *hartals* (closing of shops) against the projected visit of the Simon Commission. In November, 1927, the government of India had announced the appointment of an Indian Statutory Commission, to be headed by Sir John Simon. This Commission was to come to India, investigate the functioning of the 1919 Montagu-Chelmsford reforms, and report to the British Parliament with a view toward further improving the Indian governmental structure. The fact that no Indian was appointed to the Commission aroused widespread anger, and a movement for a Simon Commission boycott gained support among all sections of the population. At the Madras session of the Congress, S. Srinivasa Iyengar, who had served as president during the previous year, moved a resolution to boycott the Commission; the Congress accepted it although, as noted above, the Communist resolution in favor of more direct action failed.

But when the Simon Commission landed in Bombay in February, 1928, there was a nation-wide *hartal,* and violence broke out in Bombay, Calcutta, and Madras. During the remainder of the year, the Commission was an irritant that crystallized much of the growing political consciousness of the masses, and was a wedge that increased the distance between the conservatives, who were willing to accept eventual dominion status, and the radicals who demanded full independence.

---

[2] *Loc. cit.*

As Nehru's victory at the Madras session showed the growing radicalization of the intelligentsia, so popular hostility to the Commission was an indication of the growing unrest among the masses. There was evidence in other sectors as well. In the same month that the Simon *hartals* were taking place, the peasants in Bombay State began a *satyagraha,* involving nonpayment of taxes, that attracted nation-wide attention and support for several months. Since the disputed taxes were ultimately reduced as a result of the campaign, this incident made manifest the latent political power in an organized peasantry.

Growing unrest among the industrial proletariat, too, was impressively shown in the phenomenal rise in strikes during 1928–1929; there were 203 strikes in that year as against only 129 during the previous year. More than 506,851 people participated, and 31,647,404 working days were lost.[3] Of greatest importance was the general strike in the Bombay textile industry, which lasted from April 26 to October 6, 1928, and caused shut-downs in fifty mills. The Communists were active in the leadership of the Bombay strike, but many non-Communist trade unionists also took part.

Additional evidence of the growing radicalization of Indian politics was provided by nationalist reaction to the Public Safety Bill. Introduced in the Central Legislative Assembly by the government of India in September, 1928, the bill was an anti-Communist measure designed to provide the legal means for expelling foreign agitators from India. There was little doubt in anyone's mind that it was aimed specifically at Philip Spratt and Ben Bradley, the British Communists who were the actual leaders of the Indian Communist movement at the time and who had accomplished so much in the field of trade-union organization.[4]

Despite the government's attempt to raise a Communist bogey, nationalists of all shades vigorously opposed the legislation. Lala Lajpat Rai declared that the purpose of the bill was "to frighten away people who want to investigate into labour conditions in this country," and N. M. Joshi added: "Communists are not the only persons and Communist doctrines are not the only doctrines which are aimed at by this Bill."[5] Also active in the debate against the measure were S. Srinivasa Iyengar, Motilal Nehru, the conservative father of Jawaharlal Nehru, and the right-wing Congressman Madan Mohan Malaviya. The bill was defeated.

---

[3] *India in 1928–29* (Calcutta: Government of India, 1930), p. 7.

[4] That the bill was aimed at the trade-union movement is clear from the speech of the minister for industries and labor, A. C. McWatters, in *Legislative Assembly Debates* (Official Report) 1928, Vol. III (Simla: Government of India, 1929), p. 676.

[5] *Ibid.,* pp. 643, 671.

The debates on the bill in the Central Legislature had shown that the bourgeois Indian politicians were well aware of the nature of Communist propaganda and of the contempt in which it held them as a class. Why, then, were they not content to sit by and permit the enactment of a bill aimed primarily at removing the Communists from the Indian scene?

There are probably many reasons. As their statements showed, they feared the bill as a step toward greater restriction of all political freedom, including their own. Too, the laudatory comments of Nehru and Iyengar, after their visits to Russia, had aroused a certain amount of sympathy for the Soviet Union. Furthermore, some of the nationalists appeared to feel that if the Communists annoyed the British, they could well be regarded as useful allies.

In any case, the nationalist politicians were ready to overlook the Communists' avowed enmity to the point of vigorously defending them from government attack—a measure of the favorable atmosphere in which the Communists could operate during this period. Unrest and incipient rebellion in every sector of Indian society; the triumph of leftism in the National Congress; the fact that so important a leader as Nehru was already inclined toward Socialist ideas and active in a Comintern-sponsored organization; and the growing interest in and feeling for the USSR—all these were favorable factors for Communist agitators, who looked forward to eventual capture of the nationalist movement. Instead, largely because of doctrinal confusion and conflicting advice, the Communists failed for almost two years to take advantage of the situation. When at last they received a clear directive from the Comintern it required that they attack their presumptive allies, dissolve the single organization, the WPP, which was already beginning to channel the disaffections of the proletariat and peasants, and to isolate themselves from the most potentially valuable locus of discontent and rebellion, the nationalist movement.

The "Independence for India League"

Of possible allies of Indian communism, one of the most likely in the nationalist movement was the Independence for India League— the offspring of the misunderstanding at the Madras session of the Congress as to the implications of Nehru's independence resolution. Having accepted the resolution, the Madras session had decided to convene an all-parties conference which would draft a constitution for an independent India. Accordingly, representatives of numerous nationalist organizations met in Delhi in February, 1928. It was immediately apparent that there was considerable opposition to the idea of a completely independent India and that dominion status was the preferred goal of many. The question was complicated by Hindu-Muslim communalism, and it was not until May that a drafting sub-committee under the chairmanship of Motilal Nehru was appointed.

The Committee's draft, known as the Nehru report, favored dominion status rather than full independence, and this immediately precipitated a split in nationalist ranks. S. Srinivasa Iyengar, just arrived after his tour of the Soviet Union, issued a statement saying that it would be "suicidal for India to accept Dominion Status." He then joined with Jawaharlal Nehru and Subhas Chandra Bose to establish the Independence for India League. In a draft constitution promulgated at its first meeting in Delhi on November 3, 1928 the League defined its objective as "the achievement of complete independence for India and reconstruction of Indian society on a basis of social and economic equality." Speaking of the new party, Jawaharlal Nehru said: "It is a permanent organization with a definite policy and program. It will coöperate with pleasure with all other organizations which have the same objects in common with it." [6] It was planned to affiliate the Independence League with the League Against Imperialism.

To determine the extent to which the League's ideological orientation was compatible with that of communism is difficult today—as indeed it must have been at the time. This much is clear: its leaders were radical and militant, viewed the Soviet Union with some sympathy, and accepted many Socialist theories. On the other hand, they were not bound by a shared ideology but rather by common impatience with the Gandhian approach to independence, and they preached socialism less militantly than they demanded independence. Nehru's Fabian moderation is shown in a newspaper paraphrase of one of his speeches before the All-India Congress Committee:

> He believed in full-blooded socialism, but would not bring that before the Congress now because very few understood it. A time, however, would come when the Congress, for the sake of its own existence, would adopt the socialist program in full.[7]

Nehru's words were prophetic, for the "time" did indeed "come"—though not until 1955.

The Independence for India League represented the militant left of the National Congress, but it was still labile: it might move with Nehru toward independence and socialism, or it might march with

---

[6] Nripendra Nath Mitra, ed., *Indian Annual Register, 1928* (Calcutta: The Annual Register Office, 1929), II, 6, 513.

[7] *The Tribune* (Lahore), Nov. 6, 1928, p. 2.

Subhas Chandra Bose toward independence under some more authoritarian type of government. The Indian Communists eyed the new organization with considerable interest and waited to see which course it would follow.

CPI vs. Comintern

During 1928, the CPI had put much of its energy into the Workers' and Peasants' parties and continued to organize new ones. On September 28, 1928, a new branch for the Punjab was organized at Lyallpur, and on October 14, a WPP for Uttar Pradesh was set up at Meerut.[8] There were already Workers' and Peasants' parties in Bombay and Bengal; during October, preparations were announced for the first All-India Conference of Workers' and Peasants' parties.[9] It convened in Calcutta from December 21 to 24, with Sohan Singh Josh presiding.[10]

In the thesis adopted at this conference, the WPP's Communist leaders indicated that all effort was now to be directed toward strengthening this "open," legal, mass organization. The thesis ignored the CPI, but declared that the WPP was "the only organization which has a correct policy and can unite and lead all the mass revolutionary forces of the country." [11] Formerly, said the thesis, it had been appropriate that the WPP work within the national movement as a left wing of the Congress Party. Now, however, the situation had changed, and the WPP must prepare to "play a definitely independent part." Relations with the Congress were spelled out in detail:

For some time . . . the Congress will maintain its composite character, as a loose organization, with indefinite creed, under bourgeois leadership, but with a petty-bourgeois following including different social strata and different political tendencies, some of a potentially revolutionary nature. While this is the case, and while the Workers' and Peasants' Party remains relatively weak and unorganized in the country, it will be necessary to follow the traditional policy of forming factions within Congress organizations for the purpose of agitation, of exposing its reactionary leadership and of drawing the revolutionary sections towards the Workers' and Peasants' Party. This policy, however, is only temporary. The Workers' and Peasants' Party can have no intention of dominating or capturing the Congress: the function of its members within the Congress is a purely critical one. Party members cannot, therefore, be allowed to take office in [the] Congress organization (except with the special permission of the N. E. C.). The object of the Workers' and Peasants' Party can only be to build up its own independent

[8] Meerut Sessions Judgment, p. 211.
[9] See *The Tribune* (Lahore), Oct. 27, 1928, p. 3.
[10] For the names of others in attendance see *ibid.*, Dec. 23, 1928, p. 9.
[11] "The Political Situation in India; thesis of the Workers' and Peasants' Party of India," *Labour Monthly*, XI (March, 1929), p. 159.

organization so that it can as soon as possible dispense with the necessity of agitation within the Congress.[12]

Not only was this moderate position vis-à-vis the Congress contrary to the stand of the Sixth Comintern Congress, but the convening of an All-India WPP Conference was in itself directly contrary to the edict that Workers' and Peasants' parties should be liquidated. One of the reasons for this wide discrepancy may have been delayed and faulty communication from the Comintern. Philip Spratt recalls that the Indian Communists "had no direct instructions till G. M. Adhikari arrived from Europe in December, 1928"[13]—more than three months after the conclusion of the Comintern Congress. This delay he explains on the basis that the Comintern bureaucracy did not take the new line seriously:

By 1928 the Comintern had ceased to matter, except as a field for the intrigues of the Russian party factions, and the swing to the left in that year bore no relation to world politics but was merely an outcome of these factional quarrels. Probably the Comintern bureaucracy in Moscow realized this and saw that it did not matter whether the Indian party followed the new line or the old. Certainly they took no special trouble to inform us.[14]

Nevertheless, according to Spratt, he and the other CPI leaders had "sensed from the brief press reports that a change was taking place." Spratt says that, having arranged the WPP Conference:

I had to prepare the long printed resolutions ("theses") and the report. In these I changed the line somewhat, and though my efforts were overshadowed by more dramatic events at the Conference, I congratulated myself that I had been acute enough to see which way the Comintern wind was blowing.[15]

On the third day of the Calcutta conference, the Indian Communists received a letter from the ECCI addressed to the WPP, specifically prohibiting any alliance with the Independence for India League:

The main obstacle to the victorious organized struggle against British imperialism and its feudal allies in the period of increasing terrorism and bloody repression is the influence of opportunist bourgeois nationalism. . . . The greatest danger to the organization of the masses, to the creation of a revolutionary bloc of the proletariat and the peasantry and to the proletarian leadership in this bloc, consists not only in bourgeois nationalism as such, but comes from the organizations and groups of "prominent" petty-bourgeois intellectuals actually influenced by the former, the "Independence League." . . . Your Conference . . . cannot fail to

---

[12] Ibid., p. 160.
[13] Philip Spratt, Blowing Up India (Calcutta: Prachi Prakashan, 1955), p. 42.
[14] Ibid., p. 43.
[15] Loc. cit.

dissociate itself from the confusion and twaddle which characterizes the advertized League platform with its lavish promises.[16]

Despite this plain injunction to steer clear of the Independence League, some at the conference argued in favor of working with it. K. N. Joglekar, D. R. Thengdi, and S. Kumarananda even moved a resolution to this effect.[17] Although the resolution was defeated, the thesis as adopted was a considerable victory for their viewpoint and amounted to a rejection of Comintern instructions. It said:

> Although not homogeneous in membership, the Independence League has a definite policy and program. It is in essence a bourgeois organization whose policy is an insincere travesty of that of the Workers' and Peasants' Party, and whose object is in large part to prevent the independent growth of the mass movement. Workers' and Peasants' Party members cannot enter the Independence League as members, as to do so would be to attribute to it before the masses a seriousness and importance which it does not possess. The Workers' and Peasants' Party can only work with the Independence League in a united front, on the basis of its propaganda for independence, which in spite of its frivolous character has objectively some value. But it is necessary continually to expose the League's faults of program and policy, and its fundamentally bourgeois, even Fascist character, and ultimately counter-revolutionary role.[18]

Thus the WPP could criticize the League and expose its "counter-revolutionary" role, but they would still work with it in a united front for its propaganda had "objectively some value." Clearly the WPP did not agree with the Comintern that the League program was entirely "confusion and twaddle."

It may be wondered why the Indian Communists virtually ignored the Comintern letter and why, since they had the Comintern's instructions from Adhikari, they did not forthwith dissolve the WPP. They may have realized that there was still disagreement in the Comintern on basic strategy and tactics and were probably aware of the current power struggle between Bukharin and Stalin, which was not resolved for another six months. It must be remembered, too, that the CPGB which, through Spratt and Bradley was directing the CPI, had maintained its opposition to the new line on the WPP's. Indeed, in late November, 1928—almost two months after the Sixth Congress— Clemens Dutt wrote to P. C. Joshi: "I hope that you are finding it possible to draw in actual proletarian workers into the WPP Party." [19]

Furthermore, Roy's stand, after the Chinese catastrophe, could

---

[16] Letter dated December 2, 1928, Meerut Case Evidence, Exhibit No. P 334. Emphasis in original.

[17] *Ibid.*, Exhibit No. P 465.

[18] "The Political Situation in India . . . ," p. 160.

[19] Meerut Case Evidence, Exhibit No. P 345.

scarcely have been clear to the Indian Communists, since he was now vehemently supporting Stalin's coöperation with bourgeois nationalism in the Kuomintang, while opposing—but less emphatically than before —coöperation with bourgeois nationalism in India. (See chapter 6.)

During the next six months the Indian Communists continued to receive advice from the CPGB and Roy that was not only self-contradictory and mutually contradictory, but which also conflicted with the Comintern line.

Conflicting Advice from Abroad

In March, 1929, the CPGB tacitly sanctioned the CPI's maintenance of the WPP by publishing the WPP thesis in *Labour Monthly* and prefacing it with the following introduction:

This resolution will be found of great interest, not only for its estimate of the situation in India but also for its authoritative statement of the political tasks and policy of the Party. It would be easy to criticize some of the features of their view, which has clearly not taken into account the important discussions of the Sixth Congress of the Communist International on the Indian question, notably with regard to the industrialization of India and the dangers inherent in a political party, like the Workers' and Peasants' Party, based on a union of different classes. This fact only makes it the more important for us in Great Britain to pay adequate attention to the important movement now developing in India.[20]

One may suspect that this admonition to pay greater attention to Indian developments was addressed as much to Russian as to English comrades.

The head of the British Party, R. Page Arnot, implied defiance of Comintern policy on the WPP in a pamphlet published in 1929, in which he said:

This [the WPP] is a two-class party. . . . As a form of organization it was expressly condemned in the Colonial Thesis of the Sixth Congress of the Communist International as one which Communists should not attempt to build. But this Workers' and Peasants' Congress, the speeches at it, and its decisions, its resolutions, all give an unmistakable feeling of a real conscious mass movement for the first time in India, a real proletarian awakening. True, it is still only a handful of people. But in the tones of the Congress speeches there can be heard overtones, the rolling of the thunder, the noise of a great mass in motion.[21]

The CPGB did not, however, approve, any alliance with the Independence League, and here conformed to the Comintern line. Clemens Dutt wrote in *Labour Monthly* in January, 1929, that the League did not represent revolutionary socialism but reformist social democracy.

[20] "The Political Situation in India . . . ," p. 159.
[21] R. Page Arnot, *How Britain Rules India* (London: CPGB, 1929), p. 30.

In fact, he said, the League was "a challenge to the Workers' and Peasants' Party, an attempt to regain the ascendancy of the Nationalist bourgeoisie over the masses, which were in danger of escaping from bourgeois influence." [22]

In summary, then, the CPGB advised the Indian Communists to continue organizing the WPP but to avoid alliance with the Independence League.

Roy's views, during 1928 and early 1929, were not only inconsistent with the Comintern line, but were self-contradictory and, at the last, a complete reversal of his whole previous position. To add to the confusion, his articles were printed in the official Comintern journal, *Inprecor.*

In August, 1928, while the Sixth Comintern Congress was in session, Roy published an article in *Inprecor* in which he aligned himself first with Varga and the leftist ECCI document, and then with Dutt and the CPGB. (See pp. 107–110.) In the first part of the article, Roy seemed to adhere to the leftist views concerning the roles of various classes in the Indian revolution. "The possibility of class differentiation in the nationalist movement," Roy said, "the petty bourgeois rank and file breaking away from bourgeois leadership, owing to the treachery of the latter, is still remote." [23] But after saying that the petty bourgeoisie "still remains largely under the control and influence of the treacherous reformist bourgeois leaders," [24] which was in line with Varga and with the ECCI document, he then said that "the development of independent political action by the working class is splitting the petty bourgeois radical nationalists into two ever diverging tendencies. One advances towards revolutionary alliance with the working class in the Workers' and Peasants' Party; and the other moves rapidly toward Fascism" under the leadership of Subhas Chandra Bose. He concluded his article by stating that "This regrouping of class forces is a precondition for a revolutionary anti-imperialist fight for national freedom." [25]

Roy was straddling the fence. He had begun his article by saying that the possibility of "class differentiation" in the nationalist movement was remote, but he ended by describing a "regrouping of class forces" then in progress. He asserted early in the article that the petty bourgeoisie still remained "largely under the influence and control" of the bourgeois leaders, but near the end he pointed out that one

[22] Clemens Dutt, "The Indian League for Independence," *Labour Monthly,* XI (Jan., 1929), p. 27.
[23] M. N. Roy, "The Indian Constitution," *Inprecor,* VIII (Aug. 24, 1928), p. 954.
[24] *Ibid.,* p. 955.
[25] *Loc. cit.*

section of it was advancing toward a revolutionary alliance with the working class. On the one hand, then, Varga was right, but on the other hand Dutt was right. This article did not commit Roy to move in either direction, but four months later his choice became evident.

Discussing the Indian National Congress in the December, 1928, issue of *Inprecor,* Roy spoke of the "radicalization" of the nationalist movement and the "revolt of the petty bourgeois nationalist ranks against the compromising reformist policy of the bourgeois leaders." Then he added, "If the revolt of the petty bourgeois nationalist masses does not receive the leadership of a more revolutionary class, the right wing leaders will recover their control of the nationalist movement and temporarily obstruct the process of its radicalization." [26] And in the February, 1929, issue of *Inprecor* Roy continued his argument that the petty bourgeoisie could be brought under the influence of the proletariat. "They are not likely to advance in the revolutionary direction," he said, "unless the proletariat meet them half way, and make a fighting alliance with them for the realization of the program of national revolution." [27] Not only was Roy prepared to meet the petty bourgeoisie half way, but he even criticized the WPP for having failed to support the Independence League. "When the petty bourgeois left radicals are trying to oust the bourgeois leaders from the leadership of the nationalist movement," he said, "they are not supported; on the contrary, they also were condemned as the enemies of the workers and peasants, in the same breath with the representatives of big capital and landlordism." [28]

In summary, Roy, who had been a leftist during his entire career in the Comintern now found himself to the right of both the Comintern and the CPGB. The Varga articles in the spring of 1928 had indicated that the Comintern was moving left. Dutt's reply had shown that the CPGB, which then controlled the Indian Communist movement, did not want to adopt leftist tactics. As the debate progressed Roy straddled the fence. At the Sixth Congress the leftists triumphed but the right opposition was neither beaten nor silenced, and the CPGB continued to favor rightist tactics for India. After the Sixth Congress Roy began to move to the right, and by early 1929 his support of the Independence League actually placed him to the right of the CPGB.

It is interesting to speculate on the reason for Roy's change of posi-

---

[26] M. N. Roy, "The Indian National Congress," *Inprecor,* VIII (Dec. 27, 1928), p. 1733.
[27] M. N. Roy, "The Conference of the Workers' and Peasants' Party of India," *Inprecor,* IX (Feb. 1, 1929), p. 93.
[28] *Ibid.,* p. 94.

tion. It is unfair to attribute it wholly to an attempt at retrieving his position by guessing the outcome of the power struggle then going on in the Comintern. Undoubtedly, he was influenced by the fast-moving events in India and by the growing evidence that the Congress, after the triumph of the leftists under Nehru, was playing an "objectively revolutionary" role. Certainly his analysis of Indian conditions after 1928 was more in accord with political realities than was that of the Comintern.

It is also curious that Roy's rightist articles could continue to be published in *Inprecor* as late as February, 1929, although the Comintern had adopted its militant leftist policy in the summer of 1928. But it must be remembered that Stalin's struggle with Bukharin and the rightists continued for more than a year after the Sixth Congress. Roy had been friendly with Bukharin as early as 1921,[29] and Bukharin remained editor of *Pravda* until February, 1929, was head of the Comintern until April, and was not expelled from the CPSU Politbureau until November. All through 1928 and for some months in 1929, the opponents of ultra-leftism held positions of importance in both the CPSU and the Comintern.

Roy remained on good terms with G. M. Adhikari and wrote to him from Berlin on February 27, 1929: "You know I have been happily relieved of the administrative responsibility of our affairs, and therefore am not in a position to be of much practical assistance or to know why people at home are in such conditions."[30] Without doubt Roy was here referring to his former authority over Comintern activities in India. But Adhikari's reply indicates that Roy still had some authority in India, and that he was not the only Indian Communist to have fallen from grace in the Comintern. In a letter dated March 15, 1929, Adhikari wrote that Usmani had "asked me to tell you that 'your man' attacked him over there without reason. But the CI has cut his feet as well as yours. He has nothing against you. Nobody here is making any propaganda against you."[31]

The CPI is Reorganized

Although at the WPP Conference the Indian Communists had ignored the Comintern's letter regarding the Independence League and did not change the WPP thesis to conform with the new line on the Congress, they did make some effort to comply with Comintern policy on the organizational question. On December 27–29, 1928, im-

---

[29] *Roy Memoirs* (July 11, 1954), p. 330.
[30] Meerut Sessions Judgment, p. 243.
[31] *Ibid.*, p. 245.

mediately after the WPP Conference, the WPP leaders reconstituted
themselves as the CPI and convened a meeting in Calcutta. The new
Comintern line was discussed; and three days later a new CPI Central
Executive was established. It consisted of S. S. Mirajkar, S. A. Dange,
R. S. Nimbkar, K. N. Joglekar, S. V. Ghate, Muzaffar Ahmed, Abdul
Halim, Shamsul Huda, Abdul Majid, and Sohan Singh Josh. Ghate
was appointed general secretary, and the Executive decided to request
formal affiliation with the Comintern.[32]

The only available record of this meeting consists of notes made
by one of the participants, and later picked up by the police. Two
quotations from these notes show that the Indian Communists had
by no means as yet accepted Comintern formulations *in toto:*

> The thesis of the Comintern was gone into and it was decided to accept it as
> a basis for work. Possibilities of an open party were to be tested.[33]

> Discussion of thesis. [Presumably the Sixth Congress Colonial Thesis.] The inter-
> pretation is that this should be taken up as a basis and changed according to the
> conditions in India. Possibilities of an open party should be tested.[34]

Not only was the Colonial Thesis to be modified as the CPI saw
fit, but on the matter of party organization, the CPI was evidently not
yet ready to conform to the Comintern's injunction, for an "open
party" is the exact opposite of the "illegal, independent and centralized Party" called for by the Sixth Congress. Moreover, in the
WPP the CPI already had an "open" party. This suggests the possibility that the CPI was holding to Roy's earlier recommendation
to maintain an illegal elite Communist Party operating side by side
with an open, legal, mass party.

The reasons for this divergence from Comintern policy are not
clear. It may have been that the conflicting articles and letters
emanating from Roy and the CPGB had left the Indians somewhat confused, and doubtful that the Colonial Thesis was the last word on
the subject. Moreover, communication with Communists overseas was
poor. As late as March 14, 1929, Spratt wrote Dutt in England: "I
should say, by the way, that I have heard practically nothing yet of
British Party affairs, nor even anything of value about the International." [35]

The CPI met again in Bombay on March 17–19, 1929, and once
more the only record consists of fragmentary notes later picked up by
the police. These notes indicate that the Communists had not yet de-

---

[32] *Ibid.,* p. 234.
[33] *Loc. cit.*
[34] *Loc. cit.*
[35] *Ibid.,* p. 242.

cided to dissolve the WPP, and that the chief supporters of its continuance were Mirajkar and Usmani—an interesting fact in view of Usmani's prominent role at the Sixth Congress. This seems to confirm the hint contained in Adhikari's letter that Usmani was no longer in the good graces of the Comintern.

At the Bombay meeting it was decided to reorganize the CPI as "the basis of all Communist work," but to continue the WPP as well. It is significant, however, that in planning the next meeting, the first item on the agenda was "the danger of having WPP." [36]

But before the meeting could take place the government of India struck the Communists what it hoped would be a crippling blow, and in doing so resolved, for all practical purposes, the problem of the WPP.

The Meerut Conspiracy Case

On March 20, 1929, the day after the Bombay meeting of the CPI, the government arrested thirty-one Communists and trade unionists and took them to Meerut (Uttar Pradesh) to be tried on the charge of having engaged in a conspiracy to deprive the king-emperor of his sovereignty over India. Practically all leaders of the CPI were included; eight defendants were members of the All-India Congress Committee (AICC), and one was a former president of the All-India Trade Union Congress (AITUC).

The defendants gained the sympathy of Indian nationalists of all shades of opinion, and a defense committee including Dr. M. A. Ansari and Jawaharlal Nehru was immediately set up. Nehru wrote to Walter Citrine, secretary of the British Trade Union Congress General Council, saying:

I would like to point out that this trial cannot be isolated from the general situation and must be treated as one phase of the offensive which the Government here has started against the Labor movement. . . .

There is a lot of shouting about Communists and Communism in India. Undoubtedly there are some Communists in India, but it is equally certain that this cry of Communism is meant to cover a multitude of sins of the Government.[37]

Further indication of the support enjoyed by the Meerut defendants is the fact that Mahatma Gandhi himself visited the jail and offered encouragement to the prisoners.[38]

[36] *Ibid.*, p. 246.
[37] *The Meerut Trial, facts of the Case.* (London: National Meerut Prisoners' Defence Committee; 1929), p. 10.
[38] Lester Hutchinson, *Conspiracy at Meerut* (London: Allen and Unwin, 1935), p. 107. Hutchinson was also a defendant in the Meerut case, although he was arrested after the others.

The trial dragged on for three and a half years, 320 witnesses were examined, 3,000 exhibits were entered as evidence, and the total cost of the proceedings reached about Rs. 1,500,000.[39] During this long period P. C. Joshi asked to be released in order to sit for the law examinations, but this was not allowed. Instead he was transferred to Allahabad prison where he was permitted to take the examinations in confinement. According to Spratt, the defendants were not treated badly. They received books and papers almost uncensored, and were even provided with proscribed Communist literature to enable them to prepare their defense. This made it possible for them to continue their Marxist studies and to indoctrinate other prisoners.

For recreation, the Meerut defendants were allowed chess, table tennis, cricket, and volleyball, and in general, according to Spratt, "lived well." [40] Yet it was a boring existence for the most part, enlivened a bit at first by the argumentative brilliance of the government prosecutor, J. Langford James. But when James died early in the trial, the whole procedure became deadly dull. Day after day, in the sweltering heat of dusty little Meerut, the air in the steaming courtroom was stirred by nothing more refreshing than the monotonous turning of ceiling fans and the long speeches of D. R. Thengdi "on the subject of his constipation." [41]

On January 16, 1933, sentences were pronounced. Muzaffar Ahmed received life imprisonment, and Dange, Ghate, Joglekar, Nimbkar, and Spratt were all sentenced to twelve years. Bradley, Mirajkar, and Usmani received ten years; the lightest sentence was three years.[42] Most of these sentences were reduced on appeal, however, and by the end of 1933 nearly all Meerut conspirators had been released.

Since it was obvious that the CPI did in fact conspire to deprive the king-emperor of his sovereignty over British India, it is difficult to explain why the government of India found it necessary to proceed against the Communists in such a spectacular way, and why it spent so much time and effort to prove a fairly simple case. The Communists assert that the 1929 elections in Great Britain were the underlying reason. "The Meerut trial," says one Communist historian, "was designed by the Conservative Government of Baldwin to play up the 'Communist danger' which was allegedly threatening the entire capitalist world." [43] This seems far-fetched, but certainly the imprison-

---

[39] Meerut Committal Order, pp. 12 ff.

[40] Spratt, *Blowing Up India*, p. 48.

[41] Hutchinson, *Conspiracy at Meerut*, p. 165.

[42] Meerut Sessions Judgment, p. 675.

[43] N. Somin, "Meerut Trial in India and the Colonial Policy of the Labourites," *Communist*, III (July–Aug., 1950), p. 67.

ment of the Meerut defendants crippled the organizational apparatus of the Party to some extent, especially in the trade-union movement. With its leaders in jail, the WPP virtually disintegrated, although there was occasional WPP activity here and there for some time to come.

In perspective, however, the Meerut trial appears to have worked to the long-term advantage of Communist aims in India. The leniency of the prison regime made it possible for the Meerut prisoners to be consulted by their comrades on the outside, and Spratt recalls that they were able to set up "what amounted to a party office" in the Meerut jail.[44] New leaders, notably S. V. Deshpande, R. D. Bharadwaj, and B. T. Ranadive, came to the fore and worked to build the Party.

More important, however, was the fact that the publicity surrounding the trial and the prominence of the personalities assisting in the defense offered rare propaganda opportunities, of which the Communists took full advantage. Spratt recalls:

On the whole the revelation of our secret methods caused people to admire us: we had done what most young men wanted to do. . . . We had our opportunity in the sessions court to make political statements, and these were widely published in the press. Several of them were long enough to make a short book, and altogether no doubt most of what can be said in favor of Communism was said.[45]

The Meerut trial made martyrs out of the Communists, and martyrs are especially important in Indian political life. Indeed, Harold Laski wrote:

The Meerut trial belongs to the class of cases of which the Mooney trial and the Sacco-Vanzetti trial in America, the Dreyfus trial in France, the Reichstag Fire trial in Germany, are the supreme instances.[46]

Saumyendranath Tagore has said, and Philip Spratt agrees, that the Meerut Case "placed Communism on a sure footing in India." [47]

Indian Nationalism Takes the Offensive

During the years that the Meerut proceedings were dragging on, there were increasing indications of the revolutionary potential in the Indian nationalist movement. Socialist ideas, disseminated by Nehru and other left-wing leaders, had become fashionable among India's educated elite; the workers in the trade-union movement were falling more and more under the dominion of Communist and pseudo-Com-

---

[44] Spratt, *Blowing Up India*, p. 53.

[45] *Ibid.*, pp. 51–52.

[46] Preface to Hutchinson, *Conspiracy at Meerut*, p. 8.

[47] Saumyendranath Tagore, Historical *Development of the Communist Movement in India* ([Calcutta?]: Red Front Press, 1944), p. 21.

munist leaders; and mounting unrest throughout the country resulted in sporadic outbursts of terrorism.

Of these, one provided the most spectacular incident of the period. On April 8, 1929, a young Punjabi terrorist named Bhagat Singh threw a bomb onto the floor of the central legislature. He was caught, tried, and sentenced to life imprisonment. While serving this sentence he was again tried, this time for the murder of a British official committed before his arrest. He was convicted of this crime also, and was hanged on March 23, 1931. The case aroused great sympathy among all Indian nationalists, and at its Karachi session the Indian National Congress passed a resolution condemning the hanging.[48]

Bhagat Singh was not a Communist, but he was apparently exposed to Communist ideology while in jail. In his statement to the court at his trial he called for a revolution that would establish the "sovereignty of the proletariat." [49] With his martyrdom, Bhagat Singh became a national hero in India, and as recently as 1955 a movie of his life attracted large crowds at Indian theaters. Ajoy Ghosh, the present general secretary of the CPI, was one of Bhagat Singh's comrades and was also a codefendant in the murder trial. Largely on the strength of this relationship the CPI has tried to claim Bhagat Singh as a Party hero and has published two pamphlets on his life and ideas.[50]

In a similar act of terrorism, on April 18, 1930, Bengali revolutionaries raided the Chittagong armory and although the event had no great revolutionary consequences, martial law was proclaimed and troops were called out to suppress the resulting violence.[51]

But the most important development in Indian political life during this period was Gandhi's famous Civil Disobedience Campaign. Unresponsive to the moderate influence Gandhi had exercised on Congress policy since the passage of the Independence Resolution in 1928, the government of India declined to accept the eleven-point program Gandhi promulgated in January, 1930. Feeling that an impasse had been reached, Gandhi organized a group of satyagrahis to begin a civil-disobedience campaign by violating the law which reserved salt production to a government-controlled monopoly. With his band of followers, Gandhi marched across Gujerat to the sea, and with the attention of all of India focused on him, he ceremoniously broke

---

[48] Congress Bulletin, No. 1 (April 10, 1931).

[49] Text in Mitra, ed., Indian Annual Register, 1929, I, 78.

[50] See Ajoy Ghosh, Bhagat Singh and his Comrades (Bombay: People's Publishing House, 1946); and Gopal Thakur, Bhagat Singh, the man and his ideas (Bombay: People's Publishing House, 1953).

[51] For a Communist account see: Kalpana Dutt, Chittagong Armoury Raiders, Reminiscences (Bombay: People's Publishing House, 1945).

the law by preparing salt from sea water. When he was arrested a short time later, strikes and demonstrations broke out all over India, and resulted in the arrest and detention of between 40,000 and 60,000 demonstrating nationalists.

Sympathetic to Communists, if not to communism, increasingly vigorous, and radiating an atmosphere hospitable to radicalism, the nationalist movement in 1929–1931 would seem to have been a plum within easy reach of Communist hands. By the end of 1929, however, the Comintern at last issued unequivocal instructions to the CPI. They took no account of the actual situation in India; instead these instructions forced the Indian Communists to turn their backs on the fertile field of Indian nationalism and to isolate themselves from the wellspring of Indian political life.

The Comintern Line Becomes Clear

At the tenth plenum of the ECCI, held in Moscow July 3–19, 1929, Stalin solidified his leadership. All opposition to the leftist line of the Sixth Congress was submerged, and the Comintern plunged forward on its ultraleftist course. As at the Sixth Congress, Otto Kuusinen was the spokesman of Comintern policy for India. In his report to the plenum he said concerning India:

Our greatest weakness there is the fact that we are not yet firmly enough established as a Communist Party. A good many Indian Communists have worked in the ranks of the "Workers' and Peasants' Parties." We have advised them to endeavor to induce these Parties to reorganize themselves, to assume another organizational form, in keeping with the principles of Leninism. But not the two-class character of these parties was the worst thing, much worse was the fact that hardly any practical revolutionary work has been done yet among the peasantry.[52]

Another Russian delegate, P. Schubin, lamented the fact that the "liquidation" of the WPP was taking place more slowly than it should. "It is a characteristic trait of worker and peasant parties," he said, "that when they cease to live they refuse to die, clinging to the shell of their existence, hindering the development of sound forms of organization." [53]

The deliberations of the plenum were not published in *Inprecor* until August and September, although an account of the proceedings may have reached India before the official publications. In any case, by January, 1930, the Indian Communists could no longer have any doubts as to Comintern policy, for in that month *Inprecor* published

[52] O. V. Kuusinen, "The International Situation and the Tasks of the Communist International," *Inprecor*, IX (Aug. 20, 1929), p. 847.
[53] *Inprecor*, IX (Sept. 17, 1929), p. 1097.

an open letter from the Young Communist International to Indian youth, workers, and peasants. Its line was remarkably strong and straightforward. "The National Congress," declared the Letter, " . . . actually retards the revolutionary movement. . . . It has long ago betrayed the masses of the Indian people and cannot lead their struggle against British imperialism. . . . Sever your contact with the National Congress and the League of Independence [Independence for India League]," it counseled; "disclose their falseness and treachery. Show them up for what they are, as assistants of British imperialism. Drive the traitors, the phrasemongers out of your ranks." [54] The Open Letter also called upon the youth to organize strikes and help the peasants seize the land.

The CPI's course was now clearly and authoritatively mapped out: it was to dissolve any remnants of the WPP, sever connections with all elements of the bourgeoisie, and launch a full-scale attack on Gandhi, Nehru, and the Indian National Congress.

M. N. Roy's Expulsion from the Comintern

For more than a year, until the tenth plenum, M. N. Roy had been, as he later phrased it, "standing before the 'sacred Guillotine.' " [55] The tenth plenum made it clear that he was finished in the Comintern. "Roy is no longer our comrade," the Indonesian delegate, Musso, told the plenum. "He is rather the comrade of Gandhi, or at least a comrade of Brandler and Thalheimer." [56] Roy was also denounced by his erstwhile colleague, G. A. K. Luhani, who climbed on the Stalinist band wagon by ignominiously recanting the straighforward position he had taken at the Sixth Congress.[57] (See pp. 118–119.)

But though Roy was denounced at the tenth plenum, he was not formally expelled, or at any rate no report of his expulsion was published in the Comintern press. It was not until December, 1929, that *Inprecor* carried the following statement:

In accordance with the resolution of the X Plenum of the ECCI (On the International Situation and the tasks of the Communist International, Para. 9) and the decision of the Presidium of the ECCI of 19. 12. 1928 according to which adherents of the Brandler organization cannot be members of the Communist International, the Presidium of the ECCI declares that Roy, by contributing to the Brandler press and by supporting the Brandler organization, has placed himself outside the ranks

---

[54] "Open Letter from the Y.C.I. to the All-Indian Youth Congress and to All Young Workers and Peasants of India," *Inprecor*, X (Jan. 9, 1930), p. 25.

[55] M. N. Roy, *Our Differences* (Calcutta: Saraswaty Library, 1938), p. 25.

[56] *Inprecor*, IX (Aug. 21, 1929), p. 887.

[57] *Inprecor*, IX (Sept. 11, 1929), pp. 1039–1040.

of the Communist International, and is to be considered as expelled from the Communist International.[58]

Roy's break with the Communist International has been a matter of controversy for many years. His own version of the circumstances is as follows:

I was the victim of some internal intrigue, the history of which had better not yet be written publicly. The desire of the Communist Party of Great Britain to establish its protectorate over the Indian Communist movement had a good deal to do with it. The internal struggle of the Russian Communist Party also contributed to my victimization. One fact may be mentioned here. For the first time in the history of the Communist International, there appeared an Indian delegation in the Sixth World Congress. Previously, in spite of repeated efforts, no *bona fide* Communist from India could reach Moscow. The object of the first Indian delegation to the Communist International was to denounce me, obviously in accordance with a previously laid plan. Corroborating the reports of some British Communists, who had previously paid flying visits to India, the mysterious delegation told the Congress of the Communist International that I was a person completely unknown in India, having had no connection whatsoever with the revolutionary movement. The interesting fact, however, is that only one member of the delegation was allowed to return to India. It is reported that the rest were presently suspected of being British spies and dealt with as such. The one who returned to India has dropped out of politics altogether.[59]

There is certainly no doubt that at least one member of the Indian delegation, Saumyendranath Tagore, denounced Roy, although it does not seem likely that this was the result of a "previously laid plan" as Roy charges. As has been shown in chapter 4, there was some discontent in India concerning Roy's leadership, but the Indian delegates to the Sixth Congress appear to have gone off to Moscow without any definite instructions. (See pp. 110–112.) Tagore remained a bitter critic of Roy. In his subsequent explanation of Roy's expulsion he states:

It is clear that Roy's expulsion from the Communist International was not due to any political difference with Stalinism. Roy, the careerist, always served the man in power. He was always the most servile agent of Stalin and is still a Stalinist with the hope that the wheel of fortune may turn in his favor and he again may be reinstated in his former position by Stalin. Roy joined the Brandler opposition in Germany only after his expulsion from the Communist International. And he did that only to give a political coloring to his expulsion.[60]

Tagore asserts that the real reason for Roy's expulsion was indiscipline, uncomradely behavior, forgery, and misappropriation of funds.

It is not correct to say, as does Tagore, that Roy had no political

[58] *Inprecor,* IX (Dec. 13, 1929), p. 1470.
[59] Roy, *Our Differences,* p. *ii.*
[60] Tagore, *Historical Development of the . . . ,* p. 18.

differences with Stalinism. As has been shown, Roy moved to the right after the Comintern, at the Sixth Congress, moved to the left; although the Comintern adopted a strategy close to that which Roy had advocated for years, Roy himself abandoned it. On the other hand, it cannot be assumed that these political differences were alone responsible for Roy's expulsion. During his leftist period, from 1920 to 1928, the Comintern had been remarkably tolerant of Roy's basic disagreement with the accepted strategy and had even placed him on the highest policy-making body, the ECCI. Moreover, when the Comintern changed its line, Roy's deviation (this time as a rightist) was apparent for a full year before he was expelled. This suggests that his policy disagreements were not the only cause of his expulsion, if indeed they were any cause at all.

Although at the tenth plenum Roy had been charged with having contributed to the press of the Communist opposition group that had formed around Heinrich Brandler, the authors have been unable to locate any Brandlerite journal of the title given (*Volks-Recht*). Brandler's principal paper during this period was *Gegen den Strom,* but it did not contain any articles by Roy until September, 1929, when he began his long series entitled "The Crisis in the Comintern."

There is little doubt that Roy knew he was in trouble with the Russian leaders as early as February, 1928, when he fled from the Soviet Union after the ninth plenum. Still for some time he must have assumed that there was a possibility of his returning to favor and that he would be reprieved. He did not launch his public attack on Comintern policy until after the tenth plenum had made it clear that his situation was, for the time being at least, hopeless.

Again, Tagore's description of Roy as "servile" is certainly wide of the mark. Roy's 1920 debate with Lenin, the tone of his polemics, and the assessments of his personality by his contemporaries all indicate that he was proud and rebellious, not servile. But Roy was loyal to Stalin and backed him to the hilt even when it meant supporting Stalin's distorted version of events in China in contradiction to his own better judgment and earlier published views. Roy's unswerving attachment to Stalin is revealingly expressed in a letter written from an Indian jail in January, 1936:

> You see, after all, I still remain a personal admirer of my ex-friend, who used to pride over our racial affinity, and called me "gold." Now he won't appreciate me even as copper! But I have the weakness of giving the devil his due. And in my account, his due is very considerable. I was publicly castigated for this weakness once—at Weimar.[61]

---

[61] M. N. Roy, *Fragments of a Prisoner's Diary,* III (Bombay: Rajaram Panday, 1943), p. 168.

Jay Lovestone, former head of the American Communist Party, and for many years since an active anti-Communist engaged in the international affairs of the AFL and today the AFL-CIO, recalls:

> Roy was a most loyal Stalinist. In many ways, Stalin had a terrific hold on him. For years after our expulsion, I differed violently with Roy because of his attitude towards Stalin. When Roy blamed the 1927 debacle on the Chinese Communist Party, he did so in line with his loyalty to the Comintern, to the Kremlin, and to Stalin.[62]

When Stalin died in 1953, Roy wrote in his journal, *Radical Humanist,* that Stalin was "the most hated, feared and maligned man of our time." He added:

> No great man has ever been an angel. Greatness is always purchased at the cost of goodness. Stalin did not do anything worse. He certainly deserves a place among the great men of history. . . . Our plea is that some justice should be done to the most maligned man of our time. He deserves justice; because, but for his caution and wisdom, and also his fanatical faith in the inevitability of revolution, war might have already overtaken the civilized world. If the charitable obituary notices on his death do not acquit Stalin of the charge of preparing a war against the democratic world, they would be hypocritical and unrealistic. . . . He was the greatest military genius of our time. . . . Stalin was undoubtedly the tallest personality of our time, and as such is bound to leave his mark on history.[63]

For many years after his expulsion, Roy evidently hoped that his new strategical line would be accepted by the Comintern, and that he would be vindicated and restored to a position in the International. When after 1935 the Comintern had at last abandoned its ultraleftism and again embarked upon the united-front strategy, Roy published a book to show that "there are no differences any longer." "Yet, for some reason unknown to me," he said, "the Communist Party of India still carries on the crusade against me." [64]

It is not within the scope of this book, nor is it possible with the evidence presently available to the authors, to assess completely Roy's complex career in the Communist International, or to examine his motives and character. Nor is it possible to state definitively why he and the Comintern parted company. It may have been, as Tagore claims, that the Comintern lost confidence in Roy because of financial irregularities, proved or unproved, or because of his exaggerated reports of successes in India. But in view of Tagore's own self-interest in the matter and his obvious personal dislike for Roy, his testimony alone is not sufficient evidence. Moreover, financial irregularities and inaccurate reporting were so commonplace among Comintern leaders

---

[62] Letter from Jay Lovestone to Marshall Windmiller dated July 23, 1956.

[63] M. N. Roy, "The Death of Stalin," *Radical Humanist,* XVII (March 15, 1953), pp. 121, 132.

[64] Roy, *Our Differences,* p. *iv.*

that such lapses would scarcely be enough to justify the expulsion of an able and loyal Stalinist. On the question of Roy's expulsion, Jay Lovestone has written:

Everyone in the Comintern made greatly exaggerated reports as to the progress of the organization he headed. This applied not only to India and China but also to Britain and France. . . . No Communist leader in the Far East could ever show or give any receipt as to how money had been used. . . . The "revolutionists" considered it as a matter of principle to have contempt for accounting as a bourgeois instrument. . . . If there had been anything serious to the charges abovementioned, Moscow would have made a lot of noise about it during the years after Roy's expulsion. I was in the forefront of the fire as a target of Stalin and Company and I would have heard such rubbish. I do not recall it at all.[65]

In view of all these complexities, the final word on M. N. Roy's career in the Communist International must await the opening of archival material which, despite the denigration of Stalin, still remains a Communist preserve.

Ultraleftism

For nearly three years (until May, 1932), Comintern policy for India undeviatingly pursued the ultraleftist strategy mapped at the tenth plenum, and the Indian Communists loyally followed the Comintern's lead. During this period a number of articles on India appeared in *Inprecor* and in other Comintern publications. Most of them were journalistic accounts of struggles in India, emphasizing those events which seemed to bear out the correctness of Comintern strategy and glossing over those that did not. Virendranath Chattopadhyaya, in his articles in *Inprecor,* emerged as a leading Comintern expert on Indian affairs, although his statements were not of any theoretical or strategical importance. *Inprecor* also carried a series of articles on the Indian question by Karl Radek which were important for their authoritative reiteration of the Sixth Congress line but did not indicate new strategical or tactical directions.

The main characteristics of Comintern literature of this period are (1) violent opposition to Gandhi, Nehru, Bose, and the Congress Party as bourgeois and counterrevolutionary, (2) insistence that Gandhi and the Congress had been repudiated in the eyes of the masses, and (3) repeated injunctions to form a strong, illegal Communist Party.

It is evident that Comintern advice to Indian Communists during this period was strongly colored by the China experience. Having expelled Trotsky from the Comintern for leftism, Stalin had now taken over his arguments on the role of the bourgeoisie in colonial areas,

---

[65] Letter from Jay Lovestone to Marshall Windmiller dated July 23, 1956.

and his new analysis of the events in China provided the matrix for policy in India. Little allowance was made for the radically different political, social, and cultural conditions. Thus Karl Radek argued in June, 1930:

When the earnest revolutionary struggle of the workers and peasants begins, the national reformists will inevitably stand on the other side of the barricade. . . . To have even the slightest doubt of this, after what we have seen in China, and to fail to prepare ourselves and the masses for this inevitable change of front on the part of the national reformists, would mean a frivolous and criminal abandonment to defeat of the workers and peasants.[66]

And the following month *Inprecor* carried a message to the working masses of India from the All-China Labor Federation which made the parallel even more mechanical:

The Indian Nationalist Party under the direction of Gandhi is just like the Kuomintang of China. Both are the tools of imperialism. We must not have the slightest illusion toward Gandhi. On the contrary, we must oppose him in order to guarantee the victory of the revolution.[67]

The most important document of this ultraleftist period of Indian communism (1928–1934) is the "Draft Platform of Action of the C.P. of India," which was published in *Inprecor* in December, 1930. There are no indications where it originated, although it was represented as having been written by Indian Communists who wished it published in the Comintern press in order that foreign comrades might evaluate and criticize it. A few minor criticisms did appear, but none of them dealt with important questions of strategy and tactics. The Draft Platform was widely circulated among Communists in India, and for a year and a half was frequently cited in Comintern literature as the primary directive for Indian communism.

The Platform is a leftist document from beginning to end. Regarding the Indian National Congress it is unequivocal:

The greatest threat to the victory of the Indian revolution is the fact that great masses of our people still harbor illusions about the National Congress, and have not realized that it represents a class organization of the capitalists working against the fundamental interests of the toiling masses of our country.[68]

The Platform calls for "ruthless war on the 'Left' national reformists," and makes it clear that violence will be the prime tactical weapon. It declares that "the road to victory is not the method of individual ter-

[66] Karl Radek, "Problems of the Revolution in India," *Inprecor*, X (June 26, 1930), p. 545.
[67] "Solidarity with the Working Masses of India," *Inprecor*, X (July 31, 1930), p. 666.
[68] "Draft Platform of Action of the C.P. of India," *Inprecor*, X (Dec. 18, 1930), p. 1218.

ror but the struggle and the revolutionary armed insurrection of the widest possible masses of the working class, the peasantry, the poor of the towns and the Indian soldiers, around the banner and under the leadership of the Communist Party of India." Among the main objects of the present stage of revolution, the Platform lists:

> The confiscation without compensation of all the lands, forests and other property of the landlords, ruling princes, churches, the British Government, officials and money lenders, and handing over for use to the toiling peasantry. Cancellation of slave agreements and all the indebtedness of the peasantry to moneylenders and banks.[69]

A policy more likely to arouse the hostility of all politically active elements in Indian society could hardly be imagined. It was aimed at the very strata from which the Indian Communists had been recruited, and from which they had received perhaps the most sympathetic hearing. The Draft Platform was a bill of divorcement from the main nationalist movement.

Moreover, growing disagreement among the Communists themselves soon reduced whatever effectiveness the CPI might have attained in spite of its Comintern-imposed isolation. While the Communist old guard tried to direct CPI affairs from the Meerut prison, new leaders were actively working in the trade-union movement. Chief among them were Abdul Halim, in Calcutta, and S. V. Deshpande, Mrs. Shuhasini Nambiar, and B. T. Ranadive in Bombay. Both Halim and Deshpande, however, were moderates, and despite Comintern instructions to build an illegal Party, preferred to operate within the law.[70] Ranadive, on the other hand, was a leftist and argued for tactics in keeping with the militant Comintern line. While Halim and Deshpande were satisfied with publishing workers' newspapers and conducting Marxist study clubs, Ranadive wanted to foment strikes and demonstrations. The Party in Bombay split into two groups; and the major arena of their struggle, the trade-union movement, became badly riven with factionalism.

During this period, too, Virendranath Chattopadhyaya and Clemens Dutt established a secretariat in Berlin from which they attempted to guide the Indian Communist movement. When the Nazis came to power, this office was moved to Paris and later to London.[71] Meanwhile Roy attempted to organize the Indians in Europe into a Communist party under his own direction, and among those who joined forces with him were Sundar Kabadi and Tayab Shaikh; the latter became Roy's biographer under the pen name, A. K. Hindi.

---

[69] *Ibid.*, p. 1219.
[70] *India and Communism* (Simla: Government of India, 1933), p. 161.
[71] *Ibid.*, p. 172.

Roy Returns to India

To complicate matters for the CPI, in the middle of 1930 Roy began an active effort to reëstablish himself as the leader of the Indian Communists, and thus perhaps to effect a reconciliation with Stalin. His tactics, however, were directly opposed to the CPI's official policy —and a direct reversal of those he had advocated during his tenure of office in the Comintern. Whereas previously he had been opposed to any dealings with the National Congress, he now set out to work with it—a much more realistic policy than the one the Comintern had promulgated. Thus, ironically, where in the past he had advocated that the CPI capture control of the nationalist movement by working outside the Congress, he now was trying to regain control of the Communist movement by working within the Congress.

To begin his campaign he dispatched Tayab Shaikh and Sundar Kabadi to India with a manifesto. Addressed to the "Revolutionary Vanguard of the Toiling Masses of India," it declared that "in India the way to Communism lies through the national revolution." To this end, it continued, the CPI "must work through the national mass organizations—the National Congress, Youth Leagues, students' organizations and volunteer corps." [72]

Tayab Shaikh arrived in India in August, 1930; he got in touch with various leftists including Yusuff Meherally, C. G. Shah, and V. B. Karnik, and claims to have obtained sixty-five Congress signatures to the manifesto.[73] Before long he was arrested, held for a short time, and released. Sundar Kabadi returned to Europe.

It was evident that Roy could not accomplish anything through emissaries and so he decided that he himself would have to go. It was a bold decision, for he was named on the Meerut Case charge sheet and was wanted by the authorities. Moreover, in view of the hostility of some Communist leaders, there was great danger that he might be betrayed. He arrived in Bombay in December, 1930, traveling on a forged passport. For the next seven months he managed to work in the trade unions, undetected, and to further his aim of gaining influence in the Congress.

To what extent he succeeded in the latter objective is not clear. At Nehru's invitation, he attended the Karachi session of the Congress, held in March, 1931, at which the most notable event was the passage of a resolution on fundamental rights. The resolution clearly reflected Socialist thinking, and in his autobiography Nehru declares that by passing it, the Congress "took a step, a very short step, in a

---

[72] *Ibid.*, p. 163.
[73] Interview with Tayab Shaikh by Marshall Windmiller in London, January, 1956.

socialist direction by advocating nationalization of key industries and
services, and various other measures to lessen the burden on the poor
and increase it on the rich." [74]

Although it is widely believed [75] that Roy was the author of the
resolution, Nehru states that he himself drafted the resolution and
secured Gandhi's approval of it before it was presented to the Congress. Nehru says that Roy visited him at his home in Allahabad
shortly before the Karachi Congress, and that he saw Roy again for
five minutes at Karachi. He was attracted, he says, by Roy's "remarkable intellectual capacity," and sympathized with him as a "lonely
figure, deserted by everybody." He insists, however, that Roy "had
absolutely nothing to do" with the Karachi resolution.[76]

Regardless of his influence, if any, on the Karachi Congress, there
is no doubt that during the seven months he was active Roy made a
strong impact on trade unionism and radical politics. Working underground, with the police in vigorous pursuit, he succeeded in getting
a major section of the trade-union movement to abandon ultraleftism
and to adopt a more moderate policy under his leadership. He produced an enormous quantity of literature, and contributed articles
to the Communist opposition press in Germany and America. British
Intelligence described one of these articles as a "shrewd appreciation
of things as they really were," [77] and to his work in general paid
this left-handed tribute:

There is no gainsaying the fact that, in the seven months during which he was at
large in India, Roy did very considerable mischief, despite the fact that the police
were continually hot on his heels. His doctrines gained many adherents in Bombay
and the United Provinces, and at a later date also in Calcutta and its environs.
He made serious and by no means unsuccessful endeavours to impregnate the
Congress with his views and was received, and well received, by several of the
Congress leaders in different parts of India. Even Mr. Gandhi was aware of his
presence in the Congress *pandal* [enclosure] at Karachi. Judged from the intellectual
standpoint, Roy, ever a realist, stands out head and shoulders above all other
Indian Communist leaders with the possible exception of Dr. G. M. Adhikari, and
his continuous exhortations to "eschew the disastrous ultra-left policy" were calculated in the end to win over many more adherents to Communism than Deshpande's vaporous thunderings could ever have done.[78]

It will never be known how successful Roy might have been, for
he was arrested on July, 1931, prosecuted at Cawnpore as a defendant

[74] Nehru, *An Autobiography*, p. 266.
[75] *India and Communism*, p. 165.
[76] Nehru, *An Autobiography*, p. 268.
[77] *India and Communism*, p. 164.
[78] *Ibid.*, p. 168.

in the original Cawnpore Conspiracy Case, and sentenced on January 9, 1932 to imprisonment for twelve years. This was reduced on appeal, and he was released on November 20, 1936. "His conviction," says a British Intelligence document, "removed from the political arena a dangerous enemy of capitalism, landlordism, and imperialism, and struck another blow at Indian Communism generally." [79]

Emissaries from the Comintern

Having taken a firm line on policy for India at the tenth plenum, the Comintern sent a number of emissaries to the subcontinent. Their visits are chiefly of interest, however, as showing the efficiency of the British CID, for with two exceptions they were arrested and deported before they could accomplish anything of importance. One exception was a Comintern agent whose presence in India was known to the authorities, but who managed to avoid capture for six months and apparently left the country in 1930.[80]

Prem Lal Singh, who had completed a course of study at the Lenin Institute in Moscow, visited India and made contact with the Meerut prisoners, but, intimidated by the police, returned to Moscow. Two American Communists, William N. Kweit and Harry Sommers, traveled to India on false passports, evidently bringing funds to finance the Indian movement; they were caught and deported in September, 1930.[81] In 1931, Roy's former colleague, Mohammed Sipassi, tried to get into India by mingling with Indian Muslim pilgrims in Mecca. He reached Mecca after the pilgrims had already left, however, and had no alternative but to return to Moscow.[82] Another American, Henry G. Lynd, was more successful. He arrived in 1931 with funds for the CPI and met with its leaders in Bombay, but later he too was picked up and deported.

The most effective of all emissaries was Amir Haidar Khan who arrived in Madras in March, 1931, disguised as a seaman. Working cautiously he succeeded in forming Communist groups in three important textile mills, organized a Young Workers' League, and dispatched at least one comrade to Moscow for special training. He also maintained contact with both Communist factions in Bombay, each of which bid for his support. Labeled by the authorities as "a most dangerous individual," he was arrested on May 7, 1932, tried, and sentenced to two and a half years imprisonment. Upon his release in

[79] Loc. cit.
[80] Ibid., p. 175.
[81] Loc. cit.
[82] Ibid., p. 176.

1934 he immediately resumed political activity and was arrested and imprisoned again.

The most telling summary of the work of the various Comintern agents who visited India during this period can be found in the best available source of information, a report prepared by British Intelligence:

> It cannot be claimed, of course, that all of Moscow's emissaries to India have been objects of official attention, but it may be accounted fortunate indeed that so many of them have come under the watchful eye of the police. Except for Amir Haidar Khan, none has any practical achievement to his credit. This is due to a variety of reasons, not least of which is the preventive action which the authorities in India have been able to take. But another important reason is the inferior stamp of the agents themselves, and it was a strange freak of fortune which placed substantial funds in the hands of those who were incapable of spending to the best advantage but kept an energetic enthusiast like Amir Haidar Khan in penury to the detriment of all his ambitious schemes. The Meerut convicts are known to have made complaints to Moscow on this score and to have specifically asked that British citizens be sent in the future. If, therefore, the Comintern repeats its former mistakes in this respect, it will have only itself to blame.[83]

A semiofficial CPI history of the Party recounts that in 1930 one of the agents from the Comintern helped the Indian Communists to reorganize after the Meerut arrests. According to this account, he tried to form a secret central committee of the Party in Bombay, and had some contact with Party members in Calcutta.[84] The same source implies that this agent was able to operate in India until 1933, and that he took a complete report on Indian activities back to Europe with him. If this is correct, he was certainly an able conspirator, for the British authorities were unaware of his activities.[85]

Further Contradictory Advice from Abroad

By 1931 the Meerut prisoners were beginning to appreciate the catastrophic consequences of the current tactical line. "We found fault with what was being done," recalls Philip Spratt, "but we did not direct our attack at the persons really responsible, viz., the Comintern authorities in Moscow."[86] Instead they blamed the leaders outside jail, especially the warring Ranadive and Deshpande factions in Bombay. Spratt says that Joshi understood the real cause of the dif-

---

[83] *Ibid.*, p. 179.

[84] Chalasani Vasudeva Rao, *Bharatha Communist Party Nirmaana Charithrea* [History of the Formation of the Indian Communist Party], (Vijayawada: Praja Sakti Press, 1943), p. 65.

[85] Spratt refers to another Russian agent who spent a considerable amount of time in India without being discovered by the CID. *Blowing Up India*, p. 40.

[86] *Ibid.*, p. 53.

ficulties and expressed his doubts at the time. Dange may also have realized the folly of the Comintern tactical line, Spratt thinks, but he had been expelled from the Party as a result of quarrels that arose in jail. At any rate, the Party leadership in Meerut jail realized that a change in tactics was necessary and prepared analyses to this effect for the information of the Comintern. British Intelligence reports that at least three such documents were smuggled out of jail, but whether they were all delivered is not known. In one of them the Meerut leaders appealed to the Comintern to publish an open letter analyzing the mistakes of the Party and arbitrating the differences between the dissident groups in Bombay. The Comintern responded with an "Open Letter to the Indian Communists," published in *Inprecor* in June, 1932, and signed by the Central Committees of the Communist parties of China, Great Britain, and Germany. It was an extraordinary document which, in effect, scolded the Indian Communists for having followed Comintern instructions and advised the Party to ride off in all directions at once.

The Open Letter begins with the declaration that the revolutionary struggle for national and social liberation had reached a "turning point." This would seem to imply a strategical change, yet the document does not suggest that a realignment of class forces had taken place since the Sixth Congress. The bourgeoisie, it declares, "is continuing its policy of counter-revolutionary compromise with British imperialism and betrayal of the revolutionary people." [87] Yet despite this betrayal, "the bourgeois National Congress . . . has so far succeeded in maintaining influence over considerably wide masses of the workers." The task of the Communists should be "to isolate the National Congress and all the 'left' national reformists from the toiling masses." This was the prescription as before.

But then the Open Letter states that the biggest mistake made by the Indian Communists was that they "stood aside from the mass movement of the people against British imperialism." This "self-isolation" had "created confusion in Communist ranks," and must be remedied by the Communists' taking "a most energetic part in the struggle for independence." The Communists, the letter counsels, must be "in the forefront of *all* activities, demonstrations and clashes of the toiling masses with the imperialists." [88] But while doing this they must follow a policy of "definite, sharp, clear and *uncompromising* struggle and exposure of the National Congress and especially the 'left' national

[87] "Open Letter to the Indian Communists," *Communist International*, IX (June 1, 1932), p. 347.
[88] *Ibid.*, p. 350. Emphasis in original.

reformists," and should be "sharply and mercilessly exposing and struggling against the National Congress and its 'left' wing." [89]

To be at the forefront of *"all"* anti-imperialist activities, the Communists had to be at the forefront of the Congress demonstrations led by Gandhi. Just how they could accomplish this while at the same time waging an "uncompromising" struggle against the Congress, the Open Letter does not explain. In retrospect it seems incredible that such a document could be taken seriously.

The Open Letter also offered advice regarding organizational forms. It acknowledged that the Communist Party still consisted of a few "weak groups, often isolated from the masses, disconnected with each other, not politically united, and in some places not clearly differentiated from national reformism." For that reason it was *"absolutely necessary* to raise the standard of struggle for an All-Indian Communist Party. . . ." [90] The leading organs of the Party," said the Letter, "and the kernel of the Party organizations, must be in an *illegal position.*" The mixing of the open and the conspiratorial apparati of the Party is fatal, and "measures must be taken for preserving and strengthening the conspirative [sic] kernel of the Party organization." Both legal and illegal papers should be published, and legal front groups should be organized under the leadership of Party committees, but they should "under no circumstances injure the existence of the illegal cells."

About a year after the publication of the Open Letter, the government began to release the Meerut prisoners. G. M. Adhikari was among the first to be released. In November, 1933, he went to Calcutta where he organized a "nucleus of the Provisional CC of the CPI," which included S. G. Patkar, P. C. Joshi, and Abdul Halim. [91] During the same month *Inprecor* published a second Open Letter to the Indian Communists, this time from the Central Committee of the Chinese Communist Party alone.

With respect to organizational forms, the advice in the second Open Letter was similar to that in the first. "The chief decisive question," said the Letter, "is the formation of a militant *mass Indian Communist Party.*" [92] This party should be like the CPSU, "a model of Bolshevik organization and iron discipline . . . not a peaceful Party, but a militant, bold, revolutionary Party." The Chinese com-

---

[89] *Ibid.,* p. 351.

[90] *Ibid.,* p. 356. Emphasis in original.

[91] *India and Communism,* pp. 188–189.

[92] "Open Letter to the Indian Communists from the C.C. of the C.P. of China," *Inprecor,* XIII (Nov. 24, 1933), p. 1153. Emphasis in original.

rades warned: "We are becoming more and more uneasy at the slowness of the process of the formation of the Communist Party of India." The Letter welcomed Adhikari's provisional Central Committee as a step in the right direction.

Although stated in a somewhat contradictory fashion, the most important difference between the two letters concerned instructions for trade-union work. For example, the work the Communists had done in trade unions was criticized as sectarian, yet at the same time they were advised to promote more political strikes. The second letter added that the struggle against the left-national reformists "does not mean refusal to work in the reformist trade unions . . . or even the joining together of the Red and mass national-reformist trade unions." This advice to join and unite with the reformist unions appears to be a reversal of the position taken by the first Open Letter, although internal contradictions in both documents make it difficult to determine this definitely. For example, the first letter stated that "the position of the comrades who tried to secure unity with Kandalkar [a leading reformist trade-union leader] was entirely wrong." Yet it also said: "It is a great mistake to continue the practice of self-isolation from workers' meetings, and the mass trade unions which are under the influence of the reformists."

By suggesting that the Indian Communists enter reformist trade unions, the second letter was taking the initial step away from the ultraleftism that had begun with the Sixth Congress. And whereas the CPI Draft Platform had called for war on the reformists, the second Open Letter advised the Communists to join them.

Both letters represent attempts to twist reality to conform to dogma. The foreign Communist parties had to admit what was obvious to everybody: that Gandhi had fired the imagination of the Indian masses and enjoyed their confidence, and that all political activity of any consequence revolved around the Indian National Congress. Yet to concede so much to a religious prophet of nonviolence and to a bourgeois political party was more than they could bring themselves to do gracefully and clearly. It had to be explained away in Marxist-Leninist terms and made to look unimportant and temporary. It could not be admitted that Gandhi and the Congress could continue to enjoy mass support. Thus, in essence, the fraternal parties advised the CPI to win over the masses by attacking the very leaders who had earned their loyalty, and the organization that had directed their struggles. Attempting to follow this obviously futile advice, the Indian Communists continued to wander for the next four years in the political wilderness. Yet years later, in 1943, an official Indian Communist commentator said of the two letters: "They helped us to understand the immediate responsibilities of the Party. They helped to eliminate our weaknesses and form a Party to suit the Indian circumstances." [93]

On such gullible loyalty rests the foundation of international proletarian solidarity.

---

[93] Rao, *Bharatha Communist Party* . . . , p. 71.

8   THE UNITED FRONT

In the middle of 1934, at a meeting of the Institute of World Economy and World Politics, the Soviet academician Pavel Mif delivered an optimistic judgment of the Indian scene. The colonial crisis is deepening, he said, and an upsurge of working-class and peasant activity is under way. The Indian proletariat "is challenging the national bourgeoisie with increasing success," he said, and the Communist Party of India "plays a stronger role with every day." [1]

The actual situation of the Communist Party of India was less impressive than Mif's picture suggested. The CPI was indeed growing, but within narrow bounds: during 1934 it increased from about 20 members to 150.[2] It was only beginning to recover from the disruption that had followed the Meerut Trial, and it was faced with great obstacles. In July, 1934, the Party was declared illegal—a curb which was not lifted until 1942. The Red Trade Union Congress, the Workers' Publishing House, the Young Communist League of Bombay and Madras, and other subsidiary Communist organizations were also declared illegal. The CPI was, as its provisional statute described it, "a strictly underground organization." [3]

---

[1] *Kolonial'nyi Problemy; Sbornik 3–4* [Colonial Problems; Collected Volumes 3–4] (Moscow: Institut mirovogo khoziaistva i mirovoi politiki, kolonial'nyi sektor, 1935), pp. 6, 7.

[2] *India and Communism* (Simla: Government of India Press, 1935), p. 208.

[3] "Draft of the Provisional Statutes of the Communist Party of India," *Inprecor*, XIV (May 11, 1934), p. 775. This document was later published by the CPI in Information Document Number 6, Oct. 16, 1952.

Soon after the Meerut defendants had been released from prison, many of them were reärrested on attempting to renew militant trade-union activity. Under the circumstances, Party officers could serve for only short terms; in the space of one year, G. M. Adhikari was replaced as general secretary by S. V. Ghate, and he, in turn, by S. S. Mirajkar. It was impossible to form a Central Committee, and the Party published no regular journal, openly or secretly.

But there was one factor in the situation which promised to aid the Party in its recovery: the new trend in international communism toward "softening" the leftist line that had prevailed since the Sixth Comintern Congress of 1928. The consequence of the leftist line for the CPI had been isolation and impotence. But in 1933, with the Open Letter from the Chinese Party, the Indian comrades had been instructed to emerge from their isolation; they must penetrate into, and even collaborate with, "reformist" organizations in the trade-union field. At the beginning of 1933 the CPI had taken the first step in this direction and had begun to work for increased coöperation between its own Red Trade Union Congress and the non-Communist All-Indian Trade Union Congress (AITUC).

The next logical step was to penetrate into and coöperate with "reformist" political organizations. The Soviet authorities approved this move: in his Moscow speech Mif declared that, throughout the colonial countries, Communists must make contact with the "national-revolutionary" forces; and articles in *Inprecor* at about this time called upon the Indian comrades to cultivate good relations with the petty bourgeois rank and file of the National Congress, and to use the League Against Imperialism as the agency for coöperation with other leftist forces.[4] In short, the united-front tactic, which the CPI had begun to apply in the trade-union sphere, was to be extended to the political sphere. At the end of 1934 the CPI made the first tentative move in this direction by establishing preliminary contact with the newly-formed Congress Socialist Party (CSP).

The CSP had been formed in 1934 as a bloc within the Indian National Congress, and was responsive, from its inception, to the idea of leftist unity. Its foremost leader, Jayaprakash Narayan, had been a Communist during his student days in America, and though he had since renounced Bolshevism he was willing to regard the Indian Communists as good Marxists. He ardently aspired to unify all Marxist groups under the banner of the Congress Socialist Party.

---

[4] V. Basak, "A Few Remarks on the Indian Communist Movement," *Inprecor*, XIV (June 1, 1934), pp. 845–849; and L. M., "The Situation in India," *Inprecor*, XIV (June 8, 1934), p. 878.

If the CPI could continue to shed the extremism which had characterized its orientation since 1928, it had before it a promising opportunity for a united-front alliance with the CSP and other political forces in India.

The Seventh Comintern Congress

After 1933, the fundamental fact confronting international communism was the rise of a powerful enemy in fascist Germany. In response to this threat, the Soviet leadership steadily abandoned its "hard," leftist line, hoping thus to find new allies. This "softening" process culminated in 1935 when the Seventh Comintern Congress was called to announce the new policy.

In order that the colonial Parties could do their part in mobilizing greater pressure on the bourgeois governments of Europe, they must revert to the Leninist emphasis on anti-imperialist strategic goals. Hence they must renew their collaboration with the bourgeois nationalist movements in their own countries. The four-class strategy was therefore revived for the colonies and the European parties.

The main spokesman on policy in the colonies, at the Seventh Congress, was the Chinese leader Wang Ming. Soon after the Congress, he prepared for publication a general statement which enunciated the line for the colonial countries.[5] The essence of the new line was contained in his discussion of China and Brazil. In China, Wang Ming declared, the Communists sought temporary allies among militarists, national reformists, and all other anti-imperialist forces, against the reactionary Kuomintang leadership. The Chinese Party, he said, "is the party of the entire Chinese people in the struggle for their national and social emancipation." The goal of the Chinese Communists was to unite under their leadership the working class, peasantry, petty bourgeoisie, and national bourgeoisie.

In Brazil, Wang Ming stated, the Communists pursued a similar strategy of collaboration with some elements of the national bourgeoisie against imperialism. In the realm of tactics, however, the Chinese and Brazilian cases differed. Whereas the main Chinese Communist tactic was to build a Party which would incorporate the four classes within its own ranks, the Brazilian Communists sought to build a broad anti-imperialist coalition, composed of various political blocs representing the four classes.

---

[5] Wang Ming, *The Revolutionary Movement in the Colonial Countries* (New York: Workers Library Publishers, 1935), 64 pp. This is a revised and augmented version of Wang Ming's report to the Seventh Comintern Congress, delivered on August 7, 1935. The original report, which dealt only with China, is in *Inprecor*, XV (November 11, 1935), pp. 1488–1493.

Wang Ming declared that the Indian Communists must make use of both the Chinese and the Brazilian examples. The burden of his advice was that on the one hand, they must widen and strengthen the CPI by enlisting all four classes, and on the other hand, they must join forces with bourgeois nationalist blocs in a broad, anti-imperialist organization. This would mean that they must penetrate the nationalist movement and appeal directly to its rank-and-file membership, while at the same time they must promote joint action with at least some elements of the nationalist leadership. In other words, the CPI must employ both the united-front-from-below and the united-front-from-above tactics—simultaneously subverting the nationalist leadership and making common cause with it.

Wang Ming severely chided the Indian Party for its past failure to join actively in the anti-imperialist struggle. "Our comrades in India," he said, "have suffered for a long time from left sectarian errors; they did not participate in all the mass demonstrations organized by the National Congress or organizations affiliated with it." But neither did they operate effectively as an independent political force, he said, for they were too weak to organize "a really powerful and mass anti-imperialist movement."

The Indians were also sharply reminded of the need to formulate a program with a broad appeal. "Our Indian comrades can serve as an example of how not to carry on the tactics of the anti-imperialist united front," he said, since in the past they had tried to establish a united front on the basis of a program demanding a "general strike" for a "Workers' and Peasants' Soviet Republic."

Another expression of Comintern policy for India appeared in a speech by Georgi Dimitrov at the Seventh Congress. But Dimitrov's message was somewhat different from that of Wang Ming. Dimitrov declared that the CPI, while retaining its independence, must "carry on active work inside the organizations which take part in the Indian National Congress, facilitating the process of crystallization of a national revolutionary wing among them, for the purpose of further developing the national liberation movement." [6] He emphasized the necessity for a united-front-from-below tactic—that is, the need to work within the Congress in order to mobilize a left wing that would influence, and eventually oust, the Congress leadership.

This advice would appear to mean, in sum, that the CPI should ally with one element of bourgeois nationalism (the left or "reformist" wing which was assumed to be genuinely anti-imperialist) and attack the

---

[6] Georgi Dimitrov, "The Offensive of Fascism and the Tasks of the C.I. in the Struggle for the Unity of the Working Class Against Fascism," *Inprecor,* XV (August 20, 1935), p. 971.

other element (the right-wing Gandhian leadership which was assumed to represent domestic reaction). In India, then, the Comintern did not require an all-out application of the anti-imperialist strategy; it did not insist on collaboration with all shades of nationalism, and the Communists could retain some militancy.

The CPI itself was not represented at the Seventh Congress of the Comintern; the two CPI delegates, S. V. Deshpande and S. S. Mirajkar, had been arrested in Singapore en route to Moscow.[7] In their absence, British CP leaders attending the session in Moscow stepped into their usual role of mentor to the CPI. Indeed, without waiting for Comintern advice to be communicated to India, they immediately took it upon themselves to put the new policy into effect. Minoo R. Masani, one of the founder-members of the Congress Socialist Party, happened to be in Moscow at that time. By Masani's account, the British leaders—Harry Pollitt, R. Palme Dutt, and Ben Bradley—met with him and broached the question of an alliance between the CPI and the CSP. Masani suggested that the CPI dissolve itself, in order that a united Socialist party might be created. And he added that such a party should not affiliate with the Comintern.[8] At this point the negotiations broke down, but a start had been made.

The British leaders then proceeded with the task of interpreting and officially notifying the CPI of the new Comintern line. Dutt and Bradley prepared a formal statement for the Indian comrades—the "Dutt-Bradley Thesis," which was printed in *Inprecor*.[9] The thesis opened on a routine polemical note, asserting that the Indian National Congress "has given up for the time the attempt to direct the struggle" against imperialism. However, it then proceeded to establish the assumption upon which the entire document rested—the view that the Congress consisted of two wings, only one of which was reactionary. Before 1935 Dutt and Bradley had seen only "left national reformists" within the Congress, but they now perceived a progressive element pressing for "a line of irreconcilable struggle with imperialism, for an advance of the program to reflect the growing influence of *socialist ideas*." Here were fit allies for a united front.

In detailing the methods for organizing the "Anti-Imperialist People's Front" in India, Dutt and Bradley focused exclusively on the Congress. Indeed, they asked, was not the Congress already "the united front of the Indian people in the national struggle?" Heretofore, this question could not even have been conceived by the Communists, but

---

[7] "Comrade S. V. Deshpande," *New Age* (monthly), II (June, 1953), p. 2.

[8] M. R. Masani, "The Communist Party in India," *Pacific Affairs*, XXIV (March, 1951), pp. 21–22 (footnote).

[9] R. Palme Dutt and Ben Bradley, "The Anti-Imperialist People's Front," *Inprecor*, XVI (Feb. 29, 1936), pp. 297–300.

now it was answered with a qualified "yes." Dutt and Bradley declared that the Congress had performed a "gigantic task" in uniting wide elements of the Indian people for national liberation. In fact they claimed that it represented the "mass army" of the national struggle. Could it not, then, serve as the all-encompassing agency of the anti-imperialist people's front?

> The National Congress can play a great and a foremost part in the work of realizing the Anti-Imperialist People's Front. It is even possible that the National Congress, by the further transformation of its organization and programme, may become the form of realization of the Anti-Imperialist People's Front; for it is the reality that matters, not the name.[10]

Having granted that the Congress could serve as a genuine united front against imperialism, in the remainder of their statement Dutt and Bradley ignored any other possibility and concentrated on the problem of "transforming" the Congress. This was to be the task of the Indian Communists.

According to Dutt and Bradley, this transformation required four reforms: the Congress must accept "collective affiliation," that is, the collective admission of mass organization; it must democratize its Constitution in order to eliminate centralized control; it must adopt an unambiguous anti-imperialist program and demand complete national independence with a "democratic" government; and, last, it must eliminate the "dogma" of nonviolence. The first of these reforms was obviously essential to the attainment of the others, since the admission of such mass organizations as trade unions would vastly strengthen the left wing. But the left wing would have to achieve an unprecedented unity; the Indian Communists must therefore make peace with rival radical groups. Dutt and Bradley clearly specified in the thesis that left-wing unity in the Congress was to be attained through the medium of the Congress Socialist Party:

> Congress Socialists, Trade Unionists, Communists and Left Congressmen should all be able to unite on the essentials of *a minimum programme* of anti-imperialist struggle for complete independence, of organization of the masses and development of mass struggle, and of the fight for changes in the Congress Constitution, policy, organization and leadership to forward these aims. The Congress Socialist Party can play an especially important part in this as the grouping of all the radical elements in the existing Congress. It is of the greatest importance that every effort should be made to clarify questions of programme and tactics in the Congress Socialist Party.

Dutt and Bradley estimated that the Congress Socialists "represent already a substantial minority of roughly one-third of the forces, and a potential majority" in the Congress. They obviously reasoned that with the addition of the mass organizations and of the Communists, the

---

[10] *Ibid.*, p. 298.

left wing would surely constitute a majority. The goal of capturing the Congress, and optimism as to its achievement, were therefore transparently proclaimed.

Although Dutt and Bradley did not pause in their thesis for a systematic attack on the "bourgeois" Gandhian leadership of the Congress, their hostility was implicit throughout the document. Their demand that the CPI oppose nonviolence was of course incompatible with anything but forthright opposition to the Gandhian leadership. This did not, however, signify opposition to the bourgeois elements of the membership as a whole. At several points Dutt and Bradley suggested that the anti-imperialist people's front must be based on the workers, peasants, and petty bourgeoisie; but, they were careful to emphasize that the CPI, for the time being, was to maintain and broaden the scope of the Congress, not to drive out any of its components—that is, the bourgeoisie.

In sum, the Dutt-Bradley Thesis, following Dimitrov's dictum, called upon the CPI to rally the Congress left wing for an attack on the right-wing leadership. This meant an alliance (that is, a united front from above) with the Congress Socialist Party, and penetration (that is, a united front from below) of the Indian National Congress as a whole. The Indian comrades must try to isolate the national leadership from its rank and file, and must transform the Congress into a more revolutionary weapon against imperialism.

The Communist-Socialist Alliance

In January, 1936, the Congress Socialist Party met in Meerut for its second conference. On the recommendation of the general secretary, Jayaprakash Narayan, the CSP National Executive unanimously adopted a resolution to admit Communists to membership in the CSP. It specified that membership was to be granted only on individual application, which had to be submitted to the decision of the Executive. Since the CPI was illegal, the decisions had to remain secret.

Apart from British overtures in Moscow, the CPI-CSP alliance was undertaken on Socialist initiative. In his account published a few years later, Narayan states that there had been no specific request or proposal from the Indian Communists; in fact though the CPI had sent a fraternal representative to the Meerut conference, the official Communist attitude was still aloof, if not hostile toward the CSP. The decision of the National Executive was made unilaterally, Narayan reports, in the belief that "important elements" in the Communist Party were amenable to a united front.[11]

[11] Jaya Prakash Narayan, *Towards Struggle* (Bombay: Padma Publications Ltd., 1946), p. 170.

According to a CPI account of this period, the Communists were reluctant to accept the Comintern's united-front line. When, in January, they received a prepublication copy of the Dutt-Bradley Thesis, they were still prone to a "sectarian attitude" and "did not take it seriously." [12] Many members bridled at the idea of joining the "bourgeois" National Congress or of working with the despised Socialists. The notion that an anti-imperialist front could be forged with these groups was considered dangerously close to heresy. Not until March —two months after the unsolicited invitation to join the CSP—did the new CPI Central Committee, set up the year before, take formal notice of the Dutt-Bradley recommendations and consider ways and means of implementing them. And the Committee had still to contend with widespread antipathy for the new line among the CPI leftists.

The Party as a whole was therefore slow to rally for the united front and, in the absence of effective central leadership, the various factions might have quarreled indefinitely over the new line. But a potential leader was available in the person of P. C. Joshi, who was not identified with any of the CPI factions.[13] Joshi was made general secretary, and under his energetic and able direction the CPI finally grasped the opportunity thrust at it by the Congress Socialist Party.

At Joshi's order, the Communists began applying for membership in the CSP. They also set about creating an organizational apparatus with which to meet the new tasks: the CPI began publishing a secret journal, *Communist,* and established a system of Party "fractions" which would work as disciplined units within the CSP, in the Congress itself, and in other mass organizations such as trade unions and peasant unions, to which they now had free access.

So far as is known, neither the CSP nor the CPI has published any estimate of the number of Communists admitted to the CSP. Narayan has stated that the number was "large," but he could not have had exact information since some joined "secretly," that is, without making their Communist affiliation known. Moreover, known Communists were in practice accepted into the CSP without going through the formality of National Executive approval. It is thus apparent that the CPI penetrated freely into the Socialist ranks. The results provide an absorbing case study of the alliance tactic in action.

---

[12] Chalasani Vasudeva Rao, *Bharatha Communist Party Nirmaana Charithrea* [History of the Formation of the Indian Communist Party], (Vijayawada: Praja Sakti Press, 1943), pp. 116–117.

[13] Deven and Bal Krishna, "Talks With Comrade R. Palme Dutt and Other Impressions Gained Abroad by Deven and Bal Krishna," *PHQ Open Forum* (Jan. 6, 1951), p. 3.

By the second half of 1936, reports began to reach the CSP National Executive that Communist fractions were disrupting the organization; they were converting members to communism, maneuvering to capture local CSP units, or competing with Socialists in such mass organizations as trade unions. The Executive responded with no more than a word of caution to the provincial CSP committees. In some cases this warning was wholly futile, for certain provincial CSP units were already in the hands of Communists or their sympathizers. In South India, Socialist affairs were largely directed by E. M. S. Namboodiripad, joint-secretary of the CSP and leader of the Kerala provincial unit; by the end of 1936 he had placed the Tamilnad organization under the direction of P. Ramamurti and P. Jeevanandam,[14] and within a short time all three of them had openly espoused communism. The Andhra provincial unit fell under the control of the known Communist P. Sundarayya. Through the influence of these leaders, whole provincial units were gradually turned into branches of the CPI. Similar cases occurred in labor centers in North India, where open or secret Communists took over the leadership of CSP units. An important unit dealing with labor organizations in Bombay, for example, was controlled by the Communist Soli Batiwala, who later became a member of the CPI Central Committee.

Early in 1937, the CSP National Executive issued a statement taking cognizance of the CPI's disruptive activities. But the Executive merely reaffirmed a "policy of combatting such factionalism . . . if necessary by resort to disciplinary action." [15]

Thus, almost from the start of its association with the CSP the Communist Party capitalized on successful infiltration. At the same time, however, in the realm of policy the two parties coöperated to some extent on their common goal of opposing the Congress leadership. The Socialists easily found a broad measure of agreement with the mild CPI program, which was limited to anti-imperialism and anti-feudalism. The CPI faithfully obeyed the Comintern injunction on moderation—an injunction which was reiterated in the pages of *Inprecor* with the statement that it should be possible for "anyone who hates foreign oppression, who sympathizes with the sufferings of the people" to work in unison with the CPI.[16]

Indeed, when disagreement did occur between Socialists and Communists it was often because the CPI had moved too far to the right.

---

[14] "Party News," *Congress Socialist,* I (Dec. 26, 1936), p. 38.

[15] *All-India Congress Socialist Party Circular Letter Number 4 to Provincial Secretaries,* Patna, March 31, 1937, p. 2. (An inner-Party circular.)

[16] "The United National Front," *Inprecor,* XVI (Nov. 7, 1936), p. 1342.

For example, in an editorial in the March issue of *Communist,* the CPI declared its support for "the struggle of the Indian capitalists against the domination of British finance capital." The interests of all four classes converge, said the editorial, on the issue of anti-imperialism.[17] To the Socialists, this was a betrayal of Marxism.

The main source of dispute was a resolution, adopted by the CPI Politbureau in February, 1937, which was a full-dress declaration of the four-class strategy. The anti-imperialist front, said the resolution, must include not only the National Congress, the CSP, the CPI, and mass organizations of the working class and peasantry, but even "certain organizations of the Indian merchants and industrialists." [18] This resolution was hailed by the Communist leadership as a "landmark" in the Party's policy, but it touched off a furor in the CSP. The Socialists castigated the Communists as revisionists; the Communists charged the Socialists with being "left sectarian." [19]

To defend itself against the Socialist indictment, the CPI was obliged to issue several long explanatory statements of its stand vis-à-vis the Indian bourgeoisie.[20] In these statements the Communists acknowledged that the February resolution had created a stir not only in radical circles, but even in the CPI itself. They tried to ease the situation by stating that the resolution did not signify the renunciation of anticapitalist struggle, but only its postponement. Nevertheless, they did not renege on their obligation to appeal, for the time being, to the bourgeoisie: the united front, one statement asserted, must comprise all classes "including large sections of the Indian bourgeoisie and barring a small top knot section of the pro-Imperialist bourgeoisie and the big landlords and Princes." [21]

Despite these ideological differences, however, the Communists and the Socialists found common ground on such concrete issues as the questions of economic and social policy. In an account published some years later the Socialist leader, Madhu Limaye, states that the CPI and the CSP "functioned in unison"; at about the beginning of 1937, he says, the Communists seemed to have moved closer to the Socialist point of view.[22] At that time the two parties entered into the so-called "Lucknow Agreement" which, according to the Socialist interpretation, signified that they would eventually merge in a single organiza-

---

[17] *Communist,* I (March, 1937), p. 18.
[18] *Ibid.,* p. 5.
[19] *Ibid.,* I (April, 1937), p. 25.
[20] *Ibid.,* I (June, 1937), pp. 16–26.
[21] *Ibid.,* p. 25.
[22] Madhu Limaye, *Communist Party: Facts and Fiction* (Hyderabad: Chetana Prakashan Ltd., 1951), p. 31.

tion. Had their coöperation on this level been given full expression, the Indian left wing might well have exerted a very potent influence on the Congress program and on the development of the Congress itself.

But organizational and theoretical rivalries proved too great an obstacle, and the Lucknow Agreement was never implemented. Increasing friction expressed itself in a variety of complaints and counter-complaints, with interorganizational disputes providing the primary source of rancor. By June, 1937, the Communists were protesting against a "heresy hunt" in the CSP; they claimed that anyone who dared to criticize the National Executive was berated as a "disruptor" and threatened with expulsion. In fact, they said, new Communist applicants were no longer being admitted to the CSP. Accordingly, they intensified their polemics against the Socialists, claiming that "united action is practically impossible." [23]

A few months later the CPI allegation that its members were no longer being admitted to the ranks of the CSP became fact. When the National Executive met in August, there was placed before it an alleged CPI document which had fallen into Socialist hands. According to Narayan's account of this episode, the document categorically stated that the CPI was the only genuine socialist party, and that the Communists would never tolerate a rival in the field. The exposure of this document, Narayan says, caused "painful shock and great indignation" among the Socialists. The National Executive concluded that the Lucknow Agreement was dead, and it unanimously decided to halt admission of Communists. However, it chose not to expel Communists already in the CSP—a "mistaken decision," Narayan admits.[24]

The CPI responded to this affront by pleading allegiance to the Lucknow Agreement; as proof of their loyalty the Communists proposed that the two parties merge immediately. According to Narayan, the Socialists dismissed the proposal as being patently insincere. Relations between the two groups, he states, "steadily deteriorated." The CSP felt itself "increasingly paralyzed" by Communist disruption and its own inability to take decisive action.[25]

Early in 1938 Minoo R. Masani, joint-secretary of the CSP and by this time a most bitter opponent of the Communists, got possession of another confidential CPI document that described appropriate methods for capturing CSP units. Masani published this document,

---

[23] *Communist*, I (June, 1937), p. 34.
[24] Jaya Prakash Narayan, *Towards Struggle*, pp. 172–174.
[25] *Ibid.*, p. 174.

and pressed for action against the Communists.[26] But the National Executive still shrank from making a decision.

In the meantime, the Communists had almost succeeded in capturing control of the National Executive itself. At the Lahore conference of the CSP, Narayan proposed a slate of candidates for the Executive which gave one-third of the seats to the Communists. But this did not appease them, and they essayed a coup by nominating a list of candidates that would assure them a majority on the Executive. By the narrowest margin, the Conference adopted Narayan's slate.[27]

After the Lahore conference, coöperation between the two parties was maintained only in the most limited range of action, and this was achieved primarily as the result of a working agreement, on the personal level, between Narayan and P. C. Joshi. Narayan tried, with the utmost tenacity, to preserve the vestiges of unity between Communists and Socialists. He and Joshi continued to exchange views and to issue joint statements on political issues. But by now it was clear that the initiative within the CSP had passed to the Communists.

By the beginning of 1939, the Communists had gained enormous benefit from their penetration of the Congress Socialist Party, for it had given them the opportunity not only to capture units of that organization, but to influence its mass audience in India. The Communist Party had grown tremendously, multiplying its membership many times over in the space of these three years.[28] It had built up a tightly knit organizational apparatus, and could boast an impressive collection of journals. The most important benefit, however, was access to the Indian National Congress itself.

Penetration of the Congress

As the Congress Socialist Party was a constituent part of the Indian National Congress, membership in the CSP had given the Communists entry into the entire nationalist organization, from the lowest village unit to the All-Indian Congress Committee itself. The opportunity for mass contact thus afforded was of incalculable value, and the label "Congressman" gave the Communists unprecedented respectability and influence.

---

[26] M. R. Masani, *The Communist Party of India* (London: Derek Verschoyle, 1954), pp. 69–70.

[27] *Ibid.*, p. 71.

[28] No membership figure for 1939 is available, but the increase in this period may be inferred from the fact that it rose from 150 in 1934 to 5,000 in 1942. The figure for 1942 is in P. C. Joshi, "Report to the Central Committee," *People's War*, I (Oct. 4, 1942), p. 5.

The united-front-from-below tactic against the Gandhian national leadership required, above all, grass-roots activity to cultivate influence among the rank and file of the Congress. This activity served the CPI recruitment program, but it was also directed at securing representation in the top levels of the Congress; so successful was this effort that by 1939 the Communists claimed twenty members on the All-India Congress Committee (AICC).[29] There they continually pressed the issue of violence versus nonviolence in order, apparently, to force Gandhi to declare his views for the record—as though they were fully confident that the record would be his undoing. At the Faizpur session of the Congress, for example, the Communists raised the issue by introducing an amendment which asserted that self-government could be achieved "only as a result of an uncompromising revolutionary mass struggle with imperialism." It may be noted, as an index of leftist strength in the Congress at this time, that the amendment received as many as 45 votes out of 128 in the AICC, and 262 out of 713 in the full Congress session.[30]

The united-front-from-below tactic was not only tenaciously pursued but was uncompromisingly proclaimed by the Communists. In the words of a pamphlet distributed at the Faizpur session, the Party's policy was designed for "moving the active sections of the Congress rank and file out of the reactionary 'Constructive Programme' of Gandhism." [31]

This policy, however, increasingly involved the CPI in a dilemma that had been inherent in the "Anti-Imperialist People's Front," for it required that the CPI aim at unifying the nationalist movement, and at the same time try to capture it. These goals were fundamentally incompatible, and the CPI was increasingly forced to face the question as to which it should sacrifice—the campaign for a united Congress, or the campaign against Gandhi and the nationalist leadership.

In a vivid instance of this dilemma one of the foremost Communist leaders, S. A. Dange, chose to sacrifice unity. Dange was both president of the now Communist-dominated All-India Trade Union Congress (AITUC) and a member of the All-India Congress Committee. During the elections of 1937 the AITUC supported the Congress nominees for the most part, but in Bombay the two organizations ran separate candidates. Dange openly supported the AITUC candidate, and the Congress leadership threatened him with disciplinary action. He answered,

---

[29] R. Palme Dutt, *India Today* (Bombay: People's Publishing House, 1949), p. 397.
[30] *Communist,* I (Feb., 1937), p. 2.
[31] *Ibid.,* p. 7.

"my choice is with the TUC, for the workers and the national struggle," and he offered to resign from the Congress if necessary.[32]

Not long afterward, the CPI itself was required to resolve the dilemma with a choice so crucial that it brought about a fundamental change in policy.

The CPI Opts for Unity

By the end of 1938 leftist strength in the Congress had increased significantly, but the radicals had not yet found a weapon with which to unseat the dominant Gandhian leadership. Early in 1939, however, the Congress presidential election gave them an opportunity to seize the balance of power and seriously challenge the supremacy of the conservative Gandhian group.

The popular left-of-center leader, Subhas Chandra Bose, was a candidate for reëlection as Congress president. Gandhi announced that he would consider the reëlection of Bose a vote of nonconfidence —and the lines were drawn. The leftists supported Bose, and he won the election. But when the Gandhians threw down the gauntlet and refused to serve under Bose on the most important Congress body, the Working Committee, it was clear that the leftists could capture the Congress only at the cost of splitting it. They were face to face with an ultimate choice—leftist hegemony, or Congress unity. When the issue of Gandhi versus Bose came to a showdown at the Tripuri Congress session (March, 1939), the Socialists officially proclaimed their neutrality by abstaining; the Communists chose unity under Gandhi.

Explaining its position, the CPI stated in its official organ, *National Front,* that the interests of the anti-imperialist movement "demanded not the *exclusive* leadership of one wing but a *united* leadership under the guidance of Gandhi." [33] This did not signify, said the CPI, that it renounced criticism of the Gandhian leadership; it meant only that the Party recognized that Gandhi possessed "the greatest mobilizing power" for the anti-imperialist movement. Actually, the decision meant that the Indian Communists must now abandon the united-front-from-below tactic against the right-wing Congress leadership, in favor of a more docile policy of coöperation with that leadership.

This about-face not unnaturally caused great consternation in the ranks of the CPI and its sympathizers. Writing in *National Front,* Ajoy Ghosh admitted that the Communist declaration of confidence in Gandhi could reasonably be interpreted as "a repudiation of the

[32] S. A. Dange, *Statement to Pt. Jawaharlal Nehru* (Bombay: The New Manohar P. Press, 1937), p. 19.
[33] *National Front,* II (March 19, 1939), p. 96. Emphasis in original.

line we had hitherto advocated." This decision, he confessed, "has given rise to tremendous confusion in the ranks of our supporters and has definitely harmed the prestige of Communists."

Has not Tripuri meant the smashing up of the entire Left including the Communists? Did not the Communists follow a tailist policy throughout the Session? Were they not obsessed with ideas of unity and did they not, therefore, try to placate everybody and end by placating none? Did they not in their eagerness for unity vacillate at every step, renounce their entire political line and even their fundamental principles? These are the questions that are being asked.[34]

But despite obvious bewilderment in the ranks, having made the choice for unity under Gandhi the CPI leadership proceeded unabashedly to accept its implications in full. The new course required a drastic reëvaluation of Gandhi, and this was soon forthcoming.

In the April, 1939, issue of *National Front*, S. G. Sardesai explained that the Communists were extending "the hand of coöperation" to Gandhi because, under current conditions, he served a "progressive role."

It is obvious that in such conditions the Leftists not only do not need to but must not continue their old attitude towards Gandhism and Gandhian leadership. They have exposed the shortcomings of Gandhism sufficiently in the past. With the new strength at their command the time and the opportunity have come for them to weld even Gandhism with the new nationalism. . . .

This necessitates a very close study of and emphasis on every positive side of Gandhism particularly during its militant anti-imperialist phase between 1919 and 1920. . . . This is the Gandhism that we have to resurrect, burnish and replenish.[35]

The new CPI policy also, of course, required that the intensity of the attacks on the Congress right-wing be modified. The Party now expressed its dissatisfaction with the "vacillating" position of the rightist leadership, but it disavowed any intention of unseating that leadership. It was an error, *New Age* explained, "to make the Right the target of attack instead of imperialism"; in place of undermining that leadership, the Party would now endeavor only to influence it, with confidence that "the entire national forces including the national reformist bourgeoisie can be won over to struggle against imperialism." [36] And *National Front* declared that "The offensive from the Right has to be resisted, but this cannot be done by launching a counter-offensive to throw out the Right." [37]

Another striking feature of the new policy was a reduction in trade-union militancy. The Party announced that its labor policy would

---

[34] *Ibid.*, p. 101.

[35] *Ibid.*, (April 30, 1939), p. 189.

[36] *New Age* V (May, 1939), p. 501.

[37] *National Front*, II (June 18, 1939), p. 309.

be based on an attempt to "secure the coöperation and support of
Congress Committees." Any tendency to force a leftist stand upon
non-Communist labor leadership "is nothing short of disruption," it
said. "The old tradition of conducting workers' struggle in isolation
must be ended," and strike tactics must be conceived "with a view to
win public sympathy and Congress support." [38]

In seeking the reasons for this dramatic turn in CPI policy, it is
likely that factors in the international scene played a dominant role.
With the mounting danger of war against the USSR, it was more than
ever important that the CPI concentrate its attack on the enemies of
the Socialist fatherland. Since the Chamberlain government in Britain
was considered an ally of fascism, the CPI must sacrifice everything
to the cause of strengthening the anti-British movement in India. As
the Indian Communists declared, the defeat of that government was
essential to the defeat of fascism itself. An alliance with *all* anti-
imperialist forces in India—including the Gandhian leadership of
the Congress—was therefore imperative.

It is also clear that in the decision to collaborate, the Indian Communists were again coached by their British comrades. Speaking for
the British Party, Harry Pollitt dispatched a message to India on the
occasion of the Tripuri Congress session, declaring: "The question
of paramount importance in India in our view is the unity of all national forces under the leadership of the Indian National Congress." [39]

As international events moved toward a climax in 1939, the CPI
hewed to the line of strengthening international communism, even
at the possible cost of weakening Indian communism.

---

[38] *New Age,* V (May, 1939), pp. 512–513.
[39] *National Front,* II (March 19, 1939), p. 103.

9   THE IMPERIALIST WAR

In August, 1939, the Nazi-Soviet pact drastically changed the international framework of CPI policy. With the signing of the pact, the USSR secured temporary respite from the threat of its European enemies, and gained much additional territory in the bargain. The Socialist fatherland could look upon the coming war with equanimity, for it would now be an "imperialist" struggle in which the Western European powers might well destroy each other. With the temporary alleviation of pressure on international communism, the Indian Communists and their international mentors could reassess the Indian situation.

Certain aspects of the picture were encouraging. Though technically the CPI was still illegal, during the previous five years it had emerged from semiobscurity to a position of considerable strength; while its influence was still modest, that influence must have seemed formidable as compared to earlier years. Furthermore, the left wing as a whole had by now achieved a role of some importance in Indian politics: in the Congress, the Forward Bloc led by Subhas Chandra Bose had joined other radical groups, including the Socialists and Communists, to form the Left Consolidation Committee; and though the left remained a minority, it had become increasingly better organized and influential.

The progress of the CPI during these years was but one aspect of the rapidly accelerating growth of political consciousness and activity throughout India. This was shown by the increase, both in size and variety, of political movements. For example, the membership of the National Congress had increased tenfold—from 500,000 at the beginning of 1936 to 5,000,000 in 1939 [1]—and it had become far more vital a factor in Indian politics. There had been a parallel increase in the vitality of other political movements also, which showed itself in the growth of the Muslim League. As Nehru remarks in his account of this period, for the first time in its history the League "got a mass backing and began to develop into a mass organization." [2]

Finally, the growth of political consciousness was manifested by the extension of nationalist agitation and organization into a new arena, that of the princely states. In its earlier phases the nationalist movement had, by and large, been confined to British India, but by 1939 a mass "states' people's movement" had developed in the domains of the native autocrats. Though encouraging this movement, the Congress had not yet formally embraced it.

The growth and multiplication of political forces in India during this period was to a great extent an outcome of the 1935 Government of India Act. This act broadened the franchise and increased the autonomy of the provincial governments, and while it did not affect the locus of final power—the viceroy—it stimulated political controversy and activity and thus promoted the development of divers political organizations. According to Nehru, "the psychological change was enormous and an electric current seemed to run through the countryside." [3]

The Communists could expect to benefit by this striking politization, and they could look with satisfaction to its further growth. But in their view an even more substantial basis for optimism was to be found in the rapid increase in class consciousness and class organization that had also taken place since 1934. According to later Communist accounts, there had been a "new upsurge" of trade-union activity, during which the number of registered unions had increased from 191 in 1934 to 296 in 1938. [4] Among the peasants, as well, there had been a heightening of class consciousness that culminated in the formation of the All-India Kisan Sabha (AIKS); by 1939 this organization was able to boast of the "phenomenal awakening and growth" of the peasant movement, and to claim 800,000 members. [5]

---

[1] R. C. Majumdar, et al., *An Advanced History of India* (London: Macmillan and Company, Ltd., 1953), p. 989.

[2] Jawaharlal Nehru, *The Discovery of India* (London: Meridian Books Ltd., 1951), p. 366.

[3] *Ibid.*, p. 347.

[4] R. Palme Dutt, *India Today* (Bombay: People's Publishing House, 1949), p. 395.

[5] Quoted in *ibid.*, p. 258.

On the eve of World War II, then, the CPI might have regarded the Indian situation as providing grounds for optimism, as well as confirmation of the wisdom of its united-front policy. Whether that policy would be retained after war broke out depended, of course, on future developments in the international and Indian scenes. As long as the Soviet Union remained neutral the war would be "imperialist," and Communist strategy would be aimed equally against British and German imperialism. In India, this would mean continuing the strategy of uniting all anti-imperialist classes against the prevailing enemy, the British; tactics would continue to depend on the attitudes of the various Indian parties toward imperialism.

The crucial question affecting the Communists' relations with other parties would be their attitude toward India's participation in the impending war. With increasing frequency during 1938 and 1939 the National Congress had proclaimed that it was opposed to such participation; in 1938 it said that as long as the imperialist system remained, and India was held in colonial dependence, a war between Great Britain and Germany was an "imperialist" war to which India could not be a party. India would not join any war, declared the Congress, "without the express consent of its people." [6] At the beginning of 1939 the Congress went further; it stated that while it sympathized with the Western democracies, it was "opposed to imperialism and fascism alike." [7]

When the war actually broke out, however, the Congress modified its stand somewhat. In mid-September the Working Committee, meeting at Wardha, refused in principle to coöperate in an "imperialist" war, but it withheld any decision on the immediate situation. The Committee invited the British government to declare its intentions with regard to India and demanded that a pledge of future independence be included, with immediate implementation of that pledge "to the largest possible extent." [8] Thus the Congress no longer required unconditional relinquishment of British authority as a prerequisite of Indian participation in the war, and it left indefinite, in terms of immediate changes, the cost of India's coöperation.

Both the Congress Socialist Party and Bose's Forward Bloc had been even more militantly opposed to India's taking any part in the war. In the middle of 1939, majority CSP opinion had completely and unconditionally rejected the idea of entry into any European war—even

---

[6] N. V. Rajkumar, ed., *The Background of India's Foreign Policy* (New Delhi: All-India Congress Committee, n.d. [1952]), pp. 55–56.

[7] *Ibid.*, p. 58.

[8] *Ibid.*, pp. 61–67.

were India to be granted independence—and had called for immediate mass action should Great Britain seek to involve India in the hostilities. With the actual outbreak of war, however, the CSP decided to accept the Congress position, which left the door open for further negotiations. Bose, on the other hand, soon showed that he was determined to promote an immediate national struggle for independence, with or without the Congress.

In its first reaction to the outbreak of war, the British government was little inclined to concede to Indian aspirations. On September 3, the viceroy proclaimed that India was at war and issued an ordinance providing for emergency powers. Not until mid-October did Whitehall, through the viceroy, state its intentions toward India; then it merely promised that after the war there would be fresh negotiations with the Indian leaders. In the meantime it offered to establish a consultative group, representative of Indian opinion, in order that India should have some voice in war-time policy. Gandhi called this offer "profoundly disappointing." [9]

Emergence of the Comintern Line

With future developments uncertain, the Indian Communist Party had two choices. It could continue the from-above alliance with the Gandhian leadership of the Congress, attempting to strengthen its antiwar orientation. Or it could renounce that alliance tactic and, seizing the opportunity provided by Congress vacillation, attempt to lead a more aggressive movement against both imperialist rule and the war. The events of 1939–1940 suggest that the CPI increasingly turned to the latter alternative—despite the cautionings of international Communist authorities.

In their commentary on India, during the months immediately after the war began, Russian and Comintern spokesmen clearly demanded the continuation of the united-front tactic.[10] Whether in ignorance or

---

[9] Nripendra Nath Mitra, ed., *The Indian Annual Register, 1939* (Calcutta: The Annual Register Office, 1940), II, 32.

[10] The following summary of the international Communist view of India in this period is based upon these articles: V. Bushevich "Natsional'no-osvoboditel'noe dvizhenie v Indii i bor'ba rabochego klassa" [The National-Liberation Movement in India and the Struggle of the Working Class], *Mirovoe Khoziaistvo . . . ,* (Nov.) 1939, pp. 133–153; A. Dyakov, "Massovoe dvizhenie v Indiiskikh kniazhestvakh" [The Mass Movement in the Indian Princely States], *Mirovoe Khoziaistvo . . . ,* (Oct.) 1939, pp. 121–134; S. Mel'man, Indiia v bor'be za svoiu natsional'nuiu nezavisimost' " [India in the Struggle for National Independence], *Mirovoe Khoziaistvo . . . ,* (Sept.) 1939, pp. 92–104; S. Mel'man, "Stalin i natsional'no-kolonial'nyi vopros" [Stalin and the National-Colonial Question], *Mirovoe Khoziaistvo . . .* (Nov., 1939), pp. 48–64; and D. Protap, "Indiia i imperialisticheskaia voina" [India and the Imperialist War], *Kommunisticheskii Internatsional,* 1939, pp. 43–50.

through deliberate distortion, they praised the Congress as being determined to "use the war crisis for achieving complete national independence," and as having the support of "all mass organizations" in this policy. At the same time they castigated the Muslim League, the Liberal Party, and the Indian princes for supporting the war, and called them "agents of British imperialism."

Accordingly, the Congress was proclaimed to be "the organization of the anti-imperialist front, which embodies the leadership of the anti-imperialist struggle." The Congress, said the Communist spokesmen, was composed of two main factions: a left wing which represented the "progressive democratic masses" under Nehru's leadership, and a right wing which represented the bourgeoisie. But though the right wing was ready to compromise with imperialism—that is, to support the war in return for partial concessions—it was, they said, on the whole anti-imperialist. The main emphasis, therefore, in the Russian and Comintern writings was on the necessity to further consolidate and unify the National Congress. In other words, the CPI was to ally itself with the Congress leadership.

This line implied the expectation that the left forces in the Congress —including the Communists—would continue to grow stronger and could in the future capture the nationalist organization. This expectation was implied, also, in the attention that Comintern spokesmen devoted to the growth of class consciousness and class activity in India. The years since 1937, they said, had been a period of "upsurge" in the national movement; the working class had become "an increasingly strong political force" with "greater and greater influence." As evidence of the workers' increased political consciousness, a Soviet article cited an Indian police report which revealed, it said, that the Bengali workers had recently celebrated May Day, Anti-War Day, Lenin Day, November Resolution Day, Palestine Day, Spain Day, Saklatvala Day, Subhas Bose Day, and Political Prisoners Day. The CPI itself, another spokesman claimed, was "in the leading ranks" of the Congress and constituted a "significant force."

In addition to their emphasis on unifying the Congress itself, the international Communist authorities naturally laid considerable stress on the need to consolidate the radical forces within the Congress. They called for coöperation among the Communists, Socialists, and, through the Left Consolidation Committee, the followers of Bose. They referred to Bose as a "left nationalist" and viewed his defeat by the Gandhians as merely temporary.

The essence of the Russian and Comintern view of the Indian situation at this time is perhaps best expressed in a Russian article describ-

ing a working-class demonstration in Bombay against certain legislation of the Congress-controlled provincial government. According to
the Russian account, "The basic slogan of the demonstrators was a
demand for a change in the law, at the same time expressing confidence
in the National Congress as the leader of the anti-imperialist struggle." [11] The policy here described—and therefore the proper path for
Communists—was that of working within the Congress and, at the
same time as far as was consistent with unity, intensifying the pressure
on the established leadership.

Since the Congress was in fact less militantly opposed to the war
than Soviet commentators had portrayed it to be (and assuming they
knew this) it might be asked why they insisted so firmly that the Indian
Communists continue to support the bourgeois nationalist movement.
A possible reason, directly related to Soviet strategic interests, is supplied in British Communist writings of this period. An article in the
unofficial Party organ, *Labour Monthly,* declared that British plans
included war against the Soviet Union, using Iran and India as bases.
The subcontinent would therefore become a " 'jumping-off ground'
of the greatest importance." [12] Indeed, this view was expressed not only
immediately following the outbreak of the war but even as late as one
month before Germany's attack on the USSR, when R. Palme Dutt
stated that the principal danger to the Soviet Union was "the massing
of the main imperialist forces"—German and British—around its
borders.[13] The British Communist spokesmen apparently envisaged an
attack on Russia through India; this possibility required that the British be denied any support or coöperation in India itself. Hence it
would be incumbent on Indian Communists to sustain and encourage
all antiwar forces in India, including the vacillating National Congress.

The CPI Anticipates Revolution

As the previous section has shown, Russian and Comintern spokesmen clearly indicated that though the CPI was to seek greater influence
on the Congress leadership, its chief task was to maintain the united
front, giving top priority to unity against the war. Nevertheless, an
examination of Indian Communist policy and activity during this
period shows that increasingly the Party departed from the alliance

---

[11] S. Mel'man, "Indiia v bor'be . . . ," p. 93.
[12] Michael Carritt, "India Before the Storm," *Labour Monthly,* XXII (May, 1940),
pp. 294–295.
[13] R. Palme Dutt, "Notes of the Month," *Labour Monthly,* XXIII (May, 1941), pp.
209–210.

tactic and adopted the from-below tactic, attacking all other political leadership not only in the Congress but among the leftists as well. Apparently, the CPI finally chose to pursue hegemony, even at the cost of unity.

Very soon after the outbreak of hostilities the CPI demanded that the war be converted into a revolution—a classic Leninist theme that had been conspicuous by its absence from current Comintern literature. This demand was the crux of the CPI's increasingly radical line, and was unambiguously stated in an official resolution of the CPI Politbureau, adopted at its October, 1939, meeting.[14] The resolution decried the "imperialist war" and declared that the British government had no intention of granting independence to its colonies. Great Britain aimed at bolstering reaction at home and intensifying exploitation in the colonies; consequently, said the resolution, the task of the Indian people was the "revolutionary utilisation of the war crisis for the achievement of National Freedom." The resolution asserted that "capture of power is an immediately realisable goal" and explicitly called for "transformation of imperialist war into a war of national liberation."

The resolution admitted, however, that the CPI alone could not mobilize a mass struggle for freedom; the Party's aim, therefore, must be to create such an intense antiwar sentiment among the people as a whole, and among the Congressmen in particular, "as would move the Congress itself towards struggle." Although the resolution accused the Congress leaders of seeking a treacherous compromise with the British, and said that they must be "sharply criticised" and "ruthlessly exposed," it reaffirmed the necessity of working, for the time being, within the Congress.

Here, then, the CPI signified its intention to use the Congress machinery for its own revolutionary purposes. This tactic was even more clearly set forth in another CPI statement of the period declaring that the Party must "seize the initiative in making preparations for struggle through the Congress Committees" and must convert the Congress-led *satyagraha* into "mass insurrection." [15] It was admitted that this would

---

[14] The following quotations from this document are taken from extracts published later by the Party (P. C. Joshi, *Communist Reply to Congress Working Committee's Charges* [Bombay: People's Publishing House, 1945], pp. 35–39). The resolution was not available to the authors in its original version. The CPI's legal publication, *National Front,* was banned by the government at the beginning of the war.

[15] Quoted in M. Muni Reddy, *The Student Movement in India* (Lucknow: K. S. R. Acharya, 1947), pp. 9–11, Part II. The document quoted, said to have been published by the Bengal Committee of the CPI, may in fact be merely a local edition of the Politbureau resolution, since the extracts quoted by M. Muni Reddy are consistent with available extracts from that resolution, and in one sentence, identical.

take time and would depend on the Party's becoming firmly entrenched in the Congress organization. In the meantime, however, no other political organization should launch any mass action without Congress sanction, for this "becomes adventurous, disrupts the national movement and dissipates our forces." The Party statement therefore condemned the CSP and the Forward Bloc for allegedly proposing mass action that was not sanctioned by the Congress.

In the Independence Day Manifesto of January, 1940, the CPI proclaimed its new policy in what was virtually a clarion call to insurrection. The manifesto pictured the world situation as "the deepest crisis of capitalism," and declared that the European masses as "already raising the Red Banner of revolt."

> The world is on the brink of mighty upheavals. Before our very eyes the old order is tottering, shaking, falling to pieces. Caught in the vicious grasp of their own creation, the rulers of the capitalist world are seeking a way out by murdering millions, by devastating whole countries, by causing untold suffering to their peoples. . . . Democracy, Freedom and Peace have entered into decisive conflict with the forces of Imperialism, Fascism, and War. On the outcome of this conflict depends the fate of humanity.
>
> The old world is collapsing. In the midst of the horrors of war and starvation a new world is being born. We are passing through a momentous period of world history.[16]

The Indian scene, as well, was one of tremendous mass upheaval and revolutionary potential, according to the manifesto. "No longer is Britain the master of the situation, master of our destiny," it said; "we are now in a position to begin an advance which imperialism will not be able to repel," a struggle which "will draw millions of our countrymen into organized assault on the very citadel of Imperialism."

But the manifesto proclaimed the Party's loyalty to the Congress as the agency of national struggle, and it emphasized the Party's identification with the Congress by declaring: "Let us Congressmen realize that we stand on the threshhold of victory." At the same time, however, the CPI signaled that it intended to mobilize mass pressure upon the Congress leadership by calling upon workers, peasants, and students to join mass demonstrations, hold rallies, and organize marches.

These attempts to create revolutionary pressure from within the Congress itself entailed certain dangers for the CPI. Since it was not yet ready to desert the Congress, it could not unrestrainedly exploit what it saw as a revolutionary situation. Other leftist parties, however —the CSP or the Forward Bloc—might recognize the opportunity and, free to leave the Congress, they might be able to wrest the revo-

---

[16] This manifesto was published in *World News and Views*, XX (March 16, 1940), pp. 166–167.

lutionary initiative from the CPI. Faced with such a dread possibility the Party might be expected to do its utmost to weaken any other leftist groups or leaders, at the same time that it was working to displace the conservative leadership of the Congress. Events during the next year show that this was, in fact, the course the CPI followed.

The CPI Breaks with Its Radical Allies

At the end of December, 1939, the Socialist leader, J. P. Narayan, addressed a "war circular" to CSP units and members in which he declared that during the past few weeks the Communists had "left nothing undone" to destroy unity within the CSP.[17] They had, he said, propagated lies about CSP policy, setting out "to create confusion and even rebellion" in the ranks by accusing the CSP of an "adventurist" plan to launch a civil-disobedience campaign without the sanction of the Congress. The fact was, said Narayan, that the CSP policy was identical with that of the CPI—to move the Congress itself toward more decisive action.

According to Narayan, the CPI had "[torn] off its mask completely and stood as the sworn enemy of the Congress Socialist Party and of every other progressive organization with which it had worked before." [18] At its Ramgarh meeting in March, 1940, the CSP National Executive therefore decided to expel all Communist members. The decision came late, however, for by this time the Communists had captured a large part of the Socialist Party, and the Executive's action meant the expulsion, not of a handful of members, but of a substantial section of the CSP organization. Virtually the entire South Indian section (the Andhra, Tamil Nad, and Kerala branches) went over en bloc to the Communist Party, having gradually come under the influence of local leaders who were Communists openly or secretly. It was found, moreover, that many individual Socialist Party members, including even some members of the Executive, had joined the CPI secretly some time before. In the words of one Socialist leader, the CSP was "all but finished." [19]

Evaluating the CSP's experience of alliance with the Communists, Narayan wrote that "it is desirable once for all to give up vague talk of unity with the Communist Party." Collaboration with the CPI is

---

[17] J. P. Narayan, *War Circular Number 2* (Lucknow: All-India Congress Socialist Party, 1939), 5 pp. This is a mimeographed innerparty circular, addressed to provincial party secretaries and party members.

[18] Jaya Prakash Narayan, *Towards Struggle* (Bombay: Padma Publications Ltd., 1946), p. 179.

[19] Madhu Limaye, *Communist Party: Facts and Fiction* (Hyderabad: Chetana Prakashan Ltd., 1951), p. 38.

inevitably doomed, he said, by the very nature of the international Communist movement. The CPI, being a branch of the Communist International, could not genuinely unite with another party unless it too affiliated with the International. In any event, he stated, "unity is a misnomer." [20]

Thus despite the Soviet injunction to consolidate all leftist forces, the Communists had so exacerbated their relations with the Socialists as to produce a final break between the two groups. At about the same time the Communists broke with Subhas Bose also. At a meeting of the Left Consolidation Committee in December, 1939, they refused to withdraw an earlier accusation that the Forward Bloc was "counter-revolutionary," and the Committee was disrupted.[21] Uneasy collaboration continued for a few months in the Bengal Congress Committee which Bose dominated; but when, in the beginning of March, this unit was suspended by the Congress Working Committee because of its defiance of the Gandhian leadership, the Communists deserted it and joined an ad hoc committee established by the Working Committee. The Communists declined to join the Forward Bloc in its Anti-Compromise Conference later that month, and the rupture was complete.

In his own account of this episode, Bose said that the Communists had used the Left Consolidation Committee merely as a platform "for popularizing their own organization," while carrying out "reprehensible propaganda" against the Forward Bloc. "Today they have cast off all sense of shame," he concluded.[22] Thus, again, the Communists managed to alienate an erstwhile ally.

Here, however, the CPI had been faced with an interesting dilemma. When Bose and the Bengal Congress Committee defied the established Congress leadership, the CPI was forced to choose between them, for it could not support Bose in his bid to provide "alternative leadership" to the Congress, without throwing off all pretense at collaborating with the Congress. Thus the Communists could not fulfill the Soviet injunction to "consolidate the left" without at the same time disobeying the injunction to work within the Congress.

But, as has been suggested, the CPI had reason for wishing to weaken any other leftist leader; in denouncing Bose, the Party's general secretary, P. C. Joshi, revealed that the split with the Forward Bloc was part of an attempt to reduce the prestige of a rival—it had to be pre-

[20] Jaya Prakash Narayan, *Towards Struggle*, pp. 182–183.

[21] Subhas Chandra Bose, *The Indian Struggle, 1935–1942*, quoted in Sita Ram Goel, *Netaji and the CPI* (Calcutta: Society for Defence of Freedom in Asia, 1955), pp. 5–6.

[22] *Ibid.*, pp. 6, 8.

vented from seizing the opportunity to build a mass following based on a radical program:

Workers, peasants, students have already adopted the proletarian technique of struggle—mass action. They have already come under the influence of Socialism. The effort of the Forward Bloc to win over these movements for its satyagraha or political policy has to be resisted as the infiltration of bourgeois influence over the masses. Before the working class, Kisan, and student workers, the Forward Bloc has to be opposed not as being too left but as *being the disruptive agency of the bourgeoisie*.[23]

Having split with other leftist groups, the CPI also stepped up its campaign against the prevailing Congress leadership. In another policy statement of this period, P. C. Joshi declared that genuine national struggle—that is, "an explosive struggle with gloves off"—had become a "practical proposal," and he castigated the Congress elite for failing to lead it.

We do not have a national struggle because the bourgeoisie is at the top of the national movement. The obvious course would be to free the national front from the influence of bourgeois reformism and develop the political strength of the proletariat within the common front so as to develop the forces of struggle in a manner so as to make a national struggle inevitable and *overwhelm and isolate the cowardly bourgeoisie*.[24]

Like the splits with the Socialists and the Forward Bloc, this campaign culminated in March. At the Ramgarh session of the Congress, the CPI published a new statement of policy entitled, significantly, "Proletarian Path." [25] This statement demanded that India "make revolutionary use of the war crisis"; the first step toward this objective, it declared, would be a "political general strike in the major industries together with country-wide no-rent and no-tax action." Next, the national movement would enter "a new and higher phase—the phase of armed insurrection." The principal features of this forthcoming struggle, according to "Proletarian Path," would be "storming of military and police stations by armed bands of national militia in rural as well as urban areas, destruction of Government institutions, actual offensive against the armed forces of the Government on the most extensive scale."

Since the CPI could not conceivably have hoped to convert the Gandhian leadership to such a policy, it is clear that the Party's aim

---

[23] P. C. Joshi, *Unmasked Parties and Politics*, quoted in Sita Ram Goel, *Netaji and the CPI*, pp. 9–14. This CPI pamphlet, issued in March, 1940, was "a severe denunciation" of other parties of all stripes, according to Goel. It evidently represented a climax to the Party's polemics against rival political groups.

[24] *Ibid.*, p. 13. Emphasis in original.

[25] Short extracts from this document, which was not available to the authors in the

was to popularize its revolutionary policy in order to displace that
leadership at the earliest opportunity. According to contemporary
newspaper reports of the Ramgarh session of the Congress the two
Communist delegates, K. M. Ashraf and V. D. Chitale, offering an
amendment to the main Congress resolution, urged "immediate
launching of the struggle" and condemned any talk of compromise
with the British.[26] Their amendment was defeated. It may be noted
that the Socialists voted for the main resolution, giving further evidence that the CSP was not officially planning an "adventurist" action
as the Communists had claimed earlier.

The issuance of the "Proletarian Path" statement, with its bald
proposal of orthodox proletarian revolution, led to serious difficulties
for those Communists who were working in the peasant movement.
Under the from-above tactic, they had been collaborating with the
non-Communists in the All-India Kisan Sabha and had outwardly
accepted the AIKS slogan, "Kisan Mazdoor Raj," which signified that
peasants and proletariat were to be equal in the ideal state of the
future. The new Party statement was evidently taken by the non-
Communists to mean that the CPI had now abandoned its professions
of faith in peasant-proletariat equality and was, in the words of N. C.
Ranga, then vice-president of the AIKS, demanding "an undiluted
proletarian path for the achievement of freedom." [27]

Moreover, according to Ranga, the Communist delegates to the
annual AIKS session at Palasa, later in March, tried to prevent the
adoption of a resolution claiming that the peasants "are entitled to
the foremost place in the government of the country." Since contemporary newspapers report that the resolution was passed unanimously,
apparently the Communists did not carry their opposition to the point
of a vote.[28]

The other elements of AIKS policy were, in general, consistent with
the CPI position, since the AIKS condemned the war and the Congress
decision to postpone all-out national struggle. Uneasy collaboration
between Communist and non-Communist forces therefore continued
in the peasant organization.

As one of the steps toward armed insurrection, "Proletarian Path"
had called for a "political general strike in the major industries";

original, were quoted by the home minister, Sir Reginald Maxwell, in a speech to
the Central Assembly, New Delhi, on February 12, 1941. See *Legislative Assembly
Debates; Official Report*, 1941, Vol. I, No. 2 (12 Feb. 1941), (Delhi: Manager of Publications, 1941), pp. 122–123.

[26] *The Tribune* (Lahore), March 21, 1940, p. 9.

[27] N. G. Ranga, *Kisans and Communists* (Bombay: Pratibha Pubs., n.d.), p. 8.

[28] *The Statesman* (Calcutta), March 29, 1940, p. 11.

early in March the CPI showed what this meant by organizing a general strike in the textile industry of Bombay. Though the strike did not result in violence, it immobilized the majority of the textile mills in the Bombay area, and 150,000 workers joined the walkout at its peak.[29] The Communists, in collaboration with some leftist allies in the Girni Kamgar Union and other labor organizations, showed that they could disrupt a major industrial center, and thus translated into action at least part of their proposal for all-out attack on the British.

Repression of the CPI

The official British response to these CPI pronouncements and actions was exceedingly drastic. It amounted to the most effective repression yet undertaken against the Communist movement in India, although it was not so publicly dramatic as the Cawnpore or Meerut trials. Early in March, 1940, immediately after the start of the textile strike, Indian newspapers began to report the arrests of prominent labor leaders in Bombay—notably S. A. Dange, B. T. Ranadive, S. S. Mirajkar, S. V. Parulekar, and A. S. K. Iyengar. Within a few days the arrests spread to other parts of the country, and Sajjad Zaheer and S. V. Ghate were imprisoned. On March 15—at the very beginning of the Ramgarh session of the Congress—the press published a note in which the central government announced that it had determined to "pass orders for the detention of the main Communist leaders under the Defence of India rules." The Communists, the note declared, "by means of subversive propaganda and in other, organized ways, have attempted to prejudice the internal peace of India and to interfere with the efficient prosecution of the war by impeding the supply of men and material." [30] Within two weeks, other prominent Communists, including R. S. Nimbkar and S. G. Patkar, were reported to be in jail. The arrests also extended to such non-Communists as J. P. Narayan, N. G. Ranga, Rahul Sankrityayana, and Swami Sahajanand Saraswati. A substantial proportion of the officers of the Girni Kamgar Union, the All-India Kisan Sabha, and the All-India Trade Union Congress, as well as other leftist leaders, were within a month removed from the Indian political scene. The total number of arrests during the next months is not known, but by February, 1941, the home minister could report that the government had detained 480 persons who were "acknowledged Communists or else active supporters of the Communist programme of violent mass revolution." The minister, Sir Reginald Maxwell, stated that "the central directorate of the Com-

---

[29] Nripendra Nath Mitra ed., *The Indian Annual Register, 1940,* I, 47.
[30] *The Hindu* (Madras), March 15, 1940, p. 9.

munist organization in India" had been imprisoned in order to "cripple the Communist machinery." [31]

Sir Reginald declared that the Communists were detained not on suspicion alone—which would have been legally permissible under the Defence of India rules—but on the basis of concrete knowledge of their activities. They could have been brought to court in a trial such as those of the Meerut and Cawnpore Conspiracy cases, he said, but this would have involved "the disclosure of secret information" and long court proceedings, neither of which could be contemplated in time of war.

It is plain that the CPI paid dearly for its radical policy. The repressive measures of the government apparently fell more heavily on the Communists than on the other political parties, for Sir Reginald's statement revealed that the 480 Communists and their supporters constituted over two-thirds of the total number of persons detained under the Defence of India rules at that time. The CPI itself has since admitted that it was indeed crippled. A semiofficial Party history, discussing this period, states that due to inadequate preparation for underground operation "most of the important Party leaders could be arrested" and "the Party lost much of its organization." [32] This self-critical report suggests that the CPI was taken completely by surprise when the government swept its leadership into jail; the Party had not organized secret units or effective systems of communications, and indeed it was operating more openly during the months of its radical provocation than it had in the previous united-front period. It was evidently unaware that the government would not tolerate such provocation in time of war.

The CPI's policy at the beginning of the European war—a policy which brought all the consequences of what the Party itself would call "adventurism"—had thus gone far beyond anything called for in the writings of the international Communist authorities. But if there were any doubt that the Party's line was not sanctioned by international communism, that doubt was removed in May, 1940, when the Comintern published "an abridged text" of the CPI's Independence Day Manifesto of January.[33] This abridgment in fact thoroughly expurgated the Indian pronouncement and, by removing some passages and amending others, excised its revolutionary core.

---

[31] *Legislative Assembly Debates* . . . , p. 121.

[32] Chalasani Vasudeva Rao, *Bharatha Communist Party Nirmaana Charithrea* [History of the Formation of the Indian Communist Party], (Vijayawada: Praja Sakti Press, 1943), pp. 129, 151.

[33] "Vozzvanie kompartii Indii" [Proclamation of the Communist Party of India], *Kommunisticheskii Internatsional*, No. 5, 1940, pp. 127–128.

The Comintern version of the CPI manifesto omitted the three paragraphs quoted above in which the CPI suggested that world revolution was under way, and where the original manifesto had declared that the masses of Europe were "raising the Red banner of revolt," the Comintern version said merely that they were "raising the banner of struggle"—in Communist terminology a mild phrase having no genuine revolutionary overtones.

The Comintern deleted those sentences declaring that the British were no longer masters of the situation in India and that India stood "on the threshhold of victory." Where the manifesto had proclaimed that the forthcoming struggle would "draw millions into organized assault on the very citadel of imperialism," the Comintern version declared merely that the struggle would "carry the millions of our country to victory." The manifesto paragraph calling upon the workers, peasants, and students of India to organize marches and rallies was deleted. Finally, a sentence stating that obstacles to struggle were created by "the communal agencies"—an implied criticism of other political forces in India—was altered by the Comintern to read "imperialist agents, acting under the signboard of various religious organizations"—thus placing the blame on imperialism rather than on domestic reaction.

This deliberate doctoring was apparently designed to warn the CPI against overestimating the revolutionary potential in either the international situation or the Indian scene.

The same issue of the Comintern journal carried an article on India by D. Protap, that shows clearly the discrepancies between the Soviet and the CPI views.[34] Protap notes that the national-liberation movement was assuming "an increasingly wider and sharper character," but he conspicuously fails to speak of imminent revolution and instead declares that all progressive forces in India increasingly recognized the need to rally "in a united national front for struggle against British imperialism." And though he refers to "certain tendencies toward compromise" in the Congress leadership, he does not inveigh strongly against that leadership.

The British Communists, also, appeared to be cautioning the CPI in their statements on India. On the whole they withheld support of the CPI's view that revolution was around the corner; instead, they stressed the need for political unity. One article specifically enjoins the CPI to "overcome sectional differences on the Left"—by implica-

---

[34] D. Protap, "Indiiskii narod protiv imperialisticheskoi voiny" [The Indian People Against Imperialist War], *ibid.*, pp. 60–65.

tion urging the CPI to reunite with the Socialists and the Forward Bloc.[35]

Adjustments in the International Line (1940–1941)

In mid-1940, however, as if in belated adjustment to the current CPI course, the international Communist authorities began to discuss the Indian scene in more radical terms. The first hint of this new approach appeared in June when a Comintern article, listing the current tasks of the CPI, included that of destroying "the illusions of Gandhism in the masses." [36] A theme long subdued in Communist pronouncements was thus revived.

Further confirmation of this leftward turn came a month later in an authoritative article in *Bolshevik,* when Kochariants, one of the top-ranking Soviet spokesmen, put the stamp of approval on all aspects of the CPI's increasing radical course.[37] By declaring that the situation in India, especially in Calcutta, amounted to "approaching wars" he confirmed the CPI's view that revolution was pending; he cited (and thus approved) a CPI statement which had implied that the imperialist war must be converted into a revolution; he cited Communist leadership of strikes that had not been supported by the Congress, and he specifically commended such action outside the Congress orbit.

In this article, moreover, the Comintern now began to attack the Congress with real vigor. Where previously the international Communist authorities had been content merely to note the Congress leadership's tendency to compromise with imperialism, now Kochariants attacked its domestic policy as well, saying that since the war the Congress had increasingly been disposed to protect the selfish interests of the Indian capitalists, and that it represented in fact, the industrial bourgeoisie.

Kochariants explicitly approved the CPI's abandonment of Subhas Bose, claiming that the Forward Bloc could not gain mass support; he also commended the CPI's attack on "ultra-left sectarianism"—apparently a reference to the Socialists. And though he reiterated that the CPI must maintain unity with the Congress, it was clear that the CPI was to undertake a more aggressive campaign to neutralize the bourgeois Congress leadership and to eliminate other leftist rivals, in order to capture the nationalist movement.

---

[35] Michael Carritt, "India Before the Storm," p. 299.

[36] "O nekotorykh voprosakh raboty kompartii v usloviiakh voiny" [On Some Questions on the Work of the Communist Parties in Conditions of War], *Kommunisticheskii Internatsional,* No. 6, 1940, p. 114.

[37] G. Kochar'iants, "Voina i natsional'no-osvoboditel'noe dvizhenie Indiiskogo naroda" [The War and the National-Liberation Movement of the Indian People], *Bolshevik* (July) 1940, pp. 59–76.

With this article, then, the international Communist leadership confirmed the CPI line, generally and specifically. Abandoning its cautious, rather defensive attitude of the past year, the Comintern openly blessed the CPI's attempt to ride the revolutionary wave to power.

Isolation of the CPI

No sooner had the Comintern moved to the CPI position than the CPI moved still farther left.

In October, 1940, the CPI issued a statement which charged the Gandhian leadership with "bankruptcy" and "hypocrisy," and accused it of sabotaging the national struggle and "maneuvering for a suitable compromise." In this statement, moreover, the CPI not only denounced the "right wing" of the Congress, but added to its roster of enemies certain erstwhile "radical" allies within the Congress, including Nehru himself; Nehru's role, said the CPI, was "to bark at the Communists and to hang revolutionary drapings round the Working Committee resolutions." [38]

This outburst was occasioned by an incident which revealed the extent to which its policy had isolated the CPI from the rest of the Congress. In September, at the Bombay meeting of the All-India Congress Committee (AICC), the seven Communists had stood adamantly against the rest of the Committee in the debate on the main resolution relating to war policy. They alone voted against the official resolution whereupon Nehru, according to the CPI statement, had demanded "almost in a fury" that their names be recorded. The names appeared in the entire Indian press the next day.[39]

At the end of 1940, the Party took the final leftward step in one realm of activity: it completely abandoned the from-above tactic in the student movement. Communists and non-Communists, for years, had collaborated in the All-India Students' Federation (AISF), but in December, 1940, at its Nagpur session, the organization split over the question of accepting Gandhi's recommendation that students shun politics. Led by the Party's representatives in the student movement, the leftists rebelled against Gandhi's influence, although a later Communist account declares that it was the right-wing Gandhian elements that walked out.[40] In any case, the split was complete, and the Gandhian and leftist groups held simultaneous rival conferences. With

---

[38] "Bombay A.I.C.C. and After," *Communist*, II (Oct.) 1940, pp. 1–3. The sole copy of this issue of *Communist* available to the authors contained only its first three pages.

[39] *Ibid.*, p. 3.

[40] Ramen Banerji, *This is the A.I.S.F.* (Bombay: All-India Students' Federation, 1945), pp. 22–30.

this rebellion the radical tendency of Party policy reached its climax.

But the Communist student conference, led by the well-known Communists Dr. K. M. Ashraf and Professor Hiren Mukerjee, was exceedingly significant for another reason as well. At this meeting, for the first time, the Communists hinted at a new policy on the nationality question, an issue which was later of the utmost importance to the CPI.

The religious and linguistic heterogeneity of the Indian people had produced two primary issues in contemporary Indian politics: the Hindu-Muslim problem, and the linguistic-states problem, both of which revolved around the fundamental question of defining Indian "nationality." Was India as a whole one nation? Or were the Hindus and Muslims two separate nations, each entitled to separate state existence? And what about the linguistic groups such as the Bengalis or Tamils—were they, too, separate nations, each entitled to a large amount of autonomy within a federal state, or even to independent existence? In the struggle against imperialist rule, Indian leaders of almost all political or cultural affiliations had subordinated their domestic differences to the common purpose, but as the attainment of independence grew nearer these domestic issues became more urgent—particularly the Hindu-Muslim rivalry. Having grown so remarkably during the late 1930's, the Muslim League, in March, 1940, had for the first time proclaimed its demand for separate statehood for the Muslim people, and decisively challenged the right of the Congress to represent itself as the "national" organization for all India.

Up to now the Indian Communists had treated India as a single "nation" engaged in a united struggle for freedom. Tactical collaboration with the Congress had required the assumption that it spoke for the entire Indian people, and the CPI had condemned the Muslim League as a reactionary communal organization. Soviet spokesmen had been especially contemptuous of the League after the beginning of the European war, and had flayed its demand that India be divided into Hindu and Muslim nations as "politically bankrupt and reactionary." [41] In December, 1940, Dyakov and V. Bushevich published an article in which they condemned the League for disrupting "the front of struggle of the Indian people for its independence." They approvingly described a recent conference of anti-League Muslim groups which had urged that all Muslims support the Congress.[42]

---

[41] D. Protap, "Indiiskii narod protiv imperialisticheskoi voiny," p. 64.

[42] V. Bushevich and A. Dyakov, "Indiia i vtoraia imperialisticheskaia voina" [India and the Second Imperialist War], *Mirovoe Khoziaistvo* . . . , No. 12 (Dec.) 1940, pp. 53–68.

But the Indian Communists, that same month at the leftist student conference, declared in an official resolution that the Congress had failed to solve the communal problem and had been unable to achieve unity among all religious groups in India. They took the momentous step of challenging, as had the Muslim League, the right of the Congress to speak for the whole of India. The new line was embodied in a concrete political proposal: the resolution declared that the future India should be a *"voluntary* federation of regional states based on mutual confidence."* Instead of a single nation comprising a united Indian people, the Communists now implied that India would be a multinational state.[43]

The enunciation of this policy, however, was apparently embarrassingly premature, and the CPI immediately tried to undo its results. Later, recounting the development of its nationality policy, the Party admitted that the conference had "tried to put forward a correct policy, but bungled and created confusion," and that the Party "had to rectify the errors immediately afterwards."[44] The CPI sought to revive the united front in the student movement: only a month after the split the new Communist student federation, which came to be known as the "A.I.S.F. (Farooqui Group)," made overtures to the Gandhian group for reunification. But the leaders of the two groups could not come to an agreement on methods for arbitrating their differences even though the matter was taken to many national leaders, including Gandhi himself. The student movement remained divided.

During the first half of 1941, Communist policy for India remained stable. There were no major statements on the subject in the Russian and CPGB journals, nor is there evidence that forthcoming events— the Soviet Union's entry into the war and the subsequent global reversal of Communist policy—were in any way anticipated.[45]

Conclusions

In pursuing increasingly radical tactics, the CPI appears to have been responding more to its own picture of the Indian situation than to published international Communist guidance. The Indian Communists set out to capitalize on revolutionary opportunities, real and imagined, in the domestic context, while the international leadership in effect clung to the more moderate orientation which had prevailed

---

[43] Mitra ed., *The Indian Annual Register, 1940*, II, 415. Emphasis added.

[44] G. M. Adhikari, *Pakistan and Indian National Unity* (London: Labour Monthly, n.d. [1943], p. 26.

[45] Harry Pollitt, "India—A Call to the British People," *Labour Monthly*, XXIII (June, 1941), p. 265.

since 1938. Only in mid-1940, after a considerable lag, were the views of the Indian and the international Communist elites finally brought into focus with each other, and it was the international view which had been adjusted.

This adjustment may have been a necessary response to changes in the international position of the USSR. With the downfall of France and the general deterioration of the Soviet strategic position at this time, the interests of the USSR required not so much the further weakening of Great Britain, as the creation of genuine sources of support from abroad. The USSR may therefore have wished to strengthen communism in India, as distinguished from anti-imperialism, and may accordingly have spurred the CPI to improve its own position rather than lend support to the Congress.

In any event, the Communist expectation that revolution lay within reach in India came to nothing, not primarily because of events in India itself, but rather because of "Operation Barbarossa"—the march of Hitler's troops over the borders of the Soviet Union.

10 THE PEOPLE'S WAR

With the invasion of Russia by Nazi Germany, the position of the Soviet Union in the international scene—the prime determinant of world Communist policy—was altered decisively. From its neutral corner the USSR was flung into a struggle for survival together with France, Britain, and other "capitalist" states. Ironically, after decades of promoting conflict within the capitalist world, the USSR found itself fighting side by side with one capitalist alliance, against another.

Germany's attack on Russia called forth an indignant response from many nationalist leaders in India. This was expressed in an official resolution of the Congress Working Committee, which declared:

> The Soviet Union has stood for certain human, cultural and social values which are of great importance to the growth and progress of humanity. The Working Committee consider that it would be a tragedy if the cataclysm of war involved the destruction of this endeavor and achievement. They have admired the astonishing self-sacrifice and heroic courage of the Soviet people in defence of their country and freedom and send to them their warm sympathy.[1]

The nationalist leaders, according to Nehru's later account, were "stirred" by Russia's plight, and followed the development of events with "anxious interest." [2]

Britain may have hoped that the new turn in international events

---

[1] N. V. Rajkumar, ed., *The Background of India's Foreign Policy* (New Delhi: All-India Congress Committee, n.d. [1952]), p. 85.

[2] Jawaharlal Nehru, *The Discovery of India* (London: Meridian Books Ltd., 1951), p. 418.

would change the attitude of the Congress leadership toward the war, but sympathy for Russia, however ardent, did not take precedence over the cause of Indian nationalism; Nehru states that "the nationalist position, the question of India versus England, had in no way changed." [3] Indian opinion, in the main, therefore continued to address itself to the overriding nationalist objective of freedom, whatever might occur outside the limits of the subcontinent.

The International Communist Response

For several months after the USSR's entry into the war, Communist journals in Russia and England did not mention the subject of policy in India. But the general character of international Communist policy was clear enough: the defense of the Soviet Union was now the sole strategic aim, and Communist tactics were assessed solely on the basis of their contribution to a Russian victory.

The basic rationale of the new line was spelled out with reckless candor in articles appearing in the British Communist journal, *Labour Monthly,* in July and August. One particularly frank writer explained to the British comrades that the traditional Marxist-Leninist goal of converting a war into revolution could not be mechanically applied.

Obviously the first concern of the proletariat in an imperialist country fighting the Soviet Union is to procure the defeat and overthrow of its own Government, turning the imperialist war into a civil war. The first concern of the proletariat in other imperialist countries, on the other hand, must be the defence of the Soviet Union, whose defeat would be a terrible blow not only for the proletariat of all countries, but for humanity in general. Every act of the proletarian struggle has to be subordinated to this supreme aim of procuring the victory of the USSR, which would mean a great stride forward of the people's cause in every country.[4]

Acceptance of this "supreme aim" was justified, of course, by the basic assumption that the interests of the Soviet Union automatically determined those of the "people" everywhere. As this British writer put it, "The interests of the British imperialists temporarily coincide with those of the Soviet Union, and *therefore with those of the British people.*" If his stand needed further clarification, he supplied it when he took up the question whether this policy signified that the British Communists were agents of a "foreign power": he replied, "No, it does not. The Soviet Union is not a foreign power for the workers and the common people." [5]

---

[3] *Ibid.,* p. 419.

[4] "Quaestor," "Leading the World Against Hitler," *Labour Monthly,* XXIII (Aug., 1941), pp. 361–362.

[5] *Ibid.,* pp. 361–362. Emphasis added.

The question of India was finally taken up in September. Russian and British Communist declarations made it plain that notwithstanding India's colonial status, the Indian Communists were to support the British imperial government as long as it fought side by side with the USSR. The inexorable logic of the Communist view was applied to India without any important qualifications.

The Russian Party organ, *Bolshevik*, printed in its September issue an article by I. Lemin entitled "The Role of the British Empire in the Current War." [6] It was the only article on the British colonies, or on India specifically, that *Bolshevik* published during the entire war, and it was evidently intended to dispose of the subject once and for all. In it, Lemin assigned to the British Empire as a whole "the highest place side by side with the USSR" in the "great coalition of democratic peoples" fighting fascism. He offered not the slightest hint that India should demand its freedom as a condition of participating in the coalition of "democratic peoples"; in fact his treatment of India put it in the same category with the self-governing dominions, as though to conceal the fact that it was not already a free country. He affirmed that India had a "great role" to play in the war, and suggested that the Indian people were actually eager to fulfill that role.

> The attack of fascist Germany on the Soviet Union called forth huge indignation among the Indian people, who understand that this increases the menace to India itself, since German fascism always considered an attack on the Ukraine and the Caucasus as the beginning of a further attack on Mesopotamia and India.

Lemin came to the point in a single sentence; after declaring that India had not yet fully summoned its forces for the war effort, he concluded, "The further the mobilization of these forces for struggle against Hitlerite fascism proceeds, the better."

Little further attention was devoted to the Indian problem in the whole of Soviet publication throughout the war. One book, which purported to be a general reference work on the British Empire, gave a reasonably straightforward survey of Indian history instead of the usual polemic against British imperialism. And it ended with the altogether unreal assertion that "The wide masses of the Indian people are prepared to support actively the military measures of the British government." [7]

It was left to the British Communist Party to fill in the details. In

---

[6] I. Lemin, "Rol' Britanskoi imperii v sovremennoi voine," [The Role of the British Empire in the Current War], *Bolshevik* (Sept., 1941), pp. 27–37.

[7] *Britanskaia Imperiia* [British Empire], (Moscow: *Gosudarstvennyi Institut "Sovetskaia Entsiklopediia,"* 1943), p. 227.

the September issue of *Labour Monthly*, R. Palme Dutt bluntly told the Indian Communists that their support of the war was to be unconditional, and was not to rest on their achievement of independence.

The interest of the peoples of India and Ireland and of all the colonial peoples, as of all the peoples of the world, is bound up with the victory of the peoples against Fascism; that interest is absolute and unconditional, and does not depend on any measures their rulers may promise or concede.[8]

Dutt went on to demand that Britain make some concessions to Indian nationalism. This was little more than a gesture, however, for his only concrete suggestions were designed to "lessen the obstacles" to Indian participation in the war: he suggested merely that the government release Nehru and other political prisoners, and institute "direct negotiations with the National Congress." Since he failed to specify the terms of such negotiations, his demand had little meaning.

Dutt's article was most significant for its failure even to hint that the war would have revolutionary implications for India. In short, the Communist Party of India was advised to set aside all goals except that of mobilizing India's resources in the service of its British rulers in order to secure a Soviet victory.

Debate in the CPI

Rarely had the international and domestic environments so plainly pulled the CPI in opposite directions as in the months after June, 1941. The international Communist authorities served notice that the Party was required to support the war, with or without Indian freedom. But Indian nationalism demanded freedom, war or no war; any political party in India that urged temporary surrender in the anti-imperialist struggle would risk ostracism or worse.

There were at this time actually two Communist parties in India. The inner core of the Party's leadership, arrested in 1940–1941, was confined at Deoli Detention Camp in Ajmer-Merwara. Outside prison, there was a disorganized underground Party led by P. C. Joshi. These two fragments of the CPI were almost entirely isolated from each other, and each fragment was therefore on its own in reappraising CPI policy immediately after the USSR's entry into the war. Their separate deliberations resulted in two separate, and indeed antithetical, policies.

The Party stalwarts at Deoli included most of the "Old Bolsheviks" of the CPI such as S. A. Dange, Muzaffar Ahmed, and S. S. Mirajkar, as well as younger leaders like B. T. Ranadive and Ajoy Ghosh. Though

_____

[8] R. Palme Dutt, "Notes of the Month," *Labour Monthly*, XXIII (Sept., 1941), p. 381.

little is known concerning the immediate response of this group to the news of invasion of the USSR, their agitation may well be imagined. In the impassioned debates which must have ensued, the view that India owed full support to the British war effort, since this now contributed to the defense of the Soviet Union, apparently dominated. At any rate, this was the view of the so-called Deoli Thesis, propounding the "people's war" slogan, which was smuggled out of prison to the underground Party.[9]

This decision must have required months, for it was not until October that intimations of it began to appear in the clandestine Party press. It may have involved painful mental conflict for the Deoli Communists, for they were undoubtedly under considerable pressure from the numerous Congress and Socialist prisoners in the camp. As late as November, at least some of the Communists joined a group of their nationalist prison mates in a hunger strike against the British authorities, which would seem to reflect either dissent from the Deoli Thesis or an endeavor to avoid complete alienation from the nationalist ranks.[10]

Among those subscribing to the Deoli Thesis, ingrained international loyalties apparently prevailed. They arrived at substantially the same view as that set forth by the Soviet and British Communist authorities. Their decision may have been spontaneous, but it is quite possible that they were helped toward it by knowledge of the new line, obtained from *Labour Monthly* or other journals. The British authorities may have recognized the usefulness of providing such information to the Communist prisoners.

The response of the Indian Communist elements outside prison presents a dramatic contrast. Their first reaction was closely in accord with the prevailing nationalist orientation; the underground Party apparently adjusted more freely than did the Deoli group to the demands of their domestic environment. It declared that the purpose of the war was broader than the mere victory of the Soviet Union, and included "a world-wide victory of the people"—or, in short, liberation from the old order as well as from fascism. According to a Politbureau resolution of July, the Indian Party would "convert imperialist war into a revolutionary war."

The Communist Party declares that the only way in which the Indian people can help in the just war which the Soviet is waging, is by fighting all the more vigorously for their own emancipation from the imperialist yoke. Our attitude

[9] Interview with former member of CPI in India.
[10] For information on the hunger strike, see *The Hindu* (Madras) for 1941, Nov. 6, p. 6; 10, p. 2; 12, p. 8; and 24, p. 2.

towards the British Government and its imperialist war remains what it was. We must continue, nay, intensify our struggle against both. There can be no change in our policy until a real people's government which unequivocally renounces imperialist aims in this war as well as in India and in the colonies, comes to power. We can render really effective aid to the Soviet Union only as a free people.[11]

Besides asserting that it would continue to fight for Indian freedom, war or no war, the underground CPI demanded that the British Party raise a revolution against the Churchill government. Discussing the implications of its policy, the Indian Politbureau said:

This means not complacent reliance that British and American aid will bring Soviet victory and a new world, but a ceaseless struggle to expose the imperialist war aims of the British and American rulers, to isolate them and to mobilize the people for seizing power.[12]

As late as the end of October, elements of the underground Party launched a direct attack against the views of the Deoli Communists. A Party statement declared that those who urged support of the British war effort "are following an imperialist policy" and "echoing the imperialist lie."

Reliance on the people, on the working class and NOT on the imperialists, this is the core of a truly internationalist policy. . . . They are false internationalists and the deceivers of people who say that we can side [with] the Soviet or win the war for the people by aiding the British Government's war efforts.[13]

During this period (June to November) the underground CPI had suited action to words, operating in various spheres to spur the national movement forward to revolt. In the peasant movement, the Communists pressed the Kisan Sabha for more militant action, with an enthusiasm which N. G. Ranga later described as "frenzy." [14] In October, they secured the adoption of a resolution by the Kisan Executive and Standing Committee condemning the failure of the Congress to launch an active struggle for independence.[15] Communists working in the student movement were equally fervent, and the leader of the Party's wing of the All-India Students Federation, Farooqui, was arrested in September for an inflammatory anti-British speech.[16] Communists at the second annual Madras Students' Conference, at the

---

[11] *Soviet-German War: Statement of the Politburo, July, 1941* (no place, no publisher, 1941), (mimeographed), p. 6. This quotation may also be found in: Acharya Narendra Deva, *Socialism and the National Revolution* (Bombay: Padma Pub. Ltd., 1946), pp. 152–153.

[12] *Communist*, III (Aug., 1941), p. 3.

[13] Quoted in Acharya Narendra Deva, *Socialism and the National Revolution*, p. 153.

[14] N. G. Ranga, *Kisans and Communists* (Bombay: Pratibha Pub., n.d.), p. 11.

[15] *Ibid.*, pp. 10–11.

[16] *The Hindu* (Madras), Dec. 1, 1941, p. 2.

beginning of November, demanded a nation-wide student struggle for freedom; [17] and at a meeting of the Punjab Students' Conference, at the end of November, Dr. Hiren Mukerjee declared that the Indian people must "do all in their power to win freedom for the country." [18]

During November and December, judgments were handed down in two conspiracy trials, the Madras and Tinnevelly cases; the Communist defendants were found guilty of conspiracy to commit prejudicial acts against the government or to disseminate prejudicial literature. These acts had been committed before June, 1941; however, newspaper accounts of the court proceedings do not report that the defendants disavowed their anti-British purposes, as had the Deoli prisoners.[19]

It is not known when or by what means the underground CPI received information concerning the new international Communist line for India. If the Party had this news in September (the date of the articles in British Communist and Russian journals), its actions in October and November were outright defiance of the international edicts. But it is possible that circumstances prevented the immediate receipt of the news; wartime conditions may have delayed communications from abroad. And in any event, the underground Party was too disorganized to reverse its course all at once.

According to one report that was widely believed in India, the CPI was officially informed of the new line by a letter from Harry Pollitt of the CPGB, delivered to the Deoli Communists in November or December with the connivance of the British authorities.[20] It is interesting to note, although it may have no significance, that Maxim Litvinov stopped briefly in two Indian cities at the end of November, en route to his diplomatic post in Washington.[21]

Whatever the reason, by November the underground CPI had apparently begun to entertain second thoughts concerning its adamantly anti-imperialist policy. According to N. G. Ranga, in that month Communist members of the peasant movement proposed the "people's war" thesis to the Nagpur session of the Kisan Standing Committee. They were not yet ready to force the issue, however, and accepted a resolu-

---

[17] *Ibid.*, Nov. 4, 1941, p. 6.

[18] *Ibid.*, Dec. 1, 1941, p. 4.

[19] For accounts of the Madras Conspiracy Case, see *The Hindu* (Madras), for 1941, especially Oct. 8, p. 2; 10, p. 11; and 26, p. 2; and Nov. 20, p. 8. For the Tinnevelly Conspiracy Case, see *ibid.*, Dec. 20, 1941, p. 12.

[20] This explanation is given in M. R. Masani, *The Communist Party of India* (London: Derek Verschoyle, 1954), p. 80. N. G. Ranga describes it as one of the "many stories" which were current at the time, in *Kisans and Communists*, p. 13. No documentation has been offered.

[21] *The Hindu* (Madras) for 1941, Nov. 27, p. 6; Nov. 28, p. 6.

tion which declared that only after India had achieved independence would the war become a "people's war." [22]

But with the passage of another month, the underground CPI totally abandoned its anti-imperialist stand. On December 15, the Politbureau formally embraced the "people's war" policy. The Politbureau resolution explained:

> We are a practical party, and in a new situation it is our task not only to evolve a new form of struggle for it, but also to advance new slogans appropriate to the new stage, suiting the new form of our national movement. The key slogan of our Party, which guides all our practical political activity is: "MAKE THE INDIAN PEOPLE PLAY A PEOPLE'S ROLE IN THE PEOPLE'S WAR." [23]

The CPI was at last officially in step with international communism.

This episode of policy-making in a period of crisis for the CPI demonstrates with exceptional clarity both the international and the domestic influences upon the Party's operation, and the ultimate superiority of the international influence. While it was temporarily deprived of guidance emanating from Moscow and London, the Party as a whole manifested two reactions in the choice confronting it. One group, composed primarily of the more experienced functionaries of the Party, perceived and accepted the course required by their loyalty to their international community, though the policy they adopted spelled virtual political suicide at home. They probably found this decision easier by virtue of the fact that, being in jail, they were not immediately responsible for implementing it. Another group, composed of a few more youthful leaders and remnants of the rank and file, clung to a policy more compatible with domestic opinion. At one stage, this group accused the other of being out of touch with Indian realities.[24] But this was the ultimate in heresy, and could not endure. At last, when possessed of firm international guidance, the Party as a whole set aside domestic influences and domestic advantage, and accepted the demands of the international community.

It should be noted that the fact that Japan had now entered the war was not used by the CPI as a justification for its new line. But later, of course, when Japanese military advances brought the war into Indian territory itself, the "people's war" line had greater reality.

A later explanation of these events by the Communists themselves confirms both the Party's temporary sensitivity to Indian realities and its ultimate rejection of those realities.

---

[22] Ranga, *Kisans and Communists*, p. 16.

[23] Quoted in P. C. Joshi, *Communist Reply to Congress Working Committee's Charges* (Bombay: People's Publishing House, 1945), p. 45. [Capitalization in source.]

[24] Madhu Limaye, *Communist Party: Facts and Fiction* (Hyderabad: Chetana Prakashan Ltd., 1951), p. 44.

Why did the Communist Party take six months to understand that the war was a People's War for India too? This was a result of an un-Communist left-nationalist outlook. It was due to the influence of the anti-British attitude of the people on the Communists. The Indian people and their political parties had fought against the British for 50 years. They believed that the struggle for Indian independence was an anti-British struggle. Hence, they did not believe that they could acquire their independence by supporting a group which was allied to the British. The people thought that aiding the war effort meant strengthening the British Government and weakening the struggle for independence. This anti-British outlook had an influence on the Communist Party, too. It took six months to get out of this rut of nationalism, to think like a Communist, to give a new program for the struggle for independence which suited the new circumstances.[25]

As an epilogue to this narrative, it may be recorded that the Communist defendants in the Madras Conspiracy Case evidently remained adamant against the new "people's war" line for at least another six months. They were finally converted in mid-1942, it is said, by the direct intervention of the sister of one of the prisoners, who had just returned from London, fresh from interviews with R. Palme Dutt and Harry Pollitt.[26] Undoubtedly, this reluctance to accept the new policy was widespread in the CPI, but it is a tribute to the cohesiveness of the Party organization that such resistance was largely overcome.

The CPI Rallies for "People's War"

With a truly remarkable resilience, the CPI proceeded now to gather its forces for the new antifascist strategy. Making the maximum use of his flair for rendering policy in dramatically emotional or even sentimental terms, P. C. Joshi labored strenuously to popularize the "people's war" line. His first major effort was a lengthy policy statement of February, 1942.[27] To make the new policy even remotely palatable to the Indian taste, he was forced to go beyond the stark outlines of the British or Russian pronouncements, and to promise that India would secure its freedom in the course of supporting the war. To bol-

---

[25] Chalasani Vasudeva Rao, *Bharatha Communist Party Nirmaana Charithrea* [History of the Formation of the Indian Communist Party], (Vijayawada: Praja Sakti Press, 1943), pp. 167–168.

[26] Interview with former member of the CPI in India.

[27] This statement appeared in pamphlet form in India. The original was not available to the authors, and reprinted versions of the document have therefore been used. The lengthiest (and therefore presumably the most complete) is that contained in a collection of documents published by the CPI in the same year: G. M. Adhikari, ed., *From Peace Front to People's War* (Bombay: People's Publishing House, 1942), pp. 347–377. Another version is a reprint by the British Communist Party: P. C. Joshi, *The Indian Communist Party* (London: Communist Party of Great Britain, 1942), 33 pp. Brief extracts from the original document were also provided in Joshi, *Communist Reply to . . .* , pp. 45–58. Until otherwise noted, the quotations used here are taken from the version presented in the collection of documents edited by Adhikari.

ster this promise, he invoked two main lines of reasoning: (1) that the leadership and example of the Soviet Union was in itself a guarantee of world-wide liberation from the prewar order, and (2) that the creation of national unity within India for the prosecution of the war would force the British to concede its freedom.

In the first of these two arguments Joshi asserted, in effect, that the USSR would dominate the Allied camp and impose revolutionary goals upon the course of the war. Under Soviet inspiration, he said,

the peoples of the world are advancing arm in arm, with one common aim of destroying Hitler-fascism and its allies, of smashing up the very structure of world imperialism, which bred the plague of fascism and imperialist war, and of replacing it by a world of free peoples.

Within each of the capitalist countries, Joshi asserted, the balance of power among classes was shifting in favor of the progressive forces. Thus a "revolutionary situation" existed on a world-wide scale. By this Joshi did not mean, as might reasonably be inferred, that the overthrow of the governments of Britain and the United States was a part of the Communist war strategy. He avoided this uncomfortable implication by declaring that the Roosevelt and Churchill governments were themselves "more or less progressive" and worthy of serving as "instruments in the hands of the united front of peoples of the world." Setting aside the revolutionary trappings, then, the crux of his theme was the simple promise that Soviet influence and popular pressure in Britain would force the Churchill government to grant independence to India.

But Joshi supplemented this argument, which might not prove persuasive to the Indian audience, with his second premise; namely, that in the very act of uniting for war, the Indian people would achieve the strength to exact their freedom from the imperialist government. If all patriotic parties and groups rallied together, he said, they could take the war into their own hands. This argument was subsumed in the slogan "National unity for national defense and national government"—and this was to be the dominant motif of CPI policy through the war.

Having sought to popularize the "people's war" strategy, Joshi turned to the problem of its tactical implementation. His main proposal was most significant: instead of calling for unity within the National Congress, as in the years before the war, he now demoted the Congress to a position of parity with the Muslim League and demanded coöperation between these two organizations. Translating national unity as Congress-League unity, Joshi thus brought to mature and formal expression the earlier trend within the CPI toward abandoning the Congress as the main agent of Indian bourgeois nationalism.

Clarifying this new attitude beyond any doubt, Joshi defined the Muslim League as "the premier political organization of the second largest community in our country." [28] In effect he conceded the communal basis of Indian politics and relegated the Congress to the role of spokesman for the Hindus of the subcontinent. He declared that it was "wrong and unrealistic" to dismiss the League as reactionary and said that the Congress itself had "some responsibility" along with the League for the lack of communal unity. He condemned the Gandhian orientation of the Congress as "the outlook of negation, the policy of passivity and the practice of subservience," but praised the "progressive elements" of both the Congress and the League.

For achieving unity between the two parties, Joshi demanded that the Congress make the necessary concessions. It must "boldly concede the sectional demands of the Muslim League" he declared—presumably signifying that the Congress must accept the League's 1940 demand for division of the subcontinent into two sovereign states. And as the first step, he called upon the Congress to take the initiative in forming joint ministries with the League in the Indian provincial governments.

In discussing the more general features of the political program on which national unity should be based, Joshi emphatically proposed that Indian political parties reënter the provincial ministries:

We differ from those who say we must be free first before we fight freedom's war. . . . We advocate immediate resumption of Ministries to develop the popular pressure against the bureaucracy from within the constitution itself. And the great job that needs taking in hand immediately is the organization of the nation's war effort.

Specifically, Joshi called upon the ministries to organize more effective air-raid protection, a "citizen's army," a war fund, and the acceleration of industrial production. Alongside these urgent demands, Joshi also called for Indian independence and the formation of a national government. But it was clear that the goal of freedom was not the immediate and preëminent issue.

It is interesting to note that the fundamental tactic of Congress-League unity, which signified that the Indian Communists were now intent on penetrating not only the Congress but also the Muslim League, ran counter to the express recommendations for India of the British Communist leaders. Earlier pronouncements of R. Palme Dutt

---

[28] The remaining quotations from Joshi's February statement are taken from the British Communist reprint: P. C. Joshi, *The Indian Communist Party.*

and others had indicated that the Congress alone was to be regarded
as entitled to speak for all of India, and this was reiterated in the
British Party journal for some time after the CPI had contradicted it.
In the issue of *Labour Monthly* for April, 1942—two months after
Joshi's policy statement—D. N. Pritt wrote that

the British Government should recognize that Congress is entitled to be accepted
as the representative of the whole Indian people, and that any terms to which it is
ready to agree, so long as they contain provisions safeguarding minorities, should
be treated as accepted by India.[29]

Pritt condemned the Muslim League as a creation of the British
imperialists, and asserted that it had no right to speak for the Indian
Muslims. Its demand for Pakistan he dismissed as "impractical." In
May, Ben Bradley added his voice to the chorus, condemning the
British policy of treating the League as equal with the Congress,
and insisting that the Congress had the right to make a settlement "on
behalf of the Indian people." [30]

This discrepancy between British and Indian Communist policy
persisted until September, when the British comrades signaled their
adoption of the CPI's position by reprinting, in pamphlet form, Joshi's
policy statement. This pamphlet contained an introduction by Harry
Pollitt, who affirmed that Joshi's proposal had "in the light of later
developments" been demonstrated to be one of "absolute correctness." [31] At the same time, Dutt, writing in *Labour Monthly,* flatly
abandoned his previous stand that the Congress alone spoke for the
Indian people, and now called upon the British government to negotiate "equally with the Congress and with all political sections and
leaders in India." Like Joshi, he suggested that the Congress must
make "far-reaching concessions" to other political groups for the sake
of unity, and he even argued that "for present purposes we need not
concern ourselves with the representative or unrepresentative character" of these groups.[32]

Since the British and Indian Communist lines had been well co-
ordinated in certain other respects, it is not likely that the discrepancy
in their attitudes toward the Congress, from February to September,
was due to lack of communication. It seems more probable that the
CPGB, unlike the CPI, continued during these months to hope that
an honorable compromise would be reached between the British

---

[29] D. N. Pritt, "India," *Labour Monthly*, XXIV (April, 1942), p. 107.
[30] Ben Bradley, "India Threatened," *ibid.* (May, 1942), p. 146.
[31] P. C. Joshi, *The Indian Communist Party*, p. 1.
[32] R. Palme Dutt, "Notes of the Month," *Labour Monthly*, XXIV (Sept., 1942), p. 266.

government and the Indian nationalists, and that the Congress would agree to support the war.

The British Party had ample reason to believe that this was desired by progressive elements of the Congress; V. K. Krishna Menon, the official London representative of the Congress, had said as much. In three articles published in the CPGB's *Labour Monthly* for August, 1941, and January and June, 1942, Menon claimed that for the colonial peoples the character of the war had been transformed by the USSR's entry; India was eager to participate, he said, but could not do so because of its enslavement.[33] Speaking of the attitude of the colonies toward the USSR, Menon stated:

To them the victory of the Soviet Union is not merely the hope of freedom, but the guarantee of its achievement. They realize that the Soviet people have unfailingly recognized the common interests of the peoples of the world. . . .

The Soviet union has consistently championed the struggles for national independence and the autonomy of nationalities. . . . [It] has given great inspiration to the colonial peoples. . . . It has also inspired and enabled national movements of liberation to recognize their role and seek to play their part in a freer world and in the world struggle for people's freedom.

The attack on the USSR, he said, "calls for the fullest mobilization of all the forces of freedom everywhere." He declared that participation in the "world anti-Fascist front" was an "integral" part of Indian policy, but that the demand for freedom was "equally" a part of that policy.

Menon called on the British government to reopen negotiations with India on the basis of recognizing its independence. But in the meantime he approved of certain forms of Indian coöperation in the war effort. He condemned British inefficiency in mobilizing India's economic resources, and said, "Production, yet more production is now the cry." He demanded the release of political prisoners in India, stating:

A great many of them, Communists and other anti-Fascists, are the very people who, despite the obscurantism of the British Government, would rally the people in resistance and prevent a repetition of the experience in Burma.

The Communists, Socialists, and other working-class leaders were, he said, the "most pronounced champions" of antifascism in India. Again, he specifically cited the Communist Party of Malaya as the "vital" antifascist force in that country, having earlier described the Soviet Union as the "vital" element in the war. With respect to India,

---

[33] The articles by Menon are as follows: "Freedom's Battle," *Labour Monthly* (Aug., 1941), pp. 364–367; "India in the War," *ibid.* (Jan., 1942), pp. 26–28; and "India Calls for Action," *ibid.* (June, 1942), pp. 185–188. The quotations used are from all three articles.

he stated that only "the leadership of a government by the nation's most vital elements" could mobilize the country.

Finding such views put forth by the official spokesman of the Congress, the CPGB might well have been optimistic that the Indian nationalist organization would sooner or later decide to support the war. Any hopes of this were dashed, however, when the Congress served notice, with its famous "Quit India" resolution of August, 1942, that unconditional freedom must come first. And it was in the next month (September) that the CPGB approved Joshi's tactic of demoting the Congress to the status of a merely Hindu organization.

The CPI Emerges from Illegality

Having closed ranks on the new line, the CPI leadership moved to put it into effect on many fronts. One of the advantages of the "people's war" orientation, whatever its limitations, was the opportunity it gave the CPI to gain legal status in Indian politics. Having been officially proscribed by the British authorities through most of its career, the CPI would now be regarded with unprecedented favor in government circles. Recognizing this, the Party first of all set out to extract from the government the right to a legal existence.

In early 1942, the bargaining position of the CPI grew stronger with each succeeding week. The Japanese were pressing the British back throughout Southeast Asia, and the government sought support within India with increasing fervor, for the subcontinent was the final prize in the Pacific war. Soon resistance to the Japanese in Burma was crumbling, and full-scale overland and amphibious invasion of India itself was considered imminent. By February the government hinted that it was willing to release Communist prisoners. In a debate in the Legislative Assembly, Sir Reginald Maxwell stated: "If there be any person whose attitude is such that he wishes earnestly to help in the war effort, I have no desire whatever to keep him in jail." [34]

During March and April, with the Japanese already within the borders of India, the Cripps Mission began negotiations with the Indian nationalist parties. The concessions offered by the Churchill government were not great enough to satisfy either the Congress or the Muslim League, and the Cripps Mission failed to obtain their formal coöperation in the war. The CPI Politbureau, on the other hand, proclaimed its approval of the Mission's plan and appealed to the Congress and League to "achieve a settlement on the basis of the Cripps proposal." The Party "pledges its full support to such a settlement," it said.[35]

---

[34] Indian Information, X (April 1, 1942), p. 332.
[35] Party Letter, II (April 6, 1942), p. 3.

More important, the CPI made it plain beyond any doubt that it would fight to defend India against Japan. During the Cripps Mission visit, the Communist prisoners in Bareilly Jail issued a statement pledging "unflinching support to the cause of the victory over fascism. . . . We declare that with every ounce of our energy, with every drop of our blood, we shall fight and rest not till victory is won." [36] Pointing out that the regular army was too weak to resist a full-scale Japanese invasion, the CPI called upon the British authorities to "let the prison gates be thrown open," and assured them that if the people were given arms hundreds of thousands would come forward to fight.

It was widely believed in India that P. C. Joshi had secretly met with Sir Reginald Maxwell, and even with Cripps himself, to negotiate greater freedom of action for the CPI. Shortly after the Cripps Mission, the CPI circulated a private statement addressed to "friends and sympathizers," outlining its position and describing in full detail the assistance which the Party was willing to render in return for legality.[37] Conceding that "the mass of patriotic opinion" opposed supporting the war without freedom, the statement nevertheless declared that "Today all the Indian Communists, whether inside jails or outside, whether free or underground, are burning with an ardent desire to do all they can to coöperate with the existing war-effort even under the present Government, if we can do so in an honorable and effective manner." As the condition of its coöperation, the Party demanded that all restrictions on its members and publication facilities be removed. In return, it promised to undertake an extraordinary "plan of work." In addition to waging an intensive propaganda campaign to rally the people against fascism on a nation-wide scale, the CPI pledged itself to promote recruitment for the armed forces and to provide various services to the army, such as entertainment and medical duty. It promised to mobilize the student movement and, more important, to use its influence in the ranks of labor to stimulate increased industrial production; declaring that the Party would be guided by one slogan, "All for the front," the CPI said that the government would "have no need to fear strikes as far as we Communists can help it." Finally, the Party pledged itself to take up arms by recruiting "suicide squads" from among Communists and sympathizers; these units should, said the statement, "be used for service in the threatened provinces, in the

---

[36] *Loc. cit.*

[37] *Memorandum on Communist Policy and Plan of Work* (no place, no publisher, no date), 7 pp. This is a typed copy of the original, and is labeled "Confidential; Not for Publication." The authenticity of the document is not absolutely certain, but it appears likely. Its contents do not include any proposals which were not later borne out in the open policy and activity of the Party.

enemy's rear to organize sabotage, and themselves become the nuclei for guerrilla bands based upon the people."

In July, 1942, the government announced that the CPI was now legal and began releasing Communists from jail.[38] But more significantly, even before taking this step the government had seized upon the Communist offer to bear arms, and had organized a program for training a guerrilla army, to be composed largely of Communist volunteers. The British authorities no doubt understood the dangers of creating a Red army in India, and this decision was thus a calculated risk. That it was taken is a measure of the gravity of the military situation, and of the paucity of support from other elements of the Indian population.

According to the few accounts available, the training program was in operation by the beginning of June. Though security requirements presumably limited the publicity that could be given to it, the Communists advertised its existence in their own press. A general description of the program is given in "Fragments from a Guerrilla's Diary," written by one of the first trainees and published in *People's War*.[39] It said:

> True, we aren't anywhere near being full-fledged guerrillas; but we've picked up marching; we can handle our bayonets as vigorously as any soldiers; we've learnt how to ambush and snipe at the enemy, how to read maps, use the ground in operations, blow up bridges and buildings, put up barbed-wire defenses and pierce through them, throw bridges across rivers and marshes, and combat and destroy the dreaded tank. We've not only learnt how to prepare Molotov Cocktails but have proved our mettle at the firing range.

According to this diarist, his group contained about 300 volunteers from areas throughout India. The course was conducted by British officers and lasted twelve days. Another source describes a training camp in the hills near Poona, where units of fifteen volunteers each were instructed in guerrilla tactics by American and Chinese officers whose identities were kept secret.[40]

Later the threat of Japanese invasion receded, and the British authorities evidently chose to disband the guerrilla program. Nothing more was heard of it. The opportunity to organize a Red army, which might have been of incalculable significance for the future of the CPI and of India itself, was therefore snatched away from the Party. If events had taken another turn—if the Japanese had invaded India, and

---

[38] For the government announcement, see *Indian Information*, XI (Sept. 1, 1942), p. 197.

[39] Rajbans Kishen, "Fragments from a Guerrilla's Diary," *People's War*, I (Aug. 2, 1942), p. 5.

[40] Interview with a former member of the CPI in India.

the resistance movement had fallen under Communist command—
the recent history of China might well have been repeated in the subcontinent.

Advances in CPI Organization

Though its efforts on the military front were halted, the CPI made
dramatic organizational progress in other spheres. From the middle of
1942, it was aided not only by its own legality but by the illegality of
the other political organizations. As a result of the climactic events in
August, when the All-India Congress Committee challenged the
British to "Quit India," the Congress was declared illegal and its leaders
were once again imprisoned. Some elements of the nationalist movement resorted to terrorism and sabotage and other elements collaborated with the Japanese military forces. The CPI therefore had
relatively little opposition in the open political arena, and it was able
to capture or consolidate its control over mass organizations in many
spheres.

In the peasant movement, the Communists had already increased
their influence. By converting a number of non-Party peasant leaders,
such as Swami Sahajanand and Indulal Yagnik, to the main elements
of their policy, and by taking over the leadership of one after another
of the provincial units of the All-India Kisan Sabha, they had gradually
gained strength in the central councils of the organization. By the
end of 1941, the Socialist section, and then the Forward Bloc section,
had seceded from the AIKS.

The CPI consolidated its influence in the AIKS at the annual meeting of the organization in May, 1942.[41] The last organized opposition
to the Communists melted away in October, when the defeated Ranga
withdrew. Ranga took with him six provincial units, and the AIKS
was thus fragmented, but the Communists now dominated the parent
body.[42] They maintained their ascendancy throughout the rest of the
war.

In the student movement, also, the Communists succeeded in gaining
preëminence. The All-India Students' Federation had, it will be remembered, already been split into Communist-dominated and non-
Communist wings. In December, 1941, when the Communist section
met in Patna for its annual session, the Party's student leaders had
managed to convert all but a handful of delegates to the "people's war"
policy—no mean accomplishment considering the abruptness of the

---

[41] For a CPI account of the February meeting, see *Party Letter*, II (March 24, 1942).
On the AIKS session of May, see Mitra, ed., *Indian Annual Register, 1942*, I, 350–353.
[42] Ranga, *Kisans and Communists*, p. 22.

change. The leaders' enthusiasm over the achievement is reflected in a later account in *The Student,* which exclaimed: "Think of it, comrade: in three days the hundreds of students in Patna—the best and finest—are convinced, CONVINCED." [43] Converting the entire rank and file of the organization took greater effort, however, and a later issue of *The Student* stated that the new policy had been hotly discussed for at least four months.[44] By and large the line prevailed, and the Communist AISF gained steadily in organizational strength. At the end of the war it overshadowed the rival group.

This success was probably due to the Party's moderate handling of the student organization; the Communist leaders did not force a completely orthodox Party-line policy upon the AISF sessions, nor did they purge non-Communist elements altogether. By permitting a modicum of free play of opinion, the CPI was able to associate many prominent non-Communists with its student activities.[45]

The Indian trade-union movement proved only slightly more resistant to CPI penetration. The Party steadily increased its influence in the All-India Trade Union Congress, but it failed to secure immediate official adoption of the "people's war" line by the annual sessions of the organization. At the AITUC session in February, 1942, the Party, which had succeeded in dominating many local unions, encountered adamant opposition to its new line from the highest quarters.[46] Nehru himself, who inaugurated the session, expressly condemned the Communist orientation, declaring that Indians must fight for the freedom of their own country before taking up the cause of any other. The president of the AITUC, V. R. Kalappa, added his voice, asserting that "All talk of an anti-Fascist front will lead us nowhere." He condemned the demagogy of the Communists in promising freedom to India as a consequence of the war, which "their masters have not contemplated." The veteran labor leader N. M. Joshi also declared himself to be against the "people's war" line. In the face of such powerful opposition, the Communists could not altogether prevail. Although they secured majority support for their resolution, they failed to achieve the three-quarters majority required for important decisions by the rules of the AITUC.

At the next annual session, in May, 1943, the contest was resumed.

---

[43] *The Student* (Organ of the All-India Students' Federation), II (Feb., 1942), p. 15. Emphasis in original.

[44] *Ibid.,* II (June, 1942), p. 3.

[45] See, for example, the report of the 8th Session of the AISF (1944) in Mitra, ed., *Indian Annual Register, 1944,* II, 249–252.

[46] The following account of the session is from Mitra, ed., *Indian Annual Register, 1942,* I, 366–369.

According to a contemporary account,[47] Communist and anti-Communist slogans were raised in the midst of the proceedings and "feeling ran high"—so much so that there were fist fights outside the hall. On this occasion the main Communist resolution secured 424 out of 616 votes—barely short of the required 75 per cent. Another CPI resolution calling for increased production for the war effort was therefore withdrawn. Non-Communist leaders remained in the top posts of the organization, with N. M. Joshi serving in the crucial general secretary's position. But the extent of the delegate strength which the CPI was able to muster indicated its increasing dominance of local trade unions.

The Communist pattern of action in all these spheres—the peasant, student, and trade-union organizations—was to concentrate on gaining control in the local units. In this way, the CPI was able to direct concrete activity at the grass-roots level. In the top councils of these mass organizations, the Communists were cautious and moderate in demanding compliance with the Party line. The Party allowed non-Communists to remain in titular positions—even those who had publicly demurred at some elements of the "people's war" line. The Communist leadership frequently warned its members against using mass organizations solely as "Party platforms"; in other words, it did not insist on word-for-word duplication of Communist policy in the resolutions of a given organization. Party leaders constantly disavowed Communist domination of any organization, and instead called for unity of diverse political forces. These supple tactics enabled the Party to operate with greater effectiveness than might have been expected in view of the general hostility of the national movement.

The organizing ability of the CPI leadership, under P. C. Joshi, was further reflected in the creation, during the war years, of an impressive array of front groups.[48] The Indian People's Theater Association, the Progressive Writers' Association, the Friends of the Soviet Union, *Bala Sanghams* (children's societies), and *Mahila Sanghams* (women's organizations), are some examples. These organizations served, on the one hand, as useful instruments for action and propaganda, particularly where the Party's policy could be correlated with the interests of a specific profession or group. And on the other hand, they drew potential recruits or activists toward the Party—among them many who had little interest in or comprehension of the Party's ideological or political program but were persuaded that it was sympathetic to their particular interests.

---

[47] *Ibid.*, 1943, I, 357–358.
[48] For a fuller discussion of the development of front organizations, see chapter 17.

The greatest challenge to the organizing skill of the CPI leaders, however, was the task of Party-building itself, and here too they acquitted themselves surprisingly well. One index is the expansion of membership. According to the Party's claims, its membership grew from about 4,500 in 1942, to 9,200 at the beginning of 1943, 15,000 in mid-1943, and 30,000 in 1945.[49] An American government intelligence report on the CPI in this period estimated the membership at about 2,500 in 1942 and 25,000 in 1945—an increase of 1,000 per cent.[50] This rapid growth was accomplished primarily by relaxing the standards for admission; following a decision of the Central Committee to create a "mass" Party, the CPI announced it would throw off "old inhibitions," "remove all unnecessary barriers, and throw open party membership to all honest elements who have proved their worth." [51]

Other manifestations of Party growth included the expansion of propaganda activity. With legalization, the CPI began publishing a weekly newspaper, *People's War,* and a string of provincial newspapers. Within a year it claimed a total circulation of 66,350 for these organs.[52] Publication of book and pamphlet materials also increased rapidly.

Internal Party organization was taken in hand, with special attention to establishing a stable system of cadres. By 1943 the CPI claimed to have 2,637 "whole timers"—full-time salaried functionaries.[53] And there is evidence that these professionals were operating with much greater efficiency than ever before. Successive issues of *Party Letter,* a newsletter addressed to members only, contained a flood of instructions, circulars, questionnaires, charts, and other items designed to systematize operations. Lower units of the Party were tutored in the tactics to be applied in special spheres such as trade-union activity, provided with "lecture notes" for speeches at mass meetings, instructed in the preparation of cell newspapers, and furnished with models for their reports to the central office. They received questionnaires on their financial situation, their membership

---

[49] The figures for 1942 and early 1943 are contained in N. K. Krishnan, ed., *Forgery Versus Facts* (Bombay: People's Publishing House, 1943), p. 4. Approximately the same figures for these dates, and the figures for mid-1943 and 1945, are given in Joshi, *Communist Reply to . . . ,* p. 142.

[50] *The Communist Party of India* (R and A Number 2681), (mimeographed), Office of Strategic Services, Research and Analysis Branch, 1945, pp. 5, 8. This report was declassified in 1947.

[51] Quoted from *People's War* in *ibid.,* p. 9.

[52] Krishnan, *Forgery Versus Facts,* pp. 6, 8. This claim appears to be accepted in the American intelligence report cited above: *The Communist Party of India,* pp. 16–17.

[53] *Party Letter,* III (June 8, 1943), p. 3.

and its composition, their work in the food production campaign, their activity among Muslims, and many other aspects of their operation.

An illustration of the thoroughness of this organizational reform is a decision in mid-1943 which set specific goals for immediate Party expansion. According to *Party Letter,* the leadership aimed at a total of 6,020 whole timers, 260 provincial organizers, 1,720 local organizers, 6,250 cell secretaries, an over-all membership of 56,000, and a special fund collection of 500,000 rupees (about $167,000 at the current rate of exchange).[54]

At about the same time, *Party Letter* provided a detailed statement of the CPI budget. It claimed that the assets of the Central Committee, apart from those of the provincial and local organizations, amounted to 225,000 rupees (about $75,000). The Central Committee's monthly expenses were listed as 7,500 rupees ($2,500) and its regular monthly income as 5,000 rupees ($1,666).[55] Irregular fund drives covered the difference. Compared with its earlier financial position, this was no doubt heartening to the Party.

With legalization, the Party had for the first time in its history the opportunity to convoke genuinely open conferences. When an enlarged plenum of the Central Committee met in September, 1942, therefore, it was hailed in the Communist press as a historic event.[56] *People's War* pointed out, incredulously, that the meeting had even been announced in the daily press throughout India.

The plenum consisted of thirty persons, including members of the CC and "invited representatives" from provincial units. It was characterized by a mood of strenuous—perhaps even desperate—self congratulation. An official Party report of the meeting claimed that the CPI was "the third biggest party in our country" and that it had an international role "which is next in importance to that of the Communist Party of the Soviet Union and to that of the Communist Party of China"—a remark hardly calculated to please the British Communists. In his speech to the plenum, Joshi explained that the Party was now legal because it had "served the Motherland steadfastly" and "earned the love and admiration of the patriots and the people." He ended with the assertion that the CPI was the only party which could "save the nation." According to the account in *People's War,* he stressed the prominent role of the Party "again and again," in order

---

[54] *Ibid.,* p. 4.

[55] *Party Letter,* III (Aug. 12, 1943), p. 1.

[56] The following account of the September plenum is from *People's War,* I (Oct. 4, 1942), as reprinted in N. K. Krishnan, ed., *National Unity for the Defence of the Motherland* (Bombay: People's Publishing House, n.d. [1943?]), pp. 1–15.

"to inspire the delegates with confidence and courage to face the new tasks."

Another plenum met in February, 1943. It drew up plans for an even more spectacularly novel event: the First Congress of the Communist Party of India.[57] Convened in Bombay on May 23, 1943, the Congress was composed of nearly 300 delegates from all regions of India. Its week-long deliberations did not produce any radical departure from existing CPI policy, but rather served as an opportunity to rally the entire Party behind that policy. The Congress reëlected P. C. Joshi as general secretary, and on the whole approved the prevailing leadership.

It is interesting to note that the Congress was convened just one day after the formal dissolution of the Comintern; it could therefore be used as a platform from which to combat the charge that the CPI was committed to alien loyalties. In a special statement, Joshi declared the dissolution of the Comintern was a "powerful blow against all reactionary forces" which had used it as a pretext for anti-Soviet and anti-Communist activity.

In the course of these three meetings of 1942–1943, the CPI evolved an elaborate tactical line, charted within the framework of Joshi's earlier pronouncements. These tactics, which served the Party for the rest of the war, may be considered under two major headings: the "national unity" campaign, and the production campaign.

The National-Unity Campaign

As stated earlier, the main outlines of the CPI tactic for national unity consisted of an appeal for Congress-League collaboration, which would require the Congress to accept the League's right to speak for the Muslim community, and to make drastic concessions to the League's political aspirations. Pursuing such a tactic, the CPI had found it increasingly difficult to maintain even a façade of good relations with the Congress. In an attempt to appease the Congress, in July, 1942, the CPI addressed an "open letter" to the Working Committee. It claimed that "it is our birthright to remain inside our great patriotic organization [the Congress]," and continued:

You are the respected leadership of our proud national movement, represented by the great Congress, which has been built up with the blood of our martyrs, which is supported by countless millions of our people. . . . We Communists are 15 years old, born in the womb of the same broad national movement and we have endeavored our very best to strengthen it. All of us proudly carry our Congress

---

[57] This account of the CPI's First Congress is from Mitra, ed., *Indian Annual Register, 1943*, I, 304–309.

membership card, as a treasured possession of our national heritage, as a living inspiration to fight the battle of India's freedom, shoulder to shoulder with our fellow patriots.[58]

But this fulsome praise could not conceal the fundamental division between the CPI and the Congress. In August the Communists on the All-India Congress Committee in effect renounced the organization by opposing the adoption of the "Quit India" resolution. The principal Communist members of the AICC—K. N. Ashraf, Sajjad Zaheer, and S. G. Sardesai—produced amendments which embodied the "people's war" policy, and fought bitterly with the prevailing leadership of the Congress.[59]

The vast wave of nationalist sentiment which swept India following the "Quit India" resolution evidently shook the Party's confidence in its policy. Joshi later admitted that there were "vacillations" in the ranks of the CPI; as a result, he said, "our boys were bogged." [60] The Party therefore had to find new ways to conciliate the Congress. And this was the apparent purpose of one of the main elements of the national-unity campaign as it took shape in the following months: the demand that the Congress be legalized again, and that Gandhi be released from prison. The September plenum of the Central Committee defined the main slogans of the campaign as follows:

Release Mahatma Gandhi and the national leaders, stop repression, check destruction, sabotage and anarchy, lift the ban on the Congress, negotiate for an all-round settlement, set up Provisional National Government for India's defense.[61]

The CPI criticized the "Quit India" resolution as "misguided" and "pernicious," but declared the British bore the main responsibility for the errors of the Congress. It undertook an intensive campaign on behalf of Gandhi, and also soft-pedaled its criticism of the Congress. It reserved its condemnation for the "fifth column"—those elements of the Indian nationalist movement which resorted to sabotage of the British war effort in India or to collaboration with the Japanese. The Indian Socialists were described as the advance guard of the Japanese Army, and attacks on Subhas Chandra Bose and his collaborationist "Indian National Army" formed a large part of the Party's progaganda.

But a profoundly anti-Congress orientation was implicit in the CPI's increasing warmth toward the Muslim League. Having already elevated that organization to a position of parity with the Congress, the

[58] Krishnan, ed., *Forgery Versus Facts*, p. 23.
[59] Mitra, ed., *Indian Annual Register, 1942*, II, 245–246.
[60] Krishnan, ed., *National Unity for . . .* , pp. 5–6.
[61] *Ibid.*, p. 20.

Party declared its approval of the League's aspirations. In the words of the Central Committee member, Sajjad Zaheer, himself a Muslim:

It is a good and fine thing, a happy augury, for Indian Muslims and for India as a whole that the Muslim League continues to grow and gather around it millions of our liberty-loving people. . . . In the increasing strength and capacity of the League to move the Muslim masses on the path of progress and democracy lies the salvation of millions of our Muslim countrymen and the possibility of Congress-League unity.[62]

But the CPI did more than merely proclaim its general sympathy toward the League and its aims. It formulated a program for a settlement of the communal problem of India which, while appropriate to Communist theory and purposes, was also helpful to the League's purposes. The Party's "nationality" policy, which had first begun to appear in 1940, was now fully expressed.

By mid-1942, the Party was expressly committed to the general view that India was a multinational entity, and that the unqualified right of self-determination should be granted to each nationality. A Party statement of July asked: "What can be the basis of our national unity? Recognition of the principles of self-determination including the right of separation, for all the nationalities that inhabit our great subcontinent." [63]

A resolution of the September plenary meeting of the Central Committee, based on a report by G. Adhikari, definitively outlined the Party's new orientation. Its critical passage was as follows:

Every section of the Indian people which has a contiguous territory as its homeland, common historical tradition, common language, culture, psychological make-up, and common economic life would be recognized as a distinct nationality with the right to exist as an autonomous state within the free Indian Union or federation and will have the right to secede from it if it may so desire. . . . Thus free India of tomorrow would be a federation or union of autonomous states of the various nationalities such as the Pathans, Western Punjabis (dominantly Muslims), Sikhs, Sindhis, Hindustanis, Rajasthanis, Gujeratis, Bengalis, Assamese, Beharies, Oriyas, Andhras, Tamils, Karnatikis, Maharashtrians, Keralas, etc.[64]

As to whether, in the final analysis, all nationalities should separate, the Party did not give a direct answer. According to Adhikari, "The grant of the right of separation should not be confused with the actual exercise of this right, it should not be confused with the actual expediency of separation in this or that particular case." [65] But the

[62] Sajjad Zaheer, *A Case for Congress-League Unity* (Bombay: People's Publishing House, 1944), pp. 20, 36. Zaheer later became the first secretary of the CP in Pakistan.
[63] Krishnan, ed., *Forgery Versus Facts*, p. 19.
[64] Krishnan, ed., *National Unity for* . . . , pp. 24–25.
[65] G. M. Adhikari, *Pakistan and Indian National Unity* (London: Labour Monthly, 1943), p. 29.

resolution made it abundantly clear that those nationalities which were predominantly Muslim could secede: "This would give to the Muslims wherever they are in an overwhelming majority in a contiguous territory which is their homeland, the right to form their autonomous states and even to separate if they so desire.[66]

At this point the Party did not expressly provide for the right of the Muslim nationalities to coalesce in one nation-state, Pakistan. But that prospect was inherent in the nationality policy, and each succeeding resolution and pronouncement revealed more clearly that the Party approved it: The September political resolution referred, at one point, to "Muslim independence"; [67] and a manifesto, in October, used the word "sovereign" instead of the former term, "autonomous," in discussing a Muslim state.[68] By a year later, the Party was openly supporting Pakistan. Zaheer admonished the Congress that:

> Congressmen generally fail to see the anti-imperialist, liberationist, role of the Muslim League, fail to see that the demand for Muslim self-determination or Pakistan is a just, progressive and national demand, and is the positive expression of the very freedom and democracy for which Congressmen have striven and undergone so much suffering all these years.[69]

The formula which the CPI proposed for a political settlement between the Congress and the League, was, therefore, one which called for concessions on one side only. P. C. Joshi frankly admitted this:

> The Congress is the major party, it has to deliver the goods, Gandhiji's responsibility is greater. It is enough for the League to formulate its demand clearly; it is the organization of the minority, it has every right to feel suspicious of the majority. He [Gandhi] has to think harder than Jinnah Saheb. He has to work out a *new* platform for the Indian national movement which satisfies the League and leads to Congress-League United Front.[70]

The immediate purpose of the CPI's nationality policy appears to have been to befriend the Muslim League, presumably in order to enlist the support of the League and the Muslim people for the war. R. Palme Dutt later referred, in so many words, to the "tactical reasons for this sympathetic approach to the supporters of Pakistan in order to win them for the United all-India national front." [71] In all likelihood, this policy had also the long-term purpose of making it easier for the Communists to penetrate the Muslim population of the subcon-

---

[66] Krishnan, ed., *National Unity for . . . ,* p. 45.

[67] *Ibid.,* p. 21.

[68] Krishnan, ed., *Forgery Versus Facts,* p. 43.

[69] Zaheer, *The Case for Congress-League Unity,* p. i.

[70] P. C. Joshi, *They Must Meet Again* (Bombay: People's Publishing House, 1944), p. 30.

[71] R. Palme Dutt, "India and Pakistan," *Labour Monthly,* XXVII (March, 1946), pp. 88–89.

tinent. Soli Batliwala, a member of the Central Committee at that time, said after his defection that the Communists believed "that support of the League will give them a foothold in the Muslim masses, as support of the Congress from 1936 onwards gave them a foothold among the nationalist masses of this country." [72]

Yet it is inconceivable that the Communists should have failed to realize that a gain among the Muslims would inevitably result in some losses among the Hindus (that is, the majority) of the Indian population and, would, above all, worsen its relations with the Congress. Why, then, did the Party set out upon this momentous course? Several explanations may be hazarded. The Party may not have realized, first, how severe its losses would be; it perhaps did not fully comprehend the intensity of communal feeling, as indeed it would be difficult for Communists to do. Alternatively, the Party may have chosen deliberately to sacrifice its interests among the non-Muslims, in the higher interests of recruiting Muslim support for the war effort, believing that such support was more valuable than non-Muslim support. Muslim support might have been considered more valuable for the simple reason that the Muslim-majority areas of India were of the greatest military importance; these areas guarded the borders of India in both the east and the west, where any Japanese or German invasions would be expected to occur.

There may, however, be still another explanation. The policy may have been prompted in part by an intention to encourage not Muslim separatism alone but all regional particularism throughout the subcontinent. The regional linguistic units of India, while no one but the CPI termed them "nationalities," had in many cases shown strong particularist impulses on which a political party might easily capitalize. At this point the CPI may have dimly recognized that the time had come, in the political development of India, to associate itself with these impulses, as it had earlier associated itself with the nationalist impulse. Bourgeois nationalism was on the verge of achieving freedom and establishing an independent state; in preparation for its struggle against that state, the CPI could have no better weapon than regional separatism, which could weaken or even destroy a bourgeois government in New Delhi.

However, such an interpretation of the Party's war-time policy is highly speculative. During the war there were only hints that the CPI contemplated, not the partition of India into two parts, but rather its Balkanization. At one stage the Party openly proposed that Bengal be a sovereign country, in addition to India and Pakistan. It also

[72] Soli Batliwala, *Facts Versus Forgery* (Bombay: National Youth Pub., 1946), p. 19.

hinted at independent status for the Sikhs. But it was only after the war that this larger import of the Party's policy—its identification with regional particularism—emerged fully.

The Production Campaign

Like the national-unity campaign, the CPI's economic program was designed to maximize India's contribution to the war effort. As the tactic of Congress-League unity had sought to promote collaboration among the political forces of the country, so the production campaign sought to unify all economic forces: workers and capitalists, peasants and landowners, and traders. And as in the national-unity campaign, the CPI evidently aimed, as well, at strengthening the Party itself.

In the resolution on economic policy adopted by the plenum of 1942,[73] The Party sought, while proclaiming the goal of full industrial production, to retain some of its traditional concepts of working-class interests. It relinquished all mention of economic reform, much less of revolution, but it castigated the government for inefficiency and the employers for profiteering, and it put forward certain minimum demands on behalf of the workers. It declared that it would attempt to minimize strikes, but showed itself reluctant to give up this proletarian weapon altogether, specifying that strikes should be resorted to "only when we are compelled to do so."

But by mid-1943 these vestiges of conventional policy gave way altogether to the tactical necessity of promoting production. In his report to the First Congress,[74] B. T. Ranadive declared that "conditional support of production" was a "left nationalist deviation." Even though the lives of the workers were "hellish" and "intolerable," he said, "strikes should be firmly prevented." Production was a "sacred trust," and the demands for improvement of working-class conditions had their justification only so far as they contributed to increased production. For settling economic disputes, Ranadive proposed institutionalized collaboration between workers, employers, and governmental agencies, in the form of tripartite boards.

The CPI's policy for agrarian production was in the same spirit as its industrial policy.[75] The conventional demand for land reform was

---

[73] Krishnan, ed., *National Unity for* . . . , pp. 27–35.

[74] B. T. Ranadive, *Working Class and National Defence* (Bombay: People's Publishing House, n.d. [1943?]), 34 pp.

[75] See the Central Committee resolution of February, 1943, in Krishnan, ed., *National Unity for* . . . , pp. 63–69. The Party's principal spokesman on agrarian policy was S. G. Sardesai, who delivered the report on the subject to the Plenum of February, 1943: S. G. Sardesai, *People's Way to Food* (Bombay: People's Publishing House, n.d. [1943?]), 46 pp.

altogether abandoned, and the peasants were exhorted to coöperate with landlords and rural traders for full production. The Party urged the establishment of "People's Food Committees," embracing all sections of the rural population except "hoarders." It declared that agrarian policy must assure a "reasonable rate of profit" to traders and owners, as well as a reasonable price to the peasant.

The campaign for full economic production was given the greatest possible emphasis in the Party's propaganda and activities, particularly through its work in the trade-union and peasant movements. The importance of this campaign was attested by P. C. Joshi, who declared that alongside the production campaign "everything else is empty phrases," [76] as though all elements of CPI policy were ultimately aimed at a maximum economic contribution to the war. But the Party frankly stated that the production campaign also served its own partisan political purposes. Speaking of the organization of food production, Central Committee member S. G. Sardesai admitted that "the acid test of our correct lead and actual achievements on the food front is therefore the extent to which it strengthens the Party numerically and politically." He unabashedly justified this position with the argument that the Party alone had a correct policy, and continued:

> Building the Party through the food campaign, therefore, is not at all seeking a sectarian, selfish advantage for our organization at the cost of any other of our countrymen. On the contrary, the building of our Party is the highest service we render to every Indian and to every other patriotic party in the country. To build the Party is the only unfailing guarantee for the salvation of our motherland.[77]

The Fruits of Policy

Though the Communists threw all their skills and resources into the "people's war," the Party found more and more difficulty in applying its tactics and realizing its aims. The Congress, expressing general Indian opinion, continued to oppose the war effort; thus the Communist goal of national unity for the antifascist struggle was not attained. The Congress and the League remained fundamentally at odds in their aims and outlooks; thus the Communist tactic of Congress-League unity came to naught. Nor, as later years were to show, did the Party succeed to any great extent in popularizing itself among the Muslims with its nationality tactic. And although the CPI probably did contribute to increased production by abstaining from agitating for strikes or land reform, its economic tactics did not suc-

---

[76] Mitra, ed., *Indian Annual Register, 1943*, I, 305.
[77] Sardesai, *People's Way to Food*, p. 34.

ceed in permanently consolidating its position among the workers and
peasants; while it made impressive organizational gains in the trade-
union and peasant movements, as well as in other fields, these gains,
for the most part, had resulted merely from lack of opposition.

The principal fruit of CPI wartime policy was increasing alienation
from the primary nationalist agency, the Congress. One of the Party's
main concerns during the last year of the war, in fact, was an attempt
to maintain at least the fiction of cordial relations with the Congress
in the face of mounting hostility among Congressmen. Communists
still held membership and some offices in the Congress, but they were
under increasing attack. An anti-Communist pamphlet of this period
conceded that the Party had deep native roots but charged that it had
betrayed the national movement because of its "anxiety to safeguard
the interests of Russia." [78] Another, published by the Bombay Provincial Congress Committee, asserted that the Party had "persistently
and systematically vilified and slandered *every section* of the Indian
National Congress by turn, one after another." [79]

Relations with the Congress were also damaged by the suspicion
that the CPI was secretly collaborating with the British authorities. In
1942 and 1943 various Indian journals reprinted a document alleged
to be a letter from Joshi to Sir Reginald Maxwell, which revealed that
the CPI was receiving financial aid from the government, had a secret
pact with the Muslim League, and was undermining Congress activities in various ways.[80] The Party denounced the letter as a forgery,
and its authenticity is in fact very doubtful. Further grounds for popular suspicion were added in 1945 when Soli Batliwala, the well-known
defector from the Party, claimed that he had seen similar correspondence between Joshi and Maxwell.[81]

By the end of 1944 Joshi was forced to acknowledge that "anti-
Communist prejudice prevails in a majority of Congressmen." [82] In a
number of provinces Congress committees had already passed resolutions barring Communists from office. In response, Joshi dramatically
appealed for the restoration of good relations, pouring praise upon
the Congress:

---

[78] D. K. Rangnekar and S. K. Parukh, *Congress-Communist Tangle* (Bombay: National Youth Publications, 1945), pp. 16–17.

[79] A. G. Tendulkar, *Nation Betrayed? A Case Against Communists* (Bombay: Bombay Provincial Congress Committee, 1945), p. *iii*. Emphasis in original.

[80] The document was reprinted but was disavowed by the CPI in Krishnan, ed.,
Forgery Versus Facts, pp. 3–16.

[81] Batliwala, *Facts Versus Forgery*, pp. 7–10. Batliwala challenged the CPI to publish
this alleged correspondence, but he did not offer any concrete evidence of its existence.

[82] Quoted in Tendulkar, *Nation Betrayed? . . .* , p. 24.

It is the Congress that planted the banner of Indian freedom; it is from Congress leaders that we got our early lessons in patriotism and it is today Congressmen who want to deny us the privilege of fighting shoulder to shoulder with them for the cause they taught us to accept as our main aim in life. To us the Congress is our parent organization, its leaders our political fathers, its followers our brothers-in-arms.[83]

The Party's effort to conciliate the Congress culminated in an extraordinary appeal to Gandhi himself. In correspondence with him extending over a period of a year, Joshi sought to persuade him of the Party's patriotism and good faith. The Party itself published the letters, and it clearly attached the highest importance to this ultimate attempt to cut its losses.[84]

Joshi had initiated the correspondence with a brief note paying "warm homage" to Gandhi, "the most loved leader of the greatest patriotic organization of our people." A meeting was then arranged, and Gandhi put certain questions to Joshi concerning the Party's policy and activity, to be answered in a subsequent letter. Receiving no reply, Gandhi wrote to Joshi, repeating his questions. In his response, Joshi attempted to put a good face on the situation, expressing his "pleasant surprise" that Gandhi was "so eager to know more about us." He explained his earlier failure to reply by saying, "I thought I was helping the fulfillment of a big national task, your speedy recovery to normal health, by not writing to you." He then proceeded to answer Gandhi's questions.

Asked to explain the meaning of "people's war," Joshi gave a brief presentation of the CPI formula which added nothing to previous statements. To the question whether the Party's finances were subject to public audit, Joshi pointed out that the accounts of political parties are ordinarily not subject to public scrutiny but offered to let Gandhi or his representative examine the CPI's books. Asked whether the Party had assisted the government in arresting strike leaders, Joshi was evasive, refusing to give a categorical answer and asking Gandhi to rely on the judgment of N. M. Joshi as to the Party's good faith. Asked whether the CPI had penetrated the Congress with "hostile intent," Joshi again evaded the question, stating that the Communists regarded their Congress membership both as a right and as a "glorious privilege." Asked, finally, whether the policy of the CPI was "dictated from outside," Joshi asserted that while all Communist parties "have the same

---

[83] P. C. Joshi, *Congress and Communists* (Bombay: People's Publishing House, 1944), p. 2.
[84] The following account of the correspondence is based on *Correspondence Between Mahatma Gandhi and P. C. Joshi* (Bombay: People's Publishing House, 1945), pp. 1–42.

ideology," the CPI "decides its own policy as it understands the interests of its own people and of the peoples of the world."

Continuing, Joshi said that Gandhi's questions "pained us" because they suggested "pre-conceived prejudices." He dealt also with the accusation that the Party received financial support from the British government, but again evaded a categorical answer, merely citing instances of government repression of the Communists.

Gandhi's next letter characteristically mixed expressions of personal humility with a very firm political viewpoint. He admitted that he had a prejudice against accepting Joshi's answers, and said that this admission "is an appeal to you to have patience with me and to disarm my prejudices in the best manner you can."

I know your worth. You have very able young men and women, as selfless as I would claim to be. You are all hard-working and possess great energy and you impose strict discipline on your workers. All this I prize and admire. I would not easily lose such a force because of any preconceived notions of mine.

But at the same time, Gandhi, in effect, flatly rejected most of Joshi's answers. He said that the "people's war" thesis was "highly misleading," and continued, "As I am composing this letter to you, I have read and re-read your argument. Every paragraph offends for, to me, it lacks reality." He accepted Joshi's good faith on the question of Party finances, but reserved judgment on the other questions and implied that it would be necessary for Joshi to supply concrete evidence of his statements.

From this point onward, the correspondence dealt chiefly with nonpolitical matters. Joshi sought to answer charges that the CPI was guilty of immorality, meat-eating, rejection of homespun cloth, and the avowal of violence. In the end, Gandhi declined to accept the responsibility for making a decision on the status of the CPI, declaring that Congress circles must "be guided by their own knowledge and not by my judgment which may be erring from want of complete evidence."

The Party thus failed in this dramatic attempt to pacify Gandhi and, through him, the Congress as a whole. Relations between the two organizations grew steadily more bitter, and only a few months after the end of the war the Congress Working Committee took action. It appointed a top-level subcommittee, composed of Nehru, Vallabhbhai Patel, and Govind Ballabh Pant, to investigate the activities of Communists in the organization. The subcommittee quickly recommended that they be charged with acting in opposition to Congress policy and be required to show cause why they should not be subjected to disciplinary action. The CPI did not take up the challenge, and instead issued a directive instructing all Communists to resign forthwith from the Congress, with the exception of those who were members of the All-India Congress Committee. Accordingly, the Working Committee formally resolved in December to remove the Communists from the AICC or any other elective office.[85] The rupture between the Congress and the CPI was complete.

The "people's war" had been won, but it had cost the Indian Communists dearly.

[85] Mitra, ed., *Indian Annual Register, 1945,* II, 102, 112–122.

11 CONSTITUTIONAL COMMUNISM

With the end of World War II, the problem of India's future status took on increased urgency. The new British Labor government was expected to make fundamental revisions in colonial policy and to undertake a fresh approach to Indian nationalism. Moreover, the situation in India demanded such an approach; as events were to show, wartime repression had produced a bitterness in the national movement which had explosive potentialities. In the two years that followed the end of the war, therefore, both the will and the necessity for a solution of the problem existed. Events moved rapidly toward a long-awaited culmination in Indian independence.

This was a time of headlong transition—a time that saw the Indian National Congress transformed from a party in prison to a party that held formal governmental power. In such a period of flux and of opportunities, the international Communist movement might be expected to respond with forceful initiative. In fact, however, the Soviet attitude toward India was cautious and improvised. Until the very eve of independence, it evolved haltingly, trailing after events rather than anticipating them.

Hindered by lack of clear-cut guidance from abroad, by public indifference or even animosity, and by deepening internal strife, the CPI itself was reduced to erratic and belated improvisation. Its policy fluctuated and lost focus. This was a time of transition for the Party, during which it appeared, on the whole, to seek merely a respectable role as the "loyal opposition" in a free India.

Soviet Temporizing

As the war neared its end, the temper of the Indian national movement was highly inflammable. When the bulk of the Congress leadership was released in March and April, 1945, after two and a half years
in prison, the political scene was one of "frenzied excitement," as Nehru
expressed it, and of "abiding anger and bitterness" against British
policy.[1] For a time the movement cast confusedly about for a new direction, its frustration intensified by a stalemate among the principal
parties to the dispute: Congress, League, and Government. Recent conferences between Gandhi and Jinnah had failed to resolve the contradictions in Muslim League and Congress aspirations for India. A
major statement of policy from the Churchill government in June,
1945, offered no fresh lead; it merely reasserted the constitutional
proposals of the Cripps Mission of 1942.[2] Subsequent negotiations between the viceroy and the Indian leadership came to nothing; they
further inflamed, rather than pacified, Indian opinion.

The rising anger of the Indian masses focused briefly on British
attempts to court-martial captured officers of the Indian National
Army, which had fought alongside the Japanese. The intensity of
popular sympathy for men who had taken arms against the British
indicated the virulence of anti-imperialist feeling.

In the meantime, the Labor government had taken office and had
announced its intention to accord complete self-government to India
as soon as possible. As a step toward convening a constitution-making
body, the viceroy had proclaimed new elections for the central and
provincial legislatures.[3] These elections, held during the winter of
1945–46, established the supremacy of the Congress over the various
Hindu communal parties and validated the Muslim League's claim to
speak for the Muslim community. Thus the League and the Congress
confronted each other from secure positions on either side of the communal line that more and more deeply divided the Indian people.

The fact that the British promise of imminent independence had
not dissipated the mounting tensions was demonstrated in February,
1946, by an unprecedented event—a large-scale mutiny in the Royal
Indian Navy. Though this outburst was checked by the moderate
Congress leadership as well as by the British authorities, it showed
plainly the violent potentialities of the situation.

---

[1] Jawaharlal Nehru, *Discovery of India* (London: Meridian Books Ltd., 1951), p. 542.
[2] The text of the statement is in Sir Reginald Coupland, *India: A Re-statement*
(London: Oxford University Press, 1945), pp. 295–299.
[3] For the text of the viceroy's announcement, see *ibid.*, pp. 299–300.

Yet during the first months after the war's end, the Soviet commentary furnished only the most routine recognition of these tumultuous events. In the face of what might readily be interpreted as a revolutionary situation, the Soviet authorities were surprisingly passive. Far from offering a militant lead, their commentary on India was vague and cautious in the extreme.

This response was probably due to a multiplicity of factors. It was consistent with current Soviet policy of restraint whereby, for example, Communist parties in Western Europe were advised to collaborate with the postwar governments instead of attempting to seize power. With regard to India, too, Soviet spokesmen tended to adopt a wait-and-see attitude. And for India, unlike Italy or France, such an attitude was appropriate to the weakness of the Communist Party, though in the past such weakness had not hindered a call to revolution. Soviet leaders might also have been indifferent to Indian affairs, which must have had low priority as compared with the challenges of reconstructing Russia, absorbing Eastern Europe, and achieving a European political settlement.

Perhaps the clearest indication that Soviet authorities were improvising their approach to India was their willingness to consider United Nations trusteeship for the colonial areas. The first sign came from E. Zhukov, the eminent Soviet spokesman in the field of Asian studies, who acknowledged the proposal of trusteeship, though he did caution that British and American imperialist interests would attempt to pervert such a system to their own purposes.[4] But in an article on the colonial problem and the principles by which it should be settled, published almost a year later, Zhukov went further. He declared that while the U.N. Charter provisions for trusteeship were not ideal, trusteeship "can accelerate the progressive development of colonies along the path to complete independence."[5] He conspicuously abstained from the traditional Communist polemics; he referred favorably to the Anglo-Soviet-American coalition, "which led the forces of democracy," and urged that its program—presumably the Atlantic Charter—be applied to the colonies.[6]

Other Soviet writers took an equally moderate viewpoint. A. Dyakov,

---

[4] E. Zhukov, "The Colonial Question at the Present Stage," *Marxist Miscellany* (Bombay), II (May, 1945), pp. 118–119. The article is reprinted from *War and the Working Class* (Moscow), (March 15, 1945), pp. 5–10.

[5] E. Zhukov, "Porazheniie Iaponskogo imperializma i natsional'no-osvobiditel'naia bor'ba narodov vostochnoi Azii" [The Defeat of Japanese Imperialism and the National-Liberation Struggle of the Peoples of East Asia], *Bolshevik*, (Dec., 1945), pp. 86–87.

[6] *Ibid.*, p. 80.

who emerged at this time as a leading commentator on India, observed mildly that it was "paradoxical in the extreme" that India, a member of the United Nations, was not granted the right of self-determination. The fact that the colonies continued to be deprived of elementary political rights, he concluded, "creates additional handicaps" in the maintenance of international peace and security.[7]

One of the Soviet statements on imperialist policy in Asia is, however, significant as a tentative hint of future policy. Again it came from Zhukov. He cautioned that unless political independence were accompanied by economic independence, the granting of formal sovereignty to the colonies might only be a mask for continued subjugation. There is a trend, he said, toward a new type of colonial empire composed of dependencies having only the façade of sovereignty; its prototype is the relationship between the United States and the Philippines.[8] But Zhukov did not elaborate on the subject, nor did he explicitly identify India as a prospective victim.

Soviet spokesmen were equally tentative in their approach to Indian domestic issues. They did mark out the general lines of a new strategy, but they were ambiguous as to tactics. Even before the end of the war, Soviet advice had tended to suggest that the CPI revert to the prewar anti-imperialist strategy calling for collaboration with the Indian bourgeoisie;[9] this was now reiterated in many subsequent statements. All classes in India, they affirmed, had a part to play in the national-liberation movement "with the exception of the feudal princes and a section of the big landlords."[10]

As contrasted, however, with the earlier "united-front" line, the Soviet view of 1945–46 did not explicitly assert that the national-liberation movement was embodied in the National Congress. Nor did it validate the CPI tactic of "Congress-League unity." On the primary questions of tactics, therefore, the CPI could derive little clear guidance from the Soviet pronouncements.

With regard to the Congress, however, the Soviet attitude was in general cautiously favorable. Like others, Dyakov's analysis commended the heterogeneous composition of the Congress and the broad support it received from the masses. He did not identify its leadership with any single class, merely remarking that the bourgeoisie played a "large role" in it. He stated that the Congress aimed at complete independ-

---

[7] A. Dyakov, "India After the War," *New Times,* (Jan. 15, 1946), p. 10.

[8] E. Zhukov, "Porazheniie Iaponskogo . . . ," p. 86.

[9] See especially a quotation in the Indian Communist pamphlet, P. C. Joshi, *Victory . . . Whose?* (Bombay: People's Publishing House, n.d. [1945]), p. 18.

[10] A. Dyakov, "Sovremennaia Indiia" [Contemporary India], *Bolshevik* (Feb., 1946), p. 41.

ence for India, and that its social and economic program was, under Indian conditions, "progressive." [11] He described Nehru as a "progressive democrat," and praised him for his "in the main correct appraisal of the international situation." However, other Congress leaders were typified, said Dyakov, by Abul Kalam Azad, whom he characterized as far less progressive, although not an orthodox Gandhian like the "narrow nationalists" Sardar Vallabhbhai Patel and Rajendra Prasad.[12]

Soviet commentators paid more attention to the Congress than to the Muslim League, but with the latter, also, they dealt sympathetically on the whole. They termed it the "most influential Muslim organization" and implicitly justified its existence with the comment that the Congress had earlier been a narrow Hindu organization and had "paid little heed to the needs of the Muslims." [13] But they did not spell out a clear attitude toward the League.

On the crucial question of Pakistan, the Soviet view was carefully neutral. On the one hand Dyakov chided the Congress for not acknowledging, in its program, the right of secession; he pointed out that one of the most prominent Congress leaders, C. Rajagopalachari, had proposed that the Muslim areas be permitted to form a separate state, Pakistan, and that this proposal was supported by the All-India Trade Union Congress and other workers' and peasants' organizations [i.e., the Indian Communists]. On the other hand he stated that "many progressive Indian leaders consider that partition of India would not solve the Hindu-Muslim problem and would weaken India." The Congress leaders he said, believe that "the transformation of India into a federation of national administrative-political regions would contribute far more to the interests of the development of India than its division on a communal basis into two or even three separate states." [14]

In effect, Dyakov simply reviewed the positions of the various Indian parties—including the CPI. He did not expressly sanction the Indian Communist line on partition, and indeed, his words might be interpreted as implying approval of the Congress position.

Underlying any approach to Pakistan was the question of the "national" composition of India; on this issue, the Soviet spokesmen withheld judgment also. The CPI had produced a precise and comprehensive program which included a catalogue of the various "na-

---

[11] *Ibid.*, pp. 44, 51.

[12] A. Dyakov, "Indian National Congress Leaders," *New Times* (May 15, 1946), pp. 27–29.

[13] A. Dyakov, "Sovremennaia Indiia," p. 45.

[14] *Ibid.*, pp. 48–51.

tionalities." But while the Soviet authorities conceded the general principle that India was a multinational state, they declined to accept any hard and fast definitions of "nationality," much less the CPI's definitive list. In one article purporting to offer a brief geographical sketch of India, for example, a number of ethnic groups were designated as "nationalities," but the list was far from complete; moreover, the term "nationality" was not precisely defined, and such small primitive tribes as the Santals, Gonds, Oraons, and Mundas were identified as nationalities on an equal basis with the Bengalis, Tamils, and other large linguistic groups.[15] Such an unsystematic analysis of the question would seem, in effect, to be a refusal to validate the CPI program.

Soviet spokesmen were similarly cautious in dealing with specific current events in India. They offered only brief descriptions of such important political disturbances as the demonstrations against the court-martialing of the Indian National Army officers or the mutiny in the Royal Indian Navy, and noted merely that these events testified to the "extreme tension" prevailing in the Indian political scene.[16]

Finally, one of the most striking features of the Soviet commentary during this period was its almost total disregard of the CPI. Though Soviet commentators discussed the Congress and the League at length, they scarcely mentioned the Indian Communist Party, much less identified it as the vanguard of the national-liberation movement. The reason for this indifference—and the crux of the Soviet attitude toward India as a whole—may perhaps be discerned in a comment by Dyakov:

The social and political activity of the masses in India remains at a very low level, and their degree of organization is considerably inferior to that observed in democratic countries. This being so, a political party like the National Congress, embracing comparatively limited circles, is in a position to formulate in its program a number of propositions which have the support of considerably broader sections of the population.[17]

During this period, then, the Soviet authorities apparently saw little prospect of revolutionary change in India. They did not, it appears, believe that the British would surrender power, or that the prevailing Indian leadership would seize it. Since there were many imponderables in both the international and the Indian scenes, they watched and temporized. And though they vaguely prescribed a four-class "united national front" strategy, their pronouncements furnished little enlightenment or comfort to the Indian Communists.

---

[15] A. Dyakov, "India and Her Peoples," *New Times* (March 1, 1946), pp. 25–31.
[16] A. Dyakov, "Sovremennaia Indiia," p. 52.
[17] A. Dyakov, "India After the War," p. 11.

The CPI Election Manifesto

During the winter of 1945–46, the Indian Communists were in the midst of the first postwar elections for central and provincial legislatures. The many facets of the Party's campaign constitute a remarkable case study of the elaboration of strategy and tactics.

It should be noted at the outset that the CPI's election policy was formulated by the existing leadership under P. C. Joshi, without a fresh mandate from the Party as a whole. Although the CPI constitution called for an All-India Party Congress every year under normal circumstances, the last had been held in 1943 and the leadership did not choose to convene one in 1945.[18] Not until 1948 did the Second Party Congress meet; in the meantime P. C. Joshi continued to preside as general secretary. His term of office in that post—thirteen years—is the longest on record in the CPI.

In one respect, the CPI's position was refreshingly novel: for the first time it was entering an election contest as a legal party. Its new status, together wth the prevailing tension and unrest, gave the Party an unprecedented opportunity to assert a separate identity in Indian politics. It could not, however, make revolutionary use of this opportunity, since it had adopted the anti-imperialist strategy; positing the goal of class collaboration against feudalism and imperialism, this strategy required a policy moderate enough to permit an alliance with the bourgeoisie.

As on other occasions, this alliance was sought primarily through the tactic of the united front from below: thoroughly alienated from the National Congress and unsuccessful in cultivating an alliance with the Muslim League, the CPI could not contemplate a formal united front from above with the leadership of these parties, and had no choice but to appeal directly to their bourgeois followers.

In its election manifesto, issued in February, 1946, the CPI detailed the new strategy and tactics.[19] The manifesto made clear the Party's strategic orientation by calling for a "united struggle of all freedom-loving Indians" against the British "enslavers," and by confining its

---

[18] *The Constitution of the Communist Party of India* (Bombay: People's Publishing House, n.d. [1943]), Article 7. This clause was retained in the revised constitution adopted by the Party in 1948 (*The Constitution of the Communist Party of India* [Calcutta: Communist Party of India, 1948], p. 12.) In 1953 it was amended to provide for an All-India Congress "every two years" (*The Constitution of the Communist Party of India* [Delhi: Communist Party of India, 1954], p. 14).

[19] The following quotations from the election manifesto are taken from the version given in P. C. Joshi, *For the Final Bid for Power! Freedom Programme of Indian Communists* (Bombay: People's Publishing House, n.d. [1945?]), pp. 101–122.

criticism of Indian classes to the large landlords and big business. It made a clear appeal to the bourgeoisie:

> The Communist Party shall seek the whole-hearted coöperation and close alliance of the middle-class and shall struggle to build its alliance with the working-class. . . . The Communist Party appeals to the revolutionary middle-class to see in our Party the unifier of the middle-class with the working-class in the towns and the peasantry in the villages.

Furthermore, the manifesto included specific assurances to the middle-class, rural and urban, that the Party had their interests at heart. Thus in its economic proposals the manifesto called for only mild reform, and declared that state industrial planning would be implemented through "free and equal coöperation between the representatives of the State, Management, and Labor." It even made a friendly gesture to the advocates of cottage industry, proposing that small- as well as large-scale industry should achieve "maximum growth." On the subject of agrarian policy it reiterated the slogan of "abolition of landlordism" but it put the maximum land-holding at 100 acres—a very generous limitation. That there should be no doubt of its intentions, the manifesto promised that the Party would "not touch the small zamindar [landlord] or the rich peasant." Containing, of course, the usual planks shaped to attract the working class, the manifesto thus offered an election platform designed to have an exceptionally broad appeal.

In several supplementary campaign pamphlets the Party stated the class-collaboration theme even more explicitly. A statement on industrial policy, by Ranadive, called upon "workers, peasants, middlemen, employers to rally for a planned national development," [20] and another on agrarian policy, by G. Adhikari, called for unity among all sections of the peasantry and even went so far as to admit that under the CPI program the middle and rich peasant would prosper more than the poor peasant.[21]

Both Ranadive and Adhikari showed signs of uneasiness, however, at offering a friendly hand to the bourgeoisie, for elsewhere in their statements there were passages reminiscent of the old-style attacks on "vested interests," "capitalists," or "businessmen." Both agreed on the danger that British and Indian "vested interests" or "big business" would become partners in exploiting the subcontinent.

As later testimony of the Party leaders themselves shows, the ambivalence in the Ranadive and Adhikari statements on economic

---

[20] B. T. Ranadive, *Jobs for All* (Bombay: People's Publishing House, 1945), p. 30.
[21] G. M. Adhikari, *Food for All* (Bombay: People's Publishing House, n.d., [1945?]), p. 26.

policy reflected a split within the Party. By December, 1945, dissatisfaction with the moderate line of P. C. Joshi had resulted in the appearance of a "left opposition," of which Ranadive, Adhikari, and Ajoy Ghosh were the principal top-level spokesmen. In the months that followed, the CPI was increasingly divided by debates over a "soft" versus a "hard" line.[22] But for the time being Joshi remained in control.

More important than the manifesto's economic platform was its program for India's constitutional development. In this question, the CPI apparently saw an irresistible opportunity to attract all classes —especially the provincial middle-class—by a strong appeal to regional particularism.

There had previously been hints that the CPI was associating itself with the separatist impulses of the various linguistic "nationalities," seeing in this association a source of strength against the day when the major national parties would take power at the center. The manifesto confirmed this policy. Its political program constituted an express demand for the political fragmentation of India into a confederation of seventeen sovereign states, corresponding to the linguistic groups.

After making the routine demand for immediate independence, the manifesto proposed, in effect, that power be transferred not to one or even to two Indian governments (India and Pakistan) but to seventeen interim "sovereign" national constituent assemblies, corresponding to the "nationalities" as defined by the Party in 1942, with one addition —the Baluchis. The manifesto neglected to suggest how the boundaries of these states were to be delimited—though this was the crux of the problem—or how the assemblies were to be created. But it left no doubt that they were to constitute independent entities, possessing "full and real sovereignty" and enjoying the "unfettered right to negotiate, formulate, and finally to decide their mutual relations within an Independent India, on the basis of complete equality." Each assembly would send delegates to an All-India Constituent Assembly to debate the final constitutional settlement, but, the manifesto declared, these delegates should "have no more authority than that of plenipotentiaries."

The interim governmental structure which the CPI proposed was,

---

[22] For references to the inner-Party disputes of this period, see especially the main self-critical report of B. T. Ranadive to the CPI's Second Congress, 1948 (*People's Age, Supplement,* March 21, 1948, pp. 3–4). See also Prabodh Chandra [Ajoy Ghosh?], "On 'A Note on the Present Situation in our Party'," *PHQ Open Forum,* No. 12 (Oct., 1949), pp. 2–3. This inner-Party document contains a great deal of information on internal affairs in the CPI during 1945–1949.

therefore, not a federation of states on the Soviet pattern, but a confederation of independent states. The manifesto made it clear that the
Party would, moreover, argue for such a confederation in the final
constitutional arrangements. The manifesto declared that while the
National Congress would call for a single Indian federation, when the
issue was debated in the All-India Constituent Assembly, and the Mus-
lin League would demand two separate federations, the CPI would
propose "a voluntary Union of sovereign national States," democratic
and mutually helpful, "the more advanced helping the less advanced
through a common Federal Center." Though the nature of this
"Center" was not specified, it obviously could not be "Federal" if the
states were to be sovereign.

Communist nationality policy in India had reached its culmination.
Until 1940, the CPI had assumed India to be a single nation, but afterward it moved rapidly through a number of stages ending in a final
concession to regional separatism. First, it granted the *right* to self-
determination in a multinational India, but did not commit itself on
the question of secession. Then it conceded that secession was desirable for the Muslim nationalities who wished to form their own state,
Pakistan. Finally, in the election manifesto, the CPI declared that all
nationalities should form their own sovereign states.

Though it is likely that Adhikari was largely responsible for the
nationality policy itself, Joshi probably wrote the manifesto, for his
dramatic flair is discernible in its style. Nevertheless when the manifesto was published in English as a pamphlet, Joshi wrote a long introduction which was apparently designed to soften the impact of the
nationality proposals.[23] In discussing them, the introduction is remarkably ambiguous. Joshi frequently used the terms "sovereign" and
"autonomous" as though they were identical concepts and, for example, he spoke of the future India as a "willing union of sovereign
autonomous states." [24] Moreover, he condemned the Muslim League
for asserting the rights of the Muslim community in a "separatist"
manner, counterposing the Party's view that the Indian people are a
"family of nationalities," and he praised the Soviet and Yugoslav
federations as constitutional models that united various nationalities
as "brothers." Finally, he declared that the proposal for seventeen
national homelands, rather than dividing India, "creates the basis
for building a happy India." [25]

It is likely that Joshi's hedging interpretation of the manifesto was

---

[23] Joshi, *For the Final Bid* . . . , pp. 1–100.
[24] *Ibid.*, p. 34.
[25] *Ibid.*, p. 90.

an adjustment to the views of the English-speaking urban intelligentsia whose sense of the country's unity would naturally be stronger than that of the provincial intelligentsia or the illiterate peasantry. It should be pointed out, furthermore, that the constitutional arrangement which Joshi's interpretation seemed to suggest strongly resembled other compromise schemes then current in Indian political circles. For example, certain moderate Muslim leaders such as Sir Sikander Hyat Khan and Sir Muhammad Zafrulla Khan had proposed a novel type of confederation, to be united by a vaguely defined central agency which would possess only derived powers.[26] The [Tej Bahadur] Sapru Commission, and such independent British scholars as Sir Reginald Coupland, had put forward somewhat similar schemes for a loose federation under a central government possessing only very limited powers.[27] Such schemes had attracted much support, both British and Indian, as the only feasible alternative to partition, and the CPI, too, urged that its proposal was the middle way between the demands of the League and of the Congress.

However, the Communist proposal was distinguished from the others in that it was presented not merely as an expedient solution, but as the only just solution—on the assumption that the linguistic nationalities were entitled to sovereignty not as a convenience but as a right. The CPI scheme saw the "national homelands" as the only natural basis of political organization.

In any event, in its mass campaigning the Party apparently disregarded Joshi's moderate interpretation and took the extremist tone of the manifesto itself. For though the CPI's campaign activities were in general small-scale and sporadic, its press accounts show that in some areas it concentrated intensively on regional particularism. In an appeal to Telugu-speaking voters in Madras State, for example, the CPI exhorted:

If you want to rescue one-third of your Telugu brothers and two-fifths of your land from the Nizam's gulami [corruption] to build an independent VISHAL ANDHRA [Greater Andhra] of all the Andhra people then you MUST vote Communist, for our Party alone has inscribed Vishal Andhra on our banner and is fighting for it.[28]

Another facet of the CPI's campaign was apparently an effort to restore its reputation as a militant anti-imperialist force—a reputation which had been severely damaged by the CPI's support of the British war effort in India. The Communists had been clearly on the de-

---

[26] Coupland, *India: A Restatement,* pp. 271–272.

[27] *Ibid.,* pp. 266–271. See also P. N. Masaldan, *Evolution of Provincial Autonomy in India, 1858 to 1950* (Bombay: Hind Kitabs Ltd., 1953), pp. 174–176.

[28] *People's Age,* IV (March 17, 1946), p. 3. Emphasis in original.

fensive against popular hostility, which was shown not only by the
demand that the CPI be expelled from the Congress, but in violent
attacks upon Party members and offices, especially in Bombay. In
September, 1945, the Party press reported that CPI members, selling
the *People's War* on the streets, were being assaulted by organized
gangs; a week later when Communists tried to join a Congress-spon-
sored public meeting, a riot ensued.[29] In November and again in January crowds had attacked the Party's offices in Bombay, throwing stones
at Party members and damaging equipment in its printing plant.[30]
The Calcutta office was also attacked.

Soli Batliwala (formerly on the Central Committee) claimed after
his defection that in some instances these assaults were provoked by
the Communists themselves who threw stones into crowds innocently
gathered near Party offices; on the balcony of the building which housed
the Bombay headquarters, he said, the Party kept a large emergency
supply of stones and empty bottles.[31]

But the CPI insisted that it was the victim of Congress persecution,
and in March, 1946, Joshi issued a statement claiming that "today
the whole country knows that it is the Congressmen who are beating
up the Communists and not the other way around." He instructed
Party members to defend themselves "with every weapon available,"
warning that "any comrade who comes back after receiving a beating
without giving hard blows in return will be classed as a coward and
expelled from the Party." [32]

To counteract popular animosity the CPI undertook an intensive
campaign to prove that the Party was the true heir of the revolutionary
tradition in India. To do this, it published a number of pamphlets
demonstrating that the CPI was the ultimate haven of certain terrorist
heroes of the earlier decades of nationalism, and that therefore the
Party was the "rightful heir of their glorious revolutionary heritage." [33] The Party boasted that many members of famous terrorist
groups—including the Chittagong Armory Raiders and other Bengali
organizations, the Ghadr Party of Punjab, and Bhagat Singh's Hin-

[29] *People's War*, IV (Sept. 9, 1945), p. 5, and (Sept. 16, 1945), p. 4.

[30] *Ibid.* (Nov. 18, 1945), p. 4, and (Jan. 27, 1946), p. 3.

[31] Soli Batliwala, *Facts Versus Forgery* (Bombay: National Youth Pub., 1946),
pp. 16–17.

[32] *People's Age*, IV (March 3, 1946), p. 5.

[33] Niranjan Sen, *Bengal's Forgotten Warriors* (Bombay: People's Publishing House,
1945), back cover. This is one of a series which included Kalpana Dutt, *Chittagong
Armoury Raiders: Reminiscences;* Ajoy Kumar Ghosh, *Bhagat Singh and His Comrades, by One of Their Colleagues;* Niranjan Sen, *Bengal's Forgotten Warriors;* and
Randhir Singh, *The Ghadar Heroes; Forgotten Story of the Punjab Revolutionaries
of 1914–15.*

dustan Socialist Republican Association—had joined the CPI while
in prison. Indeed, at the time these pamphlets were published there
were "jail units" of the CPI, the most important of which was a special
cell called the "Communist Consolidation" made up of former terrorists then incarcerated in the penal colony on the Andaman Islands.

According to the CPI these terrorist martyrs had turned from
normal nationalist politics to terrorism only because of their frustration in the Congress noncoöperation movements; their conversion to
communism, said the Party, represented a still higher stage of political "maturity," Writing on the Chittagong Armory Raiders, for example, Joshi said:

> To read her own story [that of Kalpana Dutt, one of the Raiders] is to understand
> a living phase of our national movement, how it was that in the thirties the vast
> majority of the terrorist detenus and prisoners became Communist. Their coming
> under the banner of our Party was for them at once an easy and a difficult step
> to take. It was easy because in the policy and practice of our Party they saw the
> more scientific and successful struggle for their revolutionary dreams. It was
> difficult because they had to live down illusions and see through their own heads
> where they had gone wrong and where they had to correct themselves to be able
> to continue fighting the country's battle to which they had pledged themselves
> in their teens. These reminiscences reveal how terrorism was the infant as Com-
> munism is the mature stage of their revolutionary lives.[34]

Many of these "political prisoners" were still in prison, and although
an earlier CPI campaign to secure their release had received wide
popular support and the approval of such leaders as Gandhi, Nehru,
and Rabindranath Tagore, a new campaign launched in 1945 had
been much less successful, receiving only scattered support from lesser
Congress and Muslim League personalities and a few well-known
journalists, intellectuals, and artists.[35]

The fact that the Party sought to legitimatize itself by identifying
with the "revolutionary heritage" of terrorism does not imply that
the Party itself contemplated an imminent resort to violence. On the
contrary, when a dramatic outbreak of violence with obvious revolutionary potentialities did occur—the February, 1946, naval mutiny—
the Party was at pains to disavow any responsibility for it and to preserve the peace.

Indian naval personnel, mutinying against their British officers,
had succeeded in gaining control of a few ships and shore establish-
ments, and the imperial government was confronted with the ominous
phenomenon of destroyers and lesser naval vessels sailing from port

---

[34] Kalpana Dutt, *Chittagong Armoury* . . . , pp. 3-4. Kalpana Dutt is P. C. Joshi's
wife.

[35] Niranjan Sen, *Bengal's Forgotten Warriors*, pp. 91-93.

to port under hostile command and occasionally even shelling British-controlled shore positions. Sympathy strikes spread throughout India, extending even to the Indian personnel of the Royal Air Force.[36] But the central leadership of the CPI conspicuously refrained from encouraging violence; it merely urged all parties to unite in rousing public support for certain of the mutineers' demands—better living conditions and more privileges. Local Party units in the port cities where popular feeling ran high no doubt fretted at such moderation. But though a number of Communists among the naval personnel had taken an important part in the mutiny, the central leadership declared, in the official government inquiry held several months later, that the Party had played no role in organizing the rebellion and that Communist participants had acted strictly "on their own." [37]

In the judgment of an Indian Socialist critic of the CPI, Madhu Limaye, the Communist leadership was "confused and bewildered" in the face of the rising fever of popular discontent; committed to a collaborationist line, the Party was slow to detect, much less to seize, opportunities for more militant action. According to Limaye, it "reluctantly followed in the wake of these demonstrations, appealing for the creation of a United Front." [38]

In the early postwar period, then, the CPI was seeking not revolution but respectability in the Indian body politic. It apparently saw the elections as an important means to this end, and it took considerable satisfaction in its right to participate as a legal party. But it was most conciliatory toward the Congress and the League. For a total of 1,585 provincial legislative seats, the Party put up only 108 candidates; and it announced that where there was no Communist candidate the CPI would support the Congress candidates for general seats, and the Muslim League candidates for Muslim seats.[39] Thus the CPI gave further notice that it accepted the communal differential in legislative representation and that it regarded the League as the authentic spokesman of the Muslim community—a gesture hardly likely to endear it to the Congress.

The CPI had publicly declared that it expected to win twenty-five seats in the provincial legislatures; in fact it won only eight seats,

---

[36] For an account of the mutiny and the accompanying disturbances, see Nripendra Nath Mitra, ed., *The Indian Annual Register, 1946* (Calcutta: The Annual Register Office, 1947), I, 285–329.

[37] *Towards a People's Navy* (Bombay: People's Publishing House, n.d. [1946?]), p. 18.

[38] Madhu Limaye, *Communist Party: Facts and Fiction* (Hyderabad: Chetana Prakashan Ltd., 1951), p. 54.

[39] See "Election Policy of Indian Communists," *People's War*, IV (Oct. 14, 1945), pp. 5 ff.

representing a total of 666,723 votes. Its victories were confined to four states (Bengal, Bombay, Madras, and Orissa), and seven of the eight contests it won were for seats reserved for labor representatives. The CPI won only 2½ per cent of the total popular vote, and the Congress and the Muslim League overwhelmingly dominated the election scene.[40]

Nevertheless, the CPI was established as the third-ranking party in terms of the popular vote, and this achievement was the more encouraging in view of one serious obstacle it had faced: the conservative bias of the narrowly restricted electorate. Only about 14 per cent of the adult population was enfranchised in the provincial elections, the primary qualifications being based on property and income.[41] Moreover, according to a contemporary commentator, had a system of proportional representation been followed, the CPI would have won not eight, but fifty-one seats.[42]

Contesting an election for the first time and under serious handicaps the CPI might well have taken encouragement from its showing. Such a showing might have seemed, furthermore, to confirm the wisdom of Joshi's postwar line. However, other influences were at work that would soon produce dramatic changes in CPI policy.

Direct International Guidance

Until March, 1946, international Communist publications, Russian and British, had furnished the CPI with comparatively little useful guidance. But in March, R. Palme Dutt, the British CP official who served as the principal mentor of Indian Communism, arrived in India. Accompanying the British government's Cabinet Mission as a special correspondent for the London *Daily Worker,* he was on hand to guide the CPI through the critical months of the negotiations for a general political settlement with Indian nationalism.

Dutt's account of his Indian visit was published in his journal, *Labour Monthly,* as a lengthy series of "travel notes." At the outset, according to these notes, Dutt apparently confirmed the correctness of the current CPI strategy—collaboration of all anti-imperialist, anti-feudal classes in a "unified national front"—but suggested important tactical adjustments. Though he subscribed to a variety of Congress-League-Communist united front, in elaborating on this he urged most

---

[40] For a summary of election results, see Mitra, ed., *The Indian Annual Register, 1946,* I, 229–232. For a Socialist analysis of the election, see Asoka Mehta, *The Political Mind of India* (Bombay: The Socialist Party, 1952), Appendix IV, pp. 82–89.

[41] Masaldan, *Evolution of Provincial Autonomy* . . . , p. 109.

[42] Mehta, *The Political Mind of India,* p. 89.

emphatically—and this was the crux of his advice to the CPI—that there be a from-above alliance between the Communists and the Congress. Deploring the split between them, he wrote, "It is to be hoped that this breach may be overcome at the earliest possible moment, in view of the paramount importance of national unity in the coming period." [43]

Moreover, he described the Congress in the most sympathetic terms, reminiscent of the mood of the late 1930's, pointing out that the Congress "has a long tradition as the main uniting body of all sections of Indian progressive nationalism" and that it enjoyed the support of "the overwhelming majority of the Indian people." Though he noted that the Congress was increasingly influenced by big Indian capitalism, he did not, at this point, challenge the patriotism of the latter: they wished, he said, to "break the stranglehold of British monopoly," and to pursue "large-scale industrial development under a National Government." [44]

Dutt labored personally to effect a Congress-Communist reconciliation. In a dramatic move, he broached the problem directly, not only to Gandhi and Nehru, but to other Congress leaders such as Sardar Vallabhbhai Patel and S. K. Patil who were noted for their hostility to communism. In his account of these interviews he stated that he invariably stressed the necessity of a rapprochement with the CPI. To Gandhi he expressed the hope that existing differences could be overcome, and he sought to dispel the prevailing idea that the Communists advocated "secret force,"—an idea which, according to Gandhi, was an "impassable barrier" between the two parties. Of his interview with Patel, Dutt reported that the "iron man" of the Congress organization "expressed full friendliness to the desirability of reconciliation with the Communists and letting the past difficulties be buried." [45]

Dutt went further and pressed his Indian comrades to modify their tactics in order to propitiate the Congress—most importantly, to extricate themselves from their position of open support to the idea of Pakistan. "The unity of India is desirable from a progressive point of view," he declared, "and partition would be a reactionary step." [46] He described the Muslim League's demand for Pakistan as a "reactionary" tactic and explicitly stated that the CPI must "distinguish"

---

[43] R. Palme Dutt, "India and Pakistan," *Labour Monthly*, XXVIII (March, 1946), p. 92.

[44] *Ibid.*, pp. 91–92.

[45] Dutt, "Travel Notes Number 2," *Labour Monthly*, XXVIII (June, 1946), pp. 185, 188.

[46] Dutt, *Freedom for India* (London: The Communist Party of Great Britain, 1946), p. 15.

its policy from that of the League. The CPI, he continued, must make it clear that self-determination for the seventeen "nationalities" of India was not the same as the League's demand for a single Muslim state.[47]

Furthermore, Dutt made a constitutional proposal which was in flat contradiction to the election manifesto's demand for seventeen sovereign states based on linguistic entities. Ignoring the CPI scheme for a confederation of seventeen constituent assemblies which would send plenipotentiary representatives to a central body, Dutt proposed a central Constituent Assembly, directly elected by the people, with "sovereign" power to determine the constitutional framework of India. Before the convening of such an assembly, Dutt said, the British should turn over their power to a provisional Indian government to be composed of representatives of the Congress and of the League on a parity basis or, failing this, of representatives from the Congress alone.[48] Thus, he clearly indicated his partiality for the Congress.

In Dutt's view, then, the CPI must advocate unity, at least for the time being. That the CPI's advocacy of unity was, however, to be more a matter of appearance than of reality, Dutt hinted elsewhere in his comments. For though he indicated at one point that the ideal constitutional settlement would provide for an "All-India Union," he added that "we do not predetermine the question" of partition. "In the event of a united demand from the Congress and the Muslim League for more than one Constituent Assembly [for India and Pakistan]," he said, it "should be accepted automatically." [49] In other words the CPI should appear to be neutral, urging unity but not altogether rejecting partition, and should await the outcome of the political contest between the Congress and the League.

The first visible fruit of Dutt's counsel appeared on April 15, in the form of a CPI memorandum to the Cabinet Mission. It was equivocal: while it gave lip service to the right of self-determination, including "sovereignty" for the "nationalities" of India, it proposed that a single central Constituent Assembly be directly elected to settle the constitutional problems. The memorandum omitted any mention of Pakistan and stressed unity, declaring that the CPI "is firmly convinced that the best interests of the Indian masses will be served by their remaining together in one common Union." In the meantime, it said, the British should hand over power to a provisional Indian

---

[47] Dutt, "India and Pakistan," pp. 88–89.
[48] *Ibid.*, pp. 92–93.
[49] *Ibid.*, p. 93.

government constituted by Congress and the League on the basis of parity.[50]

Thus, with this one pronouncement, the CPI abruptly retreated from the formulations of the election manifesto and withdrew from its advocacy of confederation. Dutt himself patronizingly commended this performance: the memorandum was, he said, "a clear, practical, constructive, and (what is less usual for Communist publications here) concise document." Most significantly, he remarked that it "kills stone-dead" the "myth" that the CPI supported the League demand for Pakistan [51]—thus, perhaps, revealing the memorandum's central purpose.

Communism's Reaction to the Cabinet Mission Plan

After about two months' intensive negotiation with the Indian leaders, the British Cabinet Mission conceded its failure to obtain an agreement from the Congress or the Muslim League. The mission therefore issued its own plan, which was published on May 16, 1946. The plan provided for a federal system with a weak central government that would possess authority only in the fields of foreign affairs, communication, and defense; the remaining powers would be vested in the provincial governments. It also provided for an intermediate level of government based on regional groupings of provinces, corresponding roughly to the Hindu-majority and Muslim-majority areas—an arrangement which might satisfy the Muslim minority in lieu of actual partition.[52] In effect, however, the plan allowed partition, since it granted to each province the right to secede after a stated period.

Though both parties made use of those parts of the plan that they considered advantageous, it was soon apparent that neither the Congress nor the League was satisfied with it. The atmosphere grew increasingly bitter; when, in August, the League sponsored a "direct action day" in Calcutta, bitterness culminated in the outbreak of communal violence.

During this critical period the Soviet spokesman on India continued to temporize. The sparse commentary that did appear in Russian journals confined itself to describing the Cabinet Mission plan as a new imperialist maneuver designed to strengthen the British position in India, and to noting that the progressive wing of the Congress opposed the plan and recognized that it would not bring independence.[53]

---

[50] The text of the memorandum is in Mitra, ed., *Indian Annual Register, 1946*, I, 220–222.

[51] Dutt, "Travel Notes Number 2," pp. 189–190.

[52] The Plan is summarized in Masaldan, *Evolution of Provincial* . . . , pp. 176–178.

[53] "A New British Plan for India," *New Times* (June 1, 1946), p. 20.

It was left to Dutt, on the scene, to provide the CPI with more useful guidance. Dutt's "travel notes" show that after the Cabinet Mission failed to secure a settlement he began to have second thoughts on the Indian situation. He appeared to be increasingly sceptical as to the good faith of the Indian capitalist class, whose patriotism he had earlier affirmed. Reporting an interview with J. D. R. Tata, one of India's leading industrialists, he declared that Tata's views showed "how strongly Indian Big Business looks to the United States capitalism as the model, and how deeply anti-Soviet propaganda has bitten." [54] Moreover, he now hinted that the increasing influence of big business was tainting the Congress, and he noted that Tata had recently moved from a nonpolitical position to "a more open Congress orientation." [55]

In analyzing the Cabinet Mission plan Dutt declared that it was a maneuver devised, primarily, in response to the new "popular upsurge" that was taking place in India and indeed throughout the world. He did not explicitly define this "upsurge," nor did he indicate what action, if any, the CPI should take. But that he now had in mind a new approach was revealed by one of his last acts before leaving India: his emphatic endorsement of Sheikh Abdullah and his "Quit Kashmir" movement.

Sheikh Abdullah was the leader of the National Conference, the most important political organization of Kashmir. It was not affiliated with either the League or the Congress, but although the majority of the Conference membership was Muslim, its leadership was pro-Congress. Sheikh Abdullah, however, was predisposed to militant action, and while the Cabinet Mission was negotiating with the Congress leadership in India, Abdullah had launched a vigorous mass-action campaign. Under the slogan "Quit Kashmir," it was directed against both the princely autocracy and the imperialist authorities of Kashmir. Soon after arriving in India, Dutt had been in correspondence with Abdullah, and it is possible that Dutt and the Indian Communists participated in the planning of the campaign.

In any event, in this movement—half-way house between revolutionary action and the Congress Party's policy of restraint—Dutt apparently found a model for future Indian Communist action. After the launching of the movement and Abdullah's subsequent imprisonment, Dutt praised him in his travel notes as the "most courageous and outstanding representative of the States peoples," [56] and in June Dutt made the long trip to Kashmir and talked with Abdullah in the courtroom where he was standing trial. Dutt even met the under-

---

[54] Dutt, "Travel Notes Number 4," *Labour Monthly*, XXVIII (Sept., 1946), p. 287.
[55] *Ibid.*, p. 287.
[56] Dutt, "Travel Notes Number 3," *Labour Monthly*, XXVIII (July, 1946), p. 219.

ground leaders of the National Conference—a remarkable feat for a British journalist. In his account of the Kashmir trip Dutt declared that the "Quit Kashmir" movement was "the strongest and most militant of any Indian state," and that it should receive the "fullest possible backing." The essence of Dutt's view was summed up, perhaps, in the declaration that Kashmir was "the political storm-center of the Indian fight for freedom." [57]

That these were not idle words was made clear by later events. On his way back from Kashmir to England at the end of July, Dutt stopped in Bombay for a brief conference with the CPI Central Committee, which was then in session; [58] soon after, the Committee adopted the so-called August Resolution,—a drastic though confused reorientation of policy.[59] Evidently the radical wing of the Party, led by Adhikari, Ranadive, and Ghosh, had found in Dutt's view at least partial support for their more militant line and had therefore been able to press it on the Central Committee more effectively than in the past. But in fact, as the August Resolution shows, the radical group went much further than Dutt had gone and it must therefore have represented a strong current within the Party itself.

The August Resolution was an undigested mixture of radical and moderate views, an obvious and uneasy compromise between the Joshi and leftist factions. On balance the leftist view prevailed, though it was weakened by serious contradictions. One passage of the resolution in particular exemplifies the ambivalence of the document. It begins with a seemingly innocent statement, representing no more than the Joshi line as modified by Dutt:

> The National Congress represents the main stream of the independence movement of the country.
> The Muslim League has behind it the bulk of the anti-imperialist freedom-loving Muslim masses.
> And the Communist Party leads the bulk of the organized workers and peasants.
> A joint front of the three main patriotic parties—Congress, League, Communist Party, and other popular patriotic parties is thus essential for developing such a final struggle and guaranteeing its success.

Having dispensed with the amenities, however, the passage shifts its tone; it attacks both Congress and League leaderships, representing

---

[57] Dutt, "Travel Notes Number 5," *Labour Monthly*, XXVIII (Oct., 1946), pp. 321–324.

[58] *Ibid.*, back cover.

[59] The following quotations from the "August Revolution" are taken from the official version published in pamphlet form: *For the Final Assault; Tasks of the Indian People in the Present Phase of Indian Revolution* (Bombay: People's Publishing House, 1946), 18 pp.

the Indian bourgeoisie, as "compromising." A joint front can only
be built, it declares

by making the masses move for it in spite of the leaderships.

It is built in the measure that the Party is able to establish and extend its political leadership in the ever-widening sweep of common mass struggles, in the measure that the Party is able to dissillusion the masses about the sectarian, disruptive
and compromising policy of the leaderships, and rouse in them the will to fight
against the British Imperialist Plan and for the realization of the essential tasks
of the program of National Democratic Revolution.

The resolution itself concludes by calling for "bold and militant"
leadership of working-class action, leading to a political general strike
as part of the struggle for power; for a more powerful peasant movement; and for "broad-based struggles" on the order of Kashmir in all
princely states. The CPI must, it declares, "come forward as the organizer of this new phase of the Indian Revolution and lead it to
victory." Thus the word "revolution" resumed its place in the Indian
Communist lexicon.

Indeed, the key to the new policy was the assumption that the CPI
faced a "revolutionary upsurge." The contrast between the resolution's
term, "revolutionary upsurge" and Dutt's "popular upsurge" is an
index of the difference between the two lines.

On the one hand, then, the resolution asserted as its predominant
theme that the CPI must now capture leadership and carry the anti-
imperialist revolution to its fullfillment by opposing bourgeois nationalism, which had revealed that it was willing to compromise with
imperialism and had thus gone over to reaction. This assertion was
sound, old-fashioned leftism reminiscent of the 1928–1934 line; it implied an anticapitalist strategy, on the assumption that a new stage of
the Indian revolution had been attained. The resolution dropped the
solicitous tone toward the bourgeoisie that had distinguished earlier
policy statements.

But, on the other hand, this radical theme was damagingly qualified.
First, there were scattered suggestions that the bourgeois nationalist
leadership should be influenced rather than swept aside, implying that
the leaders were not reactionary but merely vacillating and still
amenable to reason. Moreover, in sometimes identifying the Congress
and League leadership, not with the bourgeoisie as such, but only with
the "big bourgeoisie," the resolution implied that only the latter was
reactionary. Both of these implications were consistent with the anti-
imperialist strategy, and would require a continued appeal to the
bourgeoisie.

In short, the August Resolution represented remarkably ambiguous theorizing, and the CPI could scarcely set a stable course on such a basis. Until the CPI could come to a decision concerning the fundamental strategic question—that is, define its attitude vis-à-vis the bourgeoisie—it could not formulate a coherent program for action.

Though it is unlikely that Dutt, a proficient theorist, had a hand in the final version of this document, his influence was apparent at several points. The resolution forwarded the attempt, begun at his behest, to dissociate the CPI from the Muslim' League's demand for Pakistan, for it declared that this demand reflected "the policy of the Muslim bourgeois feudal vested interests who are seeking a compromise with imperialism for a share of administration in a divided India." The resolution asserted that the masses of people supporting the Congress "rightly oppose the partition of India on a religious and undemocratic basis and correctly desire a single Union." It continued to call in vague terms for "self-determination" for the nationalities, but said that the Muslim masses should agree to Congress-League unity "without making the acceptance of Pakistan a precondition." It set the goal of "a voluntary union."

Dutt's counsel was evident at still another point: the resolution proposed mass action *à la* Kashmir in all states, thus indicating that the CPI had adopted the "Quit Kashmir" movement as a model for political action. Indeed, a few weeks after the publication of the August Resolution, the Party issued another policy statement that declared Kashmir to be the "hub of today's freedom battle" and asserted that "a *new* form of struggle" had begun there. The statement criticized the Congress leadership, including Nehru, for attempting to restrain Sheikh Abdullah; it termed Nehru's cautionary advice to Abdullah "a terrible tragedy"; and it asserted that Kashmir could not wait since it was "at war." [60]

Disruption of the CPI

The August Resolution represented only a partial—and temporary—victory for the radicals, for P. C. Joshi and his adherents continued to promulgate their moderate line. As Joshi admitted in a later statement of self-criticism, he "seized upon the weaknesses in the August 1946 resolution to work back to the old line." [61] The split in the Party grew more severe, and by the end of 1946 the central office ap-

[60] Romesh Chandra, *Salute to Kashmir* (Bombay: People's Publishing House, 1946), pp. 22–23.

[61] This statement is from Joshi's speech of recantation at the Second Congress of the CPI, 1948, and is given in: "Resolution of the Central Committee of the Communist Party of India on P. C. Joshi's Appeal Against Expulsion," June 5, 1950 [typed copy] p. 4. This is an unpublished inner-Party document.

peared to be thoroughly uncoördinated. The interim government, headed by Nehru, had taken office in September, and as the Party struggled to define an attitude toward it, contradictory statements followed one another in quick succession.

In an official policy statement by Adhikari, the radical faction had its way; the statement condemned the nationalist leadership as "appeasers of vested interests," and declared that the CPI must pave the way for a country-wide general strike, and must build the "revolutionary unity of the Indian people for the final fight for Independence and Democracy." Thus, in effect, it proposed an all-out fight against the interim government.[62]

Yet almost at the same time the Party republished Joshi's mild memorandum to the Cabinet Mission, written the previous April—a document which should have been rendered obsolete by the August Resolution.[63] Furthermore, at about this time Somnath Lahiri, the Communist member of the new Constituent Assembly, tabled a draft resolution calling upon the Indian people to "stand behind" the interim government which, he said, enjoyed "the support of the overwhelming majority of our people" and which should convert itself into a provisional government of independent India.[64] Adhikari himself, in a preface which accompanied the Party's publication of Lahiri's resolution, apparently capitulated to the moderate faction. For though he reiterated that the nationalist leadership was "appeasing the British imperialists," he accepted Joshi's assumption that it was still amenable to influence, and affirmed that the Constituent Assembly, representing the two major parties and the minorities, could "become the instrument for asserting and expressing the will of the Indian people." [65]

Adhikari's capitulation apparently reflected a general tendency within the Party, for in the following months the Joshi line of "loyal opposition" prevailed. Nevertheless, the leftist view occasionally manifested itself when local CPI units, bursting the confines of the moderate line, flared into militant action. The Madras unit, in particular, opposed the new Congress government of that province so vehemently that CPI-inspired rioting in a number of cities, including Golden Rock, Coimbatore, Madura, and Vikramsingapuram, resulted in the

[62] G. Adhikari, *Resurgent India at the Crossroads; 1946 in Review* (Bombay: People's Publishing House, n.d. [1947?]), 24 pp.

[63] *Declaration of Independence* (Bombay: People's Publishing House, n.d. [1946?]), pp. 11–16. The preface to this pamphlet is dated December 8, 1946; it is likely that it was published in that month.

[64] The text of the resolution is given in *ibid.*, pp. 5–10.

[65] *Ibid.*, pp. 2–4.

arrest of 550 workers and trade-union leaders—among them many local Communist officers.[66] In January, 1947, the Madras government declared the Party illegal in that state, and detained 160 more Communists.[67]

Indeed, the militant leftist viewpoint was so strong in one area as to produce a genuinely revolutionary situation. In Hyderabad state, notably in the Telugu-speaking Nalgonda and Warangal districts (known as Telengana), a revolutionary peasant movement had slowly been forming, in large part led by local Communist leaders. During 1947 guerrilla warfare gradually spread, and the situation steadily grew more serious. Though Adhikari, at one point, hailed this movement as "shaking for the first time that main bastion of the feudal order in India to its very foundations," [68] the central CPI leadership on the whole ignored this revolutionary opportunity.

Indeed, the Party maintained its loyal opposition to the interim government despite hostile action by that government. Indian Communists gained access to the "top secret" British plans for military action in the event of serious strikes or insurrection, and in September, 1946, the CPI published these plans in the Party press.[69] That the plans were genuine and their disclosure a serious breach was clearly indicated by the drastic police action which followed throughout the country. On January 14, 1947, raids were conducted in seventeen cities during which Party offices, front-organization offices, and the homes of important Party members were searched, presumably in an attempt to discover what other secret documents the Party might possess. According to CPI accounts, thirty-six Party leaders were arrested.[70] The Communists proclaimed their own guilt; in a public statement, Joshi declared, "It is true that we exposed certain secret military plans made by the British Army GHQ and its various commands." [71] The CPI claimed the police repression was approved by the Indian home minister, Sardar Vallabhbhai Patel, and by certain of the provincial Congress governments; it called upon the interim government to clear itself of any responsibility for the "persecution" and to punish the

---

[66] *People's Age,* VI (Sept. 14, 1947), p. 8.

[67] *Ibid.,* V (Feb. 2, 1947), p. 12.

[68] G. Adhikari, *Resurgent India . . .* , p. 14.

[69] The plans were disclosed in a series of articles entitled "Patriot's Notebook," published in *People's Age* between April and August, 1946; they were reprinted in pamphlet form in September under the title *Operation Asylum* (Bombay: People's Publishing House, 1947).

[70] *"Operation Asylum" and You* (Bombay: People's Publishing House, 1947), pp. 22–25. Those arrested included Adhikari and Romesh Chandra, editor and subeditor, of *People's Age.*

[71] *Ibid.,* p. 14.

British military authorities implicated in the disclosed plans. But it directed its main attack against the British authorities, claiming that it was they who had "initiated, planned, and organized" the raids. This police action was designed, said the CPI, to eliminate the most militant section of the nationalist movement, in order "to better combat the Congress-led movement later." It specifically commended the "progressive declarations of the Congress leadership" in the Constituent Assembly, and called upon all patriotic Indians to join the "common cause" against the British.[72]

This repression, added to the inner-Party schism, further crippled the CPI in the remaining months of India's rush toward independence. Through the crucial events of early 1947, the Communists were strangely subdued. Instead of addressing themselves to the central questions of India's future, they directed their attention to minor peripheral issues and events. During this time, the Party conspicuously refrained from issuing a major policy statement on the constitutional problem, although the election manifesto of nearly two years earlier, the last such statement, was presumably outdated.

In February, 1947, Britain announced that it would grant Indian independence no later than June, 1948, and embarked upon renewed negotiations with Indian nationalist leaders. The only response by the CPI which demonstrated a sense of urgency to match the real situation was related to the problem of the princely states, to which its attention had been turned by Dutt. Now the Party professed to see not an opportunity for revolution but a danger of British domination in the states. The British plan, declared the Party, was to encourage the more powerful princes to remain independent of both India and Pakistan, and then to convert their states to a "Princistan" which would provide economic and military bases for British control of the subcontinent.[73]

But even here, the CPI expressed confidence that the Congress leadership could be brought around to a correct policy for coping with the situation. The Congress, Joshi said, had been guilty of "appeasing the princes," but popular pressure "can and must decisively influence it." [74]

Throughout these months the CPI played the role of friend and gentle critic vis-à-vis the Congress. In discussing the United Nations, it highly praised the Indian delegation, headed by Madame Vijaya-

[72] *Ibid.*, pp. 4–7.
[73] *Down with Autocracy: Tasks Before the States' Peoples Movement* (Bombay: People's Publishing House, n.d. [1947?]), pp. 3–5. See also Romesh Chandra, *Princistan —Imperialism's Nest for Tomorrow* (Bombay: People's Publishing House, 1947), 15 pp.
[74] *Down With Autocracy . . .* , pp. 4, 6.

lakshmi Pandit and made up chiefly of Congress members: the delegation, said the CPI, was "truly representative of our country and our people, and spoke up, not at Britain's command, but in India's interests." [75] Again, in a series of statements on the situation in various provinces, the Party expressed its confidence in the Congress. These statements were usually issued in the form of memoranda to the Congress Working Committee from the various provincial Communist committees; they accused the provincial governments of "sanctioning police repression" or of allowing "free reign" to "the greedy vested interests," and appealed for the intervention of the national Congress leadership. And the memoranda invariably implied that the Congress could be persuaded to put things right.[76] One memorandum, for example, asserted, "We expect that a popular Government whose head is Pandit Nehru himself, should put a stop to this policy of the Delhi bureaucracy." [77]

Perhaps the best index to the mildness of the CPI's approach to the whole Indian situation was the fact that a statement by the Andhra Communist Committee did not even mention the peasant revolts in Telengana, and took pains to show that the Communist campaign in Andhra was, with one minor exception, completely nonviolent.[78]

Thus the CPI, in this period, tended to disassociate itself from the major problems of Indian independence by turning to international issues on the one hand, and to local issues on the other; but in both spheres, where it was not openly friendly to the Congress it was at least not irreconcilable.

Soviet Procrastination

The CPI's pronouncements in the first half of 1947 clearly indicated that P. C. Joshi had reasserted his control over the Party, though this had substantially reduced its dynamism. In his victory over the radical faction in the Party, it was probably of crucial importance that the "left opposition" found no further support in either the British

---

[75] Mohan Kumaramangalam, *India and UNO* (Bombay: People's Publishing House, 1947), introduction.

[76] Pamphlets included in the series are as follows: Andhra Committee, Communist Party of India, *Zemindar-Police Terror in Andhra;* S. A. Dange, *Under Congress Ministry! Blood Bath at Amalner;* Delhi Committee, Communist Party of India, *Who Rules in Delhi?;* Karnatak Provincial Committee, Communist Party of India, *The "Goondas" of Karnatak.* These were published by the People's Publishing House, Bombay, at the end of 1946 and the beginning of 1947. Another similar pamphlet, entitled *Travancore in Travail,* was issued by the Travancore Defence Committee, Bombay.

[77] *Who Rules in Delhi?,* p. 5.

[78] *Zemindar-Police Terror in Andhra,* p. 9.

or the Russian Communist pronouncements for taking up the banner of revolution.

The British Communist Party was all but silent: during the year following his visit to India, Dutt's *Labour Monthly* contained nothing of significance on India. The Russian authorities, apparently postponing judgment, were only slightly more helpful. In October, 1946, a major statement on the Asian situation by E. Zhukov had noted the "upsurge of the national-liberation movement," but it did not in any way suggest that the situation in India was revolutionary. Zhukov did little more than repeat the themes sounded by R. Palme Dutt in June, ignoring the CPI's August Resolution; and he concentrated most of his attention to an analysis of the British imperial policy. Its essential tactic toward the nationalist movements throughout Asia, he said, was to isolate the more militant elements and then strike a bargain with the right-wing forces. Thus, he said, the imperialist powers "utilized the steadily strengthened reactionary tendencies of Kemalism in Turkey, the influence of Gandhism among the Indian national bourgeoisie, the treachery of the counter-revolutionary right wing of the Kuomintang in China." [79]

Translated into more forthright language, this might be taken to imply that the British sought to make a bargain with the Gandhian right-wing element of the bourgeois National Congress, but Zhukov did not mention the Congress; and he did not amplify his statement beyond warning that the British imperialist policy was patterned on the relationship between the United States and the Philippines whereby the latter had received only formal independence while remaining under the economic and military control of the U.S. Moreover, Zhukov conspicuously failed to suggest that the Indian bourgeoisie, or even the right wing, was prepared to accept a "bargain" with British imperialism.

Later Soviet commentary contributed little toward filling in the gaps in Zhukov's statement, and for the most part offered not much more than a collection of clichés. But as events unfolded in India, Soviet spokesmen seemed to hint a certain warmth toward Nehru's interim government. As before, Dyakov commended Nehru as a "left-wing progressive" and noted that the Indian delegation to the United Nations included "some progressive leaders." [80] When diplomatic rela-

---

[79] E. Zhukov, "Velikaia oktiabr'skaia sotsialisticheskaia revoliutsiia i kolonial'nyi vostok" ["The Great October Socialist Revolution and the Colonial East"], *Bolshevik* (Oct., 1946), p. 43.

[80] A. Dyakov, "The Situation in India," *Soviet Press Translations*, Feb. 28, 1947, p. 6 (from *Pravda*, Oct. 21, 1946).

tions were established between India and the Soviet Union, early in
1947, the Soviet press hailed the occasion as "a sign that India is moving towards an independent policy." [81] Accounts by Soviet visitors to
India celebrated the friendship between the two countries; V. P. Volgin, returning from the All-India Scientific Conference, emphasized
the Indian government's friendship to Russia by relating that Nehru
had praised the flowering of science in the USSR. Moreover, Volgin
was able to boast that he and E. N. Pavlovsky received honorary degrees of doctor of science.[82]

More significant was the visit to India by E. Zhukov, himself, who
went as a delegate to the Inter-Asian Conference held in March-April,
1947. In general, Soviet commentary praised this conference for its
contribution to greater solidarity for genuine independence among the
Asian countries.[83] In his account of the trip, however, Zhukov gave
primary emphasis to the current CPI theme: that the British planned
to use the princely states as bases for maintaining their domination
over India. "Progressive circles" in India, he said, fear that Britain
could thus retain economic and military control even if formal independence were granted.[84]

Another Soviet comment referred to the possibility of "the dismemberment of India into a number of separate states." [85] The prospect
that the subcontinent might be fragmented in the course of attaining
independence thus received increasing emphasis in the Soviet view,
as it did in the Indian Communist pronouncements.

Apart from this, however, the Soviet interpretation of the Indian
scene continued to be noncommittal, merely posing the question
whether India would become "a genuinely independent, democratic
country," or a dependency like the Philippines.[86] An article by N.
Baltiisky, appearing at the beginning of June, referred to the necessity for a progressive policy on the part of the nationalist leaders, and
concluded: "Whether this is sufficiently understood by the present

---

[81] "Establishment of Soviet-Indian Diplomatic Relations," *New Times* (April 18,
1947), p. 15.
[82] "Eighteen Days in India," *Soviet Press Translations*, April 15, 1947, p. 11 (from
Izvestia, Feb. 2, 1947).
[83] I. Platov, "The Results of the Inter-Asian Conference," *Soviet Press Translations*,
Sept. 15, 1947, p. 95 (from *Izvestia*, May 31, 1947).
[84] E. Zhukov, "India: A Traveler's Impressions," *Soviet Press Translations*, II
(Sept. 15, 1947), pp. 100–101 (from *Pravda*, May 12 and 16, 1947).
[85] "One More Plan for India," *New Times* (March 7, 1947), p. 20.
[86] E. M. Lemin, *Britanskaia Imperiia* [British Empire], (Moscow: Izdatel'stvo
"Pravda," 1947), p. 31. This pamphlet is the verbatim report of a lecture of May 20,
1947.

shapers of Indian policy, by National Congress and Muslim League leaders, the near future will tell." [87]

The "near future" was nearer than Baltiisky knew, for within a week after the publication of his statement the long period of Soviet temporizing came to an abrupt end.

[87] N. Baltiisky, "Reply to Indian Readers," *New Times* (June 6, 1947), p. 19. For a fuller discussion of Soviet policy, see Gene D. Overstreet, *The Soviet View of India, 1945–1948* (M. A. Thesis, Columbia University, Political Science, 1953).

12 THE ROOTS OF INSURRECTION

In February, 1947, the British government had firmly committed itself to grant independence to India within sixteen months. The task of presiding over a final settlement was entrusted to Lord Louis Mountbatten, who was dispatched to India to replace Lord Wavell as viceroy. By May, it was clear that partition of the subcontinent could not be averted: [1] the Muslim League's demand for it was adamant; and the Congress leaders, in their public statements, wearily and bitterly revealed that they saw no alternative but to accept it. Mountbatten proceeded with urgent negotiations over the final details of transferring British power to the two governments.

In the first week of June, the so-called Mountbatten Plan was approved by the leaders of both Indian parties. [2] According to this settlement, the representatives of those areas that did not choose to join the existing Constituent Assembly of India could re-form into a "new and separate Constituent Assembly"—that is, Pakistan. On the day after the plan was published, it was announced that Britain would formally abdicate on August 15, little more than two months away. This afforded the Indian parties no further time for maneuver; the new dominions of India and Pakistan would be launched abruptly into an uncertain future.

---

[1] Alan Campbell-Johnson, *Mission With Mountbatten* (New York: E. P. Dutton and Co., 1953), chapters 4, 5, 6.

[2] The plan is contained in a statement by Prime Minister Attlee in the House of Commons, June 3, 1947. Reprinted in Harold Isaacs, *New Cycle in Asia* (New York: The Macmillan Co., 1947), pp. 137–143. Original in Cmd. 7136, H.M.S.O., London.

The Soviet Decision on Nehru

In the midst of this crescendo of events there were signs that a major change of policy for India might be under way in Moscow. The first intimation came in May, 1947, during the conference in which Soviet economists met to debate the views of Eugene Varga, as set forth in his recently published book.[3] In a chapter on the colonies, Varga had declared that they were becoming economically less dependent on the imperialist powers; he cited the fact that some of them had undergone substantial industrial growth and had, in a few instances, even become creditors of their imperialist rulers. This observation, which was realistic with respect to India, suggested that the colonies could achieve independence by an evolutionary process—heresy indeed. Like the decolonization theory attributed to M. N. Roy in an earlier decade, this view suffered stern Communist attack, and the meeting of Soviet economists was called, apparently at the behest of the Soviet leadership, to discredit Varga. He was condemned for his hint of an evolutionary perspective, and accused of neglecting to stress the need for revolutionary struggle in the colonies. Since, in fact, the British at that moment were preparing to surrender formal power in India, Soviet reëmphasis on revolution had an unreal but ominous ring.

Another intimation of a major change in policy lay in the initial Soviet response to the Mountbatten Plan: an article by Dyakov in *New Times*.[4] Denouncing the plan as a British maneuver calculated to perpetuate imperialist control of the subcontinent, he declared that the Indian leaders, in accepting it, had "abandoned their former position." They had done so, he said, because "the top levels of India's wealthy classes are exerting strong pressure on National Congress leaders and compelling them to agree to a compromise." Indian businessmen desired a bargain with imperialism, Dyakov said, whereby they would share the domestic market and avert revolution.

Here, then, was a hint that in the new Soviet view, the Congress represented reaction in India. But Dyakov did not expressly state this, and in fact he hedged his remarks significantly; at another point, in discussing the Congress decision to accept the plan, he said:

We still do not know what their motives were, but from the comments in the Indian press it can only be judged that certain political circles thought it better to consent without delay to at least a partial satisfaction of the demand for independence, rather than leave the whole question hanging in the air indefinitely.

[3] Frederick C. Barghoorn, "The Varga Discussion and Its Significance," *American Slavic and East European Review*, VII (Oct., 1948), pp. 223, 232.
[4] A. Dyakov, "The New British Plan for India," *New Times* (June 13, 1947), pp. 12–15.

From this passage it could be inferred that Dyakov assumed the good faith of at least some of the Congress leaders. Moreover, he commended Nehru's assertion that the Indian Constituent Assembly would act as a sovereign body and not be limited by the British proposals. The interpretation by Dyakov was plainly tentative; since he continued to assume that the Congress leadership included both progressive and reactionary wings, he could not clearly estimate the significance of the Congress decision.

This Soviet indecisiveness was, however, short-lived. In July there appeared an article on India by the ranking Soviet authority on Asia, E. Zhukov. This pronouncement signaled the birth of a new line, and with it the Soviet leadership declared cold war on the Nehru government.

Zhukov said outright that the leadership of the National Congress now represented the Indian big bourgeoisie (monopoly capitalism) and had gone over to reaction in agreeing to British terms for a political settlement.[5] The leadership had capitulated to imperialism, he said because the big bourgeoisie feared the masses more than they feared the British. They did not desire full independence, but instead were content to strike a mutually profitable deal with the British whereby formal independence would be qualified by continued imperialist economic and military connections.

The magnitude of the Soviet change of heart was perhaps best indicated by Zhukov's attitude toward Nehru himself. Formerly regarded as a progressive democrat, Nehru was now called a "rich man" and accused of moving to the right with such reactionary leaders as Patel. Nehru now supported the reactionary clique in its capitulation to imperialism, said Zhukov.

Zhukov declared, however, that the rank-and-file Congress membership still included progressive elements. Furthermore, he applied the same description to the Muslim League, asserting that though it was dominated by the reactionary big bourgeoisie, it included genuinely democratic elements. Thus he was neutral as regards the great debate between the Congress and the League. However, he implicitly approved partition with the remark that the idea of Pakistan had a different meaning for the Muslim masses than for the reactionary League leadership. Moreover, he specifically commended the CPI's program of self-determination for the "nationalities" of India, which would enable each linguistic group to join the federation of its choice or to remain independent.

---

[5] E. Zhukov, "K polozheniiu v Indii" [On the Situation in India], *Mirovoe khozia-istvo* . . . (July, 1947), pp. 3–14.

Another notable feature of Zhukov's pronouncement was his emphasis on the role of the working class, which, he said, was now more than ever the leading force in the anti-imperialist movement. As if to give further stress to the importance of the working class, Zhukov said that the peasantry by contrast was backward, being immobilized by illiteracy, the caste system, and the remnants of feudalism in the countryside.

In sum, then, Zhukov proposed the anti-imperialist strategy against imperialism and its allies, feudalism and monopoly capitalism. Though this strategy required an attack on Nehru's government, its identification of the government with the big bourgeoisie connoted a moderate program; that is, the united-front-from-below tactic designed for an appeal not only to the petty bourgeoisie, but to the middle bourgeoisie as well.

This new interpretation of the Indian scene, considered in the context of the international situation in mid-1947, was clearly tailored to the emerging cold-war policy of the USSR. Asserting that India would not in fact achieve real independence, the new line sought to mobilize Indian opinion against Western imperialism—that is, against Britain and America, the Soviet Union's antagonists in the cold war. Moreover, by assuming that only the big bourgeoisie of India had capitulated to imperialism, Zhukov's policy sought to draw the wavering bourgeoisie into the fold. The Soviet authorities might reasonably expect that British investment in India would continue to inhibit the expansion of Indian capital, and that therefore the Indian business class would continue to bear a grievance against imperialism; and in any event, they evidently thought that British influence would be perpetuated through the native princes—a situation which would keep anti-imperialist sentiment alive. The Communist movement could continue to utilize unsatisfied bourgeois nationalism even after formal power had been transferred to the new Indian governments.

The chief source of Zhukov's stand on India, then, was probably the desire to attract the widest possible support for the cold-war struggle against the Western powers. But that stand meant cold war on the Indian government, too.

Debate in the Communist Community

The Soviets had decided the question, for or against the Nehru government. But later events showed that they had not unanimously decided the underlying strategic question: for or against the bourgeoisie. This was a fundamental issue since it would determine the nature of the program by which the Communists would fight Nehru, but here there was sharp disagreement among the Soviet Indologists.

Documents published in Russia in 1949 show that the Soviet experts on India held a special session of the Academy of Sciences in June, 1947, to discuss the Indian situation.[6] The keynote statement was delivered by Zhukov. (Apparently, this speech formed the basis of the July, 1947, article by Zhukov, summarized above.) But Dyakov and Balabushevich, in their speeches, dissented fundamentally. Both declared that the Nehru government represented not only the big bourgeoisie, but the middle bourgeoisie as well, and that the latter, too, had turned reactionary.

According to Balabushevich, the partition of India was "the result of a deal of the Indian bourgeoisie and landlords with English imperialism." He declared: "The Indian bourgeoisie and the leadership of the National Congress have gone over completely to the camp of reaction and imperialism." Dyakov said that the partition of India demonstrated "that the Indian bourgeoisie, which plays a decisive role in the leadership of the Congress, came to a compromise based on the abandonment of a number of its own demands." The current situation, he declared, is a result of "the cupidity and treachery of the Indian bourgeoisie, which for the sake of its profits is prepared to sacrifice the independence of its country."

It should be noted that both Balabushevich and Dyakov condemned the Indian national leadership not only unqualifiedly, but retroactively. Balabushevich stated that the Congress had been revealed as "bankrupt" during the war, and that in the immediate postwar period "the reactionary policy of the National Congress and the Muslim League [had] only strengthened the position of British imperialism and permitted it to maneuver." In a similar vein, Dyakov asserted that the Congress interim government had begun to take a reactionary line in 1946, "coming openly to the defense of the interests of the Indian bourgeoisie." However, none of these interpretations had occurred to Soviet commentators at the time.

Balabushevich, like Zhukov, placed great emphasis on the role of the Indian working class in the national-liberation movement, and paid only brief, incidental attention to the peasantry. The working class has shown, he declared, that it has gained increasing influence

---

[6] *Uchenyi zapiski tikhookeanskogo instituta; Tom 2: Indiiskii sbornik* [Scholarly Papers of the Pacific Institute; Volume 2: Indian Collection] (Moscow: Izdatel'stvo akademii nauk SSSR, 1949), chapters 1, 2, 3. According to the introduction the paper by Zhukov had already been published. For a more detailed discussion of this debate and of postwar CPI policy, see John H. Kautsky, *Moscow and the Communist Party of India* (New York: The Technology Press of Massachusetts Institute of Technology and John Wiley and Sons, Inc., 1956), pp. 24 ff.

over the peasantry and petty bourgeoisie; he claimed that the peasantry was inspired by the struggles of the working class, and that it was most active where it had the closest contact with urban workers. And although he described at length such proletarian activity as the strikes of 1946 and 1947, he made virtually no mention of the Communist-led peasant uprising in South India, which had occurred during the same period. However, he terminated his remarks on the peasantry with a note of optimism, stating that such holidays as May Day and the anniversary of the October Revolution were "universally" celebrated in Indian villages.

At the conclusion of his speech, Balabushevich declared:

The toiling masses of India, under the leadership of the Indian working class and its party—the Communist Party of India—are conducting a resolute struggle against the reactionary bloc of imperialists, bourgeoisie, and landowners for complete independence, for liquidation of all remnants of feudalism, for people's democracy.[7]

In sum, Dyakov and Balabushevich expressed a strategic-tactical formula that diverged basically from the Zhukov line: in place of Zhukov's four-class strategy, against imperialism, feudalism, and monopoly capitalism, they proposed the three-class strategy against capitalism. Whereas Zhukov's formula called for a moderate program as the basis for opposing the Nehru government, that of Dyakov and Balabushevich required a very radical program aimed at revolution.

That such a fundamental divergence could appear in a meeting of the Soviet Academy of Sciences, apparently convened to promulgate a new line for India, is of more than passing interest. Since, in the Communist view, policy for India had never been conceived as an isolated problem but as an integral part of an international whole, a dispute over this question may have reflected a dispute concerning the whole.

Apparently the disagreement did not turn on the relevance to India of the new doctrines of Chinese communism, for though reliance on the peasantry was the heart of Chinese Communist movement, none of the Soviet spokesmen gave significant attention to the Indian peasantry. Moreover, although Dyakov and Balabushevich were saying in effect that India had passed to a higher stage of the revolution, they did not draw on the Stalinist formula for China to assert that this higher stage was that of agrarian revolution. Nor did they compare the "reactionary" turn of the Indian nationalist leadership with that of the Kuomintang leadership in 1927—an analogy which they would surely have used if they had had the Chinese context in mind.

The sources of the dispute on India must therefore be sought else-

[7] *Ibid.*, p. 28.

where. It appears likely that they lay in a debate over the new theory of "people's democracy" and its application to the colonies. Indeed, Balabushevich had used the term "people's democracy" to sum up the aims of Indian communism.

Communist regimes established in Eastern Europe after World War II had required fresh theoretical explication, for they did not fit conveniently into the standard Marxist-Leninist assumptions. As a result of Russian occupation, Communists had been given key positions in these regimes, but they did not enjoy total control. In accordance with the exigencies of the international and local situations, as interpreted in Moscow, the Communists temporarily tolerated bourgeois parties, and proceeded cautiously with the gradual expropriation of the bourgeoisie, both urban and rural. To describe these regimes, the theory of "people's democracy" soon emerged. In its essentials this rationale declared that a "people's democracy" was a new transitional state form, being neither a bourgeois nor a proletarian government. It used the parliamentary machinery of bourgeois democracy, but employed it in the interests of a worker-peasant alliance. Moreover, it directed its policy primarily against foreign capital (that is, against imperialism), the big bourgeoisie (monopoly capitalism) and the big landlords (feudalism).[8] In short, it adopted the anti-imperialist strategy.

But by mid-1947, this view of "people's democracy" was apparently under attack from at least one quarter within the Communist community: the Yugoslav Party. Judging from later declarations of Yugoslav theorists, they had already begun arguing for a more militant policy.[9] They did not say that the "people's democracy" was a transitional regime, lying somewhere between the bourgeois and the socialist revolutions; they asserted, rather, that it must combine or "intertwine" these two revolutions, in order to press on to socialism. The Yugoslav theorists therefore called for a more drastic policy aimed against the bourgeois class or capitalism as a whole, and not merely at monopoly

---

[8] A statement of this theory is continued in E. Varga, "Demokratiia novogo tipa" [Democracy of a New Type], *Mirovoe khoziaistvo* . . . (March, 1947), pp. 3–15. See also C. E. Black, ed., *Readings on Contemporary Eastern Europe* (New York: National Committee for a Free Europe, Inc., 1953), pp. 71–92. The document by Jozsef Revai, included in this work, gives an especially clear picture of the development of the "people's democracy" theory.

[9] A number of works on postwar Yugoslavia or Eastern Europe cite evidence of the "leftism" of the Yugoslav Party leadership; see especially Hamilton Fish Armstrong, *Tito and Goliath* (New York: The Macmillan Co., 1951), pp. 57–59; and Vladimir Dedijer, *Tito Speaks* (London: Weidenfeld and Nicolson, 1953), p. 304. On the basis of such evidence, Franz Borkenau in *European Communism* (London: Faber and Faber Ltd., 1953), pp. 504–522, suggests that the Yugoslavs represented a "forward" faction in the international movement, which was projected even into the Russian ruling elite.

capitalism and feudalism. And they suggested that the institutions of bourgeois democracy must be smashed and replaced by new forms of "Soviet democracy"—the forms to be determined by specific circumstances in each country.[10]

The Yugoslav leaders did not stop with a dissent as to the nature of "people's democracy" in Eastern Europe. They were apparently critical of Communist policy in other parts of the world, as was evidenced by their attack on the French and Italian parties at the first meeting of the Cominform. But more important in the present case, they had spoken out as early as the beginning of 1947 on the question of policy in the colonies, proposing a line which contrasted sharply with the temporizing in the Soviet commentary of that time. In an article published in January, 1947, in the official theoretical journal of the Yugoslav Party, Edvard Kardelj had declared the "national bourgeoisie" in the colonies was a "reactionary" agent of foreign imperialism. The working class, he said, was in many colonies moving not only toward liberation from imperialism, but also toward the defeat of the bourgeoisie, or in short toward "the victory of people's democracy." And this victory would, he implied, be achieved only through violent revolution; the colonies faced a prospect of "unrest and turmoil in which more or less sharp clashes between the imperialist reactionary forces and the democratic anti-imperialist forces will take place." Asserting that the anti-imperialist revolution would be combined with the anticapitalist revolution under a three-class strategy, Kardelj had, in effect, applied the Yugoslav version of "people's democracy" to the colonies.[11]

When the Russian Indologists gathered in Moscow in mid-June, 1947, Dyakov and Balabushevich expressed a strategic formula which was substantially the same as that given by Kardelj a full half-year earlier; the Russians omitted any mention of the need for violent revolution, but otherwise there was little to distinguish these two points of view. Zhukov's formula, on the other hand, coincided with the standard Soviet definition of "people's democracy," in which the big bourgeoisie, not the bourgeoisie as a whole, was the enemy.

It appears, then, that there was a direct connection between the

---

[10] These views are summarized from the report presented by Edvard Kardelj to the Cominform meeting held in Warsaw in September; extracts from this report were published by the Indian Communists in *Communist*, I (Jan., 1948), pp. 334–340. The differences between the Yugoslav and the prevailing Soviet concepts of "people's democracy" are described in later writings by Kardelj; see especially: Edvard Kardelj, *On People's Democracy in Yugoslavia* (New York: Yugoslav Information Center, n.d. [1949]), 97 pp.

[11] Edvard Kardelj, *Problems of International Development: A Marxist Analysis* (Bombay: People's Publishing House, 1947), pp. 28, 32.

debate on the nature and application of "people's democracy," and
the debate on Communist policy in India.

The CPI Rallies Behind Nehru

Simultaneously with the meeting of Soviet Indologists, the Central
Committee of the CPI was gathered in Bombay. It apparently worked
in complete ignorance of what was transpiring in Moscow, and it
emerged with entirely different conclusions concerning Nehru.
Whereas the Russians denounced the Mountbatten Plan as a betrayal
of the nationalist cause, and attacked the Nehru government for accepting it, the CPI in effect declared the settlement to be a step ahead
and pledged the Party to support the Nehru government.[12]

The CPI resolution began with conventional criticism of the Mountbatten Plan, saying that it did not accord full independence to India
and that it was calculated to retain as much imperialist influence as
was feasible under the new circumstances. However, the resolution
affirmed that the plan did represent "important concessions" and
"new opportunities for national advance." Thus the CPI characterized
the settlement as at least a partial satisfaction of the nationalist demands.

The British hoped, the resolution continued, to retain influence in
India through the feudal princes and landlords and also through align-
ment with Indian big business, which had "great influence" over the
"extreme Right wing of the Congress leadership." But the CPI clearly
assumed that this traitorous wing did not dominate either the Congress
as a whole or the new governments:

> The Congress is the main national democratic organization. . . .
> The Communist Party desires that the Congress leadership implement rapidly
> and consistently the declared anti-imperialist democratic programme of the Con-
> gress.
> The Communist Party will fully coöperate with the national leadership in the
> proud task of building the Indian Republic on democratic foundations, thus paving
> the way to Indian unity.

The resolution acknowledged that the Mountbatten concessions had
been "extracted through the continuous pressure of the Congress leadership for transfer of power," as well as through mass pressure. Thus
the CPI appeared to take for granted the good faith of the dominant
section of the nationalist elite. Accordingly, the resolution called for the
"fullest coöperation between the popular Governments and all popular organizations for the noble task of national liberation and reconstruction and final unification." Such coöperation, it said, should be

---

[12] "Statement of Policy," *People's Age*, V (June 29, 1947), pp. 6–7.

effected by a "joint front" of all "progressive" forces—the left elements of the Congress and the League, alongside the CPI itself.

It is of especial significance that the CPI gave only lip service, in the resolution, to the demand for self-determination on the part of the Indian "nationalities." The predominant theme of the June resolution was the aspiration toward unity—the unity of the multifarious political and religious elements of the subcontinent. The Party was "fully confident," the resolution declared, that with such unity "the imperialist intrigues can be decisively defeated" and that India could pass on to genuine national independence.

The Indian Communist response to the prospect of immediate independence was, therefore, the very antithesis of the Soviet response. The CPI response followed the earlier Soviet view, but the tone of the CPI resolution suggests that the Party was in some degree also influenced by the mood of its domestic environment—a mood compounded of exhilaration and anxiety. This mood was apparently strong enough to carry even the radical wing of the Party with it. In a subsequent *mea culpa* B. T. Ranadive admitted that the radicals on the Central Committee approved the policy of loyal opposition. "Nobody," he said, "saw the enormity of the reformist deviation" of supporting the Nehru government.[13]

The CPI was apparently confident that it was in step with international communism. Inner-Party documents of this period indicate that the Party was not immediately notified of the new Soviet line. Also, the Indian Communists had received firm support of their loyalist orientation from their British mentor, R. Palme Dutt; in June Dutt pronounced his verdict on the Indian situation, and it was almost identical with that of the CPI.[14] After expatiating upon the evils of the Mountbatten Plan, quoting Soviet authorities on the subject, Dutt nevertheless concluded that it permitted a "signal advance" and would "open the way" to future democratic progress. He declared that the plan was, in essence, an "enforced retreat of imperialism." Accordingly, he did not condemn the national leadership for accepting the Mountbatten terms, and instead called for collaboration between the CPI and the Congress:

Now more than ever the situation reveals the urgent need, increasingly recognized on both sides, to endeavour to overcome the past phase of sharp divisions between the Congress and the Communist Party in order to march forward together upon

---

[13] See Ranadive's self-critical review of Party policy given at CPI Second Congress, 1948: *People's Age: Supplement*, VI (March 21, 1948), p. 4.

[14] R. Palme Dutt, "The Mountbatten Plan for India," *Labour Monthly*, XXIX (July, 1947), pp. 210–219.

a common programme of democratic advance, for the achievement of full independence and eventual all-India democratic union, and for the fulfillment of the
economic and social demands, land reform, measures of nationalization and planned
industrial development, for which the workers and peasants and masses of the
Indian people are looking.

Dutt's statement implied throughout that the Nehru government
was progressive. Indeed, he praised the Indian delegation at the United
Nations for certain "courageous and progressive" stands, and envisaged
"the combined leadership of the Soviet Union, India, and the progressive democratic countries" in world affairs. Since to be associated with
the Soviet Union is the highest praise in the Communist lexicon, this
statement alone demonstrates the optimism with which Dutt regarded
the future of India under the Nehru government.

The CPI reprinted Dutt's statement, presumably convinced that its
own line was thereby legitimized. It could readily believe so, since the
Russians themselves did not communicate the new anti-Nehru line
to the CPI for some months. In fact, aside from the single article by
Zhukov, published Russian commentary continued to be almost as
inconclusive after the Academy session as it had been before. At a
public lecture in Moscow, delivered at the beginning of July and published immediately thereafter, V. Ia. Avarin declared that the Congress had agreed to the Mountbatten terms "in order to find a way out
of the political impasse." He added that the Congress feared the mass
movement and was "falling under the influence of elements prepared
to come to an agreement with British imperialism," but he did not
elaborate this hint, nor did he apply the epithet "reactionary" to the
Congress leaders. He concluded indecisively, saying that it was necessary "to expect new complications" in India.[15]

Dyakov himself wrote an article appearing in the July issue of
Izvestia which was even more notable for its omissions. It consisted
merely of an attack on British policy, reiterating the familiar message
that the Mountbatten Plan was calculated to perpetuate imperialism
in the subcontinent.[16] However, his article was the clearest expression
to date of the expectation that India would be fragmented in the
course of attaining formal independence. Dyakov said that seven
princely states had indicated their intention to remain separate, and
he pointed out that this would result in the Indian Union's being cut

---

[15] V. Ia. Avarin, *Politicheskie izmeneniia na tikhom okeane posle vtoroi mirovoi
voini* [Political Changes in the Pacific Since the Second World War] (Moscow:
Izdatel'stvo "Pravda," 1947), pp. 8–19. This is the text of a public lecture of July 2,
1947.
[16] A. Dyakov, "The English Plan for the Partition of India," *Soviet Press Translations,* II (Nov. 1, 1947), pp. 201–203 (from *Izvestia,* July 5, 1947).

into two parts, isolated from each other by some independent states. Thus, he declared, the subcontinent would become a "conglomeration of dominions and states." Even those princely states which would join the dominion, he said, would be "only nominally subject to its authority."

The general picture which emerges from this and earlier Soviet statements on the future of India is of a Balkanized subcontinent remaining under indirect imperialist rule.

To communism, the prospect of a weak and fragmented country would provide an extreme temptation to revolution. And it is true that when the Nehru government fell heir to power on August 15, 1947, it was gravely vulnerable because of the urgent problems confronting it. The princely states were formally separate; the challenge of integrating them was truly appalling. But more important, partition was accompanied by a sanguinary civil war between Hindus and Muslims, and the simple challenge of bringing peace strained the resources of the new government to the limits.

However, the CPI, far from turning to revolution, proclaimed its loyalty to the government with increasing zeal. On the eve of independence the Party declared that it would "join the day of national rejoicing" and would place itself "shoulder to shoulder with the national movement for full independence." [17] In its accounts of the mass meetings and demonstrations celebrating freedom, the Indian Communist press gave special emphasis to those which were jointly sponsored by the CPI, the Congress, and other "patriotic" parties. It took particular note of a meeting at which Communist and Congress speakers, overcome by the emotion of the occasion, embraced one another on the public platform.[18]

Communist willingness to pledge loyalty to the government was apparently strongly reinforced by the outbreak of the civil war between Hindus and Muslims. The Party interpreted it as "an offensive of imperialism and its agents" against the Nehru government.[19] But communalism has a "narrow social base," declared the CPI, and could be "rapidly liquidated" through coöperation among progressive forces.[20] Clearly, the Indian Communists had little comprehension of the mass irrationality underlying the Hindu-Muslim conflict in India, and may well have been bewildered and alarmed by the reality of communal carnage for which they had been ill-prepared by Marxian

---

[17] *People's Age*, VI (Aug. 3, 1947), pp. 1, 16.
[18] *Ibid.* (Aug. 31, 1947), p. 9.
[19] *Ibid.* (Sept. 14, 1947), p. 1.
[20] *Ibid.* (Sept. 21, 1947), p. 4.

notions of human motivation. Indeed, the communal riots were a major factor, Ranadive later explained, in persuading the radical wing to join Joshi and rally behind the two governments.[21] But whether the CPI's reaction was the result of confused panic or of tactical calculation, its logical course was to seek a stronger role among the anti-communal political forces. Accordingly, Joshi cast off all restraint; proclaiming to both the Indian and Pakistani governments that the CPI would support them, he declared, "It is the duty of us all to rally wholeheartedly and enthusiastically behind them and pledge them all our support." [22]

As a sign of its loyalty the Party went so far as to repress the mass agitation that it had itself set in motion earlier. The Tebhaga movement provides a noteworthy example. This movement, which the CPI had promoted in Bengal a year earlier, expressed a peasant demand for a larger share of the crops. It had gained great momentum, but in the fall of 1947 the Party's foremost Bengali leader, Bhowani Sen, declared, "We appeal to the peasants not to launch direct action this year as they did last year." Explaining, he said that the new government "must be given an opportunity of fulfilling its promises through legal channels." [23]

In general, however, it became increasingly apparent that the CPI's deference was not to the new Indian government but rather to one man: Nehru. In October, the Party called Nehru the "voice of the people," and it proposed a "joint front from Pandit Nehru to the Socialists and Communists." [24] In November the Party urged Congress's rank and file to strengthen the prime minister's hand for "progressive reorganization of the Government." [25] And on Nehru's birthday, the CPI sent greetings which asserted that he "alone kept the democratic traditions of the national movement alive" during the past months. This birthday message resounded with uncritical praise, and it concluded with the eager hope that Nehru would become "India's Premier No. 1 who set her on the road to Socialism and prosperity." [26]

Thus it became clear that the CPI distinguished between the progressive Nehru and the rest of the government, and focused all its aspirations on liberalizing the government through strengthening the prime minister. This tactic was plainly set forth in a statement attributed to R. Palme Dutt by the Socialist leader, Madhu Limaye. Ac-

---

[21] *Ibid.; Supplement* (March 21, 1948), p. 4.

[22] P. C. Joshi, "The Punjab Riots," *Labour Monthly*, XXIX (Oct., 1947), p. 315.

[23] *People's Age*, VI (Nov. 30, 1947), p. 10.

[24] *Ibid.* (Oct. 12, 1947), p. 5; and (Oct. 19, 1947), p. 1.

[25] *Ibid.* (Nov. 30, 1947), p. 16.

[26] *Ibid.* (Nov. 9, 1947), p. 3.

cording to Limaye, Dutt told him in a personal interview in November, 1947:

Your talk about leaving the Congress is untimely and mistaken and you should not only remain in the Congress but agitate for the re-admittance of the Communists into the national organization. The Congress is now divided into two camps, the progressive camp led by Pandit Nehru, Sheikh Abdulla and others, and the reactionary bloc led by Sardar Vallabhbhai Patel. It is the supreme duty of all of us to support Nehru. If Nehru offers you seats on his cabinet, you should readily accept the offer.[27]

Thus the CPI and its tutor, R. Palme Dutt, continued almost to the end of 1947 to judge Nehru worthy of left-wing support and amenable to left-wing influence. They apparently were confident that, with Communist backing, the prime minister would rout the more conservative forces in his government and bring progressive elements into the seats of power. All this, a full five months after the Soviet authorities in Moscow had pronounced precisely the opposite verdict on Nehru, shrugging him aside as a "rich man" and condemning his regime as "reactionary."

The CPI Declares War on Nehru

The surrender of the radical faction of the CPI to Joshi's moderate line proved to be only temporary. Although it was apparently inhibited by the communal civil war, the leftist element again began to grow restive soon after the achievement of independence. Joshi's line continued to prevail officially, but from about mid-August articles by Ranadive began to appear more frequently in the Party press, sounding a harsher note alongside Joshi's lyrical passages. For example, in the midst of the Party's celebrations on Independence Day itself, Ranadive warned in *People's Age* that the Nehru government was "compromising" and that it was "developing authoritarian attributes." [28]

One can only speculate about the precise reasons for the reëmergence of radical sentiment within the CPI. However, it is probably not a coincidence that in mid-August another influence, hitherto unrepresented, began to appear in Indian Communist publications—an influence bound to stir militancy. In its third issue, which appeared on about August 15, the CPI theoretical journal, *Communist*, began to print articles written by leaders of the Yugoslav Communist Party.[29]

---

[27] Madhu Limaye, *Communist Party: Facts and Fiction* (Hyderabad: Chetana Prakashan Ltd., 1951), p. 57.

[28] *People's Age*, VI (Aug. 15, 1947), p. 20.

[29] "Character of the New Democratic State in Yugoslavia," *Communist*, I (Sept., 1947). This is described as an editorial reprinted from the official organ of the Central Committee of the Communist Party of Yugoslavia, *Communist* (Jan., 1947).

From later testimony of CPI leaders, it is clear that the Party was already aware of Kardelj's radical article on Communist policy in the colonies. Indeed, by the end of 1947 the Indian Communists published this document in pamphlet form.[30] In Kardelj's view that the bourgeoisie as a whole had turned reactionary and must be met with violent revolution, the hotbloods of the CPI probably found the encouragement they needed for shaking off the uncongenial policy of loyal opposition to Nehru.

However, domestic factors were also at work in rousing radical sentiment in the CPI, and that sentiment now found much broader support among the rank and file. In the first place, it is likely that the Party's veterans were so thoroughly conditioned to militancy that they could not gracefully adjust to the role of loyal opposition in free India. In the second place, the membership as a whole evidently tended to blame the Joshi line for difficulties which confronted them in many of the Party's mass activities. In the trade-union, peasant, student, and women's movements, the CPI had seen its strength steadily ebbing since the war, as Congress and Socialist organizers returned to action after long imprisonment. The Party now faced a serious problem in these fields; in the trade-union sphere, for example, it was witnessing the formation of a rival federation, the Indian National Trade Union Congress, sponsored by the Congress with the express intent of giving battle to the Communist-dominated All-India Trade Union Congress. In these circumstances, Communist labor leaders could not be expected to enjoy turning the other cheek through a policy of loyalty to the Congress government. The natural reflex of Party stalwarts in this and other fields was to demand a more aggressive policy. Moreover it is likely that the rank and file began to perceive more sharply the revolutionary potentialities in the anxious and disordered Indian political scene.

The main factor, however, in inner-Party dissatisfaction with Joshi's moderation was no doubt the example of the success of a more militant line in Telengana. Telengana, as has been mentioned, is in the eastern half of the princely state of Hyderabad, comprising eight districts and an area of 44,000 square miles, and populated mainly by the Telugu-speaking people. Under the despotism of the Nizam of Hyderabad, a notoriously oppressive semifeudal agrarian system had been perpetuated, and as a result the peasantry was ripe for radical leadership. Beginning during the war with the capture of the Andhra Mahasabha, formerly a reformist cultural-political organization tolerated by the Nizam because of its moderation, the Telengana Communists

[30] See footnote 11.

gradually set in motion a genuinely indigenous mass campaign against the landlords and the state autocracy, concentrated in the two districts of Nalgonda and Warangal. By mid-1946 this movement assumed the proportions of active revolt in scattered localities, as armed volunteer village brigades began to form for resistance against the authority of the Nizam. It was obvious that a chain reaction of village insurrections might be ignited at any moment. Up to this point the Communists had professed moderate goals; under directions from the central CPI leadership they did not encourage outright revolt. Their demands were limited to the abolition of "illegal exactions" and other excesses perpetrated by the landlords. Moreover, they pledged to support Hyderabad's accession to India, and they maintained at least the façade of collaboration with the Congress organization in the state. Communist policy was thus aimed against the state autocracy rather than the central government. Yet the intense particularism of the Telugu-speaking people, added to the peasant discontent, made them a tempting base for an attack on the government.[31]

Whatever the reasons, a radical propensity began to reassert itself in the CPI, and Joshi found himself under increasing criticism. He was attacked as a "petty-bourgeois reformist" and accused of installing too many of his own supporters—many of them youths just back from British universities—in positions of power in the Party bureaucracy.[32] As further news of the leftist trend in the international Communist movement reached India, it found a growing faction in the CPI eager to seize upon it as sanction for ousting Joshi and reversing the Party's course.

Apparently, the first clear statement of the radical international line came to the Indian Communists in the reports of the first Cominform meeting, held in Poland in September, 1947. The major speech of the meeting, delivered by Zhdanov, gave additional support to the Indian radicals. Zhdanov asserted that the weakening of the imperialist states had aggravated the "crisis of the colonial system." In desperation the imperialist powers resorted to several devices to maintain the subjection of the colonies, he said. They had tried to crush the national movements by force, producing colonial wars such as those in Indonesia and Viet Nam. Or they had erected a Red bogey to justify their continued power; in this way, he said, "they are seeking to keep India and China under the sway of imperialism and in continued political

---

[31] This description of the situation in Telengana is drawn primarily from the following sources: "On Telengana," Information Document No. 7 (2) (Politburo, Communist Party of India, Oct. 7, 1950), pp. 1–5; and *The Hyderabad Problem: The Next Step* (Bombay: Hyderabad Struggle Committee, Socialist Party, 1948), pp. 70–77.

[32] Interview in India with a former member of CPI.

and economic bondage." In the current international situation, he declared, "the chief danger to the working class . . . lies in underrating its own strength and overrating the strength of the enemy." Communist parties must therefore lead national resistance to "the plans of imperialist expansion and aggression along every line." [33] Zhdanov said nothing more about India, but the radicals in the CPI, assuming that the Nehru government had aligned itself with imperialism, read his speech as a call to arms against that government.[34]

Zhdanov did indeed sanction an intensified anti-imperialist campaign in the colonies which, in the Russian view, meant an attack on the Nehru government, but he did not openly sanction an all-out anticapitalist strategy. In fact, he concluded his speech with emphasis on "democratic" Communist aims, and he did not specify that the bourgeoisie had turned reactionary.

But in another speech at this meeting, given by Kardelj, the Indian radicals found clear sanction for an anticapitalist strategy: in this address Kardelj made a powerful statement of the view that the democratic and socialist revolutions must "intertwine," and that the Communists must therefore attack the bourgeoisie as a whole. It was to this speech that the CPI radicals paid the most eager attention; extracts from it, together with parts of Marshall Tito's main report to the Yugoslav Party's Second Congress, were reprinted in the official CPI journal.[35] According to a later inner-Party account of this period by Ajoy Ghosh, the Indian radicals regarded Kardelj as the greatest Marxist thinker outside Russia; Ghosh claims that Kardelj's writings "most powerfully influenced me and others who were fighting against Joshism," and that Ranadive hailed them as "showing us the correct Marxist revolutionary path." [36]

The impact of Yugoslav influence on the CPI was apparently reinforced by one other event: a trip made by the Party's principal labor leader, S. A. Dange, who went to Prague for a meeting of the World Federation of Trade Unions. Little is known about Dange's activities except that he toured Eastern Europe and the U.S.S.R., but he apparently served on his return as a carrier of the Yugoslav line; R. Palme Dutt later referred to him as "one of the main vehicles for Titoite political influence" in the CPI.[37] Since Dange must have made

---

[33] A. Zhdanov, *The International Situation* (Moscow: Foreign Languages Publishing House, 1947), pp. 11, 16, 46–47.

[34] Interview in India with a former member of the CPI.

[35] *Communist*, I (Jan., 1948), pp. 313–319; 334–340.

[36] Prabodh Chandra, [Ajoy Ghosh?], "On 'A Note on the Present Situation in Our Party'," *PHQ Open Forum*, No. 12 (Oct., 1949), pp. 3–4.

[37] Deven and Bal Krishna, "Talks with Comrade R. Palme Dutt and Other Impressions Gained Abroad by Deven and Bal Krishna," PHQ Unit, Jan. 6, 1951, p. 4.

contact with other leaders of international communism, it seems likely that he received their approval for, or at least their acquiescence in, applying the "Titoite" line in India.

In any event, the CPI acted as though it had conclusive international sanction for a new line. In the second week of December, 1947, the Indian Central Committee met in Bombay, and the radical faction challenged Joshi. If the radicals had required another argument to bolster their opposition, they could have found it in the fact that the Congress government of Bombay, to which Joshi urged loyal opposition, had only a week earlier announced severe restrictions on the content of the Communist press.[38] But the radical faction was already well-armed; Ranadive secured majority support for his line and displaced Joshi as the real leader of the Party.

In a new resolution, the Central Committee announced a complete reversal of the Party's course.[39] The resolution denounced as "opportunism" the assumption made by Joshi and Dutt that the Nehru government could be influenced by popular pressure or that it might even be reorganized to include leftist forces. Instead, the resolution called for an uncompromising struggle against the government. Following Zhdanov's thesis that the world was now divided into two hostile camps, it declared that Nehru's policy "is only leading to subservience to the Anglo-American Imperialist Camp." Indian big business, it said, had come to an agreement with imperialism, and the bourgeois government was backing up this "reactionary" policy. Thus, the resolution concluded, "the national bourgeois leadership will be increasingly forced to submit to the imperialist domination and the common toiling people will be forced to submit to the leadership of the upper classes, namely the national leadership." To meet this situation, the resolution called for unity among the "workers and peasants and progressive intellectuals" in a campaign to unseat the bourgeois leadership.

So far as the CPI was concerned, then, the long debate of 1946–47 —for or against the Nehru government, for or against the Indian bourgeoisie—was concluded. The Indian Communists, though they did not seem yet to understand its full import, had made the crucial decision for an all-out political attack on Nehru under a thorough-going anti-capitalist orientation. The cold war had reached India.

The Russian academicians had long before reached agreement on the debate concerning Nehru, but the evidence suggests that at the end of 1947, and even after, they were still in disagreement on the

[38] *People's Age*, VI (Dec. 7, 1947), p. 1.
[39] *Communist Statement of Policy: For the Struggle for Full Independence and People's Democracy* (Bombay: People's Publishing House, 1947), 14 pp.

second part of the debate—for or against the Indian bourgeoisie. In December and January, 1947–48, Zhukov, Dyakov, and Balabushevich expressed their views at length in the Russian journals, and in these views there was still no agreed strategy for Indian communism.

In the December issue of *Bolshevik* Zhukov said that in the colonies as a whole it was the big bourgeoisie which had betrayed national interests by coming to terms with imperialism; therefore, he declared, "in many countries" of Asia the middle bourgeoisie could be an ally of the working class. He applied this thesis to countries such as Viet Nam and Indonesia where colonial wars were being waged, but he did not expressly apply it to India. Indeed, in discussing India his view of the bourgeois classes was ambiguous; he condemned the "Indian bourgeoisie" for aspiring to neutralism in international affairs, but in a letter passage Zhukov declared that the "bourgeois nationalists," or "national-reformists," were Britain's "second line of defence" in India. But in defining the tasks of the CPI he did not even hint at an anti-capitalist strategy, and in fact he seemed to stress the relative weakness of the Party, as though to caution it against revolutionary adventurism.[40]

Dyakov and Balabushevich both held firm to their position that the bourgeoisie had turned reactionary.[41] However, Balabushevich betrayed the fact that he was trailing behind events rather than anticipating them by declaring that the Mountbatten Plan represented a real concession and was therefore a "step ahead" for India—an echo of the Joshi line which was patently incongruous in his analysis. This fact, along with Zhukov's apparent unwillingness to commit himself, seems to indicate that the Russians did not have an agreed strategy for the Indian situation. The result, whether intentional or not, was that guidance of the CPI fell to the Cominform, and thus to the Yugoslavs.

The CPI Second Congress

With or without express sanction from the Russian authorities, the Ranadive radicals now controlled the Central Committee of the Party. On the charge of factionalism, they began to purge the Party bureaucracy of all who stood by the Joshi line. In addition, in order to formalize their control and to mobilize the Party behind the new line, they decided to hold an All-India Party Congress—the second in

[40] E. Zhukov, "Obostrenie krizisa kolonial'noi sistemy" [The Sharpening of the Crisis of the Colonial System], *Bolshevik* (Dec. 15, 1947), pp. 51–65.

[41] A. Dyakov, "Partitioned India," *New Times* (Jan. 14, 1948), pp. 3–10; V. Balabushevich, "Indiia posle razdela" [India After Partition], *Mirovoe khoziaistvo . . .* , (Dec. 1947), pp. 41–63.

the CPI's history. At the Committee's December meeting a subcommittee was appointed to draft a comprehensive political resolution for distribution within the CPI, and a list of nominations for a new Central Committee was drawn up for submission to the Party Congress. Members of the Central Committee went back to their bailiwicks and hastily convened provincial Party conferences to discuss the draft resolution and elect delegates for the Congress. Thus with strong direction from the top, the Party machinery operated rapidly and effectively to rally the organization. On February 28, 1948, only two and one-half months after the December decision, the Party Congress convened in Calcutta.[42]

Attending the meeting was the core of the Party. Of the 632 delegates on hand, according to the Party press, 565 were "whole-timers" or "professional revolutionaries"—that is, Party functionaries and organizers. A total of 919 delegates had been elected, People's Age said, but many were not able to attend. From Telengana, 75 delegates were supposed to come to Calcutta, but only four or five managed to make the trip. Also in attendance, according to the Party press, were fraternal delegations from Australia, Burma, Ceylon, and, finally, Yugoslavia. There was no official representative of the British Party and none from the Soviet Union.

Later inner-Party accounts of the Congress make it clear that the comrades from Australia, Burma, and Ceylon were merely passive spectators. However, the Yugoslav delegates—Vladimir Dedijer and Radoven Zokovic—played an exceedingly active part, as though with the authority of the international Communist movement. According to Ajoy Ghosh, they tutored the Indian delegates in the thesis of the "intertwined" revolutions under an anticapitalist strategy. They also argued, at the Congress, for the tactic of a monolithic party front in India, on the order of that created by the party in Yugoslavia. Some Indian leaders recognized that such a tactic was unrealistic in India, given CPI weakness, but as Ghosh said, "otherwise, we swallowed all that the Yugoslavs told us." Comrade Sharkey from Australia, reported Ghosh, did not object to the adoption of the Yugoslav advice; the theories of Chinese communism were mentioned by no one.[43]

Basing his line squarely on the Yugoslav views, Ranadive was in command of the Congress from the outset. The first major event of the session was his report on the draft resolution, and it established

[42] The following account of the proceedings of the CPI Second Congress, which were held in camera, is drawn primarily from the official report in the Party press: People's Age: Supplement, VI (March 21, 1948); and ibid. (March 14, 1948).
[43] Prabodh Chandra, "On 'A Note . . .' ," p. 5.

the tone of the Congress. Ranadive declared that the Indian bourgeoisie was lining up with the Anglo-American imperialist camp, which was locked in "irreconcilable conflict" with the democratic camp led by the Soviet Union. Accordingly, he said, the Party must lead the struggle for "people's democracy," in which the fight for democracy "gets intertwined with the fight for Socialism." In other words, the Party must lead the "fight for rallying the majority of the people against capitalism." Toward this end, he said, the Party must build a "people's democratic front" representing an alliance from below among the working class, the peasantry, and the petty bourgeoisie, along with the progressive intelligentsia.

Beyond reciting the anti-capitalist strategy, Ranadive strongly implied that his violent terminology would be accompanied in certain areas by violent tactics. Whereas the Joshi leadership had ignored the agrarian insurrections in Telengana, Ranadive seized on them as symbols of the new stage upon which the Party was entering. In Telengana, he said, "we took the struggle to new qualitative heights with exemplary organization." In conclusion he declared, "Telengana today means Communists and Communists mean Telengana."

In the second major speech at the Congress, Bhowani Sen, who was to become Ranadive's principal lieutenant, delivered a fuller statement of the new tactics. This speech represented a crucial revision of the nationality policy which the Party had pursued from 1942 to 1948; now the CPI declared that self-determination must be accomplished, not by the whole population of a given nationality, but by revolutionary action of the working class and its allies. Condemning the earlier policy as exemplified in Kashmir, where the Party had supported Sheikh Abdullah's pro-Indian movement and had even supported formal accession to India rather than to Pakistan, Sen asserted that Telengana provided the new model for CPI policy. Revolution must come first—not only in the princely states which had not yet been formally integrated into either India or Pakistan, but throughout the subcontinent.

The real solution to this question is on the field of battle. The heroic people of Telengana, the great example of their fight against autocracy, not only show what will happen inside the States, but also what will be the real future of India and Pakistan. That is the way the victorious people must march to freedom and real democracy. . . . We must be proud to say that here at least there is the force that will achieve Indian liberation.[44]

In fact, sentiment in favor of the Telengana movement was so strong that the delegates from that area were able to secure adoption of a

[44] *People's Age: Supplement,* VI (March 21, 1948), p. 3.

spontaneous resolution expressing full support of their ʌ

The main reports to the Congress were followed by a one·
dress in which P. C. Joshi, the deposed leader, performed the ɪ,
self-criticism. Joshi confessed that he had "confused and corrʋ
the Party, acting as a "betrayer," a "coward," a "petty-bourgeois ʋ
lator," an "arch bureaucrat," and "the embodiment of right refoɪ
ism." He denounced his entire career as a leader, even declaring thɛ
at the beginning he had been "a student intellectual thrown into
Party leadership by the accident of history." [45]

However, when the retiring Central Committee presented its official
nominations for a new Committee, Joshi's name was on the list along
with a majority of the old members and nearly an equal number of
new members. But the delegates to the Congress were evidently convinced by Joshi's self-condemnation, for he alone among the official
nominees was not elected. The new Central Committee immediately
elected B. T. Ranadive as general secretary, thereby formalizing the
change which had taken place two and one-half months earlier.

Other business transacted by the CPI Second Congress included a
long debate on the main political resolution, the "Political Thesis,"
submitted by the leadership. Already amendments had been incorporated into this resolution by the drafting commission, after inner-
Party discussion of the earlier draft. However, the Congress delegates
further criticized details of the document with "vigour and firmness,"
according to the Party press. At the end of the discussion, Ranadive
called upon the Congress to adopt the resolution without change and
to entrust the Central Committee with amending it afterward in accordance with the views expressed by the delegates. This proposal
was accepted, and the resolution was adopted unanimously. The Political Thesis ran to ninety-five pages in the pamphlet edition published
later, and it constituted a comprehensive statement of the new line.[46]
In its essentials it declared that a "revolutionary upsurge" was in motion in India, and that the final phase of the revolution, the phase of
"armed clashes," had arrived. This "people's democratic revolution," it
said, involved "the completion of the tasks of democratic revolution
and the simultaneous building up of Socialism." The Party must mobilize the working class, the peasantry, and the petty bourgeoisie against
imperialism and capitalism. The Nehru government, according to the
thesis, represented the interests of the Indian national bourgoisie; this

---

[45] "Resolution of the Central Committee of the Communist Party of India on P. C. Joshi's Appeal Against Expulsion," June 5, 1950 [typed copy], p. 4.

[46] *Political Thesis; Adopted at the Second Congress, Calcutta, February 28–March 6, 1948* (Bombay: Communist Party of India, 1948), 95 pp.

government must be attacked by a new democratic front, a "genuine fighting alliance of the masses."

If there was any doubt of the concrete meaning of this document, it was dispelled for the Congress delegates by a specific statement, made on behalf of the Central Committee in the course of the debate, to the effect that the "people's democratic state" meant nothing more nor less than "the dictatorship of the proletariat." The CPI had served notice that it was bent on orthodox revolution against the Nehru government.

As events later demonstrated, the Indian Communists were not to be alone in this intention. In 1948 Communist parties elsewhere in Southeast Asia took the revolutionary path, and violent civil war broke out in Burma, Malaya, and Indonesia. Students of international communism have speculated, without clear evidence, that these revolts were instigated on specific orders from Moscow communicated to the parties at a meeting of the Southeast Asia Youth Conference, held in Calcutta almost simultaneously with the CPI's Second Congress.[47] Russian guests attended this meeting as did delegates from India, Pakistan, Burma, Indonesia, Malaya, Viet Nam, the Philippines, and North and South Korea. But more important, perhaps, was the presence of the Yugoslav delegation, on hand for the CPI Congress. Since the Yugoslav Communists spoke with authority to the Indian Communists, whether that authority was a product of their international prestige or of concrete sanction from the Cominform, it is possible that they also spoke with authority to other Southeast Asian parties. As P. C. Joshi expressed it in a statement published later, the Telengana peasant revolution in India was conducted by the CPI leadership "on the basis of the tactical line personally given by the Titoite Yugoslav delegates to our Party Congress." [48] It is at least possible that Yugoslav directives triggered Communist guerrilla-style revolution throughout Southeast Asia.

The general secretary of the Burmese Communist Party, Than Tun, was present at the CPI Second Congress in Calcutta, and on the occasion of a speech to the Congress he hinted broadly at revolution in Burma. The Burmese Communists were making every effort to avoid civil war, he said, "but if the national bourgeoisie, backed by the Anglo-Americans, insist on having it, well they will have it." Concluding, he declared, "Comrades, 1948 is a decisive year for the libera-

---

[47] For a summary of and comment upon this speculation, see John H. Kautsky, *Moscow and the Communist Party of India*, pp. 33–34.

[48] P. C. Joshi, *Problems of the Mass Movement* (Allahabad: Adhunik Pustak Bhandar, n.d. [1951?]), pp. 76–77.

tion movements. It will decide the fate of the liberation movements in Southeast Asia." [49]

But whatever the significance of the year 1948 for other Communist parties in Asia, that year witnessed the beginning of a crisis for the CPI unequalled in its history.

---

[49] *People's Age,* VI (March 14, 1948), p. 10.

13   THE CONSEQUENCES OF ADVENTURISM

B. T. Ranadive moved into the general secretary's office at CPI headquarters in Bombay with a mandate from the Party Congress for
revolution. Above all, he had a mandate to mobilize the Party for extending the Telengana-type of agrarian revolt to other parts of India.
It soon became evident, however, that Ranadive did not have a plan
for revolutionary action to match his revolutionary phraseology; nor
had the Party, which had given the signal for violent action against
the Nehru government, built a nation-wide organization capable of
carrying out such a task. The period immediately following the Second
Congress could therefore only be one of preparation for action.

Ranadive's first concern was to complete the purge of Joshi supporters in the Party bureaucracy, particularly within the headquarters
staff itself where Joshi's influence was apparently still felt. The members of this staff played a crucial role in the CPI organization: not
only did they hold in their hands the operational instruments of the
Party, but they also had access to the most detailed information concerning Party affairs. Ranadive had therefore to assure himself of
their loyalty, and he set out to do so in a manner so authoritarian that
it aroused opposition even among other members of the Politbureau.[1]

But while Ranadive and the new Communist leadership were thus
engaged in clearing the decks, the Nehru government proved to be
well prepared for counteraction: within a month after the Second
Congress, the government anticipated Communist violence with a na-

---

[1] Prabodh Chandra [Ajoy Ghosh?], "On 'A Note on the Present Situation in Our
Party'," *PHQ Open Forum*, No. 12 (Oct., 1950), p. 5.

tion-wide program of partial repression. Nehru himself declared in
a public speech that the Communists were trying to bring chaos to
the country, and it was clear that he was prepared to assume personal
responsibility for the repression.[2] Although the central government did
not declare the CPI illegal on a national scale, Nehru's guidance was
apparent in the scope and timing of the local measures, as one after
another of the state governments took action against local Communists.

On March 26, under the Public Safety Act, the government of West
Bengal banned the Party. The state home minister, K. S. Roy, declared
that his police had located Communist arms caches and had seized
secret documents which proved that the Party was preparing for violent revolt.[3] During the following week the Party was declared illegal
in Mysore, Indore, Bhopal, and Chandernagore. Police searched CPI
offices in other major centers, such as Bombay, Madras, Patna, Allahabad, and Nagpur. The official newspapers of the West Bengal, Kerala,
and Andhra Party committees were suppressed. Scores of Party leaders
throughout India were arrested, including S. A. Dange, Jyoti Basu,
Muzaffar Ahmed, S. S. Mirajkar, Sohan Singh Josh, R. D. Bharadwaj,
and Dinkar Mehta.[4]

Thus in one coördinated sweep a large part of the CPI organization
was rendered impotent. The Party was apparently taken by surprise,
and the local units throughout the country were confused and demoralized. But the core of leadership at headquarters in Bombay was
temporarily unaffected; Ranadive, Ajoy Ghosh, G. M. Adhikari, and
others remained at liberty, and the Party continued to publish its central newspaper, *People's Age*.

The leadership's first response to this repression was a mixture of
righteous indignation and defiance. In two statements published at
the beginning of April, Ranadive denied that the Party was collecting
arms for violent uprising, and he appealed to the Congress leaders to
reëxamine their policy and to restore freedom. But he indicated that
the CPI would not retreat; if the actions of the Party are dangerous to
the government, he said, "the policy of the existing government must
change or the government itself must change." This is "the essence of
democracy," he declared.[5]

---

[2] B. T. Ranadive, *Nehru Government Declares War Against Toilers* (Bombay:
Communist Party of India, 1948), pp. 7–14.

[3] Quoted in M. R. Masani, *The Communist Party of India* (London: Derek
Verschoyle, 1954), p. 91.

[4] Ranadive, *Nehru Government Declares . . .* , pp. 16–22.

[5] B. T. Ranadive, *Open Letter to Congressmen* (Bombay: Communist Party of
India, 1948), p. 19.

The fact that the top leaders of the CPI—those most responsible for the threat of violence—were not immediately arrested led the Communists to charge that the government repression was not preventive but provocative, designed to anger the Party into action that would discredit it. The leadership reacted by going underground. Within a few months Ajoy Ghosh, S. G. Sardesai, Romesh Chandra, S. V. Ghate, S. S. Yusuf, and other Communist leaders had been arrested, and there were warrants against Ranadive and Adhikari. The central Party publishing facilities were under restriction by the Bombay State government, and many members of the *People's Age* staff, including the editor, M. B. Rao, were in jail. The newspaper continued to appear, but it was soon banned from circulation in several states. The Party was later banned in Madras, Hyderabad, and Travancore-Cochin.[6]

Sometime in August Ranadive addressed a secret letter to the Party, declaring that within six months there would be a general strike and large-scale peasant uprisings throughout the country.[7] But because of his trade-union background and his admiration for Russian-style insurrection his proclivity was to urban rather than agrarian revolution, and he concentrated more and more on mobilizing violence in the cities in order to seize power through a general strike.

This tactic required, particularly, a nation-wide railway strike; the Communists in the All-India Railway Federation (AIRF) set out to mobilize the rank and file for militant action, and sentiment for a strike mounted. But the Socialist leadership of the AIRF, under President Jayaprakash Narayan, settled with the government, and the impending strike was called off. The Communist elements defied the leadership and tried to carry the strike through, but with no success. Six months later the Communist organizers tried to bypass the AIRF leadership in order to mobilize a general railway strike, but again failed. Extremist strike tactics had also been followed in other trade unions; they had been most nearly successful in the unions federated under the Communist-controlled All-India Trade Union Congress (AITUC)—with the result that by the end of 1948 most of its Communist officials were in jail and many of its prominent non-Communist officers such as N. M. Joshi and M. K. Bose had resigned.[8]

The extent of the CPI's revolutionary tactics is indicated in a selected account of Communist activities of that period, *Communist Violence in India,* published in 1949 by the Ministry of Home Affairs.

---

[6] Details on arrests and other government measures are summarized from *People's Age,* April–December, 1948.

[7] Prabodh Chandra, "On 'A Note . . .'," p. 5.

[8] *People's Age* (Aug. 29, 1948), p. 8; and (Oct. 17, 1948), p. 2.

It quotes a Nehru speech of February, 1949, denouncing the Communists for their program of "murders, arson, and looting, as well as acts of sabotage." Nehru told of demonstrations in Calcutta in which bombs and hand grenades had been thrown at police or into public buses and tramcars. He asserted that the Party was determined to "create a chaotic state in the country" through sabotage of the railway system and other communication facilities. He even accused the Party of "deliberately seeking to create famine conditions" through paralysis of the railways.[9]

The government account included many quotations from Party documents which had been seized in police raids. Under the heading "Communists Preach Violence" it quoted a CPI pamphlet entitled "Course for the Cadres of the Shock Brigade," a manual on guerrilla warfare. This manual gave detailed instructions on the use of small arms and hand grenades; it dealt with the organization of guerrilla squads, training methods in field exercises, and questions of tactics in specific raid operations. Offering a general definition of appropriate guerrilla activities, the document listed "the raiding of the police stations, zamindar or jotedar [landlords'] houses; ambushing police parties to annihilate and to collect arms from them; sabotaging the enemy communication lines, cutting of telephone and telegraph lines for isolating the enemy." The political objective of such activity, said the manual, was to "help the mass movement developing all over the country and raise it to the higher level when the people in general will take up arms." [10]

Among other Communist documents cited by the government were a great number issued by various Communist groups in Bengal: [11] typical of these was a circular of the Bengal Provincial Committee of the CPI calling upon Indian Army personnel to "turn your guns and bayonets and fire upon the Congress fascists" and "fraternize with the revolutionary labourers in the factories and the students in the streets"; a leaflet published by the Fighting Committee of the Communist Union of the Pottery Labourers, inciting workers to "Attack the houses of the Congress dalals [agents] and drive them out by beating them. . . . Destroy the murderous Congress government"; another leaflet declaring, "Set fire to the whole of Bengal. . . . Attack the Congress brutes in all directions"; another declaring "The blood of our martyrs is calling for revenge. The gaping wounds of our prison-heroes cry for justice. Forward to unprecedented mass militant struggles. Forward

---

[9] *Communist Violence in India* (New Delhi: Ministry of Home Affairs, Government of India, 1949), pp. 3–7.
[10] *Ibid.*, pp. 8–13.
[11] *Ibid.*, pp. 13–34.

to storm the Congress Bastilles." In an appendix the government listed a number of Communist atrocities, including bank robbery; train robbery; bomb and acid-bulb attacks at public meetings (including one at which Nehru was speaking); looting; destruction of factory equipment; and murder of police, rival labor organizers, and other enemies. These instances were drawn primarily from Bengal but were recorded also from Assam, Bihar, and Madras.[12]

In later inner-Party self-criticisms the CPI freely admitted that it had carried on such activities. One such statement acknowledges:

> We attacked railway stations, we threw bombs on trains and buses, we tried to break up Nehru's meeting . . . , we set fire to Congress offices. . . . These acts, as well as the use of acid bulbs in meetings and demonstrations, were part of the old leadership's revolutionary line.[13]

But the general pattern of Communist activity which emerges from these accounts is not that of a planned and coördinated revolutionary campaign, but rather of unorganized and sporadic outbursts of desperate violence. Though, plainly, the Ranadive leadership had the will to mobilize revolt in the cities, equally plainly, it did not have the resources; and apart from general exhortations to violence wherever possible, the Party was without comprehensive tactical directives from the top.

Such "adventurism" produced increasing criticism among Party members and sympathizers, particularly from the former general secretary, P. C. Joshi. During the entire period of Ranadive's chieftainship, Joshi conducted a bold campaign against the official CPI leaders in an effort to get himself reinstated. In published polemics he cited CPI handbills and leaflets to support his contention that the Party was being led into promoting individual terrorism.[14]

When, toward the end of 1948, the Indian Politbureau met for the first time after the Party Congress, apparently it was still mainly concerned with further measures for purging the Party of its disloyal elements, rather than with drawing up a genuine blueprint for revolution.

---

[12] Ibid., pp. 59–71. For other government documents on CPI activity, see Communist Crimes in Hyderabad (Hyderabad: Government Press, 1950), 83 pp.; Communist Activity in Bombay State, 2 vols. (Bombay: Directorate of Publicity, 1950), 14 and 32 pp.; and Charge-Sheet Against the Communists (Madras: Government Press, 1949), 21 pp.

[13] Ajoy Ghosh, S. A. Dange, and S. V. Ghate, "A Note on the Present Situation in our Party," Sept. 23, 1950 [typed copy], p. 23.

[14] P. C. Joshi, Views to Comrades Abroad and B. T. Ranadive (Howrah: P. C. Joshi, 1950), pp. 4–5.

The International Communist View

Only a few weeks after the CPI Second Congress, there began, with a correspondence between Belgrade and Moscow, the excommunication of the Yugoslav Party. When, in June, 1948, it was formally expelled from the Cominform, the Yugoslavs ceased to play a role in the tutoring of the Indian Communist Party.

Nevertheless, several early international Communist reports of the Second Congress appear to endorse the strategic line which it had adopted on the advice of the Yugoslavs. In an article in *Labour Monthly*, R. Palme Dutt condemned the "Indian bourgeoisie," and declared that "the working class steps forward to take over the leadership of the battle." The Indian fight for freedom, he said, had entered "a new phase." [15] When the official Cominform journal, *For a Lasting Peace* . . . , issued an article commenting on the CPI Congress, it too castigated the "Indian bourgeoisie," as though supporting the CPI's anticapitalist orientation.[16]

These were, however, the last echoes, in the international Communist sources, of the militant Yugoslav line on India. Thereafter Russian spokesmen resumed the initiative and began to sound a note of restraint. Indeed, the Cominform article itself had seemed to hint at caution on the question of violent tactics. It declared that the CPI had "stressed the need for a democratic front to combat the American and British imperialists and the Indian bourgeoisie." [17] This emphasis on the "democratic front" appears to be a reminder to the Indian comrades that an earlier phase of intense preparation, devoted to building an appropriate mass organization, must precede violent revolution.

This cautionary tone became clearer in later Soviet commentary. In an article in June, A. Dyakov portrayed the situation in India as being far from revolutionary.[18] He did not describe the Indian scene in terms of "revolutionary upsurge," as had Ranadive, but spoke merely of the people's "deep disappointment" with the new government. He declared that the governments of India and Pakistan "are becoming more and more isolated from the masses" and "are becoming tools of the imperialists," as though to imply that this process of "becoming" would have to mature further before the masses would be disillusioned and ready for revolution.

---

[15] R. Palme Dutt, "Whither India," *Labour Monthly*, XXX (June, 1948), pp. 161–170.
[16] *For a Lasting Peace, For a People's Democracy*, April 15, 1948, p. 3.
[17] *Ibid.*, p. 3.
[18] A. Dyakov, "The Situation in India," *New Times* (June 2, 1948), pp. 14–17.

Again, a comprehensive article by M. Alexeev, appearing in a June issue of *Bolshevik,* reiterated that the CPI had emphasized the need for creating a democratic front; thus, from the pages of the official Russian Party journal the Indian comrades were reminded of the necessity for proper advance organization. Alexeev concluded his description of CPI policy with the further declaration that the Party led the masses "for final destruction of colonial rule, for liquidation of feudal remnants and the feudal dismemberment of India." [19] With this statement it should have been clear that anticapitalism had no place in the CPI's program. Nowhere in these Soviet articles was there any acknowledgment of the Ranadive thesis, borrowed from the Yugoslavs, that the democratic and socialist revolutions should be intertwined.

However, Alexeev left a significant hiatus in his discussion of the Indian situation. Though he said clearly that only the big bourgeoisie was the reactionary agent in India and the dominant force in the Nehru government, he stated with equal clarity that the classes to be united by the Indian Communists were the "workers, peasants, and petty-bourgeoisie." Thus, he ignored the middle bourgeoisie, which Zhukov had earlier included among progressive forces in some Asian countries. To justify his analysis Alexeev quoted Stalin to the effect that the bourgeoisie in India had divided into "two sections, a revolutionary section (the petty-bourgeoisie) and a compromising section (the big-bourgeoisie)." Since the quotation dated from 1925, it was not especially serviceable in clarifying the situation in 1948.

Thus the matter stood until October, 1948, when a book by Dyakov appeared in the USSR.[20] This 328-page study of the "nationality" question in India was a complete reversal of Dyakov's previous position; moreover, it filled the gap in Alexeev's analysis, and provided a major refinement and clarification of the Soviet attitude.

In the main, Dyakov's book is a comprehensive analysis of the "national composition" of the Indian people, together with an extended discussion of the policies of the British and Indian parties on the nationality question. One of its chief themes is the assertion that the Indian national movement was dominated by the big bourgeoisie, not of the country as a whole, but of a few nationalities—most notably by the "Gujerati-Marwari" business group. The latter sought, Dyakov

---

[19] M. Alexeev, "Indiiskii soiuz i Pakistan posle raschleneniia Indii" [The Indian Union and Pakistan After the Partition of India], *Bolshevik* (June 15, 1948), p. 66.

[20] A. Dyakov, *Natsional'nyi vopros i angliiskii imperializm v Indii* [The National Question and English Imperialism in India] (Moscow: Gosudarstvennoe izdatel'stvo politicheskoi literatury, 1948), 328 pp.

said, to monopolize the Indian market, in combination with the British capitalists, by inhibiting the development of other nationalities and thereby preventing the rise of rival business groups. This meant, as Dyakov said in his concluding chapter, that the Indian government, controlled by the Gujerati-Marwari big bourgeoisie in an alliance with feudal princes and landlords, "not only suppresses the revolutionary movement of workers, peasants, and petty-bourgeois strata of the people, but also acts counter to the interests of the weaker bourgeoisie of a number of the nationalities of India: the Marathis, Bengalis, Telegus, etc." [21] Although Dyakov did not on this occasion spell out the strategic implication of this formula, it was obvious: in the revolutionary movement against the government the provincial bourgeoisie among certain nationalities of India could be counted as allies. In short, he proposed to pit the Marathi, Bengali, Telugu, and other regional business classes against the dominant national business group, the Gujerati-Marwaris.

Dyakov laid out a clear program for giving tactical effect to such a strategy. He declared that though they were led by their respective bourgeoisies, the "national movements" of such peoples as the Marathis and Bengalis were "progressive," and he called upon the Indian Communists to collaborate with the middle-class linguistic movements as they had earlier collaborated with the middle-class national movement.[22]

Here at last, then, was Soviet sanction for promoting subnational particularism as a weapon against the ruling national party—a policy which the CPI had formulated in 1942. But, ironically enough, sanction came at a time when the Indian Communists had neglected that policy in favor of violent revolution.

At the beginning of 1949, Dyakov's formula received general confirmation in the pages of *Bolshevik*.[23] Reviewing the book, E. Zhukov commended Dyakov's conclusion that the Gujerati-Marwari big bourgeoisie was the dominating factor in the national leadership of India, and he did not oppose Dyakov's primary strategic implication that the bourgeoisie of the weaker nationalities was a fit ally of the progressive movement; he concluded with the statement that "the book merits positive appreciation."

Zhukov made certain criticisms of Dyakov's study—chiefly, that it neglected the agrarian side of the revolution in India. He chided

---

[21] *Ibid.*, p. 311.

[22] *Ibid.*, pp. 137–138.

[23] E. Zhukov, "Maneuvers of British Imperialism in India," *Communist*, II (June–July, 1949), pp. 123–134. Reprinted from *Bolshevik* (Feb., 1949).

Dyakov for omitting the feudal landlords in the list of class enemies, and asserted that despite its backwardness the Indian peasantry was increasingly being drawn into the struggle.

Zhukov's review, therefore, was evidence that Soviet observers were impressed both with the appeal of regional particularism and with the potentialities of agrarian discontent in India. And it may also have been a sign of another tendency. Since alliance with the bourgeoisie and emphasis on the agrarian basis of the revolution were central elements of the Chinese Communist ideas, the Soviet spokesman may already have been developing a new appreciation for those ideas.

In summary then, the Soviet commentary that appeared in the year following the CPI Second Congress contradicted much of the current Indian Communist line; the Soviet spokesmen indicated opposition to an anticapitalist strategy and warned against premature use of violent tactics. However, if a rebuke of Ranadive was intended, it was never directly expressed. The international Communist movement did not, as it had in decades before, address a public reproof to erring Indian Communist leadership. Nor, so far as is known from CPI documents available for this period, did it communicate secretly with the CPI. In fact, when opposition to the Ranadive line developed within the Indian Party, it was helpless for some time precisely because it could not produce authoritative international Communist support. It it likely, then, that the Soviet leadership, which had given ample evidence of its hostility toward the Nehru government, was willing that Ranadive should proceed with his revolution against that government as long as there was any possibility of its success.

Opposition Within the CPI

Dissent against Ranadive's leadership was not long in appearing within the Indian Communist organization. This opposition was based, first, on resentment of the general secretary's authoritarian manipulation of the Party machinery. Ranadive had secured at the Second Congress an amendment to the Party constitution empowering the Central Committee "under exceptional circumstances . . . to reconstitute itself and other committees and fractions and to frame new rules." [24] He used these and other organizational prerogatives with increasing severity, dissolving lower Party committees (such as the Bengal Provincial Committee) and expelling recalcitrant members. The case of P. C. Joshi illustrates some of the methods used against individual opponents in this purge. Having been suspended from the Party by the

---

[24] *Constitution of the Communist Party of India* (Bombay: Communist Party of India, 1948), p. 13.

Politbureau, Joshi was exiled from Calcutta where he had been working, and was cut off from contact with the Party: he was not permitted any Party activity, was refused entrance to the Party library in Bombay, and every effort was made to deny him access to Party literature. After a year of this isolation, he was formally expelled.[25]

But in addition to the opposition to Ranadive's methods, there soon emerged strong dissent against his line. This political, as distinct from personal, opposition came primarily from two quarters: the trade-union leaders in Bombay and the agrarian leaders in South India.

According to his own confidential account, after Ajoy Ghosh was arrested in mid-1948, he sent a protest from jail to Ranadive declaring that the expectation of revolution within six months was unrealistic in extreme, and that more effective organizational measures were required. Ranadive's response was an attempt to isolate Ghosh by prohibiting Party members from contact with him. As the extremism of the Party's strike tactics became increasingly apparent at about the beginning of 1949, Ghosh again sent a "very strong" protest to the general secretary, accusing him of "petty-bourgeois revolutionism." Convinced that Ranadive must be "in delirium," in May Ghosh again dispatched a note asserting that the Party's trade-union tactics were "fundamentally wrong." At this, Ranadive threatened him with expulsion.[26]

Another trade-union leader who eventually defied Ranadive was S. A. Dange, president of the AITUC. Through a long history of labor activity in Bombay, Dange had established firm personal control over at least one Bombay union, the Girni Kamgar Union (GKU). Ranadive challenged that control and tried to expel Dange's lieutenants. But the Dange faction resisted and denounced the general secretary, going so far as to issue public handbills against the "Trotskyite" Ranadive.[27]

The opposition among trade-union veterans of the CPI arose only from a disagreement on tactics; this group was concerned lest premature violence disrupt the labor organizations over which they had so long presided. But a more fundamental dissent was registered by the South Indian agrarian leaders who challenged the basic strategy underlying Ranadive's policy.

Even before the Second Congress of the CPI, the Telengana movement in Hyderabad had burst its previous moderate bounds. The

---

[25] Joshi, *Views to Comrades* . . . , pp. 31–32.

[26] Prabodh Chandra, "On 'A Note . . .'," pp. 5–6.

[27] P. C. Joshi, *Problems of the Mass Movement* (Allahabad: Adhunik Pustak Bhandar, n.d., [1951?]), pp. 37–38.

threatened chain reaction of village revolt had been touched off, and within a few months hundreds of village "soviets" had been established, seizing land and murdering or driving out landlords and local officers of the Nizam's government. A full-scale guerrilla army was quickly brought into action and virtually all of Nalgonda and Warangal districts came under Communist control.[28] The Nizam's government, which was holding firm against accession to the Indian Union, was confronted with a Communist enclave in its territory.

The Communists across the state border, in the Telugu-speaking section of Madras State called Andhra, looked upon the Telengana events as the harbinger of agrarian revolution. The organizational relationship between the Andhra Communists and the Telegana movement is not clear; technically, since the Andhra Provincial Committee embraced all Telugu-speaking people both of Hyderabad and of Madras, the Hyderabad District Committee was merely a subordinate section of the Andhra Committee. In practice, however, the Andhra and Telengana Communist groups were separate entities, divided as they were by state boundaries, and the Telengana leadership exercised a great deal of autonomy. In any event, close collaboration between Communists in Andhra and Telengana was established early in 1948, and the Andhra Communist leaders sought to extend the agrarian revolt to their area. There were combined guerrilla operations on both sides of the border, but on the Andhra side the lack of a suitable organization, as well as a lower degree of peasant discontent, meant that Telengana could not be duplicated.[29]

Nevertheless, from the outset it was the Andhra Communist leaders rather than the Telengana general staff who took it upon themselves to oppose Ranadive's policy within the CPI, speaking for agrarian revolution. In their campaign they possessed an important source of strength: a persuasive theoretical argument of external origin. As Ranadive had found sanction for his theories in the Yugoslav writings, so the Andhra leaders found their sanction in the Chinese Communist writings. Thus at the beginning of 1948 the ideas of Mao Tse-tung began to be applied in India and, indeed, to influence the formulation of CPI policy.

Though it is an oversimplification, the attachment to Maoism of the Andhra Communists seems attributable, in large part, to one factor—their social background. The Andhra CP was dominated by a group of Kamma landlords, members of the Kamma caste which

[28] *On Telengana,* Information Document No. 7 (2), (Politburo, CPI, Oct. 7, 1950), pp. 4–5.
[29] "Self-Critical Report of the Andhra Communist Committee," [typed copy, 1952?], Part I, pp. 25–31.

owned 80 per cent of the land in the fertile delta area.[30] Maoism, with its tolerance for wealthy peasant classes, suited their position admirably.

Organizationally, the Andhra Communists were very weak, for the Andhra Provincial Committee had been almost totally disrupted by government repression and only a small Secretariat remained. Despite this, only a few months after the CPI Second Congress the Secretariat began a factional campaign against the Ranadive leadership. In the so-called Andhra Letter of June, 1948, the Andhra Communists declared that Mao's "new democracy" should serve as "guidance to India." [31] They proposed a strategic formula by which the entire peasantry (including the rural bourgeoisie or rich peasants) would be united under the leadership of the working class for "guerrilla warfare (Chinese way)." For since, according to the Secretariat, only the big bourgeoisie and the big landlords had become reactionary,

the middle peasant is a firm ally in the revolution and participates in the revolution. The rich peasant who has no feudal tails can be neutralized as a class but in areas like Telengana and Rayalaseema, where feudalism is very strong, it is even possible to get sections of rich peasantry in the struggle (though vacillating).[32]

Summing up, the Andhra Secretariat said of India:

Our revolution in many respects differs from the classical Russian Revolution; and is to a great extent similar to that of the Chinese Revolution. The perspective is likely not that of general strikes and general rising leading to the liberation of the rural side; but the dogged resistance and prolonged civil war in the form of an agrarian revolution culminating in the capture of political power by a democratic front.[33]

The Ranadive and Andhra views are here clearly contrasted.

As P. C. Joshi later commented, the Andhra Communists merely replaced Ranadive's obedience to the Russian example with equal obedience to the Chinese example. And he added that "the swing-over from ignorant, insolent slandering to blind and servile idol-worship comes very naturally and easily to the Indian intellectuals with our traditional outlook determined by the caste-ridden and Brahmin-dominated feudal society." [34]

---

[30] Selig S. Harrison, "Caste and the Andhra Communists," *American Political Science Review*, L (June, 1956), pp. 380–381.

[31] "Self-Critical Report . . . ," Part I, p. 15. The original version of the Andhra Letter has not been available, but it is summarized in this document.

[32] "Struggle for People's Democracy and Socialism—Some Questions of Strategy and Tactics," *Communist*, II (June–July, 1949), p. 71. This source contains extensive quotations from the Andhra Letter.

[33] *Ibid.*, p. 83.

[34] P. C. Joshi, *For a Mass Policy* (Allahabad: Adhunik Pustak Bhandar, n.d. [1951?]), p. 15.

The CPI's advocacy of self-determination for Indian "nationalities" had evoked a greater response among the Andhras than among any other linguistic group, and it was very largely by this tactic, as well as by its land policy, that the CPI was able to implement its strategy of appealing to the Andhra bourgeoisie, both urban and rural. Hence, the Andhra Communists had made self-determination the first point in their program.[35]

In essence then, the Andhra program combined the CPI's nationality policy with the Maoist version of the anti-imperialist strategy and the Maoist tactic of agrarian revolution.

Ranadive's Response to Andhra Opposition

Whereas Ranadive had been able to counter the opposition of trade-union veterans within the Party by means of private organizational sanctions, he was forced to accord greater respect to the Andhra challenge, buttressed as it was by the mounting prestige of Chinese Communist ideas. Hence the general secretary brought to bear all the authority of his office, using the pages of the Party's official theoretical journal, *Communist,* for a powerful rebuttal in the shape of four articles in the January, February, and June–July issues.

In the first, he presented a basic restatement of his strategy, reiterating his formulation of "people's democracy" as applied to India. It involved the assumption that the time had come, in India, to pass on to the socialist revolution—that is, that the Indian economy had reached a high stage of capitalist development and was ready for conversion to socialist forms of organization. The logical implication of this stand was that the democratic revolution had virtually been completed—that imperialism had been practically eliminated and the bourgeoisie had come to power. Accordingly, bourgeois capitalism was the main enemy. Ranadive envisaged a regime, therefore, which would take power during the transition between the democratic and socialist revolutions and, under an antibourgeois strategy, would immediately undertake the struggle for socialism. He sought to show that his views merely restated the orthodox theory of uninterrupted revolution, and he supported his argument with copious quotations from Lenin and Stalin.[36]

In the second article, Ranadive specifically applied his strategic

---

[35] *On Telengana,* p. 4.

[36] B. T. Ranadive, *On People's Democracy* (Bombay: Communist Party of India, n.d., [1949?]), 12 pp. Reprinted from *Communist,* II (Jan., 1949). A longer and more detailed discussion of this theoretical debate appears in John H. Kautsky, *Moscow and the Communist Party of India* (New York: The Technology Press of Massachusetts Institute of Technology and John Wiley & Sons, Inc., 1956), pp. 61–80.

formula to the rural scene. Assuming that there was a high degree of capitalist development in the countryside, he called for an attack on the rural bourgeoisie—the rich peasantry. Only the middle peasantry (the petty bourgeois element of the peasantry), he said, could be an ally in the socialist revolution. The logical inference of this argument was, then, that feudalism, as well as imperialism, had largely been eliminated.[37]

In the third article, Ranadive was concerned to show the European source of his ideas, presumably in order to strengthen his stand by an orthodox statement of the Cominform line. He criticized the old, pre-1947 view of "people's democracy," lumping a variety of "errors" under the epithet "revisionism." [38] It is interesting that Ranadive used this opportunity to attack the Yugoslavs; like the Soviet leaders he attributed revisionist views to the Yugoslav Party, though in fact the Yugoslavs, in 1947, had been the chief opponents of such views.

In the last article [39] Ranadive reiterated, in the most extreme terms, the major points of his position. He claimed that "the entire experience of the Russian Revolution is fully valid in the case of India also"—that Russian history provided the model for India. Reviewing his strategy, he repeated that the bourgeoisie was the main enemy since it was "the leading member" of the "feudal-imperialist-bourgeois combine." Three pages later, however, he retreated a bit from this stand, conceding that the bourgeois government of India "remains tied to the imperialists" in a dependent relationship, and that imperialism was therefore the chief enemy. In general, however, his tone was harsh and violent, and scattered throughout his article was such revolutionary phraseology as "Fascist terror," "revolutionary upsurge," "wide mass battles," and "miniature civil wars."

In this article Ranadive displayed the views of the Andhra Secretariat and attacked them specifically. Quoting from the Andhra Letter, he detailed the Andhra strategy of combining four classes, including the rural bourgeoisie, for agrarian revolution, and declared that this was "reformism in its most naked and gross form," a "shamefaced theory of class collaboration." He repeated that the rich peasantry is an enemy, and he implied that the Andhra Party leaders failed to acknowledge this only because they were themselves predominantly "rural intellectuals, sons of rich and middle peasants."

If there is any doubt of Ranadive's self-confidence, it is dispelled

[37] "On the Agrarian Question in India," *Communist*, II (Jan., 1949), pp. 13-53.
[38] "Struggle Against Revisionism Today, In the Light of Lenin's Teachings," *Communist*, II (Feb., 1949), pp. 53-66.
[39] "Struggle for People's Democracy . . . ," pp. 21-89.

by another element in his last article: a broadside against Mao Tse-tung himself. Having attacked the views of the Andhra Secretariat, he did not shrink from attacking the source of those views; after stating that "this is not the place to sit in judgment over the formulations of Comrade Mao," Ranadive proceeded to do just that. Some of those formulations, Ranadive declared, were "such that no Communist Party can accept them; they are in contradiction to the world understanding of the Communist Parties." Going even further, he applied the terms "erroneous," "reactionary," "counter-revolutionary," and "horrifying," to specific ideas quoted from Mao's writings.

Ranadive's attack came on the eve of victory for the Chinese Communist revolution. There has been much speculation that Ranadive dared make so amazing a public assault at such a time only because he knew that Mao's theory of "new democracy" was already under assault from Moscow. Indeed, some Indian Communists so explained it. Ajoy Ghosh later wrote that when he and his jail mate heard of Ranadive's attack on Mao

we said that our leaders could not do this on their own. The example of Tito and Gomulka was there fresh in our consciousness and we thought our comrades [Ranadive and the Politbureau] must have received some information from the international sources that there would be some big blowup in China; that this must be the result of their discussion with the international comrades.[40]

Ghosh offers no further information to show that his own interpretation was correct. However, in another inner-Party document, the later self-critical report of the Andhra leadership itself, there is a hint of evidence for this hypothesis. This report states that in his attack on the Andhra Secretariat Ranadive made use of "the Soviet Bureau documents" which showed that the revolution in India would be a complete socialist revolution.[41] But the report does not identify the "Soviet Bureau" or otherwise elaborate on this cryptic remark, and other inner-Party documents for this period offer no further information.

On the other hand, however, with Dyakov's book of 1948 on the Indian nationality question and with Zhukov's review endorsing it, the Soviet authorities had already taken a theoretical position which contradicted Ranadive's and which may have reflected an appreciation of certain elements of Maoism. The hypothesis that Ranadive had support in Moscow for his attack on Mao must, therefore, remain at least unproven.

---

[40] Prabodh Chandra, "On 'A Note . . .'," p. 5.
[41] "Self-Critical Report . . . ," Part II, pp. 1-2.

In any event, Ranadive's articles show clearly that he was convinced he should draw guidance for India only from the Cominform. As a major argument against Mao, he said:

Firstly, we must state emphatically that the Communist Party of India has accepted Marx, Engels, Lenin and Stalin as the authoritative sources of Marxism. It has not discovered new sources of Marxism beyond these. Nor for the matter of that is there any Communist Party which declares adherence to the so-called theory of new democracy alleged to be propounded by Mao and declares it to be a new addition to Marxism. Singularly enough there was no reference to this new addition to Marxism in the Conference of Nine Parties in Europe [Cominform].[42]

That Ranadive himself should thus expose this inner-Party debate in print signifies the gravity of the dispute. It may also indicate that the Party apparatus was so badly disrupted as to prevent thorough circulation of confidential inner-Party documents, and Ranadive had no choice but to resort to the journal. Finally, it suggests the possibility that Ranadive wished to communicate his views to readers outside the Party itself—to sympathizers within India, or to advisers abroad. Conceivably, he may have hoped that fellow-travelers in India could, on this occasion as on others, have some influence on Party policy (see chapter 17); and, what was more important, he may have hoped to insure support from the authoritative sources, in London or Moscow, of international Communist policy for India.

While his campaign against the Andhra Secretariat consumed a good part of his energies, Ranadive did not neglect his effort to bestir the revolutionary masses. As the failure of his insurrectionist tactics grew more apparent, his calls to arms grew more intense. Although he was under warrant of arrest, Ranadive and a handful of the central leadership remained at large, and the Party continued to publish its journals and occasional pamphlets whose pages bristled with incitement to revolt. It is at least possible that the government chose deliberately to permit their publication in the belief that the Party would discredit and disrupt itself.

Ranadive professed to view the situation around him with satisfaction, asserting that the revolutionary upsurge had already incited the government to counterrevolutionary measures that would only inspire the masses further. The government had betrayed its weakness and its reactionary nature, he said; more, it had revealed itself as a "fascist monster rearing its head." When the new constitution of the Republic of India was promulgated at the end of 1949, Ranadive de-

---

[42] "Struggle for People's Democracy . . . ," p. 77.

nounced it as "a slave constitution," a "constitution of fascist tyranny." [43]

Casting about for signs of revolution, Ranadive was forced to turn to the Telengana movement. While on the one hand he quarreled with its policy, he had necessarily to point to the movement as the primary evidence of revolutionary upsurge. In the same months during which Ranadive attacked the Andhra Secretariat in the pages of *Communist,* the Party published a statement hailing Telengana as "the warning of the advancing floodtide of the people's democratic revolution." [44]

In fact, however, the Telengana movement itself was faltering. During the early part of 1948 the movement had waxed powerful on the strength of peasant support for a program directed against traditional local enemies, and especially the autocracy. But when the CPI, under its new policy, focused its opposition on the Nehru government, the Telengana Communists tended to restrain their action against the Nizam's regime. They declared that they would resist Hyderabad's integration with the Indian Union, and they called upon the Nizam for protection against Nehru. Indeed, in return for this apparent support the Nizam's government lifted the ban on the Party that had been in force since 1943.

When, in September, 1948, the Indian Army marched into Hyderabad to secure its integration, the Communists proclaimed an "Azad [free] Hyderabad" and called for resistance to the "fascist" troops.[45] The Telengana Communist guerrillas fought alongside of, and at times apparently in collaboration with, their former enemies, the Razakars, a private army representing extremist Muslim sentiment loyal to the Nizam.[46] Within a matter of days the Indian Army quelled all other resistance, including the Razakars, but the Communist guerrillas resorted to hit-and-run tactics and could not be crushed. The Indian government then brought in extra forces and succeeded in confining the revolt, if not in terminating it. In a confidential statement circulated within the Party, the Telengana leader Ravi Narayan Reddy

---

[43] *Manifesto of the Central Committee of the Communist Party of India on the New Constitution* (Bombay: The Communist Party of India, n.d., [1949?]), pp. 1, 4. See also, *One Year of People's Struggles* (Bombay: Communist Party of India, 1948), 16 pp.; *One Year of Freedom* (Bombay: Communist Party of India, 1948), 20 pp.

[44] *What is Happening in Hyderabad?* (Bombay: Communist Party of India, 1949), 26 pp.

[45] "Self-Critical Report . . . ," Part I, pp. 24–25; also, *On Telengana,* pp. 7–9; and Bhayyaji Kulkarni, *et al., Struggle Against Sectarian Legacy and For a New Perspective* (Poona: n.p., 1950).

[46] Alan Campbell-Johnson, *Mission With Mountbatten* (New York: E. P. Dutton and Company, 1953), pp. 325, 331.

admitted that the movement degenerated into a series of "indiscriminate and unnecessary terrorist actions against non-military individuals." This brought "much disrepute" to the leadership, he said, and as a result "we practically came to a state of liquidation." The Party was "unable to mobilize the people behind the struggle," and only tiny remnants of the guerrilla forces remained.[47]

On the Andhra side of the border, the situation was still less promising for the Communists. The attempts of the Andhra leaders to promote a Telengana-style rebellion had produced nothing; worse, it had disrupted the Party. As Andhra leaders later admitted, "the people did not join us." Since the people were not prepared, they said, "our activites proved to be like a battle in the air." Efforts to stir the masses to violence by the power of example led to individual terrorism, and this in turn resulted in further isolation and repression of the Party. By the end of 1948, the leaders conceded, "on the whole there were no struggles or strikes in the entire province." As a result, the Andhra Party membership shrank from 21,000 to 7,000; indeed, certain of its district organizations openly opposed the Secretariat's policy. In a number of areas the Party was "shattered to pieces." [48]

The views of the Andhra Communists had not therefore proved markedly successful in practice, and it is unlikely that they would have prevailed in the CPI on the strength of indigenous support. But now, in a period of declining strength, the Andhra leaders found themselves possessed of international Communist sanction.

Soviet Approval of the Chinese Pattern

If there had been Russian opposition to Mao Tse-tung, it was quickly overcome. Almost simultaneously with Ranadive's polemic against Mao, Soviet authorities bestowed official approval on the Chinese pattern of revolution. At a meeting of Soviet academicians held in June, 1949, and presided over by Zhukov, the anti-imperialist strategy of Lenin, which in its more modern version had been the heart of the early Soviet definition of "people's democracy" and of Mao's "new democracy," was promulgated for Asia as a whole—this time, without dissent.

In his opening speech Zhukov gave great emphasis to the similarity between the Eastern European and Chinese theories.[49] While there

---

[47] Quoted in O. P. Sangal, *Telengana and the Rajeshwar Rao Leadership* (Allahabad: Adhunik Prakashan, 1951), pp. 53, 55. Sangal was a colleague of P. C. Joshi in opposition to the CPI leadership at this time.

[48] "Self-Critical Report . . . ," Part I, p. 35, and Part II, pp. 12–17.

[49] E. Zhukov, "Voprosy natsional'no-kolonial'noi bor'by posle vtoroi mirovoi voiny" [Problems of National and Colonial Struggle After the Second World War],

were differences in "tempo" (that is, in levels of development), the
same general laws of development obtain in both, he said; thus "in
its basic features People's Democracy in the East does not differ from
People's Democracy in the West." The program of the Chinese regime,
Zhukov said, demonstrated that it was realizing the stage of people's
democracy appropriate to the Chinese national situation.

Defining the strategy for Asia, Zhukov said:

> In the struggle for People's Democracy in the colonies and semicolonies are united
> not only the workers, the peasants, the petty bourgeoisie, the intelligentsia, but
> even certain sections of the middle bourgeoisie which is interested in saving itself
> from cut-throat foreign competition and imperialist oppression.

Since the countries of Asia were at a lower level of economic and
cultural development than Eastern Europe, said Zhukov, the revolution in Asia must at the outset be anti-imperialist, not anticapitalist.
It is clear that India was included in this formula; Zhukov did not
specify that the strategy was applicable only "in some countries,"
and he spoke of the "big bourgeoisie" as the enemy in India, as elsewhere in Asia.

In the realm of tactics, Zhukov now appeared to give explicit sanction to violent revolt in India and throughout Southeast Asia. Hailing
"the armed struggles of the peoples of a number of colonial and dependent countries," he specifically cited "the peasant uprisings in
India" along with revolts in Indonesia, Indochina, Malaya, Burma,
and China. These struggles, he said, bore witness to the fact that the
national-liberation movement had entered a "new and higher stage."

Delivering the meeting's principal report on India, V. Balabushevich gave a full-scale presentation of the way in which the Chinese
strategy and tactics should be applied to India.[50] He stated that certain
elements of the middle bourgeoisie could be counted as temporary
"fellow-travellers" of the revolution; and he designated those elements
as including the section whose interests were violated by foreign capital, and the bourgeoisie of the more backward "nationalities" of India.
Moreover, Balabushevich followed Zhukov's lead in hailing the development of armed struggle in India. He praised the Telengana
movement as the "first attempt at creating People's Democracy in

---

Voprosy Ekonomiki [Problems of Economics], No. 9, 1949, pp. 54–62. Reprinted in
Colonial Peoples' Struggle for Liberation (Bombay: People's Publishing House,
1950), pp. 1–11.

[50] V. Balabushevich, "Novyi etap natsional'no-osvoboditel'noi bor'by narodov
Indii" [The New Stage in the National-Liberation Struggle of the People of India],
Voprosy Ekonomiki, No. 8, 1949, pp. 30–49. Reprinted in *Colonial Peoples' Struggle
. . .* , pp. 32–59.

India." It was, he said, "the harbinger of agrarian revolution" and "the most important content" of the liberation movement. He clearly indicated that this was the path that the Indian Communists must follow. Thus the program of the Andhra Secretariat, adapted from Maoism with a heavier emphasis upon cultivating subnational particularism, was clearly confirmed.

This new Soviet formula was promptly communicated to all the Asian Communist parties. Zhukov's and Balabushevich's articles were published in the Russian journal, *Voprosy Ekonomiki* [Problems of Economics]. Dyakov echoed the new line in the chapter on India in a major Soviet book on the Asian situation, *Krizis kolonial'noi sistemy* [Crisis of the Colonial System]; he observed that active peasant struggle, sometimes taking the form of armed uprising, was "the most characteristic feature" of the revolution in India.[51] Finally, the new message was delivered to the Asian parties in November when the Trade Union Conference of Asian and Australasian Countries met in Peking.[52] In his opening speech the Chinese leader, Liu Shao-chi, declared that the path followed by the Chinese revolution "is the path that should be taken by the peoples of the various colonial and semicolonial countries in their fight for national independence and People's Democracy." In summarizing that path he indicated that it should invariably be based on the four-class strategy and that it included "armed struggle" "wherever and whenever possible." Armed revolution, he said, is "the main form of struggle" in many Asian countries. He cited the civil war in Viet Nam, Burma, Indonesia, Malaya, and the Philippines, declaring that in those countries the parties "are acting entirely correctly." And in another passage, he said that "armed struggle for emancipation has started also in India." It is not clear whether he meant that armed revolt was or should be "the main form" in India, too, but this was surely not excluded. Though the manifesto of the Peking Conference did not include India in the list of countries engaged in armed revolt, the list was clearly not exhaustive for it was preceded by the phrase "for instance." In any event, Dyakov and Balabushevich had already stated that armed peasant revolts were

---

[51] *Krizis kolonial'noi sistemy* [Crisis of the Colonial System] (Moscow: Izdatel'stvo akademii nauk SSSR, 1949), p. 122. This article was later reprinted in India: A. Dyakov, *New Stage in India's Liberation Struggle* (Bombay: People's Publishing House, 1950), 48 pp.

[52] *Manifesto and Opening Speech by Liu Shao-chi; Trade Union Conference of Asian and Australasian Countries, Peking, November 1949* (Bombay: People's Publishing House, n.d., [1950?]), pp. 1–10. See also "Speech by Liu Shao-chi at the Conference of Trade Unions of Asia and Oceania," *For a Lasting Peace . . .* (December 30, 1949), p. 2. These two versions of the speech are identical in the passages cited.

"the most important content" or "the most characteristic feature" of the Indian revolution. It is therefore reasonably evident that, as circumstances permitted, violent agrarian revolution was decreed for the CPI.

Emphasizing that violent tactics must be combined with various forms of legal activity, Liu Shao-chi concluded his speech by calling upon the assembled delegates to discuss the nature of the "concrete struggle" to be waged in each country. But this was apparently not possible for India. The CPI sent no representatives to the meeting, and later events showed that no clear-cut decision was reached at Peking on a detailed tactical plan for the CPI.

In January, 1950, application of the Chinese program to underdeveloped Asian countries was formally approved in still another source—*For a Lasting Peace* . . . , the official organ of the Cominform.[53] With regard to India, however, the Cominform leadership appears to have hedged against total and exclusive application of either the strategic or tactical features of the Chinese path. Although the article gave high praise to the Chinese revolution, asserting that it was of "enormous significance" in strengthening the national-liberation movement in other underdeveloped countries, Liu Shao-chi's remarks were significantly altered: where Liu had said that the Chinese path, in its general aspects, should be taken by "the peoples of the various colonial and semi-colonial countries," seeming to mean all these countries, the Cominform's quotation changed the wording to "the people of many colonial and dependent countries." Thus whereas the Chinese leader claimed that the Chinese path was universally applicable in Asia, with the single qualification that the element of armed struggle might not be feasible everywhere, the Cominform seemed to insist on a more general qualification. Moreover, in discussing India the Cominform article declared that the CPI must draw on "the experience of the national-liberation movement in China and other countries."

It is possible, then, that the Cominform resisted a final decision on applying the Chinese model to the Indian revolution, and that this resistance reveals a jurisdictional dispute over the locus of international Communist guidance of Indian communism. The Cominform, which had in 1947–1948 exercised guidance over the CPI, may well have been reluctant to concede this prerogative to the Chinese leadership.

However, in a paragraph discussing the policy for India the Comin-

[53] "Mighty Advance of the National Liberation Movement in the Colonial and Dependent Countries," *For a Lasting Peace* . . . (Jan. 27, 1950), p. 1.

form article affirmed the four-class formula; thus there was no apparent difference between the Cominform and Chinese views in the realm of strategy. But, in sharp contrast to earlier Russian comments on the agrarian scene in India, the Cominform made no mention whatever of violent methods. On the basic tactical question, therefore, the Indian comrades were confronted with a bewildering ambiguity in the advice emanating from various international Communist quarters. But by now it was abundantly clear that the Ranadive strategy was finished.

The CPI Central Committee Reforms

After the Cominform article, the full impact of the new Soviet view made itself felt in the Indian Communist Party. Ranadive produced a self-accusation in which he admitted to "certain errors in dogmatist and sectarian directions" and swore allegiance to the new line. Nevertheless, his concessions were somewhat qualified, for though he admitted that the entire peasantry must be united, he insisted that the poor peasantry and the rural proletariat had to be weaned from the influence of the rich peasantry—a calculated swipe, perhaps, at the Andhra Communist leaders.[54] Moreover, according to a later inner-Party document Ranadive persisted in his anti-Maoism, stating in a letter to another Party leader that a certain section of the Peking Conference manifesto represented an "atrocious formulation." [55]

Ranadive's statement was reprinted in the official theoretical journal of the British Communist Party, as though he might still enjoy support in London. But R. Palme Dutt remained silent, and Ranadive could not, therefore, show that any quarter of international communism sanctioned his leadership. Only the Andhra Secretariat could claim to be the legitimate bearers of the new line. With supposed international approval, therefore, this faction took over the leadership of the Party.

At a meeting of the Central Committee in May, 1950—the first in two years—the Andhra leaders effected a palace revolution in the Party. Ironically, it was enabled to do so by an amendment to the Party constitution, secured by Ranadive himself at the CPI Second Congress, which empowered the Central Committee to reconstitute itself. The old Committee removed Ranadive as general secretary and then elected a new Committee of nine members, four of whom were

---

[54] "The Situation in India," *Communist Review* (London, June, 1950), pp. 175–184.

[55] "Letter of the New Central Committee (Reconstituted by the Central Committee Elected at the Second Party Congress) to All Party Members and Sympathizers," June 1, 1950, p. 5.

from Andhra. It is interesting to note that of the old Committee's thirty-one members, nineteen were able to attend this meeting despite government repression of the Party; only six were in jail, while one was dead, three had been removed or suspended, and two failed to appear. The new Committee completed the *coup* by electing C. Rajeshwar Rao, the leading member of the Andhra Secretariat, as general secretary.[56]

Immediately after this meeting the Editorial Board of *Communist* also reconstituted itself, and in the next issue of the journal it formally withdrew the Ranadive self-critical statement, which represented, it said, "an utterly left-sectarian line" and a "full-fledged Trotskyite thesis"; in another statement, elaborating on the first, it added the epithet "left-opportunist." And the Board sent greetings to the Communist Party of China on the occasion of its twenty-ninth anniversary, declaring that "the Communist Parties in the colonial world are looking upon the Communist Party of China as their model." [57]

Aside from these gestures, the Editorial Board offered only a vague statement of its new policy. A clearer exposition was provided in a confidential letter "to all Party members and sympathisers," circulated within the Party by the Central Committee.[58] First, the letter reviewed the internal situation in the Party. The organization had been brought "to the verge of disruption," it said, and "a stinking barrack-like atmosphere of suspicion, intrigue, and tension" had prevailed under Ranadive's control. Only international Communist intervention in the form of the new line had saved the Party, in the eleventh hour, from "total disruption." But after acknowledging that the Party was a shambles, the new Committee proceeded to outline an exceedingly ambitious program—one, moreover, in which it was abundantly clear that the Andhra Communists were determined to mobilize the Party for armed agrarian revolution.

By declaring that it based its deliberations not only on the Cominform article and the Peking Conference, but on articles by the Russians—Zhukov, Dyakov, Balabushevich, Maslennikov and others—the new Central Committee showed that it had access to all the relevant international sources of guidance. But though these sources were ambiguous on the question of armed struggle, the Committee was not. It stated that the Chinese program signified, first, a strategy of "united national front" in which the middle bourgeoisie, including the rich peasantry, would be combined with the other progressive classes. And

---

[56] *Ibid.*, pp. 13–14.

[57] *Communist*, III (July–Aug., 1950), pp. 1–26.

[58] "Letter of the New Central Committee . . . ," pp. 4–15.

secondly, it said, the Chinese program included as an "essential point" the stand that the national-liberation struggle "has to be waged by means of armed guerrilla warfare in the countryside, the formation of liberation bases and liberation armies—culminating in the seizure of power all over the country." The Committee thus asserted that armed struggle was a necessary concomitant of Maoism.

In another passage, the Central Committee acknowledged that armed struggle had been decreed only for "many," not for all, colonies. Nevertheless, the letter insisted that the international authorities had included India among those countries where conditions were ripe for violence; in support of this it could and did quote from another Cominform article, which had appeared in May, that listed India among the countries where armed struggle was in progress. This article, added to similar references in the Russian journals and in Liu Shao-chi's speech, had apparently been sufficient to convince the new Committee that it had full international approval for promoting Telengana-type revolt throughout India. Thus the Committee was able to cite "the direct political guidance of the Cominform Bureau and political assistance of the brother Parties" as a "guarantee" that its line was correct.

In addition to claiming international approval, the new Committee in its letter chided those comrades who nevertheless contended that India was not in fact ripe for armed struggle. Indeed, the Committee presented a picture of enormous revolutionary potentialities. The Indian masses, it said, had learned that the Congress government was a government of "blood-suckers"; previous illusions about this "satanic" regime had been "completely shattered," and the people wanted action. The main precondition for revolution, "the mass desire that the ruling power should go," already existed, the Committee said. "The objective conditions for starting guerrilla resistance are there, taking India as a whole, leaving aside some areas." In fact, although the Party was weak, according to the Committee the only way to strengthen and extend it was to adopt violent tactics. While the letter conceded in a passing comment that the Party must not neglect other tasks such as its own needed reorganization, the new leadership was committed, as the letter said, to put the Party "on the rails of armed struggle in the countryside."

In another significant passage the Committee served notice that the Party would renew the appeal, neglected by Ranadive, to regional-linguistic particularism. Pointing to the strength of the movements for autonomous provinces, the Committee declared that the Party must "seize the initiative and lead these movements as part of the general struggle for national independence and People's Democracy." It pointed out, as had Dyakov, that these movements were directed against the ruling big-bourgeoisie and the feudal princes, and asserted that they were "progressive."

In the following months the new CPI leaders set about realizing their goal of extending armed agrarian revolt throughout India. They prepared a confidential summary of the Telengana experience, to be used as a pattern; although this summary is almost certainly exaggerated, it provides the best evidence of the nature of Communist action there. According to this document, a total of 3,000 villages had been Sovietized, and one million acres of land had been seized by the peasants. Regular guerrilla squads numbered 2,000 members, and village squads provided an estimated 10,000 more. Before the occupation of Hyderabad by the Indian Army, the Nizam's police had "butchered" about 2,000 people, and the guerrillas in turn killed an equal number of police and landlords. In action against the Indian Army, guerrillas had killed 200 and suffered losses of more than 300.[59] Such was the movement which, according to the new leadership, had "blazed the path of Indian People's Democratic Revolution."

To encourage the adoption of this model the Central Committee subsequently dispatched reports and instructions concerning guerrilla movements developing in other isolated areas. In a report on the hill-border regions of Mymensingh (East Pakistan), for example, the Committee furnished a very detailed description of the local movement, including its tactics of guerrilla action, methods of armament manufacture, and specific raids against police units.[60]

The Andhra Communists, in a cooler mood two years later, confessed their own "mad faith in the armed guerrilla fights." [61] That faith was not shared, however, by substantial sections of the Party.

Renewed Opposition Within the Party

The revolutionary admonitions of the Rao leadership intensified the confusion within an exhausted and disorganized Party. The CPI was without effective detailed guidance from the international Communist authorities, and it seems likely that those authorities were again content, as in the early period of Ranadive's leadership, to permit revolutionary effort in India as long as it had any prospect of

---

[59] *On Telengana*, pp. 5, 9, 16.
[60] "Report on the Struggle in the Hill-Border Regions of Mymensingh, Bengal," Information Document No. 6 (1), (Sept. 30, 1950), [typed copy], 14 pp. See also "Tripura State People's Heroic Armed Resistance to Fascist Terror," C. C. Information Document No. 5 (Dec. 3, 1950), [typed copy], 10 pp.
[61] "Self-Critical Report . . . ," Part III, p. 3.

success. However, several sections of the CPI stood out as stalwart opponents of the prevailing line.

The most dramatic opposition came from P. C. Joshi. Formally outside the Party, Joshi had waged an incessant campaign against the Ranadive program, and now he was equally set against the Andhra line. He utilized the experience and skills acquired in a long career as a Party functionary, and he employed devices of opposition virtually unknown in the Communist world. Apart from his efforts to maintain contact with and influence over his former associates, Joshi published at least three known pamphlets and founded a monthly magazine to express his views.[62] In his appeal for support against the prevailing CPI leadership, he openly addressed not only the public at large but foreign Communist parties as well. Joshi's polemics were extremely indiscreet, for he was, as he expressed it, "in a very disturbed emotional state"; but he vowed that he was loyal to the Party and was doing nothing which he knew to be "unworthy of a Communist."

Joshi argued from entirely orthodox sources; he demonstrated that he was thoroughly familiar with the international Communist press and frequently showed a shrewd insight into international Communist expectations. Joshi castigated the Rao leadership for the same error that Ranadive had made: the assumption of a revolutionary situation in India. He claimed, both from a reinterpretation of international Communist articles and from pragmatic evidence, that the country was not ripe for armed violence. In one passage he drew a clear contrast between the historical development of the Indian Communist movement and that of China, to demonstrate that the Chinese path could not be mechanically applied. He argued, essentially, for a return to the "loyal opposition" of the immediate postwar period, under a four-class strategy and parliamentary tactics. So widely did Joshi make his position known that, according to Indian press comment, the government hoped that he would lead a Titoist faction out of the Party and, in order to facilitate this, did not arrest him.[63]

But more effective opposition to the Andhra line came from the Communist leaders in the trade unions. This group, too, considered the new policy to be adventurist and a threat to the Party's very existence as an organization. Since they were better able to work within the Party, their opposition was less sensational than Joshi's; nevertheless, it took unusual forms.

---

[62] See P. C. Joshi, *For a Mass Policy; Problems of the Mass Movement;* and *Views* . . . The journal which Joshi published was titled *India Today* (Allahabad). It began publication in May, 1951.

[63] The press statements are quoted in *Crossroads*, I (April 7, 1950), p. 7.

S. A. Dange was again one of the leaders of the trade-union opposition. In July, 1950, he issued a statement to the press denying that the
CPI was planning armed revolt; he said that "unfortunately that impression was strengthened to some extent by the ill-planned behavior
of some sections of the leadership of the Communist Party." He declared that his own views were not final and authoritative, and that
some questions of Party policy were still under discussion, with many
groups holding conflicting ideas.[64]

A week later the Party press reported a Politbureau statement to
the effect that Dange spoke for himself and not for the Party.[65] Con-
firming Dange's declaration that CPI policy was under discussion in
the ranks, this statement said that all members could express their
views, but that "in public statements all Party members must conform
to the line enunciated by the Central Committee." In fact, an inner-
Party debate was in progress such as the Party had never experienced
before, and Party discipline was completely shattered.

The previous April, Dange had prepared a long critical analysis of
Party policy entitled "Some Notes on the Roots of Our Mistakes After
Calcutta," [66] for circulation within the Party. Now, in September,
Ajoy Ghosh and S. V. Ghate joined him in writing another similar
statement.[67] It asserted that Party membership had dropped from
nearly 100,000 to 20,000; that Communist trade unions were in a state
of "complete paralysis and stagnation"; that peasant organizations
were "practically wiped out"; and that the Party itself was in a condition of "paralysis and disintegration." The gist of both of these statements, like those of Joshi, was an attack on the adventurism of both
Ranadive and Rao.

By the fall of 1950, the so-called Party Headquarters Unit (PHQ)
was providing a focal point from which the activities of the opposition could emanate. This unit, composed of members working at headquarters and of various types of Party leaders, served as forum for the
airing of dissident views and, indeed, printed an irregular opposition
journal entitled *PHQ Open Forum*. In October the journal reported a
speech by Ajoy Ghosh that expressed with unusual clarity the condition to which the Party had come; he declared:

Today the reality is that nobody in the Indian Party can solve this crisis. It was
the international comrades who pointed out our mistakes. Since we are not agreed
on the interpretation, only they can help us. We must, therefore, contact the inter-

---

[64] *Ibid.* (July 28, 1950), p. 2.
[65] *Ibid.* (Aug. 11, 1950), p. 5.
[66] "Some Notes on the Roots of Our Mistakes After Calcutta," 43 pp.
[67] "A Note on the Present Situation in Our Party," pp. 4–5.

national leaders. None of us is clear what the *Lasting Peace* editorial means. If anybody claims he is correct, it is arrogance on his part.[68]

New Advice from London

In the very month in which Ghosh declared that the Party faced an insoluble "crisis," a new lead came at last from abroad—this time from London. After almost three years of seeming indifference, the British Party reclaimed its role as tutor to the CPI, dispatching a confidential letter to the Central Committee from the Political Committee of the British Communist Party.

The Rao leadership, however, not only refused at first to act on the British advice, but did not even allow the letter to circulate within the Party: British counsel, ordinarily considered authoritative, was "suppressed," as later inner-Party accusations phrased it. It was not until about three months later, in December, that the document fell into the hands of the Party Headquarters Unit and became known to the Party as a whole when PHQ circulated it "on its own responsibility." [69]

In the letter, the British Party chided the Indian leadership for having neglected to make a concrete analysis of the Indian situation and for having failed to furnish any concrete proposals for reorganization of the Party. It called for solution of the Party crisis by means of "full and unfettered discussion" throughout the rank and file, and by election of a new leadership "enjoying the confidence of the membership," commenting that the method of choosing the existing Central Committee had represented a "denial of democracy." It called for a complete purging of the "Trotskyite-Titoite cancer" and recommended a Party Conference for the selection of new leaders.

Proceeding to questions of policy, the British letter noted that the CPI had apparently failed to provide "current political leadership on burning issues," having no policy on Korea, on the peace movement, on the rising cost of living, on famine in Bihar, or on other practical political questions. Instead, according to the letter, there was a "paralyzed silence." The basic source of the problem was a "distortion" of the January article in *For a Lasting Peace* . . . , by which the Rao leadership assumed that armed struggle was the main and immediate task of the Party. The tactic of armed struggle is not excluded for India, the letter explained, and that aim should be pursued "as the path to victory"; but it is not an immediate prospect in view of the

---

[68] Prabodh Chandra, "On 'A Note . . .'," p. 9.

[69] "PHQ Unit's Covering Note to the Letter of the Political Committee of the CPGB to the Communist Party of India," Dec. 6, 1950, 6 pp.

situation in the Party and in India. In conclusion, the letter urged that all opportunities for legal activity be utilized and, above all, that the CPI prepare for the coming general elections.

Within three weeks after the dissemination of this letter within the Party, the CPI Central Committee met to take stock. The task before it was appalling: to formulate a genuine political program appropriate to a peaceable party, in place of strategic abstractions or handbooks of insurrection. The Committee was forced to admit an initial defeat; it stated in the communique on the meeting that "it was not possible at this meeting to thrash out the main political differences and evolve an agreed political line." Accordingly, the Committee enlarged itself and elected a new Politbureau, "so that all major trends in the Party are represented in the leading bodies." Rajeshwar Rao continued temporarily to serve as general secretary. Finally, the Committee promised a Party Congress "as soon as possible," and it announced that it was considering the readmission of P. C. Joshi. It also passed several tentative political resolutions calling for a united front with other leftist parties and progressive elements for contesting the elections.[70]

At about this time additional counsel came from London. In answer to five questions purportedly addressed to him by the CPI, R. Palme Dutt formulated the main outlines of a policy for the new period.[71] The first question and its answer served as a device for stressing the peace movement which, Dutt said, must be mobilized against the Anglo-American imperialist bloc and for the liberation of Asia. It was the answer to the second question, however, which indicated the central feature of the new policy: asked for an appraisal of Nehru's attitude on the issues of Korea and the admission of China to the United Nations, Dutt replied that signs of a change in Indian foreign policy constituted "a very important development of the present international situation." Although Nehru's policy, Dutt said, represented only "a beginning" and was not yet a "consistent peace policy," it showed signs of "hesitant and limited" opposition to the imperialist war policy. Every step toward disentangling India from the imperialist camp must be welcomed, he indicated, and a vigorous campaign must be conducted to press for further steps toward that goal. With this single statement, the international Communist policy of irreconcilable hostility toward Nehru, maintained for three years, was replaced by a policy of qualified opposition with the possibility that common ground might be found in the realm of foreign policy. Nehru was thus recognized as a potential friend of "peace."

[70] *Crossroads,* II (Dec. 29, 1950), pp. 5–6.

[71] R. Palme Dutt, *Situation in India* (Bombay: Crossroads Pub., n.d.), pp. 2–6.

The answer to the third question elaborated on the vital role of the peace movement and stressed the necessary connection between peace and freedom. Since all wars are imperialist wars, Dutt said, anyone who is for peace is also for freedom from imperialist control. The fourth answer spelled out a new tactical line for India: a united front with leftist parties and organizations, based on a simple democratic program. This "broad democratic front" must be a united front from above, Dutt indicated, created through agreement with the leaders and representatives of other progressive parties. And it should formulate a common action program based on peace and independence, able to attract majority support, in order that the front itself might eventually furnish an alternative government. In answering the fifth question, Dutt clarified beyond doubt the inapplicability of violent tactics in the existing Indian situation. Though he specified there would be resort to armed struggle when conditions were ripe, he disqualified it as an immediate prospect.

These recommendations were further elaborated when the PHQ circulated the report of a personal interview with Dutt obtained by two unidentified Indian comrades who had traveled to London.[72] In this report the new Communist definition of the Nehru government was clarified, for Dutt had revived the idea that the Indian government contained two tendencies or wings. This he explained by saying that though it was a government of the big bourgeoisie, one part of that class, represented by Patel, leaned more heavily on imperialism, while another, led by Nehru, tended to diverge. For, said Dutt, some members of the big bourgeoisie realize that since India borders on China, a war with China might mean their own doom, and they therefore adopt a foreign policy which is not always in agreement with the imperialist camp. Thus the Indian government vacillates, he said, and popular pressure must be applied to promote the anti-imperialist tendency.

In summary, then, with these communications to India at the end of 1950 Dutt proposed the strategy and tactics of "people's democracy" or "new democracy," but he excluded violent revolution for the time being. The four classes would be united, either through united-front-from-above tactics vis-à-vis "progressive" parties or united-front-from-below tactics vis-à-vis the Congress. The tactic of armed struggle against the government was shelved.

---

[72] Deven and Bal Krishna, "Talks With Comrade R. Palme Dutt and Other Impressions Gained Abroad by Deven and Bal Krishna," PHQ Unit, Jan. 6, 1951, 6 pp.

Preparation for the Third Congress

The Central Committee had promised to hold a Party Congress, but the CPI was riven with disagreements which had to be resolved before such a gathering could demonstrate the desired monolithic unanimity. The next period in the history of the CPI was therefore one of slow organizational and ideological renewal. The Party recovered from the trauma of internal and external insurrection only through a long process of convalescence.

The first step was taken at a meeting of the Politbureau in April, 1951, at which a "Draft Programme" and a tentative "Statement of Policy" were adopted.[73] These documents were then circulated in the Party for discussion. The Central Committee met in May for further policy discussions, and it tentatively approved the Draft Programme. The Committee also received the resignation of C. Rajeshwar Rao as general secretary; for the time being a new general secretary was not designated, but Ajoy Ghosh was named secretary of the Secretariat. A few months later Ghosh was formally elevated to the general secretary's post.

In October an All-India Party Conference was convened. It received no publicity in the Party press, but was composed, presumably, of representatives from the provincial units in addition to the Central Committee. With minor amendments it approved the Draft Programme and the Statement which thus, by gradual stages, became official Party policy.

The new Programme of the CPI was a painstaking exposition of the new line as promulgated by Dutt; it made an elaborate appeal not only to the interests of the proletariat, peasantry, and petty bourgeoisie but to those of the middle bourgeoisie as well.[74] The Party assured the "democratic" bourgeoisie that while the CPI adhered to the goal of socialism, it was "not demanding the establishment of socialism in our country in the present stage of development." Accordingly, the CPI pledged itself to protect the development of private industry against foreign competition and called for a mixed economy under general government regulation and coördination. In another programmatic device, designed as an appeal to the broadest possible audience, the CPI emphasized its demand that all "nationalities" be

---

[73] *Draft Programme of the Communist Party of India* (Bombay: Communist Party of India, 1951 [April]), 16 pp.; *Statement of Policy of the Communist Party of India* (Bombay: Communist Party of India, 1951 [May]), 12 pp.

[74] *Programme of the Communist Party of India* (Bombay: Communist Party of India, 1951 [Oct.]), 20 pp.

granted the right to self-determination, calling for the reorganization of the states according to linguistic boundaries and for the creation of a "voluntary" union.

In the realm of foreign policy, however, the Programme indicates that the CPI found Dutt's views harder to swallow. The idea that a big-bourgeois government could be even potentially a friend of peace and freedom was indeed novel, and the Indian Communists were most reluctant to abandon the thesis that the Nehru government was a lackey of imperialism: in the Programme, the CPI was at pains to emphasize that the government "essentially carries out the foreign policy of British imperialism" and to assert that the government's professions of peace were belied by its acts. Moreover, the Programme declared that Nehru's government was not only subservient to British imperialism but was also permitting American imperialism to penetrate India. Since the reference to American imperialism was an amendment to the original Draft Programme, it apparently indicates a view within the Party that American imperialism was an increasing threat to India.

Furthermore, where Dutt had lumped the imperialist powers together in the "Anglo-American bloc," the CPI kept them distinct. In dealing with the goal of national freedom, the Programme treated Britain as the main enemy of the Indian people; to be truly independent, it said, India must break with the Commonwealth, remove British capital, and get rid of British advisers in government and military posts. But, dealing with the goal of peace, the Programme treated the United States as the chief enemy. It called for a complete break with the war camp led by the U.S. and reiterated its earlier claim that Nehru's policy on the issue of peace was "spurious" or "suspicious," and not in India's interests.

Like the Programme, the Statement of Policy took a less optimistic view of Nehru's foreign policy than did Dutt.[75] Moreover, both documents gave far less attention to the issue of peace than Dutt's heavy emphasis required. The CPI bridled at the prospect of losing its primary political weapon against Nehru—the charge that he was a stooge in the imperialist camp.

But there was ample evidence of continuing inner-Party dispute over the main issues of CPI policy. During 1951, the leadership had permitted the publication of a number of pamphlets in which Party members aired conflicting views. One of these pamphlets, expressly called an "open forum," was announced to be the first in a series of

---

[75] *Statement of Policy of the Communist Party of India* (Bombay: Published by Jayant Bhatt, 1951 [Nov.]), 12 pp.

similar publications.[76] A year later, an issue of *Party Letter* admitted that there were still "dissensions" within the ranks.[77]

As it entered the campaign for the first general elections in India, the Party relied heavily upon its traditional anti-imperialistic weapon. In its election manifesto, it declared that Nehru's foreign policy was "not a policy of peace." A government "tied to imperialists," it asserted, "cannot pursue an independent and progressive foreign policy, a genuine policy of peace." In general the manifesto dealt very harshly with the Nehru government, calling it a government of "national betrayal," of "landlords and monopolists, and of *"lathis* [clubs] and bullets." [78] (For a description of the Party's election campaign, see chapter 19.)

The results of the elections appeared to provide exhilarating confirmation of the tactic of uncompromising opposition, for the Party scored its greatest victories in precisely those areas where its struggle had been boldest or even most violent—and particularly in Telengana. The radicals of the CPI must have concluded that conditions were ripe for a sterner line. However, the demands of the international Communist environment bore increasingly in the opposite direction, toward a greater emphasis upon cultivating Nehru's potentialities as a partner in peace. And when the extended plenum of the Party met at the end of 1952, it criticized the neglect of the peace movement and declared that this must be the key task of the CPI.[79] However, the resolution of the Central Committee meeting of March, 1953, posed Britain as the chief target, and continued to treat the Nehru government as a collaborator with imperialism.[80]

As the CPI approached the Third Congress, therefore, a very unstable situation prevailed in the Party on the old question, for or against the Nehru government, although now the question, for or against the bourgeoisie, had been settled.

---

[76] *Nehru's Foreign Policy* (Bombay: Crossroads Pub., n.d. [1951?]), 28 pp. This pamphlet contains a reprint of an article in *Crossroads* by Romesh Thapar, and two dissenting statements—one from M. K. Rajan and another from a group of "readers in Paris." Both statements criticize Thapar for an excessively negative attitude toward Nehru's foreign policy; they are followed by a recantation by Thapar.

Another similar pamphlet is S. G. Sardesai, Subrata Sen Gupta, and Tarun Basu, *Economic Data Relating to Some Statements in the Draft Programme* (n.p., n.d., [1951?]), 58 pp. The only copy of this pamphlet available to the authors is without a title page or cover.

[77] *Party Letter* (April, 1952), p. 34.

[78] *Election Manifesto of the Communist Party of India* (Calcutta: Central Election Board of the Communist Party of India, 1951), 29 pp.

[79] *Party Letter* (Jan. 30, 1953), p. 3.

[80] *Resolutions of the Central Committee of the Communist Party of India* (Delhi: Communist Party of India, 1953), pp. 9–10.

14 THE RETURN TO CONSTITUTIONAL COMMUNISM

When the Third Congress of the CPI met in Madura (Madras State) from December 27, 1953 to January 4, 1954, the Communists found themselves still unable to agree on the role the Party should play in its Indian environment. Though since 1950 the Party had been steadily moving away from the concept of armed struggle, it was not yet ready to limit its functioning merely to that of a parliamentary opposition party. The radical function was under a cloud as a result of the adventurism of 1948–1951, but its leaders were by no means contrite and, holding positions of power in the Communist strongholds of Andhra, West Bengal, and Bombay, they were still a force to be reckoned with.

Though camouflaged by jargon and ambiguity, the issues which most agitated the delegates at Madura can be discerned by a careful reading of the official documents. Of these issues, the most controversial and important concerned the problem of organizing a united front, and the question of the Party's attitude toward the Nehru government. Indeed, until the present writing the latter issue has dominated intra-Party discussion, and disagreement has been so serious as to cause one crisis after another within the CPI.

This chapter, therefore, will describe the evolution of CPI policy toward the Nehru government, from the Madura Congress to the beginning of 1958.

At Madura, as so often before, the CPI was torn by the conflicting demands of its dual environment. On the one hand, the government of India was pursuing a neutralist foreign policy that invited Soviet blandishments. The possibility of converting India's neutralism to anti-Western sentiment suggested that the best policy for international communism vis-à-vis India would be one which not only sharpened the conflicts between India and the West, but which promoted friendly relations between India and the Communist states. The latter could scarcely be achieved, however, if a Moscow-led Communist Party was embarked on a major campaign of internal subversion. Any Soviet plan to turn India against the West demanded that the CPI refrain from indiscretions which might embarrass the Communist powers. Thus, the international situation and loyalty to the USSR required that the CPI follow a moderate policy with regard to the Nehru government—a course which the rightists in the Party had long advocated.

On the other hand, certain elements in the Indian political scene seemed tailor-made for leftist tactics. The popular agitation for the creation of linguistic states had already produced considerable violence, and governmental authority was threatened by antagonisms among India's many linguistic groups; moreover, the presence of forty million Muslims within India's borders meant that the possibility of communal violence had always to be considered. Unsettled conditions in Kashmir, and in the Naga tribal areas, constituted another major problem for the central government, while discontent among the growing masses of unemployed, and the government's slowness in solving the land-tenure problem added to the national unrest. There was plenty of troubled water in which to fish, and many delegates at Madura wanted to declare open season.

The Conflict at Madura

The Madura Congress faced the necessity of devising a formula that would satisfy both rightists and leftists. The problem hinged on a decision as to which was the major enemy, the United States or Britain. "The question who the main enemy is, is not an academic question," said Ajoy Ghosh in his review of the Congress, "for with it is bound up our entire line of action." [1]

The Andhra branch of the Party submitted to the Madura Congress a thesis which argued that Britain was the main enemy. It stated:

Now, comrades raise the questions: Is not American imperialism the spearhead of reaction and the chief enemy of the Soviet Union, People's China and other People's Democratic States? Is not American imperialism hatching conspiracies against communist parties throughout the world, our party being no exception?

[1] Ajoy Ghosh, "On the Work of the Third Party Congress," New Age (weekly), I (Jan. 24, 1954), p. 3.

Is not American imperialism trying to penetrate into our country and exploit and enslave us? When such are the facts are we not to fight American imperialism as well? These are all very pertinent questions and we have to answer them correctly. Our party, as the vanguard detachment of the Indian working class which is part of the world working class has to fight against American imperialism. This is our inviolable international obligation or rather a revolutionary duty on our part. We, as a party of the working class, as a part of the world working class have our national and international duties to discharge. Internationally speaking, America is the spearhead of world reaction as the main enemy of Peace and Freedom for all the people. We, situated as we are in a country under a particular State, have some concrete tasks to perform. The chief enemy of our national freedom today is British imperialism.[2]

The essence of this quotation, and of the Andhra thesis, was that the requirements of the Indian environment should take precedence over the requirements of the international environment; that the chief enemy of the Soviet Union and the people's democracies was not necessarily the chief enemy of the CPI; and that the needs of Soviet foreign policy should not impede the Party's bid for political power within India. Clearly, the Andhra comrades were nationalistic.

The other faction wanted, according to Ajoy Ghosh, "to make the U.S. threat the basis of our entire activity." [3] Though this was the line most suited to the current needs of Soviet foreign policy, it should not be assumed that its champions automatically placed the needs of the Soviet Union over those of the CPI. For the anti-U.S. line would tend to push the CPI into the role of loyal opposition, while the anti-British line implied mass struggle of one sort or another. Hence the faction opposing the Andhra thesis undoubtedly included many, like P. C. Joshi, who found the tactical consequences of the anti-U.S. line more to their liking.

Both factions were strong, but in numbers it appears likely that the Andhra-led group had the edge. This advantage was negated to some extent, however. First, the anti-U.S. faction had behind it the authority of the international leadership; this was dramatically evident in the presence at Madura of Harry Pollitt, general secretary of the CPGB, who made it clear in his public speeches that he was preoccupied in attacking the United States.[4] Second, the anti-U.S. faction

---

[2] *Communist Conspiracy at Madurai* (Bombay: Democratic Research Service, 1954), pp. 51–52. This collection of documents on the Madura Congress was published by the Democratic Research Service (DRS), an anti-Communist information service in Bombay. When the DRS released the documents, the CPI branded them as forgeries. However, their close correspondence to documents published in the CPI press, and the private admissions of CPI leaders, make a strong case for accepting them as genuine.

[3] Ghosh, "On the Work of . . . ," p. 3.

[4] See *Harry Pollitt Speaks* (Calcutta: National Book Agency, 1954).

gained support from the suspected intention of the United States government to extend military aid to Pakistan. A genuine fear of Pakistani aggression, especially over the Kashmir dispute, prompted the Indian government, press, and public opinion to interpret the American plan as an unfriendly act. (Military aid to Pakistan later became a popular rallying point, and presented the CPI with a patriotic issue on which to build a mass following.)

In an article reviewing the Third Congress, Ajoy Ghosh clarified the policy-alternatives concealed behind the question as to the identity of the chief enemy:

> If U.S. imperialism becomes the main enemy not only to peace but also to our freedom, then we could take up no other attitude but one of progressively lining up behind the Nehru Government on the plea of fighting the American threat.
>
> If the U.S. constitutes a danger to peace only and in no way menaces our freedom, then the struggle against it and the struggle for peace loses all sense of urgency in relation to our country.
>
> It became necessary at the Party Congress to be absolutely clear on this point. For, the way we understand this point will decide our basic attitude towards the Nehru Government itself.[5]

Ghosh stated that there were only two possible courses of action: "coöperate with the Government but criticize specific acts; or, oppose the Government but support specific acts."

With the scales so nearly balanced between the two factions, the political resolution adopted at Madura represented an uneasy compromise: the Party chose to oppose the government, but to support specific acts. "The situation," declares the resolution, "does not warrant that democratic forces should give general overall support to governmental policies even in the international sphere. This is because the Indian Government does not follow consistently a policy of peace and democracy."[6] "Our attitude towards the Government," Ghosh wrote in summary "continues to be one of general opposition."[7]

Deteriorating Indo-American Relations

That the United States was considering military assistance to Pakistan first became publicly known in November, 1953, although the actual announcement was not made until February 25, 1954.[8]

---

[5] Ghosh, "On the Work of . . . ," p. 3. When the Party reprinted this article in pamphlet form, these paragraphs were modified to make them less clear-cut. See Ajoy Ghosh, *On the Work of the Third Congress of the Communist Party of India* (Delhi: Communist Party of India, 1954), p. 6.

[6] *Political Resolution* (Delhi: Communist Party of India, 1954), pp. 6–7.

[7] Ghosh, "On the Work of . . . ," p. 4.

[8] See James W. Spain, "Military Assistance for Pakistan," *American Political Science Review*, XLVIII (Sept., 1954), pp. 738–751.

From November on, Indo-American relations steadily declined. Harsh criticism was directed against the United States by the prime minister and by many national leaders, and all over India meetings were organized to protest the "Pak-Pact." President Eisenhower's attempt to assuage Indian feelings with assurances that America was prepared to supply arms to India, also, evoked no sympathetic response from New Delhi. "President Eisenhower has done less than justice to himself or to us," said Prime Minister Nehru. "If we are objecting to military aid being given to Pakistan we will be unprincipled opportunists to accept such aid ourselves." He added that, in view of Washington's action, American military observers attached to United Nations cease-fire supervision teams in Kashmir could "no longer be treated as neutrals." [9]

Matters were not helped when the U.S. Assistant Secretary of State Walter S. Robertson was reported to have said that the United States must "dominate" Asia for an indefinite period in the interest of peace. Speaking before the Lok Sabha (House of the People, or lower house), Nehru lashed out against the United States: "Whatever their objective may be," he said, "the countries of Asia and certainly India do not accept this policy and do not propose to be dominated by any country." [10]

The Soviet Union quickly recognized that such anti-American statements from the prime minister could be useful to Soviet foreign policy. Ten days after Nehru's speech to the Lok Sabha, Georgi Malenkov, then premier of the USSR, told a Moscow audience:

A great contribution to the cause of strengthening peace has been made by the great nation of India. We welcome the vigilance displayed by the Indian leaders in connection with attempts of forces of aggression in Asia.

After the recent statement of American diplomats declaring their intention to dominate Asia for an indefinite time, the Prime Minister of India said that countries of Asia, and India among them, will not consent to this policy and are not going to fall under the rule of any foreign state.

These words are full of deep and realistic meaning. [11]

During the spring of 1954 Nehru continued to take steps in the field of foreign affairs that met with approval in the Communist countries: he called for an end to hydrogen-bomb tests; on April 29, in Peking, the Indian government signed a trade agreement with China concerning Tibet, and the next day agreed to turn over to the Chinese, without charge, its properties in Tibet. On May 23, V. K. Krishna Menon began a series of talks with Chou En-lai in Geneva, following which,

---

[9] *The Hindu* (Madras), March 2, 1954, p. 4.
[10] *Loc. cit.*
[11] *Ibid.*, March 14, 1954, p. 5.

on June 25, Chou arrived in New Delhi for further conversation with Prime Minister Nehru. These talks produced the communique embodying the now famous *Panch Shila* (Five Principles) of peaceful coexistence.

Initial Efforts to Change the Line

After Chou En-lai's visit to India in June, there was evidence in *New Age* (weekly) that the rightist viewpoint was gaining ground in the CPI. For in the July 18 issue P. Ramamurti (its editor, and a member of the Party's nine-man Politbureau) wrote that the Nehru-Chou declarations signified a "change in the relationship of forces in Asia." After using several columns to attack the United States, Ramamurti presented his conclusion that:

> All peace-loving mankind, and our people are enthused by the fact that Nehru . . . has today taken a stand against many of the U.S. machinations in Asia and against its threat to India. . . .
> Our people have warmly and enthusiastically welcomed the development of friendly relations with China. . . . Equally enthusiastically do they welcome the development of coöperation and friendship with the Soviet Union. . . .
> The more Nehru takes a forthright stand against the imperialists and by the side of the forces of peace . . . the more enthusiastic will be the support of our millions.[12]

Ramamurti then advanced the slogan of a "national platform for peace and freedom"—a phrase which fanned the fire of Party controversy.

The significance of Ramamurti's apparently inoffensive slogan is obvious when viewed in the context of statements made by Ajoy Ghosh when he moved the Political Resolution at Madura. Ghosh had said:

> The struggle for peace and the struggle for freedom are not identical. The main edge of one is against America and of the other against the British. . . . We should understand that the two movements are not coextensive. The peace movement is broader than the struggle for liberation. All those who participate in the struggle for liberation must come into the peace movement. But all those in the peace movement may not agree to participate in the struggle for liberation.[13]

But in Ramamurti's slogan the struggle for peace and the struggle for freedom—which the Madura Congress had taken pains to keep separate—were joined. If the pro-peace forces (which included the Nehru government) could be linked with the pro-freedom forces (the CPI and its allies), then where were the differences between the two?

---

[12] P. Ramamurti, "Drive U.S. Out of Asia!" *New Age* (weekly), (July 18, 1954), p. 14.

[13] Ajoy Ghosh, "Tasks Before the Communist Party of India," in *On the Work of the Third Congress of the Communist Party of India*, pp. 23–24.

Furthermore, Ramamurti plainly pointed to the U.S. as the main enemy not only of peace, but of freedom; and the logical consequence of this was, as Ghosh had pointed out, a policy of "progressively lining up behind the Nehru Government on the plea of fighting the American threat."

The Ramamurti article brought inner-Party controversy to a climax and released a storm of debate, culminating with the charge that the Politbureau was guilty of reformist tendencies. It seems probable that it was the Party crisis rather than the announced need for medical treatment which prompted Ajoy Ghosh to depart for Moscow late in July.

At a meeting of the thirty-nine-member Central Committee, held September 5–11, a majority of the Committee supported the charge of "reformism" leveled at the Politbureau. In his official report on the meeting, E. M. S. Namboodiripad said:

> After a thorough discussion, the Central Committee came to the conclusion that the slogan of a National Platform for Peace *and Freedom* which was given in Comrade Ramamurti's article . . . is a slogan which is likely to create the impression that recent international developments have made it possible for a platform of peace *and freedom* to be evolved—a platform which will include the Congress organization.
>
> As such this was a wrong slogan because the Congress organization, dominated by landlords and monopolists collaborating with British imperialism, cannot stand for a consistent policy of peace, and there is no question of a platform with the Congress organization for freedom.[14]

Namboodiripad's report indicates that the leftists had the upper hand, and that the Party's attitude toward the Nehru Government remained unchanged.

> The Central Committee discussed this question and came to the conclusion that there was no warrant for a revision of the attitude of the Party to the Congress Government or for the revision of the central political slogan evolved at the last Madura Congress. . . . There is no question of abandoning the struggle against the Congress Government or revising the slogan of replacing it by a Government of Democratic Unity. The task of the democratic forces, on the other hand, is to intensify this struggle.[15]

Advice From Abroad

Despite the rebuff administered by the Central Committee in September, Ramamurti's analysis of the trend of international Communist policy had been correct. This became abundantly clear in

---

[14] E. M. S. Namboodiripad, "Counter Seato by Asian Solidarity," *New Age* (weekly), I (Sept. 19, 1954), p. 15. Emphasis in original.

[15] *Loc. cit.*

October when the Cominform journal published an important article by R. Palme Dutt. Dutt's article argued that a change had taken place in the world scene; since the Second World War, American imperialism had intensified its efforts to penetrate and dominate the former colonies of the Western European powers including India, Pakistan, and Ceylon, and from this fact important conclusions were to be drawn:

> First, the struggle for national independence in the countries in the sphere of British imperialism is no longer only against British imperialism, but, first of all, against the direct rule of British and the growing penetration of American imperialism. Failure to recognize this new stage of the struggle can lead to the destruction and defeat of the aims of the national liberation movement, if its leadership falls into the trap of regarding the American imperialists as the rivals and enemy of the British imperialists. . . . The fight for peace against the war drive of the imperialist camp led by American imperialism is closely linked with the fight for national independence. . . . *There can be no separation of the fight for national independence from the fight for peace.*
>
> The interests of the struggle of the colonial and dependent peoples for national independence are inseparably linked with the democratic anti-imperialist peace camp and with promoting and supporting all moves which serve the cause of world peace.[16]

Dutt was thus saying precisely what Ramamurti had said in July. He was calling for a policy of collaboration with the Nehru government. When his article became available in India, the Politbureau was still highly sensitive to the charges of reformism hurled at it during the September Central Committee meeting. Determined to avoid giving cause for additional criticism of this nature, it called another Central Committee meeting for November to discuss the article. A secret Party document published by the Democratic Research Service (DRS), an anti-Communist organization in Bombay, states that the Politbureau called this meeting for the specific purpose of rejecting the Dutt article.[17]

---

[16] R. Palme Dutt, "New Features in National Liberation Struggle of Colonial and Dependent People," *For a Lasting Peace, For a People's Democracy* (Oct. 8, 1954), p. 6. Emphasis added.

[17] *Communist Double Talk at Palghat* (Bombay: Democratic Research Service, 1956), p. 92. This is one of a second collection of documents published by the Democratic Research Service. In September, 1956, Ajoy Ghosh issued a statement which challenges the authenticity of only one document in the collection, a letter purported to have been written by Dimitri Shepilov to the CPI. Ghosh ignored the fact that the DRS version of the Central Committee's Report to the Fourth Congress is more detailed than the officially published version. As for the Organizational Report, Ghosh says: "Another so-called secret document is a note on some organizational shortcomings placed before the Congress of our Party by the Politbureau. There was nothing secret about this document. It was circulated among all delegates but was not published because it was meant for discussion only and

There is no doubt that the publication of Dutt's article in the official Cominform journal strengthened the hand of the rightist faction in the Central Committee, and when it met in November there was a stalemate which necessitated the creation of a special Commission for "reassessing the situation that had developed since Madura." [18]

Ajoy Ghosh arrived back in New Delhi from Moscow in the first week of December. *New Age* (weekly) immediately carried a leading article by him which showed that as a result of his Russian visit, he had moved somewhat to the right: "Can any serious student of Indian affairs," he asked, "deny that the foreign policy of Pandit Nehru's Government has undergone a shift in the last five years? . . . [We] support this change," he said; and he outlined the new policy as "support to the peaceful aspects of Pandit Nehru's foreign policy and relentless fight against the reactionary policies internally." [19] And in a press conference on December 7, Ghosh made the Party's position even more explicit. "The internal policy of the Nehru Government does not suit the interests of the masses," he said, "while the foreign policy does." [20]

Complicating Factors

A number of developments on the Indian scene during the winter of 1954–55 further complicated the strategical problems of the CPI. Prime Minister Nehru returned from his visit to China early in November, and in a major speech on November 28 he linked praise for China's economic progress with a bitter attack on the CPI. In the same speech he referred to the scheduled visit to India by Marshal Tito of Yugoslavia who had still not made his peace with the USSR. "Yugoslavia is a strange country," said Nehru, "in this way that it is a communist country more or less. . . . The Yugoslavs have their own communist way and because of this some estrangement had developed in the past between Yugoslavia and Russia." [21] Then, on the same day that Tito addressed the Indian parliament in New Delhi, the government introduced its resolution proclaiming the goal of government policy to be the creation of a socialistic pattern of society.[22] Tito also

not for adoption by the Congress." ("Tissue of Lies," *New Age* [weekly], III [Sept. 23, 1956], p. 2.)

[18] *Communist Double Talk at Palghat*, p. 93.

[19] Ajoy Ghosh, "Communist Answer to Pandit Nehru," *New Age* (weekly), II (Dec. 5, 1954), pp. 1, 13.

[20] "Ajoy Ghosh Answers Questions on Communist Policies," *New Age* (weekly), II (Dec. 12, 1954), p. 13.

[21] *The Hindustan Times* (New Delhi), Nov. 29, 1954, p. 12.

[22] *Ibid.*, Dec. 22, 1954, p. 1.

journeyed to Madras for the annual session of the Congress Party and endorsed the government's economic policy from the platform. Yet Tito's visit was not mentioned in the Communist press.

The most important event of the period, however, was the February election in Andhra. Andhra is one of the major strongholds of the CPI and the leadership of the Party in that state is in militant hands. The Communists had done well in Andhra in the general elections in 1952, and it was widely believed that they would improve their position in the state legislature in 1955. Because of this, the Congress Party made a gigantic effort to defeat them, forming alliances with minor parties, spending large sums of money, and sending important national personalities into the state to campaign. The main theme of the Congress campaign was that the Communist Party was loyal to a foreign power. All this effort proved effective, and the Congress won a resounding victory, capturing 61 per cent of the seats to the Communists' 8 per cent.[23] One of the unique features of the Andhra election was the fact that on January 26 (India's Republic Day) *Pravda* had published an editorial which praised the Nehru government not only for its foreign policy but for its domestic policy as well.[24] Congress election strategists in Andhra made the most of this, reprinting thousands of copies of the text and circulating them throughout the state.

The Breakdown of Central Leadership

When the Central Committee of the CPI met from March 17 to 29 to analyze the causes of the defeat in Andhra, differences within the Party had reached serious proportions and the discussions "assumed the character of an acrimonious debate." [25] According to one document:

> With this meeting of the CC ended whatever there was of the PB [Politbureau] and its functioning. The differences that had appeared in the September and November meetings of the CC took clearer and sharper forms. What is worse, these differences made those who held particular views look upon those who differed from them as people who should be "fought" and "defeated." [26]

The official communique issued after the March meeting identified two shortcomings which had contributed to the defeat in Andhra. The

---

[23] For details on the Andhra election see Marshall Windmiller, "The Andhra Election," *Far Eastern Survey*, XXIV (April, 1955), pp. 57–64; and Margaret W. Fisher and Joan V. Bondurant, *The Indian Experience with Democratic Elections* (Berkeley: University of California, 1956), pp. 79–86.

[24] See text in *Current Digest of the Soviet Press*, VII (March 9, 1955), p. 33.

[25] *Communist Double Talk at Palghat*, p. 93.

[26] *Ibid.*, pp. 93–94.

first was the Party's mistake in "not placing before the people with sufficient emphasis the important part that India was playing in recent times in the international arena in favor of world peace and against imperialist warmongers." The second was the "failure of the Party to pursue correct United Front tactics." [27] But the Central Committee was unable to come to a specific decision for remedying the situation. During the following two months the situation continued to deteriorate. The Commission which had been set up in November to reassess the Party's policy split into two factions, each of which prepared a document for consideration at the meeting of the Central Committee scheduled for June.

In June, while Prime Minister Nehru was touring the Soviet Union, the Central Committee debated for a full month before finally adopting a thirty-two page political resolution. It represented a compromise between the contesting factions, for though the resolution indicated a clear-cut stand regarding the government's foreign policy, its appraisal of the government's domestic role, and the attitude the party should take toward it, was confused and contradictory.

The resolution supported the Nehru foreign policy:

India has been playing a great role in the world-wide battle for the preservation of peace—a role that has heightened India's international prestige and evoked in every patriotic Indian a sense of national pride.

The Communist Party which has been fighting for a consistent policy of peace welcomes and supports this orientation and will strive to further strengthen it.[28]

In one passage the resolution attacked the domestic policies of the government of India:

the general attitude of the Government towards the demands and struggles of the people has been one of unconcealed hostility and of full support to the vested interests. Wherever the masses have fought against worsening conditions of life, the attempt of the Government has been to suppress them with a heavy hand. The policies of the Government have thus meant attack on the standard of life of the people and their democratic rights, interruption in production, increase in police expenditure, intensification of strife and conflict all over the country.[29]

In a later passage, the resolution appeared to call for CPI penetration into government developmental schemes:

The tendency to keep away from schemes and projects sponsored or run by the Government must be given up. We have to participate in them, actively and effectively, combat corruption, inefficiency and bureaucratic practices, help to

---

[27] "What Caused the Landslide? Communique on Delhi Meeting," *New Age* (weekly), II (April 3, 1955), p. 8.

[28] *Communist Party in the Struggle for Peace, Democracy and National Advance* (Delhi: Communist Party of India, 1955), p. 4.

[29] *Ibid.*, p. 11.

implement and run them in such a way that maximum benefit is secured for the people. This must become an important part of the activity of the Party and of mass organizations where we work.[30]

The compromise represented by the June resolution did not succeed in resolving the differences within the Party but, rather, intensified them. Once again, as frequently in the past, the Party found itself divided into three groups—the centrists, who supported the resolution, and the leftists and rightists, who opposed it. According to a Party organization report:

An intense political struggle between the supporters of the Resolution and its opponents (the latter themselves divided into two categories—those from the "left" and from the "right") became the main feature of inner-Party life from top to bottom. Even the current activity of the Party came to a standstill in most of the provinces.[31]

At the June meeting, the Central Committee had decided to call a fourth Party Congress for December, and immediately after the meeting, Ajoy Ghosh suffered a recurrence of his "old ailment" and left for Moscow on July 7. He returned to India on September 6.[32]

During September the Central Committee met again, but was still unable to resolve the different points of view. A series of amendments to the Party program was adopted at this meeting, and was circulated for discussion prior to submission to the forthcoming Party Congress for endorsement. The proposed amendments suggest that the rightists had succeeded in obtaining some slight modification of the current line, but the tortured subtlety of the proposed changes indicates how closely balanced were the opposing viewpoints. For example, where the 1951 program had described India as the "biggest dependent semi-colonial country in Asia still left for the enslavers to rob and exploit," the proposed amendment described India not as a "dependent" and "semi-colonial country," but as "the biggest country in Asia with a semi-colonial economy"; it was subject not to "enslavers," but merely to "imperialist exploitation." [33]

From the proposed amendments it is evident that the Central Committee did not oppose India's foreign policy, and was agreed that it was "in the main, a policy that helps the cause of peace and national freedom, builds Asian unity and stands for friendly relations with

---

[30] *Ibid.*, p. 30.

[31] *Communist Double Talk at Palghat*, p. 94.

[32] See *New Age* (weekly), II (July 10, 1955), p. 1, and (Sept. 11, 1955), p. 4.

[33] See *Programme of the Communist Party of India* (Bombay: Communist Party of India, 1951), p. 24; and *Amendments to the Party Programme* (Delhi: Communist Party of India, 1955), p. 13.

socialist and democratic countries." [34] It may be assumed, therefore, that as early as September, 1955, disagreements within the Party were primarily focused on the attitude the Party should take regarding the government's domestic policy.

The Visit of Bulganin and Khrushchov

On October 16, *New Age* announced that the Fourth Party Congress originally scheduled for December would be postponed until February 2, 1956. It seems likely that the reason for postponement was the visit to India of Soviet Premier Nicolai Bulganin and Nikita Khrushchov. This visit was widely interpreted by the Indian press as a setback for the CPI, and on the surface it had that appearance. There was almost no contact between the Soviet Communist Party head and his Indian counterpart, the only one recorded being a brief handshake at a formal government reception. The CPI was also denied the privilege of participating officially in the ceremony which marked the arrival of the Soviet guests in India, a fact which irritated the Indian Communists in view of the participation of the Congress Party head, U. N. Dhebar. It was the government and the ruling Congress Party that derived prestige from the Bulganin-Khrushchov visit, and to this extent the CPI was hurt. But in the long view, communism as an ideology was given respectability and was to a large extent linked with socialism in the Indian popular mind. Since the government of India and the Congress Party have adopted a socialist society as a goal, this can have far-reaching implications.

The Fourth Party Congress

The Fourth Congress was postponed again on account of the Twentieth Congress of the Communist Party of the Soviet Union held in Moscow in February and attended by Ajoy Ghosh. The Congress was finally held April 19–29, 1956, at Palghat in Malabar District (now in Kerala State), a Communist stronghold. As with previous congresses, the deliberations at the Fourth Congress were secret, and the many newsmen who had journeyed to Palghat to cover the meeting were admitted only to one open session in which there was no controversy. The accounts of the Congress in the non-Communist press were generally unimaginative and of doubtful accuracy, and on such basic information as the number of delegates present, reports ranged from 400 to 460. The Communist press published very little more than the official texts of the adopted resolutions and a list of members of the new Central Committee and Politbureau.

---

[34] *Amendments to the Party Programme*, p. 11.

The debate at the Fourth Congress on the Central Committee's proposed political resolution appears to have been quite intense, and was described by the Party journal as "marked by serious and sharp expressions of the points of view of the many who spoke." [35]

According to one non-Communist account, P. C. Joshi took the unprecedented step of offering an alternative resolution to the Congress, and in a formal vote received the support of about one-third of the 400-odd delegates present.[36] The final resolution bears the imprint of his viewpoint to such an extent that one could say that the CPI's official line had become substantially rightist. Ramamurti's heresy of July 1954 was now orthodox doctrine, for the resolution states: "Life itself has shown how the struggles for peace and defence of national freedom, for democratic rights and vital interests of the masses, are inseparably linked and strengthen each other." [37] The attitude to be taken toward the government was made specific: "Every step that is taken by the Government for strengthening national freedom and national economy, against imperialist, feudal and monopoly interests, will receive our most energetic and unstinted support." [38] During this phase the CPI would conduct itself as a parliamentary opposition. The resolution declares: "In order that the Communist Party may pursue such a revolutionary and flexible policy and play its rightful role as the builder and spearhead of the democratic movement, it must come forward as an independent national force. It must act as a Party of Opposition in relation to the present Government." [39] With this tactic the Party would attempt to become the real champion of the reforms to which it accuses the Congress of rendering only lip service. Through this device it would maneuver to penetrate the governmental structure by means of coalitions at both the state and national levels.

Such a line would be difficult for the CPI to follow, for it requires a great deal of restraint and a measure of responsibility which the Party has never demonstrated. To become the leaders of the opposition in a democratic constitutional system, the Communists not only would have to work with many non-Communist leaders who have had bitter experiences with past Communist duplicity, but would have to gain their confidence as well. This requires a give and take of a kind with which the CPI has had no experience, and that a substantial seg-

---

[35] V. Hanumantha Rao, "Fourth Communist Party Congress in Session," *New Age* (weekly), III (April 29, 1956), p. 1.

[36] *The Times of India* (Bombay), April 26, 1956, p. 7.

[37] *Political Resolution* (Delhi: Communist Party of India, 1956), p. 5.

[38] *Ibid.*, p. 22.

[39] *Ibid.*, p. 24.

ment of the leadership strongly opposes. However, the political resolution adopted at Palghat made it clear that the Party would make the attempt. Referring to the ruling party the resolution says:

> Although the Congress is the political party of the bourgeoisie which has taken many landlords in its fold, it has among its members a vast number of democratic elements. It has an anti-imperialist and democratic tradition. Recent measures of the Government and its promises have helped the Congress to rehabilitate its position even among some sections that were moving away from it. Simultaneously, there has been a growth of radical and democratic sentiments inside the Congress and among masses following the Congress.
>
> Our approach towards the Congress and the method of criticism of its political policies have to be such as take into account all these factors. They have to be such as do not repel honest Congressmen but draw them towards unity. They have to be such as strengthen the fight for democratic policies inside the Congress itself, strengthen the forces that, however haltingly, are taking a relatively progressive stand.[40]

With regard to the other major left-wing parties, the Praja Socialist Party and its offshoot, the Socialist Party, the new line was purposely vague, calling for unity but failing to specify the form this should take. "The coming together of Left parties," the resolution states, "helps to unite the advanced sections of the masses and is a factor of great importance for mass struggles as well as electoral contests." [41]

The Palghat resolution was much more moderate on the question of mass struggle than was its June, 1955, predecessor, and after its adoption the Party exercised notable restraint on such issues as Goa, and the linguistic question. As the government had opposed further *satyagrahas* in Goa, the Communists refrained from overt action of any significance, and allowed the anniversary of the 1955 *satyagraha* to pass without organizing a repeat performance—for which they could have secured considerable popular support. Similarly, they noticeably toned down their propaganda on the linguistic issue, despite the fact that the reorganization of Bombay State left a residue of discontent that offered a tempting field for irresponsible political agitation. This made disciplined adherence to the national CP line very difficult for the Bombay branch. A similar situation developed in Bengal where, as a result of CPI leadership in the campaign to prevent the merger of Bengal with Bihar, the local Party was able to win an important parliamentary by-election. Because such local struggles are vitally important to the building of state-level Party organizations, constant pressure against the tactic of restraint is inevitable.

---

[40] *Ibid.*, p. 30.
[41] *Ibid.*, p. 31.

The Effects of de-Stalinization

When Stalin died in 1953, the CPI's theoretical journal published the message sent by Ajoy Ghosh, on behalf of the Central Committee, to the Soviet Communist Party. It read:

> With sorrow too deep for tears, we pay our homage to the memory of Comrade Stalin. Mankind has lost its noblest representative, the movement for human liberation its greatest leader, the cause of Peace its indefatigable champion. . . . Stricken with grief at the passing away of this titan of human thought and action, we, Communists of the present generation, shall ever recollect with pride that we have lived in the same epoch as Comrade Stalin, have been guided and led by him, have been taught by him how to serve the working class and the people to the last drop of our blood.[42]

Though there is no doubt that international communism's de-Stalinization campaign damaged the CPI's prestige and unity, it is still too early at this writing to assess its full effects. The Indian Party has reprinted most relevant international documents, and has passed two resolutions on the subject. In March 1956, a Central Committee resolution criticized the "cult of the individual" but qualified the criticism with a paragraph of praise for Stalin's contributions to revolutionary progress. It said:

> It is known to all that after Lenin's death, Comrade Stalin led the Party in the struggle for the building of Socialism in the USSR against the Right and Left deviations. He developed and further enriched the theory of Marxism-Leninism. He played a leading role in the battle against the Hitlerite aggressors. He rendered great service to the world Communist movement and in the development of the Communist Parties. Comrade Stalin was a great friend of the colonial and semi-colonial peoples and his works immensely helped them in their struggle for national liberation. All these are a part of the heritage of the world Communist movement and will always inspire the Communists all over the world.[43]

The publication by the United States Department of State on June 4, 1956, of the complete text of Khrushchov's attack on Stalin forced the CPI to take a stronger position. In July the Central Committee published a second resolution on the "cult of the individual" which stated:

> It is evident that Comrade Stalin was mainly responsible for the distortions of Soviet democracy and for the violation of inner-Party norms. It is also incon-

---

[42] "Message of the Communist Party of India," *New Age* (monthly), II (March, 1953), pp. 6–7. See also "Homage to Stalin," *New Age* (monthly), III (March, 1954), p. 1, which is considerably more moderate in its praise of Stalin and contains a reference to "harmful trends like the cult of personality," possibly explained by the Beria episode. Of interest also is a special Stalin Supplement to *New Age* (weekly) I, in its issue of March 7, 1954.

[43] "Resolutions on 20th Congress of the Communist Party of the Soviet Union," *New Age* (weekly), III (April 8, 1956), p. 5.

testable that in the later period of his life, the cult of the individual assumed enormous proportions. While fully recognizing the negative features and grave defects that developed in Stalin's methods of leadership, the Central Committee of the Communist Party of India considers that a one-sided appraisal of his role during the last twenty years of his life, years of mighty developments in the USSR and the world Communist movement, causes bewilderment among the masses and can be utilized by enemies of Communism to confuse them. . . . It is evident that a system in which such violations and distortions were inherent could not have unleashed the creative energies of hundreds of millions on a scale never known before and brought about such unprecedented social transformations. . . . The mistakes and excesses that occurred in the USSR were not due to the principles of Marxism-Leninism or the Soviet system but to deviations from them in practice in several respects.[44]

In accordance with the Soviet reversal of the de-Stalinization line, which became evident in late 1956, *New Age* (weekly) published a full-page commemorative article on the occasion of Stalin's seventy-seventh birthday. Written by Ajoy Ghosh, the article acknowledged that "a number of serious mistakes were committed by Stalin," but concluded:

Nevertheless, notwithstanding these mistakes, the name of Stalin will always be cherished by mankind as one of the greatest Marxists of all times, as a towering personality and a titan of thought and action, as a man who dedicated his life to the service of the working people and to the cause of Socialism. His contribution to the cause of emancipation of mankind will continue to inspire millions all over the world.[45]

Many Indians are highly susceptible to hero worship and often fail to differentiate between ideologies, *per se,* and the personalities of their leading advocates. Therefore, to tell a true believer that mankind's "noblest representative" was in actuality a tyrant and a murderer is to invite trauma and disillusionment with the Communist way of life.

The leadership recognized this, as is indicated by its fear that the Khrushchov report might be used to cause "bewilderment among the masses." It may be expected, therefore, that the CPI will do its utmost to conceal or explain away Stalin's crimes in an effort to preserve its pantheon intact.

Equally as damaging to the Party, and equally as difficult to assess fully, are the effects of the events in Poland and Hungary in the autumn of 1956: hardest hit were the front organizations, some of whose non-Communist members, unable to condone Soviet brutality in Hungary, resigned.

---

[44] "Struggle Against Cult of the Individual in CPSU," *New Age* (weekly), III (July 15, 1956), pp. 1, 13.

[45] Ajoy Ghosh, "J. V. Stalin," *New Age* (weekly), IV (Dec. 23, 1956), p. 3.

The Impact of New Ideas

But there has been another development on the international scene which may have greater long-range effects on Indian communism than did de-Stalinization and Hungary: this is the debate within the world Communist movement on the question of the "paths to socialism." The essence of this debate, which began with Tito's heresy, has been whether socialism may be achieved by means other than those adopted by the USSR and whether the Soviet leaders have the right to determine policy for Communist parties in other countries.[46] Certain aspects of this debate have been profoundly disturbing to the CPI leadership.

In July and August, 1956, *New Times* (the English-language journal published from Moscow), printed a two-part article by one Modeste Rubinstein. Entitled "A Non-Capitalist Path for Underdeveloped Countries," the article dealt primarily with India. Rubinstein cited with evident approbation the Indian National Congress' Avadi resolution which, in January 1955, committed the governing party to the goal of a "socialistic pattern of society." [47] Describing the Indian government's ownership of electrical-equipment factories, steel, and fertilizer, he said, "These steps to develop state industry are not, in themselves, of a socialistic character. . . . However, in India, as in other economically backward countries that have recently embarked on the path of independent development, state-capitalist enterprises assume a special character. . . . State capitalist enterprises in India, under present conditions, play a progressive part." Thus, he concluded, "given close coöperation by all the progressive forces of the country, there is the possibility for India to develop along socialist lines. . . . The economic plans now being evolved in a number of underdeveloped countries can be carried out only with the active participation of their workers and peasants, their young technical intelligentsia, scientists, students, etc." [48]

The Rubinstein article was received by the Indian Communists with profound shock. Their line had been that the Avadi resolution was a hoax perpetrated by the big bourgeoisie to deceive the masses,

---

[46] For the important documents on this controversy see: Paul E. Zinner, ed., *National Communism and Popular Revolt in Eastern Europe* (New York: Columbia University Press, 1956).

[47] For the text of the Avadi resolution and a discussion of events surrounding its adoption see: Margaret W. Fisher and Joan V. Bondurant, *Indian Approaches to a Socialist Society* (Berkeley: University of California, 1956).

[48] Modeste Rubinstein, "A Non-Capitalist Path for Underdeveloped Countries," Reprinted in *New Age* (monthly), V (Oct., 1956), p. 19–28.

but here was an article in a Soviet journal implying that under Congress leadership the country was moving toward socialism. Worse than that, the Indian Communists were being told to coöperate with the Congress toward this end—a course which would be tantamount to the proletariat's accepting the leadership of the bourgeoisie in the march toward socialism!

Ajoy Ghosh expressed the Party's dismay in the October issue of *New Age* (monthly). Referring to Rubinstein's arguments as "astounding," Ghosh asked:

> *Which class* has profited most from the economic policies of the government—this is a question which any Marxist, any serious student of economics has to examine in order to determine whether the path taken by a government is the path of socialism or even of democratic planning. Unfortunately, Modeste Rubinstein does not even pose the question.[49]

But Ghosh made it clear that the real cause of pain lay in the implications for the CPI. He quoted the Report of the Central Committee of the CPSU to the Twentieth Congress, saying:

> What is virtually ignored in the article is the profound truth that "Whatever the form of transition to socialism, the decisive and indispensable factor is the political leadership of the working class headed by its vanguard. Without this, there can be no transition to socialism." . . . The bourgeoisie, no matter how radical and progressive, cannot build socialism which is based on new property relations. Power in the hands of the democratic masses led by the proletariat—this is the essential condition for the building of socialism. The replacement of bourgeois-landlord rule by the rule of the people headed by the working class—without this, socialism is inconceivable . . . To conclude: There undoubtedly exists a non-capitalist path of development for the underdeveloped countries like India. But it would be an illusion to think that the present government, headed by the bourgeoisie, can advance on that path. The Communist Party of India does not suffer from such illusions.[50]

Although Ghosh did not use such a powerful word as "revisionist," it would surely have been appropriate in attacking Rubinstein's article. By implication the article so contradicted classical Marxism-Leninism as to repudiate the most fundamental principles of Communist strategy and tactics.

Agonizing Reappraisals

There can be no doubt that the events of 1956 forced Communists all over the world to face up to the weaknesses of Marxism-Leninism as they had never done before. In India the Communists were es-

---

[49] Ajoy Ghosh, "On India's Path of Development," *New Age* (monthly), V (Oct., 1956), p. 8.

[50] *Ibid.*, pp. 16, 17, 18.

pecially shaken by the voice of an old ally, Jayaprakash Narayan who, as the leader of the Socialist Party in the 1930's, had favored the united front with the Communists that had brought such disastrous consequences on the Socialists. Early in November, Narayan addressed a letter to the Communists, requesting the editor of *New Age* weekly, whom he addressed as "Comrade," to publish it in full. In an unprecedented step the CPI complied with his request, and the letter appeared on November 18. It was replete with questions Narayan wanted the Communists to answer. How, he asked, could all the crimes of Stalin have been concealed from Communists so long? "The 'revelations' of Khrushchov," he said, "were indeed no revelations at all. It is impossible that the Communists—at least their leadership—did not know the facts. Why then did they remain silent so long?" Again: "are the Communists going to stop where Khrushchov has led them? Are they not going further in search of the truth? Is the truth not of any service to Communism? Can Communism be built on a foundation of lies?" [51]

The following week Ajoy Ghosh took more than twice the space to reply, yet dodged most of Narayan's questions. As for Stalin's crimes, he said: "The truth is that we did not know them until they were brought to light by the CPSU leadership itself." He charged Narayan with a one-sided appraisal. "For you the abolition of capitalism and landlordism and the ending of exploitation of man by man seem to mean nothing," he said. "Nor do you seem to attach any importance to the fact that in the USSR and in other Socialist States, it is the mass of the people—the workers, the peasants and the working intelligentsia—that exercise power at all levels, through their elected organs." He called upon Narayan to "recognize, without equivocation, that the establishment of the power of the working masses in one-third of the world, is the greatest event in recorded human history."

Ghosh did make an attempt at self-criticism. He said:

We agree that we were wrong in idealizing everything in the USSR. We should have paid more attention to the criticism of the USSR made by Socialists and non-Communist democrats. We agree that among us and in other Communist Parties, the tendency developed of defending everything done by the USSR, of condemning everyone who criticized any aspect of the Soviet policy. We are deeply conscious of the damage this has done to the cause of Communist-Socialist unity and even to the cause of Socialism. We are determined to abandon this attitude.[52]

---

[51] Jayaprakash Narayan, "A Letter from Jaiprakash Narain," [sic] *New Age* (weekly), IV (Nov. 18, 1956), p. 7.

[52] Ajoy Ghosh, "Our Observations on the Jaiprakash Letter," *New Age* (weekly), IV (Nov. 25, 1956), pp. 1, 8–9.

But this statement was rendered meaningless by his continued un-critical praise of the Communist states and his straight-faced assertion that in those states it is the people who "exercise power at all levels." By such a performance, Ghosh was answering affirmatively in practice that question of Narayan's which he ignored in debate: "Can Communism be built on a foundation of lies?" But by the following month there was evidence that others in the Party could not ignore it.

In December, the CPI theoretical journal carried an article which suggested that Jayaprakash Narayan's letter had prompted an "agonizing re-appraisal" in the mind of at least one of Ghosh's comrades. Entitled " 'Tactics' or Truth?," the article was written by David Cohen, a regular contributor to the Party's weekly, whose trade mark has been an especially virulent anti-Americanism. Cohen journeyed to Helsinki in June, 1956, to attend the International Gathering of Journalists. On the return trip he attended the Poznan-riots trial in Poland and visited the Soviet Union and China.

In his December article in *New Age* monthly Cohen displayed philosophical concern as to the nature of truth, a concern which his writings up to then had never betrayed He said:

> Sometimes one hears otherwise clever people say: "Ah truth—yes, but from which angle: that of the capitalists or of the workers?"
>
> But how can there be any "angle" to the truth! Those who would seek to read apologetics for capitalism into reality would have to distort the truth. Truth is on the side of the working class as it is, or there would be no Communist movement. The working class does not need to find "angles" to the truth. . . . The cynics—and the philistines—sometimes behave rather crudely. They say: "Truth is all right, you know (e.g., for discussions, etc.) but somehow or other we have got to come out on top. We shall see about the truth and all that later."
>
> This boils down to the philosophy that you may do anything to win victory for the Communist Party, try any dirty tricks you like, the only criterion being whether you can succeed or not. If you fail, you will do "self-criticism"; if you win, then you can promise to be very truthful in the future! . . . The controversy which has been shirked for so many years should at last be resolved: ends and means. I believe it is necessary to say that bad means do corrupt what were meant to be good ends. The means do determine the ends.[53]

Cohen's article was extraordinary not only because it followed on the heels of his tour of the Communist countries, but also because no-where in the literature of Indian communism is there to be found such an honest and complete admission of communism's falsehood and deceit. There is no mistaking that when he refers to cynics and philistines, Cohen is talking about some of his Party comrades. "Unfortu-

---

[53] David Cohen, " 'Tactics' or Truth?," *New Age* (monthly), V (Dec. 1956), pp. 57-58.

nately," he adds, "the old saying that the revolutionaries of one generation become the conservatives of the next still seems to have some application."

The CPI Achieves Political Power

Before India attained independence, the Communists, together with many Indian nationalists, had believed that self-government would come only after a violent revolution. Britain's peaceful relinquishment of authority therefore came as a great surprise to them. Similarly, the Communists have long held that in independent India a Communist government could come to power only through the use of traditional revolutionary methods. Once again they have been surprised. In April, 1957, the Communists won the general elections in the State of Kerala and formed a government. It was the first time that they had ever held political power in India, and the fact that this power was secured by constitutional means has had a profound effect on Communist thinking. The arguments of the rightists in the CPI—that under present conditions parliamentary tactics are superior to revolutionary tactics—have been immeasurably strengthened.

At this writing it is too early to pass judgment on the record of the Communist government of Kerala. On the one hand it has been charged that the Communists have permitted the breakdown of law and order, especially in plantation areas, and that the People's Committees, formed in rural areas, provide the basis for totalitarian rule. On the other hand, the Communists have been forced to make concessions to the active and vocal opposition groups in the state, most notably in connection with their Education Bill which, when promulgated, was widely interpreted as an attack on Christian educational institutions. Plans for the nationalization of foreign-owned enterprises—a major election-campaign promise—have been set aside, at least temporarily, in favor of less radical steps.

The attitude of the government of India toward the Communist government in Kerala has been one of careful surveillance coupled with a demand that all legislation conform strictly to the constitution. To assure this the central government has invoked its constitutional right to review legislation passed in the Kerala legislature. In this manner the controversial education bill was held up for several months as was the land-reform measure.

While the Communists struggled hard to run their government under these restraints they have made some radical changes in their Party organization. Within a month after coming to power in Kerala the Central Committee decided to double Party membership by dropping for six months the requirement that prospective members must serve a probationary period as candidates. Plans were made for a complete revision of the Party structure, and in February, 1958, a new draft constitution was published in *New Age*. An extraordinary Party Congress was called for April.

Unlike its predecessor, the preamble of the new draft contained no reference to the "dictatorship of the proletariat" and did not describe the Party as a "monolithic fighting organization." Instead it stated the aim of the Party to be the establishment of "people's democracy" by "integrating the theory of Marxism-Leninism with the realities of the Indian situation, with the experience of India's history, with the traditions of the Indian people, with India's national peculiarities." [54] Still intact were the concepts of democratic centralism and international proletarian solidarity. The organizational structure that was outlined in the new document was more flexible and, on paper at least, more democratic.

After the 1948–1951 experience in Telengana, the government of Prime Minister Nehru realized that communism in India could not be effectively stamped out by force without great damage to Indian democracy. Since then it has concentrated on pressuring the CPI to abandon its propensity for violence and its excessive loyalty to the USSR. The Amritsar Congress momentarily convinced Nehru that this course had been successful, for during his first visit to Kerala after the Communists took over, he said in Trivandrum on April 24, 1958, that the CPI had come around to "a very reasonable approach." "If they think more of India and in Indian terms," he said, "I have no doubt that the Communists will veer around more and more and the party will cease to be Communist in international lingo." [55] Certainly such a development is possible, although, as Nehru himself has noted, CPI obedience to the fluctuating Moscow line on Yugoslavia would seem to indicate that it is still a long way off. Part Two of this study is concerned with those aspects of Party activity in which such a trend would be most easily observable.

---

[54] *New Age* (weekly), V Feb. 23, 1958, p. 7.
[55] *The New York Times*, April 26, 1958.

PART **2**

15 THE PARTY: STRUCTURE AND FUNCTION

According to the "Principles of Party Organization" of the Comintern, "The organization of the Communist Party is the organization of Communist leadership in the proletarian revolution." [1] Implicit in this statement is the idea that Party organization has an exalted purpose, for only the Party can lead the proletariat and only the proletariat can lead the world. A Communist party assumes that it has an exclusive right to political leadership and an obligation to exercise that right effectively. The Party's internal-organization system is thus of unique importance. [2]

Formal Organization of the CPI

Its exalted obligation requires that a Communist party be, above all, an "efficient instrument" of political action. It must, ideally, operate with flawless unity—a unity based on rigorous, self-imposed discipline. This is to be achieved by "democratic centralism," that is, through leadership which is at once responsible to the members and in absolute authority over them.

As a theory of party organization, "democratic centralism" is based on two main principles: (1) all policy-making agencies of the Party

---

[1] *Principles of Party Organisation* (Bombay: People's Publishing House, Ltd., n.d.), p. 2.

[2] On the general theory and practice of Communist Party organization, see Philip Selznick, *The Organizational Weapon: A Study of Bolshevik Strategy and Tactics* (New York: McGraw-Hill, 1952), 350 pp.; and Nathan Leites, *A Study of Bolshevism* (Glencoe: The Free Press), Chapter X.

are elected and must report periodically to the membership as a whole; (2) decisions of the higher agencies are absolutely binding on all agencies below, on the basis of strict discipline which ensures the subordination of the minority to the majority.[3] In theory, authority is built from the bottom up and is exercised from the top down. Centralization must be genuine, not formal; that is, the leading agencies have "the obligation of constantly directing and exercising a systematic influence over the Party work." [4] Nothing must be left to chance or "spontaneity." But at the same time, the "democratic" basis of this centralization must also be genuine; that is, authority must be based not on mere formal election but on a "living association" between leaders and led. The members must recognize the legitimacy of inner-Party leadership.

This "democracy" permits differences of opinion, before the actual making of a decision; but the expression of opinion is the prerogative only of individuals, never of organized groups or factions within the Party or within the committees. Factionalism, or a "contest for supremacy within the Party," is in theory impermissible.[5]

As concretely realized in the constitution of the CPI, "democratic centralism" results in a hierarchical system based on indirect elections.[6] At the bottom is the "cell" (or since 1957 the "branch")—a group of members in factory, village, or urban neighborhood. All cells in a locality participate in the town or local "Conference." This Conference is supposed to meet every two years; it elects representatives to a District Conference, the District Conference elects representatives to a Provincial Conference, and the Provincial Conference elects delegates to the national All-India Party Congress. At each level, the Conference elects a Committee, which in turn chooses a secretary; at the top, the Party Congress elects the Central Committee (CC), which elects the Politbureau (PB) and the general secretary. All Committees are empowered to act in the name of their respective Conferences in

---

[3] The classic statement of "democratic centralism" is in the Rules of the Communist Party of the Soviet Union; see James H. Meisel and Edward S. Kozera, eds., *Materials for the Study of the Soviet System* (Ann Arbor: The George Wahr Publishing Company, 1953), p. *xlix*.

[4] *Principles of Party Organization*, p. 7.

[5] *Ibid.*, p. 2.

[6] *The Constitution of the Communist Party of India* (Delhi: Communist Party of India, 1954). The following references to the constitution are from this source. Earlier versions, which differ in some details, include: *The Constitution of the Communist Party of India, Adopted by the Second Congress* . . . (Calcutta: Communist Party of India, 1948), 18 pp.; and *The Constitution of the Communist Party of India, 1943* (Bombay: People's Publishing House, n.d.), 12 pp. For a discussion of organizational changes in 1958, see Postscript.

the two-year intervals between sessions. (See diagram of CPI organization.)

TABLE I

ORGANIZATION CHART

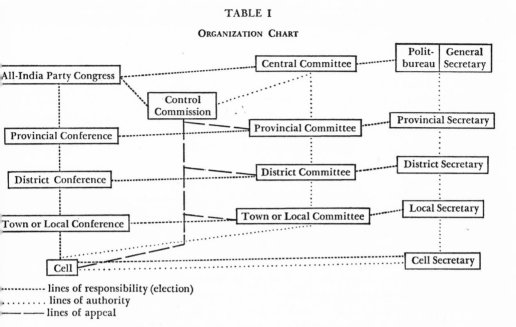

---------- lines of responsibility (election)
.... lines of authority
———— lines of appeal

The elective principle is in fact negated by other provisions of the CPI constitution. In the first place, each secretary (except the general secretary) must be approved by the Committee at the next higher level. Moreover, each Committee has the power to dissolve or even to reconstitute any Committee below it in the chain, and to postpone the convocation of a lower Conference. And at the top, the Central Committee is empowered to reconstitute itself at will. Finally, Committees at all levels possess the right of coöptation. In practice, then, the elective principle may be suspended altogether.

The principle of inner-Party discussion, formally guaranteed to the rank-and-file membership, is similarly qualified. The CPI constitution declares that "free and business-like discussion of Party policy" is an "indefeasible right" of every member. But it says that "interminable" discussion or the attempt to form factions is an abuse of this right. It concludes that "wide inner-Party discussion" is permissible only if such discussion is demanded by one or more units at the provincial level, or if it is authorized by the Central Committee itself; in short, only the top units of the Party, and primarily the Central Committee, can initiate inner-Party debate. Moreover, the constitution declares that when such debate does occur it must be conducted "under the strong leadership of the Central Committee and of the lower committees." Discussion must be based on a draft resolution furnished by the Committee and must be personally guided, as far as possible, by representatives sent from the top units to the lower bodies.

Thus the formal structure and rules of the CPI are intended to create and maintain a high degree of centralization. Indeed, the Indian Party rules allow greater formal centralization than do those of the Russian Party, which in 1939 abolished the right of coöptation, and in 1952, the right of the higher committees to dissolve the lower ones.[7]

On the other hand, the Indian Party constitution provides formal channels for the expression of rank-and-file opinion. In its definition of democratic centralism, the constitution states that every member or unit of the Party has the right to communicate "wishes, suggestions, remarks or complaints" directly to the Central Committee at any time. Moreover, it provides that members who disagree with a decision of any unit of the Party may appeal to the Central Committee or to the Party Congress. Finally, it provides for a court of appeal, in the form of the Control Commission, elected by the Party Congress and empowered to review decisions of Party units in matters relating to discipline (dissolution of lower units, expulsion of members, and the like). The Commission may hear complaints from individual members and units, or take up cases referred to it by the Central Committee. It is formally subordinate to the Central Committee, since the latter must endorse its decisions, but it has a certain claim to autonomy by virtue of being elected by the Party Congress rather than by the Central Committee.

Further comparison of the CPI constitution and the Russian Party Rules shows that the former provides more guarantees of the rights of members. The Russian Party Rules do not include, in their definition of democratic centralism, the right of members or units to communicate their wishes to the Central Committee. Moreover, the Russian Committee of Party Control (formerly called the Control Commission) is selected by the Central Committee itself, not by the Party Congress, and is strictly an enforcement agency rather than a court of appeal.[8]

---

[7] Meisel and Kozera eds., *Materials for* . . . , pp. 314, 344, *xliii, lxi.*

[8] Control Commissions or similar agencies in other CP's appear to be conceived as policing arms of the Central Committee. See Rodger Swearingen and Paul Langer, *Red Flag in Japan* (Cambridge: Harvard University Press, 1952), pp. 94–95; and Mario Einaudi, *et al, Communism in Western Europe* (Ithaca: Cornell University Press, 1951), p. 87.

The formal organization of the CPI, as summarized here, is of course only one factor in the Party's actual operation. Its behavior has frequently borne little resemblance to the model laid down in the constitution. But so far as the constitution bears any relation to the CPI's operation, it seems to suggest a combination of unusual centralization and unusual freedom of rank-and-file expression—or in other words a paradoxical combination of autocracy and indiscipline. An examination of the CPI's operation will show that these two qualities are indeed the most salient features of the Party in action.

Autocracy in the Party's Operation

As the historical survey in Part I has suggested, general authority in the CPI is vested in a very small elite at the apex of the organizational pyramid.

The CPI constitution requires that the All-India Party Congress be convened every two years, but in actuality there have been only five Congresses throughout the entire life-span of the Party—in 1943, 1948, 1953, 1956, and 1958. In the intervals between Congresses, full power is vested in the Central Committee, a body which has ranged in size from nine to thirty-nine members.

The constitution requires that the Central Committee meet every three months; full information is not available as to the frequency of its meetings, but it appears on the average to have met much less often. A Party report of 1954 states that the CC had met six times in the previous fifteen months, but describes this as a great improvement; before that, the report declares, the Committee had not met for six months.[9] In earlier periods, CC meetings have been as much as a year apart. In the intervals between meetings, full power is vested in the Politbureau, a body which has ranged in size from three to nine members.

The Politbureau must meet every month, according to the Party constitution. It too has evidently been convened, as a rule, much less frequently. In day-to-day decision-making, therefore, authority falls to the general secretary and a few other members of the Politbureau who are actually present at central headquarters.

The 1954 Party report mentioned above implies that only two or three Politbureau members were permanently attached to the Center; this tiny core of leadership, according to the report, made "vital" decisions on behalf of the Party as a whole.[10] And in 1956 the situa-

[9] *Communist Conspiracy . . .* , pp. 131–132.
[10] *Ibid.,* p. 131.

tion was virtually the same. A Party report of that year gives a detailed account of the current activities of Politbureau members, as
follows: Z. A. Ahmed was busy with his provincial organization and
was "not available for work at the Party Center except for attending
PB meetings"; Ranen Sen devoted some attention to supervision of
trade-union work but "did not pay attention to any other aspect of the
work of the Party Center"; S. A. Dange "did not take much interest in
the work of the Center"; Rajeshwar Rao "did not function in the
Center"; and Ajoy Ghosh was absent a large part of the time, for
trips abroad, and "paid no attention to specific issues and details of
organization even while at the Center." Only P. Sundarayya, P. Ramamurti, E. M. S. Namboodiripad, and Harikishan Singh Surjeet are
credited with fullfilling their general responsibilities. [11] At that time,
in other words, those four leaders virtually monopolized the day-to-day
exercise of general authority in the CPI.

But whether the leadership core of the Party be defined as this handful at the Center, or as the Politbureau, or even the Central Committee as a whole, it remains a tiny group. To this group, the rules of
the CPI grant almost unlimited formal power. In a crisis or when
dominated by a determined personality, the leadership can remake the
Party itself, in policy and personnel, at its own discretion. During
1948–1950, for example, when the crisis and the personality coincided,
authority was monopolized in practice by the general secretary, B. T.
Ranadive, together with one or two of his staunch supporters in the
Politbureau. With the aid of scattered adherents in the lower echelons
this group dissolved at least one Provincial Committee (the Bengal
Committee) and reconstituted a majority of the rest. It expelled or
suspended hundreds of members including three dissident members
of the Central Committee and even one member of the Politbureau.
Some leading Party figures were purged, among them the preceding
general secretary, P. C. Joshi, and also the following general secretary, A. K. Ghosh. Ranadive pursued a policy which increasingly departed from the mandate of the Party Congress in 1948, and he soon
encountered opposition both from the rank and file and from the international Communist authorities. But by the use of his constitutional
powers and by other devices, he was able to retain formal authority
over the Party organization for more than two years. (See chapter 13.)

In this and other crises, the Control Commission of the Party does
not appear to have served as an active check upon the central leadership. In 1950 when P. C. Joshi sought to appeal to the Control Com-

---

[11] *Communist Double Talk at Palghat* (Bombay: Popular Book Depot for the
Democratic Research Service, 1956), pp. 97–98.

mission to rescind his expulsion, the Central Committee itself decided his case. It argued that the Commission could not function since two of its members were in jail and a third had himself been purged from the Party. A new Control Commission of five members was elected in 1951, and in the next year and a half it met four times. The report of its activities indicates that it had dealt only with cases of local or provincial importance, although it had reversed a number of disciplinary decisions at these levels.[12] The Commission appears to have served as an arbiter of minor inner-Party disputes, not as a challenge to the central leadership.

Instruments of Autocracy: The Communications System

In addition to its constitutional prerogatives, the CPI leadership has certain other important instruments of authority. Chief among these, perhaps, is the inner-Party communications system.

Alongside its openly circulated journals and pamphlets, which are probably addressed mainly to the Party membership and sympathizers rather than to the public at large, the CPI maintains a regular system of private communications. One of the most important of these has been the so-called *Party Letter,* a periodical intended for the entire membership; issued from Party headquarters, it has contained detailed reports and instructions on Party policy and activity. When the Party operated normally, *Party Letter* has been issued at least once a month. In addition, the CPI has issued a periodical intended only for the Provincial and District Committees, not for the rank and file. Called the *Central Committee Information Document,* it has contained reports and instructions so confidential that Party security required their being kept absolutely secret.

There have been, of course, other irregularly issued communications such as circulars and memoranda, which frequently include statements on India by international Communist authorities. And in addition to communications flowing down, there is in theory a regular system of reports flowing up. The CPI constitution provides that each unit must submit regular reports to the next-higher unit.

In transmitting these private, inner-Party communications, the CPI ordinarily does not need to rely on the Indian postal service. The so-called "technical apparatus" or secret network has in the past provided for a monthly courier service between the Center and the provincial units, and between provincial and district units.[13] When the

---

[12] *Party Letter*, March 12, 1953.

[13] P. C. Joshi, *For a Mass Policy* (Allahabad: Adhunik Pustak Bhandar, n.d., [1951?]), p. 40. No other information is available on the subject of the organization

CPI was illegal the police disrupted this service, with great damage to Party efficiency.

Clearly, this communications system can be an important weapon in the hands of the central leadership, which controls it. In principle, communication is strictly vertical, and each unit receives information about Party activity and policy only through communications flowing down from the Center. In practice, of course, each unit gets considerable information through informal contact. But since all information converges at the Center, only the Center can properly claim to have sufficient knowledge by which to judge the over-all situation of the Party. And by its control over the distribution of information the Center can stack the cards in support of its chosen line.

The Center also possesses some degree of control over information concerning international communism's views on India. Unpublished communications from authoritative international Communist sources— for example, letters from the British Communist Party—are sent only to the Center. Moreover, the Center has readier access to the Russian-language articles in the Soviet journals, which usually contain the first expression of a change in policy and are regarded by the Indian Communists as authoritative; [14] the Center has various means for obtaining translations of the Russian-language material, but only a few of the rank and file members read Russian or can even obtain the Russian periodicals. Thus the CPI leadership can, and on occasion does, temporarily suppress news of international Communist statements, when those statements are critical and threaten its supremacy.

Of course such suppression is impossible if the statements appear in English-language journals, such as *New Times,* as they increasingly do. Further, the international Communist viewpoint is sometimes accessible to lower levels of the CPI when lesser Party leaders travel to the Communist countries; in recent years a growing number of Indian Communists, among them many secondary figures, have journeyed to the Soviet Union and to China, and have attended national congresses of foreign Communist parties. Thus the power which accrues to the Party leadership through control of the private communications system is not absolute.

---

of the CPI's "technical apparatus." A secret network presumably does exist, but the full extent and nature of its activity cannot be assessed. It should be noted, however, that the history of the CPI in its revolutionary period, 1948–1951, suggests that its underground apparatus was grossly inefficient at that time.

[14] P. C. Joshi on one occasion referred to an article on India in the Soviet Party journal *Bolshevik* (now *Kommunist*) in the following words: "The leadership of the Communist Party of the Soviet Union spoke on our Party Congress through Alexeyev's article." (*For a Mass Policy,* p. 40.)

This power is further reduced by the relative inefficiency of the system itself. In the first place, there is the obstacle of illiteracy; some Party members remain uninfluenced by the Party's communications, private or public, because they cannot read English or, in some cases, even their regional languages. A recent Party report stated that a "large number" of members are illiterate.[15] Moreover, members do not always bother to read the Party's material, as is indicated by the low circulation of the "open" periodicals. Party sources themselves complain that there is an attitude of "indifference" to Party publications within the organization, that the leaders do not take an interest either in improving the content of the journals or in writing for them, and even that the leaders themselves do not read the organs of the Party.[16] A Central Committee resolution requiring all Committee members to read certain journals was admittedly a response to the fact that some did not even read *New Age*, the official organ of the Central Committee.

Moreover, the communication system may be rendered ineffective by simple lack of response from the lower echelons. This is a frequent complaint in inner-Party literature. One such source reported that of the dozens of circulars sent out by the Central Committee in a year, only two were answered by all or nearly all Provincial Committees. It may be added that this source also complained that many reports from lower units were in the regional languages and "for obvious reasons are thus remaining in the file." [17] The language problem has apparently plagued the CPI as it has the rest of Indian politics.

In summary, the CPI's system of internal communications has certainly not been perfected as an instrument of authority. But it has been an indispensable aid to the leadership in its endeavor to create an efficient, centralized agency of political action.

The Instrument of Indoctrination

The utility of the Party's communications system lies largely in its value as a means for basic ideological indoctrination. There is abundant evidence that the Party leadership has believed that inculcating basic theory is one of the principal means of unifying and activizing the membership.

A recent Central Committee resolution stated that ideological work

---

[15] Ajoy Ghosh, *Proletarian Leadership and the Democratic Movement* (Delhi: Communist Party of India, 1954), p. 22.

[16] E. M. S. Namboodiripad, *On Organization* (Delhi: Communist Party of India, 1954), p. 74.

[17] *Communist Conspiracy at Madurai* (Bombay: Popular Book Depot, 1954), p. 133.

is of "decisive importance." For example, in discussing the usefulness of pamphlets the resolution stated that they "activize the Party ranks, sharpen their understanding of Party policy and unify them politically, thus playing a most important part in *strengthening the organization of the Party*. They make it possible to swing the entire Party into action in a disciplined and organised way." [18]

But in addition to basic ideological training, there have been several other types of indoctrination in the CPI. One is the inculcation of a spirit of military discipline within the Party. It has frequently been observed that Communist parties everywhere make intensive use of military terminology in political analysis and exhortation. This is true of the Indian Communist Party, which habitually employs such terms as "defense" and "attack," "front line" and "rear guard," "battle" and "truce," "armies" and "troops," and so on. This vocabulary arises naturally from basic Communist theoretical assumptions concerning the class struggle, but it may be that it is consciously used to reinforce discipline within the organization.

Another type of indoctrination suggested by the style of CPI literature is the creation of a family spirit in the Party; there is unusual recourse to the vocabulary used in family relationships. This is particularly apparent in the writings of P. C. Joshi. For example, Joshi described the relationship between the Congress and the CPI in terms of elder and younger brothers, and he once declared that CPI members regard the Indian people as a whole as "our real parents." On another occasion he gave a very interesting description of the Party headquarters staff as "one big joint famly"; this staff, which grew in his time from 8 to 120, was organized communally and was presided over by "one single *Mai* [Mother]." [19] These and many other similar remarks suggest that the CPI leadership has sought to reinforce the unity of the Party by emotional bonds analogous to those of the family —a device which might have special potency among the many members who have renounced their real families.

It may be added here that Communist Party discipline has embraced the personal as well as the public lives of its members. While he was general secretary, Joshi once remarked to Gandhi that "we seek to guide, criticise and mold the entire life, both personal and political, of our members." [20] A former Central Committee member, Soli Batliwala, stated after leaving the Party that the leadership could order

---

[18] *Resolution on Party Organization* (Delhi: Communist Party of India, 1954), pp. 6, 21. Emphasis added.

[19] *People's Age*, IV (Dec. 30, 1945), p. 6.

[20] P. C. Joshi, *Correspondence Between Mahatma Gandhi and P. C. Joshi* (Bombay: People's Publishing House, 1945), p. 33.

marriage or divorce, or even abortion.[21] Announcements of expulsions from the Party have occasionally ascribed the reason to "moral lapses," rather than to political error. And since the Party has endeavored to mould the total life of each member, it has tended to organize his social, recreational, and cultural activities within the fold. For example, many Party units have formed recreational and cultural groups such as drama clubs. These clubs have served the leadership not only in cementing the organization but also in providing an effective propaganda medium, since they could perform political skits or plays at mass meetings.[22]

For the ideological and psychological indoctrination of its ranks, the Party leadership does not rely exclusively on printed media. Another device is the Party school. The CPI has attempted to build a hierarchical system of schools to provide periodic instruction to members at all levels; this has included elementary education to abolish illiteracy, as well as theoretical indoctrination and organization training. Such a system is apparently not yet fully organized, but there have been occasional *ad hoc* central schools, and the lectures delivered in them have on several occasions been published to guide lower units in organizing their own schools.

A recent attempt to establish a Party school system in Bengal provides an example of the effort at the provincial level.[23] The Bengal Provincial Committee formed an education subcommittee, which set up a school system and provided syllabi and teachers. Party members and "activists" (potential recruits) were enrolled; eventually there were 550 students attending 55 regular schools. The introductory lectures gave elementary information on the role of the CPI and on its program; later classes dealt with the history of the Party and of the national movement, basic Marxism-Leninism, and the Communist view of various issues such as the agrarian problem. The Provincial Committee was eventually forced to establish a teachers' training school to meet the demand for instructors; in addition, it assembled a special series of textbooks which included the works of Stalin, Mao, Togliatti, Sobolev, Klugmann, Rostovsky, and other international Communist authorities. Public lectures and film showings were also inaugurated.

---

[21] Soli Batliwala, *Facts Versus Forgery* (Bombay: National Youth Pub., 1946), pp. 6–7.

[22] For a general discussion of the psychology of Communist Party membership, see especially Gabriel A. Almond, *et al, The Appeals of Communism* (Princeton: Princeton University Press, 1954), 413 pp.

[23] Chinmohan Sehanobis, "Some Problems of Party Education in West Bengal," *New Age* (monthly), I (Dec., 1952), pp. 76–83.

This ambitious program withered away, however, largely because the lower party units lost their enthusiasm through being denied responsibility for maintaining the schools; control and responsibility remained with the education subcommittee.[24] As in all else, centralization is a fixed principle in Party education. In the words of Ajoy Ghosh, "education has to be organised directly by the leading Committees. It has to be conducted and guided by the Party leaders."[25]

Thus ideological and psychological indoctrination constitute another valuable though imperfect instrument supporting autocracy in the CPI.

Fragmentation of Authority

From an examination of the autocratic aspect of the CPI in action, it may appear that the Party is indeed a monolith. But to stop at this point would obviously be distortion. A closer look at the internal operation of the Party will show that despite all the instruments of authority available to it, the leadership has not been able to build a genuinely united organization. It will reveal, first, that the leadership itself is fragmented rather than monolithic.

The Party report of 1956, quoted above, demonstrated that only a few members of the Politbureau were at that time available for the exercise of general authority at the Center. The gist of that passage of the report was that many Party leaders in fact shunned this authority; they "did not pay attention to" or "did not take much interest in" work at the Center. The report implied—and this is supported by other inner-Party documents—that there were two reasons for this situation. One was that many leaders were temperamentally averse to serving in staff capacities; they preferred to be on the line of action, leading strikes or demonstrations, rather than participate in general planning at headquarters. Party documents frequently complain that, throughout the Party, committees cannot function properly because many of their members are absorbed in on-the-spot political activity.

The second—and more significant—reason was the reluctance of Party leaders to neglect their individual bailiwicks. They preferred to give their attention to work in their respective spheres of interest—whether these be functional arenas such as trade-union organization or parliamentary activity, or lower levels of the Party such as provincial units. In short, these leaders preferred the exercise of *specific* authority in a subdivision of the Party, rather than the exercise of *general* authority at the Party Center.

---

[24] *Ibid.*, pp. 79–80.
[25] Ghosh, *Proletarian Leadership* . . . , p. 22.

In some instances members of the Politbureau have actually declined assignment to central headquarters. A Central Committee resolution of 1954 criticized "some of the comrades who are capable of functioning at the Center" for "refusing to shoulder their responsibility in this respect." [26] An official Party report of the same year complained that when the Politbureau attempted to relieve certain leaders of their provincial work and bring them to the Center, "either the Provincial Committees concerned or the comrades themselves, or both, were unwilling." [27] The report of 1956 states that one member of the Politbureau, Rajeshwar Rao, had even asked to be relieved of membership in that body, to avoid work at the Center.[28]

The result has been that the CPI leadership was fragmented into isolated compartments. "General" authority has become relatively meaningless, for the top echelon of the Party has become a loose confederation of department heads with each leader exercising individual control over his allotted sphere of activity. This situation was described in the report of 1956 as a "common failing" of the Politbureau.

This common failing is the failure of the individual PB members to subordinate their individual activity to the need of the common activity of the unit as a whole. This common weakness may be called individualism, a trait that is characteristic of the petty bourgeoisie.

It is this that has led to the evolution of a particular pattern of inner PB functioning, a pattern according to which (a) each PBM [Politbureau Member] "bothers" himself about that branch of PB's work (either this or that "front" or this or that Province) with which he is "specially connected" and is sunk in that job; (b) each PBM adopts an attitude of "non-interference" in the "other's jobs"; (c) both of the above attitudes together result in the PB as a whole not "bothering itself" with the main job of collective leadership.[29]

For example, the Politbureau did not function collectively in directing the Party's activities in the peace, women's, and student's movements; guidance of these spheres was "left to individual comrades." Similarly, according to this report, the Party press was guided by individuals; articles in the Party organs were "invariably" written by a staff writer after consultation with "one individual member of the PB." In the important fields of trade-union and peasant activity, the Politbureau had created subcommittees, but each of these was dominated by two or three members; problems of policy in these fields "did not become the common property of the whole PB." [30]

---

[26] *Resolution on Party Organization*, p. 9.
[27] *Communist Conspiracy* . . . , p. 132.
[28] *Communist Double Talk* . . . , p. 96.
[29] *Ibid.*, p. 101.
[30] *Ibid.*, pp. 99–100.

Thus, as is common in bureaucratic organizations, the CPI has tended to become a collection of private empires, with each leader possessing personal authority in his particular sphere of influence. The Party itself labels the situation "bureaucratism" and recognizes it as a weakness. But despite recurring self-criticism, the situation persists. The CPI is, then, not a single monolithic autocracy but rather a cluster of autocracies—functional and regional.

But this is only one of the sources of division in the Party. It is further fragmented by the "un-Bolshevik" phenomenon of indiscipline.

The Failure of Authority

The CPI has been plagued by chronic resistance to or even outright defiance of established policy, both within the leadership and in the unruly and articulate membership. Dissident elements, from top to bottom, have amply availed themselves of the opportunities provided by the constitution to express their views, and have gone far beyond the theoretical limits of properly guided inner-Party debate.

The history of the Party is replete with examples of internal dissent against the official leadership. The more dramatic cases include the Andhra Letter, which was a protest from a provincial unit against current Party policy; S. A. Dange's press conference in 1950, in which he openly opposed certain of the recent Party activities; and P. C. Joshi's campaign of opposition, conducted in public by means of a stream of pamphlets and a regular journal. It may be noted that the practice of carrying inner-Party debate into public print was sanctioned in 1950 by the CPI's mentor, R. Palme Dutt, who stated that when there was no other recourse against a "Trotskyite-Titoite" leadership, such a procedure was "not only permissible, but also necessary." [31]

Opposition to the prevailing CPI leadership has frequently arisen from the so-called Party Headquarters Unit. This unit is apparently composed mainly of junior staff members of various Party agencies in the headquarters city (now New Delhi), such as the Central Committee office, the Party press, the office of the CPI parliamentary delegation, and the headquarters of the All-India Trade Unon Congress. But it evidently includes, also, some of the important fuctionaries of these agencies, and recently even some Communist members of parliament. Composed of such elements, and situated at the center of the Party organization, this unit has been perhaps the most important "cell" in the CPI.

As has been shown (see chapter 13), the PHQ Unit played a crucial role in rallying opposition against the Party leadership in 1950–1951.

---

[31] "Talks With Comrade R. Palme Dutt and Other Impressions Gained Abroad by Deven and Bal Krishna," PHQ Unit, Jan. 6, 1951, p. 5.

To provide a platform for dissident views, the PHQ called special meetings and published a newsletter, the *PHQ Open Forum*. More recently at the CPI Third Congress in 1953–54, fourteen members of the PHQ Unit, one of whom was an M.P., moved a resolution criticizing the Central Committee for its failure to submit a report of its work to the Congress.[32]

Indeed, such has been the importance of this unit that it has recently been given official status equal to that of a provincial unit. Under the name "Staff of the CC Offices," it has held regular conferences and has been granted representation at Party congresses. At the Fourth Congress in 1956, it sent seven delegates—more than were sent by the provincial units of Delhi State, Gujerat, Karnatak, Madhya Pradesh, Madhya Bharat and Bhopal, Marathwada, or Rajasthan. This group has apparently continued in its tendency to oppose the leadership, for at its Third Conference in March, 1956, it passed a motion demanding that the Central Committee "redraft" the political resolution to be offered at the Fourth Congress and calling upon the CC to establish a special commission to formulate a new Party Programme.[33]

The expression of inner-Party opposition has never been effectively repressed in the CPI, despite the formal and informal prerogatives available to the dominant leadership. Moreover, this opposition has frequently assumed the form of organized factionalism. As the historical survey of the CPI in Part I has shown, the Party has rarely been free of serious factional disturbances that have caused continual changes in leadership. Most Communist parties in the West, and also those in the other important countries of Asia, have enjoyed relatively stable leadership for many years past—leadership that could survive changes in policy required by turns in the international line and that could, in the course of time, create an increasingly mature and efficient political organization. The Indian Communist Party has not "matured" to the same degree; it has continued to be plagued by the type of factionalism which existed in other parties in the 1920's and 1930's. A change in policy has meant a change in leadership; or rather, it has meant a change in the balance of power among the various factions within the Party.

In the CPI, as in other political parties, factionalism has tended to arise from the various special interests of different sections of the Party. There is, first, the trade-union interest. Naturally, Party members from the working class expect that the policy and activity of the Party will be oriented toward the improvement of their condition;

[32] *Communist Conspiracy . . . ,* p. 159.
[33] *New Age* (weekly), III (April 1, 1956), p. 4.

leaders who, through their work as trade-union officials, have built up a personal following among the workers, will naturally espouse this interest. Such leaders generally identify themselves with a militant policy in defense of working-class interests and sentiments, but they oppose extremes of violence which would provoke stringent governmental repression and would thereby endanger their trade-union organizations.

Another special interest is that of the peasantry. An overriding focus on the interests of its peasant following obviously motivated the formation of the Andhra faction, led by Rajeshwar Rao. Still another interest, apparently, is that of the middle and lower-middle class. Leaders whose following is based on this section of the Party would stress its interests, and would accordingly tend to advocate a more moderate ideological line based on class collaboration. In addition, it appears that the parliamentary section of the Party constitutes a special-interest group; members of this small but influential section, which has represented the Party in the central and state legislatures, may well tend to espouse whatever policy seems calculated to maintain or improve their position in their constituencies. From time to time other factions arise from other special interest groups, such as students and cultural workers.

Regional interests also contribute importantly to the formation of factions within the Party, for the demands of national Party policy may well conflict with the specific interests of a particular provincial organization. Hence the provincial leaders, including those who become members of the Central Committee, tend to embrace policies likely to forward particular regional aspirations. Though regional antagonisms appear to be less intense in the Party than in the country as a whole, they provide a source of factionalism which affects the operation of the Party. This appears to be true, also, with respect to certain other divisive factors in Indian society such as caste and communal differences.[34]

There has been no leader in the CPI, so far, who could subdue these various groups for any appreciable period, and unite the entire organization on the basis of an abiding personal authority. On the whole, the top leaders have been the representatives of particular elements of the organization, and hence have been carriers of particular political lines.

A recent example may illustrate the mechanics of factionalism and its disruptive effects. After the Third Congress, the CPI presented

[34] For example, see Selig Harrison, "Caste and the Andhra Communists," *American Political Science Review*, L (June, 1956), pp. 378–405.

a façade of unity for a few months, but by the middle of 1954 intense inner-Party debate broke out. There were deep divisions within both the Politbureau and the Central Committee, and at a meeting of the latter in September, the Politbureau presented conflicting statements, representing the right-wing and left-wing factions. Both these statements were signed by three members, while the rest of the Politbureau remained neutral. After sharp debate the Central Committee, by majority vote, reprimanded the right-wing faction as "reformist" and circulated its criticism throughout the Party.

As a result, the balance of influence in the Politbureau shifted to the left-wing section. The Politbureau then called another Central Committee meeting in November, but at this meeting the Central Committee, in effect, reprimanded the left-wing as being "extremist"; subsequently the CC circulated a resolution stating that there was serious disagreement within its ranks, without specifying the nature of the dispute. At this same meeting, the CC established a special commission to reassess the policy of the Party. But in the course of its discussions, the commission itself split into two factions, each of which drafted and presented a separate proposal to the Central Committee. In June, 1955, the Central Committee considered these proposals in a month-long meeting, and though it finally emerged with a compromise resolution adopted by majority vote, the dissension was not healed. The Central Committee therefore granted formal permission to unsatisfied CC members to oppose the resolution in the lower Party units in which they were active. Moreover, those opposing the resolution were permitted to air their views in a new inner-Party publication, the *CC Forum*. The argument raged on throughout the Party, culminating in the full-scale debate at the Fourth Party Congress in 1956.[35]

Obviously, the way in which this situation was handled constituted the grossest violation of formal rules governing inner-Party debate. But this dispute is significant for another reason: it reveals a strong tendency in the CPI toward scholasticism. The official Party report for 1956 comments that the debate had been "of an extremely abstract nature—divorced from life, divorced from problems of the mass movement." The Central Committee, it said, had functioned "not as the leader of the Party but as a debating society where abstract theoretical issues are discussed."[36] An earlier Party document gives the following description of internal disputation:

---

[35] *Communist Double Talk* . . . , pp. 91–95, 102–103. For a discussion of the policy questions involved in this debate, see chapter 14.

[36] *Ibid.*, pp. 58–59.

Comrades have been furiously discussing grave political problems and in proportion to their capacity, trying to relate them to the fundamental teachings of Marxism-Leninism. Dusty volumes of Marxist classics have been reopened to buttress one's viewpoint in the almost interminable discussions going on all round.[37]

As with Communist parties the world over, quotations from Marx, Engels, Lenin, and (formerly) Stalin are an essential part of the argument for any point of view. A somewhat more unflattering description of this state of affairs appears in still another Party source:

It has become a practice to enter into hair-splitting arguments during discussions even on small issues by the party committees, and to refer to fundamental principles. It has become a disease to call differences in opinion as reformism, sectarianism and deviationism. Consequently it has become common that even on issues wherein there was agreement, no work is done.[38]

This fondness for abstract disputation is, as one Party source puts it, "the defect of not patiently analyzing the distinctive features of the Indian situation," which it calls the "dominant defect" in the entire history of the Party.[39] The CPI seems, indeed, to exceed nearly all other Communist parties in its tendency to dwell in an ideal world of ideological formulae.

Reliance on International Authority

But factional quarrels in the CPI are not settled by quotations from Marx and Lenin. The ultimate criterion determining the factional balance of power is the current international Communist line, and in the past the faction that prevailed was the one which represented the policy line presumed to be currently sanctioned by the international authorities. It is necessary to use the term "presumed" because international guidance has not always been clear enough to eliminate any possibility of misinterpretation. At crucial times international Communist pronouncements on India have been inconsistent or vague, and have not immediately been supplemented by more conclusive private communications; as a result, an eager faction within the CPI has been able temporarily to misinterpret them and to claim a sanction from above which was, in fact, doubtful at the least.

At other times factional competition has produced a stalemate which required direct international Communist intervention. For example, the crowning act of P. C. Joshi's opposition to the Ranadive and Rao

---

[37] Sehanobis, "Some Problems . . . ," p. 76.

[38] "Self-Critical Report of the Andhra Communist Committee," [typed copy, 1952?], Part III, p. 13.

[39] Bhayyaji Kulkarni, et al, Struggle Against Sectarian Legacy and for a New Perspective (Poona: 1950).

leaderships was an appeal for such intervention. In these published pamphlets he declared that change could not come from within the CPI. Accordingly he appealed to other Communist parties: "Therefore, brothers, it is you from abroad who have to act and act quick." He continued, "since we are sincere and loyal communists we will accept our mistakes when they are authoritatively pointed out to us and struggle our hardest to correct them and get in step with International Communism." [40]

When a new policy line was announced by the reconstituted Central Committee in mid-1950, the leadership admitted that the tradition of the CPI "has been to swing like a pendulum from one extreme to the other," and that the membership was therefore "perfectly justified in feeling sceptical this time"; it therefore expressly posed the question: "What is the guarantee that this time the Central Committee has chalked out a correct path?" In answer, it listed three "guarantees," of which the first was: "The direct political guidance of the Cominform Bureau and political assistance of the brother Parties." [41]

In an inner-Party document of 1950, S. A. Dange described the crisis of that year and the Party's response to Cominform guidance:

Everyone began to feel that somewhere things were wrong, but none could say it correctly and some would not say it—until the Cominform spoke. And the whole Party felt relieved. Is it not good that we have a Cominform to tell us things and is it not good that we at least bow to the Cominform, if not the warnings of Mao, Liu Shao-chi and others? There is hope for us there; we shall correct ourselves.[42]

It is clear, then, that the CPI leadership itself has admitted privately that it was not only loyal to the international Communist movement, but abjectly dependent upon it for the settlement of inner-Party disputes. Dange has asserted that the internal Communist movement "waits a long time" before correcting a Party in the hope that it will correct itself, and intervenes only "when all hope is lost and things do not improve." [43] This interval of waiting has frequently proved painful to the CPI, for its factionalism has not found a self-corrective.

---

[40] P. C. Joshi, *Views to Comrades Abroad and B. T. Ranadive* (Howrah: P. C. Joshi, 1950), pp. 29–30.

[41] "Letter of the New Central Committee (Reconstituted by the Central Committee elected at the Second Party Congress) to All Party Members and Sympathizers," June 1, 1950, pp. 15–16.

[42] S. A. Dange, "Some Notes on the Roots of Our Mistakes After Calcutta," April 20, 1950, p. 41.

[43] *Ibid.,* p. 39.

This does not, however, exclude the possibility that a particular leader or faction within the CPI will temporarily rebel against that dependence. The CPI has on occasion complied with international Communist advice only after a period of resistance or at least reluctance. According to Dange, even so loyal a leader as P. C. Joshi at one time attempted to communicate with the editor of the Soviet journal *New Times* in order to ask that he stop publishing "embarrassing" articles which contradicted Joshi's policy.[44]

It should be stressed, however, that although factional competition has been intense in the CPI, it has not produced organized defection from the Party. The typical reaction of a dissident member or faction is to oppose the prevailing leadership vocally but to submit in action, or to abstain from any action at all. Although the Party has at times been reduced to almost total anarchy and passivity, in the past two decades no major sections have split off to form separate parties, as so often happens in Indian politics. The CPI has thus shown remarkable cohesiveness under Indian conditions.

In balance, then, although the CPI's internal mechanisms have been imperfect and inefficient in some degree, and have not prevented severe malfunctioning at times, the Party has hung together through extraordinary crises. Unifying forces have proved stronger than divisive forces. And the primary unifying factor is, it appears, the pervasive effect of ideological bonds, expressed primarily an an abiding loyalty to the international Communist community.

Party Finances

Very little is known quantitatively concerning CPI finances; needless to say, the Party does not publish an annual balance sheet. On one occasion, in 1945, when it was especially eager to disprove the charge that it received financial support from the British, the Party offered to let Gandhi or his authorized representative inspect its accounts, and even agreed to reveal the names of anonymous contributors.[45] But the offer was not accepted then, and has not since been repeated.

There have of course been persistent rumors of Moscow gold, but though it is known that in the 1920's the CPI was subsidized from abroad, there is no proof that there have been direct subsidies in recent years. The CPI receives an indirect subsidy, however, in the form of profits on the sales of books and pamphlets provided free of charge by foreign Communist governments, though the amount of this subsidy is not known. The Indian government has not cut off the supply

---

[44] *Ibid.*, p. 40.
[45] Joshi, *Correspondence* . . . , p. 9.

of foreign literature but it does not allow Communist or other party publications to be sold in bookstalls on government property, such as railway stations.

Individual contributions constitute another major source of funds. These contributions are often large, for the Party has succeeded in recruiting members from among the very wealthy who have turned over all or a large part of their incomes to the CPI. E. M. S. Namboodiripad, for example, donated Rs. 70,000 (about $14,750) to the Party. It is rumored that the CPI also receives large contributions from non-Communist sources and even from some business men.

The Party constitution requires that each member pay monthly dues but states that these monies are for the use of the committees at the district level or below. It provides that provincial and central committees may raise funds by imposing levies on the incomes of certain Party members. Members with reasonably large incomes, including MP's and MLA's, are required to turn over a fixed percentage of their salaries to the cause, and Party documents report that they occasionally object.

On the whole, the Party does not appear to have great financial resources, relative to the ruling party, the Congress, and in the past it has evidently operated close to the margin; in 1953 *Party Letter* reported that all units were in "acute financial difficulties," and that the Party's journals were "facing crises." [46] But recently the CPI has shown signs of somewhat greater affluence. According to the correspondent of the *New York Times,* in 1954 it bought nine choice office sites in Delhi and New Delhi; the known combined value of four of these properties was nearly $11,000. The monthly payroll of the central headquarters staff must be at least $5,000, the correspondent said, since there were more than two hundred full-time workers at the Center, receiving $20 to $80 per month in salaries. The total expenses of the Party throughout India, he said, must be millions of rupees monthly. (A rupee is approximately 21 cents.) The known sources of CPI funds, described above, do not "come anywhere near meeting" the Party's financial demands, he concluded. Indeed, he said, it is doubtful that the Party realizes any profit from the sale of foreign literature, because of the low prices and heavy distribution costs. But when he poses the question, "Where does the money come from?", he is unable to adduce any concrete evidence of foreign sources.[47]

If there were large-scale foreign financing of the CPI, it is likely that the government would know of it; and if the government had

[46] *Party Letter,* April 30, 1953, p. 1.
[47] *New York Times,* May 30, 1954, p. 9.

such information, it is likely that the Congress Party and Nehru himself would make use of it—especially in election campaigns in which the main argument against the CPI consists of allegations concerning its foreign connections.

There is evidence that at times central headquarters has had to depend on the lower units for operating funds. One Party document relates that in a recent period of financial embarrassment the Central Committee appealed to the provincial committees to make a special fund drive. The provincial units set their own goals and also decided what portion should be passed on to the Central Committee. The Central Committee said that it needed Rs. 100,000 for expenses in the immediate future, but in the end it received only Rs. 5,000.[48]

The financial dependence of the central headquarters may give the wealthier provincial units more influence at the Center than they would otherwise enjoy. This may be the case, for example, with the Andhra Party organization which can draw on the wealth of many landlord members.

Composition of the CPI

The Communist Party of India has on a number of occasions resolved to become a "mass party." But the standards of admission have not been relaxed to any great degree, and as long as these standards remain the Party cannot be other than highly exclusive.

The CPI constitution provides that a member "is one who accepts the programme of the Party, who works in one of the Party organizations, obeys the decisions of the Party and regularly pays the membership dues." An applicant for membership must be recommended by two Party members and accepted by the cell to which he would belong, and must be approved by the Town or Local Committee. He must serve a six-month period as a "candidate" (or twelve months if he belongs to a "landlord or capitalist" family) during which he has the duties of membership but no voting rights. Only then does the cell grant him full membership which, too, must be confirmed by the next higher unit.[49] (See Table II.)

Figures for Party membership must be treated as estimates, since they are usually from Party sources; however, they do not appear to be grossly inflated and it is likely that they reflect with fair accuracy the changes in the Party's size.

---

[48] Namboodiripad, *On Organization*, p. 72. It is of course possible that this and similar information concerning the shortage of funds is planted in CPI documents to mislead the public. But this appears unlikely, since similar comments appear in inner-Party documents not meant for public consumption.

[49] *The Constitution of the Communist* . . . , 1954, p. 5.

TABLE II

CPI MEMBERSHIP, 1934–1957

Year	Members	Year	Members
1934 [1]	150	1947 [7]	60,000
1942 [2]	5,000	1948 [8]	89,263
1943 [3]	15,563	1950 [9]	20,000
1944 [4]	25,000	1952 [10]	30,000
1945 [5]	30,000	1954 [11]	75,000
1946 [6]	53,000	1957 [12]	125,000

SOURCES:

[1] *India and Communism* (Simla: Government of India Press, 1935), p. 208.

[2] *People's War*, I (Oct. 4, 1942), p. 1.

[3] P. C. Joshi, *Communist Reply to Congress Working Committee Charges* (Bombay: People's Publishing House, 1946), p. 142.

[4] *People's War*, II (May 14, 1944), p. 1.

[5] P. C. Joshi, *Communist Reply* . . . , p. 142.

[6] R. Palme Dutt, *India Today* (Bombay: People's Publishing House, 1949), p. 401.

[7] George E. Jones, *Tumult in India* (New York: Dodd, Mead & Co., 1948), p. 178.

[8] *People's Age*, VI (March 14, 1948), p. 6.

[9] S. A. Dange, A. K. Ghosh, and S. V. Ghate, "A Note on the Present Situation in Our Party" [typed copy], p. 4.

[10] Statement by A. K. Ghosh, reported in *Hindustan Times*, Jan. 13, 1954, p. 3.

[11] *Resolution on Party Organization* (Delhi: Communist Party of India, 1954), p. 3. The figure of 75,000 includes 25,000 candidate members.

[12] *New Age* (weekly) IV (May 26, 1957), p. 5. This issue of *New Age* reports a Central Committee resolution which set the goal of doubling Party membership within six months. As the resolution indicated, this signified a determination to become a "mass" party.

An examination of these figures shows that the CPI grew steadily during P. C. Joshi's leadership. However, the essay at revolution in the years 1948–1950 caused heavy losses in membership; the Party shrank to less than a quarter of its previous size—a loss which canceled about five years' growth. In more recent years the Party has dramatically recovered, and if it pursues a moderate policy, it will probably continue to grow.

The social composition of the membership is a matter of speculation; not since 1943 has the Party published data identifying the various elements of the membership. In that year, however, the CPI did make public a detailed analysis of the composition not only of the delegates to its First Congress but also of the membership as a whole.[50]

According to this analysis, the 139 Congress delegates included 86 from the "intelligentsia," 22 workers, 25 peasants, 3 landlords, 2 petty landlords, and 1 trader. The 1943 analysis also categorized the delegates according to religious community, showing that 13 were Muslims,

[50] *People's War*, II (June 13, 1943), p. 1, and *ibid.* (Aug. 1, 1943), p. 8.

8 Sikhs, 3 Untouchables, 2 Parsis, 1 Christian, and 1 Jain. The remaining delegates were presumably of Hindu family background. It is interesting to note that the number of Untouchables was so small, for this oppressed class would seem to be a rich source of recruits for the Party.

The delegates to the First Congress were very young; almost 70 per cent were under thirty-five—and these were the leaders of the Party, not the rank and file. Almost half of the delegates were college graduates. Almost three-quarters of them had been in jail, for an aggregate of 411 years, and more than half had had experience in the underground.

With regard to the social composition of the membership as a whole, the Party stated that in a total of about 16,000 members 26 per cent were workers, 36 per cent peasants, 11 per cent students; 5 per cent were women. These categories total only about three-quarters of the whole, and the remaining were presumably of middle-class origin. Bourgeois and petty-bourgeoisie elements were thus not so predominant in the rank and file as in the leadership.

In the leadership the high proportion of middle-class intellectuals is very striking, and more recent CPI sources have continued to complain that the Party elements of nonproletarian origin are too numerous; it may be assumed, therefore, that the Party continues to draw a substantial percentage of its membership from the ranks of the bourgeois and petty-bourgeois intelligentsia. The tendency to abstract disputation, mentioned earlier, is evidence of the disproportionate number of intellectuals, and it probably encourages the recruitment of more.

The 1943 data show that 2,600 of the Party's members were "whole timers" or "professional revolutionaries who spend all their working hours educating and organizing the Party membership." Since this figure represents about 16 per cent of the total membership at that time, it indicates that the organization was comparatively top-heavy with full-time functionaries.

On only one aspect of the Party's composition—its geographic distribution—are more recent data available. The distribution of the CPI membership among the various states of India may be roughly inferred from the size of the provincial delegations to the Party Congresses, since delegation strength is supposed to be in proportion to membership. The Party did not officially report the size of the various state delegations to the Fourth Congress in 1956, but data on most of them can be derived from scattered accounts in the Party press concerning the preceding provincial Party conferences. The size of the delegations, as well as the size of some of the provincial units is shown in Table III.

TABLE III

CPI ORGANIZATION AS REPRESENTED AT FOURTH CONGRESS 1956

Provincial Committee (PC)	Membership		Dele-gates	PC mem-bers	PC Secretary
	Full	Candi-date			
C. C. Office Staff			7		
Andhra	11,700	9,000	59	35	C. Rajeshwar Rao
Assam					Phani Bora
Bihar			21	25	Yogendra Sharma
Bombay City				21	P. B. Vaidya
Delhi State	Over 500		5	12	M. Farooqi
Gujerat			4	10	Dinkar Mehta
Karnatak			5	7	N. L. Upadhyaya
Madhya Pradesh			4	15	Sudam Deshmukh
Madhya Bharat and Bhopal			4	11	L. R. Khandkar
Maharashtra	4,700		24	21	S. S. Mirajkar
Malabar	7,369	3,203	37	29	K. Damodaran
Manipur				13	Thokchom Bira Singh
Marathwada	657	184	4		C. D. Chaudhary
Orissa					Gurucharan Patnaik
Punjab			20	17	Harikishan Singh Surjeet
Rajasthan			4	9	H. K. Vyas
Tamilnad	5,700	2,000	28	25	M. R. Venkataraman
Telengana			32	31	Baddam Yella Reddy
Travancore-Cochin	11,000		33	32	C. Achutha Menon
Tripura	2,700		10	21	D. Deb Barman
Uttar Pradesh			23	31	Z. A. Ahmed
West Bengal	10,775		44	35	Jyoti Basu

NOTE: The total number of delegates to the Congress was variously reported in the Indian non-Communist press as follows: 411 (*The Statesman*, May 1, 1956); 460 (*The Hindu*, April 26, 1956); 450 (*The Hindu*, April 27, 1956). Reproduced from *Pacific Affairs*, XXIX (Dec., 1956), p. 357. Where no figure is stated, the data are not available.

Though incomplete, this analysis shows the very uneven geographic distribution of the CPI. Since, as a formality, each state was probably allotted a minimum of four delegates, it is possible that the Party was almost nonexistent in states having only that number.

It may be noted that the South Indian element (especially Andhra, Malabar, Tamilnad, Telengana, and Travancore-Cochin) predominates. With one exception—West Bengal—the six largest delegations are from areas in the South.

Some CPI Leaders

As to other attributes of the Party's leadership, the paucity of information again prevents anything like an exhaustive analysis. However, the biographical data available on some of the top leaders permits a few tentative remarks on their careers and qualities. (See Table IV.)

TABLE IV

CENTRAL COMMITTEES

PB = Politbureau,

GS = General Secretary

	Date elected					
	1943 (22)	1948 (incomplete)	1950 (tentative)	1951 (15)	1953 (39)	1956 (39)
G. M. Adhikari	X (PB)	X			X	X
Muzaffar Ahmed				X (PB)	X	X
Z. A. Ahmed				X	X (PB)	X (PB)
Aruna Asaf Ali					X	
Dasrath Deb Barman					X	X
Jyoti Basu				X (PB)	X	X
S. S. Batliwala	X					
R. D. Bharadwaj	X	X (died)				
Phani Bora					X	X
Arun Bose	X					
Romesh Chandra				X	X	X
K. Damodaran						X
S. A. Dange	X	X		X (PB)	X (PB)	X (PB)
Sudam Deshmukh					X	X
S. Y. Deshpande				X		
S. V. Ghate	X	X				
A. K. Ghosh	X	X		X (GS)	X (GS)	X (GS)
A. K. Gopalan				X	X	X
Bhupesh Gupta				X	X	X
Mohammed Ismail		X				
Sohan Singh Josh				X	X	X
P. C. Joshi	X (GS)					X
L. R. Khandkar					X	
N. K. Krishnan	X					
M. Kumaramangalam	X					
Somnath Lahiri	X	X (PB)	X			
Dinkar Mehta					X	
C. Achutha Menon					X	X
S. S. Mirajkar					X	
Biswanath Mukherji	X					
M. N. Govindan Nair					X	X
E. M. S. Namboodiripad	X	X	X	X (PB)	X (PB)	X (PB)
S. V. Parulekar		X	X			
S. G. Patkar					X	

TABLE IV (continued)

	Date elected					
	1943 (22)	1948 (incomplete)	1950 (tentative)	1951 (15)	1953 (39)	1956 (39)
Gurucharan Patnaik					X	X
P. Krishna Pillai		X (died)				
M. Basava Punniah		X	X (PB)		X	X
P. Ramamurti				X (PB)	X (PB)	X (PB)
B. T. Ranadive	X (PB)	X (GS)				X
C. Rajeshwar Rao		X	X (GS)		X (PB)	X (PB)
D. Venkatesa Rao					X	X
M. Chandrasekhara Rao			X (PB)			
M. Hanumantha Rao					X	X
N. Prasada Rao					X	X
B. Yella Reddy						X
Ravi Narayan Reddy					X	X
Manzer Rizvi	X					
S. G. Sardesai	X	X			X	X
Bhowani Sen	X	X (PB)				X
Ranen Sen	X			X	X (PB)	X (PB)
Y. D. Sharma				X	X	X
Yogendra Sharma					X	X
Iqbal Singh	X					
P. Sundarayya	X	X	X	X	X (PB)	X (PB)
Harikishan Singh Surjeet					X (PB)	X (PB)
N. L. Upadhyaya					X	X
D. S. Vaidya	X					
M. R. Venkataraman					X	X
H. K. Vyas					X	X
S. S. Yusuf		X		X	X	X
Sajjad Zaheer	X					

NOTE: Where no symbol is entered, the blank means the person was not a member of that central committee.

The Party has not, to the author' knowledge, published a list of the Central Committees of 1948, 1950, or 1951. A part of the composition of the 1948 Committee may, however, be deduced from scattered references in a variety of sources. And the whole of the 1950 Committee may be tentatively identified.

Only one known secondary source provides information on the composition of the 1950 Central Committee. An article by "Our Special Correspondent in India" in *East Europe and Soviet Russia* (London) VII (Jan. 18, 1951), pp. 1–4, lists the following: Rajeshwar Rao, "Nambudripad," "Bires Misry," "Nareyan Reddi," "Parulekar," "Marinda Singh," "Dr. Raden Sen," "Yussuf," Dange, "Ajay Gosh," and "Gatte." This list is obviously not altogether reliable; the misspelling betrays lack of familiarity with the subject, and the list does not include enough members from Andhra, whereas it does include certain persons such as Ajoy Ghosh who are known to have been in opposition to, rather than members of, the Committee.

In the "Letter of the New Central Committee" of 1950, page 13, the members of the Committee were described but not identified by name. They included: four members from Andhra; "one member of the old Politbureau from Bengal . . ."; "a member of the Provincial Committee from Bengal who had been the leader of the armed struggle in Mymensingh"; "one of the members of the Central Committee from Kerala"; "the member of the Central Committee from Assam who . . . had taken to organizing armed guerrilla struggle on the basis of his experience"; and "a member

Two distinct categories of Party leaders can be identified. One, the internal or bureaucratic leader, is typified by the general secretaries. The other, the "popular" or mass leader, is typified by the Party's elected members of parliament.

In the first category may be included all general secretaries who have served since the Party's formal inauguration in 1934. As of 1957, all of them were members of the Central Committee and continued to exercise leadership within the Party. They are: Dr. G. Adhikari, P. C. Joshi, B. T. Ranadive, Rajeshwar Rao, and A. K. Ghosh.

Among the secretaries who served before 1950 (Adhikari, Joshi, Ranadive) there are certain uniformities. First, all of them have had long experience in the Party, having been members for 25–30 years. They are all university graduates with degrees ranging from M.A. to L.L.B. and D.Sc. They all joined the Party while in university or immediately after leaving it; that is, their only experience in politics has been as Communists. All are most notable for their skill as ideologues and propagandists; all have been strongly identified with particular "lines," and all are prolific writers. None of them has a mass following of any consequence, and none of them has marked skill in such arts of mass leadership as public speaking. They are all from North India,

---

of the Central Committee from Maharashtra who had initiated the agrarian struggle in Ahmednagar, and his wide experience of Trade Union and peasant movement."

The membership of this Committee must tentatively be pieced together from these and other sources. Assuming that the "Letter of the New Central Committee" offers accurate descriptions of the members, they may be identified as follows:

The four members from Andhra are apparently C. Rajeshwar Rao (general secretary), P. Sundarayya, M. Chandrasekhara Rao, and M. Basava Punniah. Sundarayya is described as a "former" member of the Central Committee, and M. Chandrasekhara Rao as a "former" member of the Politbureau, in an article in *Crossroads* on February 8, 1952, pp. 8–9. M. Basava Punniah describes himself as a member of the CC and PB, 1950–51, in the biographical sketch in the official "Who's Who" of the Rajya Sabha.

The "member of the old Politbureau from Bengal" is identified as Somnath Lahiri, in "A Note on the Present Situation in Our Party" (page 27).

The "member of the Provincial Committee from Bengal . . ." is probably Iswar Singh. This leader was later active in Manipur and across the border in Burma, where he was killed in guerrilla fighting in 1952. He is presumably the "Marinda Singh" listed in *East Europe and Soviet Russia*.

The member from Kerala is probably E. M. S. Namboodiripad (called "Nambudripad" in the London source).

The member from Assam is probably Biresh Misra (called "Bires Misry" in the London source). Misra was secretary of the Assam Provincial Committee in 1948.

The member from Maharashtra who led an agrarian struggle in Ahmednagar is probably Parulekar. This leader is associated primarily with the movement among the Warlis, a backward group in the district adjoining Ahmednagar.

The source for the 1951 Committee is M. R. Masani, *The Communist Party of India* (London: Derek Verschoyle, 1954), p. 124.

two of the three being Maharashtrian. These three leaders seem on the whole to be representative of the "Old Bolsheviks" of the CPI. The most important of the qualities they all show are long experience, outstanding intellectual attainment, and skill in doctrine and propaganda. About their social backgrounds the available information is too vague for generalization.

The present general secretary, A. K. Ghosh, deviates from the norm in having somewhat less Party experience (about twenty years) and in having had considerable political experience outside of the Communist movement; before joining the CPI, he had been active in the Punjab terrorist movement and was associated with the Congress and with the Royist movement. He differs, also, in being primarily an organizer rather than a propagandist; though he is required by his position to write authoritatively on doctrinal quesions, he does not show an unusual flair for it. But by virtue of his broader political background, and because he is less "doctrinaire," he may represent a more "modern" type of inner-Party leader.

Rajeshwar Rao, who was general secretary from 1950 to 1951, is the only South Indian who has served in that post. He appears to be typical of the leaders from that region in that he evidently joined the CPI in the late 1930's, he is of wealthy peasant rather than urban background, and he urges a political and doctrinal line that lays greater stress on the role of the peasantry.

The South Indian contingent is underrepresented on the Central Committee. Delegation strength at the Fourth Party Congress indicates that South Indian elements accounted for more than half of the total Party membership; moreover, of the Communists who were elected to parliament in the 1951–52 general election, about 70 per cent were from South India. Yet of the Central Committee elected at the Fourth Congress, only 41 per cent was South Indian. The predominance of the North Indian section is largely due to circumstances in the early development of the Communist movement in India. The movement originated almost exclusively in the urban industrial centers of the North, chiefly because the emissaries from abroad who were instrumental in organizing it—agents of M. N. Roy and of the British Communist Party—concentrated on those centers as the best recruiting grounds. Until the late 1930's the Communist Party was insignificant in South India, and that area has therefore not produced inner-Party leaders of such long experience as the "Old Bolsheviks" from the North.

It should be noted, finally, that the top echelon leadership includes no women, for there are none in the present Central Committee. In fact, the number of women among the members of the Party as a whole, according to a recent Party document, has been "insignificant." [51]

The CPI "mass" leader is typified by its parliamentary members. The qualities of this type of CPI leader may be inferred from an analysis of the common characteristics of the following Communist MP's: A. K. Gopalan, K. C. George, Ravi Narayan Reddy, Yella Reddy, Dasrath Deb Barman, Hiren Mukherji, and Renu Chakravarty. This list includes all those M.P.'s who were in the 1956 Central Committee, plus the two prominent Bengali M.P.'s. It is striking, first, that all these leaders were attracted to the CPI during the moderate "united front" eras of 1934–1940 and 1945–1947. Nearly all had extensive political experience in the Congress and Congress Socialist parties before joining the CPI. Most of them have had professional careers (teaching or law). While information on their social origins is incomplete, most of them appear to have come from the higher social strata in their communities. Finally, most of them were elected from predominantly peasant constituencies.

In contrast to the inner-Party leaders of the CPI, these "mass" leaders have had broad political experience and have shown competence in the techniques of popular leadership. Much more than the "Old Bolsheviks," they seem to be "natural" leaders. Their backgrounds, and the fact that they joined the Party during periods when it was the moderate, "loyal opposition," indicate that they have closer bonds with their own society than do the inner-Party leaders.

It may well be that the future of the Indian Communist Party depends, fundamentally, on its ability to draw such "natural" leaders into its ranks. And as the Party has recently entered a new period of moderation, its prospects for attracting such leaders, and hence its prospects for the future, may be greatly improved.

One other CPI leader, E. M. S. Namboodiripad, who has not been either a general secretary or M.P., nevertheless deserves attention here. He appears to have a unique combination of the personal qualities which are appropriate to both inner-Party and mass leadership. As an inner-Party leader, Namboodiripad has a secure position very near the top of the Party hierarchy. His apparent dedication to the cause is strikingly evinced by his renunciation of wealth and high social position. He is an unusually skillful and prolific propagandist, and is apparently a competent administrator as well. Perhaps most important, he is noted as a moderate and has never been rigidly associated with any of the main factions of the Party; this is best demonstrated by the

---

[51] *Resolution on Party Organization,* p. 27.

fact that he is virtually the only Party leader who has served on every Central Committee since 1943 (the other is P. Sundarayya). Acceptable to all sections, he is able to mediate compromises between factions. According to unofficial sources, Namboodiripad tied for the largest number of votes in the Central Committee election at the Third Congress in 1953–54, and received the third largest number in the Central Committee election at the Fourth Congress in 1956.[52] During periods when Ghosh was in Moscow for medical treatment, Namboodiripad has served as acting secretary. There is no doubt, then, that he has in high degree the qualities necessary for inner-Party leadership.

But he also has in unusual degree the qualities needed for mass leadership. He has the social prestige of an ultra-high-caste background, for the Namboodiris are among the most select of the Brahman subcastes. He also has a background of broad political experience and popularity, having been a Congress and Socialist leader of considerable stature before his recruitment to the Communist ranks in the late 1930's. Finally, he now possesses another very important prerequisite of popular leadership in India: official government office. As chief minister of the new Communist government in Kerala, he has an opportunity unprecedented among Indian Communist leaders, past and present, to build a mass following. Among a people who tend to revere government leaders simply on the basis of their exalted office, this is a precious opportunity.

For a variety of reasons, such as the failure of his government, for example, Namboodiripad himself may fail to attain unrivaled supremacy in the CPI. However, he or another leader of similar qualities might significantly affect the CPI's development.

Such a leader might, in the first place, be able to unite and stabilize the Party on the basis of personal authority, as no one has yet been able to do. In this way the CPI might outgrow the immaturity which has characterized it, and might in some degree eliminate the weaknesses which have crippled its operation—fragmentation into a collection of personal empires, individual and group indiscipline, and scholasticism. The Party might become less abjectly dependent upon, though no less loyal to, the international Communist movement.

Moreover, such a leader might be able to popularize the CPI among the Indian voters as no other figure has been able to do. In India personal leadership has an unusually crucial role in the political process; the presence of a compelling leader at the head of the Communist Party might do more than any program or propaganda slogan to enhance its appeal.

---

[52] For Third Congress election see *Communist Conspiracy at Madurai*, p. 157; for Fourth Congress, see *Communist Double Talk . . .* , p. 155.

16 THE MASS ORGANIZATIONS

A Communist Party is an elite group which is supposed to serve as the vanguard of the revolutionary working class. Its most important auxiliaries are the mass organizations, which are the source of the Party's main political power; it is through them that the Communists endeavor to mobilize the full might of the working class and its allies for the tasks of the revolution.

The role of the mass organizations and their relationship to the Party were defined by Stalin in 1924. In *Foundations of Leninism* he said:

The Party is not the only organization of the working class. The proletariat has also a number of other organizations, without which it cannot properly wage the struggle against capital: trade unions, cooperative societies, factory and works organizations, parliamentary groups, non-Party women's associations, the press, cultural and educational organizations, youth leagues, revolutionary fighting organizations (in times of open revolutionary action), Soviets of deputies as the form of state organization (if the proletariat is in power), etc. The overwhelming majority of these organizations are non-Party, and only a certain part of them adhere directly to the Party, or represent its offshoots. All these organizations, under certain conditions, are absolutely necessary for the working class.[1]

Since these organizations serve one class, they should, according to Stalin, "work in one direction." But who is to determine the direction? The answer is obvious: the Party of the proletariat.

---

[1] Joseph Stalin, *Foundations of Leninism* (New York: International Publishers, 1939), p. 115.

The party possesses all the necessary qualifications for this because, in the first place, it is the rallying center of the finest elements in the working class, who have direct connections with the non-Party organizations of the proletariat and very frequently lead them.[2]

The Party, Stalin concluded,

is by reason of its experience and prestige the only organization capable of centralizing the leadership of the struggle of the proletariat, thus transforming each and every non-Party organization of the working class into an auxiliary body and transmission belt linking the Party with the class. . . . Members of the Party who belong to these organizations and are doubtlessly influential in them, should do all they can to persuade these non-Party organizations to draw nearer to the Party of the proletariat in their work and to accept voluntarily its political guidance.[3]

These classical principles of Communist Party organizational work have been incorporated into the constitution of the CPI. Article XI states:

Section 1. At all congresses, meetings and in the elected committees of the mass organizations, trade unions, kisan sabhas, student and women's organizations, coöperative societies, sports clubs, youth organizations, etc., and also in local self-government bodies and in legislatures, where there are not less than two Party members, Party fractions are organized which must function in a disciplined Party way. They must strive to win the support of the non-Party masses for the Party policy with a view to strengthening the unity, fighting capacity and mass basis of the organizations concerned.

Section 2. The fractions are completely controlled by the corresponding Party committees (Central Committee, Provincial Committee, District, Town or Local Committee, or Cell) and on all questions must carry out, strictly and without violation, the decisions of the Party organizations which lead them.

The fractions of higher bodies of mass organizations, by agreement with the corresponding Party committees, may send directives to fractions of the lower bodies of the same mass organization, and the latter must carry them out without fail as directives from a higher Party organ.[4]

To the CPI, the most important mass organizations have been those of the workers, peasants, students, and women. Among these the trade-union organizations have been the source of the Party's greatest political power.

All-India Trade Union Congress

Modern trade unionism had its beginning in India after World War I, and the first national trade-union federation, the All-India

---

[2] *Ibid.*, p. 116.

[3] *Ibid.*, pp. 116–117.

[4] *The Constitution of the Communist Party of India* (Delhi: Communist Party of India, 1954), pp. 17–18.

Trade Union Congress (AITUC), was formed in 1920. The organizers of the All-India Trade Union Congress were not Marxian revolutionaries, but bourgeois nationalists with close ties to the Indian National Congress. Humanitarianism as well as nationalism motivated the leadership, and one of the early leaders, an employer, explained his participation by saying: "I shall be false to myself if I do not redeem, at least in part, the debt I owe to ill-used labor." [5] The first president of the AITUC was Lala Lajpat Rai, whom M. N. Roy and his wife had known in New York in 1917. Whatever his personal friendship for Rai, Roy did not mistake him and his AITUC colleagues for Marxist revolutionaries. Reviewing the Second Session of the AITUC in *Inprecor,* Roy wrote in 1922:

> The leadership of the working-class movement in India is not all that might be desired. Most of the important unions are headed either by English skilled workers indirectly connected with the Government, or by humanitarian reformists without any conception of class struggle, or by opportunist nationalist politicians.[6]

His evaluation had not changed by the time of the Third Annual Session, which he described as a "strange conglomeration of Nationalism, Utopianism and Reformism." [7]

The Comintern clearly displayed its interest in international trade unionism when in July, 1921, it set up the Red International of Labor Unions (RILU, sometimes called the "Profintern").[8] The RILU immediately turned its attention to the Asian trade unions, an area which had been neglected by the socialist-oriented International Federation of Trade Unions (IFTU). When the AITUC held its Second Annual Session in Jharia (Bihar), November 30, 1921, the RILU sent its greetings and appealed to the Indian organization "to join in the new great world movement of international solidarity on absolutely equal terms." [9] The moderate leaders of the AITUC showed no immediate desire to affiliate with either the RILU or the IFTU, but the question remained controversial for many years.

The Indian Communists were slow in gaining a foothold in the trade-union movement, and what success they achieved in the beginning appears to have been due to the efforts of British comrades. As early as 1924 the British Communist Party began organizing Indian

---

[5] Speech of Seth T. Ramjush Agarwala, chairman of the Reception Committee, Second Annual Session, AITUC, Jharia, Nov. 30, 1921; in Mitra, ed., *Indian Annual Register, 1922,* p. 457.

[6] M. N. Roy, "The Indian Trade Union Congress," *Inprecor,* II (Jan. 3, 1922), p. 4.

[7] M. N. Roy, "Where are the Masses?" *Inprecor,* III (May 9, 1923), p. 333.

[8] See E. H. Carr, *The Bolshevik Revolution 1917–1923* (London: Macmillan, 1953), pp. 399–401.

[9] S. D. Punekar, *Trade Unionism in India* (Bombay: New Book Co., 1948), p. 91.

seamen who came to British ports.[10] That the seamen were the first to receive attention can probably be explained by the International's need for couriers who could carry messages and propaganda to the embryo Communist movement in India.

The limited evidence available suggests that the Communists in India had not engaged in any important trade-union activity before the arrival of George Allison in April, 1926. According to a colleague, Allison was sent to India by the RILU to "ginger up the Indian labor movement." [11] Within a year after his arrival the Communists were able to report some success in organizing textile workers, railwaymen, municipal workers, dockers, and pressmen, mostly in Bombay.[12]

Allison was arrested in January, 1927, but not before he had been joined in Bombay by Philip Spratt (see p. 86). Spratt was a dedicated worker and a good organizer, and Communist trade-union work received considerable impetus under his leadership. By May, 1927, Communist leaders in Bombay could record some advance in several other parts of India as well as in Bombay. An official CPI report stated that in Lahore comrades had taken "a conspicuous part in the TUC [Trade Union Congress] activities and have organized about a half a dozen unions successfully." The unions already formed in Bombay, the report said, "could command an influential position in the AITUC." [13]

It was among the cotton-textile workers and the railwaymen of Bombay that the Communists were able to organize their largest and strongest unions, the Girni Kamgar Union and the GIP (Great Indian Peninsula) Railwaymen's Union. There is very little information available concerning the early days of the GIP Railwaymen's Union. K. N. Joglekar, a Communist, was its main organizer, and for several months during 1928 he traveled up and down the GIP line recruiting members.[14] By 1929 the union had a membership of 41,000.[15]

In August 1925, a textile-workers union, Girni Kamgar Mahamandel, had been formed in Bombay under the leadership of A. A. Alve and D. R. Mayekar who served, respectively, as president and secretary.[16] A few months later, in January, 1926, N. M. Joshi led the formation of a competing union, the Bombay Textile Labor Union (BTLU). But Joshi's union was less militant than Alve's and it was to the latter,

---

[10] *Meerut Sessions Judgment,* p. 61.

[11] Philip Spratt, *Blowing Up India* (Calcutta: Prachi Prakashan, 1955), p. 32.

[12] *Meerut Sessions Judgment,* p. 179.

[13] *Ibid.,* p. 155.

[14] *Ibid.,* p. 366.

[15] Punekar, *Trade Unionism in India,* p. 326.

[16] Details on the Bombay textile unions during this period are contained in *Report of the Bombay Strike Enquiry Committee, 1928–29* (Bombay: Government Central Press, 1929), Vol. I, on which this account is based.

therefore, that the Communists gave their attention when they began to take active part in Bombay labor affairs.

In mid-1927 a number of mills in Bombay introduced an "efficiency scheme" which threatened to cut down employment. The resulting discontent among the millhands created an ideal climate for militant trade unionism, and by January, 1928 the Communists were planning to launch a general strike of textile workers. Although opposed to this, Joshi's union was forced to go along with the strike plans or be deserted by its membership. A joint strike committee was formed to represent both unions, and the walk-out began on April 26, 1928. While it was in progress, Alve and Mayekar had a falling out and the Girni Kamgar Mahamandel split in two. Mayekar's group retained the original name, and Alve registered his union as the Girni Kamgar Union (GKU); S. A. Dange was made general secretary, and Ben Bradley, S. H. Jhabwala, and R. S. Nimbkar, all Communists, were appointed vice-presidents. The general strike lasted until October 6, 1928, when the mill owners agreed to the appointment of a government committee to investigate the issues. During the six months the strike had been in progress, 22,347,620 man days were lost.[17] And by the end of the year membership in Alve's new GKU had risen from a few hundred to about 54,000, while that of Joshi's BTLU fell from 8,436 to 6,749.[18]

The Bombay textile strike was not the only manifestation of increased trade-union militancy during 1928. In its annual report to the British Parliament, the government of India noted with alarm:

During the year under review, the industrial life of India was far more disturbed than during the preceding year. The total number of strikes was 203, involving no less than 506,851 people, as compared with 129 strikes in 1927–28 in which 131,655 people were involved. The total number of working days lost was 31,647,404 which is greater than the total number of working days lost in the five preceding years taken together.[19]

There is little doubt that the Communists, especially Spratt and Bradley, were responsible for a great deal of the unrest. Indeed, it seems that the government had already recognized the Communists' role in fomenting unrest, for in its report the previous year it had said:

It is doubtful . . . whether the indigenous labor agitator is a Communist at heart. He is ordinarily a man of little education, who has acquired a smattering of Bolshevist theory, and who is able to impress the ignorant workers with

---

[17] India. Home Department. *India in 1928–29* (Calcutta: Government of India, 1930), p. 7.

[18] Morris D. Morris, *A History of the Creation of a Disciplined Labor Force in the Cotton Textile Industry of Bombay City, 1851–1951* (Ph.D. Thesis, University of California, 1954), p. 446.

[19] *India in 1928–29*, p. 7.

violent harangues inter-larded with the catch words and slogans employed by the Communist tub-thumper all over the world. He must, nevertheless, be given credit for an energy and pushfulness which is not apparent among the ranks of the "bourgeois" Trade Unionists. While pushing, on the whole, a sane course in their dealings with Labor, the Right Wing of the All-India Union Congress have remained somewhat aloof from contact with the worker himself, and have, therefore, not succeeded in "getting under his skin." [20]

It seems, also, more than a coincidence that the government should have decided to inaugurate the Communist conspiracy trial at Meerut at the height of this unrest.

Communist Infiltration of the AITUC

Communist interest in the AITUC was apparent as early as 1925 when D. R. Thengdi, a Communist sympathizer who was president at the organization's Bombay meeting, made a speech on class war which irritated the dominant moderate element. When the leftists later attempted to make the AITUC more "proletarian" by modifying the constitution, they were defeated.[21]

By 1927, the Communists began to exert considerable influence in the AITUC. Communist prestige was heightened by the fact that Shapurji Saklatvala, an Indian Communist member of the British Parliament, attended the Seventh AITUC Session in Delhi in March. A Soviet commentator, noting the resolutions passed at the Delhi meeting, wrote that a "step forward" had been taken but that it did not represent a "serious advance" as the majority of trade-union leaders in India "do not support the class struggle but still believe in class collaboration." [22]

The first real Communist challenge to the moderates came at the Ninth Session in Jharia in December, 1928. A fraternal delegate from the League Against Imperialism, J. W. Johnstone, attended the session but was arrested after the first day's proceedings. This so infuriated the delegates that they decided forthwith to affiliate the AITUC with the League, a decision which they might not otherwise have taken.[23] On the other hand, Communist efforts to affiliate the AITUC with the Comintern-controlled Pan Pacific Trade Union Secretariat (PPTUS) were defeated, and the issue was postponed for another year.

The Jharia session was also attended by another foreign fraternal

---

[20] *India in 1927–28,* pp. 341–342.
[21] M. N. Roy, "The Indian Trade Union Congress," *Inprecor,* VI (Feb. 18, 1926), p. 191.
[22] Balabushevich, "Indian Trade Union Congress Holds Seventh Session," *Inprecor,* VII (June 9, 1927), p. 714.
[23] Mitra, ed., *Indian Annual Register, 1928,* II, 503–504.

delegate who was more fortunate than Johnstone. He was the Australian Communist, Jack Ryan, who had come specifically to lobby for affiliation with the PPTUS. Assessing the Congress, Ryan later wrote in the PPTUS bulletin: "By the time the next Congress is convened there is every reason to believe that the left wing will be no longer a minority and that the old conservative leaders will be defeated." [24] This prophecy turned out to be remarkably accurate, for the first major split in the AITUC occurred at the Tenth Annual Session.

When the session convened in Nagpur, November 30, 1929, Jawaharlal Nehru was president. At some time before this session (the date is not certain) the Communists had brought their two biggest unions into the AITUC—the GKU with a membership of 54,000, and the GIP Railwaymen's Union with 41,000 members. This gave them considerably more strength than they had had at Jharia.

Before the open session, the Executive Committee had met and passed a Communist-sponsored resolution favoring affiliation with the PPTUS. Profoundly disturbed by this development, a group of leaders including N. M. Joshi, Chaman Lall, and Mrinal Kanti Bose caucused and decided not to participate in the open session. Hearing of the proposed walkout, the Communists decided to withdraw the offensive resolution at the open session in order to preserve unity. Meanwhile, the opponents of the resolution had quarreled among themselves and had split into two groups, one led by N. M. Joshi and the other by Mrinal Kanti Bose. But though the Communists were willing to withdraw their resolution, neither of these groups was willing to participate. This peculiar situation was described by Nehru in a statement after the meeting:

Although the split was likely in any event, there is no doubt that many people actively worked for it and forced the issue. On the one side, there was the youthful enthusiasm of some members of the left wing, who wanted to go ahead regardless of consequences, and on the other, the deliberate attempt to push them on so as to widen the breach and thus get additional reasons for seceding.[25]

Nehru criticized the seceders for their precipitate action because they had actually had more voting strength than those who remained. "Subsequent events showed," he said, "that had they attended the Congress, the final decisions might well have been different." "The trouble," he added, "comes from those who change color in the course of an afternoon." Nehru's testimony, therefore, does not support the frequently expressed opinion that the blame for the first major split

---

[24] *The Far Eastern Bulletin* (Jan. 16, 1930 [sic]), p. 5. This issue is evidently dated incorrectly. It probably should be 1929.

[25] Mitra, ed., *Indian Annual Register, 1929*, II, 429.

in the nation-wide trade-union movement should be placed upon the Communists.

An Opposition Communist, writing in an American Opposition journal in 1931, states that there were three main factions at the Nagpur session: the Communists (still in a minority), the reformists, and the nationalists. He contends that the election of Nehru to the presidency was the result of a deal between the Communists and the nationalists that made S. A. Dange the general secretary.[26] Whether or not there was such a deal, the Communists did capture important offices in the organization. D. B. Kulkarni, Muzaffar Ahmed, and Abdul Majid were made vice-presidents while Philip Spratt and Ben Bradley were elected to the new Executive Committee. D. R. Thengdi and K. N. Joglekar were chosen to represent the AITUC at the next world congress of the League Against Imperialism.[27]

Since 1929 the history of Indian trade unionism has been one of successive bifurcations.[28] After the Nagpur session N. M. Joshi and the moderates set up the Indian Trade Union Federation (ITUF). Meanwhile the Communist-nationalist alliance in the AITUC broke down under Communist militancy, which was dictated by the Sixth Comintern Congress. In 1931 the Communists under S. V. Deshpande and B. T. Ranadive (most of the top Communist leaders were under detention at Meerut) left the AITUC and formed the Red Trade Union Congress. They in turn fought among themselves, and their biggest unions in Bombay were riven with factionalism.

Largely because the Congress Socialist Party wanted labor unity, a joint conference on coöperation was held by the AITUC and the National Trade Union Federation (NTUF, successor to ITUF) in February, 1935. The following April, in accordance with their current united-front policy, the Communists came back into the AITUC, and in 1938 the NTUF did likewise.

When Gandhi launched the "Quit India" movement in August, 1942, most of the nationalist leaders were thrown in jail. But the Communists, because they supported the British war effort, were free and could pursue their political activities. While the nationalist leaders

---

[26] S. K. Vidyarthi, "The Trade Union Movement in India," *Revolutionary Age*, II (Aug. 29, 1931), pp. 3–4.

[27] *Meerut Sessions Judgment*, p. 227.

[28] An adequate history of the Indian trade-union movement does not exist at this writing. However, useful accounts are contained in: P. P. Lakshman, *Congress and Labour Movement in India* (Allahabad: All-India Congress Committee, 1947); Oscar A. Ornati, *Jobs and Workers in India* (Ithaca: Institute of International Industrial and Labor Relations, Cornell University, 1955); and S. D. Punekar, *Trade Unionism in India* (Bombay: New Book Co., 1948).

were in prison, the Communists gained firm control of the AITUC. After the war National Congress leaders tried to break the Communist hold on the AITUC, but failed. Unwilling to see Communist monopoly of the Indian labor movement, the Congress leaders, in May, 1947 set up their own federation, the Indian National Trade Union Congress (INTUC). The Communists were faced with still further competition when the Socialists created their national labor federation, the Hind Mazdoor Sabha (HMS).

By the 25th Annual Session of the AITUC in Ernakulam in December, 1957, the Communists had brought their segment of the trade-union movement around to the new CPI policy of conditional coöperation with Nehru's government. The main conclusion of the Ernakulam session was that the AITUC should play a positive role in national development by helping the government of India carry out the Second Five Year Plan, especially the expansion of heavy industry. To accomplish this workers were admonished not to push wage demands too hard. "Struggles will continue to be conducted," said S. A. Dange, "but every struggle need not culminate in a strike and struggles could no longer be conducted in the old way. Values are changing in our country, and in present conditions, strikes must be peaceful in order to secure the largest measure of popular support and sympathy." [29] Despite opposition from the delegates from Bengal, this new approach was adopted.

The Structure of the AITUC

The 1945 constitution of the AITUC leaves little doubt that the Communists followed the teachings of Stalin when they reorganized this particular mass organization. The AITUC constitution defines a trade union as

an organ of class struggle; its basic task, therefore, is to organize the workers for advancing and defending their rights and interests; and although collective bargaining is the necessary implication of a Trade Union and although in the transitional period to socialism, negotiations, representations, joint action and other methods of collective bargaining must remain an integral part of trade union activities, labor and capital cannot be reconciled within the capitalistic system.[30]

The amelioration of the economic and social conditions of the working classes ranks third among the objectives of the organization;

---

[29] New Age (weekly), V (Jan. 5, 1958), p. 15.

[30] All-India Trade Union Congress Constitution, 5 (a) (i). Reprinted in AITUC, Report . . . Twenty-first Session, Madras, 1945. (Bombay: AITUC, 1945), p. 96. In 1954 a committee was appointed to review the constitution and recommend changes. Any revisions that may have been made were not available to the authors.

of prior importance are the establishment of a socialist state and the nationalization of the means of production, distribution, and exchange. It is clear, therefore, that the primary function of the AITUC is political.

According to the constitution, the officers of the AITUC are elected and major policy is determined by the delegates to the annual session, which ordinarily meets in December. In practice, however, the annual session has been more nearly biennial; in the twelve years between 1942 and 1954 only six annual sessions were convened. Representation at the annual session is by union, and is determined on a diminishing scale which starts at one delegate for each five hundred of a union's members. Thus a union with 3,000 members would be entitled to six delegates, one with 12,000 would have only fifteen and one with 50,000 would have but twenty-nine.[31]

Table V shows the number of delegates registered at each of the last seven annual sessions, according to official AITUC reports; it shows as well the number of unions affiliated to the AITUC at the time of each session, and their total aggregate membership. These figures should be used with great caution, however, for not only are they undoubtedly inflated (especially those for 1949, when B. T. Ranadive controlled the CPI), but there are internal discrepancies in the official reports.

TABLE V

REPRESENTATION AT ANNUAL SESSIONS OF THE AITUC

Session	Place	Year	Delegates	Affiliated unions	AITUC membership
19th	Cawnpore	1942	168	94	
20th	Nagpur	1943	306	191	269,803
21st	Madras	1945	850	401	451,915
22d	Calcutta	1947	1,049	407	
23d	Bombay	1949	400		800,000 [1]
24th	Calcutta	1954	825	937	655,940
25th	Ernakulam	1957	1,282		

[1] The WFTU in 1949 gave the AITUC membership as 600,000. (*Report of the Proceedings of the IInd World Trade Union Congress* [Paris: WFTU, 1949], p. 360.)

It should be noted, too, that many affiliated unions are not represented at certain annual sessions. For example, the official report for the 24th Session in 1954 states that the 825 delegates who were actually present represented only 295 of the 937 affiliated unions.[32] These 295

[31] *Ibid.*, p. 100.

[32] *Twenty-fourth Session of the All-India Trade Union Congress, Report & Resolutions* (New Delhi: AITUC, 1954), p. 18.

unions had an aggregate membership of 321,932, while the total membership of the AITUC was set at 655,940. Thus 642 affiliated unions with an aggregate membership of 334,008 were not represented.

According to the constitution, at each annual session the delegates elect from among their number those who are to serve on the General Council. Membership on the General Council is by industrial category, and representation is based on a sliding scale similar to that outlined for the annual session delegates. At the 24th Session in 1954, 110 members were elected to the General Council. The national officers are *ex officio* members of the General Council.[33]

The Council has the power to coöpt additional members up to one-sixth the number of representatives of the affiliated unions. The General Council is supposed to meet "at least once a year," and although its function is not clearly outlined by the constitution, in practice it has determined or sanctioned policy during the intervals between annual sessions.

The list of General Council members elected at the 1954 annual session provides a good index to the strength of the AITUC in the various regions of India: Andhra, 5; Assam, 2; Bengal, 29; Bihar, 5; Bombay, 15; Delhi, 4; Hyderabad, 7; Karnatak, 4; Madhya Bharat, 3; Madhya Pradesh, 4; Malabar, 4; Orissa, 3; Punjab, 5; Rajasthan, 2; Tamilnad, 7; Travancore-Cochin, 5; Uttar Pradesh, 4; AITUC Headquarters, 2. The predominance of Bengal and Bombay is obvious.

Above the General Council is the Working Committee. The 1945 constitution provides that this body shall consist of the national officers of the AITUC (except the secretaries) and fifteen members elected by the General Council "by a system of cumulative voting." [34] In 1954 the number was increased to thirty, although only eighteen were elected at the annual session that year.[35] The constitution provides that the Working Committee shall meet twice a year and that it has the authority:

(i) To take all proper steps for carrying out the resolutions passed at the previous Session of the AITUC;
(ii) To deal with any emergency that arises during the year, affecting the interests of the working class; and
(iii) Generally to advance and further the aims and objects of the AITUC.[36]

---

[33] An account of the General Council meeting held in July, 1956, refers to 112 members. *New Age* (weekly), III (Aug. 5, 1956), p. 16. In 1947 there were 167.
[34] *All-India Trade Union Congress Constitution*, p. 99.
[35] *Twenty-Fourth Session of the All-India Trade Union Congress . . . ,* p. 197.
[36] *All-India Trade Union Congress Constitution*, p. 101.

Leadership

Table VI lists the top leadership of the AITUC since its 20th Annual Session in 1943. With the exception of the 1947 list, which was taken from the WFTU bulletin, all information is from official AITUC sources and the CPI press. The 1949 session took place at the height of B. T. Ranadive's leadership of the CPI and most of the top Communist trade unionists, including S. A. Dange and S. S. Mirajkar, were in jail. Very little information is available concerning the administration during this period and one may assume, from the long delay in calling the 24th Session, that the organizational structure was badly damaged.

An analysis of the table reveals several interesting facts. First, that no other person, Communist or non-Communist has held high office for so long a time as S. A. Dange or S. S. Mirajkar. Both are from Bombay and both are veteran members of the Central Committee of the CPI. From 1943 through 1947 the post of general secretary was held by the moderate non-Communist, N. M. Joshi (who died at seventy-six on May 30, 1955). Twice during this period Dange occupied the president's chair, and it may be assumed that at these times the Communists and non-Communists were fairly evenly balanced. After 1947, when many non-Communist unions withdrew from the AITUC, Dange took over the post of general secretary, and the presidency was given to V. Chakkarai Chettiar who, with B. P. Wadia had founded in 1918 the first modern trade union in India. Chettiar's age (he was born in 1881) and his poor health have prevented him from taking a really active part in AITUC affairs. He was unable to attend either the 1954 annual session or the General Council meeting in July, 1956. It may be assumed, therefore, that the office of the president during his tenure has represented no great political power.

It can be seen that as of the 1954 session, the leadership of the AITUC was firmly under CPI control. Of the top eight offices, six were held by Communist Party members. Two (Dange and Sen) were members of the CPI Politbureau, and two more (Mirajkar and Aruna Asaf Ali) were members of the Central Committee. The treasurer, K. Anandan Nambiar, was a Communist M.P. from Madras and also general secretary of the South Indian Railway Labor Union. The non-Communists, both members of the Forward Bloc (Marxist), have been close to the CPI in recent years. Satyapriya Bannerjee, a former lieutenant of the late Subhas Chandra Bose, was elected to the Council of States in 1952 with the support of the Communists in the West Bengal

LEADERSHIP OF THE AITUC

Elected at:	20th, Nagpur–1943	21st, Madras–1945	22d, Calcutta–1947	23d, Bombay–1949	24th Calcutta–1954	25th, Ernakulam, 1957
President	S. A. Dange	Mrinal Kanti Bose	S. A. Dange	V. Chakkarai Chettiar	V. Chakkarai Chettiar	S. S. Mirajkar
Vice-presidents	S. C. Sen S. K. Pramanik B. K. Mukherji Fazl-i-Ilahi Qurban Gulam Mohamed Khan	S. A. Dange V. Chakkarai Chettiar S. S. Mirajkar P. C. Bose Juggun Khan	Aftab Ali S. S. Yusuf S. S. Mirajkar K. N. Joglekar R. A. Khedgikar	Data unavailable	Ranen Sen Satyapriya Bannerji S. S. Mirajkar Aruna Asaf Ali R. K. Haldulkar	Hemanta Kumar Basu Ranen Sen P. Ramamurti Kedar Das S. S. Yusuf P. Balachandra Menon
General secretary	N. M. Joshi	N. M. Joshi	N. M. Joshi	S. A. Dange	S. A. Dange	S. A. Dange
Treasurer	R. A. Khedgikar	R. A. Khedgikar	Peter Alvarez	M. S. Bakshi	K. Anandan Nambiar	T. B. Vithal Rao
Assistant secretaries	Shanta Bhalerao S. S. Mirajkar	Shanta Bhalerao Manek Gandhi N. V. Phadke	Shanta Mukherji Manek Gandhi N. V. Phadke Dinkar Desai	Data unavailable	Maqdoom Mohiuddin P. Balachandra Menon Arvind Ghoshal S. Krishnamurthi	K. T. K. Thangamani Raj Bahadur Gour Indrajit Gupta Satish Loomba K. G. Srivastava

legislature.[37] R. K. Haldulkar was the chairman of the Forward Bloc in Madhya Pradesh and the head of a mining union there. Communist domination is also apparent from the 1957 list of officers.

The official literature indicates that the AITUC has suffered from a critical shortage of trained leaders at the secondary level. To remedy this the CPI held a convention of all Communist trade-union workers in Calcutta in May, 1952, in order to give a series of training lectures. Those by S. A. Dange were reprinted as a study guide, of which a major section was devoted to "The Make-Up and Tasks of Our TU Functionary." That the conspiratorial nature of the Party is carried over into trade-union work is made clear in this section.

> We must learn to keep some of the cadres unexposed. Or else, the victimization by the employers will throw all our best leaders and men from the real field of work that is the factory, shop and office.
> Some people think that because our unions are now legal, we bring all our cadres to the forefront. We have to remember that the unions are legal but the crisis of capitalism is not over. The bourgeoisie does not hesitate to attack us when we lead workers' struggles.[38]

A central trade-union school was also set up in Nagpur for two weeks in August-September, 1953, and it was planned to follow this up with provincial schools in all the states. But only in Gujerat, Tamilnad, and Punjab was anything done.[39]

Like the CPI itself, the AITUC must also contend with the regional loyalties of its leaders and with the consequent lack of attention to the problems of the central organization. S. A. Dange referred to this in the 1954 organizational report, saying:

> Apart from concrete guidance on each trade, we tried to visit the States and their conferences, but such visits were few and far between. For this, the Center was handicapped by lack of enough personnel and pressure of work. We could avail of the services of Comrades Satyapriya Bannerjee, Aruna Asaf Ali, P. Ramamurti, Ranen Sen, S. S. Mirajkar, and Jyoti Basu and myself for visiting the State TUCs.[40]

Finances

The financing of the AITUC is outlined in the constitution which states that each affiliated union shall pay:

(i) An annual contribution of Rs. 10 for 500 membership and below, Rs. 20 for 1,000 membership or less, Rs. 10 in addition successively for each thousand or less,

---

[37] See Satyapriya Bannerjee's statement regarding election support from Communists in *New Age* (weekly), I (March 21, 1954), p. 15.

[38] S. A. Dange, *On the Indian Trade Union Movement* (Bombay: CPI, 1952), p. 42.

[39] *Twenty-fourth Session of the All-India Trade Union Congress* . . . , p. 84.

[40] *Ibid.*, p. 85.

up to a membership of 10,000—and Rs. 5 for every additional 1,000 membership or less above 10,000.

(ii) A delegation of fee of Rs. 2 per delegate; and

(iii) Such other levy as may be fixed by a majority of not less than ⅔rds of the members at the General Council.

In 1945 these affiliation fees totaled Rs. 5,667, and in 1953 (the most recent year for which statistics have been published) they amounted to Rs. 4,925. These figures, however, do not present a complete picture of the financial status of the AITUC, for special levies are collected for special projects. The cost of the annual session, for example, is borne by the local reception committee, and for the 1954 meeting, the committee collected Rs. 18,428.[41] The constitution provides that any surplus remaining in the funds raised for the annual session will remain with the provincial unit sponsoring the session. Other levies are made from time to time. The CPI weekly in 1944 published an interesting account of collection techniques:

Collections began on December 8, the day on which the Tramway Company began to pay out wages, and the day on which union subscriptions are traditionally collected.

Outside the gate of the Kalighat Depot squat two members of the Sectional Committee. They are armed with Union and Lenin Day Fund receipt books. Two others hover just inside the gate, almost at the window of the cashier's office before which the workers are lining up for their pay. As each man gets his cash and walks up to the gate, these two immediately go up to him, one on each flank; eagerly, insistently, they remind him of the Party's needs and of the Union's pledge. Usually, the worker responds at once, and the two collectors outside the gate steadily reap their harvest.

But, just in case someone slips through, behind the collectors is yet another "defense line"—four more Sectional Committee members! They encircle the reluctant worker, argue with him, explain, persuade, until back he steps to the gate and pays his contribution. . . . At Park Circus the workers have put up a "black list" of defaulters, those who by not paying are violating their Union's solemn pledge. This exposure is working like magic—the list is thinning rapidly day by day.[42]

The total expenditure of the AITUC for 1953 as given in its published budget was Rs. 15,569.[43]

International Affiliation

The AITUC is a member of the Communist-dominated World Federation of Trade Unions (WFTU), and since 1949 S. A. Dange has been a vice-president of this international organization.[44] Although

---

[41] *Ibid.*, p. 18.

[42] Indrajit Gupta, "One Rupee Each, For the Party," *People's War*, II (Jan. 16, 1944), p. 6.

[43] *Twenty-fourth Session of the All-India Trade Union Congress . . .* , p. 201.

[44] For background on the WFTU see: Bernard S. Morris, "Communist International Front Organizations: Their Nature and Function," *World Politics*, IX (Oct., 1956),

the annual AITUC budget indicates that collections are made for the WFTU, the amount it actually contributes to international headquarters is not revealed. On the other hand, the WFTU has given financial aid to the AITUC: between July, 1950, and May, 1952, the WFTU contributed Rs. 20,000 to the defense of workers under trial for acts committed during this period of extreme militancy.[45]

In November, 1949, the Trade Union Conference of Asian and Australasian Countries of the World Federation of Trade Unions was held in Peking, but India was not represented.[46] At the suggestion of the Soviet delegate, the Conference decided to set up a permanent liaison bureau to coördinate the activities of Asian and Australasian trade unions. This liaison bureau was to consist of four members, one each from the USSR, China, India, and Australasia. The authors, however, have been unable to find any evidence that an Indian member ever served on the bureau or that the bureau ever actually functioned.[47]

In early 1952, the Chinese Communists began to show a specific interest in Indian trade unions when they invited a group of fourteen Indian labor leaders to Peking for the May Day celebrations. According to the New Delhi magazine, *Thought*, the invitations were extended to individuals rather than to any of the national trade-union federations.[48] The government of India is reported to have objected to contacts being made in this manner, and as a consequence the Chinese revised the invitation, extending it to all national-trade union organizations, including the Congress-controlled INTUC and the Praja Socialist's Hind Mazdoor Sabha (HMS). INTUC turned the invitation down, but HMS accepted. Thus, actually, the delegation that toured China contained non-Communist members whom the Chinese had not intended to invite. The following is a list of those to whom the original invitation was extended: [49]

---

pp. 76–87; and John P. Windmuller, *American Labor and the International Labor Movement 1950 to 1953* (Ithaca: Institute of International Industrial and Labor Relations, Cornell University, 1954), pp. 52–66.

[45] Dange, *On the India Trade Union Movement*, p. 60.

[46] Prabodh Chandra, "On 'A note on the present situation in our party'," *PHQ Open Forum*, XII (n.p.: 1949 [actually, 1950]), p. 9. *Crossroads*, I (Dec. 9, 1949), p. 12, states that India was represented and was given a seat on the Working Committee. No Indian delegate is named. This report must be discounted in view of the above-cited inner-Party document which categorically asserts that no Indian was present.

[47] See John H. Kautsky, *Moscow and the Communist Party of India* (New York: John Wiley, 1956), pp. 99 n, 159 n.

[48] *Thought*, IV (May 10, 1952), p. 3.

[49] *The Hindu* (Madras), April 8, 1952, p. 6.

Communist:

V. Chakkarai Chettiar, president AITUC, and head of the peace movement before its reorganization.

S. A. Dange, general secretary AITUC; member CPI Politbureau.

Jyoti Basu, member general council, AITUC; member CPI Politbureau.

Baburao Jagtap, president Mill Mazdoor Union (Red Flag), Bombay.

K. Anandan Nambiar, general secretary South Indian Railway Labor Union; Communist member of parliament.

S. S. Yusuf, vice-president AITUC; member CPI Central Committee.

V. Mukerji, possibly Biswanath (sometimes Viswanath) Mukherji, a prominent Communist of Nagpur.

T. V. Thomas, independent member of the Legislative Assembly, Travancore-Cochin.

Forward Bloc and United Trade Union Congress:

Satyapriya Bannerjee, general secretary All-India Forward Bloc (Marxist); vice-president AITUC; member of Rajya Sabha.

Sheelbhaddra Yajee, vice-chairman All-Indian Forward Bloc (Marxist).

K. T. Shah, president UTUC; Communist-sponsored candidates for president of the Republic of India. (Died, March, 1953).

Shiban Lal Saxena, member UTUC; one of the founders of the Kisan Mazdoor Praja Party in 1951.

Other:

M. A. Sayeed, general secretary United Seamen's Union, Calcutta.

Raghbir Singh, president All-India Central Public Works Department Workers' Union.

It is interesting to note that this list includes not only three key members of the Central Committee of the CPI, but also several important non-Communists noted for their willingness to coöperate with the Communists in some fields.

At least one member, Dange, was denied a passport by the government of India, and the seventeen-member delegation that finally reached Peking included only seven of those originally invited: Yusuf, Jagtap, Nambiar, Saxena, Shah, Sayeed, and Raghbir Singh.[50]

In 1955 the All-China Federation of Labor again invited a group of Indian trade unionists for the May Day festivities. The delegation consisted of thirty-two members and included many Praja Socialists and other non-Communists, although the majority were Communists or Party sympathizers.[51] On May 17, nine members of the delegation returned to Bombay, having left China two weeks early in protest against a move to organize an Asian-African Trade Union Conference "calculated to rope in all the delegates into the Communist fold." [52] The proposal for the Conference had apparently originated with a Japanese delegation, and according to Bikash Mazumdar, one of the

[50] *Survey of China Mainland Press*, No. 327, 1952, pp. 8, 9, 10.

[51] For the names see: *Trade Union Record*, XII (May 5, 1955), p. 38.

[52] *The Hindu* (Madras), May 20, 1955, p. 5.

nine who returned early, its ultimate purpose was to "initiate an Asian secretariat of the Cominform." [53] (See p. 405, for list of delegates.)

When the rest of the delegates returned to India they issued a statement acknowledging that the Japanese delegates had proposed "an informal gathering of all Asian and African countries' Trade Union representatives to discuss and exchange views on points of common interest with which the working class as a whole is concerned." [54] But, according to the statement, a proposal by the Indonesian delegates to set up a preparatory committee was dropped. All but two of the group, B. K. Mukherji and Ram Chakravarty, signed the statement.

Without more information one cannot determine whether the idea for an Asian trade-union conference really originated with the Japanese or with the international Communist leadership, perhaps through Louis Saillant, general secretary of the WFTU, who was also in Peking for May Day. Neither is it possible to understand why so many Praja Socialists were included in the delegation. It is a fact, however, that their presence proved to be a considerable embarrassment to the Communists and made it possible for the outside world to learn more than usual concerning international Communist activities in the trade-union sphere.

It is significant that in 1955 a number of AITUC leaders attended May Day celebrations in Communist countries. Six went to the USSR, two to Romania, and two to Czechoslovakia. [55] These visits of selected Indian trade unionists to China and to other Communist countries suggest that both Moscow and Peking desire to create some sort of Asian trade-union organization. Beyond this, nothing can be said at the moment. There is no evidence of Sino-Soviet competition for dominance of such a project, nor is there any indication that Peking exerts any control over the AITUC.

Overseas Communists have also maintained contact with the Indian trade-union movement by sending fraternal delegates to annual sessions of the AITUC. The 1957 session was attended by Guiseppe Casadei, secretary of the World Federation of Trade Unions; Ivan Gureev, secretary of the All Union Central Council of Trade Unions of the USSR; Liu Chang Shen, vice-president of the All-China Federation of Trade Unions; and Robert Henrio of the French CGT. [56]

---

[53] *Loc. cit.*
[54] *Trade Union Record*, XII (June 5, 1955), p. 55.
[55] *Ibid.* (May 5, 1955), p. 38.
[56] *New Age* (weekly), V (Jan. 5, 1958), p. 15.

All-India Kisan Sabha

The Comintern early recognized the political importance of the Indian peasantry and in 1926 set up a special section of the Krestintern (the Comintern's peasant international) to carry on work among Indian peasants. The Krestintern intended to work principally through the British Communists, and wrote to Arthur MacManus of the CPGB requesting the names of prominent agrarian leaders in India who could be contacted for political purposes. "Our first task," said the letter, "will be to get into touch with all the existing peasant organizations of India, even if the latter, by their programs, be at variance with our views as to the general aims and methods of work among the peasants." [57] But despite this early interest, the Communists have been much less successful in organizing the 85 per cent of the Indian people who earn their livelihood from agriculture than they have been in forming "transmission belts" to the relatively small industrial proletariat. The Communist peasant movement at this writing remains weak and, except in some areas, ineffective.

There is no satisfactory history of the Indian peasant movement, and the few available accounts are highly partisan and poorly documented.[58] Credit for starting the organized peasant movement is claimed by N. G. Ranga, a member of a wealthy landholding family of Guntur District, Andhra. Educated at Oxford, Ranga returned to India "full of admiration for the Russian experiments" and as early as 1923 began to organize a series of peasant conferences, mostly in Andhra.[59] An all-India peasant movement did not take shape until April, 1936, when the first All-India Kisan Congress was held in Lucknow under the presidency of Swami Sahajananda Saraswathi, a peasant leader from Bihar. A second congress was held in Faizpur in December, 1936, and the following national officers were elected: President: N. G. Ranga; general secretary: Swami Sahajananda Saraswathi; joint secretaries: Indulal Yajnik, B. P. L. Bedi, Bankim Mukherjee.

From the moment of its formation at this Congress, the All-India Kisan Congress was subjected to pulls and stresses from without and within. The non-Communist nationalists, like Ranga and Saraswathi, saw the Kisan Congress as a sort of auxiliary of the nationalist movement. However, their organizational work among the peasants was

---

[57] *Communist Papers,* Parliamentary Publications, 1926, Vol. XXIII (Accounts and Papers, vol. 8) Command 2682 (London: HMSO, 1926), p. 104.

[58] Some useful data is contained in N. G. Ranga and Swami Sahajananda Saraswathi, *History of Kisan Movement* (Madras: Kisan Press, n.d. [1939]), 143 pp.

[59] N. G. Ranga, *Revolutionary Peasants* (New Delhi: Amrit Book Co., 1949), p. 60.

not fully appreciated by some leaders of the Indian National Congress, especially Sardar Vallabhbhai Patel, who felt that the peasants should be organized within the Congress, not separately, and who preferred postponing certain demands for economic reform until independence had been won.[60] As a consequence, Ranga's relations with the Congress hierarchy were not always cordial.

Within the kisan movement four elements fought for control: the Communists, the Congress Socialists, and two regionally-oriented groups led by N. G. Ranga and Swami Sahajananda Saraswathi, respectively. In 1936 the Communists coöperated with Ranga to defeat the Congress Socialists.[61] Then in 1941, during the transition from "Imperialist War" to "People's War," they won over Swami Saraswathi, but lost Ranga in the process. As they gained more power in the All-India Kisan Sabha (this name had been adopted in 1938), the Communists increasingly tended to regard the organization as a subsidiary of the CPI. This irritated both Indulal Yajnik and Swami Saraswathi. Yajik resigned in July, 1943, and in a statement to the press said that because the Sabha was dominated and controlled by the Communists, there was no place in it for persons like himself.[62] Saraswathi was disturbed for the same reason, but remained in the organization for a year or so. By 1945 he too had left the AIKS, and the CPI had branded him as a renegade.[63]

At the end of the war the Communists found themselves virtually alone in the AIKS. Rival peasant organizations were being promoted by the Congress, the Socialists, and others, and although the Communists had had some success in organizing local peasant demonstrations—the Tebhaga movement in Bengal, for example—their hold in the countryside had been considerably weakened. The AIKS claim to a membership of 800,000 during this period seems highly inflated.[64]

Before the Communist peasant leaders had time to erase the odium arising from their opposition to the nationalist movement during the war, the CPI embarked on the militant leftist strategy of the Ranadive period. The resulting police repression practically eliminated the AIKS as a national organization. "Almost the entire membership of the Central Kisan Council was either in jail or underground," E. M. S. Namboodiripad recalls, and no annual sessions could be held between

---

[60] See Mitra, ed., *Indian Annual Register, 1936*, II, 286.

[61] Ranga, *Revolutionary Peasants*, p. 69.

[62] *Party Letter*, III (Sept. 13, 1943), p. 3.

[63] *People's War*, IV (Oct. 7, 1945), p. 3.

[64] E. M. S. Namboodiripad, *The Peasant in National Economic Reconstruction* (Delhi: People's Publishing House, 1954), p. 92.

1948 and 1952.[65] From the end of the war to the present writing, the AIKS has steadily declined.

Structure of the AIKS

The constitution of the AIKS is a loosely written, poorly organized, undated document of eight pages.[66] It provides for a hierarchy of three national governing bodies, and three units at the local level: annual session of elected delegates; All-India Kisan Committee; Central Kisan Council; provincial kisan sabhas; district kisan sabhas; primary kisan sabhas.

The constitution provides that any peasant of sixteen years of age or over may enroll as a member in the AIKS by joining one of the primary kisan sabhas and paying the dues fixed by the provincial unit. The relationships between the primary kisan sabhas and the provincial kisan sabhas are determined by the provincial constitutions which may differ from area to area. The provincial constitution also determines the manner in which delegates to the annual session of the AIKS are elected. Delegates are allocated on a provincial basis at the rate of one for every 2,000 primary members, subject to a minimum of five delegates per province. The number of delegates and the corresponding national membership figures as claimed by the AIKS for the last five annual sessions are given in Table VII.

TABLE VII

REPRESENTATION AT ANNUAL SESSIONS, ALL-INDIA KISAN SABHA, 1947–1956

Session	Place	Year	Delegates	Total AIKS Membership
10th	Sikandrarao	1947	700	800,000
11th	Cannanore	1953	600	1,000,000
12th	Moga	1954	258	1,087,247
13th	Dahanu	1955	over 200	1,100,000
14th	Amritsar	1956	142	693,205
15th	Bongaon	1957	about 800	599,574

These figures are useful mainly as evidence of the peculiar ratio of delegates to members, and cannot be regarded as reliably indicating the true strength of the AIKS. The figures for the number of delegates represent those who actually attended the session, and not the number authorized by the constitution. It should be noted, for example, that the greatest number of delegates attended the 10th Session, although the total membership in 1947 was less than that of the three succeeding years.

---

[65] Ibid., p. 93.
[66] Constitution of the All-India Kisan Sabha (New Delhi: AIKS, n.d.), 8 pp.

Table VIII, taken from official reports, shows the representation by province at the 1954 annual session, and the membership figures for 1954 and 1956.[67] At the 1954 session almost half the provinces were represented by less than the minimum of five delegates that the constitution provided. That so few from southern India attended is probably due, in large part, to the fact that this session was held in the extreme northwest corner of the country.

TABLE VIII

MEMBERSHIP AND REPRESENTATION AT 1954 AND 1956 ANNUAL SESSIONS, AIKS

Province	1954 Membership	1954 Delegates attending	1956 Membership
Andhra	110,074	7	20,000
Assam	15,768	8	7,788
Bihar	56,640	20	54,912
Gujerat	8,064	2	
Himachal Pradesh	1,572	3	
Karnatak	4,032	2	960
Madhya Bharat	19,152	9	7,680
Maharashtra	86,016	20	35,000
Malabar	38,400	3	116,544
Manipur	3,996	3	
Marathwada	15,000	4	
Orissa	9,234	5	6,384
Pepsu	40,704	21 ⎫	169,914
Punjab	114,336	57 ⎭	
Rajasthan	70,400	15	
Tamilnad	81,732	1	91,800
Telengana	114,000	11	
Travancore-Cochin	20,160	2	16,320
Tripura	15,760	3	3,456
Uttar Pradesh	69,888	19	19,200
Vidarbha	6,000	5	
Vindhya Pradesh	960	1	
West Bengal	185,359	37	143,247
TOTAL	1,087,247	258	693,205

NOTE: Where no figure is stated, the data are not available.

The annual session is supposed to be the primary policy-making body of the AIKS, but in practice it has generally served as a rubber stamp. After the Communists gained control, they severely limited debate and thus, except on a few issues, the annual session has merely endorsed official CPI policy.

The second largest body in the organization is the All-India Kisan

[67] *Twelfth Session of the All-India Kisan Sabha, Proceedings & Resolutions* (New Delhi: AIKS, 1954), p. 59; and *Fourteenth Annual Session of the All-India Kisan Sabha, Report* (New Delhi: AIKS, [1956?]), p. 17.

Committee, which is supposed to meet twice a year and is "the highest authority exercising all powers when the Sabha is not in session" (Article X, 1). Each province is represented on this Committee according to its strength, members being elected at the annual session from among the delegates on the basis of one member for every five delegates (Article VII, 2*a*). The Committee in turn determines the size of the Central Kisan Council and elects its members. The Council is, in effect, the executive board of the AIKS and is the primary arena for decision-making. In 1954 its number was fixed at 42, but this was reduced to 25 in 1956.[68]

Leadership

Table IX, shows the leaders of the AIKS as elected at the annual sessions from 1953 to 1957. The data for earlier sessions are incomplete. As in the AITUC, the office of president has been largely honorary, and, in recent years at least, its holders do not appear to have used it as a chair from which to influence policy. Indulal Yajnik confessed at Moga in 1954 that he had not had time to fulfill his duties as president, and asked to be relieved, but at the insistence of Sohan Singh Josh and P. Sundarayya (both members of the CPI Central Committee) he agreed to serve another term.[69] His successor, Nana Patil, who joined the CPI in 1952, had been the leader of a small group which broke away from the Peasants and Workers Party of Maharashtra, and he has been active in the struggle for a unilingual Maharashtrian state. This preoccupation with regional affairs in Maharashtra appears to have restricted his activities in the AIKS. A. K. Gopalan, who became president in 1956, has similarly been heavily occupied with other affairs. In addition to his work as a member of parliament and as a member of the Central Committee of the CPI, he has also taken an active part in the agitation for the creation of linguistic states.

The most important office has been that of general secretary, occupied since 1953 by N. Prasada Rao who is a member of the CPI Central Committee and of the dominant faction in the Andhra section of the Party. He is also a member of the Rajya Sabha. It is fitting that an Andhran holds this post, for the Andhra Communists are the chief advocates of an agrarian-based revolution, and constitute one of the largest provincial group in the CPI. After he became general secre-

---

[68] Harkishan Singh Surjeet, "Amritsar Session of the Kisan Sabha" *New Age* (monthly) V (Nov. 1956), p. 7.

[69] E. M. S. Namboodiripad, *Peasants Meet at Moga* (New Delhi: People's Publishing House, 1954), p. 16.

TABLE IX

LEADERSHIP OF THE ALL-INDIA KISAN SABHA

	11th, Cannanore, April 22–27, 1953	12th, Moga, Sept. 15–19, 1954	13th, Dahanu, May 17–20, 1955	14th, Amritsar, Sept. 28–Oct. 2, 1956	15th, Bongaon, Oct. 27–Nov. 3, 1957
President	Indulal Yajnik	Indulal Yajnik	Nana Patil	A. K. Gopalan	A. K. Gopalan
General secretary	N. Prasada Rao	N. Prasada Rao	N. Prasada Rao	N. Prasada Rao	N. Prasada Rao
Vice-presidents	Karyanand Sharma Nana Patil	Nana Patil C. Rajeshwar Rao Z. A. Ahmed	Indulal Yajnik Bankim Mukherjee Tulsidas Jadhav	Nana Patil Bankim Mukherjee	Shiban Lal Saxena Bankim Mukherjee
Joint secretaries	Jagjit Singh Lyallpuri Z. A. Ahmed S. G. Sardesai K. A. Keraleeyan	Jagjit Singh Lyallpuri B. Srinivasa Rao Yogendra Sharma Biswanath Mukherjee	Jagjit Singh Lyallpuri B. Srinivasa Rao Biswanath Mukherjee Sankar Dayal Tiwari	Jagjit Singh Lyallpuri B. Srinivasa Rao	Jagjit Singh Lyallpuri Abdulla Masool
Treasurer	Baba Gurumukh Singh	Baba Gurumukh Singh	Baba Gurumukh Singh	Baba Gurumukh Singh	A. V. Kunhambu

tary, Rao was obliged to run the AIKS almost single handed. In 1954
he claimed that he was the only official functioning from the central
office in New Delhi.[70]

The office of treasurer was held from 1953 to 1957 by Baba Guru-
mukh Singh, a Punjabi revolutionary who worked with the Ghadr
Party in California in the 1920's, traveled to the Middle East and Russia in the cause of Indian independence, and spent about seventeen
years in British and Afghan jails. His age (born about 1883) and his
long revolutionary career gave him prestige that was of great value
in soliciting contributions for the AIKS. When the AIKS was in
financial straits in 1953 he went to Jamshedpur, where the Tata Iron
and Steel Works are located, and was able to collect Rs. 2,500 for the
AIKS.[71]

Finances

The constitution of the AIKS provides that every provincial kisan
sabha shall pay an affiliation fee to the national organization at the
rate of one pie (1/192 of a rupee) per member, plus "such other quota
of financial contribution as fixed for it by the CKC or AIKC" (Article
XII, 2). In addition, each delegate to the annual session is required
to pay eight annas (half a rupee) as a delegate fee (Article VIII, 1b).
The cost of the annual session is borne by the local Reception Committee, and 25 per cent of the surplus of any money collected for this
purpose must be turned over to the AIKS office. The balance remains
with the provincial unit.

The biggest source of income of the AIKS has been its membership
fees which in 1954 (the most recent figures available) amounted to only
Rs. 4,028. Donations have provided the second most important
source.[72] But income has been woefully inadequate, and in recent years
the Sabha has found itself in one financial crisis after another. In 1954
the general secretary reported that with the exception of PEPSU, no
provincial unit had sent in any money at all, and PEPSU had sent
only a part of its quota. The total expenditure of the AIKS that year
amounted to Rs. 14,533, of which Rs. 4,950 had to be raised by loans.[73]
The situation has steadily deteriorated. The AIKS journal, the *Kisan
Bulletin,* had to be discontinued in 1954 for lack of funds,[74] and between the Dahanu (1955) and Amritsar (1956) sessions, the Central

[70] *General Secretary's Report to the 12th Session of the All-India Kisan Sabha*
(New Delhi: AIKS, 1954), p. 42.
[71] *Ibid.,* pp. 43–44.
[72] *Twelfth Session of the All-India Kisan Sabha* . . . , p. 58.
[73] *General Secretary's Report* . . . , pp. 43–44.
[74] *Ibid.,* p. 44.

Kisan Council "received no reports nor funds from the State units." [75]
Eight units had to be disaffiliated for nonpayment of dues.[76]

The poor financial condition of the AIKS is only one indication of
the organization's general decline. Meetings of the CKC have been
poorly attended. Only three were held between the 1953 and 1954 sessions, and one of those had to be postponed due to the lack of a
quorum (one-third of the members). Reporting on the period between
the 1955 and 1956 sessions, Harkishan Singh Surjeet wrote: "It was a
lamentable fact that meetings of the CKC could not be fruitful, twice
due to the simple fact of lack of quorum." [77] It was undoubtedly for
this reason that the Amritsar session decided to reduce the membership in the CKC from 43 to 25, thus reducing the quorum to nine.

In recent years attendance at the annual sessions has been corre-
spondingly poor. Reporting on the Amritsar session, *New Age* (weekly)
stated:

> Out of a total of 142 delegates, only 59 were from provinces other than Punjab.
> There were no delegates from Assam, Hyderabad, Himachal Pradesh, Gujarat,
> Maharashtra, Marathwada, Manipur, Madhya Pradesh, Orissa and Vindhya Pradesh.
> Only three delegates came from Andhra, two from UP, two from Telengana and
> four from Tamilnad.[78]

Against this background, Harikishan Singh Surjeet could hardly be
called an alarmist when he wrote in late 1956 that the "weak and un-
satisfactory state" of the AIKS was causing "justified anxiety." [79]

International Connections

The question of affiliation with international organizations, so
long a bogey in the trade-union movement, was raised as recently as
1954 in the AIKS, and the manner in which it was answered provides
some insight into the workings of the organization. In October, 1953,
Indulal Yajnik, then president of the AIKS, was in Vienna attending
the meeting of the World Federation of Trade Unions. At this meeting he announced the affiliation of the AIKS to the Trade Union International of Agricultural and Forestry Workers, a section of the
WFTU. At the 1954 annual session of the AIKS, Yajnik appeared before the All-India Kisan Committee and requested that body to ratify
his action. He was supported by P. Sundarayya, but someone suggested
that this was a matter for the full delegates session, then already ad-

---

[75] Surjeet, "Amritsar Session . . . ," p. 6.
[76] *New Age* (weekly), IV (Oct. 7, 1956), p. 2.
[77] Surjeet, "Amritsar Session . . . ," p. 6.
[78] *New Age* (weekly), IV (Oct. 7, 1956), p. 2.
[79] Surjeet, "Amritsar Session . . . ," p. 5.

journed, and the discussion was accordingly postponed.[80] However, CPI press accounts of the succeeding Dahanu and Amritsar sessions make no mention of this question, and the public record of AIKS activities gives no hint that any action has been taken.

In the AIKS, as in the trade unions and front organizations, a common device for maintaining contact with the international Communist movement is the traveling delegation. In August, 1955, nine leaders of the AIKS toured Hungary and Czechoslovakia for seven weeks as the guests of agricultural workers unions in those countries. They were: [81]

Dasrath Deb, Communist M.P. from Tripura; member Central Kisan Council; member Central Committee, CPI.

K. P. R. Gopalan, veteran Kerala Communist leader and peasant organizer.

K. R. Patil, member Madhya Pradesh Legislative Assembly and a leader of the Peasants and Workers Party.

Nana Patil, president, AIKS; Maharashtrian peasant organizer.

B. Srinivasa Rao, joint secretary, AIKS; Tamilnad peasant organizer; manager of CPI monthly in 1938–39; defeated candidate for Central Committee, CPI, 1953.

Y. V. Krishna Rao, general secretary, Andhra Provincial Ryot's Association; member Andhra Provincial Committee Secretariat, CPI.

Mohamed Abdulla Rasul, president, West Bengal Kisan Sabha.

Yogendra Sharma, general secretary, Bihar State Kisan Sabha; member Central Committee, CPI.

Harikishan Singh Surjeet, member Punjab Legislative Assembly; member Central Kisan Council; member Politbureau, CPI.

It is obvious that this delegation was more representative of the CPI than of the Indian peasantry in general. At least six of the delegates were veteran Communists with long records of Party activity. One was a member of the Politbureau and three others were members of the Central Committee. It seems highly unlikely that such a group would confine its discussions in Moscow exclusively to problems of the peasant movement.

Weaknesses

The growing weakness of the AIKS is clearly shown in the figures on membership in Table VIII. In only two areas, Malabar and Tamilnad, did the Sabha increase its membership between 1954 and 1956. In most others there was a startling decline, and some important provinces did not even report to the central organization.

It is not within the scope of this study to inquire into the reasons for the decline of the AIKS during recent years, and it should be pointed out that the weakening of the AIKS does not necessarily mean

---

[80] *Twelfth Session of the All-India Kisan Sabha . . .* , p. 14.
[81] *Trade Union Record*, XII (Aug. 20, 1955), p. 104.

a diminution of Communist influence in rural India. There are factors which can weaken a national organization—linguistic regionalism, for example—which may not adversely affect the position of the Communist groups in smaller areas. That a provincial unit fails to contribute funds to the central headquarters, or even to report, does not necessarily indicate that it is defunct. And there may be a grain of truth in the continual protestations of its leaders that despite the national deterioration in AIKS functioning, the CPI's influence among the peasants is growing.

On the other hand, it is possible to point to some factors which have seriously hurt both the Party and the AIKS in the countryside. When the Communists parted company with the Socialists they lost the large rural followings of many Socialist leaders. This was especially true in Bihar. In February, 1938, the AIKS claimed a total membership of 546,800. Of these, 250,000—almost half—were from Bihar.[82] (No other province had a third that many members.) In 1954 the membership in Bihar was given as 56,640, trailing far behind Andhra, Telengana, West Bengal, Punjab, Maharashtra, and many others.[83]

Rural Bihar continues to be a stronghold of Socialist influence, and the Praja Socialist Party has worked hard there to organize the peasants. This state has also been one of the main targets of Vinoba Bhave's "Bhoodan Yagna" movement, and the fact that the veteran leader of the Praja Socialists, Jayaprakash Narayan, has actively participated in the Bhoodan movement has done much to undermine Communist influence among the rural population.[84] Narayan and Bhave have concentrated on appealing to the conscience of landholders to give land to those who have none, but other Praja Socialist leaders, while paying respects to *Bhoodan*, have organized more militant movements in support of various peasant demands. Wherever the Socialists have provided an organized vehicle for peasant discontent, the Communists have had difficulty competing.

Another factor limiting Communist success among the rural elements has been the Party's quandary with regard to the landless agricultural workers. They constitute, in some areas, as much as 37 per cent of the total agricultural population,[85] and are employed, frequently at starva-

[82] P. C. Joshi, "Comilla Kisan Congress," *National Front*, I (June 5, 1938), p. 1.
[83] *Twelfth Session of the All-India Kisan Sabha* . . . , p. 59.
[84] For a Communist account of the Party's competition with the Praja Socialist Party in Bihar, see: Indradeep Sinha, "Bihar Peasants Struggle Against the Rise in Water Rates," *New Age* (monthly), III (May, 1954), pp. 32–37.
[85] See Thomas Shea, "Agrarian Unrest and Reform in South India," *Far Eastern Survey*, XXIII (June, 1954), p. 83.

tion wages, by the peasants and landlords. But the effective organizing
of these landless laborers to obtain higher wages would hurt the
peasant far more than it would the wealthy landlords. A Communist
party which brought this about could hardly expect the support of
the small landholder, let alone that of the more prosperous peasants
and landlords upon whom the Party is so dependent in areas such as
Andhra.[86] The question of caste further complicates matters. Most
landless laborers are "untouchables" or of low castes, and therefore
considered inferior and ritually impure by the peasantry. Thus the
interests of the landless workers do not coincide with those of the peasantry, and on the all-important question of wages are actually opposed.

On the other hand, the CPI recognizes them to be "the most militant
section of the agricultural population." [87] The problem then is to
capitalize on their militancy without alienating the important land-
holding element. To date, the Party has been unable to organize this
vast army of indigent laborers, or even to agree on a *modus operandi,*
though it has tried various means.

In April, 1954, a Central Committee resolution declared that the
Party and the kisan movement "must vigorously take up and champion
the immediate demands of the agricultural laborers." [88] But this was
to be done outside the AIKS:

> Agricultural laborers should be organized separately in independent class organ-
> izations apart from the peasant organizations, because, firstly, they have their own
> separate demands of wages, hours of work, holidays, etc. Secondly, most of these
> agricultural laborers are from socially backward or even so-called "untouchable"
> (Harijan) castes and it will be more difficult to draw them and activize them in
> Kisan Sabhas directly along with the other caste peasants or even if we succeed in
> drawing them in, it may lead to the other peasants not joining the Kisan Sabha in
> large numbers. Thirdly, agricultural laborers will become the leading force if they
> are organized separately and at the same time brought into the Kisan Sabha.[89]

While these seems to be general agreement among the Communists
that the agricultural laborers should be organized in separate unions,
there is considerable controversy over whether these unions, once organized, should be affiliated to the AIKS. The following is a revealing account of the debate on this question at the 1954 Annual Session:

> Com. [Mohamed] Abdulla Rasul of Bengal moves an amendment saying that efforts
> should be made to affiliate them [the agricultural-laborer unions] to the Kisan Sabha

---

[86] See G. S. Bhargava, *A Study of the Communist Movement in Andhra* (Delhi:
Siddhartha Publications, 1955), and Selig S. Harrison, "Caste and the Andhra
Communists," *American Political Science Review,* L (June, 1956), pp. 378–404.

[87] *Our Tasks Among the Peasant Masses* (Delhi: CPI, 1954), p. 14.

[88] *Loc. cit.*

[89] *Our Tasks* . . . , p. 16.

in all those cases where such efforts at affiliation would not harm the cause of organizing the agricultural laborers. Com. Sundarayya [P. Sundarayya, member of the Central Committee, CPI, from Andhra] opposes it saying that making such efforts at the present stage will do more harm than good; he is of the opinion that such efforts at affiliation should be made only at a stage of the development of the movement when agricultural laborers themselves feel its necessity and ask for affiliation. Com. Rasul's amendment is pressed to vote and is defeated by 115 votes against 50. Twenty remained neutral.[90]

There have been no indications in recent years that the Communists have found a way to take advantage of the militancy of agricultural laborers without losing support among the peasants. Thus the matter stands.

All-India Students' Federation

After the first world war students began to be an important factor in Indian politics, and Gandhi's civil-disobedience campaigns drew thousands away from their studies to participate in the struggle for independence. During the 1920's student organizations sprang up at various colleges, but only in the next decade was an attempt made to form an all-India organization. In August, 1936, the first All-India Student Conference was held in Lucknow on the initiative of the United Provinces Student Federation. Jawaharlal Nehru inaugurated the conference, and Mohammed Ali Jinnah, leader of the Muslim League, presided.[91] Attending the conference were 986 delegates from 210 local and eleven provincial student organizations, and from this meeting the All-India Students' Federation (AISF) later emerged.[92] There was some difference of opinion among the delegates to the Lucknow conference as to whether the proposed organization should take part in politics. That the initiators of the conference viewed the proposed organization as political seems clear from the welcoming address of Prem Bhargava, chairman of the Reception Committee, who said:

While any deep political coloring need not be an inevitable characteristic of our movement, I for one cannot understand how in the rapidly changing conditions of our country we can keep altogether away from it unless, of course, the sole purpose of our educational institutions is merely to produce "Chorus boys" of British Imperialism.[93]

---

[90] Namboodiripad, *Peasants Meet at Moga*, p. 34.

[91] Prabodh Chandra, *Student Movement in India* (Lahore: AISF, 1938), pp. 53–54. The author should not be confused with Prabodh Chandra, the pseudonym used by Ajoy Ghosh. See Bibliography.

[92] *Ibid.*, p. 53.

[93] Mitra, ed., *Indian Annual Register, 1936*, II, 503.

A compromise was finally reached between those who wanted militant participation in politics and those who did not. A statement was adopted which declared that one of the aims and objects of the organizations was "to prepare the students for citizenship, in order to take their due share in the struggle for complete national freedom, by arousing their political, social, and economic consciousness." [94]

Three months after the meeting in Lucknow, a second conference was held in Lahore under the presidency of the Bengali nationalist, Sarat Chandra Bose. Bose's presidential address dealt exclusively with politics and called attention to "the coming proletarian revolution." "It is your duty," he told the assembled students, "to see that the activities of the intellectuals are linked up with those of the proletarian workers." [95] The Lahore meeting adopted a constitution and the All-India Students' Federation was formally launched.

Although there is no evidence in the available CPI literature that the Communists had selected the student movement as an important target for penetration, there are indications that by 1938 a substantial percentage of the federation was pro-Soviet if not pro-Communist. At the third AISF conference in Madras, in January, 1938, a markedly pro-Soviet resolution was presented:

> This conference is of emphatic opinion that Soviet Russia is the one country in the whole world which is consistently following the policy of Peace and Progress, whilst its very existence serves as a beacon-light to the oppressed of all nationalities in general and the International Student movement in particular. It calls upon all students in the different countries of the world to emphatically condemn any aggression by fascist or capitalist countries on the Soviet Union and help it morally and materially in the event of any attack. This conference congratulates the Union of Soviet Socialist Republics on its successful completion of twenty years of Socialist construction in Russia and views with great satisfaction the inauguration of the new Constitution, the most democratic in the world. [96]

The resolution produced a vigorous debate and considerable confusion. At one point the mover attempted to withdraw it but was prevented by a vote of the house. Upon the demand for a formal poll, it was discovered that only two of the eleven provincial delegations had paid the delegate fees. Thereupon Minoo R. Masani, the president, adjourned the meeting until the following day. When it was resumed he immediately declared the conference dissolved; a rump session formed, elected a new president, and declared a vote of no confidence in Masani. The differences were later patched up and the

[94] Chandra, *Student Movement* . . . , pp. 54–55.
[95] Mitra, ed., *Indian Annual Register, 1936*, II, 508.
[96] *Ibid., 1938*, I, 413–414.

precarious unity which had been established between the Communists and the Congress Socialists during the united-front period continued for another two years in the student movement.

The AISF continued to draw the attention of prominent personalities in the nationalist movement, and when the AISF held its fourth conference in Calcutta, January 1–2, 1939, Sarat Chandra Bose opened the conference and Jawaharlal Nehru once again addressed it. In the presidential chair was K. M. Ashraf who later became a well-known leader of the CPI, though he may not actually have been a CPI member at the time of the Calcutta meeting. At the fifth conference held in New Delhi, January 1, 1950, Subhas Chandra Bose presided. During this period, Communist strength in the organization grew.

At the end of 1940 the Communists decided to capitalize on Britain's preoccupation with the war and seize the opportunity to overthrow the Raj in India. When the AISF held its sixth session in Nagpur, December 25, 1940, the Communists carried their new militancy into the student movement over the issue of Gandhi's "individual satyagraha" campaign, launched in October, 1940, to oppose the British war effort. Because it was not militant enough, the Communist students opposed the campaign, while most of the non-Communists supported it. Unable to reach agreement, the organization split and two separate sessions were held. K. M. Ashraf and Hiren Mukerjee led the Communist section, with Ashraf describing the *satyagraha* as "a very poor protest against the imposition of belligerency on India." M. L. Shah and Arabind Bose led the non-Communist group. Efforts by the vice-chancellor of Nagpur University to mediate between the opposing factions failed, and since then the national student movement has been seriously split.[97]

The non-Communists later organized a new national federation, the All-India Students' Congress. This organization functioned until 1948 but was then disbanded because political rivalries had rendered it ineffective. It was succeeded by the National Union of Students (NUS) which was founded in September, 1950, with the blessings of such notables as the prime minister and Jayaprakash Narayan. It is, at this writing, the largest and most representative national student organization in India. The Communists managed to retain the name of the original All-India Students' Federation, but since the formation of the NUS their influence in the organized student movement has steadily declined.

---

[97] *Ibid., 1940*, II, 414.

Organization

The AISF claimed a membership of 60,598 in 1946 and 74,000 in 1947.[98] At the 13th Annual Session in Hyderabad in January, 1953, a figure of 100,000 was given, but the *New Age* report of the 14th Annual Session (Lucknow, January 4–9, 1955) conspicuously omits figures on membership.[99]

Official membership figures, even if they were reliable, could not be regarded as valid indicators of the strength of the AISF or of its utility as an instrument of CPI policy. Indeed, the inadequate data concerning the organization and functioning of the AISF in recent years permits very little generalization on this important subject. A few observations can be made, however.

The leaders of the AISF appear to be dedicated, well-indoctrinated, and relatively competent. Many of them joined the CPI while students. Others joined the Party after ceasing to be active in the student movement. Indeed, many of the Party's present leaders received their early organizational training as student leaders (Jyoti Basu, Phani Bora, Basava Punniah, Y. D. Sharma, and others). In 1955 two of the top leaders of the AISF, Sukhendu Majumdar (the general secretary) and Krishna Anand (a joint secretary), were widely known to be full-time CPI workers, and according to a leader in the NUS, had ceased to be students several years earlier.[100] It is evident then that the AISF is both a recruiting and a training organization for the CPI.

The policies of the AISF have closely paralleled those of the other Communist-dominated mass organizations. On international questions the AISF has taken a pro-Soviet, anti-American line, and on domestic issues it has attempted to become a militant champion of political reform and of better facilities for students. It has been active in the many student strikes that have taken place in India since independence, some of which have resulted in violence and police-firings. It would be a mistake, however, to place the blame for student unrest on the AISF. The causes are much more complex, and the AISF has, apparently, only tried to capitalize on existing grievances. When a student demonstration against increased bus fares erupted in violence and police-firing in Patna in August, 1955, Prime Minister Nehru journeyed to that city and in an irate speech blamed the disturbances

---

[98] *People's Age*, IV (Feb. 24, 1946), p. 10, and V (Jan. 26, 1947), p. 12.
[99] *New Age* (weekly), II (Jan. 16, 1955), p. 16.
[100] Chandra Bhal Tripathi, *Presidential Address,* First Conference of NUS, Dec., 1955 (Lucknow: C. B. Tripathi, [1956?]), p. 17.

on the Communists. Commenting on these charges in a lengthy press statement, the Praja Socialist leader, Jayaprakash Narayan said:

> The Prime Minister indulged in a lot of Communist baiting. He was no doubt told that the whole trouble was the making of Communists. . . . As everyone knows, I am not an admirer of the Communists, but I have no hesitation in saying that their role throughout the recent disturbance has been restrained. They have never encouraged or countenanced violence of any sort. The Communists have many failings, but they are an organized, disciplined lot. They are following a particular political policy at the present in which there is no room for violence. And on this occasion in Bihar they have followed that policy in a disciplined manner.[101]

There can be little doubt, however, that the AISF tries to make the most of student unrest by attempting to infiltrate student strike committees whenever they are formed and by giving the widest publicity to disturbances, when they occur. In dealing with the Bihar episode, for example, B. Narsing Rao, then president of the AISF, published an article in *New Age* (weekly) that was accompanied by gory photographs of mutilated corpses, and the CPI People's Publishing House came out with a thirty-eight-page pamphlet on the struggle.[102] Similar publicity was given to the Lucknow students' strike in October, 1953, in which AISF leaders took an active part.[103]

International Affiliations

Like the other Communist-dominated mass organizations, the AISF has maintained contact with the appropriate international Communist groups. The AISF has affiliated with the International Union of Students (IUS), the international Communist student organization. From time to time AISF leaders have traveled abroad to IUS conferences and to other international Communist gatherings, but in view of the declining influence of both the AISF and the IUS, these contacts do not appear to have produced any significant results.[104]

The most important international activity in which the AISF participated was the so-called Little Bandung Conference of Asian and

---

[101] Reproduced as an appendix to Girija Kumar Sinha, *Bihar Diary* (New Delhi: People's Publishing House, n.d., [1955]), p. 36.

[102] *New Age* (weekly), II (Sept. 4, 1955), p. 3; and Sinha, *Bihar Diary*.

[103] *New Age* (weekly), I (Nov. 8, 1953), p. 16, and Nov. 15, 1953, pp. 8–9. For a non-Communist account of the AISF role in the Lucknow strike see Chandra Bhal Tripathi, *Presidential Address*, pp. 15–16.

[104] For a useful survey of the international student movement since World War II see "Students in World Politics," *World Today*, VII, No. 8 (Aug. 1951), pp. 346–356, and "The International Student Conference," *World Today*, XII (Sept., 1956), pp. 371–378. For details on the IUS see Evron M. Kirkpatrick, *Target: The World* (New York: Macmillan, 1956), pp. 142–144.

African students held in Bandung, Indonesia, May 30–June 7, 1956. The idea for a conference of Asian and African students originated with the Perserikatan Perhimpunan Mahasiswa Indonesia (PPMI), the Indonesian national student organization, and first took shape at its annual conference in April, 1953.[105] The IUS took an immediate interest in the proposal, and made a concerted effort to gain control. When the International Preparatory Committee was formed in September, 1955, it consisted of members from the People's Republic of China, Japan, the Philippines, India, Indonesia, Burma, Iran and Lebanon. All were Communists except the Filipino representative.

To control the Indian delegation the AISF took the initiative, in February, 1956, in forming a national preparatory committee. But by this time a number of non-Communist student leaders were interested, and were prepared to challenge the AISF's domination of the Committee. In mid-February the presidents of the university unions at Delhi, Aligarh, Benares, Lucknow, and Allahabad issued a circular requesting the presidents of all other university unions and of the state units of the NUS to attend a meeting in Lucknow for the purpose of setting up a more representative preparatory committee. The meeting was held in March, and a new twenty-two-member committee was created. It included two known Communists, the presidents of the Andhra and Vishwabharati university unions, but was far more representative than its AISF-dominated predecessor.[106] The Indian delegation which went to Bandung consisted of eight non-Communists led by Pran Sabharwal, president of the Delhi University Union, and four Communists or pro-Communists led by Sukhendu Majumdar, general secretary of the AISF.

It is evident that the Communists had two major aims at the Little Bandung Conference. They wanted to push the Conference into taking a strongly anti-Western stand, and they wanted to establish some sort of Asian-African student federation under IUS hegemony. They failed in both these aims. Due to the activity of the non-Communist delegates, especially of Pran Sabharwal and the Filipino delegate, Guillermo De Vega, the final resolutions condemned colonialism "in all its manifestations," and called for abolition of nuclear-weapons

---

[105] This account of the Little Bandung conference is based on various foreign and American newspaper sources together with the following: Chandra Bhal Tripathi, "The Asian-African Students' Conference," *Janata*, XI (May 20, 1956), pp. 11–13; Willard A. Hanna, "The Little Bandung Conference," American Universities Field Staff Report, July 5, 1956; Harry Lunn, *Asian-African Students' Conference* (n.p., n.d.) mimeographed. Lunn, a former American student leader, was a free-lance correspondent who attended the meetings.

[106] Tripathi, "The Asian-African Students' . . . ," p. 13.

testing "in all parts of the world"—neither of which excluded the USSR.[107]

Though the Communist delegates, aided by the Egyptians, were skillful and energetic and did their best to capitalize on nationalism and on racial prejudices, their opponents were equally resourceful. The net result was a conference that evinced suspicion of both major world power blocs, and insisted on freedom from foreign domination. In this respect, Little Bandung accurately reflected its more important predecessor.

The AISF learned important lessons at this conference, and it will doubtless support more activities of this sort. There is no question that the CPI is interested in encouraging the AISF to develop contacts with other Asian student organizations. In line with this, the AISF has shown a keen interest in Nepal. In December, 1953, the AISF demanded that the Indian military mission be withdrawn from Nepal, and Nepalese students have attended several AISF conferences as fraternal delegates. These students may provide valuable contacts for the CPI in this delicately balanced and strategic border region in which Communist China has shown such a keen interest.

From the limited evidence available, it seems that the AISF has neither been strong as an organization, nor effective as an instrument of CPI policy. This has probably been largely due to the nature of communism itself and to the obvious linkage between the AISF and the CPI. Indian students are undoubtedly more inquiring and better informed than the general population, and it has been very difficult to induce them to swallow the gyrations of Communist policy or to see the AISF as anything but an appendage of the CPI. For the AISF to become more influential in the Indian student movement, two changes seem to be necessary: it must develop more student and fewer professional leaders, and it must become more independent of Soviet and CPI policy. Neither appears likely at this writing.

Other Mass Organizations

The major mass organizations, then, are those of workers, peasants, and students. There have also been efforts to create youth and children's organizations as, for example, the Bombay Youth Conference held in November, 1952, for "working class youth from mills and factories, young middle-class employees from offices and firms, 'displaced' youth from the 'refugee' camps, teachers and students." [108]

---

[107] The resolutions of the Little Bandung conference appear in consecutive issues of *Student Mirror* beginning with No. 109 (July 15, 1956).

[108] *Crossroads*, IV (Nov. 30, 1952), p. 16.

Young non-Communist Indians have also been attracted to the various Communist-sponsored World Youth congresses. In August, 1956, nine Indians attended the Moscow meeting of the International Preparatory Committee for the World Youth Festival to be held in that city a year later. According to *New Age,* one of these was a deputy minister of the Punjab government and another was a member of the All-India Congress Committee's youth section.[109] But none of these activities has resulted in the creation of a mass organization comparable to those already described.

Mention should be made, however, of the Communists' efforts to establish a mass organization for women. This work has met with greatest success in West Bengal where the Communists control the active Paschim Banga Mahila Atma Raksha Samity (West Bengal Women's Self-Defense Association, MARS). In 1943, discussing MARS and its corresponding Muslim women's organization, *People's War* said: "These organizations which have today created such a mighty upsurge among Calcutta's womanhood have been built up on the initiative of the Communist Party. It is the work of 30 women Communist Party members and 33 women Party sympathizers." [110] On the initiative of this organization the "first convention of toiling women" was held in Calcutta, November 3–6, 1948. Attended by about one hundred delegates, the conference protested the Indian government's ban on the Asian Women's Conference called by the Communist-controlled Women's International Democratic Federation.[111] By April, 1954, MARS claimed a membership of 18,000, the majority of whom were peasants and workers in the jute industry.[112]

In June, 1954, a National Federation of Indian Women (NFIW) was organized at a National Congress of Women held in Calcutta. The founding congress was attended by 830 delegates from eighteen states and about 50 fraternal delegates from such organizations as the YWCA. There were also several foreign fraternal delegates including 23 from Nepal. Because non-Communist participation was desired, the Communists were careful to keep the political content of the meeting at a moderate level. Most of the resolutions dealt with women's problems, but one protested the United Nations' termination, at the "instigation of U.S. diplomats," of nongovernmental-organization status for the Women's International Democratic Federation.[113] The Con-

---

[109] *New Age* (weekly), IV (Oct. 7, 1956), p. 7. 450 Indian delegates attended the Moscow Youth Festival in July, 1957. See *ISCUS* IV (special number 4, 1957), p. 67.
[110] *People's War,* I (April 4, 1943), p. 1.
[111] *People's Age,* VII (Nov. 21, 1948), p. 13.
[112] *New Age* (weekly), I (April 18, 1954), p. 6.
[113] *New Age* (weekly), I (June 13, 1954), p. 13.

gress elected a twenty-nine member Executive Committee and the following officers: Puspamoyee Bose, president; Anasuya Gyan Chand and Hajrah Begum, joint secretaries. Hajrah Begum, an active Communist organizer, is the wife of Z. A. Ahmed, member of the CPI Politbureau.

In addition to Hajrah Begum, a number of other women have been leaders in Communist and Communist-sponsored organizations. Best known is Aruna Asaf Ali, a former Socialist, and from 1954 to 1956 a member of the CPI Central Committee. Also well-known is Renu Chakravarty, a Communist M.P. from West Bengal. Educated at Cambridge, she is the niece of the Congress chief minister of West Bengal, B. C. Roy, a fact which does not appear to cause embarrassment to either of them. Another woman M.P. who has taken an active part in Communist-sponsored movements is Kumari Annie Mascarene from Trivandrum. A long-time Congress worker, Miss Mascarene was elected to the Lok Sabha in 1952 as an independent. She was a member of the Indian Preparatory Committee for the World Congress of Women held in Denmark in June, 1953. Two other Communist Party members deserve mention, although their activities have been confined primarily to Party work rather than to the mass organizations or front groups. They are Perrin Chandra, wife of Central Committee member Romesh Chandra, and Kalpana Dutt, a former Bengali terrorist and now wife of P. C. Joshi.

The second conference of NFIW took place in Vijayawada (Andhra) in June, 1957, with 353 delegates attending from Delhi, Tamilnad, Kerala, Tripura, West Bengal, Bihar, and Andhra. In addition to Monica Felton from Great Britain, there were fraternal delegates from the USSR, Rumania, and Czechoslovakia. Most resolutions dealt with economic and social questions effecting women, but a demand was also made for the cessation of nuclear weapons testing.[114]

Traditionally, Hindu society has relegated women to a socially inferior status. This situation, however, is undergoing rapid change, and India's constitution gives them equal rights, including the right to vote. Women thus constitute an important factor in Indian political life, a situation of which the Communists are well aware. As E. M. S. Namboodiripad has said: "A contemptuous attitude towards the women's movement by the working class . . . in effect means *renunciation of the struggle for proletarian hegemony* in one of the most vital spheres." [115]

---

[114] *New Age* (weekly), IV (June 23, 1957), p. 16.
[115] E. M. S. Namboodiripad, "Women's Movement for Democracy," *New Age* (monthly), V (Feb., 1956), p. 30.

Conclusions

The story of Communist-dominated mass organizations in India in recent years appears to be one of decline. Since these organizations constitute the Party's main link with the masses, one is tempted to conclude that Communist influence with the masses must also have declined. The results of the 1957 elections, however, indicate that such a conclusion would be a mistake.

It must be remembered that during World War II the Communists had almost no competition in the major mass organizations, for the Congress leadership was in jail and the Socialists were underground. Under the organizing genius of P. C. Joshi, the Party was able to build the trade-union, peasant, and student movements with an almost free hand. When competition began to develop around 1947, the task became more difficult. To this was added the disastrous extremist line pursued by B. T. Ranadive, which hurt the mass organizations more, perhaps, than it did other satellites of the CPI. During this period many second-rank leaders were killed as the result of senseless violence and in jail strikes, and many others left the Party in disgust and disillusionment. It would appear that most of the difficulties that beset the mass movement today can be traced to the period between 1948 and 1951 when Ranadive and Rao controlled the CPI.

There has been a growing realization in the CPI that it is extremism or "sectarianism" that has weakened the mass organizations. This has been most evident in the AIKS where too close an adherence to Communist Party policy has meant the loss, from time to time, of important peasant leaders like Yajnik and Saraswathi. It is also evident in the student movement, and to a lesser extent in the trade unions. Reporting on the decisions of the Central Committee in May, 1954, Ajoy Ghosh wrote:

> Mass organizations, the Central Committee stressed, have to be built and run as real non-party united organizations, organizations which the masses consider to be their own and in whose functioning they have live interest. Such is very often not the case today, not merely in relation to organizations which are led by reformists but also in relation to organizations led by Communists. Sectarian methods of running these organizations harm both the Party and the organizations and weaken the movement of the masses.[116]

The conduct of the AISF in preparing for Little Bandung indicates that the Party has not yet learned this lesson.

But though the mass organizations appear to be weak when viewed from a national perspective, they are undoubtedly strong in certain

---

[116] Ajoy Ghosh, "On the Decisions of the Central Committee," *New Age* (weekly), I (May 2, 1954), p. 4.

areas. West Bengal is one state in which the AITUC, the AIKS, the AISF, and the NFIW are all strong; indeed, in no other area do all of these organizations together have such a broad base. This provides the Communists with a vast army which can be mobilized for strikes, demonstrations, and electioneering—an army which they have used with telling effect. In addition, the AIKS and the AISF are strong in Andhra, and the Communists have good peasant organizations in Kerala, Maharashtra, and Punjab.

A proper appraisal of the Communist-dominated mass organizations requires that they be compared with the organizations dominated by the Congress and by the Praja Socialists; such a task requires much more than a listing of membership figures, and is beyond the scope of this study. Only when better analyses of such organizations as the INTUC, the HMS, and the NUS are available and can be correlated with the behavior of the Indian electorate, will it be possible to evaluate the political significance of the Communist-dominated mass organizations.

INDIAN TRADE-UNION DELEGATION TO PEKING MAY-DAY CELEBRATION, 1955

All-India Trade Union Congress: Jyoti Basu, V. D. Deshpande, Mohamed Elias, Gulab Rao Ganacharya, S. G. Lokare, B. N. Mukherjee, K. Ramani (Raman?).

United Trade Union Congress: Waman Bhalerao, Sushil Bhattacharya, Pritish Chandra, Khemesh (Kamlesh?) Chatterjee.

Post and Telegraph Associations: **B. K. Mukherji, A. S. Rajan, Kabal (Kabul?) Singh.

All-India Bank Employees' Association: A. C. Kakkar, *F. M. Pinto.

All-India Insurance Employees' Association: R. M. Pananjpe.

All-India Port and Dock Workers' Federation: Makhanlal Chatterji, *W. T. Pinto.

All-India Federation of Educational Workers' Associations: D. H. Sahasrabudhe, M. K. Bannerji.

All-Indian Petroleum Workers' Federation: G. Sundaram.

All-India Seafarers' Federation: Sohrab Ali, *Bikash Mazumdar, *J. D. Randeria, Dilip Roy, *Abdul Khadar Sarang (Serong?).

Hind Mazdoor Sabha: *R. J.Mehta, *Gangadhar J. Ogale, *Baswan Singh.

Railway Unions: *Jagdish Ajmera, **Ram Chakravarty.

---

* Delegates who returned to India two weeks early in protest against efforts to form an Asian-African trade-union organization.
** Delegates who remained in China for the scheduled period but who did not sign the statement denying the allegations of the nine early-returnees.

17   FRONTS AND FELLOW TRAVELERS

Just as the mass organizations serve as "transmission belts" between the Party and the working class at large, so "front" organizations link the Party to "progressive" elements of other classes. The idea of transmission belts extending into all classes of society to mobilize such diverse elements as shopkeepers, landlords, professionals, clerks, and aristocrats in support of Communist aims is a concept that dates back to Lenin's time, but its vigorous application is a fairly recent development.

The Communist "front" as we know it today is seldom a working-class organization, but is primarily petty bourgeois and bourgeois. Its origin as a tactical device can probably be credited to Willi Münzenberg, the German Communist who in 1921 founded in Berlin an International Workers' Aid Society for the primary purpose of collecting relief supplies for famine areas in Russia. Not only were important sums collected and dispatched to Russia, but Russian films were shown and pro-Soviet propaganda was widely distributed in the process.[1] Münzenberg also founded the Communist Youth International, but more important so far as India is concerned was his brain child, the League Against Imperialism which from 1927 to 1931 could boast of the presence of Jawaharlal Nehru on its Executive Committee. (See p. 96.)

Since World War II Communist fronts have appeared in India in

---

[1] E. H. Carr, *The Bolshevik Revolution, 1917–1923* (London: Macmillan, 1953), III, p. 404.

abundance. In accordance with policy established in the Comintern as early as 1926, there has been created "a whole solar system of organizations and smaller committees around the Communist Party, so to speak, smaller organizations working actually under the influence of our Party (not under mechanical leadership)." [2] These fronts serve two primary purposes. As propaganda forums, they help to create a climate of public opinion favorable to Party activities, and as sources of recruitment they provide a sphere where political activists of all sorts can be observed, influenced, and drawn into the Party apparatus.

The Communist fronts in India can be conveniently grouped into three categories. First, the international-issue fronts, organizations formed to deal with specific international issues such as world peace or Indo-Soviet relations. Second, the professional fronts which aim at organizing specific occupational groups into societies that support the broad aspects of Communist policy. And, finally, the regional fronts, promoted to capitalize on the militant regionalism found in such areas as Andhra and Maharashtra.

INTERNATIONAL ISSUE FRONTS

The All-India Friends of the Soviet Union

The first important front organization to appear in India was the All-India Friends of the Soviet Union (AIFSU). Like so many other Indian political movements it had its origin in Bengal. In 1941 a Bengal Friends of the Soviet Union was organized "with the blessings of Rabindranath Tagore." A second annual conference was held in Calcutta in April, 1944, under the leadership of an "eminent Congresswoman," Mrs. Nellie Sen Gupta.[3] The organization became national when on June 3 and 4, 1944, the first Congress of the All-India Friends of the Soviet Union was held at Bombay University's Convocation Hall. Approximately 2,000 people from all parts of India attended the meeting, 100 of them being delegates.[4] The affair was a huge success in terms of the prominent non-Communist personalities who had been induced to participate. Vijayalakshmi Pandit, sister of Jawaharlal Nehru, presided, and the Chairman of the Reception Committee was Syed Abdulla Brelvi, editor of the *Bombay Chronicle*. Sarojini Naidu, the most important woman in the Indian nationalist

---

[2] "Report of the Commission for Work Among the Masses," *Imprecor*, VI (April 15, 1926), p. 429.

[3] *People's War*, II (May 14, 1944), p. 4.

[4] A. S. R. Chari, "Indo-Soviet Friendship," *People's War*, II (June 18, 1944), pp. 4–5.

movement, was elected President of the new organization but could not attend the meeting because she was then under detention for nationalist political activity.

These personages lent great prestige to the organization, but their presence certainly did not indicate that real control was not in the hands of the CPI. Communist speakers (B. T. Ranadive, Hiren Mukerjee, R. M. Jambhekar) dominated the proceedings, and Party members or reliable sympathizers were placed in strategic offices in the Executive Committee. The officers elected at the Congress were as follows: President: Sarojini Naidu; vice-presidents: Mahakavi Vallathol (67-year-old Malabar poet who has become a permanent fixture in Communist fronts), Syed Abdulla Brelvi (editor, *Bombay Chronicle*), Bhupendranath Datta (one of the members of Virendranath Chattopadhyaya's delegation to the third Comintern Congress, a confirmed Marxist if not a Party member), K. Srinivasan (editor, *The Hindu,* Madras); general secretary: R. M. Jambhekar (if not a Party member, at least a reliable sympathizer); joint secretaries: Hiren Mukerjee (later leader of the Communist Party in parliament), Dr. Junankar (no data available); treasurer: Mahendra Shah (later active in other fronts).

The war period was an ideal time to start such an organization, since the USSR was still regarded by Britain as a staunch ally, and the heroic defense of Stalingrad had inspired world-wide admiration for the Soviet people. This favorable atmosphere was fully appreciated by the then general secretary of the CPI, P. C. Joshi, who referred to it in the *Party Letter,* saying:

> This is why today the past achievements of the Soviet Union as well as its role in the present war give us the biggest weapon whereby we can educate our own people to Socialist consciousness, create the strongest revolutionary bonds between our people and the Soviet people. . . . This is why FSU [Friends of the Soviet Union] work today becomes one of the most important branches of work for our Party. To fail to see this is to fail to understand that one of our fundamental tasks as Communists is to build the broadest possible solidarity of our people with the Soviet Union as a prime means of furthering our national and international cause. . . . It is true that the FSU has to unite all patriotic sections of our people on the basis of a bond of friendship and solidarity with the Soviet Union IRRESPECTIVE OF THE PARTICULAR POLITICAL AFFILIATION of these sections. But this does not and should not mean that the FSU is a NON-POLITICAL organization.[5]

Here then is a clear description of a front: it is a political organization uniting all "patriotic" sections of the people in a way that furthers the Communists' national and international causes.

---

[5] *Party Letter,* IV (Jan. 25, 1944), pp. 2–3. Emphasis in original.

The AIFSU appears to have dropped out of sight almost immediately after its creation, and except for a few minor references to the Bombay branch, there is almost no mention of it in the Communist journals after 1944. It is probable that because of the general anti-Communist feeling that prevailed during 1944 and 1945 the organization lost its non-Communist supporters and thus merely withered for lack of "patriotic" elements that could be manipulated for Communist ends. Front organizations suffered another eclipse during the leftist period of Communist strategy between 1948 and 1951, and it was only when the Party began to change its attitude toward the bourgeoisie that such groups once again came into prominence.

In February, 1952, a group of fellow travelers in Bombay formed a preparatory committee for an Indo-Soviet Festival and Convention to be held in that city the following month, simultaneously with the visit to India of a Soviet delegation led by the Russian writer, Nikolai Tikhonov.[6] The Convention took place on March 14, 1952, and from it emerged the Indo-Soviet Cultural Society (ISCS). Dr. A. V. Baliga, a Bombay surgeon, was elected president, and S. Venkataraman was made general secretary.[7] Baliga had headed a medical delegation which visited the USSR the previous summer.[8]

The new organization has attempted to appear nonpolitical. Its journal says:

Our Society and its official journal ISCUS stand wholeheartedly for cultural exchanges, cultural understanding and cultural ties between Soviet Russia and India. As we have already declared we are unconcerned with politics. It is from the cultural platform that we appeal to the millions in India and the Soviet Union to come together and strive for cultural understanding, work for cultural progress and through this liquidate unnecessary ignorance, distrust and fear in international dealings.[9]

The techniques by which the Society seeks to promote these aims have frequently been set forth on the back cover of its journal. They are:

a) holding meetings, lectures, discussions, and study circles;
b) facilitating exchange of delegations and study tours between India and the USSR;
c) staging plays and organizing poetical symposia and poetry-reading groups;
d) arranging exhibitions of art, photography, stamps, manuscripts, etc.;
e) organizing reading rooms and libraries;
f) assisting persons interested in learning each other's languages;
g) arranging the exchange of students, scholars, artists, and professors between Indian and Soviet cultural institutions;

---

[6] *ISCUS*, II (Spring, 1955), p. 84.
[7] *Crossroads*, III (March 21, 1952), pp. 8–9.
[8] *Ibid.* (Aug. 10, 1951), p. 16.
[9] *ISCUS*, I (July, 1954), p. 3.

h) procuring the translation into Indian languages of books and publications relating to Soviet culture;

i) publication and distribution of books, journals, etc. relating to Indian and Soviet culture;

j) developing pen-friendships; and

k) other similar activities in furtherance of the aim of the Society.[10]

Any person over fifteen years of age who accepts the aims of the Society is eligible for membership.

The second ISCS conference was held in Delhi, November 26–28, 1954. It was inaugurated by Sardar Teja Singh, a former chief justice of the PEPSU High Court and the leader of a 35-man delegation, the majority of whom were Society members, which had just returned from a visit to the Soviet Union. A new National Council of ninety-eight "prominent" Indians was elected; A. V. Baliga was reëlected president, and S. Mahmuduzzafar, a veteran CPI member (died August 24, 1956) replaced S. Venkataraman in the key post of general secretary.

In the period between the two conferences, branch chapters of the cultural society had been formed in Madras, Hyderabad, Calcutta, Delhi, Bangalore, Andhra, Meerut, Amravati, Gwalior, Indore, and Patna, and some units of the defunct Friends of the Soviet Union came to life and affiliated with the Society.[11]

The report on activities presented to the Delhi conference lists an impressive number of projects carried out by the various branches. During the first sixteen months, for example, the Bombay group claims to have presented 320 showings of Soviet films to audiences totaling more than 100,000 people in the Bombay area. Numerous discussion groups and exhibitions had been arranged in many cities, and reading rooms containing Soviet publications set up in some. The Bombay chapter arranged to send India's chess champion, Ramachandra Sapre, to the USSR in March, 1954, to witness the world chess championship. Upon his return, he helped organize a chess circle in Bombay.

By the time of the third National Conference, held in Calcutta in December, 1956, ISCS was able to report the existence of 42 branches scattered all over India. The total membership of the 21 branches that sent figures to the central headquarters was 7,670.[12]

In January, 1954, the Society began publishing a quarterly journal called *ISCUS*. It is, by Indian standards, an impressive publication,

[10] *Ibid.*, I (Jan., 1954), back cover.

[11] *Ibid.*, II (Spring, 1955), pp. 85–86.

[12] *Ibid.*, III (Winter, 1956), pp. 1, 69.

competently edited and well printed. Its content is a shrewd combination of unsubtle flattery of things Indian and glowing praise of the Soviet Union—all of it dressed up with footnotes and the paraphernalia of scholarship. For example the spring, 1955, issue contains one article which gives the impression that there is an enormous enthusiasm in Russia for Indian literature, art, languages, and motion pictures, while in another article, D. N. Pritt tells *ISCUS* readers that Western-style civil liberties are unnecessary in the USSR because the Soviet citizen "feels that the Government is *his* government . . . that it is his friend, and will stand by him." [13]

One can only speculate as to the effectiveness of the Indo-Soviet Cultural Society. As of 1957 it had been unable to draw into its organization any persons of prominence comparable to those who supported its predecessor in 1944, and this would seem to indicate that it is not making a great impression on India's ruling elite. On the mass level, its work may have greater impact. When Nikita Krushchov and Nicolai Bulganin visited Bombay during their tour of India in November, 1955, the Society sponsored a dinner attended by the state's governor, chief minister, chief justice, and other dignitaries. Their presence not only greatly enhanced the prestige of the organization and its leaders, but gave the Soviet Union a respectability which it had not previously enjoyed in the eyes of the Indian masses.

The Peace Movement

Of all Communist fronts in India, the most elaborate and most effective have been the various organizations set up to advance the theme that the Soviet Union is the leading champion of world peace. The origins of the international Communist peace movement can be traced to the World Congress of Intellectuals held in Breslau (Wroclaw), Poland, in August, 1948, and to the famous Waldorf-Astoria Conference in New York the following March. Leading Indian fellow travelers were present at both of these gatherings—the writer Mulk Raj Anand, at the first, and the mathematician D. D. Kosambi, at the second. Subsequently, a formal World Peace Committee was set up at a Peace Congress held in Paris in April, 1949, and a twelve-member Permanent Bureau was created with the French scientist, Frederic Joliot-Curie, as president. No delegation was sent from India because the government of India refused passports to the delegates. However, India was represented at Paris by a number of Indians who happened to be in Europe at the time, and one among them, R. M. Jambhekar

---

[13] *Ibid.*, p. 18.

of Bombay (general secretary of the original Friends of the Soviet Union), became a member of the World Peace Committee. D. D. Kosambi was elected to the Permanent Bureau.[14]

In November, 1949, the official journal of the Cominform announced that "the organization and consolidation of the forces of peace against the forces of war should now become the pivot of the entire activity of the Communist Parties and democratic organizations" around the world.[15] What was obvious had now become explicit: that the peace movement's primary purpose was to supply the Soviet Union with another instrument of foreign policy.

The Paris Peace Congress took place at a time when the CPI was deeply committed to the antibourgeois strategy and violent tactics of B. T. Ranadive. The Party, therefore, was hardly conditioned to lead a broadly based popular movement designed to enlist middle-class elements in an international cause. Nevertheless the effort was made, and shortly after the Paris Congress the AITUC announced its intention to convene an All-India Congress for Peace "in coöperation with all progressive and democratic organizations of the toiling people in India." [16] In preparation for the national meeting, preliminary conferences were held in Bombay, Assam, and West Bengal between June and October, 1949.

The First All-India Peace Congress was eventually convened in Calcutta, November 24–27, 1949, with V. Chakkarai Chettiar, president of the AITUC, as chairman of the Reception Committee. The official report claims that 3,000 delegates, representing 250 mass organizations with an aggregate membership of two million men and women, attended the conference.[17] An All-India Peace Committee was set up with Chettiar as president and D. N. Gavankar as secretary.

Since the Communists during this period were engaged in an all-out assault on the Congress Party, the Socialists, and all representatives of the bourgeoisie, it is not surprising that the First Peace Congress turned out to be little more than an assembly of the mass organizations and affiliates under Communist control: the AITUC, the All-India Students' Federation (AISF), and the All-India Kisan Sabha (AIKS). The pro-Soviet, anti-American tone of Chettiar's presi-

---

[14] *Crossroads*, I (May 6, 1949), p. 10; April 14, 1950, p. 15. The official record of the Congress lists no Indians as members of the Permanent Bureau. *Pervyi Vsemirnyi Kongress Storonnikov Mira; Parizh-Praga, 20–25 aprelia, 1949 goda (Materialy)* [First World Congress of Partisans of Peace; Paris-Prague, 20–25 April, 1949 (Materials)] (Moscow: State Publishing House, 1950), p. 500.

[15] "Defense of Peace and Struggle Against the Warmongers," *For a Lasting Peace for a People's Democracy*, no. 28 (Nov. 29, 1949), p. 1.

[16] "Review of the All-India Peace Congress," *Communist*, III (Jan., 1950), p. 52.

[17] *Ibid.*, p. 46.

dential address is evidence that there was no effort to draw non-Communist elements into the movement. "The Soviet Union does not and cannot want war," he told the delegates, "and our people know this perfectly well and [they know] that the Anglo-American imperialist Powers are the real instigators of a war." [18]

This emphasis tended to exclude from the Indian peace movement anyone who had not already subscribed to the Soviet view of the cold war, and consequently weakened the potential propaganda value of the peace theme among the non-Communist middle classes. In terms of the aims of international communism, therefore, the Indian peace movement got off to a very poor start.

It was only two months after the Calcutta Peace Congress that the Cominform began to make known to the Indian Communists that B. T. Ranadive's leftist strategy did not enjoy the support of the international Communist leadership. (See chapter 13.) The CPI was slow in responding, however, and because leftists continued to dominate the Party until May, 1950, the peace movement suffered.

From March 15 to 19, 1950, the World Peace Committee held its third session in Stockholm and launched the now famous Stockholm Peace Appeal. R. M. Jambhekar attended the meeting as India's representative, and reported on the proceedings in the CPI weekly, *Crossroads*. In his report he made a point of quoting the remarks of Jean Laffitte, general secretary of the Permanent Committee of the World Peace Council, who said:

Our movement cannot be regarded as a co-ordinating body of the already existing democratic organizations. Neither can our movement be regarded as merely the sum total of existing democratic organizations for this would contribute nothing. Our movement must be something much more extensive.[19]

The remarks were especially applicable to India. In April the British scientist, J. D. Bernal, a member of the Permanent Bureau of the World Peace Council, visited India to attend the Indian Science Congress. While there he took the trouble to observe the progress of the peace movement, and he reported his findings to the All-India Peace Council in a letter published in *Crossroads*. Indian peace workers, said Bernal, "are all too few and I feel that they have demanded of their followers perhaps too much understanding and too far-reaching political agreement." [20]

Although no specific quota was announced when the campaign was begun in India in April, the AIPC and *Crossroads* spoke of col-

---

[18] *Ibid.*, p. 58.
[19] *Crossroads*, I (April 14, 1950), p. 15.
[20] *Ibid.*, II (May 5, 1950), p. 7.

lecting "millions" of signatures endorsing the Stockholm Appeal.[21] But by June it was apparent that things were not going well. On June 16 *Crossroads* carried a page-one notice appealing for more signatures and admitting that the "signature campaign in India is lagging behind the world movement." By September dismal failure was conceded in an inner-party document which stated that less than 300,000 signatures had been collected.[22]

When the Permanent Bureau of the World Peace Committee met in May, 1950, it decided to hold a second World Peace Congress, this time in Sheffield, England. These plans were ultimately scotched when the British government refused visas to more than 200 delegates, and at the last minute the venue of the Congress was switched to the more hospitable climate of Warsaw.

As the time for the second Congress approached, the necessity of overhauling the Indian peace movement became more and more apparent. This, however, was not an easy thing to do, for even though B. T. Ranadive had been ousted as general secretary of the CPI, the Party was still controlled by militant elements who looked upon the peace movement as merely another instrument with which to promote insurrection.

Changes first became evident in Bombay. "In view of serious defects of the peace movement in Bombay," said *Crossroads* in October, "where only 50,000 signatures to the Stockholm Appeal have been collected so far, a new Bombay Peace Committee was elected at a public meeting . . . October 22." [23] Mulk Raj Anand was made president; R. K. Karanjia (editor of *Blitz*) and K. A. Abbas became vice-presidents; Krishan Chandar was made general secretary; and Raj (Romesh?) Thapar became treasurer.

On October 28–29, 1950, an All-India Peace Convention was held in Bombay and the struggle between the leftists and the moderates came into the open. F. A. Kazmi from Lucknow "demanded close identification of the peace movement with the daily struggles of the people, and the pinning down of the Anglo-American imperialists as the aggressors and warmongers." [24] S. A. Dange replied that "the peace movement was not the labor movement" and cautioned against labeling the United States as an aggressor lest many potential supporters be frightened off. The Bengal delegation asked that the Calcutta Peace Con-

---

[21] *Ibid.*, I (Special Peace Issue, April 21, 1950), p. 14.

[22] *A Note on the Present Situation in Our Party* (n.p.: Communist Party of India, 1950), p. 38.

[23] *Crossroads*, II (Oct. 27, 1950), p. 3.

[24] *Ibid.* (Nov. 3, 1950), p. 16.

gress manifesto be withdrawn because it "deviated from the policy and program of the world movement and restricted the scope of the movement in India by giving wrong slogans." The Convention, however, declared that it was not constitutionally empowered to withdraw the manifesto, but instead it issued an appeal to guide the movement until a second All-India Peace Congress could be convened. A preparatory committee of fourteen was formed with power to coöpt. Dr. Madanlal Atal, who had served with the International Brigade during the Spanish Civil War, was elected president, and author Krishan Chandar was designated secretary. It was declared that the Committee did not supersede the old All-India Committee and would coöperate with it in planning the second national Peace Congress.

When the Second World Peace Congress was held in Warsaw, November 16–22, 1950, India was represented by a thirty-seven-member delegation headed by Dr. Madanlal Atal and including Harindranath Chattopadhyaya, independent M.P. and brother of the late Sarojini Naidu, and Romesh Thapar, editor of the Communist weekly, *Crossroads*.[25] D. D. Kosambi was unable to attend, but was elected to the Bureau of the World Peace Council (which replaced the World Peace Committee).

It will be remembered that in November, 1949, the Cominform journal had referred to the peace movement as the "pivot of the entire activity of the Communist parties" around the world. Sometime between October and December, 1950, two leading Indian Communists journeyed to Europe to seek advice concerning the crisis in the CPI. In an interview with R. Palme Dutt they specifically asked his view on whether the peace movement should be the "pivot" of all the activities of the Indian Party. A detailed report of the interview was circulated within the CPI in January, 1951, and it quotes Dutt as saying:

It is clear that the Peace movement presents the Party with one of the most important weapons for building a broad front of all sections of the Indian people. The recent experience after the war in Korea shows what immense possibilities exist in India for building this Front. If we recognize that the building of the national Democratic Front is the key task for the national liberation struggle, then it should be obvious that leaving aside the word "pivot" for the time being, the Peace movement must become the main activity of the Party—the broad front that will emerge out of the Peace movement may lay the basis for the formation of the National Front for national liberation.[26]

[25] *Ibid.* (Dec. 15, 1950), Supplement, p. 4. Harindranath is a brother of Virendranath
[26] Deven and Balkrishna, *Talks with Comrade R. Palme Dutt and Other Impressions Gained Abroad by Deven and Bal Krishna* (n.p.: Communist Party of India, 1951), p. 2. "Deven" and "Balkrishna" are pseudonyms. A non-Communist source

By early 1951, then, it should have been clear to any Indian Communist that the international Communist leadership regarded the peace movement as a matter of primary importance and disapproved of the sectarian manner in which it had been managed by the leftist leadership of the CPI. By the time the Dutt interview was circulated, however, the leadership of the peace movement had been taken out of the hands of the leftists by the more moderate elements that had organized the Bombay convention.

Meanwhile the World Peace Council, which had been created in Warsaw, held its first meeting in Berlin from February 21 to 26, 1951, and called for a new signature campaign. This time the appeal was for a pact of peace between the five great powers.

On March 3 and 4, 1951, the Preparatory Committee for the Second All-India Peace Congress met in New Delhi to draw up final plans for the Congress. Although only twenty-three members attended the Delhi meeting, the total membership of the Preparatory Committee at this point was sixty-one, and it included a number of fairly prominent non-Communists.[27] Among them was Dr. Saifuddin Kitchlew, a Muslim who had been a general secretary of the Indian National Congress in 1924 and had a long record of Congress activity.

The Preparatory Committee meeting in Delhi revealed that although the peace movement was now functioning more in line with Cominform policy, the radical CPI leadership, under General Secretary Rajeshwar Rao, was still reluctant to go along with the new peace policy. This problem occupied the attention of the Committee which "took serious note of the still persisting failure in certain states and districts to understand the necessity to preserve the really broad character of the peace platform and prevent its misuse for sectional, narrow, party slogans and resolutions."[28] Singled out for specific criticism were the branches in Andhra, Rajeshwar Rao's home region, where peace committees had tried to link the peace movement with a campaign against the Preventive Detention Act under which numerous Andhra Communists had been incarcerated.

Another problem confronting the Preparatory Committee concerned the venue of the proposed Congress, for C. Rajagopalachari, the home minister of the government of India, had declared that it could not be

states that S. A. Dange, Ajoy Ghosh, Rajeshwar Rao, and Basava Punniah went secretly to Moscow early in 1951. *Communist Conspiracy in Madurai* (Bombay: Democratic Research Service, 1954), pp. 19–20.

[27] *Crossroads*, II (March 9, 1951), p. 16.

[28] *Ibid.*, II (March 30, 1951), p. 8.

held in Delhi. Kitchlew headed a delegation which tried to persuade him to lift the ban, but the home minister was adamant.[29]

It is necessary at this point to mention the role played in the peace movement by P. C. Joshi, the former general secretary of the CPI who had been expelled from the Party during B. T. Ranadive's leadership. When Ranadive was replaced by Rajeshwar Rao in July, 1950, Joshi tried to get back into the Party but was turned down on the grounds that his political line was still reformist. As has been shown in chapter 13, Joshi had interpreted the directives of the Cominform more correctly than had the official leadership. Now, he immediately appreciated the importance which the international Communist leadership attached to the peace movement, and it did not take him long to recognize its potential utility as a lever with which to dislodge Rajeshwar Rao.

There is no published record that Joshi played any role in initiating the reorganization of the peace movement that had culminated in the Convention at Bombay in October, 1950. But by the time the Preparatory Committee met in Delhi in March, 1951, Joshi was a member.[30] When he launched his own magazine, *India Today,* in May, 1951, the first issue was a special "Peace Number" containing a long analysis by him of Indian foreign policy. The article took note of a "series of initiatives for peace by the Indian Government in the recent past" and described them as "a reflection of the contradictions in the camp of Imperialist reaction." Then, obviously addressing his erstwhile comrades, he added:

Lenin, the greatest revolutionary strategist of our age, proclaimed the tactical axiom that the proletarian and the people's movement which cannot exploit the contradictions in the enemies' camp and [which] fails to win allies however vacillating and weak, will never successfully fight forward to victory.

The right attitude for Indian progressives towards Nehru's foreign policy will be to:

Boldly support all his specific peace moves; they objectively aid the anti-imperialist peace camp;

Sharply expose all the weaknesses, vacillations and contradictions of his policy. . .

Tirelessly work to establish a Government that will . . . completely break Indian ties with the Imperialists and whole-heartedly join the anti-imperialist peace camp.[31]

Of even greater importance than Joshi's article was another in the same issue by Krishan Chandar, the secretary of the Preparatory Com-

[29] The Communists charge that the home minister had been influenced by Philip Spratt's pamphlet, *The Communist Peace Appeal* (Bombay: Democratic Research Service, 1951).

[30] *Crossroads,* II (March 9, 1951), p. 16.

[31] P. C. Joshi, "India in the Battle for Peace," *India Today,* I (May, 1951), pp. 14–15.

mittee. By writing for Joshi's magazine, Chandar was throwing the prestige of his key position in the peace movement behind a Communist who had been expelled from the Party and was still condemned as a renegade by the official CPI leadership. "The Indian peace movement is a recent growth," Chandar wrote, "and it has got nothing to do with the old peace movement which was mainly confined to one political party and its close associates and friends. It was a very exclusive movement; it had a very exclusive growth and ultimately it died of its own exclusion [sic]." [32] Other prominent members of the Preparatory Committee, including Mahakavi Vallathol, Ali Sardar Jafri, and D. D. Kosambi, also contributed to Joshi's publication.

Unable to secure permission to hold their Congress in Delhi, the Preparatory Committee selected Bombay. The All-India Peace Convention (the word "Congress" was dropped temporarily) met there May 11–13, 1951, attended by 288 delegates coming from all parts of India.[33] The Preparatory Committee was dissolved and an All-India Peace Council of 150 members, with unlimited powers of coöptation, was created. Dr. Kitchlew, much better known than Dr. Atal, became the new president, but Krishan Chandar remained as general secretary. The Convention ratified the appointments of Dr. Atal and D. D. Kosambi to the World Peace Council, and recommended that Kitchlew, Chandar, Prithvi Raj Kapoor (a Bombay film actor-producer and member of the Rajya Sabha), and Mulk Raj Anand also be accepted on the Council.[34]

Toward the goal of broadening the movement, the Convention resolved "to make special approaches at all organizational levels to all sections of opinion which are still outside the movement, including the large body of pacifist opinion, led by the close Ashram disciples of Mahatma Gandhi, and to the various religious bodies which stand for Peace." [35]

Responding to the call of the Berlin meeting of the World Peace Council, the Bombay Convention endorsed the appeal for a five-power peace pact and set a target of more than eleven million signatures to be collected before September 1. The total was broken down on a province-by-province basis, and even India's *sadhus* (holy men) were assigned a quota—200,000 signatures.[36] The goal was not reached,

[32] Krishan Chandar, "Peace in Our Time," *ibid.*, p. 34.
[33] *Peace and the Indian People* (Bombay: All-India Peace Council, 1951), p. 24. This source gives a breakdown of delegates by provinces.
[34] *Ibid.*, p. 10.
[35] *Ibid.*, p. 18.
[36] *Ibid.*, pp. 21–22.

and in September, 1952, a year after the target date, only two and a half million signatures had been collected.[37]

P. C. Joshi was pleased in general with the results of the Convention although he was a little disturbed that in eliminating the ultra-left mistakes of the past, the movement might have gone too far to the right. "Right mistakes," he said, "were being committed from above, by some responsible leaders [i.e., Communists] and one or two eminent intellectuals who were piloting the proceedings." [38] The rightist trend, he stated, manifested itself in the following way: "They [the rightists] switched on the spotlight on the positive peace efforts of the Nehru Government but switched it off on its pro-imperialist, aiding-the-war-maker acts." It was correct to praise the constructive actions of the government, Joshi continued, but it was wrong to avoid criticizing Nehru's "pro-imperialist" moves because this would "disrupt the Left Unity embodied in the existing Peace Movement." [39] Whether or not this "rightist" trend really upset Joshi is of no consequence, but it does seem likely that the success of the Bombay Convention influenced the situation in the CPI. At any rate, within three weeks after the conclusion of the Convention, the CPI headquarters in Bombay announced the resignation of Rajeshwar Rao as general secretary (June 4, 1951).[40]

After the Bombay Convention, a long procession of cultural, scientific, and economic delegations began moving back and forth between India and her two Communist neighbors to the north. On June 19, 1951, a thirteen-member delegation of writers, journalists, doctors, and engineers, led by Harindranath Chattopadhyaya left Delhi for Moscow via Kabul.[41] Most members of the delegation had been associated with one or more Communist front organizations. Five Chinese organizations had extended an invitation, through the New Delhi Chinese embassy, to the AIPC and the Bombay and Calcutta branches of the India-China Friendship Association, and in September, 1951, an unofficial delegation headed by Pandit Sunderlal left for China.[42] Earlier (in July) an Indian Preparatory Committee

---

[37] *Crossroads*, IV (Sept. 21, 1952), p. 2. In a speech in Moscow, January 5, 1953, Kitchlew claimed that three million signatures had been collected. *Hands Across the Himalayas* (New Delhi: All-India Peace Council, 1953), p. 139.

[38] P. C. Joshi, "India Can Halt War," *India Today*, I (June, 1951), p. 20.

[39] *Loc. cit.*

[40] *The Hindu* (Madras), June 5, 1951, p. 5.

[41] *Ibid.*, June 22, 1951, p. 6.

[42] Sunderlai, *China Today* (Allahabad: Hindustani Culture Society, 1952), pp. 1–2.

for the Moscow Economic Conference had been set up by the All-India Peace Council, and when the Conference met in April, 1952, twenty-eight Indians were present as participants.[43] While the Moscow Economic Conference was in progress, the government of India announced that a fourteen-member cultural delegation led by Mrs. Vijayalakshmi Pandit would leave for China on April 27.[44] The next day *The Hindu* in Madras learned that fourteen Indian trade unionists had been invited by the All-China Federation of Labor to visit China and attend the May Day celebrations in Peking.[45] Ultimately, seventeen trade unionsts made up the delegation, and it toured China simultaneously with Mrs. Pandit's cultural delegation.

While traveling delegations were becoming such a noticeable aspect of Sino-Indian relations, a group of eleven prominent Chinese intellectuals met with Soong Ching-ling (Madame Sun Yat-sen) in Peking in May, 1952, and issued a call for an Asian conference on peace.[46] On June 3, forty-seven delegates from twenty countries convened in Peking in a preparatory conference to make definite plans for a full-scale Asian meeting.[47] The Indian delegates were D. D. Kosambi, Sardar Gurbax Singh (a Punjabi litterateur and editor of *Preet Lari*), and Indulal Yajnik. Apparently, Yajnik had journeyed to Peking from Russia after having attended the Moscow Economic Conference. S. S. Yusuf, who had been a member of the trade-union delegation, signed the final communique as an observer on behalf of the AITUC.[48]

The Indian peace movement responded immediately to the Chinese proposal, and in August *Crossroads* announced that a series of provincial peace conferences would be held to raise funds and to select delegates to go to Peking.[49]

The Third All-India Peace Congress was held in Jullundur (Punjab), September 13, 1952. Notable among the new faces appearing at the Congress was that of American-educated Dr. J. C. Kumarappa (B. Sc., Syracuse; M.A., Columbia), a widely-known "Gandhian economist" and president of the All-India Village Industries Association. Kumarappa had been a member of the September, 1951, cultural delegation to China, and had repaid the Communist investment handsomely in

---

[43] *Crossroads*, III (July 27, 1951), p. 9. The names of the Indian participants are given in: *International Economic Conference in Moscow* (Moscow: Committee for the Promotion of International Trade, 1952), pp. 321–322.

[44] *Indian Press Digests*, I (March, 1953), p. 19.

[45] *The Hindu* (Madras), April 8, 1952, p. 6.

[46] *China Monthly Review*, CXXIII (July, 1952), p. 66.

[47] *Ibid.* (August, 1952), pp. 122–125.

[48] *Survey of China Mainland Press*, 1952, no. 346, p. 9; no. 349, p. 2; and no. 350, p. 6.

[49] *Crossroads*, IV (Aug. 24, 1952), p. 11.

the number of laudatory statements he made about China after his return. From then on he committed himself wholeheartedly to the Communist campaign of glorifying the Communist countries while villifying the United States.[50] Since the Third Peace Congress, Kumarappa has been a fixture on the platforms of Communist-sponsored meetings.

The Asian and Pacific Peace Conference met in Peking October 2–12, 1952, with 367 delegates from 37 countries participating in the deliberations. A Soviet writer fixes the Indian group at 39 delegates and 12 observers, but more than 65 Indians were named in the Chinese press reports of the conference.[51] Romesh Chandra claimed that more than 20 prospective delegates were denied passports by the government of India.[52]

Very little publicity was given to the delegation in either the Communist or non-Communist press in India. Only the names of the most prominent delegates were published. Much, however, was made of the participation of Chatur Narain Malaviya (a Congress M.P. from Bhopal), Ravi Shankar Vyas ("a renowned and respected follower of Mahatma Gandhi from Gujerat"), and Govind Sahai (member of the Legislative Council of Uttar Pradesh and former parliamentary secretary to the chief minister of that state).[53] The presence of CPI members on the delegation was minimized, but among those who went to Peking were A. K. Gopalan, Y. D. Sharma, Romesh Chandra, P. V. Raghavaiah (M.P.), Sardar Prithvi Singh, Karyanand Sharma, and Mrs. Sarla Gupta. Romesh Chandra was appointed deputy secretary general of the Conference, and Kitchlew, Gyan Chand, and Vyas were elected to the Presidium.

As was to be expected, the Conference approved a series of documents condemning the United States for aggression in Korea and for the use of bacteriological warfare. A declaration of scientists and doctors concerning germ warfare was signed by A. J. Faridi, Arvind Mehta, and Amiya Mukerjee for the Indian delegation.[54] Much fuss was made over a joint declaration of the Indian and Pakistani contingents concerning Kashmir, signed amid "thunderous applause"

[50] See Kumarappa's foreward to L. Natarjan, *American Shadow over India* (Bombay: People's Publishing House, 1952).

[51] A. Popov, "The Peoples of Asia Speak Out for Peace," *News* (Nov. 1, 1952), p. 15. *Crossroads*, IV (Oct. 12, 1952), p. 8, fixes the Indian contingent at 60, but the Nov. 9, 1952 (p. 8) issue states it was 54.

[52] Romesh Chandra, "At Peking in the Service of Peace," *New Age* (monthly), I (Dec., 1952), p. 25.

[53] *Ibid.*, p. 27.

[54] *Survey of the China Mainland Press*, 1952, no. 432, p. 24.

while the Indians and Pakistanis embraced one another on the dais. The declaration, however, merely called for the peaceful settlement of the dispute and criticized the United Nations and the "Anglo-American powers" whose "unmistakable purpose" was "to intensify the Indo-Pakistan conflict with a view to making both countries subservient to them." [55] No suggestions were made regarding the thorny questions of troop withdrawal and a plebiscite.

At the conclusion of the conference a Peace Liaison Committee of the Asian and Pacific Regions was set up. Four Indians were elected to this body: Saifuddin Kitchlew as one of the vice-chairmen; Romesh Chandra as one of the deputy secretaries general, and Gyan Chand and Ravi Shankar Vyas as members. [56]

In terms of its implications for the Communist movement in India, the most significant document to emerge from the Peking Conference was the report on its proceedings by Romesh Chandra, published in the third issue of the CPI's new theoretical journal, *New Age*. Chandra saw in the Peking meeting a strategic mandate for the Indian peace movement, and by implication, for Indian communism. He said:

> In discussions with delegates from other countries, we saw they were faced with similar problems as us in India. In all countries, the main danger to guard against inside the Peace movement is that of making the tone too sharp—the "left" danger—for the less politically advanced sections to understand and grasp. Naturally the other danger of running behind the advancing consciousness of the people is also there, but the main danger is the first—going too left. [57]

Thus more than a year after the CPI had replaced its radical general secretary and Central Committee with more moderate elements, the party member in charge of the peace movement still found it necessary to point out in the party journal that there was danger from the left.

The Peking meeting was in October, 1952. During December 12–19, the Congress of Peoples for Peace was held in Vienna, and thirty Indian delegates journeyed to Austria to attend. The delegation was led by Dr. Kitchlew and included a number of interesting non-Communist figures. The Gandhian element was strongly represented by J. C. Kumarappa, Mahesh Dutt Misra, and Vinubhai G. Shah, the latter identified as a well-known member of Vinoba Bhave's *Bhoodan Yagna* movement. Tulsidas Jadhav, leader of the Peasants' and Workers' Party, was also present. Of those who attended the Vienna meet-

---

[55] The texts of all documents can be found in the supplements to *News* (Nov. 1, 1952), and to *People's China*, Oct. 23, 1952, and Nov. 1, 1952.

[56] Supplement to *People's China*, Nov. 1, 1952, p. 3.

[57] Chandra, "At Peking . . . ," p. 31.

ing, only Kitchlew, Romesh Chandra and his wife, and Nandlal Dhar had been present at the Peking Peace Conference, although Gurbax Singh had been in Peking in June.

The most noteworthy fact about the delegation, however, was the inclusion of P. C. Joshi, whose status in the Party was still vague. Moreover, he was one of the twenty-six Indian delegates who, immediately following the Vienna meeting, journeyed to Moscow where Kitchlew was awarded a Stalin Peace Prize.[58] Among those who went, four (Romesh Chandra, Perrin Chandra, Hajrah Begum, S. K. Acharya) are identifiable as Communist activists, and can be classified as rightists in the CPI. S. K. Acharya, like Joshi, had even been expelled from the party by the Ranadive leadership in January, 1949.[59]

During 1953 the World Peace Council met in Budapest in June, and in Vienna in November.[60] The Budapest meeting marked the entry into the Indian movement of Major-General Sir Sahib Singh Sokhey, a nominated member of the Rajya Sabha (Council of States) and an assistant director general of the World Health Organization from 1950 to 1952. According to Crossroads, Sokhey had wanted to serve on the Chinese-approved "scientific commission" that investigated the germ-warfare charges in Korea, but had been prevented from doing so by the government of India.[61] In April, 1953, he spoke at a reception held upon Dr. Kitchlew's return from the USSR, and in June he led the Indian delegation to Budapest. When the AIPC launched its journal, Peace, in September, Sokhey was listed as a member of its board of consulting editors. As a result of these activities he became the second Indian to receive a Stalin Peace Prize, which he accepted in Moscow in July, 1954.[62]

At the Vienna meeting of the World Peace Council (November, 1953), it was decided to try to broaden the peace movement by obtaining the support of non-Communist organizations for a massive international peace gathering. This decision, reported Romesh Chandra, raised the peace movement to "a qualitatively different level." "We seek now," he wrote in New Age (monthly), "not merely contacts and discussions with parallel organizations and movements but united action with them." [63]

---

[58] For an account of the visit, see Hands Across the Himalayas.

[59] People's Age, VII (Jan. 23, 1949), p. 3.

[60] Partial lists of delegates were published in the Communist press. See Crossroads, V (June 21, 1953), p. 7; and Peace, I (Jan., 1954), pp. 17–18.

[61] Crossroads, IV (Dec. 28, 1952), p. 7.

[62] New Age (weekly), I (July 25, 1954), p. 15.

[63] Romesh Chandra, "Towards Great National and World Peace Meetings—New Stage in Peace Movement," New Age (monthly), III (March, 1954), p. 45.

It was shortly after the Vienna meeting that the Indian peace movement was given an unexpected boost by the decision of the United States government to extend military assistance to Pakistan, with whom India had long been bitterly feuding over Kashmir. This American action was widely interpreted in India as unfriendly interference in South Asian affairs, prejudicing the peaceful settlement of the outstanding problems between the two nations. A wave of anti-American sentiment swept the country, alienating many segments of public opinion which had previously been sympathetic to the United States. Taking advantage of this, the Communists designated February 14 as "Anti U.S.-Pak Pact Day" and organized demonstrations in various parts of the country, securing coöperation from elements of the ruling party in some areas.[64] Subsequently, American aid to Pakistan became the major theme of the peace movement.

Although this new international development greatly aided the Communists in their organization of a broader peace front, it brought a complication in its wake: any agitation directed against Pakistan, as this one perforce had to be, ran (and runs) the risk of inciting communal difficulties between India's majority Hindu population and her forty million Muslims. "In some states," Romesh Chandra reported, " 'all party' campaigns against the U.S.-Pak Pact, led by Peace Committees, had become communal and anti-Pakistan meetings and rallies. We had forgotten the very purpose of the campaign in the joy of securing unity, and the communal and reactionary forces seized the opportunity to utilize the U.S.-Pak Pact for their own ends." [65]

The movement continued to suffer from other difficulties as well. In some states the Party members insisted that the peace movement endorse the "most advanced slogans of Left and opposition parties," and in others they had difficulty in preventing their peace meetings from giving unconditional support to the government.

The greatest problem, however, was a general apathy among Party members toward the peace campaign. In his summary of the work of the Party's Third Congress, Ajoy Ghosh wrote in January, 1954, that there had been "a very serious under-estimation inside the Party about the importance of the peace movement" and that "the whole peace movement has been neglected by the Party." [66] Chandra reported in March that in some states there was still a tendency to take a "purely

[64] New Age (weekly), I (Feb. 21, 1954), p. 16.
[65] Chandra, "Towards Great National . . . ," p. 49.
[66] Ajoy Ghosh, On the Work of the Third Congress of the Communist Party of India (Delhi: Communist Party of India, 1954), p. 7. Published previously in New Age (weekly), I Jan. 24, 1954, pp. 3-4 ff.

formal" approach to the peace movement and to look upon it as a "waste of time." He drew particular attention to "the failure of the mass organizations to give it adequate support and attention." [67] The "mass organizations" of course referred to the Communist-dominated trade unions, kisan, and student organizations. Ghosh had hinted at the same thing.[68]

However, the peace campaign received a welcome stimulus with the visit to India, in June, of the Chinese Premier Chou En-lai. His meeting with Nehru produced the communique enunciating the famous "Five Principles of Coexistence," subsequently referred to in India as "Panch Shila." When the All-India Peace Council met in Calcutta in late July it called for a "united campaign for Asian solidarity based on the acceptance of the five principles." [69] By October, Chandra was able to note some improvement in the response of the mass organizations to the peace campaign. He reported that several trade unions had pledged active suport, and that special peace resolutions had been adopted by the AIKS at its twelfth annual session in September. Nevertheless, he said, it would be wrong to conclude that the mass organizations were "throwing all their weight into the Peace Movement. This is far from the reality. There are several provinces where the mass organizations have done little more than pay formal support, through a circular or a statement, to the Asian solidarity campaign." [70]

Although response from the mass organizations may not have been satisfactory to the peace organizers, they had reason to be pleased with the number of important non-Communist political figures associated with them. They had particular reason for satisfaction because in May, 1953, the Congress Working Committee had met in New Delhi and had pointed out that "certain peace organizations, though ostensibly working for the promotion of peace, are designed to further certain political purposes." Congressmen were advised not to join such organizations nor to go abroad to attend any of their conferences, and these instructions were reiterated in February, 1954.[71] Yet by October, 1954, several prominent Congressmen had been attracted to the peace movement, the most notable being S. K. Patil, the president of the Bombay Pradesh Congress Committee, who had in fact been present as an invitee at the Delhi meeting of the Working Committee where

---

[67] Chandra, "Towards Great National . . . ," p. 51.

[68] Ghosh, On the Work . . . , p. 24.

[69] New Age (weekly), I (Aug. 8, 1954), p. 16.

[70] Romesh Chandra, "Build a Broad Platform for Peace and Asian Solidarity," New Age (monthly), III (Oct., 1954), p. 31.

[71] Congress Bulletin, no. 5 (May, 1953), p. 144; and no. 2 (Feb.–March, 1954), p. 78.

Congressmen had been advised to avoid such associations.[72] Other Congressmen who were taking an active part in the peace campaign were Giani Gurmukh Singh Musafir, an M.P. from Amritsar, a member of the Congress Working Committee, and president of the Punjab Provincial Congress Committee; Syed Nausher Ali, a member of the Rajya Sabha from West Bengal; and Dr. Anup Singh, American-educated member of the Rajya Sabha and Indian representative on the United Nations Korean Commission from 1949 to 1951.

The importance attached to the Indian peace movement by the international leadership was evident in late December when the All-India Congress for Peace and Asian Solidarity convened in Madras; in attendance were several foreign fraternal delegates, not the least important of whom were Jean Laffitte, general secretary of the World Peace Council; J. D. Bernal; and Mrs. D. N. Pritt, wife of the British lawyer noted for his defense of the Mau-Mau terrorists in Kenya. Pritt himself was already in India helping to form a front organization of lawyers. The Madras conference was, in effect, the Fourth All-India Peace Congress, and elections were therefore held: Saifuddin Kitchlew was reëlected president; Romesh Chandra remained general secretary; and Chatur Narain Malaviya, a Congress M.P., became treasurer.[73]

The first important project undertaken after the Madras meeting was the Conference of Asian Countries, held in New Delhi on April 6, 1955. Two hundred and fifty delegates from sixteen countries participated, including a thirty-nine-member delegation from China headed by Kuo Mo-jo. Perhaps because the government of India had been willing to grant visas to these visitors and to those attending the previous Madras conference, it was widely thought that the Conference of Asian Countries enjoyed the approval of the prime minister.[74] At any rate, until the last minute several very important Congressmen were associated with the Conference, most notable of whom was again S. K. Patil, who had agreed to head the delegation from Bombay. Patil had held a press conference in Bombay on April 4, where he discussed plans for the Conference.[75] On April 6 he attended a meeting of the Preparatory Committee in Delhi, but he did not attend the inaugural plenary session of the Conference on the same day. On April 7 he was back in Bombay explaining with evident embarrassment that it was incorrect to say he "withdrew" from the Congress;

---

[72] Chandra, "Build a Broad Platform . . . ," p. 33.
[73] *New Age* (weekly), II (Jan. 9, 1955), p. 13.
[74] *The Hindu* (Madras), April 8, 1955, p. 5.
[75] *Times of India* (Bombay), April 5, 1955, p. 3.

he merely didn't attend because officials in Delhi doubted that the Conference would "create the proper atmosphere for the forthcoming Bandung talks." "We should," he said, "have ascertained the views of the Congress High Command in regard to the Delhi conference; since we did not do it, the fault is ours." [76]

The Conference proceeded as scheduled, and served mainly to provide a forum for Kuo Mo-jo and other Communist delegates to attack the "ruthless and aggressive actions of the American war cliques." [77] But the withdrawal of prominent Congressmen weakened the impact on public opinion. The Communist press accounts of the Conference conspicuously fail to name the Indian participants although much is made of the presence of Mrs. Rameshwari Nehru and Dr. Anup Singh, two important Congress personalities who remained. Mrs. Nehru presided over the main meeting, and Anup Singh presented the report on political questions on behalf of the Indian delegation. The report corresponded with the international Communist line on atomic energy, Formosa, SEATO, and other questions, although to no greater degree than did the contemporary policy of the government.[78]

Since the Delhi conference, the AIPC has placed greater emphasis on drawing into the peace movement a larger number of Gandhian and Christian pacificists and important members of the Congress Party. By August, 1956, there were indications of some notable successes along this line. In that month, Kakasahab Kalelkar, a venerable Gandhian and a member of the Rajya Sabha, presided over the meeting of the AIPC National Executive in Delhi.[79] In September, C. Rajagopalachari, abandoning the hostility he had shown toward the peace movement when he was home minister, addressed the second Madras Peace Conference.[80] In the same month, Romesh Chandra announced plans for the Fifth All-Indian Peace Congress scheduled for November, stating that it would be "of a very different nature from the point of view of participation in it, from the four Congresses which have preceded it." [81]

Before the Fifth Peace Congress could be held, the international peace movement was faced with the problem of deciding what stand it would take on the revolution and Soviet intervention in Hungary. The World Peace Council met in Helsinki November 18, 1956 and issued a communique which admitted that "there exists on this ques-

---

[76] *Ibid.*, April 8, 1955, p. 3.
[77] *New Age* (weekly), II (April 17, 1955), p. 7.
[78] *Ibid.*, p. 6.
[79] *Ibid.* III (Sept. 9, 1956), p. 3.
[80] *Ibid.* IV (Oct. 14, 1956), p. 14.
[81] *Ibid.* IV (Sept. 30, 1956), p. 14.

tion in the World Council, as in national peace movements, serious
divergences and that opposing theses have not permitted the formulation of a common opinion." [82] This disagreement in the world organization was undoubtedly responsible for the postponement of the congress in India, and it was not until May 24, 1957 that the National
Peace Convention was held in Bangalore. By this time the peace
movement had succeeded in focusing attention on a campaign to stop
the testing of nuclear weapons.

TABLE X

OFFICERS ALL-INDIA PEACE COUNCIL, 1952–1957

	3d Congress, Jullundur, 1952	4th Congress, Madras, 1954	5th Congress, Bangalore, 1957
President	Saifuddin Kitchlew	Saifuddin Kitchlew	Saifuddin Kitchlew
General secretary	Romesh Chandra	Romesh Chandra	Romesh Chandra
Vice-presidents	Mulk Raj Anand M. L. Atal Prithvi Raj Kapoor D. D. Kosambi J. C. Kumarappa Vivekananda Mukherji G. M. Sadiq Gurbax Singh Rana Jang Bahadur Singh K. Subramaniam	T. M. Krishnaswamy Aiyar Mulk Raj Anand M. L. Atal Satyapriya Bannerjee (died, 1957) Prithvi Raj Kapoor D. D. Kosambi J. C. Kumarappa Vivekananda Mukherji G. M. Sadiq Gurbax Singh Rana Jang Bahadur Singh S. S. Sokhey K. Subramaniam Pandit Sunderlal Omkarnath Thakur Indulal Yajnik	Mulk Raj Anand M. L. Atal K. Bashyam (Miss) P. Bose J. C. Kumarappa Vivekananda Mukherji Joseph Mundassery G. M. Sadiq Gurbax Singh Rana Jang Bahadur Singh S. S. Sokhey Pandit Sunderlal Omkarnath Thakur Indulal Yajnik
Secretaries	not available	Bala Kondaiah K. Madhavanar Mahesh Dutt Misra V. Parameswaran Lajpat Rai	Dilip Bose K. Madhavanar Chatur Narain Malaviya V. Parameswaran A. Sen
Treasurer	not available	Chatur Narain Malaviya	not available

The events in Hungary neither modified the pro-Soviet orientation
of the All-India Peace Council nor caused any major defections from
its ranks. Indeed, the press accounts of the Bangalore convention sug-

---

[82] The New York Times, Nov. 26, 1956, p. 5.

gest that the pro-Soviet, anti-American emphasis was intensified and support from important non-Communist personalities increased. C. Rajagopalachari, who had only addressed the Madras Peace Conference in September, 1956, inaugurated the Bangalore convention with a speech which concentrated its attack on the Western position on the nuclear issue and called for India's withdrawal from the Commonwealth.[83]

The peace movement has proved to be an effective device with which the Communists can gain influence among the non-Communist intelligentsia and the middle class in general. As long as the threat of nuclear war persists, the All-India Peace Council can perform a useful service for the world Communist movement.

The India-China Friendship Association

The India-China Friendship Association (ICFA) is the youngest of the international-issue fronts, but it may prove to be the most important. The organization originated in Bombay when a local India-China Friendship Association was founded there on May 15, 1951, at the initiative of R. K. Karanjia, editor of the Bombay tabloid *Blitz*. Among the sponsors of this first meeting were Aruna Asaf Ali, then a leader of the Socialist Party, later a member of the Central Committee of the CPI; P. R. Lele, a writer on the staff of *Blitz;* and M. D. Japeth. The blessings of the Chinese government were conveyed by the presence of Ken Mao-ch'ou, first counselor to the Chinese embassy in Delhi. A provisional committee of seven, including Karanjia, Lele, and Amalendu Roy, was set up to carry on the work of the new organization.[84]

Plans for a nation-wide India-China organization did not take shape, however, until May, 1953, when a preliminary India-China Consultative Conference was held in New Delhi. The meeting attracted a number of well-known personalities including N. V. Gadgil, Congress M.P. from Poona and former minister for works, production and supply in the government of India (1947–1952); Dr. Anup Singh, M.P.; and J. C. Kumarappa. Dr. Gyan Chand, former chief of the Financial Division of the International Monetary Fund, was chairman of the Reception Committee, of which Dr. V. K. R. V. Rao, director of the School of Economics of Delhi University, became a member. The meeting was

---

[83] *The Hindu* (Madras), May 26, 1957, p. 5 and *New Age* (weekly), IV (June 2, 1957), p. 16.

[84] *Crossroads*, III, May 18, 1951, p. 16. A year after the Bombay meeting, while Mrs. Vijayalakshmi Pandit's cultural delegation was touring China, a Chinese counterpart organization was set up in Peking, and Mrs. Pandit addressed the inaugural meeting. *Survey of China Mainland Press*, 1952, no. 338, p. 7.

addressed by Mrs. Lakshmi Menon, parliamentary secretary in the Ministry of Foreign Affairs.[85]

The First National Conference of the India-China Friendship Association was held December 11–13, 1953, in Delhi, and was addressed by Ting Si-ling, leader of a Chinese cultural delegation then touring the country. The Conference attracted the support of a number of leading non-Communist figures including Ananthasayanam Ayyangar, deputy speaker of the Lok Sabha; Brahm Prakash, chief minister of Delhi State; and Miss Lilamani Naidu, joint secretary, Ministry of External Affairs. The presidium included Gyan Chand, Saifuddin Kitchlew, General S. S. Sokhey, Gurbax Singh, and Mulk Raj Anand —giving the meeting a strong resemblance to the peace movement. In addition to an Executive Committee of twenty-one and a national council of more than one hundred, the following officers were elected: [86] President: Pandit Sunderlal; chairman, Executive Committee: Gyan Chand; vice-presidents: R. K. Karanjia, Tripurari Chakravarty; general secretary: Chatur Narain Malaviya.

When the Second National Conference of the Association was held in Calcutta, April 20–23, 1955, the Chinese ambassador attended. The following officers were elected: [87] President: Pandit Sunderlal, vice-president AIPC; chairman, National Council: Gyan Chand, former head, Economics Department, Patna University; chairman, National Executive: K. M. Panikkar, former ambassador to China; vice-presidents: Syed Mahmud, minister for external affairs, government of India, (Mrs.) Uma Nehru, Congress M.P. from Uttar Pradesh, Saila Kumar Mukherjee, speaker, West Bengal Legislative Assembly, Tripurari Chakravarty, R. K. Karanjia, editor, *Blitz;* general secretary: Chatur Narain Malaviya, Congress M.P. from Bhopal; secretary: Dwijendra Nandi; treasurer: K. A. Damodara Menon, M.P. from Malabar (elected on the KMPP ticket).

The notable feature of this second Conference is the participation of so many prominent Congressmen and members of the government, and their willingness to accept office in the organization. That persons such as Panikkar and personnel from the Ministry of External Affairs occupied key positions suggests that the government had not only bestowed its good will, but also wanted to keep a close check on the organization's policies. A complete roster of the twenty-one-member National Executive Committee is not available, but in checking over the list of Association officers one is struck by the absence of

---

[85] *Crossroads*, V (May 17, 1953), p. 14.

[86] *New Age* (weekly), I (Dec. 20, 1953), p. 16.

[87] *Ibid.*, II (May 1, 1955), p. 3.

well-known CPI leaders. In both the Indo-Soviet Cultural Society and the AIPC, a known Communist Party leader holds the office of general secretary, but in the ICFA the post is held by a Congress member of parliament, albeit one who has a long record of association with Communist-organized activities.

The speeches and resolutions of the second Conference called for: the withdrawal of the United States from Taiwan; the admission of Communist China to the United Nations; the acceptance of Panch Shila by all states; and free economic and cultural interchange between India and China—all of which are elements of the official policy of the government of India. There was no evidence, in the press reports of the meetings, of a direct attack on the United States.[88]

Precise membership figures for the organization are not available, but *New Age* claimed that there were 60 branch chapters in October, 1953, and 135 in September, 1955, and 140 district and primary branches in February, 1958.[89] The function of these chapters is to disseminate literature concerning China, to arrange for showings of films about China, to entertain visiting Chinese delegations, and in general to perform for Indo-Chinese relations the same services that its sister organization performs for Indo-Soviet relations. Between 1954 and 1958 40 Indian delegations visited China and 30 Chinese delegations visited India.[90]

The Bombay chapter is the most active, due largely to the efforts of R. K. Karanjia who has given the organization enormous publicity in his newspaper, *Blitz*. When the Bombay group held its second conference early in 1956, it was inaugurated by the governor of the state, Harekrushna Mahtab, and was given a special exemption from the ban on public meetings then in force because of the linguistic disturbances. Also present at the meeting were Murarji Vaidya, president of the Indian Merchants' Chamber; Bakshi Dalip Singh, sheriff of Bombay; and Professor C. N. Vakil, director of the Bombay School of Economics and Sociology.[91]

Despite the success of the Bombay branch, the national organization progressed slowly. Karanjia's lieutenant, P. R. Lele, complained in April, 1955, that coördination between the branches was poor and

---

[88] See *Amrita Bazar Patrika* (Calcutta), April 22, 1955, p. 10; April 24, 1955, p. 7; April 25, 1955, p. 5. The conference was ignored by most of the press, which was preoccupied with reporting the Asian-African conference at Bandung that met at the same time.

[89] *New Age* (weekly), I (Oct. 18, 1953), p. 10; II (Sept. 4, 1955), p. 13; and V Feb. 16, 1958, p. 16.

[90] *Blitz*, Feb. 8, 1958, p. 12.

[91] *Blitz*, Feb. 18, 1956, pp. 8-9.

that each knew little of what the others were doing. He also bemoaned the fact that the government of India was "not extending that help to ICFA organization which is its due and without which it cannot do as much as it has the will and potentiality to do." [92] By 1958, however, the ICFA had no reason to complain about the attitude of the government, for when the third national conference was held in Bombay in February, V. K. Krishna Menon, minister of defense, delivered a major policy address from its platform. In the presence of the Chinese ambassador, Menon called upon China to release the six Americans still held prisoner, and at the same time criticized the policies of Western nations which deprived China of her seat in the United Nations.

The main action of the 1958 conference was a decision to circulate a petition calling upon the United Nations "to take immediate steps to ensure that China is represented in the General Assembly, the Security Council and all other bodies of this organization by its rightful representatives—the Government of the People's Republic of China." [93] The following officers were elected: President: Pandit Sunderlal; chairman, National Executive: (Mrs.) Uma Nehru; vice-presidents: Syed Mahmud, Gyan Chand, R. K. Karanjia, Tarachand, M.P., V. H. Krishnan Iyer, Nageshwar Prasad, S. S. Mirajkar; general secretaries: Ch. Brahm Prakash, M.P., Dwijendra Nandi; treasurer: M. Govinda Reddy, M.P. Details of the organizational changes evident in the addition of a second general secretary and the dropping of a chairman of the National Council are not available at this writing.

THE PROFESSIONAL FRONTS

The All-India Progressive Writers' Association

The most important front organization created for specific professional groups is the All-India Progressive Writers' Association (AIPWA). It was organized at a national conference held in Lucknow in 1935 under the presidency of the well-known Hindi writer, Prem Chand. Sarojini Naidu was also present. A second national conference took place in Calcutta in December, 1938, with Rabindranath Tagore presiding, but shortly thereafter the organization disintegrated. [94] The movement was resuscitated in Bengal in April, 1942, when the Anti-

---

[92] P. R. Lele, "Consolidate India-China Friendship Movement," *Blitz*, April 23, 1955, p. 14.

[93] *New Age* (weekly), V (Feb. 16, 1958), p. 16.

[94] Hiren Mukerjee, "Bengal Progressive Writers Get Together," *People's War*, I (Nov. 15, 1942), p. 8.

Fascist Writers' and Artists' Union was formed at a meeting presided over by Ramananda Chatterjee, "doyen of Indian journalism." [95] But the following month S. S. Chauhan, editor of the Hindi monthly, *Hans,* was arrested while in the process of reactivating the national organization.

When the CPI once again received legal status in 1942 a fourth all-India conference was scheduled to meet in Bombay concurrently with the First Congress of the Party. The main purpose of the meeting was to mobilize writers in support of the war effort. The Conference met May 22–25, 1943, with S. A. Dange as president. It was decided to shift the organizational headquarters from Lucknow to Bombay, and a new set of officers was elected. Sajjad Zaheer, an Oxford-educated Communist from Uttar Pradesh, replaced Dr. Abdul Aleem of Lucknow University as general secretary. Bishnu Dey and K. A. Abbas became joint secretaries, and Mama Warerkar was elected treasurer.[96]

In accordance with CPI's emerging strategy of cultivating influence in India's Muslim population, the All-India Conference of Urdu Progressive Writers was held in Hyderabad, October 14–17, 1945. Sarojini Naidu inaugurated the Conference; also present was Maulana Hasrat Mohani, who had been on the periphery of the Communist movement since his association with Satya Bhakta's Indian Communist Party back in 1925. Krishan Chandar and Mulk Raj Anand, also, were present and spoke.[97] Lest this conference appear to give undue emphasis to Urdu, the All-India Conference of Hindi Progressive Writers was held two years later (September 6–9, 1947) in Allahabad.[98] Due to "bitterness and bickerings," the Hindi writers have been unable to form a stable organization, although a second conference was held in Allahabad in December, 1957, and was well attended.[99]

The Fifth Conference of the AIPWA convened in Bombay, May 27–30, 1949, during the time when the CPI was following the leftist strategy of B. T. Ranadive. The Conference had to be held in Bhivandi, outside the city, because permission to hold the meeting within Bombay had been denied; and a delegation of Soviet writers was unable to attend because the government of India had refused to grant them visas. A new executive committee was elected, and Dr. Ram Bilas Sharma, head of the English Department of Balwant Rajput College, Agra, became general secretary.[100]

---

[95] *Loc. cit.*
[96] *People's War,* I (June 6, 1943), p. 6.
[97] *Ibid.,* IV (Nov. 18, 1945), p. 12.
[98] *People's Age,* VI (Oct. 5, 1947), p. 11.
[99] *New Age* (weekly), V (Jan. 12, 1958), p. 15.
[100] *Crossroads,* I (June 10, 1949), p. 14.

Sharma was an appropriate person to head the AIPWA during the period of Ranadive's leadership of the CPI which is evident from the report he prepared for the Sixth AIPWA Conference in 1953, more than two years after leftism had been discredited. "The basic task of progressive writers," he said, "is to defend and enrich our national culture by our literary work. Against what do we defend our national culture? First and foremost, we defend it against the influence of the corrupt and alien culture of the British imperialists." [101]

Sharma also had something to say about the culture of the United States "which seeks to smother the voices of Paul Robeson and Howard Fast." "The culture of the U.S. imperialists means naked and unashamed war propaganda," he said. "We seek to defend our national culture from this foul contagion." Lest this lead his readers to suspect the influence of a particular political party, Sharma hastened to add: "There is no such thing as Communist domination over the PWA. Things are decided here by mutual discussion among writers whether Communist or non-Communist." [102]

The Sixth Conference of the AIPWA met in Delhi, March 6 to 8, 1953. Sharma's report was debated, amended, and adopted, and although the revised version was not published in the Communist press, there is no doubt that his strong language was toned down considerably. The more moderate Krishan Chandar took over the office of general secretary and a new executive committee of twenty was elected.[103] The Conference concluded by passing a resolution of condolences on the death of Stalin and then marching to the Soviet embassy to pay homage to the departed Soviet leader.

The most important project undertaken by the AIPWA in recent years has been the Asian Writers' Conference, held in New Delhi in December, 1956. Under the leadership of Mulk Raj Anand and Congress M.P. Benarsidas Chaturvedi, a preparatory committee was formed in Delhi March 25, 1956, on which numerous writers from the various Indian language regions agreed to serve.[104] When the Committee met with its foreign members for the first time in July, the meeting was addressed by V. K. Krishna Menon, and the members were later received by the president and the prime minister.[105]

The conference was held in New Delhi from December 23 to 28, 1956, and was attended by writers from Burma, Ceylon, China, Japan, Korea, Mongolia, Nepal, Pakistan, Syria, USSR, and Indochina. There

---

[101] Ram Bilas Sharma, *Draft Report to 6th All-India Progressive Writers' Association* (New Delhi: Preparatory Committee, 6th AIPWA, 1953), p. 2.

[102] *Ibid.*, pp. 4, 10.

[103] *Crossroads*, IV (March 22, 1953), p. 11.

[104] *New Age* (weekly), III (June 17, 1956), p. 3.

[105] *Ibid* (Aug. 12, 1956), p. 14.

were thirteen members in the Soviet delegation, and the Chinese delegation included Mao Tun, president of the Chinese Writers' Union and Yeh Shen Tao, vice-minister of education. A number of prominent Indians participated including Humayun Kabir, secretary of the ministry of education, and Prabhakar Padhye, secretary of the Indian Committee for Cultural Freedom and an outspoken critic of communism. Padhye engaged a Chinese delegate in lively debate concerning literary freedom under totalitarian regimes. At the close of the conference the delegates were addressed by the president and vice-president of India and by Prime Minister Nehru himself who had just returned from his visit to the United States and Canada.

Lack of unity has characterized the AIPWA from the outset, and Party-press reports of Communist-sponsored writers' meetings suggest that controversy gets out of control more often than not. Literary questions of form and content, as well as political and social matters, are hotly debated. A report of the Malabar District Progressive Writers' Conference held in May, 1955, states that "some interested quarters were straining their nerves to turn this controversy [over the writings of Sankara Kurup] into unhealthy channels of parochialism and communalism." [106] Ilya Ehrenburg, who was present at this Conference, sat "with a smile on his face when delegate after delegate came on the rostrum to make tearing criticism of his works." Although this incident was related as evidence of Mr. Ehrenburg's good nature, it probably serves better as an indication of his unfamiliarity with the Malayalam language. *New Age* summed up the Conference as having taken steps "to clear the muddled waters" and "to end the mud-slinging in Malayalam literature which passed for literary criticism," and as having opened the way "for principled controversies, criticism without malice and evaluation without prejudice." [107]

The CPI's purpose in the AIPWA and the conferences it sponsors is to infuse contemporary Indian literature with Communist content. Speaking at the Urdu Progressive Writers' Conference in Hyderabad in 1945, Krishan Chandar stated: "I believe that every progressive writer must now, with all the power at his command, support the Communist system of life." [108] This aim has become less explicit in recent years, but remains unchanged.

The Indian People's Theater Association

The Indian People's Theater Association (IPTA), like the AIPWA, was set up to inject Communist ideology into Indian cul-

---

[106] *Ibid.*, II (May 29, 1955), p. 15.
[107] *Loc. cit.*
[108] *People's War*, IV (Nov. 18, 1945), p. 12.

tural life. It was organized in Bombay in May, 1943, when the CPI was holding the First Congress. Traveling dance and drama troupes were organized and sent to many parts of India to perform ballets and plays dealing with Marxian and nationalist themes. The Party claimed that one troupe that toured the country in 1943–44 collected Rs. 200,000 for Bengal famine relief.[109] In 1947 the IPTA reported that during the previous year its 44 branch organizations had presented 52 stage productions and 800 new songs, and had entertained audiences numbering more than five million.[110]

When the IPTA held its seventh conference in Bombay early in 1953, 600 delegates from all parts of the country attended. The following all-India officers were elected: [111] President: Bimal Roy, film producer; vice-presidents: Anna Bhau Sathe, poet and composer, K. Subramaniam, film producer, K. A. Abbas, writer, Abdul Malik, professor and writer, (Mrs.) Surinder Kaur; general secretary: Niranjan Sen, joint secretaries: Jaswant Thakkor, Nirmal Ghosh; treasurer: Sachin Sen Gupta, playwright.

There was an interesting exchange in 1946 between K. A. Abbas and Soli Batliwala concerning the CPI's relationship to the IPTA. Batliwala had been elected to the CPI Central Committee at the First Congress in 1943, but severed his connections with the Party in 1945 because of its interference in his private life. He charged that the IPTA was under Communist domination, saying:

None of your [i.e., Abbas's] colleagues in the IPTA has chosen the IPTA work as a free person, but is under the strictest discipline of the member in charge of IPTA work in the Central Committee. I do not know if you have Com. Krishnan in your executive. But not a single one of your communist colleagues can endorse a single amendment in any discussion however secret that your executive may undertake before having received the sanction of Com. N. K. Krishnan. This applies to persons who act in your plays, who work full time for the organization in varied and different capacities.[112]

Abbas replied that the number of non-Communists, among whom he included himself, whose works had been performed by the IPTA proved the charge hollow.[113]

Nevertheless, the content of IPTA dramas, the political views of its leaders, and the manner in which it is publicized in the Party press leave no doubt that the IPTA is a CPI front. As in other fronts,

---

[109] *People's Age*, IV (Jan. 6, 1946), p. 12.

[110] *Ibid.*, V (May 18, 1947), p. 13.

[111] *Crossroads*, IV (April 26, 1953), p. 9.

[112] Soli Batliwala, *Facts Versus Forgery* (Bombay: National Youth Pub., 1946), pp. 30–31.

[113] *Ibid.*, p. 24.

however, a greater effort has been made in recent years to obscure this fact, and at the 1953 conference the drama commission's report stated only that "broadly speaking, we must glorify those who are on the side of social progress and condemn those who impede this progress." [114] When in late 1957 the CPI line had swung far to the right, *New Age* proclaimed:

> In the new phase of national and international achievements, IPTA has to declare its ideals anew and clarify that it is not a wing of any party and that it cannot be utilized by any party to serve its own interests. Its single aim is to serve the common interest of people's culture, and persons having different political leanings are welcome to join it. This principle has to be realized in practice to leave no doubts in the minds of the people.[115]

New Age announced in December, 1957, that IPTA had been extended temporary recognition by the Ministry of Education's Sangeet Natak Akadami.

All-India Association of Democratic Lawyers

Although no nation-wide front organization for lawyers was established in India before 1954, some activity had already taken place. In August, 1953, the Indian Initiating Committee was formed to help promote the International Conference of Lawyers scheduled to be held in Brussels in November of that year.[116] A Bombay State branch of the International Association of Democratic Lawyers apparently came into existence early in 1954, and at a meeting held in Bombay City an executive council of eight was elected. A. S. Badhan, former Advocate General of Baroda State, was elected president and Daniel Latifi was made secretary.[117]

The All-India Association of Democratic Lawyers was formed at a conference in Calcutta, September 27, 1954, attended by delegates from various parts of the country. The meeting was inaugurated by S. C. Talukdar, president of the Calcutta High Court Bar Association, and resolutions were passed supporting Panch Shila and advocating a ban on the H-bomb and the separation of the executive and judiciary branches of government.[118] Some of the aims of the Association were declared to be that "of defending the status of India as a sovereign democratic Republic, of striving for the preservation, enlargement and extension of the rights and liberties of the people, of

---

[114] *Crossroads*, IV (April 26, 1953), p. 18; see also "IPTA Manifesto," *Indian Literature*, no. 3 (1953), pp. 95–96.

[115] *New Age* (Weekly), V (Dec. 22, 1957), p. 12.

[116] *Crossroads*, V (Aug. 2, 1953), p. 6.

[117] *New Age* (weekly), I (April 25, 1954), p. 8.

[118] *Ibid.*, II (Oct. 17, 1954), p. 10.

defending, both in the courts and outside, persons victimized by un-democratic laws or arbitrary and illegal executive action, and of de-fending rights and liberties and safeguarding world peace." [119] P. R. Das of Patna was elected president, and Daniel Latifi and S. K. Acharya were elected joint secretaries.

The first major project of the new Association was an Asian Law-yers' Conference which was held in Calcutta January 25–30, 1955. About 300 lawyers from 28 countries attended, and all countries of Asia were represented except South Korea, the Philippines, and South Viet Nam.[120] S. M. Bose, former advocate general of Bengal, presided, and the prestige of the meeting was enhanced by the presence of H. C. Mookerjee, governor of West Bengal. The importance attached to the meeting by the international Communist leadership is indicated by the fact that top officials of the International Association of Demo-cratic Lawyers attended: it was represented by its president, D. N. Pritt; its secretary general, Matre Joe Nordmann; and its secretary, Istvan Kovacs.[121]

REGIONAL FRONTS

The strong sentiment in favor of the creation of single-language states, which developed in India after independence, has provided a fertile field for Communist agitation and one in which the device of the front organization is particularly appropriate. Such organiza-tions have functioned with noticeable effectiveness in Andhra, Ma-harashtra, and West Bengal, although it would be a mistake to assume that these were as firmly controlled by the CPI as some of the other front organizations. Indeed, so great is the popular enthusiasm for the causes advocated by the regional fronts that the leaders of various parties are drawn into participation to an extent that makes the locus of power difficult to detect. In Maharashtra, for example, the Com-munists were active in the creation of the Samyukta Maharashtra Samiti (United Maharashtra Society), but the post of general secretary of the Samiti was handed to the Praja Socialist legislator, S. M. Joshi, a man whose political record does not suggest the tractability that the Communists prefer in those who hold office in their fronts. The action committee set up by the Samiti in February, 1956, was composed of two representatives each from the CPI, the Socialist Party, the PSP, the Mazdoor Kisan Party, and Peasants' and Workers' Party, the Revolutionary Socialist Party, the Hindu Mahasabha, the

---

[119] Loc. cit.
[120] Ibid., II (Feb. 6, 1955), p. 15.
[121] Ibid. (Feb. 13, 1955), p. 11.

Bolshevik Party, the Lal Nishan group, and the right-wing Jan Sangh and Ram Rajya Parishad parties.[122] This was hardly a group that could be expected to yield to Communist discipline.

The regional front over which the Communists have been able to secure the most complete control has been the Andhra Mahasabha, an organization which agitated for the inclusion of all Telugu-speaking areas (known as Andhra or Andhradesh) in one state. The Mahasabha, sometimes called the Vishalandhra Mahasabha, was organized in the northern coastal districts of Madras State in 1913 by leaders of the Congress Party. It was primarily a cultural organization concerned with improving the educational standards among the Telugu-speaking people. "It was dominated at that time," a 1950 Communist report on the organization states, "by educated persons from [the] feudal hierarchy." [123]

During the early 1940's, when the Indian nationalist movement began to press the advantage afforded by Britain's preoccupation with the war, political leaders in the Telugu area of Madras State took a more active interest in the Telugu-speaking population across the border in princely Hyderabad. "It was in the beginning of 1940," according to the above-quoted report, "that the Communist Party in Andhra coastal districts established links with the progressive workers and leaders of AMS [Andhra Mahasabha] and won them over to the Communist Party." [124] After the "Quit India" movement in 1942, most leaders of the Congress Party were in jail, and in their absence the CP gained complete control of the Andhra Mahasabha. When the Congress leaders from Andhra were released, beginning in 1943, they immediately set about recapturing the organization. Eventually the movement split, and by the time the State of Andhra was created by the government of India in November, 1953, at least three organizations claimed legitimate descent from the old Andhra Mahasabha. They were the Congress-dominated Vishalandhra Mahasabha, headed by A. Kaleswara Rao from Vijayawada; the Andhra Mahasabha, headed by G. V. Punnaiah Sastry from Guntur; and the Andhra Mahasabha, controlled by the Communist Ravi Narayan Reddy from Hyderabad.

It was through the Andhra Mahasabha that the Communists, in 1948–1950, had organized the agrarian revolt in Telengana which, in some areas, succeeded in replacing governmental authority with

---

[122] *The Hindu* (Madras), Feb. 10, 1956, p. 12.

[123] *On Telengana* (Information Document no. 7 [2]) (n.p.: Communist Party of India, 1950), p. 1.

[124] *Loc. cit.*

peasant soviets. The above-quoted 1950 report states: "Now, AMS had become a mass organization, having one lakh [100,000] members and the old feudal leadership was replaced in 1944 by the younger elements who were won over to the Party." The report continues:

Up to 1947 end [sic], repeated efforts by the Party, under the then reformist leadership, were made to arrive at understanding with . . . Congress leaders to merge AMS under our leadership with the State Congress, through the intermediaries Swami Ramananda Tirth and Marathwada Congress group of Govindas and Bindu. But all these efforts broke down because of their insistence on our giving up anti-feudal struggles and our refusal. Finally, when the All-India States People's Conference banned Communists from being in the States People's organization, these talks ended. It was our carrying on independently partial struggles and exposure of State Congress leaders that ultimately during 1946–47 made the Party the recognized leader of Telengana people's movement.[125]

Here then is a successful example of the type of front organization the Communists would have liked to create in various parts of India among the groups agitating for linguistic states. Their initial success in Telengana was due to timing and to a number of complex factors not present elsewhere. Nowhere else have they been able to establish such complete control over a similar type of organization, although they have certainly made the effort in Maharashtra and in West Bengal.

It is impossible to predict the effect of the reorganization of states, which took place by act of parliament on November 1, 1956, on the political attitudes of specific language groups. If feelings of injustice and discrimination persist they will provide opportunities for further front organization by the Communists. If they do not, it is likely that this area of activity will receive less attention.

"FELLOW TRAVELERS"

The term "fellow traveler" has found great favor among publicists concerned with communism. It is a term which, in the United States, has become a convenient weapon for character assassination, largely because its lack of precision makes legal redress difficult for those to whom it has been unjustly applied.

In this study, the term "Communist" has been reserved for those who have taken an active part in the Party organization and have submitted to its discipline. So limited a definition creates the need for another term to describe the many who accept Communist ideology, support a large measure of Party policy, or frequently join known Party members in common political activity. The term "fellow trav-

---

[125] Ibid., p. 2.

eler" is the most obvious choice to describe such a person, but it is a term which should be used with caution, and with a degree of judgment for which it is difficult to establish criteria. For example, S. K. Patil could hardly be called a fellow traveler merely because he appeared two or three times on Communist peace-movement platforms; but J. C. Kumarappa, on the other hand, despite his long-standing Gandhian associations and his well-known disagreement with Marxism, has been associated with so many Communist-sponsored activities that the label is appropriate.

The natural abode of the fellow traveler is, of course, the front organization. This is not to say that all members of fronts are fellow travelers, for some may be thoroughly anti-Communist while others may actually be Party members. But the front is a body toward which fellow travelers gravitate; it is a school where they receive advanced indoctrination; and it is a missionary society through which they endeavor to increase their numbers.

The data on Indian fellow travelers suggest a few comments which may provide an insight into Indian political processes. The first concerns the reasons why some Indians become fellow travelers.

Examination of the background of non-Communists who are regularly associated with various front organizations shows that many of them have been unable to achieve sufficient recognition in their chosen fields of professional or public endeavor or, having once achieved it, have been shunted aside because of age or other circumstances. For such people, the front organization can often fill a definite need. The organization can confer a sense of importance by sending them abroad to international conferences. It can give them extensive publicity in the Communist press, and can mobilize crowds to hear them speak. Such recompense is attractive to those who feel themselves deprived of proper status in the conventional areas of public life. To those who have already won national recognition, the front may provide a means of remaining a little longer in the limelight.

If membership files were open for examination, one might draw useful conclusions about the professional groups represented. But in spite of the limited information available, one fact emerges: that a large number of writers and journalists have joined front organizations. No doubt this may be ascribed to the deliberate CPI policy of proselytizing the "communicators" in the society, through whom they hope to broaden the audience for their propaganda. This explains why so many motion picture personalities—actors, producers, directors, screenwriters—have also been associated with the various fronts.

Another element underlying their participation in front activity is the idealism unaccompanied by political sophistication which appears to characterize many Indian fellow travelers. Among them may be found, for example, a number who call themselves Gandhians. This is a vague term, and there is much controversy among Gandhi's followers as to who is correctly pursuing the goals of the Mahatma. But in general the term has been freely used in India to designate those who subscribe to Gandhi's views on nonviolence and economics and who have worked in one of the organizations set up to foster his teachings. Since Gandhians are pacifists, they are susceptible to Communist peace campaigns. To them, the abolition of military alliances and the banning of nuclear weapons have seemed aims worthy of support regardless of the implications for world politics—even when the implications are understood, and often they are not. Among the Gandhians who have actively supported the peace movement are Pandit Sunderlal, J. C. Kumarappa, Mahesh Dutta Misra, Mrs. Rameshwari Nehru, Chatur Narain Malaviya, Ravi Shankar Vyas, and Vinubha G. Shah. It should be added, however, that the importance of some of them in the Gandhian movement would be questioned by certain of the Mahatma's disciples. But there is little doubt that their reputation as Gandhians is sufficient to give the peace movement an aura of legitimacy valuable at the mass level.

Judging from their speeches and writings, the intellectual caliber of the Indian fellow traveler is not impressive. For example, most members of front-sponsored delegations to Communist countries have shown a singular inability to give a balanced account of what they saw. Many have written romanticized reports that claim for China and the Soviet Union virtues even beyond what those countries claim for themselves. "Many of them gape with overawed eyes at whatever they see in the country they happen to be visiting," complained one of the more sophisticated fellow travelers. At the same time they "make ill-informed remarks about the alleged backwardness of their own country, often to the acute embarrassment of their hosts." It was a mistake, he concluded, to send on these delegations "Marxist intellectuals who know more about the Soviet First Five Year Plan than about India's Second Five Year Plan." [126]

Together with this general fatuity, many Indian fellow travelers are characterized by a saccharine romanticism. Their speeches are overdramatized, heavy with platitudes and clichés. Self-praise is com-

---

[126] K. A. Abbas in *Blitz*, Sept. 15, 1956, p. 16. For an interesting analysis of the observations of Indian visitors to China, see Margaret W. Fisher and Joan V. Bondurant, "The Impact of Communist China on Visitors from India," *Far Eastern Quarterly*, XV (Feb. 1956), pp. 249–265.

mon and unsubtle, and they frequently labor at creating a heroic image of themselves.[127]

On the other hand, there are a few intellectuals who are well-informed and shrewdly aware of the international and domestic political implications of the organizations in which they participate. Of this group, the most important are in Bombay, notably Mulk Raj Anand, R. K. Karanjia, K. A. Abbas, and P. R. Lele, the last three associated with the tabloid *Blitz*. There is no evidence that any of them are Communists in the sense of actively participating in the Party as such, but they all have long records of association with Communist causes. Karanjia has been a leader in the ICFA and the peace movement, and has shown a remarkable ability to anticipate the international Communist line, on occasion in advance of the CPI leadership. Yet despite his obvious sympathy for international communism he has managed to remain on reasonably good terms with the government of India. This suggests political skill of a highly developed sort, and prompted K. M. Panikkar, himself a dexterous politician, to say of Karanjia that he was a man "who had an appreciation of some of the essential issues of politics." [128]

More interesting than Karanjia, however, is K. A. Abbas, journalist, author, and film scenarist, who has been associated with many Communist-front groups for years. Abbas describes himself as a non-Communist, yet there is no doubt that he tries to play a role not only in determining CPI policy, but in influencing the international Communist movement as well. The most interesting evidence of this is an article he wrote for J. B. Powell's *China Monthly Review* when he visited China as a member of Pandit Sunderlal's 1952 delegation. There are several remarkable points in the article, especially the criticisms of the Chinese regime. Abbas speaks of the "vicious circle of secrecy, censorship, and secrecy, and the limitation of personal liberties" in China; of the official indifference to China's cultural traditions; and of the "drab uniformity of the blue trousers and coats that men and women, boys and girls are wearing in China today." These criticisms obliged the editor to preface the article with a long rebuttal, and at least two subsequent articles in the magazine were labeled as replies to Abbas. But the article was most significant for its main thesis:

The daring experiment of "People's Democracy"—i.e., the working class leading a coalition of different parties, united on a patriotic "Common Program"—appears to us as far more significant than many people in China seem to imagine. It sets a new

[127] See biographical sketch of Prithvi Raj Kapoor in *Who's Who*, Indian Council of States (New Delhi: Council of States Secretariat, 1952), p. 76.

[128] K. M. Panikkar, *In Two Chinas* (London: Allen & Unwin, 1955), p. 138.

pattern of social revolution that is as different from the orthodox concept of revolution as Marxism was different from the Eighteenth Century liberalism of England.
. . . The Chinese people have confounded and disproved the orthodox theorists of
revolution who have laid down that peasants, simply because they were peasants,
would never be able to be the vanguard of a revolution—a privilege that they reserved for the industrial proletariat, and by implication, for the industrially advanced
countries of the West. They have proved that the farmers of Shensi and Hopeh and
Hunan, though they may have never handled machinery in a factory, when properly
led, can be greater revolutionaries than the highly industrialized workers of England
and America.

So I look at China's revolution not only in terms of what it has achieved for China
but also in terms of the path it has blazed for other countries, particularly of Asia.
The Chinese people have revolutionized not only a vast country but the whole continent of revolutionary thought—they have revolutionized the very concept of revolution!

These wider implications of their revolution, if they will permit me to say so,
confer historical privileges as well as impose historical responsibilities on them. Will
they be able, for instance, to expand the concept of "People's Democracy" to the international field—to bring together the various countries professing or practicing different ideologies on a "Common Program" of peace? [129]

It requires little imagination to see that when Abbas refers to "orthodox theorists" he means Russian theorists. By telling the Chinese that
they had revolutionized revolution, he was going far beyond what
Chinese theorists were themselves prepared to claim, however true
it might have been. That Powell's journal would print such blatant
heresy is testimony to the important role of men like Abbas in the
scheme of international communism.

Abbas, then, is a prime example of the fellow travelers who are by
no means mere puppets of the Central Committee and who, since
the Party cannot ignore them and needs their support, may exert
considerable influence on Communist policy. They may also influence
factional disputes within the Party—the *Blitz* group frequently attacks
the leftists in the CPI, and Karanjia has referred in print to "the saner
fringe of the Communist Party led by P. C. Joshi." [130] Hence when the
fronts, as often happens, become arenas for intra-Party competition,
non-Party members may help bring about a change of leadership in
the Party itself. Certainly Joshi's non-Communist friends in the peace
movement were useful to him in his bid to get back into the CPI.

Thus, although the front organization is one of the tools with which
the Communists hope to achieve their ends, it may also provide a
means by which those who are not Communists, or not even sympathetic to communism, can influence Communist policy. This may be

[129] K. A. Abbas, "Discovery of China," *China Monthly Review*, CXXII (Feb.,
1952), pp. 157–158.
[130] *Blitz*, Feb. 4, 1956, p. 3.

the aim of a few shrewd politicians among the Socialists, as well as of those naïve Gandhians who regard love as their primary political weapon. Certainly, if one regards Communists as being amenable to education in democracy, the front organization might seem a useful forum from which to begin. Moreover, non-Communists could conceivably become influential enough in the front organizations to wrest control from the Communist elements, or at least force them to modify their policies. This may already have happened in the ICFA.

In summary, then, the front is a weapon with which the CPI hopes to force entry into the upper classes and the intelligentsia. But it is double-edged, and if clumsily employed can endanger the Party itself. Thus the success of the front organizations is one of the most useful indices of the status of communism in India.

18 THE AGIT-PROP INSTRUMENT

The term "propaganda," relieved of pejorative connotations, may properly be used to signify any partisan communication intended to influence attitudes and beliefs. Thus defined, propaganda is an instrument of any political party, in any time and place. But Communist parties, which by their nature are compelled to proselytize, have used propaganda with remarkable determination and design. For them, the art of persuasion has become a crucial element of political action.

This compulsion to proselytize is the product of several inherent necessities. There is, first, a doctrinal necessity. It was pointed out earlier that the assumptions of a Communist party as to its destiny lay upon it a sacred obligation to create an effective organization; in the same way these assumptions oblige it to make effective use of propaganda. Secondly, there are certain practical necessities. A Communist party is often unable or unwilling to use other normal forms of political operation such as parliamentary or electoral activity; propaganda may therefore appear to be the best available substitute. And finally, there may be a personal necessity. A Communist is commonly a zealot, moved by the intensity of his faith or of his personal commitment to the Party to assume the mantle of the prophet.

In Communist usage the term "propaganda" has a specialized meaning and is differentiated from "agitation." The distinction is, in the broadest terms, between the general and the specific. Propaganda is the dissemination of complex ideas to select audiences; agitation is the dissemination of simple ideas, often in the form of mere slogans, to a mass audience. (In this chapter, the over-all program of propaganda and agitation will be referred to as "agit-prop.") In theory, every Party member is a full-time agitator and propagandist. As an agitator, he must, through the spoken or written word, make daily contact with the masses, stimulating them to action with elementary political slogans related to immediate issues. And as a propagandist he must address a reasoned exposition of the Party's policy to smaller, more sophisticated groups, with the aim of a fuller conversion.

Detailed examination of Communist propaganda and agitation at the grass-roots level in India must await further research on politics in that country. At present it is necessary to focus on the most striking —and probably the most important—feature of the CPI's activity in this sphere: its publishing program.

The CPI Press

PUBLICATIONS

Throughout its history the Indian Communist movement has devoted a large part of its resources, human and material, to maintaining an official Party press. Even in the early stages of its development, when its membership and organization were negligible, the CPI could boast an impressive array of publications. Propaganda seemed almost to take precedence over organization. Later, whether the Party's fortunes rose or fell, it consistently sustained an impressive publishing program; even in periods of disruption, such as the years 1949–1951 when the Party could carry out little organized activity, it usually maintained a steady flow of publications. Examination of the history and scope of the CPI's publishing apparatus shows how intensely and persistently the CPI has applied itself to publishing as a means of agit-prop.

The CPI has published two types of official central organs—a weekly newspaper intended largely for mass agitation, and a monthly theoretical journal serving as a "propaganda" medium.

Central newspapers:—The earliest Communist periodicals in India were S. A. Dange's *Socialist* in Bombay, Ghulam Hussain's Urdu weekly, *Inquilab* (Revolution), and the Bengali organ of the Labor Swaraj Party, *Langal* (The Plough). But these were the mouthpieces of localized Communist nuclei and could not claim to be central Party organs.[1]

---

[1] For a survey history of the CPI press, see the inaugural issue of *New Age* (weekly), I (Oct. 4, 1953), p. 3.

The functions of a central organ were first filled by the newspapers published abroad by M. N. Roy (see table). Published in various European cities and relatively free of censorship or financial problems, Roy's newspapers appeared with impressive regularity and penetrated India in substantial volume despite British efforts to impound them at the ports of entry.

But it was not until the latter half of the 1930's that the CPI possessed a central newspaper, *National Front,* originating in India itself. Since the Party was illegal, it could not openly identify *National Front* as an official Communist publication, but the paper served that function. When the Party was legalized in 1942, it inaugurated the weekly *People's War.* And from that date, with only one interruption of six months in 1949, the CPI has maintained a central newspaper, although it has appeared under various names.

The central newspaper has ordinarily been published in an English edition and in a number of Indian language editions as well; *People's War* and *People's Age* were issued in Hindi, Urdu, and Marathi, and *New Age* has appeared in an increasing number of special language editions.

TABLE XI

Central Newspapers, CPI

Name	Place	Dates	Editor
Vanguard of Indian Independence (also called *Advance Guard*)	Berlin, Zurich, Annecy	May, 1922–Dec., 1924	M. N. Roy
Masses of India	Paris	Jan., 1925–1928	M. N. Roy
National Front	Bombay	Feb., 1938–(1940?)	P. C. Joshi
People's War	Bombay	Aug. 2, 1942–Nov. 18, 1945	P. C. Joshi, G. Adhikari
People's Age	Bombay	Nov. 25, 1945–Feb. 20, 1949	G. Adhikari, M. B. Rao, V. M. Kaul
New Age, Current Affairs, People's Herald *	Bombay	Feb. 27, 1949–April 13, 1949	V. M. Kaul, G. S. Byndor, Y. M. Rao
Crossroads	Bombay	April 29, 1949–Sept. 27, 1953 **	Romesh Thapar, V. M. Kaul
New Age	Madras, Delhi	Oct. 4, 1953–present	P. Ramamurti, Bhupesh Gupta

* These name changes resulted from government efforts to ban the CPI press.
** Interrupted by government ban, July 22–December 9, 1949.

The Party has rarely revealed the circulation of its central organs. At the beginning of 1943, *People's War* claimed a circulation of 33,000 in all editions,[2] *Crossroads*, in 1949, claimed only 10,000,[3] and in 1954 the circulation of the official Party organ had dropped still further, for according to Party sources the circulation of *New Age* was only about 8,000.[4] But this decline presumably resulted from the instability of the Party in the crisis period 1949–1953; the circulation of *New Age* has probably increased considerably in more recent years. In any event, circulation statistics are inadequate as an index to the penetration of CPI publications; actual readership figures would be many times larger, due to the Indian practice of passing newspapers from hand to hand.

The technical quality of the CPI's central newspapers has been uniformly high. They have been produced with impressive typographical competence, and in this respect compare well with the commercial press of India. They are profusely illustrated with cartoons and photographs, and in size and layout resemble an American tabloid.

The content of the official newspaper has been aimed chiefly at "agitation." It has been the Party's principal carrier for slogans on the issues of the day, and much of its space is devoted to presenting the Party's interpretation of current events—local, national, and international. Major articles are often written by Party leaders themselves, although the bulk of the material is provided by staff journalists or by local correspondents. In addition, articles by foreign Communist leaders, interpreting international issues or affairs of their countries, are common features. Some space is given to reports of internal Party developments, such as local and provincial conferences or expulsions and suspensions of members. In sum, the CPI's weekly organ is primarily designed to mobilize the public and the Party rank and file to political action.

Theoretical journals:—A CPI theoretical journal first appeared in about 1937, under the name *New Age*, published monthly and edited by S. V. Ghate. It was suspended during World War II, but reappeared in 1945 as *Marxist Miscellany*, edited by G. Adhikari and issued irregularly for several years. In 1947 it was replaced by a new journal, *Communist*, although several issues of *Marxist Miscellany* were pub-

---

[2] N. K. Krishnan, *Forgery Versus Facts* (Bombay: People's Publishing House, 1943), p. 8.

[3] *Crossroads*, I (July 22, 1949), p. 1.

[4] E. M. S. Namboodiripad, *On Organization* (Delhi: Communist Party of India, 1954), p. 68.

lished later. Under the editorship of an unidentified Editorial Board, *Communist* appeared almost monthly until the end of 1950; then, after a lapse of about two years during which no theoretical journal was published, it reappeared under the earliest title, *New Age*. It is properly designated *New Age* (monthly) to distinguish it from the weekly newspaper, *New Age*. Up to the time of writing, it has been edited by A. K. Ghosh, general secretary of the Party.

The CPI's theoretical journal primarily prints general pronouncements on the fundamentals of Party policy, along with frequent expositions of Marxist-Leninist philosophy. Reprints from the foreign Communist press, and particularly from the Russian journals, have consistently formed a substantial part of its content, and in many issues they fill most of its pages. The journal is plainly designed to educate a small audience of Party members and intellectual sympathizers in the basic features of CPI strategy and tactics.

Books and pamphlets:—The third element of the CPI central press— and agit-prop—is comprised of books and pamphlets. The Party maintains its own publishing company, the People's Publishing House, Ltd. (PPH), located in a modern office building next door to the Central Committee offices in Delhi. The PPH has its own printing facilities through a subsidiary, the New Age Printing Press, housed in the same building.

By keeping prices as low as possible the CPI tries to insure that its publications will reach a broad audience. The average pamphlet, plainly but competently printed and containing between 15 and 30 pages, costs from three to five cents; booklets of 80 to 100 pages cost about 25 cents; and a book running to 350 or 500 pages costs between $1 and $1.50. The subscription rate for the weekly Party newspaper is Rs. 12 per year, and that for the monthly theoretical journal Rs. 6 (about $2.62 and $1.26).

Although comparisons can be based only on estimates, the CPI appears to produce a greater volume and variety of partisan books and pamphlets than any other Indian party. Only the Indian National Congress rivals it, although the Praja Socialist Party has also issued a substantial number of publications.

The extent and diversity of the CPI's output may be inferred from the PPH catalogues. The 1954 catalogue, for example, offers seventy-five major approved publications, including five published under another imprimatur but distributed by the PPH. The categories, according to subject matter, include India, China, the Soviet Union, World

Affairs, History and Biography, Art and Literature, Economics, and Marxism.[5]

One of the most striking features of the list is the fact that only a small proportion of the publications are by Indians about India: of the seventy-five titles, only twenty-three are on Indian subjects, and several of these are by foreign authors. Two-thirds of all items listed are by non-Indians.

Only English-language materials are included in this catalogue. But the CPI also produces a great number of vernacular pamphlets and books; not only does the PPH print vernacular editions of the works published in English, but the provincial units publish their own materials in their own languages.

The vernacular press:—The newspapers and journals published by the provincial units of the Party in the various regional languages constitute another important element of the CPI publishing program.

These publications appeared earlier than the central newspaper. By the late 1920's, many branches of the Workers' and Peasants' Party were putting out regular weekly newspapers: the Bengal unit produced *Ganavani,* edited by Muzaffar Ahmed; P. C. Joshi edited a Hindi journal, *Kranti Kari,* for the branch in United Provinces; the Bombay branch published *Kranti* in the Marathi language; and the Punjab unit produced *Mehnat-Kash* in Urdu. Other local Communist newspapers in this period included *Payam-e-Mazdoor* in Urdu, *Kirti* in Punjabi, and *Jagaran* in Bengali.

---

[5] *Catalogue of Books, 1954* (Bombay: People's Publishing House, n.d.), 41 pp. The following are representative of the publications offered:

India: R. Palme Dutt, *India Today* (2d revised Indian edition), 590 pp.; Indrajit Gupta, *Capital and Labour in the Indian Jute Industry,* 64 pp.; Kartar Singh, *Kashmir and Imperialist Intervention,* 40 pp.

China: Mao Tse-tung, *China's New Democracy* (4th Indian edition), 44 pp.; *Stalin on China,* 106 pp.

The Soviet Union: W. P. and Zelda K. Coates, *Soviets in Central Asia,* 240 pp.; *Soviet Cinematography,* 244 pp.; E. Frolov, *Industrialization Without Foreign Loans,* 40 pp.

World Affairs: Joseph Starobin, *Viet-Nam Fights for Freedom,* 62 pp.; T. Ganesh, *Colonialism in Africa,* 16 pp.

History and Biography: Alexander Trachtenberg, *History of May Day* (2d Indian edition), 26 pp.; Emi Siao, *Mao Tse-tung: His Childhood and Youth,* 76 pp.

Art and Literature: G. V. Plekhanov, *Art and Social Life,* 252 pp.; Harindranath Chattopadhyaya, *I Sing of Man,* 74 pp.

Economics: Leo Huberman, *Man's Worldly Goods* (3d Indian edition), 280 pp.

Marxism: Maurice Cornforth, *Dialectical Materialism,* 172 pp.; J. Stalin, *Marxism and the National and Colonial Question,* 258 pp.; Liu Shao-chi, *On the Party,* 116 pp.

These journals were discontinued as a result of the government repression which accompanied the Meerut Conspiracy Case. Some of them reappeared briefly in the 1930's under different names, but were again suspended because of government repression; these included *Din Mazur, Marx-Panthi,* and *Gana Sakti* in Bengali, *Prabhatam* in Malayalam, *Kranti* in Marathi, *Navasakti* in Telugu, and *Janasakti* in Tamil.

With the legalization of the Party in 1942, the CPI began to build a systematic array of official provincial newspapers. The first were *Janayuddha* in Bengali, *Prajasakti* in Telugu, *Deshabhimani* in Malayalam, *Janasakti* in Tamil, *Muktiyuddha* in Oriya, and *Jange-e-Azadi* in Punjabi. In 1943 their total circulation was 34,350, according to the Party.[6] To this list was soon added *Janasakti* in Kannada.

Other provincial journals were inaugurated after World War II, but in 1948–1949 the CPI provincial press was yet a third time temporarily silenced by government bans; by this time, however, it had shown marked growth, as is indicated by the circulation of some of the papers at the time of their suppression. The Bengali newspaper, then called *Swadhinata,* claimed 100,000 "effective" circulation; the press-run of *Prajasakti* was 15,000, that of *Deshabhimani* was 15,000, that of *Janasakti* was 10,000, and *Munnani,* another Malayalam newspaper, had a circulation of 5,00.[7] Three of these were daily newspapers and two were weeklies.

By 1953, the vernacular Communist press had again been revived. It now included five dailies (*Swadhinata, Vishal Andhra, Desabhimani, Navalokam,* and *Naya Zamana*) and nine weeklies (*Naya Hindusthan, Janyug, Janasakti, Navayugam, Jana Shakti, Aruna, Navi Dunia, Janasakti* of Bihar, and *Matamat*). Most of the important regional languages were represented, including Hindi, Urdu, Bengali, Telugu, Malayalam, Tamil, Kannada, and Oriya.

The later growth of the provincial press has been similarly erratic, and financial crises have occasionally forced temporary suspension. But on the whole, this section of the CPI press has continued to expand.

Very little recent data are available on these vernacular publications, and because they are issued in such a wide variety of languages, a thorough analysis of their contents is impossible here. But their significance should not be underestimated, for they reach a much broader audience than the English-language publications of the central press. Moreover, to the extent that the provincial press is not a

---

[6] Krishnan, *Forgery Versus Facts,* p. 6.
[7] *People's Age,* IV (July 4, 1948), p. 6.

mere carbon copy of the central press, and devotes itself to the provincial scene, it has more intimate meaning for that audience. To the outside observer who naturally focuses on the national level of CPI policy and activity, the Party's English-language publications may appear to be the most important instruments of its agit-prop apparatus. But further study of the provincial press may well show that it is a more effective medium.

Front publications:—In addition to the open or official CPI publications, there are the publications of the Communist-influenced mass organizations and front groups. While these publications are not all equally subject to CPI discipline, they must be counted among the channels through which the Party disseminates significant parts of its message to the Indian public.

Most of the mass and front organizations maintain regular journals: the All-India Peace Council publishes the monthly magazine *Peace;* the now-defunct All-India Friends of the Soviet Union produced the *Indo-Soviet Journal,* and its successor, the Indo-Soviet Cultural Society, publishes *ISCUS;* the Progressive Writers' Association publishes *Indian Literature;* the Indian People's Theater Association publishes *Unity;* and the All-India Students' Federation has produced a regular journal, *Student.* The All-India Trade Union Congress has in several periods published a *Trade Union Record.*

Many of these organizations also issue pamphlets and brochures, the content of which depends of course on their "clientele" (see chapters 16 and 17). These publications are distributed through the regular sales agencies for CPI publications, as well as through facilities provided by the mass and front organizations themselves. Systematic data on the volume or circulation of these publications is not available, but it is certain that they importantly complement the Party's output.

DISTRIBUTION FACILITIES

For the promotion and distribution of its publications the CPI makes use of both conventional and unique devices.

The Party does not neglect the usual commercial channels; wherever possible it consigns its publications to ordinary book dealers, and in order to make its wares more attractive it offers a discount which is considerably higher than the standard rate. While the largest book stores, which cater primarily to a foreign clientele, ordinarily eschew partisan publications, the ubiquitous bazaar book stalls often display Communist materials.

Alongside these commercial outlets, the CPI has built its own distributive network consisting of a chain of official Party book stores established in many Indian cities, large and small. These stores are agents for the People's Publishing House and deal exclusively in approved Communist publications. Perhaps the best known of these is the Delhi Book Center, which in location and appearance compares favorably with all but the best of the capital's book stores.

Furthermore, the CPI can and does use every Party member as a salesman for its literature. Local units are periodically required to organize "literature sales squads" to peddle Party publications on the city streets, at factory gates, or from door to door. Even Party leaders participate in these special campaigns; Communist members of parliament have on occasion appeared as salesmen on the sidewalks of New Delhi's main shopping center.

Other distribution devices include mobile book shops and temporary stalls set up for special occasions. In many local units it is customary for members to make regular rounds to the bazaars and outlying villages with "shops" mounted on bicycles or motorcycles. And where large crowds gather for a fair or a festival, or even at centers of religious pilgrimage, there can often be seen a book stall erected and manned by members of the local CPI unit. After the Kumbh Mela in 1954, a rare religious gathering which drew enormous masses of Hindu worshippers to Allahabad, the CPI reported that it had sold Rs. 1,500 (about $315) worth of Party literature—representing many thousands of booklets and pamphlets costing a few cents each.[8]

It is evident, then, that the Party seizes every opportunity to bring its literature directly to the public, in order to disseminate its message as widely as possible.

ADMINISTRATION OF THE PARTY PRESS

For administering its publishing activities, the CPI has set up a special organization designed to insure centralized control. The CPI constitution requires that the Party's publication program be directed by the Central Committee and that its members shall "divide among themselves" such responsibilities as that of "Editor of the central Party organ and central Party publications" and "Party press and distribution of literature." [9] The constitution also provides that the Central Committee must approve the editors of the provincial organs, and that these editors must be selected from among the members of the provincial committees. Moreover, it states that the provincial units of

---

[8] *New Age,* I (April 4, 1954), p. 12.
[9] *Constitution of the Communist Party of India* (Delhi: Communist Party of India, 1954), p. 17.

the Party may produce and distribute literature only "if allowed by the Central Committee." [10]

As a rule, the editors of the CPI's central organs have been members not merely of the Central Committee but of the Politbureau (exceptions include M. B. Rao, V. M. Kaul, and Romesh Thapar, who were apparently not even members of the Central Committee); in several instances the general secretaries themselves have served as editors.

Moreover, in order to institutionalize central supervision of the Party press as a whole, the Politbureau has formed an Agit-Prop Subcommittee from among its members, and the Central Committee, also, chooses an Agit-Prop Committee.[11] In actual practice the work of supervising the Party press has evidently fallen to interested persons rather than to a unit of the Party, and effective coördination is a goal rather than a reality (see chapter 15). But centralization remains a fixed principle of the CPI's agit-prop program, as it does in other spheres of its activity.

The mechanics of central control of the CPI press are illustrated by several instances when the Party took disciplinary action. In one case, Ali Sardar Jafri, of the editorial staff of *Indian Literature,* was censured by the Central Committee for permitting the publication of heretical material—a poem by Sri Sri entitled "Salute to Russia" which stated that the ideas of "Marx, Engels, Bakunin, Bukharin and Kropotkin" were fullfilled in the USSR. According to the Central Committee, by ignoring advice to refrain from publishing the poem, Jafri had "failed to discharge his political responsibilities" as a member of the CPI.[12]

In another case, Govind Vidyarthi, of the staff of *Crossroads,* was punished by the Central Committee for his part in publishing an unauthorized book that was judged "an anti-Party work." He and his associates in this enterprise were debarred from responsible Party positions for various periods.[13]

As the above examples suggest, the CPI agit-prop organization does not operate with flawless effectiveness. Its apparatus has been impaired by certain internal weaknesses, and Party publications themselves are replete with self-criticism on this score.

A Central Committee resolution of 1954, for example, contains a

---

[10] *Ibid.,* p. 13.
[11] In 1951 this Committee was said to include S. A. Dange, S. V. Deshpande, Ali Sardar Jafri, Romesh Chandra, and Victor Kaul. See M. R. Masani, *The Communist Party of India* (London: Derek Verschoyle, 1954), p. 124. More recent data are not available.
[12] *Party Letter,* April 30, 1953, p. 3.
[13] *Ibid.,* p. 4.

number of specific complaints.[14] It declares, first, that Party propaganda and agitation tend to be "extremely general and diffused"
and are characterized more by "vehemence" than by "effectiveness."
Thus the tendency toward scholasticism—toward an avoidance of
real grass-roots Indian issues—has admittedly affected CPI agit-prop
as it has inner-Party debate. Moreover, the resolution acknowledges
the parrotlike quality of Party agit-prop, noting that it is marked by
"repetitiveness and hurling of slogans." Finally, it chastizes members
for insufficient attention to their duties in this realm, claiming that
propaganda and agitation constitute "one of the most neglected spheres
of our activity." It notes, in particular, that agit-prop activity had been
confined to the press and to public speeches, while the technique of
"individual verbal propaganda" was neglected.

But such self-criticism, while revealing certain flaws, also serves
to underline the persistent determination with which the CPI addresses itself to the problem of making the best possible use of the
agit-prop weapon.

Foreign Communist Propaganda

Viewed in a broader perspective, CPI agit-prop is merely part of
the stream of international Communist agit-prop that daily flows into
India. In order to see the whole picture of Communist efforts at persuasion in India, it is necessary, therefore, to examine the means by
which international communism carries its message to the Indian
public.

RADIO, FILMS, PUBLICATIONS

International Communist agit-prop uses two media which are
inaccessible to the CPI: radio and films. The Indian radio network is
nationalized and has thus far refused to broadcast paid political messages, but Radio Moscow, using transmitters in Central Asia, can be
heard on most radios in India. By 1955 Soviet stations were broadcasting music and political commentary to India for a total of 15¾ hours
a week in English, 5¼ hours in Hindi, and 8¾ hours in Bengali.[15]
These broadcasts were listed in the radio logs of many Indian newspapers, along with the Voice of America and other foreign broadcasts.
Peking Radio, also, broadcasts to India, but only in English and on
a smaller scale.

---

[14] *Resolution on Party Organization* (Delhi: Communist Party of India, 1954),
p. 16.
[15] Evron M. Kirkpatrick, ed., *Target: The World; Communist Propaganda Activities in 1955* (New York: The Macmillan Company, 1956), p. 239.

Soviet films are also available to Indian audiences. A total of fifty-six films, including twenty full-length features, entered India from Communist countries in 1954.[16] Like American and British films, which are imported in far greater numbers, the Communist films must be approved for exhibition by the Indian government. According to the CPI press, in 1953 six foreign Communist films were denied exhibition certificates.[17]

There are theaters in the major Indian cities which regularly show Communist-bloc films, and special front organizations have been set up to promote private showings. An example is the People's Educational Film Center in Calcutta, formed in 1952, which arranged showings of Communist films to trade unions, youth groups, and other audiences.[18]

In addition, the Communist-bloc countries have made intensive efforts to promote their films at international film festivals in India, and the Soviet Union is one of the few countries which have been willing to reciprocate by promoting Indian films in their own theaters. Moreover, in 1956 the Soviet government was instrumental in promoting a joint venture between Mosfilm Studios and K. A. Abbas in India, to produce a film on the life of Afanasy Nikitin, the fifteenth-century Russian traveler to India.

It is on the field of publications, however, that the Communist-bloc countries place the greatest emphasis in their agit-prop program. Soviet and Chinese journals in English, such as *Soviet Russia, New Times,* and *People's China,* are available in book and magazine stalls throughout India, as are international Communist publications such as *For a Lasting Peace . . . .* Also available is a Hindi edition of *Soviet Land,* entitled *Soviet Bhumi.* The Indian Communist Party receives, free of charge, a flood of books from the Communist countries, and these are distributed through its regular channels at very low prices. The foreign Communist material is supplemented by the publications of the Soviet news agency, Tass; its New Delhi office not only issues official press releases to Indian newspapers, but also produces occasional pamphlets for general circulation.

Delegations

Still another channel for agit-prop has become increasingly important in recent years—the "live" media, consisting of delegations to and from the Communist-bloc countries. Many of these delegations

---

[16] *Ibid.,* p. 242.
[17] *New Age,* I (Dec. 13, 1953), p. 14.
[18] *New Age,* I (Jan. 17, 1954), p. 11.

serve the normal ends of cultural, diplomatic, or technological exchange, but they frequently cannot avoid serving, also, as instruments
of Communist public relations. Thus—wittingly or unwittingly—
delegations often act as carriers of Communist agit-prop to the Indian
public.

COMMUNIST DELEGATIONS TO INDIA

There has been an increasing flow of delegations to India from
the USSR, China, and other Communist countries; these constitute
one of the most formidable of the agit-prop media and, due to the
potency of personal communication, may in the long run prove much
more effective than the "canned" media—radio, movies, or the printed
page.

Whether the Communist-bloc delegations consist of government
officials, academicians, film stars, authors and artists, or athletes, they
seldom hesitate to advertise Communist progress or to expound Communist policy at public meetings and press conferences. Delivered in
person, their message has far more impact than similar messages conveyed by the pages of the local Communist press. Moreover, since
their visits are newsworthy events, their words and actions arouse great
interest and are reported throughout the non-Communist press.

But even without any open proselytizing, these delegations have an
inherent propaganda value, for their members ordinarily represent
a level of technical attainment in their various fields that Indians find
most enviable; each delegation contributes further to the picture, in
the Indian mind, of a highly developed Communist civilization. Such
delegations effectively counteract the anti-Communist thesis that the
Soviet Union or other Communist countries are hopelessly backward
and benighted. They demonstrate, on the contrary, that India may
be able to learn, in technical fields at least, from the Communist countries. And since technical achievement is one of the supreme goals of
the political elite in India, this is a very significant accomplishment.

The delegations counteract another extreme notion held by some
anti-Communists: that foreign Communists are bomb-carrying bogey
men. By their geniality and calculated use of flattery, at every opportunity praising all things Indian, the delegations generally evoke a
warm personal response in India; this is made the more easy by the
Asian tradition of hospitality which may sometimes appear excessively
cordial to Western observers.

According to a recent compilation, during 1955 alone 58 delegations
visited India from the Communist countries: 22 were from the USSR,
22 from Eastern Europe, 10 from China, and 4 from other Asian Com-

munist countries such as North Korea. Classified according to type, there were 16 cultural groups, 5 athletic teams, one peace delegation, one delegation in the field of labor, agriculture and coöperatives, 13 trade or commercial missions, 15 scientific, professional or technical groups, and 7 official government missions.[19] India ranked eighth among the non-Communist countries in the number of delegations received.

Description of a few Communist delegations will show how they operate. The most spectacular were the official state visits of the Soviet leaders, Bulganin and Khrushchov, and of the Chinese Premier Chou En-lai. (See chapter 14.) Widely reported throughout the world, these visits represented an intensive effort at ingratiation, both personal and political, on the part of the Communist governments. But isolated political missions of this sort, however dramatic, may be of less consequence in the long run than the steady stream of "nonpolitical" delegations.

The most-publicized of these was a special Russian cultural delegation which toured India in 1954, giving performances in the major cities. Led by the Deputy Minister for Culture N. N. Bespalov, the delegation included some of the Soviet Union's outstanding musicians and dancers: Maxim Mikhailov and Leokadia Maslennikova, opera stars of the Bolshoi Theater; Maya Plisetskaya and Yuri Gofman, leading figures in the Russian ballet; Yuri Bryushkov, pianist; Olga Kaverzneva, violinist; Mukuram Turgunbaeva, folk dancer; folk musicians, and other dancers. In New Delhi, Calcutta, Madras, Bangalore, and Bombay, the performances of this troupe excited great public interest and acclaim; according to the *Times of India,* the Russians "have endeared themselves to everyone" and trailed "clouds of glory" wherever they went.[20] Audiences were particularly charmed by the fact that several Russian artists performed Indian songs or dances— a gesture which "delighted the doting Indian crowd," in the words of the *Hindustan Times.*[21] The artists were official guests of the Indian government, and during their tour were greeted by such Indian dignitaries as the central minister of health, the chief minister of Madras, and the chief justice of the Bombay High Court. All proceeds from the performances were turned over to Prime Minister Nehru's National Relief Fund. The group was entertained throughout its tour at a variety of official and nonofficial receptions, including a number by the Indo-Soviet Cultural Society; at one of the latter Mr. P. V. Raja-

---

[19] Kirkpatrick, *Target: The World . . . ,* p. 107.
[20] *Times of India* (New Delhi) Feb. 4, 1954, p. 3.
[21] *Hindustan Times* (New Delhi) Feb. 2, 1954, p. 4.

mannar, chief justice of Madras and president of the National Academy of Dance, Drama and Music, declared that "the future of Indian culture lies in the same way as the Soviet culture has developed," meaning that culture should be a national activity but that the individual cultures of various regions should grow freely.[22] The leader of the Russian group, Mr. Bespalov, used these and other public occasions to urge further development of cultural bonds between the USSR and India in the service of greater understanding and friendship between the two countries. He constantly paid tribute to Indian culture, which he said has "greatly influenced the development of world culture." [23] At a press conference in New Delhi, as well as on other occasions, he paid considerable attention to describing the great material and social benefits accorded to artists in the Soviet Union, and to pointing out that there was no dearth of criticism and self-criticism in Soviet cultural circles.[24]

About a year later, a similar Chinese delegation visited India. Led by the Vice Minister for Cultural Affairs Cheng Chen-to, it comprised a troupe of sixty-seven and included folk singers and dancers, a classical Chinese orchestra, and leading performers of the Peking Opera. The group toured India for six weeks as guests of the Indian government; the reception committee which arranged for the tour was headed by the prime minister's daughter, Mrs. Indira Gandhi. Like its Russian predecessor, the Chinese troupe staged a program of high quality and aroused great interest and admiration. But interwoven with the excellent entertainment were strands of obvious propaganda: the performance opened with a song "Indo-China Friendship," which celebrated the good will between the two countries and called this friendship a "great force of peace"; this was followed by a song entitled "Our Gardener," which according to the official printed program "expresses the ardent love and gratitude" of the people of Sinkiang Province toward Mao Tse-tung and reflects "their happy and colorful life." [25] In a farewell message at the close of the tour, Cheng Chen-to praised India's "vast and beautiful land," "ancient and rich culture," and "love for peace." He promised that along with their souvenirs and gifts, the troupe would take back to China songs and dances which they had learned.[26]

Other Communist delegates representative of various types may be

---

[22] *Ibid.*, Feb. 20, 1954, p. 8.
[23] *Ibid.*, Jan. 18, 1954, p. 1.
[24] *Times of India*, Feb. 3, 1954, p. 4.
[25] Cultural Delegation, People's Republic of China, *Programme, Dec. 12, 1954, National Stadium, New Delhi* (New Delhi: Ministry of Information and Broadcasting, Government of India, 1954), p. 1.
[26] *Times of India*, Jan. 20, 1955, p. 3.

mentioned more briefly. A nonperforming cultural delegation from Russia visited India in 1955; led by Alexey Surkov, poet and winner of the Stalin Prize, it also included drama and music directors, an expert on Oriental architecture, several journalists, an official of the Anti-Fascist Committee of Soviet Youth, several authors from Soviet central Asia, and the deputy chairman of the All-Union Society for Cultural Relations with Foreign Countries (VOKS). The delegation toured India for more than a month, visiting the major cities and the standard tourist attractions. In the course of many public speeches or interviews, Surkov praised Indian culture, economic progress and "peacemindedness." [27] He stressed the similarity between Indian and Russian conditions, asserting that India was now passing through the same stage of development that the Soviet Union had undergone several decades earlier.[28]

In 1953 the Soviet deputy minister for health, Madame M. D. Kovrigina, visited India for three weeks at the invitation of the Indian government. In her public statements she was largely concerned with portraying the progress of women in the USSR.[29] Her visit coincided with a visit by the Chinese minister of health, also a woman, Madame Li Teh-chuan.

In 1954 India entertained a high-level trade delegation from China headed by the vice-minister of foreign trade, Kung Yuan; [30] in 1955 a Czech trade mission led by the vice-minister of foreign trade, the director of the Czechoslovak Chamber of Commerce, and the vice-minister for cultural affairs arrived in India in connection with a Czech Industrial Exhibition in Bombay, which was called the largest display of industrial products from a single country ever assembled in India.[31] (By the middle of 1955, the Soviet Union had opened a permanent showroom for industrial products in Bombay, displaying more than 150 types of machinery and equipment.[32])

In 1954 an eleven-man Russian delegation, led by Dr. G. F. Alexandrov, attended the Indian Science Congress in Hyderabad. In a number of speeches inside and outside the Congress sessions, the delegation leader expounded a variety of Soviet propaganda themes; he detailed Russian social and economic progress, praised the "absolute freedom of scientific research" in the USSR, explained the harmony of public and private interests in the Soviet political and social order, and condemned Western population policy as being a justification

[27] *Ibid.*, Jan. 29, 1955, p. 3.
[28] *Hindustan Times*, Feb. 24, 1955, p. 6.
[29] For example, see *Times of India*, Dec. 26, 1953, p. 10.
[30] *Indian Express* (New Delhi) Sept. 18, 1954, p. 5.
[31] *Times of India*, Feb. 5, 1955, p. 10.
[32] *Ibid.*, April 18, 1955, p. 10.

for continued war.[33] At least one Indian newspaper commented, however, that these speeches were "blatant propaganda" and that the
Russian contribution at the Congress was "more on the political than
the scientific level." [34] The next session of the Indian Science Congress,
a year later, was again attended by a Russian delegation, headed this
time by Mr. Ostrovityanov, vice-president of the Soviet Academy of
Sciences.

Other Communist delegations have included: a Chinese trade-union
mission led by the president of the All-China Federation of Trade
Unions; a team of Russian economists and statisticians; Russian soccer
and volley-ball teams which toured India for a series of matches; and
Russian, Chinese, and Czech film delegations sent to India on the
occasion of the International Film Festival in 1952. (Of the foreign
delegations at this festival, the Soviet Union's was the largest and was
led by a deputy minister.)

In sum, India is visited each year by a great variety of delegations
from the Communist countries, and while these groups are often agents
of normal political, cultural, and economic relations, they serve also
as agents of ideological and psychological persuasion. In the absence
of systematic public-opinion surveys on the subject, their impact upon
Indian attitudes can only be a matter of speculation. It should not
be assumed that they invariably produce a significant effect, or that
that effect is necessarily favorable. Moreover, their influence is perhaps counterbalanced by delegations from the Western countries.

It may be noted, however, that an opinion poll conducted in three
areas of India just after the visit of Bulganin and Khrushchov showed
a significant change in attitudes toward the USSR and toward communism itself. Asked whether their opinion of the Soviet Union had
altered in the past months, and if so, how, respondents answered as
follows (in per cent): [35]

	favorably	unfavorably	unchanged
Calcutta	62.0	0.0	38.0
Delhi	22.5	0.4	77.1
Travancore-Cochin	42.3	0.8	56.9

Questioned further as to whether their opinion of Communism had
altered, and how, the respondents answered as follows (in per cent):

	favorably	unfavorably	unchanged
Calcutta	16.0	0.0	84.0
Delhi	5.7	1.3	93.0
Travancore-Cochin	10.6	1.7	87.7

[33] *Hindustan Times,* Jan. 7, 1954, p. 12; and Jan. 26, 1954, p. 3.
[34] *Ibid.,* Jan. 18, 1954, p. 6; and Jan. 24, 1954, magazine section, p. 3.
[35] *Monthly Public Opinion Surveys,* nos. 7, 8, 9, 1956. This journal is published
by the Indian Institute of Public Opinion, New Delhi.

The figures in the "unchanged" column were not included in the source, but have been added here by the authors to give a clearer picture of the change or *lack of change* in attitudes.

There is evidence, then, that Communist delegations serve both an immediate and a long-range political function, creating a more cordial climate of opinion which is useful to the USSR now and to the Indian Communist movement later. Thus, this element of international Communist agit-prop activity is an exceedingly helpful supplement to the CPI's program of persuasion.

INDIAN DELEGATES TO THE COMMUNIST COUNTRIES

In 1955 there were 126 Indian delegations to the Communist countries—more than twice as many as the number traveling in the opposite direction.[36] Indeed, India sent more delegations to the Communist orbit than any other non-Communist country except England and France.

Of the 126 Indian groups, 46 traveled to the USSR, 43 to Eastern Europe, 35 to China, and 2 to other Asian Communist countries (Tibet and North Viet Nam). Classified according to type, there were: 22 cultural; 10 sports; one in the women's field; 4 "peace and friendship"; 8 youth and students; 14 labor, agriculture and coöperatives; 11 trade and commerce; 40 technical, professional or scientific missions; and 16 official government missions.[37] It is noteworthy that the broadly "technical" delegations (including those in the labor, agriculture and coöperative fields, the trade and commercial groups, and the technical, professional, or scientific groups) accounted for more than half of the total—a larger proportion than was true of the Communist delegations to India. Indian emphasis, therefore, has been upon technological exchange.

These Indian groups, like their Communist-bloc counterparts, often serve as useful vehicles for Communist agit-prop in India. The activities and impressions of these delegations while abroad are front-page news in India; if a Communist government succeeds in evoking favorable opinions from the delegation members, those opinions are soon echoed in Indian newspapers. Moreover, after the delegates return, their views are further disseminated via press conferences and public lectures. These views may significantly influence Indian attitudes toward the Communist powers.

As for pro-Communist Indian delegations sponsored by front organizations (such as the peace movement), the Communist governments have little difficulty in making a favorable impression; Communist

---

[36] Kirkpatrick, *Target: The World . . .* , p. 106.
[37] *Loc. cit.*

propaganda enters the Indian press almost unchanged. Many examples may be found in the statements of delegates from the Indian peace movement. For instance, Mr. Govind Sahai declared in a public report on his trip to the Vienna meeting of the World Peace Council in November, 1953, that the Russian people "have put their country on the right path to progress." He claimed that the Russians are so much attached to their system of life that they sincerely attempt to achieve the production targets set by the government. Perfect harmony has been achieved between science, art, and culture in Russia, he said.[38] Another peace leader, M. Atal, stated after his tour of the USSR that standards of individual liberty in the Soviet Union compare favorably with those in any Eastern or Western country, and that tremendous progress is being achieved in all aspects of life there.[39] Similar statements could be cited almost without end, from the pages of the non-Communist Indian press.

The CPI press, of course, heavily plays up such sympathetic views, and the front organizations spread them further in their own publications. For example, the pamphlet *Hands Across the Himalayas,* published by the All-India Peace Council, describes the visit to the USSR of the Indian delegation to the 1952 Vienna Peace Congress. An attractively printed booklet of 156 pages, profusely illustrated with photographs, it is a detailed panegyric in the form of a travel diary. Its political bias may be inferred from its account of the delegates' visit to the birthplace of Stalin: according to the booklet, the group was inspired by a "feeling of homage" toward this "dauntless fighter for freedom," which it sought to express in the following statement recorded in the visitor's book:

We, the Indian delegates to the Congress of the Peoples for Peace at Vienna, are deeply moved to see the footprints on time left by Comrade Stalin. It is an inspiration to future generations to know what real fighters for the liberty of a nation have to do. It is the path strewn with thorns. Sacrifice spells liberty. May we the younger ones in the field follow this noble example. Lives of great men all remind us we can make our lives sublime.[40]

The pro-Communist delegations thus serve, in effect, as mouthpieces for the CPI. So too, albeit unintentionally, do some of the non-Communist groups invited to tour the Communist countries. Although some delegates return with critical attitudes,[41] others have patently

---

[38] *Times of India,* Jan. 4, 1954, p. 12.

[39] *Hindustan Times,* Jan. 9, 1954, p. 5.

[40] *Hands Across the Himalayas; Indians in the Soviet Union* (New Delhi: All India Peace Council, n.d., [1953]), pp. 4–5.

[41] See for example the report of her visit to the USSR by Sucheta Kripalani, in *Times of India,* July 16, 1954, p. 3.

been influenced. An extreme example is a labor delegation, representing the Socialist trade-union federation, which toured the USSR and China in 1954. The Indian Socialists are in general strongly anti-Communist, but several prominent members of this delegation apparently revised their opinions. An article in the *Indian Express,* reproduced here in full, gives the following summary of their report of the trip:

KANPUR, Aug. 30.—Mr. Raja Ram Shastri, General Secretary of the All-India Hind Mazdoor Sabha, said here yesterday that the fundamental set up of national life in Russia and China was based on the closest coordination between the Government, the people and the trade union leaders.

Mr. Shastri and Mr. Virendra Bahadur Singh, Secretary of the Kanpur PSP, who were jointly addressing a press conference on their return from a two-month visit to Russia and China, added that in every walk of life people showed tremendous enthusiasm and devotion for their Governments, and the Governments in return were earnestly devoted to the welfare of the people.

Referring to the political conditions in those countries, Mr. Shastri said that people had the full right to criticise their Governments but their criticism was very healthy and bound by certain discipline.

He said that there was perfect freedom of religion also. He saw mosques, temples and churches packed by devotees in Moscow, Tashkent and many cities of China.

Mr. Shastri said that the total picture which a foreigner got both in Russia and China was that the people in these countries were very happy. Their standard of living was very high. Cities were well planned, neatly kept and well managed.

Mr. Shastri said that in Russia there were small railways run by boys aged from eight to 15 in the city itself. Small stations named "victory" and "freedom" were built in the city. There were boy engine drivers, station masters, guards and even railway mechanics.

Mr. Virendra Bahadur Singh said that both in China and Russia the trade union movement was organized on scientific lines. There was no clash between the workers and the employers. He said that trade unions which acted as a link between the employees and the employers exercised a very healthy influence.

Cases of retrenchment and dismissals were so few that only two workers were dismissed during the last five years in a private mill at Shanghai.

Mr. Shastri said that he was highly impressed to note that Russians and Chinese had a great respect for Prime Minister Nehru and his policies. They looked to India with respect and admiration, he added.[42]

It would be difficult to find in the Communist press itself a neater summary of the chief themes of international Communist propaganda in India.

One such enunciation of the Communist message from the lips of a non-Communist, in the pages of the daily press, probably accomplishes more than would a thousand pages of propaganda in the Party press. Thus the "live" media, imported and domestic, add immeasurably to the effectiveness of the CPI's already powerful agit-prop weapon.

---

[42] *Indian Express,* Aug. 31, 1954, p. 6.

19 THE PARLIAMENTARY ARENA

In the classic Marxist view, bourgeois-democratic parliaments do not qualify as agencies for effecting genuine political change. The legislative machinery of the bourgeois state, in this view, is nothing more than an instrument of the ruling capitalist class, and this ruling class will never voluntarily abdicate power; it is fruitless, therefore, to seek either reform or revolution through the legislative process.

If Communists can neither influence nor overthrow a capitalist government by parliamentary means, should they not boycott parliaments altogether? Many Communists in the early decades of the twentieth century said "yes." During the 1905 Russian revolution, Lenin had held this view and had scorned legislative action, believing direct mass action to be the only effective way of changing the social and economic system. But later he approached the question from a more pragmatic tactical perspective. While affirming the general Marxist position, he contended that in circumstances which made direct revolutionary action impracticable, participation in bourgeois legislatures could be a most useful auxiliary weapon: Communists could not gain power by parliamentary means alone, he said, but they could win greater influence with the masses, which would be of inestimable help as a step toward the final goal.

In an essay, "Should We Participate in Bourgeois Parliaments?" Lenin summarized his position, hammering home the point that so long as elements of the masses had faith in parliaments, parliamentary activity was obligatory—in order to destroy that faith. For, he said, participation in bourgeois-democratic parliaments helps "to *prove* to the backward masses why such parliaments deserve to be dispersed; it *helps* their successful dispersal, and helps to make bourgeois parliamentarism 'politically obsolete.' " Addressing European Communist Parties, he said:

Precisely because the backward masses of the workers and—to an even greater degree—of the small peasants are in Western Europe much more imbued with bourgeois-democratic and parliamentary prejudices than they were in Russia, precisely because of that, it is *only* from within such institutions as bourgeois parliaments that Communists can (and must) wage a long and persistent struggle, undaunted by any difficulties, to expose, dissipate and overcome these prejudices.[1]

In short, the purpose of Communist parliamentary activity was to utilize yet another opportunity to address and "educate" the masses. A parliament provided a platform for propaganda and agitation, and no platform should be scorned. This tactic was entirely consistent with Lenin's general dictum to work within the enemy camp. And it is interesting to note that, in defending Bolshevik participation in the Russian Constituent Assembly, he used a military analogy; the existence of a Bolshevik group within the Constituent Assembly helped in the liquidation of the Assembly, he said, just as the existence of a Bolshevik opposition within the White Russian camp helped in its defeat in the Civil War.[2]

In accordance with the decision to fight in the parliamentary arena, the Russian Bolsheviks contested elections and worked within the State Duma in the years 1907–1915—roughly the period from the failure of the first revolution to the onset of the second. As a result of this practical experience, they became accomplished parliamentarians. The nature of their activity—and the tactical principles guiding it—are neatly summarized in the official history of the Russian Party, which gives the following account of Bolshevik work in the Fourth Duma:

At first the Bolsheviks and Liquidators [another Socialist faction] formed a joint Social-Democratic group in the Duma. In October, 1913, after a stubborn struggle against the Liquidators, who hampered the revolutionary work of the Bolsheviks, the Bolshevik deputies, on the instructions of the Central Committee of the Party, withdrew from the joint Social-Democratic group and formed an independent Bolshevik group.

The Bolshevik deputies made revolutionary speeches in the Duma in which they exposed the autocratic system and interpellated the government on cases of

---

[1] V. I. Lenin, *"Left-Wing" Communism, An Infantile Disorder* (Moscow: Foreign Languages Publishing House, 1950), pp. 74, 81–82. Emphasis in original. This work was written in 1920.

[2] *Ibid.*, p. 76.

repression of the workers and on the inhuman exploitation of the workers by the
capitalists.

They also spoke in the Duma on the agrarian question, calling upon the peasants
to fight the feudal landlords, and exposing the Constitutional-Democratic Party,
which was opposed to the confiscation and handing over of the landed estates to the
peasants.

The Bolsheviks introduced a bill in the State Duma providing for an 8-hour working day; of course it was not adopted by this Black-Hundred Duma, but it had great
agitational value.

The Bolshevik group in the Duma maintained close connections with the Central
Committee of the Party and with Lenin, from whom they received instructions. . . .

The Bolshevik deputies did not confine themselves to work within the Duma, but
were very active outside the Duma as well. They visited mills and factories and toured
the working-class centers of the country where they made speeches, arranged secret
meetings at which they explained the decisions of the Party, and formed new Party
organizations. The deputies skilfully combined legal activities with illegal, underground work.[3]

From this account of Bolshevik parliamentary practice it is possible to abstract, paragraph by paragraph, the working principles—
the *modus operandi*—of Communist parliamentary behavior.

1. Ally with (but fight against) other friendly legislative groups.
2. "Expose" government policy at every opportunity.
3. Assert, first, the interests of the working class and, second, those
   of allied classes such as the peasantry.
4. Propose legislation for its propaganda value.
5. Observe strict Party discipline.
6. Combine work in the parliament with political action outside—
   including illegal action where necessary.

This code of behavior is distinguished from that of other political
parties, then or now, not so much by its specific principles as by its
underlying assumption: that parliamentary activity is subordinate and
ancillary to other forms of political action. In Stalin's words, "the
parliamentary struggle is only a school for and an auxiliary in organizing the extraparliamentary struggle of the proletariat," since "the
fundamental problems of the working-class movement are solved by
force, by the direct struggle of the proletarian masses, their general
strike, their insurrection." [4]

This, in essence, was the original Communist parliamentary code,
and it was inherited by the Indian Communist movement, as it was by
all others.

---

[3] *History of the Communist Party of the Soviet Union (Bolsheviks); Short Course*
(Moscow: Foreign Languages Publishing House, 1951), pp. 241–242.

[4] J. Stalin, *The Foundations of Leninism; On the Problems of Leninism* (Moscow: Foreign Languages Publishing House, 1950), p. 29.

Early CPI Parliamentary Policy

Though it was accomplished by slow and measured steps, responsible parliamentary institutions were gradually implanted on the subcontinent under British rule. Indians found the process far too slow, but they rarely questioned that these institutions should be closely modeled on Western prototypes; they fought British overlordship, but by and large they demanded British-style government.[5]

A start had already been made in the latter half of the nineteenth century when the British conceded to the Indian demand for a greater role in the administration of the country. In the consultative "legislative councils" to which Indians were admitted in 1861, there lay at least the seeds of responsible government. Through a series of reforms in 1892, 1909, and 1919, these councils grew steadily in size, influence, and responsibility; the Indian element increased, the councils were granted additional prerogatives, and the elective principle was gradually applied. But these councils were still not representative, since they were elected by a miniscule part of the adult population; and they were not sovereign, since they remained subject to the viceroy's overriding power.

In 1919, however, a closer approximation to responsible government was introduced at the provincial level; provincial ministries, responsible to the elected legislatures, were granted considerable autonomy in certain "transferred" fields such as health and education, though the ministries were still subject to restraint exercised through a British-appointed governor.

In the Act of 1935, which embodied a new constitution, the principle of provincial autonomy was further extended; the number of "transferred" fields was increased and, most important, the franchise was widened to include about 14 per cent of the population.[6]

To the dominant body of opinion in the Indian National Congress, the reform of 1935, whatever its faults, came to mean the first acceptable opportunity to participate in parliamentary institutions. The Congress decided to contest the provincial elections of 1936–37, though it did not then commit itself to coöperate further with the new governmental scheme. Subsequently, having won a majority or plurality vote in eight of the eleven provinces, the Congress decided after long

---

[5] For an excellent summary of the development of parliamentary government in India, see W. H. Morris-Jones, *Parliament in India* (Philadelphia: University of Pennsylvania Press, 1957), pp. 43–73.

[6] P. N. Masaldan, *Evolution of Provincial Autonomy in India, 1858 to 1950* (Bombay: Hind Kitabs Ltd., 1953), p. 109.

debate to accept office. Congress Party members took their seats in the provincial legislatures, and formed ministries in the eight provinces where they prevailed. These Congress "governments" held office until 1939, when they resigned *en bloc* in protest against India's participation in World War II.

But to the Indian Communists, who had entered the Congress in accordance with their current united-front tactics, the question of whether to participate in the provincial governments was largely academic. The Party was illegal, and the Communists formed too small a group to have much influence on the Congress's parliamentary role. Hence, the reform of 1935 did not provide an opportunity for the CPI, as such, to make use of the parliamentary arena. And in any event, the Party was unable to share the prevailing bias in favor of British-style political institutions. Accordingly, it declared itself "utterly opposed" to the Act of 1935. The Act bestowed a "slave constitution," designed to establish "the dictatorship of the capitalist class" upon India. In the provincial elections the CPI said it would support only those candidates who were "honestly intent on wrecking the Constitution and replacing it by a Constituent Assembly." And it would oppose the formation of ministries, since to accept office was "to join the ranks of the slave masters." [7]

Communist influence in the elections was, as the Party itself was quick to admit, "insignificant." [8] And, unable to prevent the Congress decision to form ministries, the CPI's only recourse was to maintain its opposition role outside the legislative halls. A Politbureau resolution of 1937 declared that accepting office signified an effort on the part of the Congress right wing to "divert the national movement to the plane of mere parliamentarism," and called for a "determined fight" against this tendency: "We must explain to the masses that Congress ministries do not mean a people's government. Not a single demand can ever be enforced until the people are prepared to organize and to fight against Imperialism." [9]

The CPI and the Constituent Assembly

Almost immediately after World War II, in September, 1945, the British government inaugurated the final stage in the constitutional development of India. The viceroy announced his intention to con-

[7] Bakar, "The Indian People in the Slave Market," *The Communist*, I (Feb. 1937), pp. 10–16.
[8] Chand, "Into Action, Comrades," *The Communist*, I (Feb. 1937), p. 9.
[9] "Resolution on the Congress Ministries," *The Communist*, I (July, 1937), pp. 8–11.

vene a central constituent assembly that would debate the country's future political form and promulgate a new constitution. So long as the British retained sovereignty, such an assembly could only make proposals, but the way to an Indian constitution of Indian making was at least half-open.

The Cabinet Mission Plan of mid-1946 provided that the Constituent Assembly was to be composed of representatives chosen by the new provincial assemblies elected in the winter of 1945–46, along with a group of delegates from the native states. In the provincial elections the CPI had participated for the first time as a legal political party. It had won only eight seats in provincial assemblies; but in the Bengal Assembly it succeeded in securing the election of one of its leaders, Somnath Lahiri, to the Constituent Assembly. Thus when the Assembly convened in New Delhi in December, 1946, a Communist took his seat in Parliament House and the Party was launched upon a parliamentary career.

Lahiri's contribution to the work of the Constituent Assembly was a forthright application of Leninist parliamentary tactics. While he adhered to conventional parliamentary etiquette, his speeches were redolent with disrespect for the purposes of the Assembly. It was his intention to make propaganda, not a constitution.

In his opening address, Lahiri condemned the "illusion" that India could achieve independence by negotiation rather than by mass action.[10] In another speech three days later he expressed his regret that the Congress had chosen to coöperate with the British plan by participating in the Assembly, and he announced that he felt grave "doubt" that the Assembly would be able to succeed in its task of constitution-making. In his words: "I don't think you will be able to get any independence out of it." He ended his speech by saying that freedom would be secured only through "the revolutionary seizure of power." [11]

In substance, then, Lahiri demanded that the Assembly abandon its task and dissolve itself. This demand was made openly in a draft resolution which he submitted on behalf of the CPI in the opening days of the Assembly. In the resolution the Party called upon the Constituent Assembly to adopt a declaration of independence, conferring sovereign power on an interim government to be made up of Congress and League representatives. This provisional government, "backed by the entire people in revolt," would forthwith convene a

---

[10] *Constituent Assembly Debates; Official Report*, I, no. 3 (Dec. 11, 1946), (Delhi: Manager of Publications, 1947), p. 45.

[11] *Ibid.*, I, no. 9 (Dec. 19, 1946), pp. 130–131.

new Constituent Assembly, based on universal franchise. In effect, the CPI draft resolution was a vote of nonconfidence in the existing Constituent Assembly.[12]

Lahiri's draft resolution was never debated in the Assembly, for it was ruled out of order by the chairman.[13] But it served as useful propaganda, as did the other proposals put forward later by Lahiri in the Assembly debates. In January, 1947, for example, he submitted an amendment to the budget that called for drastic reductions in the salaries of ministers and other high officials, and equally drastic increases in the pay of low-level government employees. It called, also, for reduction of the expense allowances for members of the Constituent Assembly itself, and in his speech Lahiri challenged his colleagues to renounce material privileges and live in the style of the people.[14]

Lahiri's parliamentary tactics also included "exposure" of dominant Congress policy in the Assembly. In a major speech, in April, 1947, he castigated the Congress proposals for a constitutional bill of rights, asserting that the proposals set such limitations upon civil liberties that the bill was a mockery. If such a definition of fundamental rights were adopted, he said, "we will simply make ourselves a laughing stock before the whole democratic world." [15]

The government obviously suspected—though it did not prove—that from the very start of his participation in the Assembly Lahiri had been applying the final element of Leninist parliamentary tactics —the combining of illegal with legal activity. About a month after the Assembly convened, police searched his residence in Calcutta and seized certain of his papers. This action was allegedly connected with the "Operation Asylum" episode (see chapter 11, pp. 246–247), but it was probably also a general precautionary measure. Lahiri protested against the action in a letter to the Assembly chairman.[16]

As the deliberations of the Constituent Assembly wore on in 1947, Lahiri's name appeared less frequently in the official record. Within the CPI a radical wing was growing increasingly restive with parliamentary tactics, and Lahiri himself was evidently associated with this faction. At the end of the year, this faction came to power in the Party, which then opted for revolution. Taking a place on B. T. Ranadive's Politbureau, Lahiri presumably went underground. The Assembly sat for four more years, but Communist participation was clearly

[12] Declaration of Independence; Communist Party Resolution for the Constituent Assembly (Bombay: People's Publishing House, n.d. [1947?]), pp. 5–10.
[13] Constituent Assembly Debates; Official Report, I, no. 6 (Dec. 16, 1946), p. 80.
[14] Ibid., II, no. 4 (a), (Jan. 22 and 24, 1947), pp. 7–10.
[15] Ibid., III, no. 2 (April 29, 1947), pp. 384–386.
[16] Ibid., II, no. 5 (Jan. 25, 1947), pp. 340–341.

superfluous, if not impossible. The CPI's parliamentary career was voluntarily interrupted.[17]

The Communist Attitude to the Constitution

When the Constituent Assembly promulgated the new constitution of the Republic of India, to take effect on January 26, 1950, the CPI was in revolt. Scorning to work within the legal political framework, the Party greeted the constitution with a hostility exceeding even that displayed toward the British Act of 1935. A Central Committee manifesto again described it as a "slave constitution" representing a conspiracy on the part of "the Indian capitalist class" and British imperialism. But now the manifesto anathematized it as "a constitution of fascist tyranny," "a constitution of national oppression," "a monstrous constitution," a "fraud." Praising Communist-led uprisings against the Nehru government in Telengana and other areas of India, the manifesto ended with the revolutionary slogan, "forward to a people's constitution." [18]

The Soviet press took a similar view, castigating the constitution as a variant of "bourgeois pseudo-democracy." [19] Soviet criticism was exceedingly specific: the constitution "perpetuates the dominant position of the foreign imperialists" through the provisions guaranteeing the inviolability of property; it restricts "the right of the working people to fight against exploitation" through an inadequate bill of rights; it "retains the administrative divisions introduced by the British oppressors" through its failure to reorganize the states on a linguistic basis; it embodies an undemocratic method of indirect election for the upper house and accords that house dominant power over the popularly elected lower house (the House of the People, or Lok Sabha); it maintains the "monarchist regimes" in the native states; and it accepts obligations which "run counter to the interests of the Indian peoples" through continued membership in the British Commonwealth.

In another Soviet comment, the Indian government was accused of "throwing aside the fig leaves of bourgeois democracy" and resorting to "openly fascist and terrorist methods." [20]

---

[17] In 1950 the Assembly converted itself into a parliament and served as the central Indian legislature until 1952.

[18] *Manifesto of the Central Committee of the Communist Party of India on the New Constitution* (Bombay: Communist Party of India, n.d. [1949]), 8 pp.

[19] T. Yershov, "Indian Version of Bourgeois Pseudo-Democracy," *New Times*, (March 15, 1950), pp. 3–7.

[20] E. Zhukov, "Voprosy natsional'no-kolonial'noi bor'by posle vtoroi mirovoi voiny" [Problems of the National-Colonial Struggle Since the Second World War] *Voprosy Ekonomiki*, 9 (1949), pp. 54–61.

The First General Elections

With the failure of the Indian revolution of 1948–1951 in Telengana and elsewhere, the CPI was forced again to alter its tactics. At the end of 1950, its British Communist mentors counseled the Party to resume legal operations and, in particular, to prepare for the general elections to be held in the winter of 1951–52. The elections are "a very serious testing for the political position and influence of the Party," they said, and the CPI's failure to formulate an election program is an "extremely serious political weakness." [21]

The CPI groped unsteadily toward a fresh policy. Its election manifesto, issued in August, 1951, provided few clues as to what Party election tactics would be. The manifesto condemned everything about the Nehru government, and promised everything to the voters. The clearest hint was a vague gesture toward unity with other "democratic" political forces.

The Communist Party appeals to all democratic forces in the country to realize that the building of the democratic unity of the people is the supreme need of the hour. The task of each democratic party is not to paint alluring pictures of what it would do if the people vote it to power but to develop a powerful mass movement which alone can break the power of those who rule over us all.[22]

The manifesto did not specify what it meant by "democratic parties," but it carried its conciliation of these undefined allies to extreme lengths: it called upon the people to vote, not for the CPI alone, but for "the candidates of the progressive and democratic parties," and more, it announced that the CPI would support any government formed by a "united front of genuine democratic parties."

This could lead to only one conclusion: rather than give exclusive emphasis to the positive aim of maximizing its own electoral strength, the CPI apparently concentrated on the negative aim of turning out Congress governments.

Communist electoral tactics took shape slowly in the campaign. It was soon evident, first, that the Party would join forces with virtually any amenable ally, short of "communal" groups like the Akalis of the Punjab or the extremist Hindu parties (Jan Sangh and Ram Rajya Parishad). The Communists opened united-front negotiations with such diverse groups as the Dravida Kazhagam, an anti-Brahmin organization championing South Indian separatism in Madras state, and

---

[21] "PHQ Unit's Covering Note to the Letter of the Political Committee of the CPGB to the Communist Party of India," Dec. 6, 1950, p. 6.

[22] *Election Manifesto of the Communist Party of India* (Calcutta: Central Election Board of the CPI, 1951), pp. 24–25.

the local elements of the Kisan Mazdoor Praja Party (KMPP), a recent offshoot of the Congress led by the Gandhian, Acharya J. B. Kripalani.

As electoral negotiations with other parties proceeded, it became evident, further, that the CPI did not want to ally itself with any national party, but wished rather to make alliances with regional or local units of the national parties. For example, the Communists attacked the national leadership of the KMPP but indicated their willingness to negotiate with "elements or individual leaders in the Praja Party or even with units of the Praja Party." [23] Eventually they reached agreements with KMPP units in Andhra and in Malabar. Again, the Communists attacked the national leadership of the Socialist Party but announced that in Hyderabad, for example, they would support several Socialist candidates.[24]

More important for the Communists than alliances with units of national parties, however, were alliances with the multitude of regional parties. In two states—Hyderabad and Travancore-Cochin—where the CPI itself was illegal, the problem was especially urgent. In Hyderabad the Communists succeeded in establishing a formal coalition party, the People's Democratic Front, with local leftist elements; in Travancore-Cochin they achieved a formal alliance with the Kerala Socialist Party and the Revolutionary Socialist Party, which functioned under the name of the United Front of Leftists.

Elsewhere the CPI negotiated less formal bilateral electoral agreements with a great variety of regional parties. According to a later Party document, the parties included the following: the Left Socialist group, led by Aruna Asaf Ali, in Bombay State; the Forward Bloc (Marxist) in Bengal, Bihar, and Orissa; the Kamgar Kisan Party in Bombay State and part of Hyderabad; the Peasants and Workers Party in the city of Sholapur; the Revolutionary Socialist Party in Uttar Pradesh; the Lal Communist Party in the Punjab; the Toilers Party in Madras State; and the Dravida Kazhagam in parts of Madras.[25]

The CPI later expressed dissatisfaction that it had not achieved broader alliances; most, though not all, of the electoral agreements were achieved with left-of-center parties. But the CPI had at least made an impressive start toward covering India with a web of united-front agreements with other regional political groups.

[23] *Crossroads,* III (Aug. 3, 1951), p. 5.
[24] *Crossroads,* III (Jan. 11, 1952), p. 9.
[25] *Party Letter* (April, 1952), pp. 18–20.

The Communists in Parliament: The Early Years

The election returns showed that the CPI had done remarkably well. Concentrating its efforts at strong points, the Party had contested only 49 seats in the Lok Sabha; it won 16, with 3.3 per cent of the popular vote. The Socialist Party, by contrast, had contested 256 seats and won only 12, with 10.6 per cent of the popular vote. If to the CPI total were added the 7 seats won by the People's Democratic Front in Hyderabad and the 3 won by independent Communists in the United Front of Leftists in Travancore-Cochin, the total was actually 26 seats. Though the Congress dominated parliament with 364 seats, gained with 45 per cent of the popular vote, the Communists were the largest opposition group in the legislature.[26]

The Communist M.P.'s were a striking group in many respects. Most notable, perhaps, was their youth; 58 per cent were under forty, whereas only 27 per cent of parliament as a whole was in this age bracket. Accordingly, the Communist members lacked legislative experience; only 4 per cent of them had served in central or state assemblies, as compared with 51 per cent of the parliament as a whole. In occupational background, they were primarily from the professions (education, law, journalism) or "public work"; only 17 per cent of them had land or business interests, as compared with 38 per cent of the parliament as a whole. Their educational level, however, did not differ from that of the average M.P.'s; 56 per cent were college graduates, as against 58 per cent for parliament as a whole.[27]

A spectator in the visitors' gallery during a sitting of parliament would have been struck by another characteristic of the Communist group: the intensity with which they participated in the proceedings. Whether in repose, or in action during the debates, they presented an exceedingly purposive and earnest appearance. And they showed external evidence of very systematic preparation for debates: in the volume of papers they carried with them to their seats they exceeded all others. The research staff of the Communist Parliamentary Office in New Delhi served increasingly well to arm them for effective participation in the business of parliament.

The Communist parliamentary group did not join a formal bloc with any other group. Immediately after the elections the CPI Central

---

[26] For a summary of election results, see Margaret W. Fisher and Joan Bondurant, *The Indian Experience with Democratic Elections*, Indian Press Digests–Monograph Series, no. 3 (Dec. 1956), (University of California, Berkeley), pp. 39–53. The term "parliament" as used hereinafter means the Lok Sabha. The Rajya Sabha, which is indirectly elected, is not considered.

[27] W. H. Morris-Jones, *Parliament in India*, pp. 115–123.

Committee declared its willingness to form a "United Democratic Opposition" with other democratic parties in parliament, but it specified that such a bloc must not restrict the CPI's freedom of expression, and it provided also that the Communists would join as a Party rather than as individuals.[28] A meeting of opposition M.P.'s, called at Communist initiative in May, 1952, failed to produce agreement on the creation of a formal bloc.[29] The CPI was later criticized by its erstwhile allies in the Hyderabad People's Democratic Front for its refusal to merge with a larger parliamentary bloc; in response, the Party claimed that it had tried to create a "coördinating committee" among various opposition groups, but it continued to insist that the Communist group must function in its own name.[30]

Although it did not formally ally itself with other friendly groups, the Communist Party otherwise implemented Leninist parliamentary tactics during its first years in parliament. Its members were quick to learn the complex devices of parliamentary procedure, and they used every opportunity to expose government policy, to champion popular grievances, and to propose legislation with propaganda value.

One parliamentary device for effective confrontation of the government is the question period. As in the British House of Commons, the proceedings of the Indian house normally begin with the question hour, in which government ministers answer written queries put to them in advance by individual members. The answers may be followed by a limited number of "supplementaries"—that is, further oral questions pursuing the subject—and a sharp give-and-take frequently ensues. The question hour thus provides the Opposition with a continuous opportunity to challenge and possibly embarrass the government. The Communists used this device with great skill and persistence. Their questions usually ranged over a wide spectrum of subjects pertaining to government policy and operations, probing constantly for weaknesses which would lend themselves to effective propaganda. The CPI later boasted that in proportion to its size the Communist parliamentary group had posed a far greater number of questions than had any other group, and that one Communist M.P. had the distinction of asking the largest number of questions among all members.[31]

Another device for challenging the government is the adjournment

[28] *Party Letter* (April, 1952), p. 40.
[29] M. R. Masani, *The Communist Party of India* (London: Derek Verschoyle, 1954), pp. 169–170.
[30] *Communist Conspiracy at Madurai* (Bombay: Popular Book Depot, 1954), pp. 147–148.
[31] A. K. Gopalan and Hiren Mukerjee, *Communists in Parliament* (New Delhi: Communist Party of India, 1957), p. 7.

motion—that is, a motion that the scheduled business of the house be postponed in order to permit the discussion of some urgent public question. Such motions are common in the Indian parliament, but they are rarely admitted by the speaker, who decides whether the question is of sufficient importance and relevance to justify a special debate. Of the 122 adjournment motions proposed in the House up to 1957, the Communists claimed fully half. The questions frequently concerned instances of public outbreaks or disasters in which some governmental fault could be alleged.[32]

Other devices include nonofficial resolutions and special "discussions" of a half-hour or longer on matters of public importance—either of which provides the opposition with the opportunity to initiate debate. The Communist group claimed the initiative in 29 out of 61 discussions, covering subjects ranging from mine and flood disasters to the problems of the cement industry, from the conduct of the deputy shipping master of Calcutta port to irregularities in the national savings scheme.[33] The Communists proposed many nonofficial resolutions, covering more general subjects such as the nationalization of the coal mines, the linguistic reorganization of states, and the right of collective bargaining.[34]

Communists in Parliamentary Debate

But it is in legislative debates of the house, perhaps, that the features of Communist participation in the first years may best be seen. A few examples of significant debates may illustrate the Party's methods.

A dramatic case is the debate on the Preventive Detention (Second Amendment) Bill. The original Preventive Detention Act had been passed in 1950 and was extended by the interim parliament in 1952. It was based on constitutional provisions enabling either the central or the state governments to detain persons without trial, subject to specified limitations. That it was aimed primarily against the Communists was indicated by the home minister's report to parliament that of 1,641 persons detained up to the end of 1951, 1,160 were Communists.[35] Shortly after the new parliament met in May, 1952, the government introduced the Preventive Detention (Second Amendment) Bill to provide minor changes and to extend the life of the Act.

---

[32] Ibid., p. 6.

[33] Ibid., pp. 7, 52–53.

[34] Ibid., pp. 49–50.

[35] Parliamentary Debates, Parliament of India; Official Report, Vol. I, no. 18, Feb. 28, 1952 (Delhi: Manager of Publications, 1952), column 1544.

Few items of legislation could so arouse the CPI. It should be noted, however, that a large body of non-Communist opinion in India opposed the Act as an unnecessary infringement of civil liberties.

Debate began with a speech by the home minister, K. N. Katju, defending the bill. Interrupted repeatedly by more than the customary heckling from the Opposition benches, Katju retaliated by accusing the Communists of aiming to create "havoc and chaos" in the country.[36] Later in his speech he reiterated his accusation against the Communists and added the charge that they had collaborated with the British during the war and were now collaborating with communalists against the bill under debate.

The resulting disorder on the floor of the House caused the speaker to rise—an act which in parliamentary usage obliges all members to be seated and remain quiet. Some Opposition hecklers remained on their feet, whereupon the speaker threatened to expel those who did not take their seats forthwith. S. S. More (of the Peasants and Workers Party, a small party in Bombay state) evidently refused to comply, for the speaker then declared that he "had better leave the House just now," and More departed.

The deputy leader of the Communist group, H. N. Mukerjee, came to More's defense, and there was a barbed exchange between him and the speaker. Following this, the speaker accused another Communist member, K. A. Nambiar, of excessive interruptions, to which Nambiar retorted that the speaker was "unfair." Told to leave the house for this gross breach of parliamentary etiquette, Nambiar refused to do so and was approached by the marshal (sergeant-at-arms)—a very rare event in Indian parliamentary history.

At this point Mukerjee rose and apologized for Nambiar's action. But he implied that the speaker was somewhat less than impartial, and he announced that the Communist group was leaving the floor *en bloc* until tempers had cooled, with the implication that it was a protest action. The prime minister came to the defense of the speaker, and threatened to suspend any member who repeated Nambiar's behavior.

A few hours later, Mukerjee returned to the floor and delivered the main Communist speech against the bill. He declared that it "stinks from every pore" and was prompted by "viciousness." But such police-state legislation was in the nature of bourgeois democracy, he said, for the capitalist system requires that real power be retained in the hands of the "vested interests." He challenged any Congress

[36] *Ibid.*, Vol. III, no. 11, July 17, 1952, columns 4067–4068.

member, including the prime minister himself, to resign his seat and contest an election on the issue of preventive detention. And he defended the "birthright" of the people to disobey laws which are so "pernicious" that they cannot be accepted. Concluding, he taunted the government with the remark that the people still had "certain illusions about your leadership" and should not be goaded "into fury." In any event, he said, there was no reason for the government to be as "panicky" as the emergency nature of preventive detention suggested. Though the dominant tone of Mukerjee's speech was obviously provocative, this was alleviated by learned references to historical or legal precedent, along with quotations from Coke, Thoreau, and George Bernard Shaw.[37]

The debate continued for five more days, at a lower pitch of excitement. The Communists proposed an amendment requiring that the bill be circulated to elicit public opinion. This amendment was defeated by a vote of 312 to 68. In a final speech, the leader of the Communist group, A. K. Gopalan, declared that passage of the bill would represent the "death-knell of the Government." But it was carried by a vote of 296–61.[38]

This was by no means an "average" debate, but it does demonstrate one aspect of Communist parliamentary activity in the early period. Walkouts and disorders were not uncommon, though they were not the prerogative of the Communists alone.

Another example of Communist behavior may be seen in the first general debate on the budget. The main Communist contribution, again by Mukerjee, reveals both the provocative style and the heavy propaganda content of the Party's speeches. He began by admitting that he felt a certain "weariness of spirit," at rising to speak in the "gas chamber" created by the "fumes" exuded by the Congress member who preceded him. For this sarcasm Mukerjee was chastized by the deputy speaker, who was then in the chair. The remainder of the speech was a detailed enumeration of faults in government policy, in which he made, *inter alia,* the following charges: that taxation policy was characterized by "softness" toward the "big money interests"; that the country's defense forces were "hopelessly dependent" upon "junk" from Great Britain and the United States; that the government displayed "bankruptcy" in dealing with the problems of unemployment; and that the government perversely refused to take advantage of the benefits of trade with the Communist-bloc countries. Concluding, he defined the government as "men of clay, of putrescent

---

[37] *Ibid.,* Vol. III, no. 12, July 18, 1952, columns 4070–4174.
[38] *Ibid.,* Vol. IV, no. 7, Aug. 6, 1952, column 5753.

clay," and asked, what are these men doing "under the mantle of our freedom?" [39]

From these cases it is apparent that the Communist role in the Indian parliament was, in the beginning, characterized not only by disrespect for the government party, which is natural in a parliamentary opposition, but also by disrespect for the governmental framework. The CPI was using parliament, not as an agency for achieving peaceful political change, but rather, in accordance with Stalin's dictum, as a training ground for mass struggle.

The CPI in the States

In the general elections of 1951–1952, the CPI emerged with several dense clusters of strength in the state assemblies. With a total popular vote amounting to only 4.4 per cent of the total for the assemblies, it nevertheless managed to secure large representation in at least four states: Madras (62 seats), West Bengal (28 seats), Hyderabad (42 seats for the People's Democratic Front), and Travancore-Cochin (32 seats for the United Front of Leftists). It also won a scattering of seats in the Assam, Bombay, Mysore, Orissa, PEPSU, and Punjab assemblies, as well as strong representation in the Manipur and Tripura electoral colleges. Its total (194) was higher than that of any other party except the Congress.[40]

In several assemblies, Communist strength was so great as to place Congress control in severe jeopardy. This, as well as its success in the central elections, gave the CPI reason for exulting. A confidential Central Committee report evaluating the election results declared that the Congress had "suffered the biggest political and moral defeat in its entire history." The report predicted that a "coalition of democratic parties including the Communists as its major constituent party, can replace Congress rule in a number of States." Thus at the state level the Party saw the prospect of power before it. Whereas its preëlection aim had been the negative one of voting *out* Congress governments, in favor of any "democratic" coalition, it now turned to the positive goal of voting *in* Communist-dominated governments.[41]

Probing for the reasons for its unexpected electoral achievements, the CPI Central Committee noted, first, that the Party had done well where it had earlier led mass struggles "in the face of terror and repression," or in plain words where it had organized armed revolt— referring chiefly to the Telengana area of Hyderabad. But since the

---

[39] *Ibid.*, Vol. I, no. 15, March 3, 1953, columns 1405–1417.
[40] Fisher and Bondurant, *The Indian Experience . . . ,* pp. 50, 53.
[41] *Party Letter* (April, 1952), pp. 1–11.

Party was for the moment eschewing armed revolt, it could not use that device to increase its electoral strength further. The Central Committee noted, secondly, that the Party had done well where it had succeeded in organizing peasant support, whereas it had done poorly in most industrial areas. Nevertheless, it affirmed that the Party "cannot become a national political force without becoming the major political force in these cities, in the working class of these cities." Thus the report tended to minimize the significance of the peasant factor as an explanation for its new strength.

Continuing, the report noted thirdly, the success of flexible united-front tactics, with their emphasis upon an appeal for unity. Fourth, it recognized the utility of the slogan of an alternative government. And finally, it noted that the Party had flourished where it made effective use of the "national" factor, that is, of linguistic particularism.[42]

The three last points were apparently the more meaningful to the Party. Woven together in an electoral tactic for the future, they signified a program of coöperation with regional parties and units, based upon an appeal to particularist loyalties and grievances. In this tactic, the CPI possessed an exceedingly effective means of challenging the Congress. Here was the primary device for giving effect to the Party's general strategy, that of uniting the four main classes in the provinces of India, against imperialism and monopoly capitalism at the center.

Prospects in the States

Pursuing this electoral tactic after 1951, the CPI Central Committee declared that, while in the Hindustani-speaking areas of North India the Party's basic task was to promote peasant support, in the rest of India it must intensify the campaign for linguistic provinces and take up other regional causes. And it must form closer ties with other regional political forces. This meant formal agreements with other parties and groups, not a united-front-from-below appeal to individuals, as was made clear by another Central Committee resolution of this period. There would be no individual membership in the "democratic front," it said. Individuals from other parties might, however, join mass organizations such as trade unions, which would in turn join the front as constituent units.[43]

Almost immediately after the elections, the Communists saw the first possibility of gaining power at the provincial level. In the Madras

---

[42] *Ibid.*, pp. 15–24.
[43] *Ibid.*, pp. 37–49.

State Assembly, the Congress Party lacked a majority; the Communists, seizing the opportunity, formed a bloc with other leftist parties—the United Democratic Front—in the hope of taking power in a coalition government. Under the leadership of C. Rajagopalachari, however, the Congress succeeded in drawing sufficient strength from the independents to form a government.

In the new state of Andhra, established a year later, the Communists saw even better prospects. In the Assembly, composed of members who had formerly represented the area in the Madras Legislature, the Communists actually outnumbered the Congress, though neither party had a majority. But here again, it was the Congress which managed to build the coalition necessary to form the government. When, about a year later, the Congress government fell and a new state election was held, the Communists had a second chance. But this time the Andhra Communists not only failed to create a broader united front but lost some of their existing strength through individual and group defections. This, combined with special features of the local situation, produced an unexpectedly weak showing for the Andhra Communist Party in the 1955 election.[44]

In discussing this setback, the CPI Central Committee attributed it primarily to a failure to employ flexible united-front tactics. The Andhra Party had stood alone, since the Congress outmaneuvered it in obtaining agreements with other parties and groups.[45] The Andhra election thus gave further impetus to the new CPI tactic of conciliating other provincial political forces.

In Travancore-Cochin the united-front alliance tactic produced more success. After a period of unstable Congress government following the first general elections, a new election was necessary. The Communist Party succeeded in holding together the United Front of Leftists, and in addition secured an electoral agreement between the Front and the Socialist Party, to the effect that neither would pit candidates against the other. Thus, in virtually all constituencies the Congress was confronted by one or the other of the left parties in a straight contest. This situation was generally acknowledged to be a political "landmark," and the election campaign was watched with intense interest.[46]

The outcome was, however, a stalemate, with relative party strength

---

[44] Marshall Windmiller, "The Andhra Election," *Far Eastern Survey*, XXIV (April, 1955), pp. 57–64.

[45] *New Age*, II (April 3, 1955), p. 8.

[46] *Times of India* (New Delhi), Dec. 28, 1953, p. 4.

remaining approximately the same. The Socialist Party succeeded in forming a ministry, with temporary support from the Congress, but the Communist Party still had reasonable hope of obtaining power after another period of instability.

Recent CPI Parliamentary Activity

In the year or two preceding the second general election in 1957 the Communist Party in parliament perceptibly mellowed its attitude and behavior, in accordance with the new international Communist line of qualified friendship toward the Nehru government. The change was apparent in both the tone and the content of the Communist contribution to parliamentary debate.

As an example, Hiren Mukerjee's speech in the general debate on the Budget in 1954 may be contrasted with his speech of 1952, described above. First, the sarcasm was moderated. Mukerjee opened his 1954 speech with a statement which was more flippant than barbed, declaring of the finance minister that this was "perhaps his worst budget, which is saying a lot." And Mukerjee added, "We all like the Finance Minister." Moreover, the content of the Communist criticism was milder. Instead of defining the budget as evil or corrupt, Mukerjee termed it "damp and dismal." In general, his critique took the form of recommendations to the government, warning that the present budget "cannot ignite that exhilaration which is absolutely necessary if our people are to build a brave new world nearer to their heart's desire." [47]

The nature of the Communist proposals in parliament appears also to have changed. Recent nonofficial bills presented by the Party have the appearance of being genuine legislation rather than mere propaganda material. In 1956, as reported by *New Age* (weekly), the Communists presented serious, detailed proposals for amendments to the Mines Act, the Motor Vehicles Act, the Workmen's Compensation Act, and the Factories Act, as well as bills to nationalize the coal and tea industries.

Obviously it would be rash to infer that the CPI has abandoned the Marxist-Leninist view of the auxiliary role of parliaments and parliamentary activity. But the Party has apparently found it necessary at least to act as though it were a responsible and loyal opposition.

Yet beyond this, there is at least the possibility that the present ideological ferment in the international Communist community, focusing particularly on the question of new paths to socialism, will

---

[47] *Parliamentary Debates, House of the People; Official Report,* Vol. II, no. 24, March 16, 1954, columns 2338–2349.

produce a fresh view of the role of parliamentary action in countries like India. The events of 1957 and 1958 tend to support this possibility.

The Second General Elections and Kerala

As the CPI prepared for the general elections of 1957, it redoubled its efforts to find allies in several key states where it saw hope of forming an alternative government. In Bengal it managed to secure an unprecedented electoral agreement among the CPI, the Praja Socialist Party, the Revolutionary Socialist Party, and the Marxist and Ruiker elements of the Forward Bloc, by which the parties agreed not only on candidates but on a common program. In Andhra the CPI renovated the People's Democratic Front and secured a partial electoral agreement between it and the Praja Socialist Party. In Bombay the CPI worked with a variety of political forces within the Samyukta Maharashtra Samiti.[48]

Once again the election results were reason for exultation on the part of the Indian Communists. While they gained modestly in the central parliament, securing four additional seats, they had extraordinary success at the state level. First, although they lost strength in a few areas such as Madras, they became a party to reckon with in many areas where they had been virtually non-existent before: in Uttar Pradesh, Rajasthan, Mysore, Madhya Pradesh, and Bihar, they made their first substantial showing; and they gained in other states such as Punjab and Orissa.

Their achievement in Kerala, however, eclipsed all others. In this state, formed by the union of Malabar and Travancore-Cochin in the reorganization of states, the Communists emerged from the election as the strongest single party. By making an alliance in the Assembly with five independents whom they had supported for election, they secured a clear majority. Accordingly, the state governor called upon the Communist leader, E. M. S. Namboodiripad, to form a government. The first Communist ministry in India—and the first democratically elected Communist government in the world—took office.

The events in Kerala might well have a profound effect upon the CPI—and, perhaps, upon the international Communist movement as a whole. The earlier Indian Communist experience with parliamentary activity had confirmed merely that such activity could be a useful auxiliary weapon for strengthening the Party, presumably in preparation for a seizure of power. But the Kerala experience demon-

---

[48] *New Age*, IV (Jan. 6, 1957), *passim*, and IV (Jan. 20, 1957), *passim*.

strated that parliamentary activity could itself be a direct path to power. The impact of this lesson is no doubt limited by the fact that Kerala is but one state in the Indian Union and by the fact that the Communist government there has not yet proved that it can retain power. But the experience nevertheless poses a clear challenge to Marxist-Leninist orthodoxy.

Basic doctrinal adjustments would come much later, if at all. But in the meantime, the CPI is likely to focus its energies increasingly on the parliamentary arena, particularly at the state level of Indian politics.

20   THE NATIONALITY QUESTION AND NATIONAL UNITY

Bolshevik Policy on the National Question

To Lenin and the Russian Bolsheviks the "nationality" question was not an exercise in abstract theory, but was rather a crucial issue of domestic policy. The Russian empire under the tsars was a multinational entity, composed of a medley of peoples ranging from the European Slavic groups in the Ukraine or Byelorussia to the Turkic peoples of Central Asia. United by conquest and dominated by a single nation—the Muscovite Great Russians—this empire was ethnically almost as diverse as were the global empires of Britain or France. Like them the Russian empire entailed the subordination of weak and backward nationalities who had profound grievances against imperialist rule. To any political party setting itself against the tsarist government, this situation obviously represented a challenge and an opportunity; such a party was obliged to offer a fresh solution to the nationality problem, and it could make political capital of the discontent bred by the old situation. Accordingly, the early Bolshevik program included not only the usual appeal to the oppressed classes as a whole, but also an appeal to oppressed nationalities of the tsarist empire. That is, the Bolshevik program combined an anticapitalist and an anti-imperialist orientation.

However, this combination did not make for an altogether harmonious blend and it involved the Bolsheviks in some awkward ideological questions. To Marxists, nationalism was in essence a bourgeois phenomenon; it arose with the development of capitalism, and was primarily an expression of the rivalry over markets among the new entrepreneurial classes of various ethnic groups or "nations." It might manifest itself within a feudal empire, in which a new national bourgeoisie demanded independence from the dominant landlord nobility at the center; or it might appear in a capitalist empire, in which the local bourgeoisie demanded independence from the dominant bourgeoisie at the center. Bourgeois nationalism, which had its origin in the desire for exclusive domination over an economic market, naturally led to political separation, or to the fragmentation of empires into their national constituents; the "nation" became a nation-state.

But according to Marxism, the prime movers of history were not nations but classes. The interests of the proletariat were the same everywhere, and they required international unity, not national separation. Why, then, should the proletariat support nationalism, since this simply meant supporting one bourgeois ruling class against another?

In 1912 Lenin assigned the young Georgian Bolshevik leader, Stalin, to write a definitive statement on the nationality question; Stalin's article has been, since that time, the touchstone for this aspect of Communist policy.[1] Addressing himself first to defining the concept of nationality, Stalin declared that a nation must possess the following features: a common language, a common territory, economic cohesion, and a common culture or "psychological make-up." Only when all these characteristics are present, he said, does a nation exist.

But having granted the existence of nations, Stalin accorded them only such rights as conformed with the aims of the proletariat, which are to minimize national consciousness and maximize class consciousness. Nevertheless, the oppression of one nation by another is undesirable, Stalin said, because by arousing national strife and animosity it inhibits the development of proletarian class consciousness and solidarity. Equality among nations is therefore in the interest of the proletariat; accordingly, all nations must have the right of self-determination. This right includes the right of secession, Stalin said, but the question whether a nation should in fact secede must be determined, again, by the criterion of proletarian class interest.

On this basis the pre-Revolutionary Bolsheviks were able to justify

---

[1] J. Stalin, *Marxism and the National Question* (Moscow: Foreign Languages Publishing House, 1950), 115 pp.—Parts of this chapter were included in a paper read by Mr. Overstreet at the meeting of the Association of Asian Studies, April, 1956.

the appeal to national particularism, which took the form of promising self-determination—including the right of autonomy or separation. Thus the Bolsheviks joined forces with the subject nationalities of the empire against the tsarist government.

But after they had come to power at the center of the empire, following the November Revolution, the Bolsheviks had a natural interest in holding it together. For domestic purposes, therefore, they stressed national unity; they asserted that it was in the interest of any given nationality to remain in a union governed by the proletarian Communist Party. Outside Russia, however, they had the opportunity to apply the pre-Revolutionary nationality policy with very potent effect, and in all parts of the world Communists joined forces with subject nationalities against the Western imperialist governments.

At the Second Comintern Congress in 1920, Lenin spelled out the global application of Bolshevik nationality policy. (See chapter 2.) In the colonies, he said, nationalism was a progressive force so long as it was directed against imperialist rule. The Communists among those subject peoples must therefore collaborate with bourgeois nationalist movements, while at the same time building their own independent strength toward the ultimate goal of capturing the leadership of the nationalist forces. Lenin argued that the strategy of supporting bourgeois nationalism would be advantageous to the Communists in the colonies, since it would enable them to make contact with the masses on the basis of an appeal to nationalist aspirations. Of greater importance, probably, was the fact that such a strategy was advantageous to the Communists in Russia, since it would undermine the capitalist powers which menaced the new Bolshevik government.

During the struggles for independence in the various colonial countries, Communist parties flourished to the extent, mainly, that they succeeded in identifying themselves with local nationalism. In China and Viet Nam they were able to capture the nationalist movement, as Lenin had hoped, and became the chief spokesmen of the demand for political and economic independence. Elsewhere, however, they failed in this ultimate goal and, as in India, saw national independence achieved under the traditional "bourgeois national" leadership.

In the new states established in South and Southeast Asia after World War II, the Communists have continued to appeal to vestiges of nationalism by claiming that the new governments are "lackeys" of imperialism and that their countries are still subservient to Western political and economic interests. So far as these governments have failed to fulfill the expectations of social reform and economic betterment—thought to be the fruits of independence—this strategy has succeeded in some degree.

But the appeal to old-style nationalism has been supplemented by a new variation on the theme: an appeal to ethnic or subnational particularism *within* the new states, again patterned after the Bolshevik appeal to the subject nations of the Russian empire.

Whereas the Communists formerly had regarded each of the Asian colonies as a single nationality, in later years they have redefined many of them as multinational entities. A number of the new countries are indeed ethnically diverse, being composed of heterogeneous subnational elements; the Communists have raised these elements to the status of "nationalities" and have supported their particular aspirations against the new central governments. In Burma, for example, the Communists have given sporadic support to the Karen and Kachin rebellions, and to the Arakanese demand for autonomy. In Thailand they have sought to promote the irredentist demands of the Muslim Malays. In Ceylon they have associated themselves, on the whole, with the Tamils.

India provides the best example of this new policy. In the historical survey of Indian communism in Part I of this book, the development of this policy has been sketched; in this chapter it will be discussed in greater detail.

The Emergence of the CPI's Nationality Policy

Though the cultural multiplicity of the Indian subcontinent offered a natural basis for a variety of particularist currents, the Indian National Congress had for many decades succeeded in unifying most of the cultural elements of British India under a single political agency which articulated the common desire for freedom from alien rule. But this unity was increasingly challenged by two main sources of division: linguistic regionalism and religious communalism.

There was in the subcontinent a proliferation of languages and dialects, of which about twelve could be considered major languages —Hindi, Urdu, Punjabi, Marathi, Gujerati, Telugu, Tamil, Bengali, Kannada, Malayalam, Oriya, and Assamese. To these might be added other important tongues such as Kashmiri, Sindhi, Bihari, and Rajasthani. With the exception of Urdu, which was associated with the Muslim community, each of these was the vehicle of a specific regional culture.[2]

With the early decades of the twentieth century many of these

---

[2] On this subject see especially Marshall Windmiller, "Linguistic Regionalism in India," *Pacific Affairs*, XXVII (Dec., 1954), pp. 291–318.

regional ethnic groups had grown markedly more self-conscious; this was shown by the Bengali agitation against Curzon's partition of that region, by increasing cultural organization among the Telugu-speaking Andhra people, and by sporadic agitation on behalf of "linguistic provinces." In 1920 the Congress itself recognized the linguistic principle as the basis of its own organization and established twenty-one party subdivisions, or "Congress Provinces," coinciding in the main with the regional linguistic groups. Throughout India sentiment in favor of a similar reorganization of governmental subdivisions grew apace. Regional particularism thus constituted a significant force. However, it should be stressed that this sentiment did not reach the point of separatism; the regional groups aspired to cultural and political autonomy, not to full independence.

A more threatening source of division, however, was religious communalism. Despite the claim of Congress to be a secular organization, the Muslims turned in growing numbers to the Muslim League. Although the League did poorly in the elections of 1937, securing only a small fraction of the Muslim votes, it later showed clear signs of vigor. In March, 1940, it dramatically bid for wider mass appeal when it formally adopted a resolution asserting that the Muslims were a nation and demanding separate Muslim statehood, or "Pakistan." Muslim particularism, therefore, developed into outright separatism.

The Muslim League's adoption of the Pakistan slogan apparently aroused great interest in the CPI. Within a few months it was evident that a major process of adjustment was underway among the Indian Communists. Though signs of it emerged haltingly, this process eventuated in a sweeping reconsideration of the Party's attitude on the question of India's national composition and, thus, on the character of Indian nationalism.

The first step in this process was the emergence of the view that the Indian National Congress had conclusively failed to unify the Hindus and Muslims of the subcontinent in a single national movement, or in other words, to solve the communal problem in India. This view was expressed in June, 1940, in an unofficial statement by the CPI leader, Dr. K. M. Ashraf, a Muslim Communist member of the All-India Congress Committee.[3] Noting that the fascination of the Pakistan slogan "grows and develops among the Muslim masses," Ashraf asserted: "I have no hesitation in repeating that responsibility lies almost wholly with the leaders of the National Congress." The rise of separatist Muslim aspirations, he said, resulted from the fact that the Congress leadership had conceived of Indian self-government

---

[3] Dr. K. M. Ashraf, *Pakistan* (Delhi: Adabistan, 1950), pp. *ii–v.*

in terms of reactionary Hindu principles rather than in terms of progressive social ideals. This bourgeois leadership, he said, had proved itself incapable of leading the Indian revolution any further, and therefore the Muslim League leadership had no difficulty in persuading the Muslim masses that the Congress could not fulfill their aspirations.

Ashraf condemned the Pakistan slogan, calling it a product of a "medieval outlook." But it was clear that while he rejected the League's version of Muslim self-determination, he did not reject Muslim self-determination itself. Indeed, he himself seemed to be fascinated by the idea. The question of a sovereign Hindu, Muslim, or Sikh state does not arise, he said, *"except* in relation to the tactics and strategy of a revolutionary political party."[4] The slogan of self-determination, he said, "can only be meant to mobilize the backward masses of the communities for an anti-Imperialist struggle." There is in Ashraf's remarks, then, a hint that he was acutely aware of the expediency of an appeal to Muslim particularism, and that he would approve its use by a "revolutionary" party.

This view apparently spread within the CPI, and particularly among the Communist elements of the student movement, in which Ashraf was active. At the end of 1940 his view was again expressed at the annual session of the All-India Students' Federation. Led by Ashraf himself the Communist faction in the AISF, after splitting with the non-Communist element, passed a resolution declaring that the Congress had failed to solve the communal problem, and proposing that free India be a "voluntary federation of regional states." (See chapter 9.)

The CPI as a whole had not yet officially embraced the idea of Muslim self-determination. To do so would appear to do great violence to its ideological system, for in Leninism-Stalinism self-determination was the prerogative of nationalities, not of religious communities. To use this appeal the CPI would have to establish that the Muslims constituted a nation. Or, alternatively, it would have to establish that the Muslims were a group of nations—and this is what it proceeded to do. The CPI broached the view that the Indian people were not a single nation but rather a collection of nations, some of them Muslim and some of them Hindu.

The first signal of this step came in the form of a party letter circulated within the CPI in May, 1941, which pronounced the new

---

[4] *Ibid.*, p. *iii*. Emphasis added.

concept of a multinational India.[5] But as the Party leadership later admitted, the new line met with widespread opposition within the CPI; the letter raised "misconceptions and doubts," and some comrades argued against it by citing the authority of earlier writings of R. Palme Dutt to the effect that India would be a single nation.[6] For the time being, therefore, the new line was not publicly promulgated.

It was not until a year later, in mid-1942, that the CPI openly and officially espoused the view that India was multinational. This line was then widely disseminated by means of the Party's publications, and in September it was fully elaborated in a Resolution adopted at a plenary meeting of the Central Committee. (See chapter 10.) The resolution, after repeating almost verbatim Stalin's definition of the concept of nationality, classified sixteen Indian "nations": "the Pathans, Western Punjabis (dominantly Muslims), Sikhs, Sindhis, Hindusthanis, Rajasthanis, Gujerathis, Bengalis, Assamese, Beharies, Oriyas, Andhras, Tamils, Karnatikis, Maharashtrians, Keralas, etc." [7] For the most part, the CPI's catalogue of Indian "nations" followed the established linguistic-cultural groupings.

The resolution was significant primarily, of course, because it elevated these groups to the status of full-fledged nationalities, entitled to outright independence. But its most striking and important feature was its great flexibility. First, the catalogue of nations ended with "etc." and was clearly not meant to be exhaustive. Moreover, the classification of the Bengalis as a single nation was contradicted elsewhere in the resolution by a provision that the Bengali Muslims, who constituted a majority in the eastern and northern districts of the region, were entitled to a separate state. But the resolution's flexibility was shown, above all, by its attempt to satisfy both particularist and unitary interests; it promised the right of secession, but claimed that since this gesture would reassure the Muslims, it would be sufficient to guarantee unity.

This adaptability was clearly evident in the explanatory introduction, said to represent the "full text" of a speech made by G. Adhikari when he introduced the resolution at the Central Committee session.[8] In his speech, Adhikari stated that it was unnecessary to "make detailed ethnographic surveys" or to provide rigid proposals as to the nature

---

[5] This document was not available to the authors, and its existence is known only through secondary references; see G. Adhikari, *Pakistan and Indian National Unity* (London: Labour Monthly, [1943?]), pp. 16–17.

[6] *Ibid.*, p. 17.

[7] *Ibid.*, pp. 30–32.

[8] *Ibid.*, pp. 5–30.

of a future political settlement among them. All that is needed, he said, is "a general approach." His meaning is clearer in his discussion of specific cases.

> Take Sind. The question arises here: are the Sindhi Muslims a nation or are the Sindhis, as a whole, a nation? I think that the Sindhis as a whole form a distinct nationality. Granting them the right of self-determination of course satisfies the aspirations of the Sindhi Muslims [who formed the majority]. A stickler for arguments might here ask: When a plebiscite comes up regarding the issue of separation, do the Sindhis as a whole vote, or do only the Sindhi Muslims vote? The answer is that this question must be *settled by negotiation*. The question does not arise to-day, it all depends on the way in which the *movement* arises, and can be developed. Ours is *not* a constitutionalist approach; granting the Sindhis the right of self-determination is enough to *settle the problem of unity and united struggle to-day*.[9]

In short, the *promise* of self-determination was sufficient for the Party's purpose, which was summarized in the term "unity." The meaning of this "unity" was further clarified in Adhikari's discussion of the Bengali nation. It is true, he said, that "the Bengalis form a nation"; but on the other hand, the Muslim-majority area of Eastern Bengal has a "special cultural complex" and is a "separate entity." He concluded that it was unnecessary to resolve this contradiction: "The crux of the problem is: *how best can we unify the oppressed peasantry of Eastern Bengal for the common struggle?*" The goal, it would appear, was a "revolutionary" unity under Communist leadership. As Adhikari elsewhere expressed it, the first of the fundamental criteria for applying the CPI's new policy was the question, *"Do we get a weapon in our hands in order to unite with the Muslim masses here and now and isolate the separationists?"* [10]

But revolutionary unity was not the same as national unity. Although the Party persistently claimed that the mere promise of self-determination would lead to a united India, implying that the CPI would tend to oppose separation when the time came, the second of Adhikari's "fundamental criteria" suggests otherwise. This criterion was the question: "Do we define nationalities in such a way that in a federated democratic India every nationality will be able to develop fully and freely?" Elsewhere he asserted, "We should so demarcate the nationalities that in a free and democratic India, the nationalities will *grow and flower, will develop towards Socialism*." Thus the CPI announced that it intended to encourage particularist sentiment; moreover, the Party refused to commit itself to opposing secession in the future. For although Adhikari condemned the "separatist tendency" of the bourgeoisie of each nationality, and spoke in passing of "unity

---

[9] *Ibid.*, p. 28. Emphasis in source.
[10] *Ibid.*, pp. 29–30. Emphasis in source.

for common revolutionary struggle," he omitted any reference to the primary unifying device of classic Communist nationality theory: the principle that the right of self-determination can be exercised only in the interests of the proletariat. He concluded:

> The question of how, when, whether, etc., to separate, cannot and must not be decided to-day. The grant of the right of separation should not be confused with the actual exercise of this right, it should not be confused with the actual expediency of separation in this or that particular case. This latter question can only be decided at any particular moment, in any particular case, in terms of whole social development.[11]

In summary, then, it appears that the CPI's new nationality policy, as it emerged in 1940–1942, was calculated to enable the Party to forge a "revolutionary" unity among the Muslim groups and eventually among all regional ethnic groups of India.

Tactical Flexibility

As CPI policy evolved during World War II, its nationality program showed growing partiality to the Muslim League and open acceptance of the League's case for Pakistan. This was illustrated by the Party's stand in the Congress-League dispute over the fate of two important regions, Bengal and Punjab. The CPI line offered major concessions to the League, and was declared in two extraordinary articles by P. C. Joshi, which appeared in mid-1944 and were later published as a pamphlet.[12] In these articles Joshi advocated, not two independent countries, India and Pakistan, but three, for he proposed that Bengal also be given sovereignty.

In Bengal as a whole the majority of the population was Muslim but only by a slight margin, the eastern and northern districts being predominantly Muslim while the others were predominantly Hindu. Earlier, the Party had proposed that Bengal be partitioned accordingly, but the League demanded that Bengal go to Pakistan. Now Joshi declared that Bengal should be a united "sovereign and independent state," which would maintain "relations of mutual assistance and friendly economic collaboration" with both India and Pakistan. This solution was clearly advantageous to the League since thus it would gain influence over all of Bengal rather than over the Muslim-majority districts only. In fact, the new state would probably make common cause with Pakistan, but this Joshi did not mention.

An independent Bengal, in Joshi's proposal, would be established

---

[11] *Ibid.*, p. 29. [This passage is in italics in the source.]
[12] P. C. Joshi, *They Must Meet Again* (Bombay: People's Publishing House, 1944), 44 pp.

not by plebiscite but by Congress-League agreement, which would determine as well the new state's relation to India and Pakistan. The internal communal problem would be solved, he said, by a bicameral legislature on the Soviet model. He ignored the earlier Party decision that Hindu and Muslim Bengalis were different nationalities with different cultures; instead he asserted that "Bengalis, both Hindus and Muslims, realize in their heart of hearts that the free Bengal will have to be a United Bengal."

With regard to the other disputed area, the six eastern districts of Punjab ("Central Punjab"), Joshi proposed a solution which was equally advantageous to the Muslim League. In all the disputed districts the Sikhs constituted a large minority, and in all but one the Sikhs and Hindus together formed a majority; in but one were the Muslims in the majority, and that by only a small margin. Yet Joshi declared that the best solution would be to give all six districts to Pakistan, adding the suggestion that there be a "Muslim-Sikh Pact" which would guarantee the rights of the Sikhs under a Muslim government. "The Sikhs have nothing to fear," he declared.

> There is no doubt that a settlement is possible on the basis of the League recognising the self-determination of the Sikhs if they in their turn recognise the self-determination of the Muslims and are willing to create a United Punjab based on the joint will of the two peoples.

Joshi thus conceded that a plebiscite would be necessary for Punjab; but elsewhere he readily admitted that this would not satisfy the demand for a Sikh homeland. The Party had defined the Sikhs as a "nation," one of the necessary attributes of which was occupancy of contiguous territory. But now Joshi admitted that in fact the Sikhs were dispersed and did not constitute a majority in any significantly large area. "A Sikh homeland therefore cannot be carved for them," he said. (It should be added that in the final territorial settlement between India and Pakistan in 1947, all these districts in fact went to India. And in view of the hideous civil war between Sikhs and Muslims which accompanied that settlement, the Communist proposal of 1944 seems grotesquely unrealistic.)

In these articles Joshi not only offered important territorial concessions to the League; he also virtually accepted the League's thesis that the Muslims as a whole constituted a single nationality—a stand radically inconsistent with the previous Communist position. He admitted that the Muslims could not be regarded as a nation "on the basis of their common religion," but asserted that this was "only half the truth," and that the various Muslim groups shared a common political aspiration, a common culture and, except for the Eastern Bengalis, a contiguous territory. In the last analysis, however, he evaded the question of Muslim nationhood, declaring at the end of one of the articles that "The problem cannot be whisked away by the 'either-or' trick, more precisely, that either the Muslims are a nation or they are not!"

These articles evidently represented the high-water mark in the Communist campaign to conciliate the Muslim League. Afterward the Party had to retreat from Joshi's position, particularly with respect to the Sikhs; the forthright admission that this group could not have a "homeland" had evidently been a serious political blunder. In 1945, G. Adhikari proposed a different solution for the disputed districts of the Punjab, a compromise which he claimed would satisfy legitimate Sikh demands.[13] Adhikari abandoned the previous CPI stand that "Central Punjab" should go to Pakistan, and instead stated that it should establish a separate constituent assembly which would decide the future status of the region. He asserted that under such an arrangement the Sikhs would have "an effective share in the administration." However, he did not clearly specify how this was to be guaranteed to a group constituting only about one-third of the population.

Joshi had provided for a plebiscite in the Punjab, but Adhikari did not; Joshi had not provided for a plebiscite in Bengal, but Adhikari did. Listing Bengal as one of the national units, Adhikari stated that there should be "previous agreement for plebiscite of the Hindu and Muslim areas," implying the possibility that the state might be partitioned. Yet he declared elsewhere, quite inconsistently, that "United Bengal—formed by an agreement between the Hindus and the Muslims," would, like Punjab, settle its future status by decision of a constituent assembly.

By 1945, therefore, Communist nationality policy had been so frequently revised that its original tenets were sometimes lost from sight. This evolution had brought the Party to the position of supporting partition of the subcontinent. However, the Party went to considerable lengths to create the opposite impression; for example, in the second edition of the pamphlet containing the Central Committee resolution of 1942 on nationality policy, the resolution was doctored by the insertion of a phrase declaring "the urgent need to stick together." [14] In this and other ways the CPI stressed the claim that its policy would produce Hindu-Muslim unity.

With the election campaign of 1945–46, the CPI broadened and

---

[13] G. Adhikari, *Sikh Homeland Through Hindu-Muslim-Sikh Unity* (Bombay: People's Publishing House, 1945), 20 pp.

[14] G. Adhikari, ed., *Pakistan and National Unity* (2d rev. ed.; Bombay: People's Publishing House, 1944), p. 16.

intensified its appeal to regional particularism. It now advocated that the subcontinent be fragmented according to the various "nationalities" which it had previously defined. In its election manifesto, the CPI proposed that each of these nations be "sovereign," and that the future India be a confederation of free nation-states (see chapter 11). With this Manifesto the evolution of the Party's nationality policy reached its apogee. No later statement has approached it as an open appeal to outright separatism.

The International Communist View

Within a few months after publication of the election manifesto the CPI was obliged to retreat somewhat from its extreme stand on separatism, as a result of the express disapproval of R. Palme Dutt. Later it was further cautioned by an article on the nationality question in India by the Soviet spokesman, A. Dyakov.

Dyakov's article, published in mid-1947, supported the main principles of the CPI's nationality policy but contradicted it in its details.[15] He agreed that India was a multinational entity, but did not concur with the CPI's catalogue of nationalities. After a lengthy linguistic and historical analysis, he arrived at a list of twelve Indian nationalities which were already "more or less formed"; these were the Andhra (Telugu), Tamil, Kannada, Malayali, Marathi, Gujerati, Sindhi, Bengali, Oriya, Assamese, Pathan, and Kashmiri nations. The formation of these nationalities was "in the main already completed" he stated; with regard to the Kashmiris he added a qualifying "perhaps."

As Dyakov himself pointed out, this was far from being a comprehensive catalogue of national groupings, since these twelve "nations" constituted, then as now, only about 45 per cent of India's population. Another 50 per cent of the population is located in two traditional centers of Indian culture, Punjab (the basin of the Five Rivers) and Hindusthan (the Ganges plain). The national relationships in these two most important areas were distinguished, according to Dyakov, by "great complexity and obscurity," and the formation of nationalities was retarded, he said, by strong remnants of feudalism in the shape of territorial parceling and religious influences.

In Hindusthan, Dyakov concluded that no single nationality had developed; economic progress might lead to the full formation of a single nation in a large part of the area, he said, but on the other hand

---

[15] A. Dyakov, "K voprosu o natsional'nom sostave naseleniia Indii" [On the Question of the National Composition of the People of India], *Uchenye Zapiski Tikhookeanskogo Instituta* [Scholarly Papers of the Pacific Institute], (Moscow: Isdatel'stvo Akademii Nauk SSSR, 1947), I, 223–330.

a number of smaller nationalities could result. The Punjab, he said, constitutes "an equally complex picture," but in this area there was a stronger basis for believing that a single nationality would develop in the future; he did not consider the Sikhs to be a separate nation.

In granting the existence of only twelve Indian nationalities, by implication Dyakov scolded the CPI for a premature "solution" of the national question. Indeed, in his entire article he did not even mention the CPI program, in existence since 1942, much less sanction it.

A year later in 1948, however, Dyakov revised his view of the national composition of Punjab and Hindustan, asserting that four more nationalities—the Punjabi, Rajasthani, Hindustani, and Bihari nations—were "on the point of stabilizing" there.[16] Thus, according to Dyakov, the number of Indian nations, formed and in the process of formation, totalled sixteen. But by this time the CPI's catalogue numbered eighteen; in addition to those sanctioned by Dyakov, it included the Baluchi and Western Punjabi nations.

However, these differences in detail now paled into insignificance, for the main import of Dyakov's 1948 message was full sanction for the CPI's appeal to regional particularism. Declaring that the linguistic movements were progressive, Dyakov called upon the Indian Communists to lend them all possible support. He incorporated this tactic into an over-all strategic formulation which would pit the provincial bourgeoisie of the weaker nationalities against the ruling big bourgeoisie at the center. Through the device of regional particularist movements, the CPI could mobilize all four classes in the provinces— proletariat, peasantry, petty-bourgeoisie, and middle-bourgeoisie—in the struggle against the Nehru government. (See chapter 13.)

In 1949–1952 this line was broadcast throughout the Soviet press. It was typified in another statement by Dyakov in 1952:

On the nationality question there is a sharp contradiction between the monopolist Indian bourgeoisie, landlords, and princes, on the one hand, and the masses of people of the Indian Union, including the bourgeoisie of a number of nationalities, especially the Andhras, Bengalis, Kannarese, Malayalis, and Marathis, on the other. . . .

Thus in the struggle against the reactionary national policy of the central government and the leadership of the National Congress, the bourgeoisie of a number of nationalities of India . . . is an ally of the toiling masses, although not a steadfast ally, and this ally must be taken into account despite its weakness and unreliability.[17]

---

[16] A. Dyakov, Natsional'nyi vopros i angliiskii imperializm v Indii [The National Question and English Imperialism in India], (Moscow: Gosudarstvonnoe izdatel'stvo politicheskoi literatury, 1948), pp. 89–90.

[17] A. Dyakov, Indiia vo vremia i posle vtoroi mirovoi voiny, 1939–1949 [India During and After the Second World War, 1939–1949], (Moscow: Isdatel'stvo Akademii Nauk SSSR, 1952), pp. 216–217.

In the Soviet view, then, regional particularism had come to play a crucial role; it had now replaced anti-imperialism as the chief device for obtaining the collaboration of the bourgeoisie in independent India. Whereas the CPI had formerly allied with the national bourgeoisie against foreign rule, it now must ally with the provincial bourgeoisie against central rule.

Moderation of the Nationality Tactic

Ironically, almost as soon as this line achieved full expression, political circumstances required that it be tempered. Recently, as the international Communist community has endeavored to cultivate friendship with the Nehru government, it has deëmphasized the nationality tactic as a weapon of aggressive opposition to that government. This change is particularly well-illustrated in the development of Communist policy on a related issue: the question of a national language for India.

The language question took on increased importance in India in 1948–1949, as the Constituent Assembly debated the new constitution. The Assembly was generally agreed on the aim of replacing English as the *lingua franca* of the country, but no single one of the regional Indian languages was so predominant as to have an undisputed claim to this status. The most widely used regional language was Hindi, but it was confined to a minority of the population and was inferior in literary development to certain other languages such as Bengali, Marathi, and Tamil. It was, however, the only feasible choice, and the constitution as finally adopted provided that Hindi was to be the official state language—though it would share this position for fifteen years with English. Subsequently the Congress government pursued a policy of promoting Hindi as the national language, despite intense opposition among other linguistic groups.

Commenting on this issue, Soviet spokesmen took a forthright stand against Hindi. Writing early in 1949, Dyakov asserted that the promotion of Hindi as an official language constituted a violation of "equality" among the various "nationalities" in the Indian union.[18] A year later, T. Yershov condemned the new constitution for failing to recognize the "equality of languages." [19] In the Soviet view, then, India should not have a single common language. As the Communists them-

---

[18] A. Dyakov, "The Indian National Congress in Power," *New Times* (January 12, 1949), p. 9.

[19] T. Yershov, "Indian Version of Bourgeois Pseudo-Democracy," *New Times* (March 15, 1950), p. 6.

selves were later to admit, such a policy plainly had divisive or "separatist" implications. It was tailored neatly to the over-all nationality tactic: the program of supporting regional particularism now included defense of all regional languages against the supremacy of any one of them (that is, Hindi) as an all-India language.

In 1948–1949 there were both pro- and anti-Hindi factions within the CPI. But by the end of 1949 the dominant sentiment in the Party was one of vehement opposition to the promotion of Hindi as the national language, either official or unofficial. This view was expressed in a forceful statement in *Communist*, which was, however, subtitled an "article for discussion," indicating that the issue was not finally settled.

The author of this article, Ram Bilas Sharma, castigated those comrades who were protagonists of Hindi for "opportunist concessions to great-national chauvinism." [20] He directed his criticism particularly at an article in the weekly Party journal *Janashakti*. Against the view that Hindi could and should become an all-India language through a natural process of development, Sharma declared that neither it nor any other existing Indian language could ever fill the role of a *lingua franca* for the country as a whole. In the distant future, he said, the various Indian languages will ultimately fuse into one common language, unlike any one of them. But in the meantime, "it is not possible to have a single language for the whole of the country." [21]

In defense of this position, Sharma cited the model of the USSR, in which, he claimed, there was no attempt to impose a single state language upon the various national groups. He quoted Stalin's thesis that the Russian language, rather than dominating the Soviet nationalities, would eventually fuse with other languages in the USSR into a single common tongue unlike any one of them.

But Sharma's attack on Hindi rested primarily on other grounds. The promotion of Hindi as a national language was, he asserted, merely another weapon of Indian big business in its drive for domination of the country. The big bourgeoisie, drawn mainly from a few dominating national groups of India, seeks to impose a single language on the country as a means of consolidating its economic and political control over other nationalities, he asserted. Since the principal rivals of the big bourgeoisie are the bourgeois classes in the non-Hindi nations such as the Tamils and Telugus, the imposition of

---

[20] Ram Bilas Sharma, "On the Language Question in India—An Article for Discussion," *Communist*, II (Sept.–Oct., 1949), p. 51.

[21] *Ibid.*, p. 51.

Hindi would inhibit their growth in the all-India market. Thus the promotion of a single national language serves "the class interests of the dominating bourgeoisie of India." [22]

By 1951 the anti-Hindi faction had obviously prevailed in the CPI. Its view was officially incorporated into the Draft Programme of April, which stated that "The use of Hindi as an all-India State language will not be obligatory." [23] But by this time a complicating factor had arisen.

In the same year, the Soviet academician Madame N. Sosina, published a monograph on the language question in India. She declared that the promotion of Hindi as a national language was a "reactionary" policy, prompted by "the desire of the ruling elements of the bourgeoisie to strengthen their control over the all-India market." [24] Thus far, then, her interpretation corresponded to Sharma's. But elsewhere in the monograph she manifested a certain indecision concerning the future evolution of languages in India. She stated that the question was "extremely complex" in a multinational country, and unlike Sharma she appeared to concede the possibility that Hindi might eventually assume the role of a national language. "The common language, whether it be Hindi or some other, will be promoted by the practice of life itself," she said.[25]

If this affirmation appeared to contradict Stalin's thesis that no single existing language, but rather a fusion of languages, would ultimately prevail in a multinational environment, it was probably because Stalin himself had recently revised his views on the subject. In 1950 the Soviet leader had issued a major pronouncement on the language question, apparently intended to produce a drastic change in Soviet linguistics. Among other points made by Stalin was the assertion that the conflict or "crossing" of national languages in the presocialist epoch resulted not in their fusion but rather in the displacement of one by the other. Thus some languages emerge victorious in the process of cultural accommodation, enriched by the partial absorption of those tongues which are displaced, he said. Elaborating his views further, Stalin declared that in the socialist epoch itself, a process of accommodation among national languages would result first in the

---

[22] *Ibid.,* p. 43.

[23] *Draft Programme of the Communist Party of India* (Bombay: Communist Party of India, 1951), p. 10.

[24] N. Sosina, "K voprosu o gosudarstvennom iazyke v Indiiskom soiuza" [On the Question of the State Language in the Indian Union], *Ocherki po novoi istorii stran srednego vostoka* [Essays on the Recent History of Countries of the Middle East], (Moscow: Isdatel'stvo Moskovskogo Universiteta, 1951), p. 18.

[25] *Ibid.,* p. 19.

emergence of a number of enriched "zonal languages" and then in their ultimate fusion into a common international language.[26]

Applied to the Indian linguistic problem, Stalin's formulations might appear to lay the theoretical basis for the expectation that one of the regional languages (presumably Hindi) would eventually assume the status of an all-India language. It might do so either through "crossing" of languages under a nonsocialist regime or through the emergence of a "zonal language" under a socialist regime. The Indian Communists, on the basis of this reasoning, would be forced to concede the prospect of Hindi as the national language.

For some time, however, Soviet Indologists did not openly draw this conclusion from Stalin's pronouncement. At one of the many meetings in the Institute of Asian Studies devoted to recasting linguistic research in the light of the new dispensation, Dyakov delivered a report on India which added nothing new to the Soviet image of that country. According to the published report of the meeting, he merely presented an account of the rise of regional "nationalities" and avoided the subject of a state language altogther.[27] Although the scholarly journals of the Institute were soon replete with fresh studies of other Asian languages, such as Japanese and Chinese, there was no immediate sign of a reëvaluation of Hindi.

However, political conditions were growing ripe for such a reevaluation. As the international Communist community gradually revised its view of the Nehru government, it had to moderate its attitude toward the language policy of that government. The theoretical basis had been laid by Stalin's pronouncement, and now the indispensable political basis was maturing.

At its Third Congress at the end of 1953, the CPI took the crucial step. In accordance with the increasing Communist endeavor to find areas of agreement with the Indian government, the Party announced its qualified support of Hindi. In the only amendment made in the Draft Programme, it stated: "Use of Hindi as an all-India state language will not be obligatory but will be encouraged as a means of intercourse between governments of different states and between people of different states."[28] Defending this decision in a later public

---

[26] J. V. Stalin, *Concerning Marxism In Linguistics* (New Delhi: Published by the Tass Representative in India, 1953), 48 pp.

[27] "V institute vostokovedeniia akademii nauk SSSR" [In the Institute of Asian Studies of the Academy of Sciences of the USSR], *Kratkie soobshcheniia instituta vostokovedeniia* [Brief Communications of the Institute of Asian Studies], III (1952), pp. 65–66.

[28] *Programme of the Communist Party of India, Adopted by the Third Party Congress* . . . (New Delhi: Communist Party of India, 1954), p. 12.

statement, Ajoy Ghosh explained that a common language was necessary for the creation of closer relations among the various nationalities
of India. In a most revealing discussion, he condemned the policy
of opposition to a national language (which the Communists had pursued up to that point) as "separatism." [29]

Several other events coinciding with the Third Congress of the CPI
suggest strongly that the Party's decision was coördinated with Soviet
policy. In the same month as the convening of the Congress, the Tass
office in New Delhi published a pamphlet containing Stalin's statement on linguistics.[30] And in the month after the Congress, Radio
Moscow announced the publication of the first Russian-Hindi dictionary, compiled by the Institute of Asian Studies.[31] It may be noted
that the preparation of such a dictionary was not mentioned in a report on the activities of the Institute in 1951; this project was therefore presumably initiated after that date.[32]

In any event, Soviet Indologists abandoned their opposition to the
promotion of Hindi. The change was dramatically demonstrated on the
occasion of the visit to India of Bulganin and Khrushchov in 1955. The
Soviet leaders met in New Delhi with the Parliamentary Association
for Promotion of the Hindi Language, and in an address to this group
Khrushchov praised its work as "highly useful and fruitful for the
Indian people and their cultural advancement." He promised that
the Soviet government would provide its own people with "greater
opportunities to learn the Indian languages, Hindi in the first place."
And he indicated that his government would use Hindi, along with
Russian, in diplomatic relations between the two countries.[33]

However, as in other aspects of their attitude toward India, this
statement made in New Delhi by the Soviet leaders is likely to give an
exaggerated impression of their warmth toward the policy of the
Nehru government. In fact, while the Indian Communists have
tempered their former wholesale opposition to Hindi as a national

---

[29] Ajoy Ghosh, *On the Work of the Third Congress of the Communist Party of
India* (Delhi: Communist Party of India, 1954), p. 18.

[30] J. V. Stalin, *Concerning Marxism in Linguistics.* The pamphlet is dated December, 1953.

[31] *Times of India,* February 16, 1954, p. 4.

[32] "Perspektivnyi plan raboty instituta vostokodeniia akademii nauk SSSR v
blizhaishee piatiletie" [Prospective Plan of the Work of the Institute of Asian
Studies of the Academy of Sciences, USSR, in the Coming Five-Year Plan], *Kratkie
soobshcheniia instituta vostokovedeniia,* I (1951), pp. 3–16. This article lists a number of projected dictionary projects, including the Korean, Afghan, Annamese, and
Turkish languages, but none for Indian languages.

[33] *Visit of N. A. Bulganin and N. S. Khrushchov to India* (Moscow: Foreign Languages Publishing House, 1956), pp. 146–147.

language, they have not abandoned this tactic altogether. They have continued to demand that, in the states, the regional languages be used in all official institutions of government and as the medium of instruction in all levels of education. They have participated actively in the literary development of the various languages. Although their policy has been relatively restrained, as compared with the years 1949–1953, they have persisted in the support of regional languages of India.

Recent CPI Policy

In the broader issue of the national question, as in the language question, the CPI has recently reduced its appeal to regional particularism, though it has by no means abandoned this tactic altogether.

The Party's Third Congress marked the adoption of the more moderate line. As Ajoy Ghosh expressed it, the CPI corrected a "bourgeois-nationalist deviation" on the national question.[34] In other words, it checked an excessive emphasis on support of the particularist claims of the provincial bourgeoisie in the various linguistic groups. These claims had frequently been mutually antagonistic, because of rivalries among the groups in cultural, economic, and political matters; therefore collaboration with the provincial bourgeoisie might involve setting provincial CPI units at odds with one another. The Party now affirmed that support of linguistic-group demands must not go so far as to jeopardize its own internal unity. As Ghosh put it, the unity of the working class among all the nationalities was more important than the unity of all classes in a given nationality. The implicit assumption was that India itself should remain united, rather than be fragmented into its various constituent "national" elements. Thus the CPI abandoned the open appeal to separatism which had earlier characterized its policy.

But the Party did not completely disown particularism. It has continued to associate itself consistently with the provincial bourgeoisie against the ruling big bourgeoisie, through support of regional political movements. In particular, it has joined wholeheartedly in the agitation for reorganization of the Indian states on a linguistic basis. In the program adopted at the Third Congress, the Party devoted considerable space to its demand that state boundaries in the Indian union be recast "according to the principle of common language." [35]

Actually, however, in its concrete proposals for the state boundaries, the CPI has departed significantly from the linguistic principle. In

---

[34] Ajoy Ghosh, *On the Work of the Third Congress* . . . , p. 17.
[35] *Programme of the Communist Party of India,* p. 12.

a 1954 memorandum to the government-appointed States' Reorganization Commission the Party urged, not sixteen or eighteen states corresponding to the number of nationalities which it had earlier listed, but twenty states.[36] This decision does not represent disenchantment with the linguistic principle as a whole; in most cases where the CPI memorandum did not strictly follow this criterion, states on India's northern borders were involved. This suggests that the Party may have special aims in the region bordering the Communist countries to the north.

The CPI's current restraint on the question of regional particularism is perhaps best illustrated by its stand on the dispute concerning the city of Bombay. Two linguistic groups, the Maharashtrians and Gujerathis, demanded the control of the city. The CPI supported the Maharashtrian claim, and local Communist leaders joined the Samyukta Maharashtra Samiti, a coalition organization of diverse political forces. But when discontent among the Maharashtrians in Bombay reached the point where it exploded in riots against the Congress government, the central CPI leadership shrank from the opportunity of seizing leadership of the movement. Though the local Communist organization apparently wanted to exploit the situation fully, the central leaders called for a peaceable settlement of the dispute.[37]

Regional particularism has been, and remains, a potent source of strength for the CPI. According to one informed observer, the Indian Communists are at present "deeply rooted only where they have become the political custodians of regional patriotism." [38] The Party has other pockets of strength which appear to be based primarily on the more orthodox Communist appeals to underprivileged socioeconomic classes. But it has unquestionably gained where it could supplement its program with an appeal to "under-privileged" linguistic groups. By utilizing regional grievances as well as socioeconomic discontent, it could evoke a greater response among workers and peasants, students, and shopkeepers, in such areas as Andhra and Bengal. Moreover, it could evoke a response even among local businessmen and landlords, and thus extend its influence to embrace the four major classes of the body politic.

The natural processes of political maturation in India may well

---

[36] *Memorandum of the Central Committee of the Communist Party of India to the States Reorganization Commission* (Delhi: Communist Party of India, 1954), 10 pp.

[37] Marshall Windmiller, "The Politics of States Reorganization in India: The Case of Bombay," *Far Eastern Survey*, XXV (Sept. 1956), pp. 129–143.

[38] Selig S. Harrison, "The Challenge to Indian Nationalism," *Foreign Affairs* (July, 1956), p. 9.

result in the reduction of particularist impulses within the country. But for the time being, regional particularism is a vigorous force. If the Nehru government were to fall from grace in the eyes of the international Communist leadership, this force would again provide the CPI with a very powerful weapon for more aggressive action.

21   THE CHALLENGE OF GANDHI

In evaluating the role of an individual political leader or historical personage, Marxists seek first to identify him with a particular class. This cannot be done merely by determining his economic background, for a leader may come from one class but in his political activities may actually represent another. Nor can the identification be based exclusively on what the leader says or writes, for he may appeal to one section of the population while actually serving another. As a rule, therefore, Marxists try to determine "objectively" which class derives the greatest benefit from the activities of the leader in question, and they then evaluate him on the basis of their attitude toward that class. Thus, if the leader advances the interests of the proletariat, he is revolutionary. If he advances the interests of the big bourgeoisie, he is reactionary.

Even here, however, there are complications, for Communist theoreticians frequently do not agree either on the definitions for the various classes or on the attitude that the Party should take toward them. Thus Communist literature speaks not only of the bourgeoisie, but of the "big bourgeoisie," the "petty bourgeoisie," the "comprador bourgeoisie," and the "nationalist bourgeoisie." These terms are rarely defined, and are often used inconsistently. Moreover, when strategy changes, the attitude toward the various classes changes, and with these adjustments must come a new appraisal of political leaders. It is for this reason that Communists must rewrite history with every major change of line, and the evaluations of Communist historians are only as durable as the contemporary strategical approach of the Party.

Perhaps nowhere is this better illustrated than in Mohandas Karamchand Gandhi, whose role in Indian politics has been a continual source of frustration for Communist theoreticians. Gandhi was bound to trouble the Communists, for he stood for everything the Communists opposed. He was a religious Hindu who believed not only in the basic philosophy of Hinduism, but also in the social structure which had evolved from it. He recognized its evils, especially untouchability, and he called for reform. But his reform was designed to strengthen the basic system, not to overthrow it. Love, he argued, not struggle, was the natural relationship between classes.

Gandhi's ideas also clashed with those of the Communists on economics and science. He opposed modern medicine, birth control, the factory, and the industrialized society that had developed in the West. He advocated a simple agrarian social order, based on decentralized cottage industries and organized with a minimum of central planning and control. He was an ascetic, and the high living standards of the West were to him the product of a materialism from which he wished to save India. Spiritual values, he felt, must take precedence over creature comforts. By developing the technique of *satyagraha* (nonviolent direct action) he challenged the concept that violent struggle was the only effective weapon of the oppressed, and thus attacked a basic tenet of Communist doctrine.

For all these reasons the teachings of Gandhi were incompatible with the theories of Marx and Lenin. But worse, as far as the Communists were concerned, was the realization that were the masses to accept his ideas of love and nonviolence, they could never be persuaded to wrest power from the exploiting classes and set up a dictatorship of the proletariat. Gandhism, therefore, was both theoretically reactionary and tactically menacing to the Communists. It had to be combatted.

But Gandhi was enormously popular with the masses, and to oppose the Mahatma was to risk the enmity of millions who adored him and responded to his political bidding. How then could the Communists attack Gandhism without appearing to attack Gandhi himself? This was a formidable dilemma, and they never resolved it satisfactorily. They were so blinded by their own dogma that they often turned their backs on political realities and pretended that Gandhi's influence was dead or declining. "The imminent collapse of Gandhism," wrote M. N. Roy as early as 1922, "will close a romantic and exciting chapter of the Indian national movement. It will demonstrate that a socially revolutionary movement cannot be influenced by reactionary forces." [1] And in 1931 R. Palme Dutt said: "Gandhism is already dying; Gandhism has reached the full exhaustion of its possibilities." [2]

But Ghandhism did not die, and as will be shown, even now the ghost of the Mahatma continues to haunt Marxist theoreticians, exposing the tortured logic in their "scientific" approach to history. "Gandhian ideology," E. M. S. Namboodiripad reluctantly conceded in 1954, "is still a very strong influence among large sections in our country who are genuinely anxious to serve the people." [3]

Early Attitudes Toward Gandhi

The first Communist writer to present a detailed Marxist analysis of Gandhi was M. N. Roy, and to a large extent it was his appraisal which determined the Comintern view in the early period. In his first book, *India in Transition*, published in 1922, Roy discussed Gandhi at some length and clearly identified him with the feudal classes. He had an "unerring instinct for safeguarding class-interest," said Roy.

This strong instinct of preserving property rights above all betrays the class affiliation of Gandhi, in spite of his pious outbursts against the sordid materialism of modern civilization. His hostility to capitalist society is manifestly not revolutionary, but reactionary. He believes in the sanctity of private property, but seeks to prevent its inevitable evolution to capitalism.[4]

Roy's conclusion was that Gandhism was "the acutest and most desperate manifestation of the forces of reaction." [5]

Roy's wife Evelyn also made a major contribution to the early Communist literature on Gandhi. In a series of articles written under the pen name Santi Devi, she produced one of the best-argued critiques of Gandhi ever published in Communist literature. These articles appeared during 1922 in various publications, including *Vanguard* and *Inprecor,* and three of them were later reprinted in a collection of essays on India that Roy published from Berlin. Evelyn Roy was not niggardly in her praise of Gandhi as a man and a saint. She declared him to be:

[an] idealist and ascetic who has cheerfully given his whole life to the service of his fellows, upon whose personal character no faintest blemish rests, whose fearless courage and love of truth stand proven before the whole world and who combines the naive purity and innocence of a child with the iron will and unbending principles of

---

[1] M. N. Roy, *India in Transition* (Geneva: J. B. Target, 1922), p. 208.

[2] R. Palme Dutt, "India," *Labour Monthly,* XIII (May, 1931), p. 263.

[3] E. M. S. Namboodiripad, "The Birth of Gandhism," *New Age* (monthly), III (July, 1954), p. 43.

[4] Roy, *India in Transition,* p. 236.

[5] *Ibid.,* p. 205.

a man, such a character will go down to history with the same moral force upon posterity as his saintly prototypes of the past, Thomas Aquinas, Savonarola, and Saint Francis of Assisi.[6]

But to follow Gandhi's doctrine of non-violence would require, she said with bitter sarcasm:

that three hundred million Indians will cheerfully endure all kicks and insults, all hunger and nakedness, all poverty and wretchedness at the hands of their exploiters, until these, touched and overcome by such a demonstration of man's innate divinity, will respond to it by throwing away their machine-guns and flesh-pots, their treasure hoards and princely power, and will welcome their three hundred million brethren to a new Fraternity of Man where Liberty and Equality will rule the human race under the aegis of Perfect Love. . . . Non-violence, resignation, perfect love and release from the pain of living—this is the substance of Indian philosophy handed down through the ages by a powerful caste of kings, priests, and philosophers who found it good to keep the people in subjection. Mr. Gandhi is nothing but the heir of this long line of ghostly ancestors—he is the perfect product of heredity and environment. His philosophy of Satyagraha is the inevitable fruit of its spiritual forbears. What is unfortunate is that Mr. Gandhi's revived philosophy of otherworldliness coincides with a most unprecedented growth . . . of a spirit of revolt against material privation, on the part of the Indian masses.[7]

In discussing the shortcomings of Gandhism, Evelyn Roy pointed first to its lack of an economic program and to Gandhi's "obstinate and futile desire to unite *all* the Indian people, landlords and peasants, capitalists and proletariat, Moderates and Extremists, in a common struggle for an undefined goal. Oil and water," she said, "cannot remain mixed; the lion and the lamb do not lie side by side; each man follows his own material interest, even in the fight for a spiritual Swaraj [self-rule]." Another defect of Gandhism was "the intrusion of metaphysics into the realm of politics" and the consequent "obstruction of the dynamic play of mass-action by religious scruples and moral cowardice."

As for Gandhian economics, Evelyn Roy called them reactionary and asserted:

To run from the Machine-age back to the Stone-age may appeal to romantic poets and religious visionaries, but the mighty process of natural evolution cannot be checked by sentimental imagination. Mankind has progressed by painful stages from being the slave of Nature to be the slave of the Machine, which his own intelligence has invented to conquer natural forces. We must go forward with this intelligence that has carried us so far, to the day when Mankind will use the Machine and Nature for his own welfare and enjoyment, instead of, as now, for the selfish profit of the few and the enslavement of man by man. To go "back to the Vedas," back to the

---

[6] M. N. Roy and Evelyn Roy, *One Year of Non-Coöperation from Ahmedabad to Gaya* (Calcutta: Communist Party of India, 1923), p. 45.

[7] *Ibid.*, pp. 48, 50.

Charka [spinning wheel], is to put away the progress of two thousand years and all the bright hopes of a future age when all men will be free to cultivate their spiritual side, because they have conquered, not run away from, the tyranny of material laws.[8]

And finally she concluded: "Gandhism is not revolutionism, but a weak and watery reformism, which shrinks at every turn from the realities of the struggle for freedom." [9]

The second important Communist to discuss Gandhi was R. Palme Dutt who, in his *Modern India*, published in 1927, analyzed the Mahatma's class orientation. Dutt declined to identify Gandhi with feudalism, as Roy had done, or with the big bourgeoisie. Though Dutt said that Gandhi "could not cut himself loose from the upper-class interests and prejudices," and charged him with looking upon workers only "as instruments of labor to be kept in their place," [10] he conceded that "the Congress leadership of Gandhi was not the direct leadership of the big bourgeoisie." He added: "It was a leadership of petty bourgeois intellectual elements, who wished on the one hand to stand forward as leaders of the masses, but who feared to break with the propertied interests of the bourgeoisie." [11]

Thus Dutt appears to have been uncertain as to which class interests Gandhi's activities were advancing. He agreed with Roy that Gandhi was certainly not helping to advance the working class, and he tended to link Gandhi with "petty bourgeois intellectual elements," which might be looked upon as revolutionary allies. There was, however, no doubt where Dutt stood with reference to Gandhian ideology. "The spiritually reactionary propaganda of Gandhism," he said, "is an enemy of the interests of the masses." [12] But he had a realistic appreciation of Gandhi's impact on the nationalist struggle:

The central significance of this period [1919–1922] consisted in the fact that the national movement became a mass movement. The achievement of Gandhi consisted in that he, almost alone of all the leaders, sensed this and reached out to the masses. This was the first great achievement of Gandhi. He did—at one point—reach the masses.

This positive achievement of Gandhi is bigger than all the idiosyncrasies and weaknesses which may be brought against him, and constitutes his real contribution to Indian Nationalism. . . .

The second great achievement of Gandhi consisted in this, that he brought before the masses a policy of action, of action of the masses.[13]

----

[8] *Ibid.*, pp. 56, 57.

[9] *Ibid.*, p. 58.

[10] R. Palme Dutt, *Modern India* (London: Communist Party of Great Britain, 1927), p. 80.

[11] *Ibid.*, p. 81.

[12] *Ibid.*, p. 113.

[13] *Ibid.*, p. 72.

Although these writings of Dutt and the Roys were hedged, imprecise, and frequently self-contradictory, it is possible to discern important divergences in viewpoint. While all three were agreed that Gandhian ideology was reactionary and should be counteracted, Dutt appears to have believed that Gandhi's political activities could have an objectively revolutionary effect. He may have been prepared to make the most of it during the bourgeois, anti-imperialist phase of the revolution. The Roys, on the other hand, believed Gandhi to be profeudal in effect as well as in outlook, and to be an impediment even to the bourgeois democratic revolution. Of course it must be pointed out that the Dutt appraisal quoted here was written in 1926, four years after Roy had published *India in Transition*. Roy did not comment much on Gandhi after 1923 but he did continue to attack what he called "the cult of non-violence," and in the *Future of Indian Politics*, published in 1926 he referred to "the counterrevolutionary political antics of Gandhi." [14] Consistent with his general opposition to the bourgeois Indian National Congress and his belief in the necessity for armed struggle, he opposed the notion that Gandhi could play a revolutionary role.

Disagreement on the Class Orientation of Gandhi

During the 1920's indecision and lack of unanimity concerning Gandhi prevailed in the Comintern. Interesting evidence for this can be found in the article on Gandhi in the *Large Soviet Encyclopedia*, published in 1929. Citing both Roy and Dutt as bibliographical references, the article refers to Gandhi as a "spokesman of petty-bourgeois ideology" who represented "the interests of the propertied circles." [15] The article does not identify Gandhi with feudalism as Roy had done, but in a vague and tentative manner appears to accept Dutt's estimate that Gandhi was linked to the petty bourgeoisie. Such a view, as has been pointed out, did not preclude a temporary alliance with Gandhi during the bourgeois stage of the revolution.

By the time the *Large Soviet Encyclopedia* had appeared in print, however, the Comintern line had changed and the International was embarked on a leftist strategy. It is not surprising, therefore, that the role of Gandhi should have come up for reëxamination. The most detailed statement on Gandhi to appear in Comintern literature during the leftist period was an article by Valia in *Communist Interna-*

---

[14] M. N. Roy, *The Future of Indian Politics* (London: R. Bishop, 1926), p. 47.
[15] *Bol'shaia Sovetskaia Entsiklopediia* [Large Soviet Encyclopedia], (1st ed.; Moscow: Aktsionernoe obshchestvo "Sovetskaia Entsiklopediia," 1929), Vol. XIV, columns 514–517.

tional in June, 1933. Noting that Indian comrades still persisted in identifying Gandhi with the petty bourgeoisie, Valia said:

> This leads us to one of the chief problems, on which a clear answer will have to be given—what is the class character of Gandhism and what is its evolution. The answer has a direct relation to preparation of a correct Bolshevik policy, the question of the hegemony of the proletariat, and the estimate of national reformism and its evolution. . . .
>
> An estimate of Gandhism as petty bourgeois philosophy . . . still finds support among some of the followers of the revolutionary movement and is extremely harmful, hindering the process of the development of revolutionary Marxism. . . .
>
> The starting point in determining the class essence of Gandhism is the statement of Comrade Stalin in his report at the XVI Congress of the CPSU:
>
> > "As for assistants (*i.e.*, of imperialism) of the type of Gandhi, Tsarism had shoals of them in the form of liberal conciliators of every kind, from which, however, nothing but confusion arose." . . .
>
> Gandhism is now again demonstrating its liberal anti-revolutionary nature. . . .
>
> Thus, *Gandhism was, and is, the philosophy of the bourgeoisie and the landlords. It is not right to state that its drawback consisted and still consists in reactionary, utopian petty bourgeois principles, because it was and is the teachings of the cowardly anti-revolutionary bourgeoisie, linked up with the landlord system and in deadly fear of a national revolution. This is the essence of the matter.*[16]

Valia made no distinction between Gandhi and Gandhism. He condemned both unequivocally.

It is interesting to compare his analysis with that which M. N. Roy had written in 1922.[17] Ironically, Valia had adopted Roy's main arguments at the moment when Roy, in disgrace with the Comintern and imprisoned in India, had reversed his stand and now looked upon Gandhi and the Indian National Congress as useful allies for the revolution.

Differing Viewpoints on Gandhi

From 1929 until 1948, when Gandhi was assassinated, there was no major change in the international Communist line on Gandhi. There had been some indication that a reëvaluation was under consideration in 1939, but nothing came of it. (See pp. 169–170.) Even during the united-front period the Communists continued to attack Gandhian ideology and to look upon the Mahatma as the defender of the propertied classes. As late as 1942 R. Palme Dutt referred to Gandhi as "the pacifist evil genius of Indian politics," [18] which was

---

[16] Valia, "The Constitution for the Enslavement of the Indian People and the Policy of the Indian Bourgeoisie," *Communist International*, X (June 15, 1933), pp. 388, 389–390. Emphasis in original.

[17] Roy, *India in Transition*, pp. 205–241.

[18] "India—What Must Be Done," *Labour Monthly*, XXIV (Sept., 1942), p. 264.

hardly a departure from his 1931 position that "to all that is young and generous in India the name of Gandhi is an object of cursing and contempt, the name of Judas." [19] Also in 1942, shortly after the ban on the CPI was removed, the rightist general secretary, P. C. Joshi, wrote:

Gandhism is the path of negation. This creed which has dominated the national leadership in the past, fails now to answer their needs. It has become the ideology of blank negation which satisfies the ethical needs of Gandhi and his immediate followers, but fails to offer an explanation of changing reality. . . .

The outlook of negation, the policy of passivity and the practice of subservience—this is Gandhism today.[20]

The first important signal that a new line on Gandhi was under consideration came in March, 1948, two months after Gandhi's death and, paradoxically, the very month when the CPI launched its leftist strategy under B. T. Ranadive. "His [Gandhi's] detractors," wrote Dutt in *Labour Monthly*, "can with ease pick out his weaknesses and inconsistencies in a manner which only reveals their own pettiness and inability to understand the greatness that was in him." [21] Dutt reiterated that Gandhi lacked a clear social theory and that he was used by propertied interests to serve their own ends but, he insisted, Gandhi's "greatness of spirit, his honesty, courage and love of humanity shine through and transcend the many inconsistencies and contradictions." Then, referring to Gandhi's efforts just before his death to quell communal violence, Dutt hinted at a new tactic—that Gandhi's martyrdom be utilized by the Communists. For Dutt said that in his efforts to quell the communal violence, Gandhi had

worked in close association with the Communists. At the last Gandhi and the revolutionary working class began to find one another in the common fight for democratic unity of the people. . . . The need for democratic unity of the left is greater than ever.

The democratic forces of India will carry forward the fight to see that Gandhi's death shall not be in vain, that the fight shall go forward to the victory of true independence and democratic unity for India." [22]

From the way he praised Gandhi and, further, linked Gandhi with the concept of democratic unity, it appears that Dutt was not only counseling moderation with regard to Gandhi but was suggesting

---

[19] R. Palme Dutt, "India," *Labour Monthly*, XIII (May, 1931), p. 264.

[20] P. C. Joshi, *The Indian Communist Party; its policy and work in the war of liberation* . . . (London: Communist Party of Great Britain, 1942), p. 26. Emphasis in original.

[21] R. Palme Dutt, "Gandhi—The Last Phase," *Labour Monthly*, XXX (March, 1948), p. 84.

[22] *Ibid.*, pp. 87, 88.

that the Communists use him as a symbol in building their own mass movement. This, however, was not the advice that came from Moscow.

The Pacific Institute of the Soviet Academy of Sciences had met in Russia during 1949 and the more important papers were published that November. (See chapter 13.) These papers were considered of such importance that they were translated into English for the benefit of the Indian Communists and were published in April by the People's Publishing House in Bombay. In the paper on India, A. M. Dyakov, a leading Soviet Indologist, dealt specifically with Gandhi:

> The attempts to utilize the authority of Gandhi for a "defense of democracy" in India are extremely harmful and dangerous. Gandhi has never headed the armed struggle against imperialism and has never come out against traitors from among the Indians. On the contrary, he has always been the principle traitor of the mass national liberation movement. The struggle against Gandhism—the ideology of the counter-revolutionary bourgeoisie of India—is impossible without a struggle against the authority of Gandhi, against the Gandhi cult, without an exposure of all the activities of Gandhi who has constantly betrayed the popular movement and by this rendered tremendous services to the British enslavers of India.[23]

Here, then, was a direct contradiction of Dutt. Dutt had claimed that Gandhi had "incarnated the Indian national movement," had "kindled the flame of revolt against imperialist domination," and had "brought out the national movement from the narrow circles of liberal constitutionalism to the masses." But the Russians insisted that he had "never headed the armed struggle against imperialism" and had "never come out against the traitors." This gave the Indian Communists three clear-cut alternatives: they could follow Dutt, follow the Russians, or come up with a line of their own. They decided to follow the Russians.

This is clearly indicated by the fact that two months after the Dyakov article had been published in Russia, an article on Gandhi appeared in the CPI theoretical journal, *Communist*. It was a long diatribe, following closely the line laid down by Dyakov. Had Gandhi led the nationalist struggle? No; during the 1920 campaign he had "decapitated the revolutionary mass movement." [24] "The theory and tactics of Gandhi," the author charged, "have played a *hampering and reactionary role* in the development of the national liberation movement." [25] Should the Communists make Gandhi a symbol of leftist unity as Dutt appeared to have suggested? No. "The paramount task

---

[23] A. M. Dyakov, *Crisis of the Colonial System* (Bombay: People's Publishing House, 1951), p. 32.

[24] S. M. Vakar, "The Class Essence of Gandhism," *Communist*, III (Jan., 1950), p. 15.

[25] *Ibid.*, p. 23. Emphasis in original.

of the Indian proletariat at this stage," said the article, "consists in the emancipation of the millions of peasant masses from the ideological and political influence of the bourgeoisie and particularly from the influence of Gandhian ideology." [26]

During the next four years the CPI virtually ignored the problem of Gandhism. It was not until the summer of 1954, when the CPI was in the midst of a crisis concerning policy toward the Nehru government, that Gandhi's role was reëvaluated in public print. In the July issue of *New Age* E. M. S. Namboodiripad began a series of articles on Gandhi, based on Tendulkar's eight-volume biography of the Mahatma, that ran for more than a year. Examining Gandhi's part in the national liberation movement and discussing his economic and social theories, these articles represented a considerable softening since 1950. Namboodiripad recognized Gandhi to have been an important leader in the national struggle, but unequivocally linked him with the bourgeoisie:

> Gandhi had no personal axe to grind; he represented the bourgeois class as a whole and not an individual or group among the bourgeoisie; he, therefore, was able to look at every problem from the point of view of the long range interests of his class as a whole, rather than from the narrow, petty, personal or group interests of sections of the bourgeoisie. He therefore was able not only to see the main sources of the instability of the new state [communalism] with a certain amount of objectivity, but also to do his utmost to remove these sources of instability. Herein lies the greatness of Gandhi as the typical ideological-political leader of the Indian bourgeoisie.[27]

Namboodiripad was obviously using great care to be less offensive to the general public than earlier Communist commentators had been. But at the same time he was making it quite clear to Marxists that the line had not changed and that the Party still regarded both Gandhi and his ideology as furthering the interests of the exploiting classes.

Meanwhile, more important adjustments of the Communist line were being made in the Soviet Union. Due perhaps to the impact which the Bandung Conference had had on international affairs, Soviet theoreticians began a major reinterpretation of recent Asian history, and this included a more favorable view of Gandhi.[28] Criticizing the general status of Oriental studies in the Soviet Union, an editorial in the May issue of *Kommunist* made a special reference to Gandhi: "In considering the role of Gandhi in the struggle with imperialism our Asian scholars have not always taken as their point of

---

[26] *Ibid.*, p. 7.

[27] E. M. S. Namboodiripad, "August 15: Gandhism's Triumph or Defeat?" *New Age* (monthly), IV (June, 1955), pp. 21–22.

[28] See Walter Z. Laqueur, "The Shifting Line of Soviet Orientology," *Problems of Communism*, V (March–April, 1956), pp. 20–26.

departure the concrete historical circumstances in India itself." [29]
Then, in a spectacular gesture timed to coincide with Prime Minister
Nehru's June visit to the Soviet Union, 100,000 copies of a Russian
translation of Nehru's *Discovery of India* were rushed through the
presses in less than a month.[30] Dyakov and Balabushevich, the most
important Indologists among the Soviet orientalists, reviewed the book
in the June issue of *Kommunist*. Though Nehru sometimes exaggerated the importance of Gandhi's role, said the reviewers, it was
"entirely proper" to give Gandhi, as Nehru did, a great place in the
national liberation movement.[31]

Additional evidence of the new Soviet line on Gandhi was provided when N. A. Bulganin and Nikita Khrushchov, visiting India in
November, 1955, made several references to Gandhi, each of them
short and very carefully phrased: On November 21 Bulganin told the
parliament: "We know how greatly important in that struggle [for
independence] were the ideas and guidance of the distinguished leader
of the Indian national movement, Mahatma Gandhi." [32] Khrushchov
told the same audience that Russian translations had been made of
the writings of Gandhi "who had such a thorough knowledge of his
country and its great people, and who played such a big part in your
history." [33] Then, speaking in Bombay on November 24, Bulganin
said:

> You had an outstanding leader who did much for your country. I am speaking of
> Mahatma Gandhi, who is held in high esteem in your country as a glorious patriot
> and friend of the people. We pay due tribute to his memory and to the work of his
> successor, Jawaharlal Nehru. (Applause). . . .
> We, Lenin's pupils, do not share Gandhi's philosophical views, but we consider
> him an outstanding leader who did much for the development of a peace-loving
> attitude in your people and for their struggle for independence.[34]

From the popular Indian point of view these statements by no means
adequately recognized the importance of the "father of the nation."
But to the Indian Communists they indicated a significant adjustment.
To appreciate this one need only refer to the article on Gandhi in
the second edition of the Soviet Encyclopedia, published in 1952 and

[29] "Za dal'neishii pod'yom sovetskogo vostokovedeniia" [For the Further Advance
of Soviet Asian Studies], *Kommunist*, no. 8 (May, 1955), p. 78.
[30] *Blitz* (Bombay), June 25, 1955, p. 16.
[31] V. Balabushevich and A. Dyakov, "Kniga o velikom indiiskii narode" [A Book
About the Great Indian People], *Kommunist*, no. 9 (June, 1955), p. 103.
[32] *Visit to India of N. A. Bulganin, Chairman of the USSR Council of Ministers,
and N. S. Khrushchov, Member of the Presidium of the USSR Supreme Soviet,
Speeches and Official Documents* (Moscow: Foreign Languages Publishing House,
1956), p. 33.
[33] *Ibid.*, p. 55.
[34] *Ibid.*, p. 76.

at this writing still unrevised (unlike the Beria article). The Encyclopedia identifies Gandhi as the "author of the reactionary political doctrine, the so-called Gandhism." Describing his career it declares:

In the years of the first World War Gandhi, as before, supported British imperialism. . . . At the same time he conducted agitation for the extension of the political rights of the Indian big bourgeoisie and landlords. The role of Gandhi in the development of the national liberation movement reflected the traitorous position of the big Indian bourgeoisie and liberal landlords.[35]

When the movement began to convert itself into revolution, he betrayed the people and helped the imperialists suppress the uprising. The Encyclopedia article further states that Gandhi played on the religious superstitions of the masses and "demagogically posed as an advocate of Indian independence." Gandhism, it says, "became the ideological weapon of the Indian big bourgeoisie, closely connected with feudal landlords and money lenders." [36]

Shortly after Bulganin and Khrushchov visited India, E. Zhukov, the leading Soviet expert on Asian affairs, published a letter in *New Times* in which he went even further than had Dyakov, Balabushevich, Bulganin, and Khrushchov in their previous cautious statements on Gandhi. Referring to Bulganin's Bombay speech, Zhukov wrote:

Unfortunately, Soviet historical literature has failed to give a clear and lucid appraisal of the part played by Gandhi. Moreover, certain Soviet studies contain an incorrect assessment of his activities.

What is the explanation?

It is, I believe, that until quite recently we did not possess sufficient knowledge of the facts of Indian history. As a result, the characterization of so complex a figure as Gandhi was bound to be one-sided. Our authors concentrated on criticizing certain aspects of the Gandhi philosophy, regarding his activities in complete divorcement from the concrete conditions and level of the anti-imperialist movement in India. And it must be admitted that most Soviet oriental scholars, myself among them, at one time shared these views, which found expression in the press.

In this connection, I should like to emphasize once again the vast importance of Premier Nehru's books for a correct understanding of many specific features of the national-liberation movement in India, and notably the part played by Gandhi.[37]

Zhukov's "explanation" was a rather lame excuse for past mistakes, since earlier Russian scholarship on India shows adequate factual knowledge, though not great objectivity.[38] But it is most significant that Zhukov was willing to accept Nehru as a source for "correct un-

---

[35] *Bol'shaia Sovetskaia Entsiklopediia* (2d ed.; Moscow: Gosudarstvennoe nauchnoe izdatel'stvo "Bol'shaia . . . ," 1952), X, 203.

[36] *Ibid.*, p. 204.

[37] E. Zhukov, "Gandhi's Role in History," *New Times* (Feb. 2, 1956), pp. 15–16.

[38] See for example A. Dyakov, *Natsional'nyi vopros i angliiskii imperializm v Indii* [The National Question and English Imperialism in India], (Moscow: Gosudarstvennoe izdatel'stvo politicheskoi literatura, 1948).

derstanding" of Indian history—significant not only for the Communist line on Gandhi, but for the whole question of doctrinal authority in the international Communist world. For Nehru's books are filled with un-Leninist views on history and socialism, views which Communists cannot accept without abandoning basic ideological principles. But if Communists could derive from the non-Communist Nehru a "correct understanding" of so complex and so often-debated a question as the Indian national liberation movement, would not his approach to other questions also have value? Thus the Soviet government's hasty gesture in publishing Nehru's book could have far-reaching consequences.

It is ironical that at the Twentieth Party Congress of the CPSU in February, 1956, the task of rehabilitating Mahatma Gandhi was assigned to Otto Kuusinen who, in the 1920's, had championed an anti-Gandhi line. Said Kuusinen at the Congress:

> The great political importance of the fact that in their statements in India Comrades Khrushchov and Bulganin justly acknowledged the prominent role played in the history of the Indian people by Mahatma Gandhi should also be noted. . . . By so doing Comrades Khrushchov and Bulganin actually took the initiative in correcting those sectarian errors which have found reflection in recent years in some of the statements made by Soviet Orientalists in the publications of the Communist International. Solely on the basis of criticism of Gandhi's philosophical views, which as is known, are at great variance with the views of Marxism-Leninism, some of our publicists were at that time so one-sided that they totally denied that Gandhi played a positive role in history.[39]

There is no doubt that this reëvaluation of Gandhi arises from the fact that Soviet foreign policy needs to promote friendly relations with India, where Gandhi's name is sacred. This reassessment is probably intended only as a tactical move, but it is likely to result in compromising basic Marxist-Leninist doctrine—and this the Indian Communists appear to recognize. Writing after the Bulganin-Khrushchov pronouncements, but before the Zhukov letter was published, Namboodiripad restated the CPI position in the Party's weekly journal. He paid tribute to Gandhi's skill in uniting the Indian people "in one solid anti-imperialist front." But he emphasized the negative aspects of this unity, saying:

> This passion for the unity of the entire nation proved, in practice, to be a force which retarded the further development of the national democratic movement. For, one of the most important articles of faith which the Mahatma developed as part of

[39] Speech of O. V. Kuusinen at the 20th Congress CPSU, *Pravda*, Feb. 20, 1956, as quoted in *Current Digest of the Soviet Press*, VIII (April 18, 1956), p. 24. Compare with his "The Indian Revolution and Gandhi's Maneuver," *Inprecor*, X (March 20, 1930), pp. 241–242.

his program of building national unity was that the oppressed and exploited classes (the workers and peasants) are the brothers and partners of the classes which are oppressing and exploiting them. . . . It was this Gandhian conception of national unity that prevented the full unleashing of the revolutionary energies of the common people—an unleashing which he denounced as "violence."

We Communists, therefore, cannot forget that it is our duty even today to carry on a systematic struggle against all manifestations of this essential class basis of his philosophy and program of action. At the same time, we cannot forget that Gandhiji's was a national and democratic leadership.[40]

Namboodiripad's article showed that there was disagreement between the Indian Communists and the Russians on the question of Gandhi. It is not surprising, therefore, that toward the end of 1956 the Russians felt obligated to make a detailed and authoritative theoretical pronouncement on the subject. This was done in an article appearing in *Sovetsko Vostokovedenie,* the leading journal of Soviet orientalists. Written by A. M. Dyakov and I. M. Reisner, the article boldly confronted the main theoretical question:

The question concerning which class Gandhi represented in his ideology has aroused great discussions both among Indian and English authors and among Soviet students of India. The following points of view have been held: Gandhi was a representative of the landowners; Gandhi was a representative of the national bourgeoisie; Gandhi was a representative of the peasants. This is a very difficult question to decide. Gandhi was an extremely complicated figure.[41]

With equal boldness the answer was given:

If one approaches Gandhi as a political leader and ideologist, then one must recognize that he acted as a representative of the national bourgeoisie. . . .

The fact that all the political activity of Gandhi was mainly concerned with his striving for the independence of India testifies also to the fact that he could in no case have been a representative of the landowner class.

In summing up, we should say the following. Basically, Gandhi played a positive role in the development of a national liberation movement. It was precisely as a result of Gandhi's activity as a leader of the National Congress that that organization transformed into a mass party. Our unconditionally negative attitude towards Gandhi's non-violent tactics have been refuted by the facts. The National Congress, adopting those tactics under conditions of a general stirring of the anti-imperialist movement, succeeded in inspiring very broad—and also backward—masses for the struggle.[42]

---

[40] E. M. S. Namboodiripad, "Mahatma Gandhi," *New Age* (weekly), Jan. 29, 1956, p. 2.

[41] A. M. Dyakov and I. M. Reisner, "Rol' Gandi v natsional'no-osvoboditel'noi bor'be narodov Indii" [The Role of Gandhi in the National-Liberation Struggle of the People of India] *Sovetskoe Vostokovedenie* [Soviet Asian Studies], no. 5 (1956), p. 29. A complete translation of this important article appeared serially in *Thought* (New Delhi), IX (March 23, 1957), (March 30, 1957), and (April 6, 1957). The quotations cited here have been taken from the *Thought* translation and have been checked against the original.

[42] *Ibid.,* pp. 30, 34.

It will probably not be long before Indian Communist theorists fall in line. Indeed, as will be shown, signs of an adjustment at a very practical level are already apparent.

Violence versus Nonviolence

The Indian Communists have a long-standing attachment for the basic Leninist principle that the overthrow of the exploiting classes can be accomplished only by violent struggle. In its 1930 platform, the CPI stated:

The Communist Party declares that the road to victory is not the method of individual terror but the struggle and the revolutionary armed insurrection of the widest possible masses of the working class, the peasantry, the poor of the towns and the Indian soldiers, around the banner and under the leadership of the Communist Party of India.[43]

In 1923, M. N. Roy said: "If India will not have freedom conquered by violent means, she will have to go without it." [44] And at the Meerut trial, Philip Spratt was quoted as saying:

It seems to me that we who are Communists need not apologize, we need not be careful to disguise the brutal blood-thirsty side of our proposals. We say these things are inevitable. Modern society is based upon fierce brutality, and if we want to get rid of it, we have to use fierce brutality. . . .

We shall not also disguise the fact that in the course of attainment of our aims and the establishment of Communism, we shall have to indulge in brutal dictatorial methods. We shall have to indulge in civil wars in most countries.[45]

Though in recent years the CPI has been less forthright in stating its position on violence, there is no doubt that violence remains in the CPI arsenal, ready to be employed whenever the situation seems to warrant it. The Party's 1951 policy statement declared:

The main question is not whether there is to be armed struggle or not, the main question is not whether to be non-violent or violent. It is the reactionary ruling classes who resort to force and violence against the people and who pose for us the question whether our creed is violence or non-violence. Such a poser is a poser of Gandhian ideology, which, in practice, misleads the masses and is a poser of which we must steer clear. Marxism and history have once for all decided the question for the Party and the people of every country in the world long ago. All action of the masses in defense of their interests to achieve their liberation is sacrosanct. History

---

[43] "Draft Platform of Action of the Communist Party of India," *Inprecor*, X (Dec. 18, 1930), p. 1219.

[44] M. N. Roy, *The Aftermath of Non-Coöperation* (London: Communist Party of Great Britain, 1926), p. 118. The introduction (p. 5) states that the book was written in 1923. Actually some of it was written in 1922.

[45] *Judgment Delivered by R. L. Yorke . . . in the Meerut Communist Conspiracy Case . . .* (Simla: Government of India Press, 1933), p. 225.

sanctions all that the people decide to do to clear the lumber-load of decadence and reaction in their path to progress and freedom.[46]

It is against the background of this doctrinal commitment to violence that the Indian Communists have had to decide what to do about the Gandhian *satyagraha* technique. *Satyagraha* has generally meant defying state authority by open and organized infraction of the law. With such action the Communists could hardly disagree. But *satyagraha*, conducted according to Gandhi's teachings, requires avoidance of violence, and this has frequently been maintained with truly extraordinary discipline. But because this technique is based on nonviolence, the Communists could never approve it. For they argued that *satyagraha* mobilizes the masses against injustice and then frustrates their natural impulses, stopping them short of true revolutionary action.

To be consistent with Communist doctrine, the CPI should have held to a policy of totally opposing *satyagraha*. Unfortunately for the Party, however, the technique has been much too popular in India, and one Communist leader has complained: "We give a call for struggle but soon the struggle transforms into satyagraha." [47] *Satyagraha* is a revered technique and to stand aside from *satyagraha*-type movements is to be separated from one of the main focal points of political action in post-independence India.

There has not been much discussion in the Party press as to the best way to solve this dilemma, but an occasional reference has been made to it. In 1952 S. A. Dange, writing on the trade union movement, commented:

Importation of Satyagraha forms in strike struggles should not be encouraged, though today in some cases, the worker and the middle-class employee under the influence of past traditions easily takes to such suggestions. If in certain circumstances such forms can help to initiate mass mobilization, we should not hesitate to use them, but with caution and care.[48]

And in 1954, reviewing the work of the Third Party Congress, Ajoy Ghosh wrote:

In Calcutta, different Left parties launched a satyagraha for food, but we kept out of the whole struggle on the ground that satyagraha is a Gandhian form of struggle; and since we could not go in for general strikes, we stayed away from it. This was a mistake, and was corrected.

[46] *Statement of Policy of the Communist Party of India* (Bombay: Communist Party of India, 1951), p. 7.
[47] *General Secretary's Report to the 12th Session of the All-India Kisan Sabha* (New Delhi: All-India Kisan Sabha, 1954), p. 37.
[48] S. A. Dange, *On the Indian Trade Union Movement* (Bombay: Communist Party of India, 1952), p. 56.

Subsequently, at some places the deviation developed of looking upon satyagraha as the main form of struggle.

The Party Congress made it clear that satyagraha is a form of struggle which disrupts mass participation and brings only some pressure upon the enemy. In fact, it is a counterpart of terrorism, relying on the same principles of heroes leading passive masses and reducing the people to the role of spectators. While in some backward areas satyagraha may become necessary at the first stage, it should not be allowed to become a substitute for mass action.[49]

Satyagraha, then, may be employed "to initiate mass mobilization," but once initiated there is little doubt that the Communists would work to turn such mobilization toward its "historically inevitable" path of violence. This has generally been recognized by those who organize such movements, especially by the Praja Socialist Party (PSP). In 1953 when the PSP organized *satyagrahas* for land reform in Azamgarh (Uttar Pradesh) and Pardi (Bombay), the Communists attempted to infiltrate the movements. The PSP was fully aware of the consequences should the Communists gain a foothold, and went to considerable lengths to keep them out. The PSP succeeded in frustrating the Communists in both places, but the Communists in Azamgarh decided to organize a separate land-reform movement of their own.[50]

It may be expected, then, that the Indian Communists will continue to view *satyagraha* expediently. They will probably eschew it for themselves, but wherever it is successfully employed by others they will attempt to join it and to channel it into Leninist forms of revolutionary struggle.

Vinoba Bhave's "Bhoodan Yagna"

Since Gandhi's death the best-known Gandhian leader in India is bespectacled 61-year-old Vinoba Bhave, one of the Mahatma's closest associates. Bhave's name has received world attention since 1951 when he launched his now-famous *Bhoodan Yagna,* or land-gift movement, in an effort to solve India's land problem. *Bhoodan,* like *satyagraha,* is essentially an appeal to conscience.[51]

Bhave started the movement in the Telengana area of Hyderabad where, in 1948–1950, the Communists had established virtual peasant soviets, and where for more than two years poverty and violence had

---

[49] Ajoy Ghosh, *On the Work of the Third Congress of the Communist Party of India* (Delhi: Communist Party of India, 1954), pp. 16–17.

[50] See *Indian Press Digests,* II, pp. 63–76, 89–90.

[51] For a sympathetic description of Bhoodan, see Margaret W. Fisher and Joan V. Bondurant, *Indian Approaches to a Socialist Society* (Berkeley: University of California Press, 1956), pp. 35–105. For a critical view see C. R. M. Rao, "The Decline of Bhoodan," *Eastern Economist,* XXVII (Sept. 14, 1956), pp. 397–399.

been the main political determinants. Bhave would hold prayer meetings and would then ask for donations of land to be distributed to the landless. The movement immediately attracted considerable publicity with the result that Bhave received and distributed several thousand acres of land. He then organized *Bhoodan* on an all-India basis and set a land-collection target of two and a half million acres. As the movement evolved, other *dan* concepts were incorporated into the movement: *Koopdan* (gifts of wells), *Baildan* (gifts of bullocks), *Sampattidan* (gifts of wealth), and *Jeevandan* (dedication of one's life to Bhoodan). Lately the emphasis has been on *Gramdan* (gifts of villages), the idea being that all villagers should pool their property and work it collectively.

In general, *Bhoodan* has operated in a very sympathetic climate. The Congress Party and the government have expressed approval of the movement, though in solving the land problem they have relied less on Bhave's ability to change the hearts of landlords and more on legislation aimed at reorganizing the land-tenure structure. Although *Bhoodan* enjoyed an initial success, public enthusiasm for it was soon dissipated, chiefly because the movement was poorly organized and because land-collecting quotas were not met. As its inadequacy in solving the land problem has become increasingly apparent, *Bhoodan* has moved toward religious revivalism, concerning itself more with improving the character of man than with solving the agrarian problem.

The Communist reaction to *Bhoodan* has been negative. The most authoritative statement of the Party position was made in 1953 by P. Ramamurti in *New Age* weekly. *Bhoodan,* said Ramamurti, "is no movement of the people. It is charity—charity in land—just like charity for any other purpose." [52] The speeches of Bhave and others, he argued, made it clear that "their primary and main aim is not the solution of the land problem, but preventing the strengthening and development of the organization and struggle of the peasant masses for their just demands." [53] This stand was reiterated a year later in a *New Age* article on the *Bhoodan* campaign in Bihar. But a new note was added. The emergence of Bhave as a new Gandhi, "is being watched with eagerness and expectation in the American camp. The whole 'American Lobby' pays homage to the new 'messiah'." Concluding, the article declared that:

Herein lies the significance and the basically reactionary character of the Bhoodan stunt. Its reverses and setbacks should not blind us to its utility as a weapon in the

---

[52] P. Ramamurti, "What is Bhoodan Yagna?" *Crossroads,* May 3, 1953, p. 10.
[53] *Loc. cit.*

hands of the ruling class—a weapon to sidetrack and disrupt the developing movement of the peasantry. It is being brought forward at a time when the shining example
of the emancipation of his Chinese brother strikes deep chords in the heart of the
Indian peasant.

In essence, Bhoodan seeks to erase these new impressions and desires from the
heart of the Indian peasant. It is his heart against which the campaign has been
launched.[54]

Gandhi's leadership in the struggle against British imperialism could
not be ignored, but the political consequences of Bhave's campaign to
change the hearts of India's landlords are, to say the least, of smaller
dimensions.

Amidst reports that Gandhian "constructive workers" had become
disillusioned with the Congress Party and had worked against Congress
candidates in the elections, there were interesting indications by the
middle of 1957 of a possible rapprochement between the Communists
and *Bhoodan*. In April, just a few months after the Communists
formed their government in Kerala, Vinoba Bhave entered the state
on a 54-day walking tour. Communist Chief Minister E. M. S. Namboodiripad journeyed to the border to receive Bhave and the two had
long private talks. Namboodiripad also attended one of Bhave's prayer
meetings and asked the *Bhoodan* leader to autograph one of his books
for him.[55]

The next month the nation's leading Gandhians, including Jayaprakash Narayan, convened their annual *Sarvodaya Sammelan* (gathering of constructive workers) in Kerala. At a public meeting Bhave remarked that Namboodiripad formerly had misunderstood the *Bhoodan*
program. This, he said, was before the two had met, and he now excused the chief minister. Bhave then appealed to his *Bhoodan* workers
to make the people understand that communism and socialism, like
the Jumna and Ganges rivers, could join together in the ocean of
Sarvodaya (literally, "welfare of all").[56] In his concluding speech he
said:

Many people feel that the Communists are a destructive force. No doubt we have
differences of opinion on many points. Communism by itself is not destructive. By itself Communism is an ideology worth consideration. . . .

No Communist, in the final analysis, believes that man is not essentially good. They
accept that after a certain stage, the State will disappear. I say that a person who
has this conviction undoubtedly entertains in himself a faith in human nature. . . .

Communists . . . say that we are Utopians. They say that today, if it is necessary,

[54] Girija Kumar Sinha, "The Bhoodan Movement in Bihar," *New Age* (monthly),
III (June, 1954), p. 76.

[55] *The Hindu Weekly Review* (Madras), April 29, 1957, p. 2.

[56] *The Hindu* (Madras), May 13, 1957, p. 10.

we should be prepared to take to violence, but ultimately, of course, we will have non-violence. In other words, for the ultimate establishment of non-violence, they want that today we must have the courage to take to violence. But I believe that today if the heart is bent upon violence and if after this you expect that non-violence will appear at a certain stage in the future, the possibilities are that it will never come. These are some of the basic differences. . . .

The land problem will be solved only when we can get 5 crore [50-million] acres of land as donation. But then this huge figure created doubts and fears in my mind. It appeared almost impossible to believe that we will get 5 crore acres of land, and so when I became doubtful I thought of the Communists. They were also doing some work in that area. And then I thought that if I cannot believe that we shall get enough land through love and persuasion, then there is no alternative for me but to have faith in the Communist ideology. If this work of non-violence and Sarvodaya has no effect, then you will have to take to Communism. Such is the nearness between the two ideologies. . . . Communism believes in violence but there can be no doubt that it is generated by compassion. This is a strange paradox.[57]

Illogical as it might seem to students of the two ideologies, one should not rule out the possibility of a working arrangement between Communists and Gandhians in India. There can be no doubt that such an arrangement is desired by the Communists. Not only have they reprinted lengthy statements by Bhave in their theoretical journal, they have opened the pages of that journal to a discussion by Party members of the compatibility of the *sarvodaya* concept with Marxism. These articles make it clear that the CPI hopes to make use of Bhave's prestige. "The fact that people of the stature of Acharyaji are criticizing the CPI, and constructively too," says one writer in *New Age* monthly, "is not only welcome but demonstrates that Communists are no more a 'splinter group determined to create trouble,' but a party strong enough and with its roots firm in the Indian people." [58]

Mahatma Gandhi's name is still an important political symbol in India, although most of his social and economic ideas are being altered or set aside in a national commitment to industrialization. The essence of Gandhi's ideology—his concept of service to the people—has remained untouched. If the Communists can gain a reputation for loyalty to this ideal, they may be able to do what they like with many other elements of his teaching and still find devoted Gandhians to carry their red banner.

---

[57] *AICC Economic Review*, IX (May 25, 1957), p. 31.
[58] *New Age* (weekly), VI (Dec., 1957), p. 40.

22 CONCLUSIONS: TRENDS AND PROSPECTS

Future historians will probably regard the year 1956 as a great watershed in the Communist movement and, by consequence, in world politics. It was in 1956 that Nikita Khrushchov stunned the delegates to the Twentieth Congress of the Communist Party of the Soviet Union with an account of the crimes of Joseph Stalin, and it was in that year that the workers of Hungary rose in angry revolt against a tyrannical Communist regime, exposing for all who would look the oppressive nature of the so-called people's democracies. Allen Dulles, chief of the American CIA said, as early as November, 1956, that the Stalin era was dead and that it was not too much "to predict that the Soviet Union can never be the same as it was in the days of Stalin." [1]

This book was begun in 1954, after Stalin's death but before the full impact of that event was apparent to the non-Communist world. Much of the research and writing, therefore, has been done during this tumultuous transition period when Communist leaders all over the world, many of them troubled by the inconsistencies between theory and reality, were trying to preserve their organizations under the contemptuous ridicule of the general public and the disillusionment of their own rank and file. It was a time of great change, a time of debate and of confusion. New ideas appeared and old canons were questioned.

The dust has not yet settled, and it will be some time before one

---

[1] *The New York Times,* Nov. 28, 1956, p. 16.

can analyze with any confidence what has happened to communism in these two or three years.

It is possible that the conclusions which may be drawn from the evidence assembled for this book no longer apply, that the Communist movement has become quite different. Yet the attempt to draw conclusions is worthwhile, for there is surely a continuity in the Indian Communist Party. At this writing, the men who established the Party in India still lead it. Some of them may be flexible, while others are set in their ways. But these are the men who led the Party into the United Front, who opposed the Congress "Quit India" movement in 1942, and who went underground from 1948 to 1951. With the monolithic unity of the "socialist" world now shaken by the great heresies of Tito and the small heresies of Gomulka and Mao, the CPI leaders must function under circumstances different from any they have experienced. Nevertheless, their past behavior should provide clues to the course they will take in the future.

Alternative Trends in the CPI

The history of the Communist Party of India may be summed up as a series of alternations between "left" and "right" policies—that is, anticapitalist and anti-imperialist strategies. Originally expressed in the theses of M. N. Roy on the one hand, and of Lenin at the Second Congress of the Comintern, on the other, these strategies have provided the broad alternatives of Indian Communist policy since that time.

The difference between these two strategies lies in the attitude toward bourgeois nationalism. The "left" strategy, aimed against capitalism *in toto,* regards bourgeois nationalism as an enemy. The "right" strategy, aimed against imperialism, feudalism, and monopoly capitalism regards bourgeois nationalism as an ally. As the CPI followed one or another of these strategies, it found itself alternately locked in battle with the Indian National Congress—the primary agent of bourgeois nationalism in India—or joined with the Congress (with its leader or only with its membership) in battle against British imperialism.

From the beginning of the Indian Communist movement, therefore, the choice between these two strategies depended fundamentally upon the goal the CPI set for itself at the moment. When it aimed merely at freeing the country from British rule, it would work with the Congress; when it aimed at achieving power in a socialist revolution, it would work against the Congress. But the goals of Indian communism have always been conditioned by the goals of the international Communist movement. The Russian leaders, interested above all in undermining British power through destroying its colonial props, naturally proposed the anti-imperialist strategy of working with bourgeois nationalism; Indian revolutionaries, such as Roy, interested above all in converting a free India into a socialist India, favored the anticapitalist strategy of working against bourgeois nationalism.

Despite Roy's influence as a highly placed Comintern official in charge of the Indian movement, the anti-imperialist Leninist strategy prevailed in official Comintern policy up to 1928. After 1928, Comintern choice was complicated by numerous challenges confronting Soviet foreign policy, but invariably it was dictated by the relative external security of the Soviet regime. When the regime considered itself menaced by a dominant "imperialist" power among the capitalist states, it reacted with a "right" anti-imperialist strategy, in order to mobilize a broad range of allies to its side. When it regarded itself as more secure against such threats, the Soviet leadership was free to adopt the "left" anticapitalist strategy.

By 1928, having been more firmly consolidated under Stalin, and being comparatively secure against its former imperialist enemy, Great Britain, the Soviet regime could call upon the Comintern to swing over to the anticapitalist strategy. But by 1933, another "imperialist" threat had arisen, in the form of fascist Germany, and within two years the Comintern was required to reverse itself as the Soviet regime sought bourgeois allies against this threat. With the conclusion of the Nazi-Soviet Pact, the Soviet regime again assured itself of temporary security, and the Comintern tentatively turned its attack against all capitalist states. World War II of course required the total mobilization of allies against the "imperialist" threat; and this phase of collaboration with bourgeois allies persisted for some time after the war, while the Soviet regime set about reconstruction and reconsolidation. But in 1947, Cominform leaders again saw an opportunity for a general assault on capitalism, and despite disagreement they set out to disseminate the "left" strategy throughout the Communist community. By about 1951, this strategy (supplemented by military aggression in Korea) had failed to overcome the capitalist camp, and the United States had emerged stronger than ever as the dominant antagonist of the Soviet Union. The Soviet leadership once more reverted to the "right" strategy, in order to draw strength from anti-American bourgeois allies.

In recent years, the "right" strategy has been refined for use in the underdeveloped countries. Patterned after "people's democracy" in Eastern Europe and "new democracy" in China, it calls for collaboration with the bourgeoisie against imperialism abroad and monopoly capitalism at home; in India it has produced an alliance be-

British occ.
- temp. gain (comm. obj.)
Communism today due to which strategy?

tween the CPI and the provincial bourgeoisie against the big bourgeoisie in the central and state Congress governments. As in other periods (1935–1939 and 1945–1947), this strategy was realized by united-front-from-above or from-below tactics, according to circumstances.

As the CPI moves increasingly to a position of supporting the "progressive" (that is, socialist) features of the "bourgeois" Nehru, it tends toward a basically new strategy of allying with the bourgeoisie against capitalism. But whether such a strategy matures depends mainly on the status of Soviet security, which determines CPI policy.

Outside forces on policy

But while the formal policy of the Indian Communist Party mirrors the prevailing strategy of international communism, it seldom completely suppresses the alternative strategy. "Left" and "right" factions have always existed; factional opposition to the formally prevailing policy has never been fully obliterated. Such opposition has sometimes delayed the adoption of a new policy; it has also produced misinterpretation or blurring of that policy; and it has occasionally produced temporary departures from that policy in the official pronouncements of the Party.

The early period of CPI history presents a particularly clear illustration of erratic deviation in official policy. The writings of M. N. Roy alternated between affirmations of the anti-imperialist strategy of the Comintern and conflicting affirmations of the anticapitalist strategy preferred by Roy himself. But other instances could be cited from virtually every phase of the CPI's history, to demonstrate official deviation in defiance of international Communist policy. The August resolution of the Central Committee in 1946 is but one case in point.

More important, factional opposition to formal CPI policy has produced unofficial deviations in the actual operations of the Party or of particular units. The established Indian Communist leadership has repeatedly complained of indiscipline within the ranks, and such resistance to official policy has more than once taken the form of open revolt against the leadership. The divisions in the Party under Ranadive in 1948–1950 are the most dramatic example of this general phenomenon.

So acute and so abiding have been the factional divisions within the CPI that they could rarely be resolved except by international Communist edict. The Party has frequently welcomed or even invited international Communist intervention as the only way out of a factional impasse. But the resolution achieved by foreign edict has invariably been uneasy and temporary, and defiant factional indiscipline has persisted.

The CPI has thus shown both extreme dependence upon and continuous factional resistance to international Communist guidance. The fundamental cause of this situation lies in the fact that, like the nation of which it is a part, the Indian Communist movement has been very imperfectly unified. To a greater extent than is apparently true of other Communist parties, the CPI has reflected, in its own internal divisions, the divisions in its domestic environment. Each faction in the Party has ordinarily been a microcosmic projection of a separate element in the Indian body politic—either ideological, social, or regional. The present study of the Party has offered glimpses of these factions, and they have been identified tentatively. Throughout its history the CPI has evidently contained a radical, revolutionary faction, a projection of the terrorist tradition in India; and a moderate, gradualist faction, a projection of the wider Marxist tradition in India. It has at times contained a peasant faction, specifically identified with the interests of that class, as well as a trade-union faction, a middle-class intellectual faction, and other factions having their roots in various social levels of the body politic. And it has contained factions based in various areas of the country and identified with their particular interests.

These factions have reacted with one another, producing various combinations which are never clearly defined and are always in flux. In their quarrels each faction has constantly resorted to theoretical point-scoring, in the manner of the scholastics. And their attitudes frequently do appear to have their origin in dogma. But it is also evident that factional attitudes derive from concrete Indian conditions and needs to which they are responsive. A striking example of the conflict between dogma and reality occurred in June-December, 1941, following the Nazi invasion of the USSR: one group of the Party, isolated in some degree from Indian realities by jail walls, followed the dogmatic imperative to support the war-effort at any cost; another group, working underground in the midst of a tense political situation, was clearly influenced by the dominant Indian sentiment of opposition to the war effort. This conflict within the Party was eventually resolved by recourse to the international Communist line, but the earlier sentiment, which in effect defied that line, was not suppressed; as Joshi admitted, it reëmerged strongly in August, 1942, and temporarily diverted the Party from its course. Loyalty to the international Communist community (that is, to the interests of the Soviet Union) in this instance provided the dominant motive behind CPI policy, but it was not the only motive and did not convert the Party into a monolith in the ideal image of Communist organization.

Sources of Strength and Weakness

Both the international and the domestic environments of the Indian Communist Party have served as sources of strength and of weakness. The Party's loyalty to the international Communist leadership has in one way strengthened it, for that loyalty has provided internal bonds which enabled the CPI to avoid the splits and defections so common in other left-wing parties in India. In a sense, Soviet leaders and R. Palme Dutt have performed for the CPI the same service which Nehru performs for the Congress—they have been the umpires and arbiters who hold the Party together primarily by prestige. At crucial moments, as in 1950, they have actually saved the Party from disaster.

But the known reliance of the CPI on foreign guidance has adversely affected the Party, as well. In the first place it has stigmatized the Communists as agents of a foreign power, as being less loyal to Indian interests than to those of the international Communist movement. Party leaders go to great lengths to prove that the charge of foreign loyalties is ill-founded. Nevertheless, enough facts are known about the relationship between the CPI and Moscow to make the charge a damaging one. In the second place, the guidance and advice given to the Indian Party has generally been formulated primarily to advance the aims of international communism or, to be more realistic, the aims of Soviet foreign policy, and for this reason it has not always been aimed at bringing the CPI closer to political power. Indeed, more often than not Soviet advice has failed to incorporate a realistic view of Indian conditions and has called upon the Indian Party to follow a policy which has seriously damaged its chances of gaining political power. The most flagrant example occurred during the leftist period of 1928–1935 when, at the call of the international leadership, the CPI attacked Gandhi, the Congress, Nehru, and the "reformist" trade unions, and in so doing cut themselves off completely from the main stream of Indian politics. The 1948 ultraleftist strategy is another example, although this was less clear-cut.

Indeed, it is probably not an exaggeration to say that the greatest obstacle to the success of the Communist movement in India was Joseph Stalin. Stalin used the Comintern as an arena for struggle against his Russian party enemies, and in so doing imposed upon the other constituent parties policies which rarely corresponded to local political realities and needs. How different the history of communism in India might have been had the Comintern recognized the revolutionary qualities in Gandhi, and had it played upon the socialist ideas of

Nehru in such a way as to draw him into leadership of all the leftist forces in the country. Instead, at the direction of Joseph Stalin, the Comintern opposed Gandhi and turned its back on Nehru. Had the Comintern formed a firm alliance with either, the CPI might possibly have shared power when India became independent in 1947.

While the concrete application of international Communist policy in India has frequently proved grossly unrealistic, the ideology which supposedly underlies that policy has provided certain psychological advantages to the CPI. The possession of a cohesive world view endows the Party worker in India, as elsewhere, with an unusual degree of militant zeal. Gandhi himself has recorded his admiration for the ability, energy, and dedication of the Indian Communists. Although a large part of this militancy is spent in internal disputes, enough remains to provide a source of positive strength to the Party and grounds for envy to even the most confirmed anti-Communists.

In addition, this ideology has a potential attraction for a large segment of the Indian population—a body of alienated intellectuals who are contemptuous of the traditional scheme of values, and who bitterly distrust the Western liberal system. The CPI reinforces this appeal by its attractive organizational features; the Party itself, as a social institution, offers a new sense of personal identification to those who have renounced old social bonds.

Related to this is the potential attraction provided by the Communist states. In its propaganda in India, the Soviet Union sedulously creates the image of a powerful and prosperous system, wherein material abundance is achieved without materialist vulgarity or acquisitiveness. An even more effective appeal, perhaps, is that associated with China, which to many Indians appears as a state which is dynamic but intensely civilized, supported by an orderly and civic-minded population.

Thus while the CPI's association with the international Communist community imposes certain severe handicaps, it also offers certain very real advantages. It is impossible to assess the balance between the resulting weaknesses and strengths, but in any event it cannot be assumed that the CPI is incapable of achieving power in India because of its alien loyalties. Indeed, in Kerala the Party has demonstrated that it can rise to power by democratic processes, despite those loyalties.

The CPI has also derived strength and weakness—again in uncertain balance—from its domestic environment.

One of the Party's chief sources of strength has been the deep-seated Indian suspicion of the West, often combined with sympathy toward and identification with the Soviet Union. These feelings have been explained best by Jawaharlal Nehru who in 1928 said:

And Russia, what of her? An outcast like us from the nations and much slandered and often erring. But in spite of her many mistakes she stands today as the greatest opponent of imperialism and her record with the nations of the East has been just and generous. . . .

Russia goes to the East as an equal not as a conqueror or a race-proud superior. Is it any wonder that she is welcomed?[2]

Nehru never lost sympathy for the Soviet Union nor for the idealistic element of Communist doctrine. But his has been, for the most part, a balanced view. He has recognized the signs of Soviet expansionism despite the fact that for the greater part of his life he was preoccupied with freeing India from Western imperialism. And the speeches he has made on the "Communist way" after trips to the Soviet Union and China in recent years make it clear that he is well aware of the totalitarian content of communism and opposes its dissemination in India. Despite his occasional lapses, he appears to have a deep emotional commitment to the freedoms embodied in British-type parliamentary democracy.

But for Nehru, as for a large body of the Indian intelligentsia, this commitment also embraces the economic freedoms believed to be enshrined in the ideas of "social democracy," or democratic socialism. Several variants of Marxism are widely espoused in India, and this circumstance narrows the distance between the Westernized Indian leadership and the Indian Communists. If the Communists themselves were to espouse parliamentary methods, the gap would be almost altogether closed, and it is thus not inconceivable that the CPI might form a coalition with socialist elements of the Congress. The Party will, in any event, draw some support from the widespread acceptance of socialist ideas in India.

Gandhian ideas, especially the concept of nonviolence, have been an obstacle to the CPI, but here too the prospect of ideological rapprochement is not altogether impossible. It should be remembered that Gandhian political tactics were not passive; rather, they created a habit of direct mass action, a habit which benefits the Communists as it does any other political party.

The primary feature of the living Gandhian tradition in India appears to be the ideal of social service. This too may be a source of strength to the CPI, to the extent that the Party succeeds in identify-

---

[2] Nripendra Nath Mitra ed., *Indian Annual Register, 1928*, (Calcutta: Indian Annual Register, 1928), I, 461.

ing itself with that ideal. Recent Communist gestures of coöperation with the *Bhoodan* movement indicate an appreciation of this potential advantage. The CPI may, through welfare activities in its mass and front organizations—and above all through the peace movement—draw support by appearing to espouse the *sarvodaya* goal of selfless service.

A final source of strength in the Indian environment is the tendency toward regional particularism. The CPI has shown great adaptability in identifying with this impulse; indeed, it may have drawn greater strength from regional consciousness in India than from class consciousness. The CPI tactic of forging united-front agreements with regional parties, as a means of challenging the Congress's near-monopoly of power both at the state and the central levels, is a very forceful political weapon.

To many Western observers Nehru's foreign policy has appeared to have a pro-Soviet bias, and in the eyes of some Americans his aim seems to be the creation of a Communist state in India. AFL-CIO President George Meany said in December, 1955: "Nehru and Tito are not neutral. They are aides and allies of Communist imperialism—in fact and in effect, if not in diplomatic verbiage." Some who hold this view even go so far as to assert that Nehru may be party to a secret conspiracy aimed at bringing India into the Soviet system of satellites. Certain aspects of Indian foreign policy—V. K. Krishna Menon's behavior in the United Nations on the Hungarian question, for example—seem to lend credence to these theories.

It is not within the scope of this book to analyze Indian foreign policy. Nevertheless it does appear that the attitudes taken by the government of India toward the Communist movement *within* India give some clue to that government's attitudes toward world communism and the leading Communist governments. In surveying the government's behavior toward the CPI from independence to 1957, one cannot escape the conclusion that it has been as anti-Communist as the rules of the parliamentary system would permit, and on a few occasions has breached the spirit if not the letter of those rules in an effort to inhibit the activities of the CPI. To this end it has pursued a policy which has included: (1) close police surveillance of the CPI, its auxiliary organizations, and their foreign contacts; (2) restriction of travel of Communists going to and from India; (3) restriction and limitation of delegations to international Communist front organizations; (4) prompt prosecution when Communists break the law, and extensive use of preventive detention when it is anticipated they might; (5) control and sometimes limitation of public meetings held by Communists; (6) intensive anti-Communist propaganda by government and Congress Party leaders; (7) creation of mass organizations to compete with Communist-controlled mass organizations; (8) infiltration by government and Congress Party personnel of some front organizations to such an extent that the Communists are unable to control organization policy; (9) stringent repressive measures when the CPI adopts a policy of armed struggle; (10) pursuit of a foreign policy which, as a by-product, makes it advantageous to the Soviet Union to instruct the CPI to follow a policy of constitutional moderation; (11) extension of full constitutional rights to the Communists including office holding, thus giving the Party a vested interest in the existing governmental system.

As of 1958 this policy appears to have been successful, and the Communist Party does not seem to be in a position to overthrow the present system of government. Moreover, there are indications that the CPI itself, in response to internal and external pressures, may eventually so modify its philosophy as to blur the distinction between itself and other leftist parties.

The Decline of Dogma

Communism in India was founded on dogma, and dogma has held it together. This dogma has had many facets—among them that the proletariat is infallible, that the international leadership is infallible, that the Party can do no wrong, that parliaments are the instruments of the exploiting classes, and that the inevitable sweep of history will bring the Party to power. Whenever reality contradicted dogma, the Communists have often turned their back on reality. They were able to do this without disastrous consequences to the Party only because they were always a relatively close-knit, well-disciplined band; and conversely they were able to remain close-knit and well-disciplined because they held to their dogma with fanatic devotion.

The rapid changes taking place in India and in the world today raise the question as to whether dogma can continue to play the role in the Indian Party that it has traditionally played. The spread of literacy and knowledge, and the competitive propaganda of the great powers, have tended to throw dogma into disrepute and to clear a path by which reality can more easily enter men's minds and regulate men's actions. The Stalin idol has been dashed to the ground and can never again be raised in the same form, and although dictators will surely come and go, one questions whether large masses of people can still be kept from the realization that "international proletarian solidarity" is only a myth designed to justify foreign domination just as "the white man's burden" was used by imperialists to justify colonial exploitation.

There are glimmerings of change within the CPI itself. Men like David Cohen and Romesh Thapar, while they are not prepared to relinquish all dogma, have nevertheless struck hard at some of its most fundamental premises. They have attempted to bring the Party back to a more realistic appraisal of the Indian environment, and such attempts cannot help but have a profound effect. One suspects that more Communists will ask more questions in the future, and that the clever manipulation of hallowed slogans and the ritualistic quoting of Lenin will be less and less effective.

One of the factors which has strengthened Communist dogmatism and exclusiveness has been the frustration engendered by the unlikelihood of their achieving power in India through democratic election procedures. But the Party's victory in Kerala in 1957 has demanded a revised approach to the parliamentary system. Success in Kerala has had two important effects: first, it has opened the prospect of repeating the victory in other states and, in the now imaginable future, at the center; and, second, it has given the Communists who now for the first time enjoy the prestige and perquisites of public office a vested interest in the parliamentary system. So long as the prospect of further electoral successes exists, the CPI is likely to exploit the parliamentary tactic to the fullest.

Factionalism is bound to continue within the Party, and the present moderate parliamentary policy will be attacked by leftists on the grounds that the leadership has abandoned the Party's revolutionary goals. These allegations will lean heavily on sacred text for support, and it is possible that the left wing will become the main custodians of dogmatism while the rightists turn more wholeheartedly to "objective reality."

If the rightists gain control, the CPI will no longer be the Party described in this book. It is not likely that in the foreseeable future they will relinquish altogether the totalitarian ideology or the extra-territorial loyalty which are the essence of communism; but they have shown a tendency to moderate these qualities.

At the present writing, in spring, 1958, the CPI is as yet some distance from the achievement of power in all of India. Its chances for success depend upon many variables including the durability of popular confidence in parliamentary government, the ability of the Congress Party to recruit young dedicated leaders, the role of Prime Minister Nehru, and the international situation, especially relations with Pakistan. The CPI is neither monolithic nor unchanging, and it is sure to be shaped by future events in India and elsewhere. Up to now, its nature has been more Communist than Indian. But it has shown some flexibility and adaptability—especially in the realm of tactics. Should it become even a little more Indian, it will be truly a force to be reckoned with.

POSTSCRIPT

The years 1957–1958 witnessed a number of apparent changes in the nature of the Communist Party of India and in its prospects. Certain critical events of this period, therefore, deserve comment before this study is closed.

The CPI Congress: Organization Reforms

The most dramatic event in the recent development of the CPI was the Extraordinary Congress held at Amritsar in March–April, 1958.[1] As Party leaders themselves said, their primary intent in calling an extraordinary congress was to deal not with issues of policy but with problems of organization. The more significant accomplishments of the meeting, therefore, were in this field, although Indian and world press coverage of the occasion tended to focus on certain supposed policy changes.

The principal product of the Congress was a revised Party constitution.[2] Unlike earlier revisions, this one represented a thorough rewrit-

---

[1] The Party announced at this time that membership had increased to approximately 230,000. It did not publish figures on the composition of Party membership, but it did for the first time since 1943 publish a report on the composition of the delegates to the Congress. According to this report, the CPI leadership continues to be predominantly nonproletarian. Approximately 67 per cent of the delegates were from classes other than the proletariat and the peasantry (middle class, landowning class, and "small traders"), 72 per cent had some college education, and 78 per cent were under 45 years of age. See *New Age* (weekly), V (April 27, 1958), p. 6.

[2] The Draft Constitution was published in *New Age*, V (February 23, 1958), pp. 7–12. Discussion of the Draft Constitution at the Congress, where it was amended

ing of the document rather than a few amendments. While practice alone will show the full significance of the changes, they create at least an appearance of wholesale Party reform.

Perhaps the most striking changes, on first glance, are those in terminology. The name of the basic Party unit is changed from "cell" to "branch." The name of the Central Committee is changed to "National Council," the Politbureau becomes the Central Executive Committee (CEC), and the names of lower committees are similarly altered. These changes signify nothing in themselves, but they may well contribute to an appearance of "Indianization" of the Party.

More significant than changes in name are the ones in the size of the leading units of the Party. The CC, or National Council, which has never before exceeded 39 in number, is to be composed of "not more than 101 members." Whereas the Politbureau has never exceeded 9, the CEC is to hold "not more than 25" persons. Moreover, whereas the Party has heretofore had only a single general secretary, it is now to have five to seven secretaries in addition to the general secretary— these together to constitute the "Secretariat." The size of provincial and district committees is similarly increased.

By thus enlarging its leading units, the Party clearly incurs the risk of paralyzing them. If factionalism persists within the Party in anything like the degree witnessed earlier, it is now all the more likely to be reflected in the upper levels of the organization. And indeed when the time came, at the Extraordinary Congress, to elect the new members of the enlarged central units, it became obvious that all elements of the Party elite, past and present, were to be represented. To the Secretariat, along with the incumbent general secretary Ajoy Ghosh, were elected Z. A. Ahmed, M. Basava Punniah, S. A. Dange, Bhupesh Gupta, A. K. Gopalan, P. C. Joshi, and B. T. Ranadive. A more heterogeneous collection would be difficult to imagine. Evidence of its political diversity is the inclusion of Joshi and Ranadive, the two main antagonists in the 1930's and 1940's, and Basava Punniah, a leading spokesman of the Andhra group. Its geographic diversity is striking, too, for it includes two from South India, two from North-Central India, two from Maharashtra, one from Bengal, and one from Punjab. Finally, it is functionally diverse, for it includes prominent trade-union and peasant leaders, parliamentarians, and propagandists.

---

in minor details, is described in *New Age*, V (April 13 and 20, 1958). For the document as adopted, see: Communist Party of India, *Constitution of the Communist Party Adopted by the Extraordinary Congress at Amritsar* (New Delhi: People's Publishing House, 1958). This pamphlet was not available to the authors, and the following discussion of the Constitution is therefore based on information in *New Age*.

To the new Central Executive Committee were elected the full 25 members. In addition to those named above, they include E. M. S. Namboodiripad, C. Rajeshwar Rao (the former general secretary), P. Ramamurti, S. G. Sardesai, Sohan Singh Josh, Bhowani Sen, and others. If to this are added the 101 members of the newly elected National Council, there is scarcely a familiar name from the Party's history that is not included.[3] It is likely that one of the principal objects of enlarging and diversifying the new central agencies was to create an impression of unity. But if in fact such unity does not exist, this arrangement seems unlikely to facilitate effective leadership.

---

[3] The full membership of the Central Executive Committee is as follows: Ajoy Ghosh, S. A. Dange, Bhupesh Gupta, Dr. Z. A. Ahmed, B. T. Ranadive, P. C. Joshi, A. K. Gopalan, M. Basava Punniah, S. G. Sardesai, Jyoti Basu, Bhowani Sen, Harekrishna Konar, C. Rajeshwar Rao, Ravi Narayan Reddy, E. M. S. Namboodiripad, M. N. Govindan Nair, K. Damodaran, Romesh Chandra, N. Prasada Rao, Phani Bora, Gurucharan Patnaik, P. Ramamurti, M. R. Venkataraman, Harikishan Singh Surjeet and Sohan Singh Josh.

The full membership of the National Council is as follows:

Andhra: P. Sundarayya, C. Rajeshwar Rao, M. Basava Punniah, Ravi Narayan Reddy, Makhdoom Mohiuddin, T. Nagi Reddy, M. Hanumantha Rao, T. Satyanarayana, Y. V. Krishna Rao, N. Rajesakhara Reddy, D. Venkateshwara Rao, G. B. Panayya, K. L. Narasimhan, B. Yella Reddy and M. Chandrasekhara Rao.

Assam: Phani Bora and Achintya Bhattacharya.

Bihar: Yogendra Sharma, Indradeep Sinha, Jagannath Sarkar, Ali Ashraf, Sunil Mukherjee and Karyanand Sharma.

Gujerat: Kindar Mehta and Chiman Mehta.

Kerala: E. M. S. Namboodiripad, C. Achutha Menon, M. N. Govindan Nair, K. Damodaran, S. Kumaran, C. Unni Raja, P. K. Vasudevan Nair, K. K. Warrier, Smt. Rosamma Punnoose, E. K. Imbichi Bava, T. C. Narayanan Nambiar, K. A. Keraleeyan, P. Balachandra Menon, C. H. Kanaran, C. Janardanan and V. S. Achutanandan.

Madhya Pradesh: L. R. Khandkar and B. K. Gupta.

Maharashtra: S. G. Sardesai, Sudam Deshmukh, B. T. Ranadive, S. G. Patkar, Chandra Gupta Choudhury and G. Adhikari.

Manipur: Th. Bira Singh and Thien Meghchandra.

Mysore: N. L. Upadhyaya and B. V. Kakkilaya.

Orissa: Gokul Mohan Rai Chudamani, Ramakrishna Pati and Gurucharan Patnaik.

Punjab: Sohan Singh Josh, Harikishan Singh Surjeet, Jagjit Singh Lyallpuri, Avtar Singh Malhotra and Master Hari Singh.

Rajasthan: H. K. Vyas and Mohan Punanmia.

Tamilnad: P. Ramamurti, M. R. Venkataraman, M. Kalyanasundaram, N. Sankarayya, P. Jeevanandam, B. Srinivasa Rao and K. Ramani.

Tripura: Dasrath Deb and Biren Dutt.

Uttar Pradesh: Kali Shankar Shukla, Shankar Dayal Tiwari, S. S. Yusuf, Shiv Kumar Misra and Jai Bahadur Singh.

West Bengal: Jyoti Basu, Ranen Sen, Muzaffar Ahmed, Bhowani Sen, Jolly Kaul, Indrajeet Gupta, Harekrishna Konar and Somnath Lahiri.

Delhi: Y. D. Sharma and M. Farooqi.

Center: Ajoy Ghosh, S. A. Dange, Bhupesh Gupta, Dr. Z. A. Ahmed, Romesh Chandra, N. Prasada Rao, P. C. Joshi, Renu Chakravarty, Hiren Mukerjee, Parvati Krishnan, Sajjad Zaheer, S. V. Ghate, Hajrah Begum and A. K. Gopalan.

The constitution does, however, try to overcome certain chronic obstacles to effective central leadership. The creation of the Secretariat is one step; this agency is evidently meant to be an "inner cabinet" designed to ensure continuous and coördinated direction of the various spheres of Party activity. The constitution provides that members of the secretariats at both the central and state levels shall devote themselves exclusively to the work of those agencies—clearly an attempt to eliminate the tendency of Party leaders to neglect staff work in favor of line activity or attention to their particular bailiwicks. Moreover, the constitution states repeatedly that these agencies must "function collectively"—clearly an attempt to eliminate the tendency toward fragmentation of authority. It also provides that a specified share of revenues from members' dues be allocated to the central units —thereby eliminating the center's dependence on irregular sources of funds.

These changes, which seem to strengthen the instruments of central authority in the Party, are, however, overshadowed by changes of opposite import. There are several reforms reducing central authority. For example, the new constitution eliminates the right of the Central Committee (or National Council) to coöpt new members or to reconstitute itself. It also reduces the Central Committee's control over the Control Commission, providing that the CC may over-rule decisions of this appeal agency only by a two-thirds majority vote. More significant, there are reforms constituting a transfer of powers from the center to the lower units: The right to dissolve or reconstitute lower committees, formerly held by the Central Committee as well as the provincial committees, is now assigned to the provincial committees alone; the authority to supervise inner-Party debate, formerly vested in the central organs, is now assigned to the provincial units in cases involving issues of state or local importance; disciplinary authority, formerly vested primarily in the Control Commission and other central units, is now partly transferred to new provincial control commissions—the decisions of the state commissions will be "ordinarily final" although recourse to the central agencies is provided for.

Apart from these specific transfers of authority, the constitution enunciates a general division of powers between the central and the state units. Defining democratic centralism, it states that while issues of all-India importance should be decided by the central organs of the Party, issues of state or local importance "shall be ordinarily decided upon by the corresponding Party organizations." The central agencies are supreme, in that no local decision shall run counter to central policy; but on the other hand, the central agencies are required to consult the appropriate state agencies when deciding an issue of particular importance to a state.

In effect, then, the new CPI constitution introduces a considerable degree of formal decentralization in Party organization. Indeed, it embodies the rudiments of a federal structure, in place of the severely monolithic structure of earlier constitutions. The significance of this fact is clearer when it is remembered that federalism, as a principle of party organization, is vehemently condemned in Lenin's and Stalin's writings. Its appearance in the CPI constitution runs counter to long-standing tradition in the international Communist community.

There is ample evidence that the new constitution is designed largely for the purpose of rendering the Party more attractive to potential recruits and followers. The CPI has on a number of earlier occasions determined to become a mass party or to mobilize a mass electoral following, but it has never before taken any action to reduce the obvious obstacles to such a goal—one principal obstacle being the forbiddingly autocratic organization of the party itself. Now it has taken such action. As G. Adhikari expressed it in his report to the Extraordinary Congress, the new constitution is "bound to have a powerful appeal to all democratic and patriotic people who sincerely want to work for socialism, and move them to either join or support our Party in that endeavor." [4]

It should be added that although the formal powers of the central agencies of the Party have been reduced, they remain sufficient as a basis for effective control. If the actual instruments of power in the Party are strengthened through other less dramatic reforms, and if unity is secured within the central agencies, then the leadership may be more rather than less effective. In this event, decentralization in the CPI constitution of 1958 will be of little significance. It is likely that the men at the top—who are the same men who have led the Party since its origin—hope and expect this to happen.

But if unity is not secured, and if the new members or followers attracted to the party demand real changes to match the formal changes, then the basic operation of the CPI may be fundamentally altered.

The CPI Congress: Revisions of Policy

Intriguing as these organizational changes were, they received less attention in India and abroad than another aspect of the new constitution: the revised statement of principles in the preamble to the document. The preamble first reiterates the conventional statement

[4] *New Age,* V (April 13, 1958), p. 4.

that the Party's aim is the achievement of power by the working people led by the working class, in a regime of "people's democracy" which would realize socialism and communism. But it then proceeds to make a dramatic gesture toward "Indianizing" the Party's creed. After declaring that the basis of the Party's policy is the philosophy of Marxism-Leninism, it asserts that that philosophy must be integrated "with the realities of the Indian situation, with the experience of India's history, with the traditions of the Indian people, with India's national peculiarities." And, rendering this more concrete, it asserts that the CPI "strives to achieve full democracy and socialism by peaceful means." Moreover, it says, under the proposed "people's democracy," there will be "the widest possible extension of individual liberty, freedom of speech, press and association, including the right of political organization." The essence of the preamble, then, is a deep bow to the nonviolent and democratic traditions of India.

The meaning of the new preamble was clarified by General Secretary Ajoy Ghosh, in a public statement issued after the Congress.[5] Asked whether the CPI had adopted peaceful methods as a creed or as a maneuver, Ghosh answered, "neither." The preamble does not constitute deception, he said, but on the other hand it does not constitute an acceptance of the principle of nonviolence. The Party cannot guarantee that violence will never be required, he said; the preamble merely means that the Party perceived a "possibility" that the working people (that is, the CPI) could achieve power through a parliamentary majority, without having to defend itself by force against a counterrevolution on the part of the old ruling classes. "And we shall try our utmost to make this possibility a reality in our country," Ghosh said. The CPI's adherence to peaceful methods is clearly temporary and conditional; the preamble has nothing in common with the *sarvodaya* philosophy, Ghosh concluded.

The CPI might appear, in this instance, again to run counter to established tradition in the international Communist community. But in fact it has merely incorporated into its own formal platform a principle already well established in that community. At the Twentieth Congress of the Communist Party of the Soviet Union, in 1956, the Russian leaders optimistically proclaimed that the working class might, in contemporary circumstances, achieve power by parliamentary means. On the crucial question as to where this might occur, Khrushchov himself was vague; he asserted merely that it was possible in "many capitalist and formerly colonial countries." But Mikoyan, in his speech at the Congress, was more specific; he declared that it was possible in

[5] *Ibid.*, (May 18, 1958), pp. 7–10.

"certain countries" located near the Communist states; peaceful socialist revolutions in these countries could, he said, be supported by "victorious socialism in neighboring countries." [6]

It was to be expected, then, that the Communists in India should soon incorporate into their program an acknowledgment of the possibility of a peaceful path to socialism.

Summarizing the import of the new constitution, both in its organizational and policy aspects, Adhikari declared that the CPI was now more national and popular in form, but no less Communist in content. Paraphrased from the conventional Bolshevik definition of nationality policy, this statement revealed the tactical character of the reforms. It would be rash indeed to interpret the new CPI constitution of 1958 as a revolutionary change in the nature of the Party. However, it would be equally rash to dismiss it as of no consequence, or to deny that in the long-run "form" may influence "content."

In any event, the constitution represented a step in the maturation of the CPI, for it demonstrated an increased capacity to adjust—if only in appearance—to the diverse and decentralized political environment of India.

Recent Evolution of CPI Policy

Apart from the revisions in the preamble to the Party constitution, the Extraordinary Congress of 1958 did not mark a major change in Indian Communist strategy and tactics. The Congress adopted a lengthy political resolution, but it served merely to reiterate the main lines of existing policy.[7] Focusing its attack upon the United States as the "most aggressive force in the world," it calls for unity among all "democratic" forces in struggle against imperialism and its reactionary domestic allies, feudalism, and monopoly capitalism. For implementation of this strategy, it prescribes a flexible combination of united-front-from-above and from-below tactics vis-à-vis other opposition parties; the CPI should, the resolution says, seek "common actions with these parties and their followers." Elaborating, it praises coalitions with other parties, principally at the state level (such as the Samyukta Maharashtra Samiti and the Maha Gujerat Parishad), while on the other hand it speaks of the need to mobilize a mass movement uniting progressive elements from all opposition parties. As to tactics vis-à-vis the Congress, it calls for coöperation with progressive elements within the organization, which means in essence a policy of qualified support

---

[6] The speeches of Khrushchov and Mikoyan appear in: Leo Gruliow, editor, *Current Soviet Policies—II* (New York, 1957), pp. 29–38, 98–103.

[7] *New Age*, V (April 20, 1958), pp. 4 ff.

of the Nehru government at the center (where the progressive element is temporarily in the ascendancy) and attack on Congress governments in the states (where the reactionary elements are in power). It acclaims certain "socialist" measures undertaken by the Nehru government, but concludes that full socialism can be achieved only by a government of the working people.

As Ajoy Ghosh subsequently expressed it, the political resolution of the Extraordinary Congress did not change the policy adopted at the Palghat Congress "in any important respect." [8] A fuller understanding of this policy depends, however, on a closer examination of the Party's more concrete pronouncements and activity.

The CPI's attitude toward Nehru is perhaps exemplified in its reaction to the prime minister's threat to resign in the spring of 1958. Whatever its private attitude may have been, the Party did not publicly rejoice at this prospect. It observed that Nehru's attitude was a reflection of the rising influence of reactionary forces inside and outside his own government, and it called upon him to meet this challenge boldly. "The country looks forward to Pandit Nehru and progressive Congressmen," the CPI said, "to advocate a fight for the solution of the crisis through concrete measures." Should Nehru take a firm position, it said, "he will have the support and coöperation of all patriotic and democratic elements including our Party." [9]

This statement, it may be noted, bears a striking similarity to statements appearing in 1947 when the CPI under P. C. Joshi proclaimed its loyalty to the new Indian government under Nehru. And it should be added that by mid-1958 Joshi had been named chief editor of the CPI's weekly organ, *New Age.* Following closely upon his elevation to the Party's Secretariat, this suggests increasing influence on his part, and, perhaps, on the part of the moderate wing within the Party as a whole.

Evidence of more conciliatory tactics toward other opposition parties is provided by the CPI's activity in the trade-union sphere. In the early part of 1958 the Communist-led All-India Trade Union Congress coöperated with national labor federations led by the Socialists and other leftist organizations in the joint formulation of a "Charter of Demands." March 27 was proclaimed a day of "National Rally" in support of the Charter, and mass meetings were organized jointly in many cities throughout India.[10] But while the Communists have collaborated with other federations, they have utilized the good will

---

[8] *Ibid.,* (May 18, 1958), p. 8.
[9] *Ibid.,* (May 11, 1958), p. 2.
[10] *Ibid.,* (March 27, 1958), p. 6.

thus achieved to consolidate and expand the AITUC. In 1957 the membership of the AITUC was well in excess of that of the Socialist-led Hind Mazdoor Sabha and was gaining rapidly on that of the Congress-led Indian National Trade Union Congress.[11] By the fall of 1958 the AITUC claimed to be the largest federation in the country.

Other apparent benefits accruing to the CPI from its conciliatory tactics included certain important electoral successes. The Party's alliance with various Maharashtrian organizations in the Samyukta Maharashtra Samiti resulted in the election of a Communist, S. S. Mirajkar, as mayor of Bombay; by an earlier agreement, the official candidate of the Samiti is chosen from one of the constituent parties, in rotation, and in 1958 it was the turn of the Communists.[12] And in Delhi, the CPI coöperated with other leftist forces to accomplish the election of Aruna Asaf Ali, former member of the Central Committee, as mayor of that city.

But the principal index of the CPI's recent policy, and the principal test of that policy, is to be found in another arena, the state of Kerala.

The Communist Government in Kerala

At the Extraordinary Congress of the CPI, the delegation from Kerala was the largest. It was also the principal object of interest, among both participants and spectators. A considerable part of the proceedings was taken up by reports and discussions concerning the program of the Namboodiripad government. And when, on the closing day of the Congress, the delegates paraded through the city of Amritsar, the biggest ovation, according to *New Age,* was for Namboodiripad; to see him "seemed to be the one privilege the people who were awaiting in the hot sun wanted." [13] It is likely that the prestige associated with governmental office was of benefit to the CPI throughout India, just as in Amritsar. But the record of the Communist government in Kerala had brought certain negative consequences.

Reviewing that record after about one year in office, Namboodiripad was eager to portray his government as a respectable rather than revolutionary one.[14] It is indistinguishable in its program, though not in its

---

[11] *Christian Science Monitor,* July 8, 1958, p. 6.

[12] *New Age,* V (April 13, 1958), p. 2.

[13] *Ibid.,* (April 20, 1958), p. 1.

[14] *Ibid.,* (April 6, 1958), pp. 1 ff. On the situation in Kerala see especially: Marshall Windmiller, "Constitutional Communism in India," *Pacific Affairs,* XXXI (March, 1958), pp. 22–36; Seyom Brown, "Kerala: An Indian Bear Walks the Tightrope," *The Reporter,* XIX (August 7, 1958), pp. 30–34; Arthur Bonner, "Communist by Choice," *Saturday Evening Post,* (May 31, 1958), pp. 36 ff. The authors are indebted to Mr. Bonner, who is the Columbia Broadcasting System correspondent in India, for information on recent developments in the CPI, obtained through correspondence.

spirit, from any other state government in India, he said. For example, he contended, its Agrarian Relations Bill is based upon the land-reform proposals of the Congress Agrarian Relations Committee and the Planning Commission's land-reform panel. Communist and Congress policy are therefore the same, he implied; what distinguishes the Communist government in Kerala is that it gives effective implementation to that policy.

Namboodiripad's outline of the goals of his government reflects clearly the general aim of respectability. The government is trying, he said, to begin "breaking the barrier" between the Communists and the mass of the people in other parties. Its aim is "a united front, or if you like, a coalition, of all those parties and elements in our public life who accept the objective of socialism." Rather than celebrate the existence of an exclusively Communist government, he asserted that the goal of the Kerala Communists was and is a "government of coalition" including the Praja Socialist Party, the Revolutionary Socialist Party, and leftist Independents, along with the CPI.

The fundamental purpose of the Kerala Communists, he said, is simply to demonstrate that the CPI was willing and able to coöperate with other political groups in such a coalition.

The modesty of Kerala Communist goals may well have been in part a result of anxiety concerning the future. As he spoke, Namboodiripad faced a by-election which, if lost, would probably result in the downfall of that government. And in actuality the record of the government had aroused considerable opposition in the state. Although greater working-class and peasant support should be forthcoming because of the government's land-reform measures and, in particular, because of its policy of police noninterference in industrial or agrarian disputes, those and other measures had evidently embittered the business and landed elements and, above all, the large Catholic community. Moreover, there were reports of corruption in the Communist government: opposition sources in the state had alleged that the law minister and other ministers, themselves landlords, had sought to evade redistribution of their property by converting it to private trusts, or that certain ministers and their relatives had derived private gain from government contracts for the purchase of rice or of textbooks.[15]

The Kerala by-election, held in May in Devicolam constituency, was a rigorous test of the Communist record. In preparation for the election the major opposition parties (Congress, Praja Socialist Party, and Muslim League) achieved a united front and proposed a single

---

[15] B. K. Desai, "Kerala After One Year," *Thought,* X (April 19, 1958), pp. 5–7.

candidate. The Revolutionary Socialist Party supported an independent candidate, who was expected to attract part of the leftist vote. The majority of the voters were plantation laborers, who might be disposed toward the government, but in fact the main opposition candidate had the support of the leaders of four out of five of the plantation-worker unions in the constituency. Moreover, the majority of the voters belonged to the Tamil minority group, which might be disposed against any Kerala government.

The result of the election, despite these unpromising circumstances, was a victory for the Communist candidate, Rosamma Punnoose, who received 48.5 per cent of the vote.[16] The opposition parties registered charges of electoral malpractices on the part of the Communists, but the government had gained at least a temporary reprieve. And the election might appear to many in India a crucial vote of confidence.

Maintaining its position in Kerala has had its costs, however, both in the internal and external relations of the CPI. Some elements of the Party have grown restive at the goal of respectability. Said to be represented by S. A. Dange, among others, these elements were especially incensed by the Kerala government's efforts to attract capital investment in the state. When the government negotiated an exceedingly liberal agreement with an outstanding Indian "monopolist," G. D. Birla, for the establishment of a rayon-pulp plant, dissent was reportedly expressed in informal meetings of Party leaders in New Delhi.[17]

The external opposition to the Kerala government also has stiffened. Prime Minister Nehru in August made one of his most unambiguous statements to date against communism.[18] And in Kerala itself opposition parties have evidently adopted more militant tactics. Activity of these parties among student and labor organizations has recently mounted, and in the months of July and August there were a series of mass demonstrations and general strikes in various cities and towns of the state. On several occasions the police used tear gas or fired into crowds, and in the view of some observers a situation dangerously close to civil war developed. Ultimately Namboodiripad was quoted in a threat of civil war "paralleling earlier developments in China," and Nehru was quoted in condemnation of "curtailment of freedom" by the Communists in Kerala. The situation in the state was debated in Parliament, with the agreement of S. A. Dange, now the leader

---

[16] *New Age,* V (May 25, 1958), p. 1.

[17] *New York Times,* July 12, 1958, p. 7.

[18] Published originally in the journal of the Congress Party, *Economic Review,* August 22, 1958, this statement is reprinted in *The New York Times Magazine* (September 7, 1958), pp. 13 ff.

of the Communist parliamentary bloc. Dange declared that the CPI would ask the Kerala government to resign if it could not restrain the police from firing on demonstrators. Namboodiripad subsequently condemned the parliamentary debate as an infringement of states' rights under the Indian constitution.[19]

This crisis receded, but it had provided further evidence of discord within the CPI and between the Communist government in Kerala and the Congress government at the center. Despite the fact that the cost of maintaining power in Kerala has risen, the CPI has not yet been deflected from the "peaceful" path which, it anticipates, will carry it to other state capitols and, eventually, to New Delhi.

---

[19] *Christian Science Monitor,* July 31, 1958, p. 6; August 23, 1958, p. 2; and September 4, 1958, p. 5.

Biographical Dictionary

BIOGRAPHICAL DATA ON SOME LEADING INDIAN COMMUNISTS

Accurate biographical information on the prominent figures of a political party is important for any valid generalizations about the relationship of that party to other political movements and to the society from which it emerges. Unfortunately, such information is not readily available concerning the leading Indian Communists, and their political histories must be pieced together from scattered sources.

Most of the information presented here has been taken from the CPI press, which frequently publishes short biographies of the Party leaders, especially when they are standing for public office. Some data could be checked against directories (e.g., *House of the People, Who's Who*) and other non-Communist sources, but in most cases it was not possible. This is especially true for birth dates, background, and early careers of the persons listed. Moreover, since both the biographical sketches and the other scattered fragments are frequently contradictory it is impossible to collate full and accurate information. Students of comparative elites will therefore find this biographical material inadequate. But because of the mentioned difficulties, its presentation can be justified by the time it will save those interested in verifying and expanding it.

Although this list contains the names of most top national and provincial CPI leaders, those acquainted with Indian politics will notice certain omissions. Some names have been left out only because no data were available. No fellow travelers were included. Because of his great importance as an adviser to the CPI, R. Palme Dutt has been included although he is a British, and not an Indian Communist.

Note.—For additional data on some of these personalities see Postscript.

If a pattern of behavior has been apparent to the authors, they have noted it; thus certain CPI leaders are described in these sketches as "moderates," "leftists," or "centrists." It must be borne in mind, however, that such identifications are rarely made in Party literature, and that they represent the judgment of the authors.

Adhikari, Gangadhar M. (Dr.)

Studied at the University of Berlin in the 1920's, receiving a doctorate of science in engineering. During that period became acquainted with M. N. Roy. Returned to India in December, 1928, bringing news of the Comintern's new leftist line. Attended the CPI and WPP conferences held in Calcutta in December, 1928. In 1929 was arrested, tried, and jailed with other Communist leaders in connection with the Meerut Conspiracy Case. Was released in the summer of 1933 and went to Calcutta where he helped to reorganize the CPI. Was active in trade-union work in Bombay in the 1930's, and was for a period interned by the authorities in the small town of Bijapur in southern Bombay. Editor of the CPI weekly paper during the 1940's, and author of numerous pamphlets and articles. The CPI's position on the Pakistan question during the 1940's is reputed to be largely his work. Was a member of the CPI Politbureau from 1943 to 1950; this included the ultraleftist period of 1948–1951, under the leadership of B. T. Ranadive. Served on the Central Committee from 1943 to 1950 and from 1953 to the present.

Ahmed, Muzaffar

Born 1893 into an impoverished Muslim farm family in southern Bengal. Attended high school in Noakhali and entered Hooghly College in 1913, later transferring to Bangabashi College in Calcutta where he became interested in Bengali literature and wrote many articles. Terminated his formal schooling when he failed his intermediate examinations. In 1920–21 was involved in the noncoöperation movement and the Khilafat agitation, and shortly thereafter became interested in Marxism through contact with Indians returning from the Communist school in Tashkent. Became active in the WPP in Bengal and edited its journal, *Ganavani*. In 1923 was sentenced to four years' rigorous imprisonment in connection with the Cawnpore Conspiracy Case, but was released on medical grounds in September, 1925. Immediately resumed Communist activity; in 1929 was again arrested and convicted in the Meerut Conspiracy Case. Remained in jail or under village internment until 1936, when he returned to Calcutta to resume kisan, trade-union, and Party work. Has been a member of the CPI Central Committee since 1951, serving on the Politbureau from 1951 to 1953. One of the Party's foremost leaders in Bengal.

AHMED, ZAINUL ABEDIN (Dr.)

A Muslim; former teacher in Sind Province (now in Pakistan). Active in Congress Party politics in the 1930's; elected to the Sind Provincial Congress Committee in 1936 and to the AICC in 1937. As a member of the AICC's Political and Economic Information Department, he was the author of a number of published reports on economic problems. A Communist organizer, he has concentrated his activity in Uttar Pradesh where he has long been the secretary of the Uttar Pradesh Provincial Committee of the CPI. Has been active in both trade-union and kisan work, and has spent considerable time underground and in jail. Member of the CPI Central Committee since 1951; served on its 1953 and 1956 politbureaus. Has recently taken a leftist position in inner-Party debate. Married to Hajrah Begum, a leader of the CPI women's movement.

ASAF ALI, ARUNA (Mrs.)

Born Aruna Ganguli, member of a Hindu family of Bengal. Her desire to become a nun, while attending the Convent of the Sacred Heart in Lahore, prompted her family to remove her from this school and send her to a Protestant school in Nainital. Unwilling to accept an arranged marriage, she later went to Calcutta and taught school at the Gokhale Memorial School for Girls. In 1928 married Mohamed Asaf Ali (now deceased), a young Muslim barrister who was later to become free India's first ambassador to the United States. Entered politics at the time of Gandhi's salt *satyagraha* and was for many years active in the Indian National Congress and in the Congress Socialist Party. When the Congress leaders were arrested after the launching of the "Quit India" movement in 1942, she went underground and traveled all over India directing violent anti-British activity. By 1945 her emphasis on violence had placed her at odds with the main leadership of Congress; Gandhi, in a public controversy with her over the RIN strike, said: "Aruna would rather unite Hindus and Muslims at the barricades than on the constitutional front." Although her tactical ideas resembled those of the Communists, she did not immediately forgive them for having opposed the "Quit India" movement and for "siding with the British" in 1942. "They are nothing else but traitors," she said.

Remained active in the Socialist Party after it broke away from the Congress in 1948, but by the following year began disagreeing with its leadership and was dropped from the National Executive in 1950. In 1952 she attacked the merger of the Socialist Party with the KMPP and joined the CPI, taking her personal following of leftist Socialists with her. Was elected to the CPI Central Committee in 1953, but dropped in 1956. A vice-president of the AITUC in 1954. Left CPI in 1957, and was elected mayor of New Delhi in 1958 with both Congress and Communist support.

ASHRAF, K. M. (Dr.)

A Muslim; holds a doctorate from London University. Active in Indian National Congress during the 1930's, and in charge of its Political and Economic Information Department in 1937. Was one of the eight Communists expelled from the AICC in October, 1945. Played a major role in the formulation of CPI policy on the Muslim question in the 1940's.

BARMAN, DASRATH DEB (See Deb, Dasrath)

BASU, JYOTI

Came in contact with the British Communist Party while a student in England in the 1930's; joined the British CP in 1937. Active in the India League and the Indian Seamen's Club in London. On his return to India in 1940 joined the CPI and became active in its Bengal branch. Secretary of the Bengal and Assam Railway Workers' Union in 1944. In 1946 defeated Humayun Kabir for the Railway seat in the Bengal Legislative Assembly. Has been a vice-president of the All-India Railwaymen's Federation, and secretary of the Bengal Provincial Trade Union Federation. A member of the CPI Central Committee since 1951, and of the Politbureau from 1951 to 1953. Has been secretary of the Bengal Provincial Committee for several years. Elected to the West Bengal Assembly in 1957.

BORA, PHANI

Entered the CPI through the student movement in Assam. Secretary of the Assam Provincial Committee of the CPI, and member of the CPI Central Committee since 1953.

CHAKRAVARTY, RENU (Mrs.)

Born in Calcutta, 1917. Educated in Calcutta, and in Cambridge, where she received her B.A. Was attracted to communism at Cambridge where she was secretary of the Federation of Indian Students. A lecturer in English at Calcutta University, she helped to organize students in political activity and was one of the founders of the Mahila Atma Raksha Samiti. In 1948 went underground for three years. Married Nikhil Chakravarty whom she met in England. (A Communist, he is a member of the *New Age* [weekly] editorial staff.) She is also the niece of Dr. B. C. Roy, the Congress chief minister of West Bengal State. Elected to the Lok Sabha from West Bengal in 1952 and reëlected in 1957.

CHANDRA, ROMESH

Born approximately 1914, a journalist frequently associated with the central Party organs. His main activity has been the All-India Peace Council of which he is general secretary; in this capacity has made several trips abroad to international Communist gatherings. A member of the CPI Central Committee since 1951; is generally associated with its centrist faction.

CHARI, A. S. R.

Began his political life when he resigned a government job to join the 1930–1934 Civil Disobedience Movement. After a period in jail he passed his law examinations and began working with Communists in Bombay. Arrested and jailed while defending Communist leaders in cases arising from strike activity. Released in 1942, he gave up his law practice to become a full-time Party worker, primarily as a writer for the CPI press and for Communist publications abroad. Again imprisoned for two and a half years during the ultraleft period (1948–1951); later assisted D. N. Pritt in preparing the defense of Communists sentenced to death for activity during the Telengana struggle. In recent years has been active in the organization of front groups in the legal profession, and has defended Communists and others who run afoul of the law as a result of political activity. Author of *Law and Justice in the Soviet Union, Lid Off Andhra Anti-Communism,* and other pamphlets and articles.

DAMODARAN, K.

Secretary of the Malabar Committee of the CPI, and member of the CPI Central Committee since 1956. Has been active in the All-India Progressive Writers' Association.

DANGE, SHRIPAT AMRIT

Born in 1899, he became interested in politics while a student. His 1920 pamphlet, *Gandhi and Lenin,* attracted the attention of M. N. Roy and the Communist International. Under the patronage of a wealthy Bombay flour-mill owner, and with advice from M. N. Roy, he helped organize Marxist study groups and publish Marxist tracts. One of the founders of the CPI, editor of its first important paper, and a defendant in both the Cawnpore and Meerut Conspiracy cases. His main center of activity has been among the trade unions of Bombay; has been either president or general secretary of the AITUC since 1945, and is also a vice-president of the World Federation of Trade Unions. Has spent at least thirteen years in jail and several more years underground, and has made many trips abroad to attend international Communists gatherings. Generally regarded as a leftist within the Party, although he helped to remove the leftists from control during the Ranadive-Rao periods, and favored participation in the general elections. Elected to the Bombay Legislative Assembly in 1948, defeated in the parliamentary election of 1952, but elected to Lok Sabha in 1957 with the largest vote polled by a single candidate in all India; leader of the Communist bloc in parliament. Author of numerous pamphlets and articles on trade unions and on other subjects. Except for the period 1950–1951, has been a member of the CPI Central Committee since the founding of the Party. Politbureau member since 1951, although trade-union activity has prevented his devoting much time to work at the Party center.

DEB, DASRATH (DASRATH DEB BARMAN)

Born in Khowai (Tripura), 1920, into a poor peasant family. Educated in Tripura and at Calcutta University. Attracted to the Communist Party during student days; active in Tripura State Trade Union Congress and other regional organizations. Was underground from July, 1948, to May, 1952, during which time he was elected to the Lok Sabha from Tripura East constituency. For many years secretary of the Tripura branch of the CPI; has served on the CPI Central Committee since 1951. One of the nine kisan leaders who toured the Soviet Union in August, 1955. Reëlected to the Lok Sabha in 1957.

DESHMUKH, SUDAM

Secretary of the Madhya Pradesh Provincial Committee of the CPI; elected to the Central Committee of the CPI in 1953 and again in 1956.

DUTT, RAJANI PALME

Born in 1896 in Cambridge, England, the son of an Indian doctor and a Swedish writer; attended Balliol College, Oxford, where in 1914 he joined the Independent Labor Party. A draftee during World War I, his antiwar agitation resulted in imprisonment and discharge. Returned to Oxford but was expelled in 1917 for political activity; later permitted to sit for the examinations, which he passed with high marks. In 1919, began working in the labor movement in London; 1919–1922 was international secretary of the Labor Research Department, then connected with the Labor Party. One of the founders of the British Communist Party in August, 1920; in July, 1921, started his theoretical journal, *Labour Monthly,* which he has edited ever since. Elected to the Central Committee and the Politbureau of the British Communist Party in 1922, and has served on these two bodies continuously since that time. As a member of the Executive Committee of the London India League, was closely associated with V. K. Krishna Menon, who contributed to his journal in the early 1940's. From the inception of the CPI, has been its major overseas adviser, and his views are greatly respected by Indian Communists. On several occasions his advice has resulted in tactical changes by the Party, most notable being the 1936 Dutt-Bradley thesis. First visited India in 1946 when he covered the Cabinet Mission for the London *Daily Worker.* A prolific writer, his *India Today* is regarded as the basic Communist primer on Indian politics. In general his analyses of Indian politics have shown less dogmatism than the writings of other Communists, and he has generally opposed the leftism which on occasion has separated the Communists from the principal Indian national leaders.

GEORGE, K. C.

Born 1903, of a Syrian Christian family in the then princely state of Travancore. Studied at Madras and Lucknow universities, and holds the B.A., M.A., and law degrees. Elected to the AICC while still a student; practiced law in Trivandrum and was elected to the Trivandrum Municipal Council in 1934. Entered the CPI as a member of the Congress Socialist Party, and was one of the founders of the Communist Party in Kerala. Elected to the Rajya Sabha in 1952 and to the Travancore-Cochin Legislative Assembly in 1954; as of 1957, a member of the Kerala State Committee of the CPI and of the Central Control Commission. Named minister for food, civil supplies, and forests in the 1957 Communist government of Kerala.

GHATE, SACHIDANAND VISHNU

One of the founders of the CPI. Active in the Bombay trade-union movement in the 1920's. Jailed in the Meerut Conspiracy Case in 1929. After his release worked in Madras for four years. Again imprisoned from 1940 to 1944, and yet again during the Ranadive-Rao period. A member of the CPI Central Committee from 1943 to 1950; party treasurer in 1953; elected to the Control Commission in 1956.

GHOSH, AJOY KUMAR

Born in 1909; holds a B.Sc. from Allahabad University. Began his political career as a terrorist in the Punjab and helped organize the Hindustan Socialist Republican Association in Lahore in the early 1920's. With Bhagat Singh, was one of the defendants in the second Lahore Conspiracy Case in 1929. In the early 1930's began trade-union work in Cawnpore, where he met S. G. Sardesai who instructed him in Marxism. Arrested in 1931, and by coincidence was jailed with Sardesai under whose influence he had become a confirmed Communist by the time he was released in 1933. Rose rapidly in the CPI and became a member of its Central Committee about 1934. In 1947 he disagreed with the moderate policies of P. C. Joshi and helped bring B. T. Ranadive to power, but later led the group that brought about his downfall. General secretary of the CPI in 1951, a post he has held ever since; editor of the Party's theoretical journal, *New Age* (monthly). Has made many trips to the Soviet Union for "medical treatment" at moments of crisis within the CPI.

GOPALAN, AYILLIATH KUTTERI

Born 1904 in north Malabar; matriculated from Mission High School in Tellichery in 1921, and for the next eight years taught in various secondary schools. Was attracted to Gandhi's movement in the late 1920's, and by 1935 had served three and a half years in jail for political activity. Joined the Congress Socialist Party in 1935; was elected president of the Kerala Provincial Congress Committee, and from 1936 to 1939 served on the AICC. Joined the CPI in 1939 and was jailed in 1941, serving six months before his escape. Jailed again in 1946 and was not released until 1951. Elected to the Lok Sabha in 1952, reelected in 1957; led its Communist bloc until 1957, when he became deputy leader under S. A. Dange. During 1952–1953 spent seven months in the USSR, where he represented the CPI at the Nineteenth Party Congress of the CPSU, and at Stalin's funeral. Has served on the CPI Central Committee since 1951, and has been especially active in the movement for the creation of linguistic states. Attracted nation-wide attention in 1956 when he was arrested in Ahmedabad where he had gone to observe the agitation for the creation of a separate Gujerat state. That same year he was elected president of the All-India Kisan Sabha.

Gopalan, K. P. R.

Peasant organizer from Malabar. For activity in the 1931 Civil Disobedience Movement was imprisoned in Cananore jail with P. Krishna Pillai and A. K. Gopalan, as a result of which he "parted ways with his old outlook and accepted the path of revolution." Nevertheless, remained active in the Congress Party, being a member of its Kerala Provincial Congress Committee (1930–1940), and twice its secretary (1935, 1940). Sentenced to life imprisonment in 1941 but released in 1946. One of the nine peasant leaders who toured the USSR in August, 1955.

Gupta, Bhupesh

Born in Mymensingh, East Bengal (now Pakistan), in 1914. Educated at Scottish Church College, Calcutta, and at University College, London, where he received a law degree. Several times arrested in the 1930's for alleged terrorist activity. Detained without trial from 1933 to 1937, during which time he passed B.A. examinations, and was converted to communism. Worked in the underground for the CPI in 1941 and 1948; was arrested in May, 1951, and detained for eleven months. Elected to the Rajya Sabha in 1952, and to the CPI Central Committee in 1953 and 1956; became editor of *New Age* (weekly) in August, 1956.

Hajrah Begum (Mrs. Z. A. Ahmed)

Wife of Z. A. Ahmed and a prominent leader of the Communist women's movement. Member of the Indian delegation to the Vienna Peace Congress (1952) and of the delegation of the Women's International Democratic Federation, which toured Egypt and the Sudan in January, 1957. Contributes frequent articles on the women's movement to CPI publications. Was defeated for election to the CPI Central Committee in 1953.

Ismail, Mohammed

Born about 1912 in Unao District, Uttar Pradesh, of Muslim parents. His father, a weaver, died when Mohammed was three months old, leaving him in the care of an elder brother who was a railway employee. After much moving about he and his brother settled in Calcutta where Mohammed became an apprentice in a motor engineering works and entered politics in 1926; was active in the Khilafat movement and in the Congress Party. Began organizing trade unions in 1929, and beginning with the tramway strike in 1933, was repeatedly arrested. Joined the CPI in 1934; elected to the Calcutta Municipal Corporation in 1944, and to the CPI's Bengal Provincial Committee in 1946. Has served continually on that body except for one year's absence. A member of the CPI Central Committee during the ultraleftist period 1948–1951. As of January, 1957, was president of the Tramway Workers' Union, the Motor Transport Workers' Union, the Biri (cigarette) Workers' Federation, and the Fruit Sellers' Union; was vice-president of the All-India Motor Transport Workers' Federation; was general secretary of the Bus Workers' Union, and of the West Bengal Federation of Motor Transport Workers' Unions. A member, also, of the Working Committee of the All-India Trade Union Congress. During the 1957 elections stood for the West Bengal Legislative Assembly against the chief minister, B. C. Roy, but lost by a narrow margin.

JEEVANANDAM, P.

Active in the non-Brahman movement in Madras during the 1930's, and later joined the CPI. Held in Vellore jail during the 1948–1951 ultraleftist period; his refusal to obey a Party order to "fast unto death" resulted in his expulsion from the Party, but was later readmitted. Elected to the Madras Legislative Assembly in 1952.

JOSH, SOHAN SINGH

Active in Punjab terrorist movement during World War I. Presided over the first All-India Workers' and Peasants' Party conference in 1928; convicted in the Meerut Conspiracy Case in 1929. Has served on the AICC, and was one of the eight Communists expelled from that body in 1945. A member of the CPI Central Committee since 1951, but his advanced age limits him to the role of elder statesman.

JOSHI, PURAN CHAND

Born in 1907 in Almora, Uttar Pradesh, the son of a school master. Became interested in communism while a student at Allahabad University, but his admission to the CPI was delayed because of his excessive youthful enthusiasm. He holds the M.A. and LL.B. degrees. In 1928 organized the Uttar Pradesh branch of the Party; in 1929 was convicted in the Meerut Conspiracy Case and was jailed until 1933. He passed his law examinations while in jail. Was elected general secretary of the CPI in 1935 "as a representative of the younger comrades who were outside the factional groupings," (Deven and Balkrishna, *Talks with Comrade R. Palme Dutt*, p. 3); he displayed exceptional organizing ability and held this post until 1948.

When the CPI adopted its ultraleftist line in 1948 he was first removed from office and then expelled from the Party. Unable to gain readmittance for several years, he was active in front organizations, especially in the Peace Movement, which gave him contacts with former comrades as well as a means of access to the international Communist leadership. During this period he published a series of pamphlets and a journal, attacking the leftist Party leadership with considerable effectiveness and showing great sensitivity to new turns in international Communist policy. Readmitted to the CPI in 1951, but was defeated as a candidate for the Central Committee at that Congress; in December, 1952, visited the USSR after attending the Vienna Peace Congress. Elected to the Central Committee at the Fourth Congress in 1956.

Joshi is an able theoretician; an admirer of Mao Tse-tung, and a keen student of his writings, he was one of the three CPI leaders who attended the Eighth Congress of the Chinese Communist Party in September, 1956. Generally regarded as the leader of the rightist faction within the Party. Became editor of *New Age* (weekly) 1958.

KALYANASUNDARAM, M.

A former railway clerk, he became a railway union organizer; also organized the textile and tobacco workers. Joined the CPI in 1938, but was active in the Congress Party as well. Spent considerable time underground and in jail. He was president of the South Indian Railway Labor Union when he was elected to the Madras Legislative Assembly in 1952. Has served three years on the CPI Central Committee, but was defeated for election to that body at the Third Congress in 1953. Reëlected to the Madras Legislative Assembly in 1957.

KHANDKAR, LAXMAN R.

Elected secretary of the Madhya Bharat and Bhopal Provincial Committee of the CPI in October, 1953; elected to the CPI Central Committee in December of that year. Was not reëlected to the Central Committee in 1956.

KRISHNAN, N. KALYANA

Jailed in 1940 for Communist activity, he was released in 1942 and did propaganda work in the Party headquarters in Bombay. Was also interested in organizational work in Karnatak, Kerala, and Madras. After the leading Madras Communists were arrested in January, 1947, he took over the work of the Party office there. Regarded as an opportunist by many top Party leaders, his name now appears infrequently in the Communist press. A member of the Central Committee 1943–1948.

LAHIRI, SOMNATH

A graduate of Calcutta University, he has been active in the trade-union movement in that city. Elected to the CPI Central Committee in 1943, to the Calcutta Municipal Corporation in 1944, and to the Constituent Assembly in 1946. When the CPI adopted an ultra leftist line in 1948 he was regarded by the new leadership as a rightist. Later joined the leftists, "going even to more extremes than some others," according to an inner-Party document. Served on the Central Committee until 1951. When the moderates came to power he was branded as an opportunist, and his name seldom appeared in Party literature between 1951 and 1956. In 1956, after an absence, he was again elected to the West Bengal Provincial Committee of the CPI. Elected to the West Bengal Legislative Assembly in 1957, where he sits as a Communist member.

MFHTA, DINKAR

Entered politics at the age of 14 as a participant in Gandhi's Civil Disobedience Movement, and was arrested in connection with the Bardoli *satyagraha* in 1928. Active in the Congress Party during the 1930's; was a joint secretary of the Congress Socialist Party; joined the CPI in 1939; one of the founders of its Gujerat branch. Imprisoned in 1948, he escaped the following year and remained underground until 1951 when he emerged to participate in the general elections. Was again arrested but released on bail. Member of the CPI Central Committee, 1953–1956.

MENON, CHELAT ACHUTHA

Born in 1913 into an aristocratic Nair family of Trichur, Kerala State. Received the LL.B and practiced in Trichur. Began his political activity in 1935 as a Congress Party worker; helped organize the Cochin Congress of which he became the secretary. For several years a member of the Kerala Provincial Congress Committee; arrested and detained for three years during World War II. Joined the CPI in 1942 and worked underground from 1948 to 1952; while underground was elected to the Travancore-Cochin Legislative Assembly, but was defeated in the Legislative Assembly elections in 1954. Elected to the CPI Central Committee in 1953 and in 1956; as of 1957 secretary of the Kerala Provincial Committee of the Party. In 1957 was named minister of finance in the first Communist government in Kerala. Has written extensively in the Malayalam language.

MIRAJKAR, S. S.

A Bombay trade-union leader, was one of the founders of the CPI. Convicted in the Meerut Conspiracy Case; spent more than ten years in jail. Elected several times to the Bombay Municipal Corporation on a CPI ticket. A vice-president of the AITUC since 1947 or earlier; for some time secretary of the Maharashtra Provincial Committee of the CPI, and recently a leader in the agitation for a separate Maharashtrian state. Member of the CPI Central Committee, 1953–1956; not reëlected in 1956. Became mayor of Bombay in 1958.

MOHIUDDIN, MAQDOOM

Formerly a lecturer in City College, Hyderabad (Andhra). Became a full-time Communist Party worker in 1942, was active in trade-union work in Hyderabad, especially among the railway workers, and became a vice-president of the Nizam's State Railwaymen's Union. Defeated for election to the Lok Sabha in 1952. A Muslim, he is better known for his Urdu poetry than for his political work.

MUKERJEE, HIRENDRA NATH

Born 1907; educated at Calcutta University, Oxford, and London; holds B. Litt. and M.A. degrees. A lawyer and an educationist, he was senior lecturer in history and politics at Andhra University from 1934 to 1935, and later head of the Department of History, Surendranath College, Calcutta. Active in trade-union work; a founder member of the All-India Progressive Writers' Association, in 1936, and of the Friends of the Soviet Union in 1941; has been active in other front and mass organizations including the Indian People's Theater Association and the AISF. In 1938–39 a member of the Executive Committee of the Bengal Provincial Congress Committee, member of the AICC, and joint secretary of the Bengal Congress Socialist Party. Member of the Goodwill Mission which the British government permitted to visit the USSR in 1942. Member of the Bengal Provincial Committee of the CPI in 1947. The author of numerous publications in English and Bengali, in 1954 he was once found to have plagiarized the work of a Communist comrade for which he apologized in the CPI theoretical journal. (*New Age* [monthly] III, December, 1954 inside back cover.) Elected to the Lok Sabha in 1952 and reëlected in 1957; has served as a deputy leader of the Communist Party in parliament.

MUKHERJEE, BANKIM

Entered politics and trade-union work in the 1920's; was active
in the Civil Disobedience Movement and in jute-workers' strikes in
Bengal. Joined the CPI in 1936 and was elected to the Bengal Legislative Assembly in 1937. Has served on the CPI's Bengal Provincial
Committee but never on the Central Committee. A member of the
1942 Goodwill Mission to the USSR. Has been active in kisan work,
and has been both president and general secretary of the AIKS.
Elected to the West Bengal Legislative Assembly in 1957.

NAIR, M. N. GOVINDAN

Attracted to politics by the personality of Mahatma Gandhi, he
spent some time in Gandhi's ashram. Active in the former Travancore
State Congress organization and in youth work. Married to Devagi
Panikkar, daughter of K. M. Panikkar, formerly Indian ambassador
to China, Egypt, and (1957) France. A member of the CPI Central
Committee since 1953.

NAMBIAR, K. ANANDAN

Born in Malabar in 1918 and educated at Malabar Christian College, Calicut. General secretary of the South Indian Railway Labor
Union since 1943. Member of the Madras Legislative Assembly from
1946 to 1952, when he was elected to the Lok Sabha. One of the Indian
trade unionists who attended the 1952 May Day celebrations in
Peking. Was elected treasurer of the AITUC in 1954, and has served
on the CPI Central Committee since 1953.

NAMBOODIRIPAD, ELAMKULAM MANA SANKARAN

Born in 1909 of a wealthy Namboodiri Brahman family of Malabar, he began his political activity as a college student in Trichur. In
1932 quit his studies and entered the Disobedience Movement, for
which he was jailed by the British. In jail he came in contact with
Krishna Pillai, A. K. Gopalan, and K. P. R. Gopalan and was converted to Marxism. When the Congress Socialist Party was formed in
1934 he became one of the joint secretaries; was also secretary of the
Kerala Provincial Congress Committee. In 1939 was elected, unop-
posed, to the Madras Legislative Assembly on a Congress ticket, and
during that year was also a member of the AICC. Although he was
probably a secret member earlier, he openly joined the CPI in 1940
and brought the majority of the Kerala members of the Congress Socialist Party with him. In 1947, after a brief detention, went under-

ground, and during this period unsuccessfully contested the 1952 elections. Was elected to the Central Committee of the CPI in 1943. He is one of the two persons to have served on that body continuously until the present. Has been a member of the Politbureau since 1950, and has usually allied himself with the centrist faction.

Namboodiripad is the author of innumerable articles and pamphlets on a broad variety of topics, but especially on the agrarian question; also one of the CPI's leading Marxist theoreticians. Has shown a great interest in China, and was one of the three CPI leaders to attend the Eighth Congress of the Chinese Communist Party in September, 1956. In 1957, when the Communist government was formed in Kerala State, he became the first Communist chief minister in India.

PATKAR, S. G.

Born of a poor peasant family in Maharashtra, he went to Bombay at the age of 13 and began working in a tailor shop. Began his political activity during the agitation against the Simon Commission in 1927, and was active in the trade-union movement during the textile strikes of 1928 and 1929; led textile strikes in 1932 and 1934. Active in the Indian National Congress as a member of the Bombay Provincial Congress Committee for seven years and of the AICC for six. Elected to the Bombay Municipal Corporation on a Communist ticket in 1940, but was forced to go underground shortly afterward. Secretary of the Girni Kamgar Union from 1937 to 1942, and general secretary from 1942 to 1951. Expelled from the CPI in 1950 because of his opposition to its ultraleftist line. Later readmitted, in 1953 he was elected to the Central Committee on which he served until 1956. Elected to Bombay Legislative Assembly in 1957.

PATNAIK, GURUCHARAN

Secretary of the Communist Party in Utkal (Orissa). Elected to the CPI Central Committee in 1953 and again in 1956.

PUNNIAH, MAKINENI BASAVA

Born in a village in Guntur District, Andhra State, he was educated at Noble College, Masulipatam, and at Andhra Christian College, Guntur. General secretary of the Andhra Provincial Students' Federation from 1937 to 1939, and secretary of the Guntur District Communist Committee from 1940 to 1942. Served on the CPI Central Committee, 1948–1951 and from 1953 to the present. Member of the Politbureau in 1950. When the Vishalandhra Provincial Committee of the CPI was formed in 1956 he became a member of its thirteen-man secretariat. Was elected to the Rajya Sabha in 1952 but lost his bid for a seat in the Andhra State Legislature in 1955.

RAMAMURTI, P.

A leading trade unionist of Madras State, he was active in the Congress and in the Congress Socialist Party during the 1930's; was a member of the AICC for eleven years. Joined the CPI in 1936. Was elected to the Madras Legislative Assembly in 1952 where he led the Opposition until 1957 when he was defeated as a candidate for a seat in the Lok Sabha. One of the CPI's leading publicists and theoreticians; editor of its Tamil paper, *Janasakti*, during the 1940's, and editor of the national weekly, *New Age*, from its founding in 1953 until 1956. Was elected to the CPI Central Committee and to the Politbureau in 1951 and has since served continuously on both.

RANADIVE, BHALCHANDRA TRIMBAK

Holder of a research scholarship in economics at Bombay University from 1925 to 1927, he was awarded the M.A. degree with distinction for his thesis on India's population problem. He became a Communist shortly afterward; during the time the Party's leaders were imprisoned in connection with the Meerut Conspiracy Case, he rose to prominence in the Party in Bombay as the leader of an ultra-leftist faction. He criticized the Dutt-Bradley thesis calling for a moderate line, and as a result was temporarily suspended from the Party for factionalism. Visited the USSR in 1942 as a member of the six-man Goodwill Mission; was elected to the CPI Central Committee and to the Politbureau in 1943. He led the movement against the moderate policy of P. C. Joshi, and in 1948 displaced him as general secretary. Under his leadership the CPI followed an ultraleftist line which resulted in widespread violence and in severe government repression. He was removed from office in 1950 after his tactics had been censured by the international Communist leadership. In eclipse for several years, in 1956 he was elected to the Maharashtrian Provincial Communist Committee and was a delegate to the CPI's Fourth Congress where he was once again elected to the Central Committee. Generally reputed to be the leader of the leftists on that body.

RAO, CHANDRA RAJESHWAR

A veteran Communist leader of Andhra, he comes from a wealthy peasant family. Led the opposition to the leadership of B. T. Ranadive in 1949, using Mao Tse-tung as a doctrinal authority, and succeeded in replacing Ranadive as general secretary of the Party. He continued to pursue ultraleftist tactics and was removed from office in 1951 when the Party line shifted. Member of the CPI Central Committee from 1948 to 1951 and from 1953 to the present. Defeated for election to the Andhra Legislative Assembly in 1955. He is generally regarded as a proponent of an agrarian-based revolution, and an advocate of insurrectionary tactics. Although a member of the CPI Politbureau since 1953, he has been unable to give much time to Party work at the center, preferring to concentrate his efforts in Andhra. When the Vishalandhra Provincial Committee of the CPI was formed in 1956 he was elected secretary.

Rao, D. Venkatesa

A Communist leader from Telengana, he has served on the CPI Central Committee since 1953. When the Vishalandhra Provincial Committee of the CPI was formed in 1956 he became a member of its thirteen-man secretariat.

Rao, Moturu Hanumantha

A veteran member of the CPI from Andhra. Member of the Andhra State Legislative Assembly in 1953 and 1954, he was defeated for reëlection in 1955. Was elected in 1956 to the thirteen-man secretariat of the Vishalandhra CPI Provincial Committee; member of the CPI Central Committee since 1953.

Rao, Nandoori Prasada

Peasant leader from Andhra and one-time general secretary of the Andhra Provincial Ryots Association. General secretary of the All-India Kisan Sabha, and a member of the CPI Central Committee since 1953.

Reddy, Ravi Narayan

Foremost leader of the CPI in Telengana; elected to the Lok Sabha in 1952, polling more votes than any other candidate in India. His reports on Party losses in Telengana during the 1948–1950 armed uprising were instrumental in bringing about the removal of B. T. Ranadive as general secretary and in modifying the Party line. Member of the CPI Central Committee since 1953, and member of the Vishalandhra Provincial Committee secretariat since its creation in 1956. Was elected to the Andhra Legislative Assembly in 1957.

REDDY, T. NAGI

Standing for the Madras Legislature in 1952, he defeated his brother-in-law, N. Sanjeeva Reddy, and when Andhra broke away from Madras in 1953 he became leader of the Opposition in the first Andhra State Legislative Assembly. (Sanjeeva Reddy, a Congressman, became deputy chief minister.) Member of the secretariat of the Vishalandhra CPI Provincial Committee when it was created in 1956. Was elected to the Lok Sabha in 1957.

REDDY, BADDAM YELLA

Communist leader from Telengana, and for many years secretary of the Telengana Provincial Committee of the CPI; member of the thirteen-man secretariat of the Vishalandhra CPI Provincial Committee. Was elected to the Lok Sabha in 1952, and to the CPI Central Committee in 1956.

SANKRITYAYANA, RAHUL

Professor of Sanskrit and of Pali in Ceylon in 1926–1928, he has traveled extensively in Tibet and Southern China. Joined the CPI in 1939; was elected president of the All-India Kisan Sabha in 1940, but was imprisoned along with other Communist leaders in Deoli detention camp. In 1944 was appointed professor of Oriental languages at the Leningrad Academy of Sciences where he remained until 1947, making an extensive study of Soviet Asia. *New Age* announced in February, 1955, that he had rejoined the CPI. Has written extensively on the compatibility of Marxism with Oriental religions, especially Buddhism.

SARDESAI, S. G.

Active in the Indian National Congress in the 1940's, he was one of the eight Communists expelled from the AICC in 1945. A leading trade unionist in Bombay, and secretary of the Mill Mazdoor Union. Served on the CPI Central Committee from 1943 to 1950 and from 1953 to the present. Active in the agitation for the liberation of Goa from Portuguese rule.

SEN, RANEN (Dr.)

A trade unionist from Bengal, he has been active in politics in Calcutta since his student days. Joined the CPI in 1930; served on the Central Committee from 1943 to 1948 and from 1951 to the present. Is secretary of the Bengal Provincial Trade Union Congress and a vice-president of the AITUC; most of his time is taken up by work for the AITUC and the CPI's trade-union subcommittee. His wife, who was active in the women's movement, was killed in a police firing during the CPI's period of ultraleftism, 1948–1951.

SHARMA, KARYANAND

Born in 1900 in Monghyr District, Bihar, of poor peasant stock. Left college in 1920 to join the Civil Disobedience Movement and was jailed the following year. After his release in 1922 worked for the Congress, organizing schools and ashrams for political activists, was jailed several times during the 1930's, and became a militant leader of the peasants in Bihar. Like many other Communists, he entered the CPI from the Congress via the Congress Socialist Party, and was one of the eight Communists expelled from the AICC in 1945. Has been president of the Bihar Provincial Kisan Sabha and of the All-India Kisan Sabha. Delegate to the Peking Peace Conference in 1952; in 1956 was elected to the CPI's Bihar Provincial Committee secretariat, and to the Party's All-India Control Commission.

SHARMA, YAG DUTT

Born about 1910, he entered politics as a student leader and in the 1930's became a secretary of the All-India Students' Federation. Has served on the CPI Central Committee since 1951; attended the Peking Peace Conference in 1952 as an observer.

SHARMA, YOGENDRA NATH

General secretary of the Bihar State Kisan Sabha, he was one of the nine AIKS leaders invited to tour the USSR in August, 1955. Has served on the CPI Central Committee since 1953; secretary of the Bihar Provincial Committee in 1956.

SINGH, BABA GURUMUKH

Born in 1883 in Ludhiana District, Punjab, into a poor peasant family. After visiting California he returned to India in 1914 and was arrested and sentenced in the Lahore Conspiracy Case. Imprisoned in the Andaman Islands, he escaped in 1922 while being transferred to a mainland jail, and made his way to Afghanistan and eventually to the USSR. In 1932, while attempting to return to India, he was arrested by the Afghan government and detained until 1934. After a brief return visit to the USSR he proceeded to India in 1935 using a false passport. In India he started a revolutionary newspaper and contacted the CPI. He was again arrested in 1936 and was held in prison in the

Andamans and on the mainland until 1946. Has been treasurer of the AIKS for several years, and is generally regarded as an elder statesman among Communists and other revolutionaries.

SUNDARAYYA, PUCHALAPALLI

Born in 1913 into a prosperous peasant family of Nellore District, Andhra, he attended college in Madras and Bangalore but left school to go into political work before obtaining a degree. Attracted by Gandhi's political activities, he worked in the villages and helped organize *satyagrahas* during the 1930's. Joined the CPI in 1932 but remained active in the Indian National Congress. Has been a member of the Andhra Provincial Congress Committee, a delegate to the 1934 annual session of the Congress, and served on the AICC from 1938 to 1939. Was also active in the Congress Socialist Party and eventually led its Andhra branch into the CPI. Member of the CPI Central Committee since 1934 and of the Politbureau since 1953; generally regarded as a militant leftist. Elected to the Rajya Sabha in 1952 and to the Andhra Legislative Assembly in 1955; a member of the Vishalandhra CPI Provincial Committee secretariat. In 1956 he was one of the three CPI leaders who attended the Eighth Congress of the Chinese Communist Party.

SURJEET, HARIKISHAN SINGH

A Punjab peasant leader, he was elected to the Punjab Legislative Assembly in a 1952 by-election. Member of the AIKS Central Kisan Council; has served on the CPI Central Committee and on the Politbureau since 1953. Is reputed to be the Party's leading authority on Kashmir politics.

THOMAS, T. V.

Born 1921 into a Christian family in Kerala, he entered the national movement as a student in 1938. In 1940 he became active in trade-union work and was elected president of the Allepy Coir Factory Workers' Union. Joined the CPI in 1943. Arrested and detained in 1946 and 1948, and while still under detention was elected to the Travancore-Cochin Legislative Assembly in 1952. President of the Travancore-Cochin State Transport Employees Union; in 1954 he fasted on the steps of the state government secretariat in support of workers' demands. He was chairman of the Allepy Municipal Council, where the Communists achieved a majority in 1952. In April, 1957, became the minister for transport, labor, municipalities, sports and sport associations in the Communist government of Kerala. The following month he married K. R. Gowri, the revenue minister, and the only woman in the Kerala cabinet.

UPADHYAYA, N. L.

Secretary of the Karnatak Provincial Committee of the CPI, he has served on the Central Committee since 1953.

VENKATARAMAN, M. R.

For many years secretary of the Tamilnad Provincial Committee of the CPI, he has served on the Central Committee since 1953.

VYAS, HARI KRISHNA

As of 1955 he was the only Communist member of the Rajasthan Legislative Assembly. Secretary of the CPI's Rajasthan Provincial Committee; has served on the CPI Central Committee since 1953.

YUSUF, S. S.

Born 1911, he has been active in trade-union work in Delhi, Bombay, Ahmedabad, and Cawnpore. His main center of activity has been Uttar Pradesh, and for seven years he was a member of the Uttar Pradesh Congress Committee. Has spent 17 years in 14 different jails, and it was during incarceration in 1930 that he was converted to Marxism. On at least two occasions he has undertaken fasts while in jail. Has held high office in the AITUC, and in 1952 was one of the Indian trade unionists who attended the May Day celebrations in Peking. Leader of the Cawnpore textile strike in 1955; member of the CPI Central Committee from 1948 to 1950 and from 1951 to the present. Although a leftist during the early period, has recently been associated with a more moderate line.

Selected Bibliography

SELECTED BIBLIOGRAPHY

The following list of books and documents is limited to those which the authors believe are of special significance in understanding communism in India, and does not include all materials cited in footnotes. Students interested in a more comprehensive bibliography on this subject or on Indian government and politics in general should refer to the indispensable bibliographical study by Patrick Wilson, *Government and Politics of India and Pakistan 1885–1955: A Bibliography of Works in Western Languages* (Berkeley: Institute of East Asiatic Studies, University of California, 1956. 356 pp.)

COMMENTARY ON THE CPI

Batliwala, Soli S. *Facts versus forgery* . . . Bombay, National Youth Publication, 1946. 33 pp.
Important, but undocumented, account of CPI policy during World War II, by a defector formerly a member of the Central Committee.

Goel, Sita Ram. *Netaji and the CPI.* Calcutta, Society for the Defence of Freedom in Asia, 1955. 72 pp.
A polemic, useful as a source of extensive quotations from CPI documents now inaccessible.

Hutchinson, Lester. *Conspiracy at Meerut.* London, G. Allen and Unwin, 1935. 190 pp.
An account of the Meerut Conspiracy Case by one of the defendants.

Kautsky, John H. *Moscow and the Communist Party of India.* New York, The Technology Press of Massachusetts Institute of Technology and John Wiley and Sons, Inc., 1956. 220 pp.
A penetrating study of postwar Communist theory on India and of the relations between the CPI and its international Communist environment.

Limaye, Madhu. *Communist Party: Facts and Fiction.* Hyderabad (Deccan), Chetana Prakashan, 1951. 100 pp.
A short survey of the history of the CPI, by an Indian Socialist leader.

Masani, Minocheher Rustom. *The Communist Party of India: A Short History*. London, Derek Verschoyle, 1954. 302 pp.
The first general history of the CPI by India's leading anti-Communist publicist. Valuable in particular because of the author's personal experience with the CPI during the 1930's and his sources of intelligence within the Party since that time.

Ranga, N. G. *Kisans and Communists*. Bombay, Pratibha Publications, 194–? 127 pp.
A valuable survey of Communist agrarian policy and activity in India, by a prominent non-Communist peasant leader. Deals with the 1930's.

Roy, M. N. *Memoirs*. Published serially in *Radical Humanist* from February 1, 1953 to September 5, 1954.
An important account of Roy's early career despite gaps and inaccuracies.

———. *Our Differences*. Calcutta, Saraswaty Library, 1938. 184 pp.
This book provides some background on why M. N. Roy parted company with the Comintern.

Spratt, Philip. *Blowing Up India*. Calcutta, Prachi Prakashan, 1955. 117 pp.
Reflections of the most important of the organizers sent to India by the British Communist Party.

Tagore, Saumyendranath. *Historical Development of the Communist Movement in India*. Calcutta, Red Front Press, 1944.
A detailed account of Indian Communist activity in the 1920's. Only a typed copy, loaned by Robert C. North, Stanford University, was available to the authors.

Tendulkar, Ayi Ganpat. *Nation Betrayed? A Case Against Communists: their Own Evidence*. 2d ed. Bombay, Bombay Provincial Congress Committee, 1946. 25 pp.
A characteristic statement of nationalist opinion of the CPI's wartime policy, with extensive quotations from CPI publications.

Yajnik, Indulal. *Life of Ranchoddas Bhavan Lotvala*. Bombay, Atmaram Dixit, 1952. 87 pp.
A valuable account of the beginnings of the CPI in Bombay, focusing on the financial assistance given to early Communists by a wealthy Bombay mill owner.

GOVERNMENT DOCUMENTS

Great Britain. *Communist Papers*. London, HMSO, 1926. 132 pp. (Cmd. 2682; Parl. Pap. 1926: XXIII)
A collection of documents seized during a raid on British Communist offices in 1925. Several relate to the Communist movement in India and the leadership role of the CPGB.

India. Home Department. *Communism in India, 1924–27*. Calcutta, Government of India Press, 1927, 415 pp.
A British Intelligence report containing detailed information on Communist activities. Summarizes Kaye report (see below) and is better organized.

India. Kaye, Sir Cecil. *Communism in India*. Delhi, Government of India Press, 1926. 154 pp.
A British Intelligence report giving great detail about the period 1920–1924.

India. *King-Emperor vs. Nalini Bhushan Das Gupta, Muhammad Shaukat Usmani, Muzaffar Ahmad, and Shripat Amrit Dange*. Allahabad, Superintendent Government Press, 1924? var. pag.
A collection of the exhibits used in the Cawnpore Conspiracy Case including much correspondence between Communists in India and abroad.

India (Dominion). Ministry of Home Affairs. *Communist Violence in India*. New Delhi, Government of India Press, 1949. 71 pp.

Official government account of Communist conspiracy and violence during the Ranadive period.

Meerut. District Court. *Meerut Communist Conspiracy Case: Magistrate's Order of Committal to Trial.* Meerut, Saraswati Press, 1929? 287 pp.

A summary of evidence adduced at the Meerut Conspiracy Case.

Meerut. Sessions Court. *Judgment delivered by R. L. Yorke . . . in the Meerut Communist Conspiracy Case.* Simla, Government of India Press, 1932–33. 2 vols. 676 pp.

A useful summary of evidence adduced in the Meerut Conspiracy Case. Very detailed but difficult to use if the printed volumes of evidence with full texts of quoted documents are not available.

Meerut. Sessions Court. *Proceedings of the Meerut Conspiracy Case . . .* Meerut, Saraswati Press, 1929. 11 vols.

Most of the documents, letters, articles and pamphlets used by the Government of India to convict the CPI of conspiracy were printed for the use of the court. This is probably the most important collection of materials concerning Communism in India prior to 1929.

United States. Office of Strategic Services. Research and Analysis Branch. *The Communist Party of India.* Washington, D.C., 1945. 73 pp.

Although it was originally a classified intelligence report, this survey of the CPI is based largely on published materials. It focuses on the Party's wartime role, and contains a useful appendix of biographical sketches.

INDIAN COMMUNIST PUBLICATIONS

Adhikari, Gangadhar M. *Food for all.* Bombay, People's Publishing House, 1945?. 32 pp.

Election pamphlet on agrarian policy, for general election of 1945–1946.

———. ed. *From Peace Front to People's War.* 2d enl. ed. Bombay, People's Publishing House, 1944. 444 pp.

Useful collection of documents of CPI and Comintern, 1935–1943.

———. *Pakistan and Indian National Unity.* London, published by *Labour Monthly,* 1943. 32 pp.

Basic statement of CPI's nationality policy. Contains Adhikari's report to the Central Committee, as well as the Committee's resolution. Original edition published in India unavailable.

———. *Pakistan and National Unity.* 2d rev. ed. Bombay, People's Publishing House, 1944. 54 pp.

Revisions offer interesting example of doctoring of documents.

Communist Party of India. *Communist Statement of Policy: For the Struggle for Full Independence and People's Democracy.* Bombay, People's Publishing House, 1947. 14 pp.

Resolution of Central Committee, December 7–16, 1947. Marks official adoption of "people's war" policy.

———. *The Constitution of the Communist Party of India, 1943.* Bombay, People's Publishing House, n.d. 12 pp.

Adopted at First Congress of the Party, 1943.

———. *Constitution.* Bombay, V. M. Kaul for the Communist Party of India, 1948. 15 pp.

Adopted (with significant amendments) by the Second Congress of the Party, 1948.

———. *The Constitution of the Communist Party of India.* Delhi, CPI, 1954. 20 pp.

As amended by the Third Congress of the Party, December, 1953, to January, 1954.

——. *Declaration of Independence: Communist Party Resolution for the Constituent Assembly.* Bombay, People's Publishing House, 1946. 16 pp.

Contains memorandum by P. C. Joshi to the Cabinet Mission.

——. *Draft Programme of the Communist Party of India.* Bombay, CPI, 1951 [April]. 16 pp.

Preliminary statement of moderate policy following 1951 (see CPI, *Programme* . . .).

——. *Election Manifesto of the Communist Party of India.* Calcutta, Central Election Board of the Communist Party of India, 1951. 29 pp.

Basic statement of CPI policy in general election of 1951–1952.

——. *For the Final Assault: Tasks of the Indian People in the Present Phase of Indian Revolution.* Bombay, CPI, 1946. 18 pp.

This is the radical "August Resolution" of the CPI Central Committee, 1946.

——. *Memorandum of the Central Committee of the Communist Party of India to the States Reorganization Commission.* Delhi, CPI, 1954. 10 pp.

An important document in the evolution of the CPI's nationality policy.

——. *Political Thesis: Adopted at the Second Congress, Calcutta, February 28–March 6, 1948.* Bombay, CPI, 1948. 95 pp.

Basic statement of policy for period of Ranadive's leadership.

——. *Programme of the Communist Party of India.* Bombay, CPI, 1951 [Oct.]. 20 pp.

Revised statement of moderate policy following 1951.

——. *Programme of the Communist Party of India, Adopted by the Third Party Congress, Madurai, December 27, 1953 to January 4, 1954.* New Delhi, CPI, 1954. 20 pp.

Revised version of 1951 *Programme.*

——. *Resolutions of the Central Committee of the Communist Party of India.* Delhi, CPI, 1953. 55 pp.

Important resolutions on policy and organization, adopted March, 1953.

——. *Resolution on Party Organisation.* Delhi, CPI, 1954. 32 pp.

Important self-critical report on CPI operation and organization, adopted by Central Committee in April, 1954.

——. *Soviet-German war: Statement of the Polit Bureau.* no place, no pub., 1941. 7 pp. (Mimeo.)

Represents initial reaction of CPI to the entry of the USSR into World War II.

——. *Statement of Policy of the Communist Party of India.* Bombay, CPI, 1951 [May]. 12 pp.

Preliminary statement of moderate policy following 1951. Complements *Programme* of same year. Compare with later revision of November, 1951.

Dutt, Rajani Palme. *India Today.* 2d rev. Indian ed. Bombay, People's Publishing House, 1949. 581 pp.

Comprehensive statement of the Communist view of India, by the principal international Communist spokesman on the subject. *India Today* is periodically revised to conform to new policy lines.

——. *Modern India.* London, Communist Party of Great Britain, 1927. 174 pp.

For a description of this book see p. 84 of the present study.

——. *Situation in India: Answers to Five Vital Questions on India.* Bombay, R. Thapar, 1950. 7 pp.

Important example of Dutt's guidance of CPI.

Ghosh, Ajoy. *On the Work of the Third Congress of the Communist Party of India.* Delhi, Communist Party of India, 1954. 30 pp.

The general secretary's explanation of the line adopted at Madura.

Gopalan, A. K. and Mukerjee, Hiren. *Communists in Parliament.* New Delhi, Communist Party of India, 1957. 54 pp.

A convenient survey of Communist activity in the Central Parliament, written by the leader and deputy leader of the Communist bloc.

Joshi, Puran Chandra. *Communist Reply to Congress Working Committee's Charges.* Bombay, People's Publishing House, 1945. 2 vols.

A lengthy rebuttal to the accusation of betrayal of national interests by the CPI during World War II.

———. *Correspondence Between M. Gandhi and P. C. Joshi.* Bombay, People's Publishing House, 1945. 63 pp.

A fascinating exchange of letters, illuminating the political and personal factors in relations between the Communists and the Congress.

———. *For a Mass Policy.* Allahabad, Adhunik Pustak Bhandar [1951]. 85 pp.

A revealing factional document, published for Party members and sympathizers following Joshi's expulsion.

———. *For the Final Bid for Power! The Communist Plan Explained.* Bombay, People's Publishing House, 1946? 122 pp.

A comprehensive statement of CPI policy in the general election of 1945–1946.

The Party's Election Manifesto is included as an Appendix.

———. *The Indian Communist Party: Its Policy and Work in the War of Liberation.* Introduction by Harry Pollitt. London, Communist Party of Great Britain, 1942. 32 pp.

A basic statement and rationale of the CPI's "people's war" line. This version, published by the British Party, is abridged from the original Indian version which appears in part in Adhikari's *From Peace Front to People's War.*

———. *Problems of the Mass Movement.* Allahabad, Adhunik Pustak Bhandar, 1951? 85 pp.

Another of Joshi's criticisms of CPI policy written during his period of expulsion.

———. *Views Under the Red Banner.* [Howrah, P. C. Joshi, 1950.] 65 pp.

P. C. Joshi's polemic against B. T. Ranadive written while outside the Party. *Views* was intended to be a periodical, but only one issue was published. Valuable for what it reveals on how policy is made within the CPI.

Krishnan, N. K. [ed.] *Forgery versus Facts: Communist Party Exposes the Fifth Column.* Bombay, People's Publishing House, 1943. 51 pp.

The CPI's answer to allegations of undercover collaboration with the government during World War II. The "forgery" is a document circulated by anti-Communist elements in India, in which the CPI allegedly admitted such collaboration; this document is reprinted in the pamphlet.

———. *National Unity for the Defence of the Motherland.* Bombay, People's Publishing House, 1943. 72 pp.

Resolutions of the two plenums of the Central Committee of the Communist Party of India held in September, 1942, and February, 1943.

Namboodiripad, E. M. S. *On Organisation.* Delhi, Communist Party of India, 1954. 96 pp.

A series of lectures delivered at the Central Party School, Delhi, on July 13–15, 1954.

Ranadive, Bhalchandra Trimbak. *Jobs for All*. Bombay, People's Publishing House, 1945. 30 pp.
A basic statement of the CPI's economic policy in the general election of 1945–1946.

———. *On People's Democracy*. Bombay, Communist Party of India, 1949? 12 pp.
A basic statement of Ranadive's theoretical line, reprinted from the monthly journal *Communist*.

Roy, M. N. *The Future of Indian Politics*. London, R. Bishop [1926]. 118 pp.
For a description of this book see p. 83 of the present study.

Thapar, Romesh, et al. *Nehru's Foreign Policy*. Bombay, Crossroads Publication, 1951. 28 pp.
An interesting reflection of inner-Party debate on the subject.

Vasudeva Rao, Chalasani. *Bharatha Communist Party Nirmaana Charithrea* (History of the Formation of the Indian Communist Party). Vijayawada, Praja Sakti Press, 1943.
A semiofficial history of the CPI based on lectures given at a party training camp. A translation of a part of the Telugu original is on file at the University of California Library, Berkeley.

Workers' and Peasants' Party of Bengal. *A Call to Action*. Calcutta, Sri Gourganga Press, 1928. 58 pp.
Detailed information on the early development of communism in Bengal.

Zaheer, Sajjad. *A Case for Congress-League Unity*. Bombay, People's Publishing House, 1944. 45 pp.
An exposition of Communist policy on the nationality question, by the Party's leading Muslim.

CPI INNER-PARTY DOCUMENTS

Chandra, Prabodh (pseud.). *On "A Note on the Present Situation in our Party"* (PHQ Open Forum no. 12). No place, no pub., 1950.
Incorrectly dated 1949. A detailed account of how the CPI was taken over by B. T. Ranadive and later abandoned his ultraleftism.

Communist Conspiracy at Madurai. Bombay, Democratic Research Service, 1954. 159 pp.
A collection of documents on the CPI Third Congress uncovered and published by an anti-Communist information center in Bombay.

Communist Double Talk at Palghat. Bombay, Popular Book Depot for the Democratic Research Service, 1956.
Documents connected with Fourth CPI Congress.

Communist Party of India. *Letter of the new Central Committee (Reconstituted by the Central Committee Elected at the Second Party Congress) to All Party Members and Sympathisers*. No place, no pub., 1950. 18 pp.
A report on policy and organization by the Rajeshwar Rao Central Committee after its assumption of power in the Party.

———. *Memorandum on Communist Policy and Plan of Work*. No place, no pub., 1942? 7 pp.
Statement describing proposed program of collaboration with government during World War II.

———. *On Telengana*. Information document no. 7 (2). No place, no pub., 1950. 29 pp.

Written by an unidentified member of Andhra Provincial Committee, this document provides a detailed account of armed revolt in Telengana.

———. *Report on the Struggle in the Hill-border Regions of Mymensingh, Bengal.* Information document, no. 6 (1). No place, no pub., 1950. 14 pp. (Mimeo.)
A report on revolutionary activities in Mymensingh District, on the border of India and Pakistan.

———. *Resolution of the Central Committee . . . on P.C. Joshi's Appeal Against Expulsion, June 5, 1950.* No place, no pub., 1950. 5 pp.
A detailed explanation of why P. C. Joshi was expelled from the party.

———. *Tripura State People's Heroic Armed Resistance to Fascist Terror.* Information document no. 5. No place, no pub., 1950. 10 pp.
A detailed account of revolutionary activities in Tripura.

Dange, Shripad Amrit. *Some Notes on the Roots of Our Mistakes After Calcutta.* No place, no pub., April 20, 1950. 43 pp.
An attack on the leftist policies of the Party leadership.

Deven and Bal Krishna. *Talks with Comrade R. Palme Dutt and Other Impressions Gained Abroad by Deven and Bal Krishna.* No place, no pub., Communist Party of India, 1951. 6 pp.
Distributed by opposition elements, this document reports the advice given by Dutt in London to two CPI emissaries.

Ghosh, Ajoy, S. A. Dange, and S. V. Ghate. *A Note on the Present Situation in Our Party.* No place, no pub., 1950. var. pag.
An important factional document which helped discredit the policies of leftist leaders.

Indian Communist Party Documents 1930–1956. Bombay, Democratic Research Service and Institute of Pacific Relations, 1957. 345 pp.
A valuable collection of public and secret documents concerning the CPI. Some of these documents appear in other Democratic Research Service publications.

PHQ Unit's Covering Note to the Letter of the Political Committee of the CPGB to the Communist Party of India. No place, no pub. December 6, 1950. 6 pp.
A message from the CPI's British mentors which had allegedly been suppressed by the existing CPI leadership.

Self-Critical Report of the Andhra Communist Committee. No place, no pub., 1952? var. pag.
An inner-Party document, providing valuable information on the policy and activities of the Communist movements in Andhra and Telengana.

SOVIET AND INTERNATIONAL COMMUNIST PUBLICATIONS

Dyakov, A. *Indiia vo vremia i posle vtoroi mirovoi voiny, 1939–1949* (India During and After the Second World War, 1939–1949). Moscow, Isdatel'stvo Akademii Nauk SSSR, 1952, 259 pp.
Comprehensive statement of Soviet view of India during early post-Independence period, by the most prolific Soviet spokesman.

———. "K voprosu o natsional'nom sostave naseleniia Indii" (On the Question of the National Composition of the People of India) in *Uchenye Zapiski Tikhookeanskogo Instituta, Tom I.* Moscow, Isdatel'stvo Akademii Nauk SSSR, 1947. Pp. 223–330.
Preliminary statement of Soviet attitude on nationality question in India.

———. *Natsional'nyi vopros i angliiskii imperializm v Indii* (The National Question

and English Imperialism in India). Moscow, Gosudarstvennoe izdatel'stvo politicheskoi literatury, 1948. 328 pp.
  Comprehensive statement of Soviet attitude on nationality question.
Krizis kolonial'noi sistemy (Crisis of the Colonial System). Moscow, Izdatel'stvo
Akademii Nauk SSSR, 1949. 289 pp.
  Comprehensive statement of Soviet policy in South and Southeast Asia, including
a chapter on India.
Ming, Wang. *The Revolutionary Movement in the Colonial Countries.* New York,
Workers Library Publishers, 1935. 64 pp.
  A revised and expanded version of the author's report on colonial policy at the
Seventh Comintern Congress, 1935. Contains important observations on India.
Uchenye zapiski tikhookeanskogo instituta; Tom 2: Indiiskii sbornik (Scholarly
Papers of the Pacific Institute; Vol. 2: Indian Collection). Moscow, Izdatel'stvo
Akademii Nauk SSSR, 1949. Chapters 1, 2, 3.
  Collection of papers read in the debate on Soviet policy for India at a meeting of
the Academy of Sciences, June, 1947.
Zhukov, E. M. "Obostrenie krizisa kolonial'noi sistemy" (The Sharpening of the
Crisis of the Colonial System) in *Bolshevik*, December 15, 1947. Pp. 51–65.
  Basic statement of Soviet policy in South and Southeast Asia, 1948–1950.

Index

INDEX

NOTE.—The Postscript is not indexed.